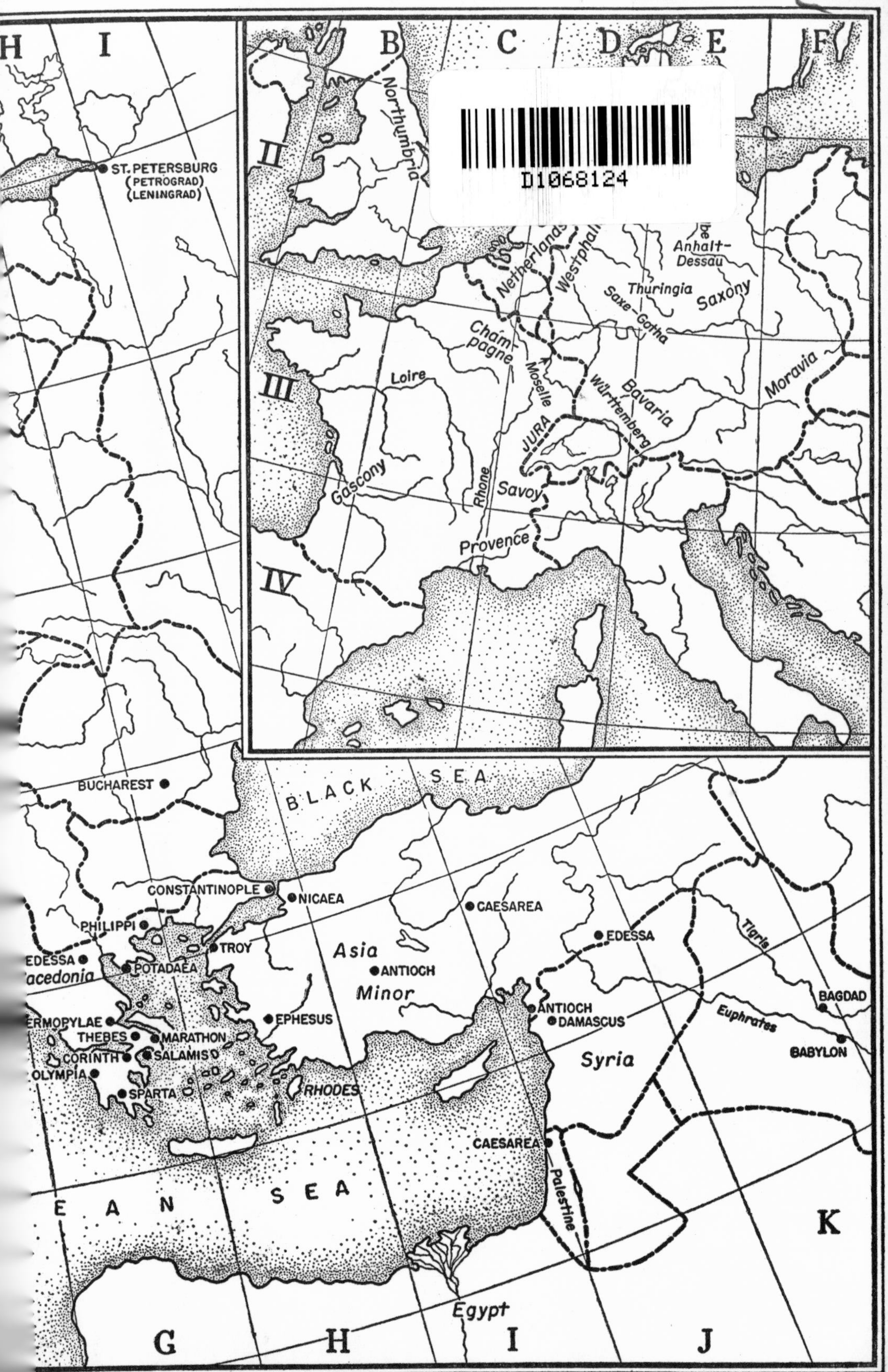
H
I
B
C
D
E
F
II
III
IV
ST. PETERSBURG
(PETROGRAD)
(LENINGRAD)
Northumbria
Netherlands
Westphalia
Anhalt-Dessau
Thuringia
Saxe-Gotha
Saxony
Champagne
Moselle
Bavaria
Württemberg
Moravia
Loire
JURA
Gascony
Rhone
Savoy
Provence
BUCHAREST
BLACK SEA
CONSTANTINOPLE
NICAEA
CAESAREA
PHILIPPI
TROY
EDESSA
Macedonia
POTADAEA
Asia Minor
ANTIOCH
Tigris
BAGDAD
Euphrates
BABYLON
DAMASCUS
Syria
ERMOPYLAE
THEBES
MARATHON
CORINTH
SALAMIS
OLYMPIA
SPARTA
EPHESUS
RHODES
CAESAREA
Palestine
EAN SEA
Egypt
K
G
H
I
J
D1068124

A HISTORY OF EDUCATION

Socrates to Montessori

A HISTORY OF EDUCATION

Socrates to Montessori

BY LUELLA COLE, Ph.D.

HOLT, RINEHART AND WINSTON · NEW YORK

21509–0510

January, 1962

Printed in the United States of America

To

ROBERT H. LOWIE

PREFACE

Many years ago in my own college days I was given the following examination in a history course:

> Suppose you were to teach this course (a) to a group of fifteen-year-old, Jewish, immigrant boys from the East Side of New York City and (b) to a group of eighteen-year-old girls in a private, fashionable, girls' "finishing" school. What materials would you use, what methods, what readings? Give sample lesson plans to show how you would handle some single unit of material for each group.

Up until that moment it had never crossed my mind that there might be more than one way of presenting historical material or that the nature of the audience was a factor in determining methodology. The seed planted by this truly educational examination has finally matured in the present volume, which contains a history of education written specifically for the average, American undergraduate. Because this book is something of a departure from the traditional history of education it needs a word of explanation and justification.

Most current texts in the field have one or both of two characteristics which make them less valuable than they should be, in view of their often excellent scholarship and clear presentation. Practically all of them are too hard for undergraduates, and some of them lack liveliness and reality. There are at least three reasons why many texts are hard. First, the scope is too great. The writer sometimes begins with ancient Egypt, ends with the modern progressive movement, and tries to cover all educational developments in between. The inevitable result is an impressive accumulation of bare facts so closely packed that the book is too difficult for students, no matter how well it is written.

The type of material in many histories of education introduces a second difficulty, because it emphasizes the growth of educational thought or educational philosophy rather than the nature of schools and methods at various times in the past. The student is told who wrote what about education, but he may read through an entire text without finding out what the daily teaching in any classroom in any century was like. The number of references to people who actually taught in school may be less than half as large as the number to those who wrote about education but either did not teach at all or merely tutored a few children. Descriptions of methods used in the classroom are not as numerous as presentations of philosophies and theories. There is, naturally, a place in a student's training for a course in the history of thought in his field, but the place is near the end of his advanced training rather than in his early undergraduate years.

Most texts are too hard also because they assume too much as known. The average student who reads them has had a course in high school American history and a little world history in the "social studies" of the lower grades. He may or may not have had a college course in history; and if he has, it is as likely to have been in the American as in the European field.

For many students the history of education is the first contact since grammar school days with Europe or the ancient world. Consequently, when a textbook writer refers to the Sophists, the battle of Salamis, the Investiture Controversy, the Edict of Nantes, Humanism, or the Bill of Rights the student has only the vaguest idea—if any—of what is meant. A condensed historical summary that assumes an already acquired foundation can be read intelligently only by a person who has the information for filling in the background as he reads. This knowledge is precisely what the undergraduate does not have.

Most existing texts are, then, unduly hard for three reasons: they cover too much ground, they contain too much that is abstruse, and they assume too much as known. A few are also lacking in interest, partly because they are hard, but largely for three other reasons.

The typical history of education is not primarily about people; it is about ideas, trends, and movements. To the average human being a depersonalized history is simply not interesting. Students like to read about people, and they will attend reasonably well to whatever material can be attached to a person, but only a handful of them will read willingly a book without characters. Especially in an introductory course is it essential to reduce impersonal data to a minimum and to keep closely connected with individuals such facts or theories as are presented.

To be sure, some existing texts mention a host of characters by name, but they remain names instead of becoming people. Thus the average number of printed lines used in the description of the individuals mentioned in five widely used histories of education is less than one line devoted to personality and slightly more than three to activities. Nearly 80 per cent of all the individuals are not described at all, and nearly 60 per cent are mentioned only once. In one of the five texts, more than 1,500 persons appear, most of them for only a few seconds. It is not surprising that historical characters make about as much impression upon the mind of the ordinary student as would be made by a glimpse of people riding by in a crowded bus. A second reason for the dullness of some texts is, then, the overabundant use of personal names, many of which appear only once and most of which are without adequate characterization or explanation.

A third reason has already been hinted at. So little information is given about most of the characters that they are only automatons. The great teachers of the world emerge as drab and boring people. Such a result is deplorable. Since histories of education are read primarily by prospective teachers, the masters among the world's teachers should appear in so interesting a light that the student will be inspired by them. And in any case, great teachers are not dull; if they were, they would not be great. A condensed presentation makes them appear uninteresting because it robs them of their delightful human traits. The cleverness of Socrates, the serene dignity of Quintilian, the lovableness of Alcuin, the flashing charm of Abélard, the moral strength of Vittorino, the courtliness of Ascham, the power and pathos of Melanchthon, the discouragements and maladjustments of Comenius, the fiery fanaticism of Loyola, the earnest disorderliness of Pestalozzi, or the mystical ecstasies of Froebel are usually lost. These men seem as alike as peas in a pod and not much more interesting. In the typical condensed and comprehensive survey of the world's thought about education there is no room for the intriguing character traits that clothe mere names with flesh and blood and thus keep the dry bones of history from rattling.

The net result of these various characteristics is, in some instances, a text that—no matter how good its scholarship—is both lifeless and difficult. The extreme condensation has squeezed out the human characteristics of the actors and has reduced them to the level of Mr. A and Mr. B of an arithmetic problem. The crowding of facts and more facts has sometimes obscured logical developments, and the concentration upon theory has resulted in subject matter of too great intrinsic difficulty. Most of the standard texts are well organized and well written, but they are not especially well adapted to the undergraduate mind.

The present book is frankly an effort to write an introduction to the history of education that undergraduates can read and will want to read. It is written in terms of student needs, student interests, and student abilities. It has a different kind of organization from that of texts now in existence, a different approach, a different style, and a much less generous scope.

First, as to organization. The book opens with a capsule of history and an even smaller dose of geography—just enough to call attention to the necessity for adequate background and to tell the student how to acquire one. This introductory chapter culminates in a timetable and a map especially designed to assist the student in reading this particular text. Since many students will need a systematic discussion of historical developments, I have listed at the end of each chapter a few references from standard texts in the history of various periods. The student is urged to read such of the references as he needs, and he may be further stimulated if the instructor assigns these or other equivalent materials as part of the required reading in the course. There is no space in this text for the inclusion of pages devoted to background, nor am I competent to write a general history, even if there were room. Moreover, there seems no reason for so doing when many sound and well-written history texts are already available in college libraries.

The main part of the book contains brief life histories of twenty-two men and one woman, all of whom lived somewhere in what is now Europe[1] at some time between 500 B.C. and the present. The series begins with Socrates and ends with Mme. Montessori. All but three of the main characters were regularly engaged in teaching school. One of the exceptions, Socrates, undertook to educate all the citizens of Athens and to this end taught constantly, but not inside a school. The second, Loyola, taught at intervals, but his main concern was with the organization of Jesuits, who were for two centuries Europe's finest schoolmasters. The third was Binet, who spent as much time in school as out, but taught very little; instead, he was studying children to find out how they think and at what rates they develop intellectually. Because these men had much influence upon schools and methods of teaching,

[1] Except for the two teachers in early Christian schools, Jerome and Origen, who spent part or all of their lives outside of Europe.

they have been included, even though they were not teachers in conventional schoolrooms.

The description of each teacher tells what manner of man he was, when and where he lived, in what schools he taught, what methods he used, what his pupils thought of him, and why he is to be regarded as either typical of his times, or great, or both. In so far as lies within my abilities, the historical figure is presented as a live, interesting, exciting human being, with virtues and faults, hopes and disillusionments, idiosyncrasies and foibles, logical ideas and irrational inspirations. Whenever possible I have let my characters speak for themselves through their own writings, through the writings of contemporaries and pupils, through anecdotes and incidents. The number of dates and of secondary characters has been reduced to a minimum. As a result of these efforts some sections of the book have a semipopular tone that may not please those who think history has to be dull and ponderous in order to be accurate. I have approached education through the personalities of great teachers with the dual objectives of creating an enthusiasm for things educational and of developing a profound respect for the profession of teaching.

The second section of each chapter contains a description of a school or schools. In some cases, the second section describes schools that existed during a particular period; others concentrate upon a single school with which one of the great teachers was connected; a few illustrate instructional materials. In these sections about a certain school or schools I have included description of the schoolroom, and discussion of the curriculum, the discipline, and the methods of instruction; there are also comments upon the position and training of the teacher. If coexistent schools of different levels are described, the interrelation among them is shown. I have introduced pictures, examples, anecdotes, and quotations, in order to give as lively, real, interesting, and specific a description as possible.

In the last section of the book I arrive at some consideration of educational thought and theory, for which the students should by now have acquired a moderate background. Wherever it can honestly be done, a connection is made between theories and people or theories and schools, partly in the interests of clarity and partly in order that students may transfer to the last section any enthusiasm that they may have generated during their reading of earlier chapters. This final section contains also a very short chapter on the growth of the curriculum through the centuries and a concluding chapter, in which I have pointed out a few agreements and disagreements among the great teachers of the past in regard to traits of personality, methods of teaching, and basic attitudes on such matters as discipline, adjustment to individual differences, or motivation. The book ends with a word about the value of history to the prospective teacher.

Two further points should be mentioned. I have realized too well my own limitations to attempt the production of this book without a great deal of aid. For each chapter there has been an advising expert. This collaborator first told me what to read. Then he went over the first draft, blue-pencilled it generously, suggested additions, criticized implications, and generally tore the copy to pieces. I then retired for a period while I read some more and rewrote the chapter. This second form was submitted, as were also as many successive forms as were necessary before the expert was satisfied. The critics were a harsh lot, with high standards of scholarship and accuracy, but without them the book could not have been written. I wish to express my great indebtedness to those who would not let me keep my favorite mistakes.

Another feature of the book is its glossary, which includes technical words, foreign words, unusual words, geographical place names, and the names of minor characters. The first time such a name or word appears in the text, it is marked with an asterisk. The student has therefore a small combined dictionary and encyclopedia to help him in his reading. Use of many special terms and of some characters other than the main one in each chapter is, of course, unavoidable; and it is not always desirable to halt in mid-career to explain words or allusions. The student who does not bring to the reading sufficient information can, by use of the glossary, build up his vocabulary and to some extent his background as he goes along.

In closing my preface I would like to express a hope that this book may help students to love history, to feel its throb of life, to be thrilled by its interesting characters, to enjoy its color and variety, and to see wherein the thoughts of yesterday contribute to a better judgment of today's bright ideas. All great teachers were exciting people who exerted a natural fascination over their followers. Those from the past were, by modern standards, sometimes right and sometimes wrong, and a few of them were more than a little odd; but they were not colorless and they did not bore their students.

LUELLA COLE

Berkeley, California
May, 1950

CONTENTS

PART SEVEN: THE NINETEENTH CENTURY

PART EIGHT: CONCLUSIONS

GLOSSARIES

ILLUSTRATIONS

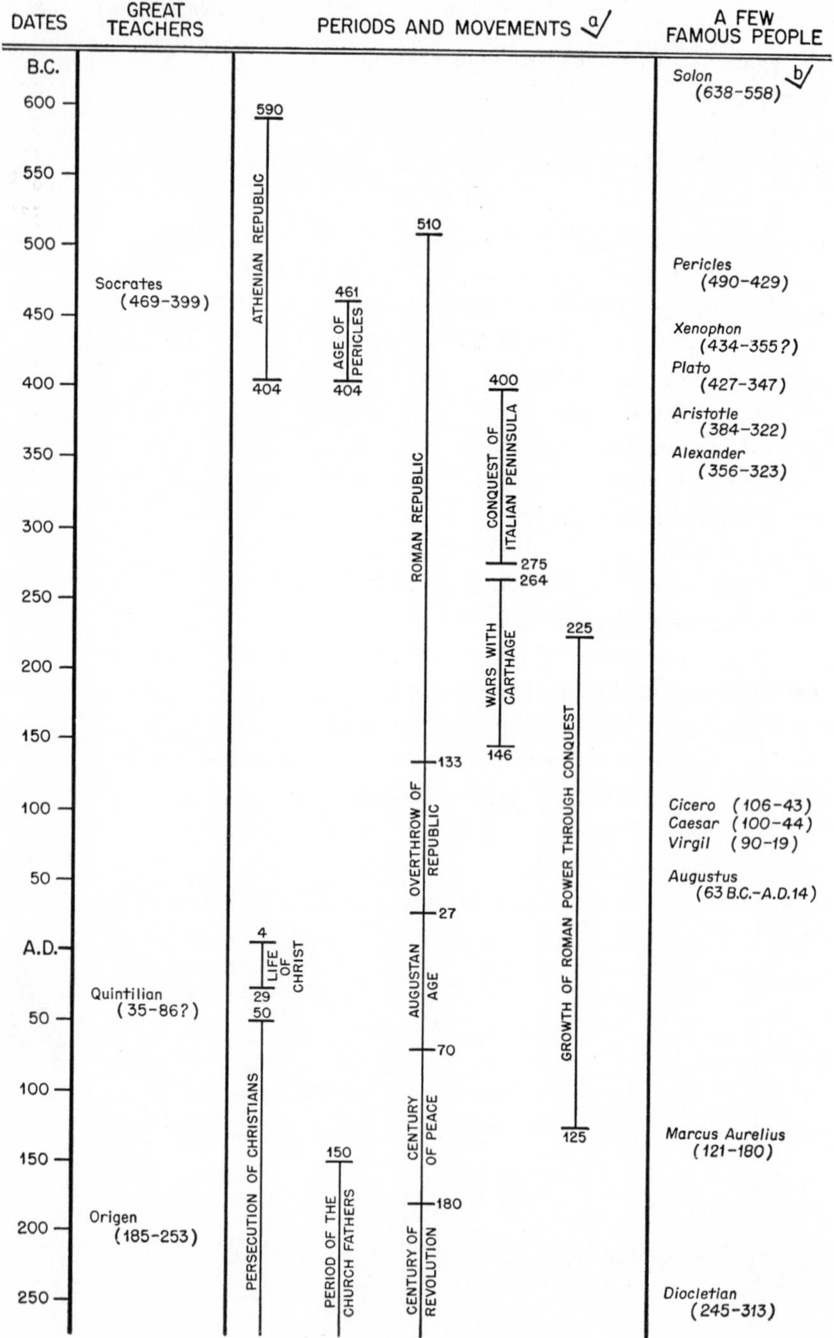
DATES
GREAT TEACHERS
PERIODS AND MOVEMENTS a/
A FEW FAMOUS PEOPLE
B.C.
600
550
500
450
400
350
300
250
200
150
100
50
A.D.
50
100
150
200
250
Socrates (469-399)
Quintilian (35-86?)
Origen (185-253)
590
ATHENIAN REPUBLIC
404
461
AGE OF PERICLES
404
510
ROMAN REPUBLIC
133
OVERTHROW OF REPUBLIC
27
AUGUSTAN AGE
70
CENTURY OF PEACE
180
CENTURY OF REVOLUTION
400
CONQUEST OF ITALIAN PENINSULA
275
264
WARS WITH CARTHAGE
146
225
GROWTH OF ROMAN POWER THROUGH CONQUEST
125
4
LIFE OF CHRIST
29
50
PERSECUTION OF CHRISTIANS
150
PERIOD OF THE CHURCH FATHERS
Solon (638-558) b/
Pericles (490-429)
Xenophon (434-355?)
Plato (427-347)
Aristotle (384-322)
Alexander (356-323)
Cicero (106-43)
Caesar (100-44)
Virgil (90-19)
Augustus (63 B.C.-A.D.14)
Marcus Aurelius (121-180)
Diocletian (245-313)

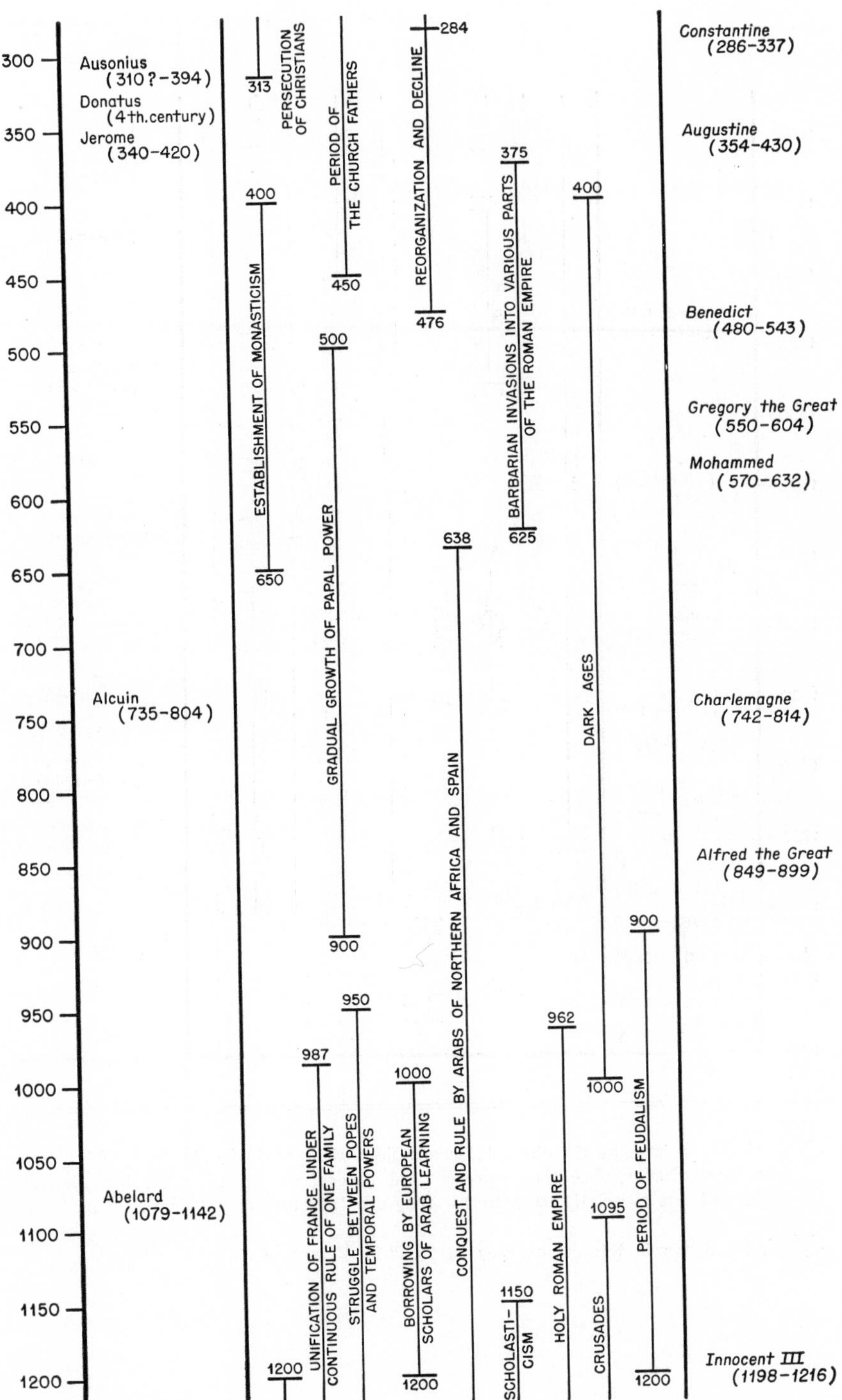
300
350
400
450
500
550
600
650
700
750
800
850
900
950
1000
1050
1100
1150
1200
Ausonius (310?-394)
Donatus (4th.century)
Jerome (340-420)
Alcuin (735-804)
Abelard (1079-1142)
PERSECUTION OF CHRISTIANS
313
ESTABLISHMENT OF MONASTICISM
400
650
PERIOD OF THE CHURCH FATHERS
450
GRADUAL GROWTH OF PAPAL POWER
500
900
REORGANIZATION AND DECLINE
284
476
BARBARIAN INVASIONS INTO VARIOUS PARTS OF THE ROMAN EMPIRE
375
625
CONQUEST AND RULE BY ARABS OF NORTHERN AFRICA AND SPAIN
638
DARK AGES
400
1000
1200
UNIFICATION OF FRANCE UNDER CONTINUOUS RULE OF ONE FAMILY
987
STRUGGLE BETWEEN POPES AND TEMPORAL POWERS
950
BORROWING BY EUROPEAN SCHOLARS OF ARAB LEARNING
1000
1200
SCHOLASTI-CISM
1150
HOLY ROMAN EMPIRE
962
CRUSADES
1095
PERIOD OF FEUDALISM
900
1200
Constantine (286-337)
Augustine (354-430)
Benedict (480-543)
Gregory the Great (550-604)
Mohammed (570-632)
Charlemagne (742-814)
Alfred the Great (849-899)
Innocent III (1198-1216)

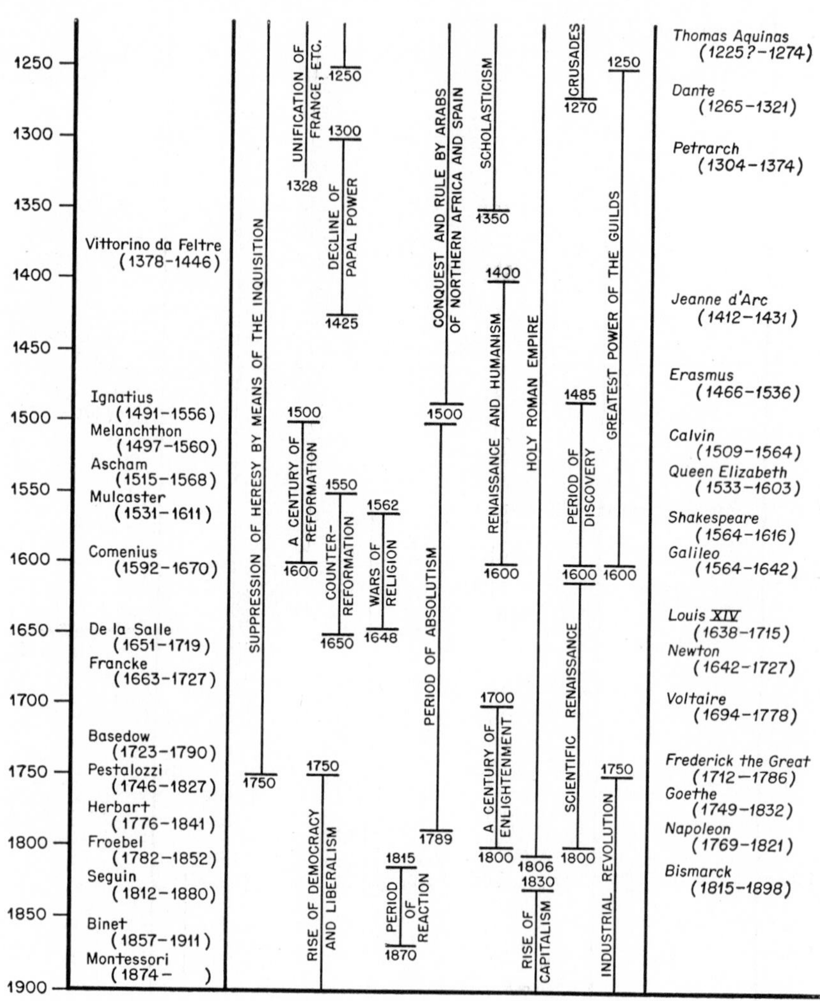

[a] Most of the dates of the above table are given whole centuries, half-centuries, or quarter-centuries, since they represent the general period during which a given movement was especially important. They are therefore only approximations.

[b] All the names in this column may be found in Glossary A.

PART ONE

INTRODUCTION

CHAPTER I

OF TIME AND SPACE

Historical characters, unlike fictional ones, actually lived in a particular time and in certain particular places. They were influenced by the dominant forces of their environment. The great teachers of yesterday did not exist in a vacuum, any more than living people do. Because both time and place are important in understanding their work and their contributions to education, it is essential that students develop a sense of chronology and an adequate historical background. Almost no student will have had courses that covered all periods in the history of Europe from 500 B.C. to A.D. 1900—the centuries included in this text. The overwhelming majority of undergraduates will, therefore, come to this course with an inadequate supply of information. Since, in the present text, there is no space for a presentation of background, the student will have to make some kind of adjustment, assuming that he has not already completed such courses in history as would give him the necessary facts. The easiest course to pursue is to do nothing and hope for the best! The drawback to this simple solution lies in its inefficiency, and the student who chooses it will not understand his text as well as he should, or enjoy the course as much as he might, or receive at the end as high a mark as he could have earned. It is a far better procedure for each student to read from the references listed at the end of each chapter whatever selections may be needed to fill in the lacunae*[1] in the knowledge that he brings to the course. A student may thus acquire background as he proceeds, and he should certainly do so if he wishes to derive from his work in the history of education profits that are commensurate with his efforts.

The average undergraduate has a relatively poor mastery of "place" geography and is lucky if he knows on which continent a given country is located. The customary deficiency in this field is, however, quite easy to remedy, in so far as this text is concerned, because all but two of the important places are located within a strip about 1200 miles long and 700 miles wide. The area thus delineated is approximately equal to that included in the adjoining north-

[1] Words that are followed by an asterisk are listed with definitions and explanations in the back of the book. Glossary C contains words that are difficult, unusual, foreign, technical, or often misunderstood. Glossary A contains the names of individuals; Glossary B, the names of places. The asterisk appears only once for each word, but the student is advised to look up any word or name that seems to him unusual, since he may have missed the asterisk when it was first used.

western states of Washington, Oregon, Idaho, Montana, Nevada, Utah, Wyoming, North Dakota, South Dakota, and Nebraska. Any student can surely learn in an hour, at the most, the location of about 30 cities and towns within such a relatively small compass. This preliminary work will be well worth the effort involved.

Suggestions to the Student for Use of the Map and the Timetable: On the front inside cover of this book you will find a modern outline map that shows the boundaries of countries as they are at the present time. This type of map was used because it is familiar to most students. You should ignore the boundary lines, except as they may help you in locating places. Throughout the text the countries are called by their modern names, in order to make the work easier. On the map you will see numbered dots, marking the places where some great teacher of the past lived and taught. You will note that the dots do not refer to the place of birth but to the place of work. In a few cases a teacher was associated with more than one place, so there is more than one dot bearing the same reference number. You should understand that these are the *main* scenes of each man's teaching career. In practically all cases, he traveled more or less, attended different schools, and taught briefly in one or more places before he settled down to his longer periods of residence; and he often spent his declining years away from the place or places in which he had worked. You are advised to study the map, to note what the marks refer to, and to associate as soon as possible each place with its appropriate person or persons. The twenty-three great teachers who are described in this text, their main places of work, and their reference numbers appear in the list on page 4:

The calendar or "timetable" is included, beginning on page XVIII. You will see at the left a column of dates, listed by centuries; this series is to be used for locating men in their proper period. The second column contains the names of the various teachers to be described in the text. These names appear beside their appropriate centuries, as listed in the first column. You will see that approximately 500 years elapsed between Socrates and Quintilian, from 150 to 300 years between Quintilian and the next group of four names, about 400 between these and Alcuin, and a similar interval between Alcuin and Abélard. Then, the intervals become approximately 200 years between individuals or pairs of individuals, then 100 years, then 50, and finally 25 or less. The dates of birth and death appear in parentheses after each person's name.

In the third column the period during which each of a number of movements was operative is shown by a line. The approximate dates appear at the tops and bottoms of the lines. Thus the Athenian republic began in 590 B.C. and continued till 404 B.C. Farther down the chart a long line shows the Dark Ages to extend from A.D. 400 to 1000. Other lines are to be read in similar

Chapter	Teacher	Place	Reference Number	Map A[a]
2	Socrates	Athens (Greece)	1	F, IV
3	Quintilian	Rome (Italy)	2	D, III
4	Donatus	Rome (Italy)	3	D, III
	Ausonius	Bordeaux (France)	4	A, III
5	Origen	Alexandria (Egypt)	5	G, V
	Jerome	Bethlehem (Palestine)	6	H, V
6	Alcuin	Aachen (or Aix-la-Chapelle) (Germany)	7	C, I
7	Abélard	Paris (France)	8	B, II
8	Vittorino	Mantua (Italy)	9	D, II
9	Melanchthon	Wittenberg (Germany)	10	D, I
10	Ascham	Oxford, London (England)	11	A, I
	Mulcaster	London (England)	12	A, I
11	Loyola	Rome (Italy)	13	D, III
12	Comenius	Lissa (Poland)	14	E, I
13	De la Salle	Rouen, Paris (France)	15	B, II
	Francke	Halle (Germany)	16	D, I
14	Basedow	Dessau (Germany)	17	D, I
16	Pestalozzi	Burgdorf, Yverdon (Switzerland)	18	C, II
16	Herbart	Königsberg, Göttingen (Germany)	19	F, I; C, I
17	Froebel	Keilhau, Bad Liebenstein (Germany)	20	D, I
18	Seguin	Paris (France)	21	B, II
	Binet	Paris (France)	22	B, II
19	Montessori	Rome (Italy)	23	D, III

[a] The capital letters and Roman numerals in this column refer to the divisions on Map A. The letters from A to I appear across the top of the map, the numerals from I to V down the left margin. Thus, Athens (F, IV) will be found in column F and across from the number IV. Find F at the top of the map and follow it down till you come to row IV. In this square you will see a dot with the number 1 beside it. This dot shows the location of Athens, where Socrates lived, taught, and died.

fashion. Naturally, whenever the beginning and end of a movement or period can be stated with exactness—as, for instance, the time during which Christians were persecuted by government decree—the dates are exact; in this case, from the first known persecution in A.D. 50 to the last one in 313. Often, however, the dates have to be approximations.

In the fourth column appear the names of prominent individuals, most of whom will be mentioned in the text. All of them are so famous that you will probably know something about them already. They are listed to help you to develop a proper sense of chronology.

Before you begin to read the chapter in the text concerning any given teacher's life and work, you should locate him on the map and in the time-table. Associate him with his proper period of history, his century,[2] and his

[2] You should remember, when considering dates, either B.C. or A.D., that the century is named for the 100 years *beyond* the actual dates, whether you are going forward into

contemporaries. To refresh yourself on what was going on in the world during the various periods, read or review a general history of the times. You would do well to memorize the timetable, section by section, as you read about each man in turn. If you do not, the tide of history is likely to wash some of the characters a few centuries up- or downstream. The recommended review and the secure anchoring of each man in time and space will prevent many errors of comprehension and will contribute greatly both to your understanding and to your enjoyment of this text.

---

the A.D.'s or backward into the B.C.'s. Thus, the 1492 is in the fifteenth, not the fourteenth. This peculiarity of English usage is unfortunate, but it cannot be helped, except by using foreign words, which, in their turn, introduce difficulties of their own. You will therefore have to reconcile yourselves to such equivalent phrases as "He lived in the 1200's," or "He lived in the thirteenth century"—two remarks which mean precisely the same thing.

PART TWO

ANTIQUITY

CHAPTER II

SOCRATES AND THE SCHOOLS OF ATHENS

This history begins in the fifth century before Christ, over twenty-four hundred years ago. At that time Greece was the most cultured country in the area now known as Europe, and Athens was the most remarkable city of Greece. The present chapter will tell the story of a famous Greek teacher and will then describe the schools of Athens.

Socrates was the first great teacher to be adequately recorded in history. He is important not only because he was the first but because he developed a method of teaching that has survived for more than two thousand years and is still in use. Moreover, he was the most commanding single educational figure of antiquity.

It is difficult for modern students to get a clear picture of Socrates as a person or as a teacher because he is known only through the writings of pupils and contemporaries. Since each of these people had his own bias and his own traits of personality one must hunt for the true Socrates among the many accounts about him. To one of his students, Xenophon,* he was a model of all the virtues; to another, Plato,* he was a great teacher and a martyr; to a contemporary comedian, Aristophanes,* he was a dangerous, advanced thinker and sophist*; to Aristotle*—a generation later—he appeared a gifted and great but sometimes mistaken philosopher; to Diogenes Laërtius,* the Walter Winchell of antiquity, he was a subject for amusing stories and anecdotes. Thus Socrates is seen only through the screen of another man's personality and known only through his effect upon other people. Behind all of the sometimes contradictory evidence, however, no one doubts that there was a real, flesh-and-blood Socrates, any more than one questions the existence of a real, flesh-and-blood Jesus behind the four gospel* accounts of his life.

A. SOCRATES: HIS LIFE AND WORK

1. The Life of Socrates[1] Socrates was born about 470 B.C. in the immediate neighborhood of Athens. With the exception of a few brief trips, chiefly

[1] The main secondary sources for this section were: A. Busse, *Sokrates,* Reuther & Richard, 1914, 248 pp.; R. N. Cross, *Socrates: The Man and His Mission,* Open Court Publishing Company, 1914, 344 pp.; E. C. Osborne, *Socrates and His Friends,* Hodder & Stoughton, 1930, 542 pp.; C. Ritter, *Sokrates,* Tübingen University, 1931, 87 pp.; and A. E. Taylor, *Socrates,* Peter Davies Ltd., 1933, 182 pp. References to primary sources will appear whenever they are quoted.

on military expeditions, he never left the city. Indeed, he was as much a city sparrow as any cockney* who has never been outside London. His father was a stoneworker—a craft in which Socrates was trained and at which he worked for some years. Presumably he went to the kind of elementary school that will be described in a later section, although this fact is not actually known.

In his early manhood Socrates began to read and study the various philosophers and scientists who had preceded him. At first he seems to have been sure that by enough such study he would sooner or later understand the riddle of life. For some years he pursued first one subject or line of thought and then another, never satisfied and always seeking for a wisdom he did not find. Although the conflict within him is lost in the fogs of antiquity, one may suppose that he traveled the same slow, painful, *via dolorosa** along which all independent thinkers sooner or later have to proceed. Socrates emerged from these years with two firm convictions: that no one as yet knew much and that the way to real knowledge lay through an intensive study of one's self and of the mind of man. As a means to this study he devised a method of analysis and questioning that is still called "the Socratic method." Since he was convinced that nothing was known, equally certain that he had the correct method for making the necessary investigations, and even more aware that he had a divine "call" to undertake the work, he ceased to be a stonemason and began a constant inquiry into what he regarded as the important things of life. He talked with everyone who would listen, he waylaid and questioned the unwary, he cornered the experts and made them admit their ignorance, he reduced the proud by first leading them into extreme assertions and then deflating them with irony. In short, he staged a one-man crusade against ignorance.

Three brief descriptions of his usual mode of life appear below:

> Socrates lived ever in the open; for early in the morning he went to the public promenades and training grounds; in the forenoon he was seen in the market; and the rest of the day he passed just where most people were to be met: he was generally talking, and anyone might listen.[2]
>
> His own conversation was ever of human things. The problems he discussed were, what is godly, what is ungodly; what is beautiful, what is ugly; what is just, what is unjust; what is prudence, what is madness; what is courage, what is cowardice; what is a state; what is a statesman; what is a government, and what is a governor;—these and others like them, of which the knowledge made a "gentleman," in his estimation.[3]

[2] E. C. Marchant, *Xenophon, Memorabilia and Oeconomicus,* Loeb Classical Library, Harvard University Press, (531 pp.), IV, 7. This passage and subsequent ones from this reference are reprinted by permission of the publishers.

[3] *Ibid.*, p. 11.

. . . he showed himself to be one of the people and a friend of mankind. For although he had many eager disciples among citizens and strangers, yet he never exacted a fee for his society from one of them, but of his abundance he gave without stint to all. Some indeed, after getting from him a few trifles for nothing, became vendors of them at a great price to others, and showed none of his sympathy with the people, refusing to talk with those who had no money to give them.[4]

It will be noted at once that Socrates taught, but not in a school. It was in the market place, in the gymnasiums, and in the streets that Socrates carried on his lifework of teaching young and old Athenians to know themselves, to know what was good, and to know what conditions influenced the development of virtue. He did not withdraw from life in order to study it under carefully controlled laboratory conditions but rather went joyfully out to meet it where it was whirling along at its busiest.

From his own point of view Socrates spent his life going about Athens and doing good to his fellow man, even though the object of his concern did not always appreciate his efforts. As he himself once said:

Accordingly I went to one who had the reputation of wisdom and observed him—his name I need not mention. As we talked I could not help thinking that he was not really wise, although he was thought wise by men, and still wiser by himself. And then I tried to show him that he only thought he was wise but was not really. And the consequence was that he hated me, and his enmity was shared by several who were present and heard me. So I left him, saying to myself, as I went away: Well, although I do not suppose that either of us knows anything really beautiful and good, I am better off than he is—for he knows nothing, and thinks that he knows: I neither know nor think that I know. In this latter particular, then, I seem to have slightly the advantage of him. Then I went to another who had still higher pretensions to wisdom, and my conclusion was exactly the same. Whereupon I made another enemy of him, and of many others besides him.[5]

Such reactions were only to be expected. In another passage, Socrates likened himself to a gadfly that stung the people into thinking about themselves, their way of life, their government, their concepts of right and wrong, their ideals, and their destiny. The role of apostle at large was not likely to endear him to the many people whom he annoyed.

In addition to his activities as self-appointed critic and reformer Socrates was a remarkable leader of youth, and it was this power over young men that lead indirectly to his eventual arrest, trial, and execution. In order to under-

[4] *Ibid.*, p. 43.

[5] From *The Dialogues of Plato,* translated and edited by Benjamin Jowett (Clarendon Press, Oxford), (3d ed., 576 pp.), II, 113–114. This passage and subsequent ones from this reference are reprinted by permission of the publisher.

stand why he should have been arrested at all, it is necessary to look briefly at the history of Athens in the period between Socrates' birth and death. His life span covered the decades during which Athens reached the height of its power and continued on through thirty years of war, decline, betrayal, and increasing weakness. From the time of Socrates' early manhood until he was about forty years of age Athens enjoyed security under the great leader Pericles.* Even before the death of Pericles, however, Athens had entered into a long and exhausting war with Sparta.* For a while during the second decade of the war the Athenians put their faith in a brilliant, unstable, charming, and thoroughly bad young man named Alcibiades*—a nephew of Pericles. Perhaps Athens in any case could not have emerged from twenty-seven years of war as still the leading city of Greece, but the machinations of Alcibiades did much to hasten the debacle.* He urged his fellow citizens into undertakings that they could ill afford, went into exile, and betrayed them to their enemies; later on he was again trusted by the Athenians, and again made trouble for them. At the end of the war Athens was not only defeated but bankrupt and exhausted. Moreover, the Athenians were coerced by their conquerors into accepting a group of reactionaries called the Thirty Tyrants* as rulers of the city. Among the Thirty, and possibly the most infamous of them, was a man named Critias,* who was, in a different way, as evil as Alcibiades. The Tyrants instituted a reign of terror, not unlike similar periods of fierce repression in Europe during the last few decades, and caused many of their opponents to be executed.

Socrates was a friend and teacher of both Alcibiades and Critias, just as he was a friend of practically everyone. Although the two younger men listened sometimes to his public discussions, their presence did not make Socrates responsible for them, in the way that a tutor is responsible for his charges, but the general public did not so view the relationship. People hated Alcibiades for his treason and Critias for his cruelty. After both men were either dead or in exile the people turned upon Socrates, whom they regarded as the teacher and inspirer of these two evil characters, and made of him a scapegoat* for their own defects and disillusionments.

After enjoying a lifetime of the greatest freedom of speech, Socrates was arrested in 400 B.C. on a charge that amounted to treason. The exact wording of the accusation has been preserved:

> Socrates is guilty of rejecting the gods acknowledged by the state and of bringing in strange deities: he is also guilty of corrupting the youth.[6]

The first part of the accusation—that Socrates did not pay respect to the

[6] Marchant, *op. cit.*, IV, 3.

gods of the city—does not seem to have been borne out by his overt behavior. He is described as a scrupulous observer of religious rites. Moreover, he spoke of the gods reverently enough, although he did say that there were many things about them that no man could ever understand; concerning these matters he saw no value in discussion. Socrates was accused also of introducing new gods. This complaint came almost certainly from the frequent allusions he made to his "inner voice." For instance, at the trial which grew out of the above accusation he said:

> You have heard me speak at sundry times and in diverse places of an oracle or sign which comes to me. . . . This sign, which is a kind of voice, first began to come to me when I was a child; it always forbids but never commands me to do anything which I am going to do.[7]

Whether Socrates meant that he actually heard a voice or that he merely dramatized his own conscience or feelings is difficult to tell. Perhaps he did not know himself. In any case he seems to have talked much about this inner counsel and even to have called his mentor a "divinity." Such remarks overheard and taken out of their original setting would be evidence to a Greek mind—already full of many gods—for accrediting Socrates with the intention of introducing still another, and his personal deity at that.

The second part of the accusation—that Socrates was guilty of corrupting youth—can be understood only by realizing the almost irresistible attraction that Socrates had for young men and the nature of their reactions to him. The old man and his clever talk had captured the youthful imagination to an alarming degree. If these young enthusiasts had always understood what their teacher said, matters would not have been so serious, but many of them only superficially grasped the points discussed and rushed off at once to broadcast their own interpretation, just as students of today spread a half-understood, garbled account of what their teachers have said. The followers of Socrates probably repeated, in and out of season and with an infinitude of variations, every clever saying they had heard, until their elders were alarmed alike at what Socrates appeared to have said and at his power over their sons. Even a bad young man like Alcibiades gave testimony on this matter of attractiveness:

> When we hear any other speaker, even a very good one, he produces absolutely no effect, upon us, or not much, whereas the mere fragments of you and your words, even at second-hand, and however imperfectly repeated, amaze and possess the souls of every man, woman, and child who comes within hearing of them . . . My heart leaps within and my eyes rain tears when I hear them. And I observe that many others are affected in the same

[7] Jowett, *op. cit.*, II, 125.

manner. I have heard Pericles and the other great orators, and I thought that they spoke well, but I never had any similar feeling; my soul was not stirred by them, nor was I angry at the thought of my own slavish state. But Socrates has often brought me to such a pass that I have felt, if I did not shut my ears against him, and fly as from the voice of the siren, my fate would be like that of others—he would transfix me, and I should grow old sitting at his feet. . . .[8]

Socrates was well aware of this power of his. In his own words, given by Plato, he says:

There is another thing:—young men of the richer classes, who have not much to do, come about me of their own accord; they like to hear the pretenders examined, and they often imitate me, and proceed to examine others; there are plenty of persons, as they quickly discover, who think that they know something, but really know little or nothing; and then those who are examined by them instead of being angry with themselves are angry with me: This confounded Socrates, they say; this villainous misleader of youth!—and then if somebody asks them, Why, what evil does he practice or teach? they do not know, and cannot tell; but in order that they may not appear to be at a loss, they repeat the ready-made charges which are used against all philosophers about teaching things up in the clouds and under the earth, and having no gods, and making the worse appear the better cause; for they do not like to confess that their pretence of knowledge has been detected—which is the truth.[9]

In referring to the possibility of exile as punishment for him after he had been voted guilty at his trial, Socrates exclaimed.

What a life should I lead, at my age, wandering from city to city, ever changing my place of exile, and always being driven out. For I am quite sure that wherever I go, there, as here, the young men will flock to me; and if I drive them away, their elders will drive me out at their request; and if I let them come, their fathers and friends will drive me out for their sakes.[10]

It was this power as a leader that frightened people even more than any particular ideas that were discussed. It is the same power that makes any great teacher great.

It is not surprising that Socrates was considered a subversive influence. He was an outspoken critic, and he could not be restrained by threats or pressure. Moreover, he managed to be so amusing that people, especially young people, who began by laughing at him ended by laughing at the people or institutions about which he spoke. His accusers said of him, he made "the worse seem the

[8] *Ibid.*, I, 586–587.
[9] *Ibid.*, II, 115–116.
[10] *Ibid.*, pp. 130–131.

better way"—that is, he so charmed people that they could no longer judge for themselves what was right and what was wrong.

At his trial upon the accusation recorded above, Socrates was found guilty by a vote of 280 to 220.[11] Socrates was then asked if he cared to propose a penalty for himself as an alternative to the death sentence. Presumably the court would have been satisfied with banishment, but Socrates insisted that he had done only good to Athens and that he could not conscientiously propose for himself any real evil such as banishment would be. He did mention a fine as a possibility, although most of it would have to be paid by his friends; however, he does not seem to have meant the fine to be taken seriously. The whole tenor of his speech was so uncompromising that a larger majority[12]—360 to 140—than had found him guilty voted the death sentence. At the close of his trial Socrates addressed to his fellow citizens a dignified and serene farewell speech, ending with the words:

> The hour of departure has arrived and we must go our ways—I to die, and you to live. Which is better, God only knows.[13]

Between the trial and the execution, the friends of Socrates bribed his jailers to let him escape, but Socrates would not go. In the first place he said that it would be undignified; in the second, it would nullify all the teachings of a lifetime; in the third, it would be a crime against the state—and Socrates was unwilling to buy his freedom at the cost of breaking laws. In the end, therefore (399 B.C.), he drank the poison by which malefactors were executed and died with the same serenity with which he had lived.

Many people have seen similarities between the life and character of Socrates and the life and character of Christ. Both were martyrs, both were teachers, and both felt definite missions to reform mankind. Moreover, their ideals and conduct were remarkably alike. Socrates exemplified, for instance, the teaching of Jesus: "Love your enemies, bless them that curse you, do good to them that hate you, and pray for them which despitefully use you, and persecute you." [14] To the moment of his death Socrates continued to love Athens and the Athenians, in spite of the treatment he had received. Both he and Jesus had the same inner consciousness of being right and could consequently face the world serene and unafraid.[15]

[11] As given in Taylor, *op. cit.*, p. 118.
[12] *Ibid.*, p. 120.
[13] Jowett, *op. cit.*, II, 135.
[14] Matt. 5:44.
[15] For an excellent discussion of further similarities see G. H. Macurdy, *The Quality of Mercy; the Gentler Virtues in Greek Literature.* Yale University Press, 1940 (185 pp.), chap. 13.

2. *The Character of Socrates* The essential traits of Socrates' character emerge quite clearly from the various accounts of his life and work, in spite of some minor contradictions. Perhaps the most outstanding was his absolute fearlessness when he believed he was right. One example is given below in part of a speech he made in his own defense at his famous trial.

> At the trial of the generals you proposed to try them in a body, contrary to law, as you all thought afterwards; but at the time I was the only one who was opposed to the illegality, and I gave my vote against you; and when the orators threatened to impeach and arrest me, and you called and shouted, I made up my mind that I would run the risk, having law and justice with me, rather than take part in your injustice because I feared imprisonment and death. This happened in the days of the democracy. But when the oligarchy* of the Thirty was in power, they sent for me and four others and bade us bring Leon from Salamis,* as they wanted to put him to death. . . . And then I showed, not in word only but in deed that, if I may be allowed to use such an expression, I cared not a straw for death, and that my great and only care was lest I should do an unrighteous or unholy thing. For the strong arm of that oppressive power did not frighten me into doing wrong; and when we came out the other four went to Salamis and fetched Leon, but I went quietly home. For which I might have lost my life, had not the power of the Thirty shortly afterwards come to an end.[16]

A second trait was his complete incorruptibility. Temptation tempted him, just as it does anyone else, but he had the power to resist and to emerge from one episode after another as the victor. This trait of his was admired equally by his two chief pupils, Xenophon and Plato. As Socrates is reported to have said of himself at his trial:

> For I do nothing but go about persuading you all, old and young alike, not to take thought for your persons or your properties, but first and chiefly to care about the greatest improvement of the soul. I tell you that virtue is not given by money, but that from virtue comes money and every other good of man, public as well as private. This is my teaching, and if this doctrine corrupts the youth, then I am a mischievous person. But if any one says that this is not my teaching, he is speaking an untruth. Wherefore, O men of Athens, I say to you,—either acquit me or not; but whichever you do, understand that I shall never alter my ways, not even if I have to die many times.[17]

In all the accounts of him Socrates is shown to have been a man of great serenity of mind and great strength of purpose. These traits are especially well shown in the simple and moving description given by Plato of the last hours in Socrates' life.

[16] Jowett, *op. cit.*, II, 125–126.
[17] *Ibid.*, pp. 122–123.

Now the hour of sunset was near. . . . Soon . . . , the jailer . . . entered and stood by him, saying:—To you. Socrates, whom I know to be the noblest and gentlest and best of all who ever came to this place, I will not impute the angry feelings of other men, who rage and swear at me, when in obedience to the authorities, I bid them drink the poison—indeed, I am sure that you will not be angry with me; for others, as you are aware, and not I, are to blame. And so fare you well, and try to bear lightly what must needs be—you know my errand. Then bursting into tears he turned away and went out.

Socrates looked at him and said: I return your good wishes, and will do as you bid. Then turning to us, he said, How charming the man is: since I have been in prison he has always been coming to see me, and at times he would talk to me, and was as good to me as could be, and now see how generously he sorrows on my account. We must do as he says, Crito [a friend of Socrates]; and therefore let the cup be brought, if the poison is prepared; if not, let the attendant prepare some.

Yet, said Crito, the sun is still upon the hilltops, and I know that many a one has taken the draught late, and after the announcement has been made to him, he has eaten and drunk, and enjoyed the society of his beloved; do not hurry—there is time enough.

Socrates said: Yes Crito, and they of whom you speak are right in so acting, for they think they will be gainers by the delay; but I am right in not following their example, for I do not think that I should gain anything by drinking the poison a little later; I should only be ridiculous in my own eyes for sparing and saving a life which is already forfeit. Please then to do as I say, and not to refuse me.

Crito made a sign to the servant, who was standing by; and he went out, and having been absent for some time, returned with the jailer carrying the cup of poison. Socrates said: You, my good friend, who are experienced in these actions, shall give me directions how I am to proceed. The man answered: You have only to walk about until your legs are heavy, and then to lie down, and the poison will act. At the same time he handed the cup to Socrates, who in the easiest and gentlest manner, without the least fear or change of colour or feature, looking at the man with all his eyes, as his manner was, took the cup and said: What do you say about making a libation out of this cup to any god? May I, or not? The man answered: We only prepare, Socrates, just as much as we deem enough; I understand, he said: but I may and must ask the gods to prosper my journey from this to the other world—even so—and so be it, according to my prayer. Then raising the cup to his lips, quite readily and cheerfully he drank off the poison. And hitherto most of us had been able to control our sorrow; but now, when we saw him drinking, and saw too that he had finished the draught, we could no longer forbear, and in spite of myself my own tears were flowing fast; so that I covered my face and wept, not for him, but at the thought of my own calamity in having to part from such a friend. Nor was I the first; for Crito, when he found himself unable to restrain the tears, had got up, and I followed. . . . Socrates alone retained his calmness: What is this strange outcry? he said. I sent away the women in order that they might not misbehave in this way, for I have been told that a man should die in peace. Be quiet then, and have patience. When we heard his words we were ashamed, and restrained our tears; and he walked about until, as he said, his legs began to fail, and then lay on his back, according to the direction and the man who gave him the poison now and then looked at his feet and legs; and after a while he pressed his foot hard, and asked him if he could feel; and he said, No; and then his leg, and so upwards, and showed us that he was cold and stiff. And he felt himself, and said: When the poison reaches the heart, that will be the end. He was beginning to grow cold about the groin, when he uncovered his face, for he had covered himself up, and said—they were his last words—he said: Crito, I owe a cock to Asclepius; will you remember to pay the debt? The debt shall be paid, said Crito; is there anything else? There was no answer to this question; but in a minute or two a movement was heard, and the attendant uncovered him; his eyes were set, and Crito closed his eyes and mouth.

Such was the end of our friend; concerning whom I may truly say, that of all the men of his time whom I have known, he was the wisest and justest and best.[18]

These characteristics of courage, incorruptibility, and serenity are the common traits of the reformer, but not all reformers have the humanness of Socrates. Although his fundamental attitude was serious, he had an excellent sense of humor and an appreciation of human frailty. Many of the anecdotes told about Socrates may not have been true, but most of them fit in well with his known character and are therefore worth presenting. For instance:

1. Upon beholding a multitude of things for sale in the market, Socrates murmured to himself, "My, my, what a lot of things I don't need."

2. When he was asked whether one should marry or not he replied: "Whichever you do, you will regret it."

3. He used to say he marvelled that those who made stone statues took such pains to make the stone as like the man as possible, but took no pains with themselves that they might not be like the stones.

4. When he had invited some rich people to dinner and his wife Xantippe* was ashamed of the meal, he said, "Don't be troubled; if they have good sense they will adapt themselves to us, and if they do not have good sense we shall care nothing for them anyway."

5. Socrates is credited with having been the first to say: "Most men live to eat, but I eat to live."

6. When his friends came to him in great excitement and said, "The Athenians have condemned you to death," he answered, "And nature has condemned them to death also."

7. When his wife cried, "But you die innocent," he answered, "Would you rather I should die guilty?"

8. Just after he had drunk the poison, a friend tried to give Socrates a

[18] *Ibid.*, pp. 264–266.

handsome cloak to wrap himself in but he replied, "Is this coat of mine good enough to live in, but not good enough to die in?"

9. When Xantippe had reviled him, then thrown a pail of water on him, Socrates remarked, "Didn't I tell you Xantippe was thundering and that it would soon rain?"

10. Upon being asked what he thought of a certain philosopher's writing he answered, "What I understood was fine, and I suppose what I did not understand was also fine, but I need a diver to go down and fetch up the meaning."[19]

Even though some of these stories are apocryphal* they are of the type that cluster about the memory of a thoroughly human and lovable man, with a reputation for quick wit and good nature. They would never have been told about a misanthrope.

Some definite facts are known about the appearance and general physique of Socrates. He was almost the exact opposite of the Greek ideal of beauty. In the first place he was short, stout, and clumsy. He had a round face, bulging eyes, flat nose, thick lips, and a protuberant belly. As if these natural oddities were not enough, Socrates added to them by going barefooted and by wearing only a shabby cloak winter and summer. Despite his lack of physical beauty, however, Socrates had both charm and dignity. In the statuette, a view of which appears here, both these traits are clearly revealed.[20]

Socrates was a man of great physical strength and superb health. During his lifetime he was thrice sent out to fight in defense of Athens and added to his excellent record as a soldier a reputation for both courage and ability to withstand severe hardships. He was apparently never sick, not even during the terrible plague that killed hundreds, including the great Pericles. He ate enough to keep himself nourished, he took regular exercise, he condemned excesses, and

[19] All anecdotes are from Diogenes Laërtius, *Excerpts from the Lives and Opinions of the Philosophers.* Translated by W. C. Lawton in the *Library of the World's Best Literature,* Henry Holt and Company, 1896, VIII, 4711–4720.

[20] I have been criticized for saying that statues and portraits reveal the traits of character shown by their subjects in life. I am well aware of modern research into the unreliability of pictures. It is entirely possible to select pictures of six criminals and six successful businessmen, mix them in a random order, and discover that no one can sort them out successfully. To me, however, such an experiment is irrelevant to the present situation. For one thing, the experimenter purposely selects faces of criminals that do not look like criminals and faces of businessmen that are not typical of businessmen. Moreover, the pictures were usually taken for purposes of identification—passport or prison pictures—and were not supposed to do more than to show the features clearly. Portraits are, however, quite different in their purpose. They are supposed to reveal character; and if they do not, they are bad portraits. After a person has lived behind the same face for a lifetime, some traces of his personality should be revealed in it, and an artist should be able to create a likeness that will preserve and even emphasize the nature of the person behind the face. Therein lies the difference between a portrait and a picture taken by a prison or a passport photographer.

Fig. 1. Socrates. From a statuette in the British Museum.

he lived a joyful life full to the brim of sheer good health and satisfying mental activity. Socrates made no fuss about poverty. He took it in his stride as being nothing to worry over and put his attention upon matters that seemed to him more important.

3. The Socratic Method According to Aristotle the contributions made by Socrates to human knowledge were two—the "universal definition" and the "dialectical argument." The former phrase means that Socrates tried to establish definitions of justice, right, nobility, and so on that would be true under all conditions. The "dialectic argument" is the question-and-answer technique that comprises the Socratic method. It should be noted that both of these permanent contributions have to do with methods of attack upon problems rather than with actual knowledge. The conclusions Socrates reached through his methods were by no means as important as his methods.

Below appear three samples of the Socratic method. All are excerpts from longer discourses and cover only a single point. They should, however, serve to illustrate the essential nature of the method. In the first sample Socrates uses his question-and-answer technique for taking the conceit out of a young man who admired himself for his ability to recite Homer.* In the second he shows another young man that he is not yet ready to undertake serious civic duties. In the third he is trying to help a student find universal definitions of truth and falsehood.

FIRST DIALOGUE

Soc: Do you not remember that you declared the art of the rhapsode* to be different from the art of the charioteer?

Ion: Yes, I remember.

Soc: And you admitted that being different they would have different subjects of knowledge?

Ion: Yes.

Soc: Then upon your own showing the rhapsode, and the art of the rhapsode, will not know everything?

Ion: I should exclude certain things, Socrates.

Soc: You mean to say that you would exclude pretty much the subjects of the other arts. As he does not know all of them, which of them will he know?

Ion: He will know what a man and what a woman ought to say, and what a freeman and what a slave ought to say, and what a ruler and what a subject.

Soc: Do you mean that a rhapsode will know better than the pilot what the ruler of a sea-tossed vessel ought to say?

Ion: No, the pilot will know best.

Soc: Or will the rhapsode know better than the physician what the ruler of a sick man ought to say?

Ion: He will not.
Soc: But he will know what a slave ought to say?
Ion: Yes.
Soc: Suppose the slave to be the cowherd; the rhapsode will know better than the cowherd what he ought to say in order to soothe the infuriated cows?
Ion: No, he will not.
Soc: But he will know what a spinning-woman ought to say about the working of a wool?
Ion: No.
Soc: At any rate he will know what a general ought to say when exhorting his soldiers?
Ion: Yes, that is the sort of thing which the rhapsode will be sure to know.
Soc: Well, but is the art of the rhapsode the art of the general?
Ion: I am sure that I should know what a general ought to say.
Soc: And judging of the general's art, do you judge of it as a general or a rhapsode?
Ion: To me there appears to be no difference between them.
Soc: What do you mean? Do you mean to say that the art of the rhapsode and the general is the same?
Ion: Yes, one and the same.
Soc: Then he who is a good rhapsode is also a good general?
Ion: Certainly, Socrates.
Soc: And you are the best of Hellenic rhapsodes?
Ion: Far the best, Socrates.
Soc: And you are the best general, Ion?
Ion: To be sure, Socrates; and Homer was my master.
Soc: But then, Ion, what in the name of goodness can be the reason why you, who are the best of generals as well as the best of rhapsodes in all Hellas,* go about as a rhapsode when you might be a general? Do you think that the Hellenes want a rhapsode with his golden crown and do not want a general? [21]

SECOND DIALOGUE

Next Socrates asked, "Well, Glaucon, as you want to win honour is it not obvious that you must benefit your city?"

"Most certainly."

"Pray don't be reticent, then; but tell us how you propose to begin your services to the state?"

As Glaucon remained dumb, apparently considering for the first time how to begin, Socrates said:

"If you wanted to add to a friend's fortune, you would set about making him richer. Will you try, then, to make your city richer?"

"Certainly."

"Would she not be richer if she had a larger revenue?"

"Oh yes, presumably."

[21] Jowett, *op. cit.*, Vol I. condensed from pp. 508–510.

"Now, tell me, from what sources are the city's revenues at present derived and what is their total? No doubt you have gone into this matter, in order to raise the amount of any that are deficient and supply any that are lacking."

"Certainly not," exclaimed Glaucon, "I haven't gone into that."

"Well, if you have left that out, tell us the expenditure of the city. No doubt you intend to cut down any items that are excessive."

"The fact is, I haven't had time for that yet either."

"Oh, then we will postpone the business of making the city richer; for how is it possible to look after income and expenditure without knowing what they are?"

"Well, Socrates, one can make our enemies contribute to the city's wealth."

"Yes, of course, provided he is stronger than they; but if he be weaker, he may lose what he has got instead."

"True."

"Therefore, in order to advise her whom to fight, it is necessary to know the strength of the city and of the enemy, so that, if the city be stronger, one may recommend her to go to war, but if weaker than the enemy, may persuade her to beware."

"You are right."

"First, then, tell us the naval and military strength of our city and then that of the enemies."

"No, of course I can't tell you out of my head."

"Well, if you have made notes, fetch them, for I should greatly like to hear this."

"But I tell you, I haven't yet made any notes either."

"Then we will postpone offering advice about war too for the present. You are new to power, and perhaps have not had time to investigate such big problems. But the defence of the country, now I feel sure you have thought about that, and know how many of the garrisons are well placed and how many are not; and you will propose to strengthen the well-placed garrisons and to do away with those that are superfluous."

"No, no; I shall propose to do away with them all, for the only effect of maintaining them is that our crops are stolen."

"But if you do away with the garrisons, don't you think that anyone will be at liberty to rob us openly? However, have you been on a tour of inspection, or how do you know that they are badly trained?"

"By guess-work."

"Then shall we wait to offer advice on this question too until we really know, instead of merely guessing?"

"Perhaps it would be better."

"Now for the silver mines. I am sure you have not visited them, and so cannot tell why the amount derived from them has fallen."

"No, indeed, I have not been there."

"To be sure; the district is considered unhealthy, and so when you have to offer advice on the problem, this excuse will serve."

"You're chaffing me."

"Ah, but there's one problem I feel sure you haven't overlooked: no doubt you have reckoned how long the corn grown in the country will maintain the population, and how much is needed annually, so that you may not be caught napping should the city at any time be short, and may come to the rescue and relieve the city by giving expert advice about food."

"What an overwhelming task, if one has got to include such things as that in one's duties!"

"But you know, no one will ever manage even his own household successfully unless he knows all its needs and sees that they are all supplied. Seeing that our city contains more than ten thousand houses, and it is difficult to look after so many families at once, you must have tried to make a start by doing something for one, I mean your uncle's? It needs it; and if you succeed with that one, you can set to work on a larger number. But if you can't do anything for one, how are you going to succeed with many? If a man can't carry one talent, it's absurd for him to try to carry more than one, isn't it?"

"Well, I could do something for uncle's household if only he would listen to me."

"What? You can't persuade your uncle, and yet you suppose you will be able to persuade all the Athenians, including your uncle, to listen to you? Pray, take care, Glaucon, that your daring ambition doesn't lead to a fall!"[22]

THIRD DIALOGUE

"I propose, then, that we write "J" and "I", and then proceed to place under these letters "J" and "I", what we take to be the works of justice and injustice respectively."

"Do so, if you think it helps at all."

Having written down the letters as he proposed, Socrates went on: "Lying occurs among men, does it not?"

"Yes, it does."

"Under which heading, then, are we to put that?"

"Under "I.""

"Deceit, too, is found, is it not?"

"Certainly."

"And what if he deceives the enemy when at war?"

"That too is just."

"And if he steals and plunders their goods, will not his actions be just?"

"Certainly; but at first I assumed that your questions had reference only to friends."

"Then everything that we assigned to injustice should be assigned to justice also?"

"Apparently."

"Then I propose to revise our classification, and to say: It is just to do such things to enemies that it is unjust to do them to friends, towards whom one's conduct should be scrupulously honest."

[22] Marchant, *op. cit.*, Vol. IV, condensed from pp. 205–213.

"By all means."

"Now suppose that a general, seeing that his army is downhearted, tells a lie, and says that reinforcements are approaching, and by means of this lie checks discouragement among the men, under which heading shall we put this deception?"

"Under justice, I think."

"Suppose, again, that a man's son refuses to take a dose of medicine when he needs it, and the father induces him to take it by pretending that it is food, and cures him by means of this lie, where shall we put this deception?"

"That too goes on the same side, I think."

"And again, suppose one has a friend suffering from depression, and, for fear that he may make away with himself, one takes away his sword or something of the sort, under which heading shall we put that, now?"

"That too goes under justice, of course."

"You mean, do you, that even with friends straightforward dealing is not invariably right?"

"It isn't, indeed! I retract what I said before, if you will let me."

"Why, I'm bound to let you; it's far better than getting our lists wrong. But now, consider deception practiced on friends to their detriment: we mustn't overlook that either. Which is the more unjust deception in that case, the intentional or unintentional?"

"Nay, Socrates, I have lost all confidence in my answers; for all the opinions that I expressed before seem now to have taken an entirely different form. Still I venture to say that the intentional deception is more unjust than the unintentional." [23]

It is essential to the Socratic method that the series of questions lead to a definite point. The questioner often begins by asking the pupil to express his opinion on a given matter. The pupil commits himself to some point of view, and then the examiner starts to question him in detail, usually beginning with some point apparently so remote from the subject that the student does not see how he is being led into a complete contradiction. He admits one point after another, until suddenly he finds himself arriving at a conclusion which disagrees completely with his original assumption. Thus, for instance, a student may remark rashly that Luther* and Savonarola* have almost identical personalities. The teacher begins by asking him what Luther did on this and that occasion, and what traits these reactions show. Then follows a similar series of specific queries about Savonarola's behavior under this or that stimulus. Each successive, specific point seems in itself to be so clear and so harmless that the student readily agrees with it. With all the facts brought out, the teacher comes back to the original statement and wants to know if the pupil still thinks

[23] *Ibid.*, condensed from pp. 277–283.

the two men exactly alike. The student then discovers for himself that he has described two people who share a few traits and interests but who have more dissimilar than similar characteristics. He is therefore forced, upon logical grounds, to recant.* Unless the questions asked are organized to carry the pupil forward to a conclusion, the teacher is not using the method devised by Socrates.

A second element in the Socratic method is the use by the examiner of only those facts that his pupil already knows. If the examinee has to go to a library and collect more data before he can reach his new conclusion, the teacher has brought in a factor not included in the original technique. For true use of the method the examiner needs only to organize familiar facts and ideas in such a way as to bear upon the matter in hand. This characteristic should be noted in the above examples.

Throughout the world there are teachers who use the Socratic method. In the United States the proportion is perhaps smaller than elsewhere because most college classes are too large for much individual work, and the Socratic method cannot easily be employed with large groups, although some famous teachers have succeeded in so using it, by carrying on a typical discussion with one or two students while the others formed an attentive audience. Such a semi-dramatic situation probably duplicates the group environment of the original Socratic dialogues. It is, however, in small classes in small colleges that one generally finds the best exponents of the method. Not every teacher can use the Socratic approach successfully, even under the best of conditions, and many college teachers never try it extensively—perhaps because telling a student a conclusion is much simpler than drawing it out of him! However, as long as a few teachers continue to use the Socratic method for making students think, Socrates will still live, even though he has been dead for more than two thousand years.

B. THE SCHOOLS OF GREECE [24]

Ancient Greece was composed of many small city-states,* to each of which belonged the freemen within the city and those from its immediate neighborhood outside. Since the social units were so small, each city had distinguishing characteristics of its own; and each varied from the others more or less in its educational practices. The description below will be restricted mainly to

[24] The chief authority for the material in this section is K. J. Freeman, *The Schools of Hellas,* The Macmillan Company, 1922, 299 pp. See also T. Davidson, *The Education of the Greek People,* Appleton-Century-Crofts Company, 1894, 229 pp., and G. L. Dickinson, *The Greek View of Life,* Doubleday & Company, 1927, 261 pp., for admirable summaries of the ideational setting in which Greek education developed.

those features that were as nearly universal as any, although it applies more to Athenian schools during the period from 500 to 300 B.C. than to those of any other one period or city. It does not, however, refer to the education of boys in Sparta.

Until the age of about six, children remained at home and received no formal education, although they were presumably told stories about the gods and heroes of Greece. The boys from well-to-do families entered school at six, but the sons of artisans did not usually come for a year or two later. Girls did not attend school at any age. Indeed, for women, anything beyond training in household affairs was considered unseemly. The good wife and mother was supposed to be virtuous and respectable but not necessarily interesting. The ordinary woman received no education outside the home, and she spent her life in almost Oriental seclusion.

1. Elementary Schools The first school to which the Athenian boy was sent had a curriculum that consisted of the following three subjects: literature—which included reading and writing; music—which consisted of learning to play the lyre* and sing to it; and gymnastics. In the fourth century some work in drawing and painting was added. There were not only different teachers for each subject but also different schools. The teachers of Athens opened their schools as purely private enterprises, apparently fixing all fees and deciding upon what subjects they would offer. The parents then sent a boy to one school or another according to their means, the nature of the work given, and the ability of the teacher. The entire arrangement was just about what it is today if parents wish to select a private school for their children.

In the schoolroom, the master sat on a chair that had a back, while the assistants and pupils sat on chairs without backs. There were no desks. On the walls hung manuscript rolls, each one labeled with its author's name. These rolls constituted the school library. The boys had their own wax tablets for writing and their own lyres. In later centuries the rooms were decorated with busts of gods or heroes and with beautiful vases.

Reading in the Greek school started with learning the alphabet and learning to spell. For this purpose a queer sort of charades was invented. Each of several children represented a certain letter. These letters, taken in order, made a word. The children who were acting the scene sang a song that told about the letters. As each letter was described, the appropriate child assumed the shape of the letter he was representing. Then the letters took their places in pairs until all combinations were exhausted. The other pupils formed the audience, calling out the letters as they identified them and eventually discovering the word also. A sample from one of these songs appears below:

First such a circle is measured out
By compasses, a clear mark in the midst.
The second letter is two upright lines,
Another joining them across their middles.
The third is like a curl of hair. The fourth,
One upright line and three crosswise infixed.
The fifth is hard to tell: from several points
Two lines run down to form one pedestal.
The last is with the third identical.[25]

Even before the boys could read they listened to and memorized excerpts from Homer* and Hesiod.* As soon as they could recognize the letters they began to write. For this purpose they used a wax tablet that was hinged in the middle so that the two waxed halves could be folded against each other and thus protected when not in use. On this they wrote with a stylus or metal rod about as long as a pencil. One end was pointed for writing and the other flat for smoothing out the wax—that is, for erasing. In later centuries parchment* and papyrus* were used more or less, but the wax tablet was universal for practice work. The pupil held it on his knees. As soon as he could write, the teacher dictated passages for him to put down and memorize. The Greeks did not have any stories written especially for children; so the boys plunged at once into Homer. Presumably they did not understand every word, for Homer's Greek was already archaic, but they could have had little trouble with getting the meaning. They acted out scenes as they went along, and they discussed the background in great detail, thus learning history, geography, and philosophy. As much as possible was memorized. There were men who knew all of Homer by heart. In this task of rote* learning a boy had help outside school from the rhapsodes—men who went about the country singing the *Iliad** and *Odyssey*.* The Greek boy read little prose but much poetry and drama.

In the music school a pupil learned to play the five-stringed lyre, to tune it, and to sing to it. Sometimes he learned the flute also. In ancient Greece, as in any other cultured civilization, singing and playing instruments were looked upon as pleasant and desirable accomplishments.

Many details of the average boy's life in school are known from the pictures painted on vases that have been dug up in excavations throughout Greece. A few of these pictures appear on the following pages. In one of them, two classes are in progress. At the left is a boy having a lesson on the flute. In the middle sits a teacher with a tablet and stylus showing a boy how to write. The paidagogos* sits on a stool watching the boys. In the second pic-

[25] From K. J. Freeman, *The Schools of Hellas,* p. 90. Used by permission of The Macmillan Company, publishers. The original authorship is obscure.

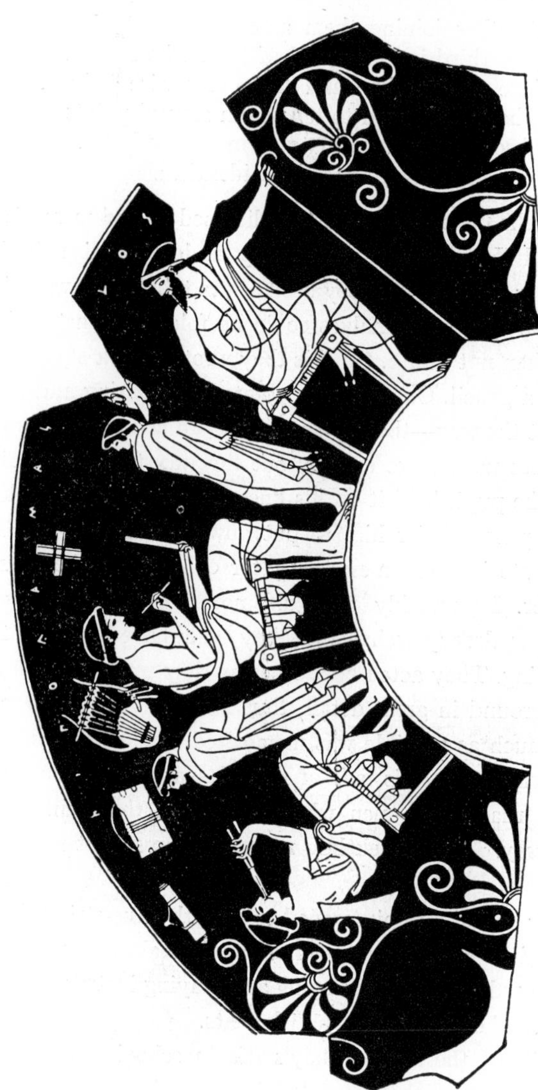

Fig. 2. School Scene (a). From the kulix of Douris, No. 2285, now in Berlin; *Monumenti dell' Instituto*, ix, Plate 54.

FIG. 3. School Scene (b). From the kulix of Douris, No. 2285, now in Berlin; *Monumenti dell' Instituto*, ix, Plate 54.

Fig. 4. School Scene (c). From a hydria in the British Museum; E. 172.

ture, one boy is playing the lyre under the observation of a teacher. Another is reading poetry. At the right sits the inevitable slave. Both pictures show the wall of the schoolroom, on which a number of things are hanging. There is a writing roll, a folded tablet, a lyre, and a T-square upon one wall, and two lyres, a shallow dish, an ornamental basket for carrying the writing rolls, and a flute upon the other. A third picture shows another scene in a music school. One boy is taking his lesson, another, accompanied by the slave, is just approaching to begin his, while a third is leaving, and a fourth sits on a chair awaiting his turn. From these pictures it is clear that instruction was individual.

The work in gymnastics was given in an open space called the palaistra. Every city had such a space set aside for exercise and physical education. It was used not only by schoolboys but by men throughout their lives. Grown men were, however, forbidden to enter beyond the dressing rooms when the boys were exercising. The palaistra was a fundamental institution. It was not merely a place for exercise but a place for bathing, for relaxation after exercising, for walking about, for discussion, and for meeting friends. Indeed, the educated Greek man spent much time there daily. Since palaistrai were built at public expense, every citizen might go and take what exercise he chose. There were seats for spectators as well as space for games. After the boys had reached military age they received training in the public palaistra at the expense of the state, but schoolboys generally had their work in private palaistrai that were owned and operated by special teachers of gymnastics.

At the palaistra the young boy learned to stand up straight, to walk gracefully, to sit down and get up smoothly, and to execute rhythmic dance steps. Simple calisthenics were soon added. All such exercises were done to the music of a flute. Later on, the boy learned to run, jump, box, wrestle, and throw both discus and javelin. The boys took all exercises in the palaistra naked, so that the sun would tan their bodies and keep them healthy. No lifeguard of today values his tan any more than a Greek gentleman did.

Typical scenes from the palaistra also appear upon Greek vases. At the left of one such picture, two young men are wrestling, under the supervision of a teacher, while a boy prepares the ground. In the second, two men are boxing, and the teacher is supervising, while a younger man is taping his hands with string preparatory to his boxing lesson. In the third picture, one boy is taking off for a broad jump and another is throwing a javelin. A teacher watches each. In the round insert two older lads are practicing with the javelin and the discus.

The teacher in the lower schools was paid very little for his services and was not held in much respect. To call a person an elementary school teacher

Fig. 5. Scene in Palaistra (a). From E. Gerhard, *Auserlesene Vasenbilder*, 1840, cclxxi, Fig. 2.

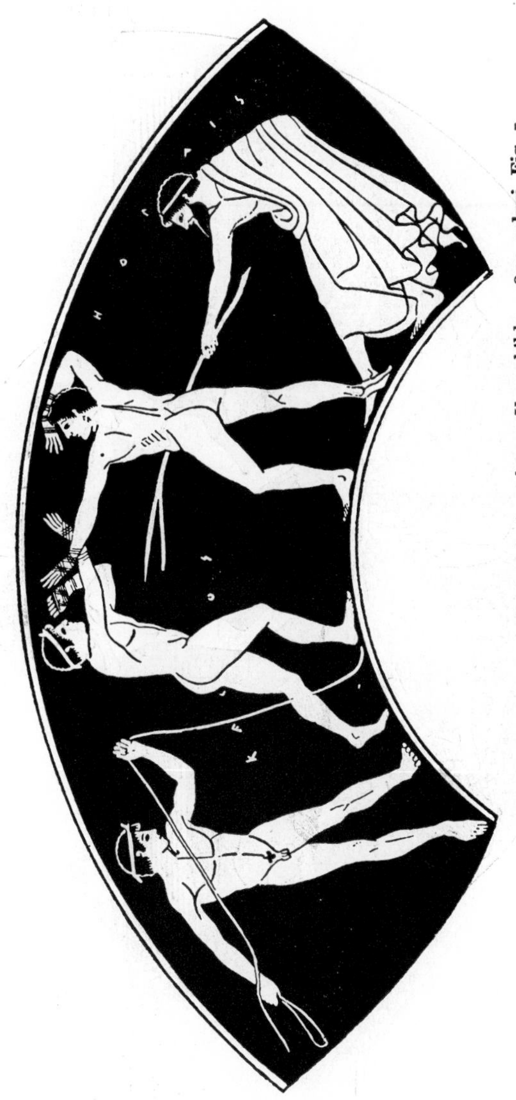

FIG. 6. Scene in Palaistra (b). From E. Gerhard, *Auserlesene Vasenbilder*, 1840, cclxxi, Fig. 1.

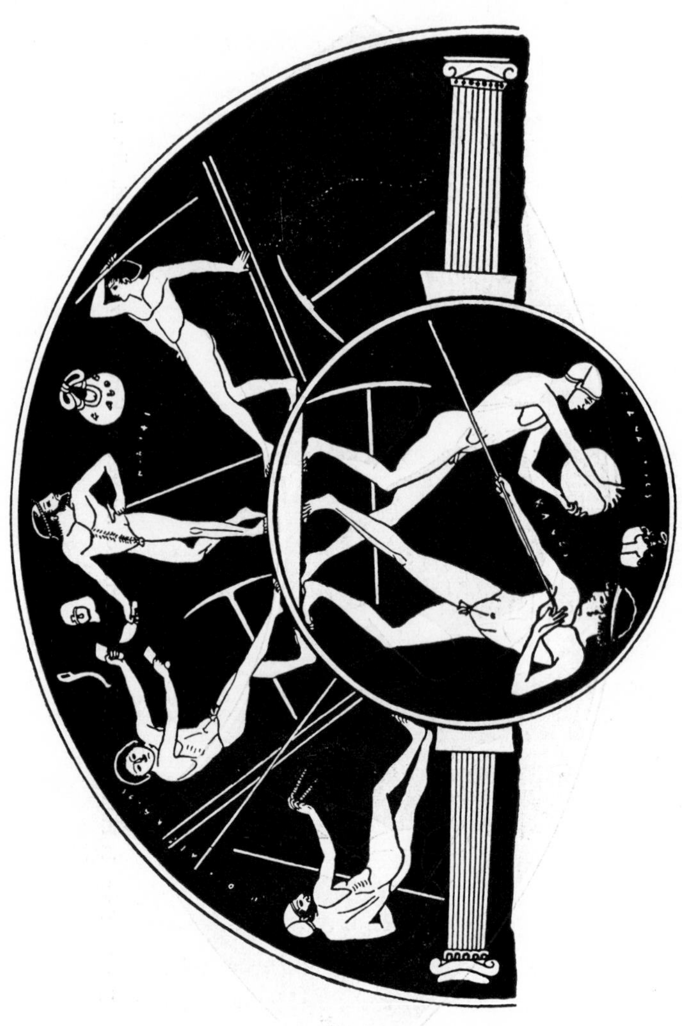

FIG. 7. Scene in Palaistra (c). From the *Archäologische Zeitung*, 1878, Plate II; kulix now in Munich.

was almost an insult. The fees charged could not have been large because even the poorest people could afford to send their sons for a few years to the elementary school.

A good description of a schoolboy's day, though actually written at a later period, appears below:

He gets up at dawn, washes the sleep from his eyes, and puts on his cloak. Then he goes out from his father's house, with his eyes fixed upon the ground, not looking at any one who meets him. Behind him follow attendants and paidagogoi, bearing in their hands the implements of virtue, writing-tablets or books containing the great deeds of old, if he is going to a musical school, the well-tuned lyre.

When he has laboured diligently at his intellectual studies, and his mind is sated with the benefits of the school curriculum, he exercises his body in liberal pursuits, riding or hurling the javelin or spear. Then the wrestling-school with its sleek, oiled pupils, labours under the mid-day sun, and sweats in the regular athletic contests. Then a bath, not too prolonged; then a meal, not too large, in view of afternoon school. For the schoolmasters are waiting for him again, and the books which openly or by allegory teach him who was a great hero, who was a lover of justice and purity. With the contemplation of such virtues he waters the garden of his young soul. When evening sets a limit to his work, he pays the necessary tribute to his stomach and retires to rest, to sleep sweetly after his busy day.[26]

This program went on every day except for feast days. There was no week-end respite from learning; in fact, there was no week end. The schoolboy was always accompanied to school by a slave who carried his material for him, remained with him every minute during his hours in school, and accompanied him home again. This slave was called the paidagogos—the word from which pedagogue is derived. A picture of a boy on his way to school, followed by his paidagogos, is shown in Figure 8. The paidagogos was a mixture of nurse, chaperon, and tutor. He had to follow his master's sons about and never let them out of his sight. He waited on the boys at home, walked to and from school with them, sat with them in the classroom, and guarded them against any persons who might corrupt either their manners or their morals. In fact, the chief care of the slave was to safeguard the morals of his charges. Boys in Athens were as carefully chaperoned as are girls in Spain. If there were more than one boy in a family, all of them had to go to the same school and the same palaistrai at the same time. In the case of unruly youngsters this stewardship must have been extremely difficult.

The same care for morals appears in the laws. Unauthorized persons were not allowed in the palaistrai when the boys were there. The hours during

[26] Lucan, *Loves*, 44–45.

which schools could be open were restricted to daylight hours, so that the boys might be safely home before dark. The lawgivers did not dictate what was taught in school or by what methods it was presented, but on the subject of morality they were explicit. The laws remained as stringent as ever, during the life of Socrates, but there appeared in the writings of the period some

FIG. 8. A Boy and His Paidagogos. From Th. Schreiber, *Atlas of Classical Antiquities,* 1895, Plate XL, No. 9.

This picture, reproduced from a red figured vase painting, shows a boy on his way to school accompanied by an aged paidagogos, who carries his young master's lyre.

complaints about the "modern" boy who is described as lacking in modesty, self-control, and good manners. The nostalgia for the "good old days" when boys were properly modest and docile was a favorite theme with the dramatists. A few lines from the famous "Clouds" of Aristophanes express the idea:

> To hear, then prepare of the Discipline rare which
> flourished in Athens of yore,
> When Honour and Truth were in fashion with youth and
> Sobriety bloomed on our shore;
> First of all the old rule was preserved in our school
> that "boys should be seen and not heard":
> And then to the home of the Harpist would come
> decorous in action and word
> All the lads of one town, though the snow peppered down,
> in spite of all wind and all weather;
> And then sang an old song as they paced it along, not
> shambling with thighs glued together:
> "O the dread shout of War how it peals from afar" or
> "Pallas the Stormer adore,"
> To some manly old air all simple and bare which their
> fathers had chanted before.

And should anyone dare the tune to impair and with
intricate twistings to fill,
Such as Phrynis is fain, and his long-winded train,
perversely to quaver and trill,
Many stripes would he feel in return for his zeal,
as to genuine Music a foe.[27]

2. *Secondary and Higher Education* For some centuries general schooling stopped at a relatively elementary level. Even before the age of Pericles, however, a desire for further schoolwork developed. Private secondary schools were therefore opened. Most of these were short-lived because the teachers moved about from city to city, but a few were permanent. Attendance was purely voluntary. These schools were intended for carrying on a boy's education during the years until he was eighteen. The sons of poor parents probably stopped their formal education at about the age of thirteen or fourteen and were apprenticed to a trade, often their father's; but if parents could afford it, boys continued their studies in the more advanced type of school about to be described.

The subjects taught, whether the school was permanent or temporary, varied with the interests of the teacher. Any one or more of many subjects might be discussed in public or private lectures. Mathematics included plane and solid geometry, the theory of numbers, and arithmetic. Pupils learned to reckon dates, to weigh and measure, and to use the abacus*—the adding machine of antiquity. Some teachers talked of astronomy and physics, but there was no experimentation or laboratory work. There was usually further study of music and literature, a great deal of rhetoric, some composition, and oratory. The latter was useful because men frequently made speeches—if not in public, then at the houses of friends. Some study of history and law might be included. And there was always exercise to be taken at the palaistra.

Secondary education in Greece had a peculiarly fluid quality because it depended in the main upon wandering teachers. These men simply arrived in a community and lectured. When a sufficient number of prospective pupils had become interested, the teacher retired to a private room and charged admission. These teachers remained in a given place for a while—probably until they had said all they had to say and their enrollment began to fall off—and then moved on to another city. As a teacher Socrates was unusual because he did not wander about, except within the confines of Athens, and he did not accept fees. These itinerants exerted a great influence upon both the tone and the nature of education, at the secondary and higher levels. They dealt with

[27] Aristophanes, *The Clouds,* translated by B. B. Robers, G. P. Putnam's Sons, 1930, p. 256, lines 960–973.

many different subjects and were immensely valuable in disseminating culture and spreading ideas throughout Greece.

Although the state used no compulsion except for military training, it did hold competitions and give prizes. The honor and prestige incident to winning these prizes were sufficient to make any boy do his best and go to school as long as he could. A few lists showing the results of these competitions have come down from antiquity. It should be noted that the boys were grouped by ages before entering the competition: [28]

Senior Class

For rhapsody,* Zoilus
For reading, Zoilus

Middle Class

For rhapsody, Metrodorus
For reading, Dionusikles
For general knowledge, Athenaias
For painting, Dionusias

Junior Class

For rhapsody, Herakles
For reading[a]
For calligraphy*
For torch race
For playing lyre with fingers
For playing lyre with plectron
For singing to lyre
For reciting tragic verse
For reciting comedy
For reciting lyric verse

[a] From here on, the names of the winners are missing.

This competition was a strictly intellectual one. Others gave prizes mainly for races of different length, boxing, and wrestling. A picture of a contest, as shown upon a vase, appears in Figure 9.

The schools of philosophy belong partly to secondary, partly to higher, and partly to adult education. Attendance was limited by ability and interest rather than by age. The philosopher usually taught in his own home or garden, or in a borrowed room. Aristotle lectured for a few students in the morning and gave a public lecture in the afternoon. Plato walked up and down his garden as he talked to a small band of the chosen.

The wandering philosophers were even more casual about where they taught. The teacher of antiquity carried his total equipment in his head and was ready for action at practically any time and in any place.

3. Military Training At the age of eighteen the boy had to go through two years of military training, the first in Athens and the second on the borders. This third level of training was controlled by the state. It was, indeed, the only part of a boy's education that was required. The seriousness of these years is reflected by the wording of the oath taken by the prospective soldier:

[28] Bockh, 3088, quoted in Freeman, *op. cit.*, p. 63.

I will not disgrace my sacred weapons nor desert the comrade who is placed by my side. I will fight for things holy and things profane, whether I am alone or with others. I will hand on my fatherland greater and better than I found it. I will hearken to the magistrates, and obey the existing laws and those hereafter established by the people. I will not consent unto any that destroys or disobeys the constitution, but will prevent him, whether I am alone or with others; I will honour the temples and the religion which my forefathers established. . . . So help me Zeus.*[29]

FIG. 9. A Foot Race. From a Panathenaic amphora, Museum Antiker Kleinkunst, Munich.

Originally the training given was exclusively physical, but after Athens ceased to be a military power and military duties became voluntary, this single type of work was replaced to some extent by courses in philosophy and literature.

The city-states needed loyal and well-trained soldiers, as may be deduced from the frequency with which Athens required military service. In the 166 years from the beginning of Athenian supremacy to its end, there were 116 of war and 45 of peace. To be sure, the Athenian citizen army did not usually fight in winter; the service was not, therefore, continuous. The Athenian citizen

[29] Pollux, *Onomasticon,* book viii, ll. 105–106

fought at least part of three years out of every four. The extraordinary stress put upon citizens in all Hellenic cities to keep themselves in good physical condition is quite understandable. The effects of such training were dramatically demonstrated at the battle of Thermopylae,* when 300 Spartan citizen soldiers stood shoulder to shoulder in a narrow defile, fought off thousands of Persian attackers, were not overcome until a traitor showed the Persians a path around to their rear, and then died in their tracks to the last man—still fighting.

Greek education has thus many elements that, fused together, produced the educated man of ancient Athens. In summary, one can perhaps do no better than to quote a famous passage from Plato on the subject of the educational process from birth to maturity:

> Education and admonition commence in the first years of childhood, and last to the very end of life. Mother and nurse and father and tutor are quarreling about the improvement of the child as soon as ever he is able to understand them; he cannot say or do anything without their setting forth to him that this is just and that is unjust; this is honorable, that is dishonorable; this is holy, that is unholy; do this and abstain from that. And if he obeys, well and good; if not, he is straightened by threats and blows, like a piece of warped wood. At a later stage they send him to teachers, and enjoin them to see to his manners even more than to his reading and music; and the teachers do as they are desired. And when the boy has learned his letters and is beginning to understand what is written, as before he understood only what was spoken, they put into his hands the works of great poets, which he reads at school; in these are contained many admonitions, and many tales, and praises, and encomia* of ancient famous men, which he is required to learn by heart, in order that he may imitate or emulate them and desire to become like them. Then, again, the teachers of the lyre take similar care that their young disciple is temperate and gets into no mischief; and when they have taught him the use of the lyre, they introduce him to the poems of other excellent poets, who are the lyric poets; and these they set to music, and make their harmonies and rhythms quite familiar to the children's souls, in order that they may learn to be more gentle, and harmonious, and rhythmical, and so more fitted for speech and action; for the life of man in every part has need of harmony and rhythm. Then they send them to the master of gymnastic, in order that their bodies may better minister to the virtuous mind, and that they may not be compelled through bodily weakness to play the coward in war or on any other occasion. This is what is done by those who have the means, and those who have the means are the rich; their children begin education soonest and leave off latest. When they have done with masters, the state again compels them to learn the laws, and live after the pattern they furnish, and not after their own fancies; and just as in learning to write, the writing master first draws lines with a style for the use of the

young beginner, and gives him the tablet and makes him follow the lines, so the city draws the laws, which were the invention of good lawgivers who were of old time; these are given to the young man, in order to guide him in his conduct whether as ruler or ruled; and he who transgresses them is to be corrected, or, in other words, called to account, which is a term used not only in your country, but also in many others.[30]

READING REFERENCES

In this list and in those at the close of subsequent chapters the full citation is given for only those books that do not appear in the footnotes of the chapter; for these books it is given only at their first appearance. The lists include some rather old books as well as new ones, since the former are often still good and are available in small libraries that do not have the newer ones. Moreover, a contemporaneous description of a school is often better than anything written later is likely to be. The last section in each list, that on translations of primary sources, is sometimes shorter than desirable because certain works have not been translated or else have appeared in such obscure places that they are not accessible.

A. General Histories of the Period

Botsford, G. W., and C. A. Robinson, *Hellenic History,* The Macmillan Company, 1939 (398 pp.), chaps. 4, 7, 9, 12, 14, 25.

Breasted, J. H., *Ancient Times: A History of the Early World,* Ginn and Company, 1916 (742 pp.), chaps. 10–16, 21.

Caldwell, W. E., *The Ancient World,* Rinehart & Company, 1937 (590 pp.), chaps. 11–13.

Jardé, A., *Formation of the Greek People,* Routledge and Kegan Paul, Ltd., 1926 (359 pp.), part iv, chaps. 1, 2, 4.

Laistner, M. L. W., *History of the Greek World from 479–323 B.C.,* Methuen & Co., Ltd., 1936 (492 pp.), chaps. 20–22.

Prentice, W. K., *The Ancient Greeks,* Princeton University Press, 1940 (254 pp.), chaps. 5, 6.

Reisner, E. H., *Historcial Foundations of Modern Education,* The Macmillan Company, 1927 (513 pp.), chaps. 3, 4.

B. Other Texts in the History of Education

Boyd, W., *The History of Western Education,* A. and C. Black, Ltd., 1932 (4th ed., 452 pp.), chaps. 1, 2.

Cole, P. R., *History of Educational Thought,* Oxford University Press, 1931 (316 pp.), book i, pp. 3–54.

[30] Plato, *The Protagoras* (translated by B. Jowett) Clarendon Press, 1924 ed., pp. 146–148. Used by permission of the publishers.

Cubberley, E. P., *History of Education,* Houghton Mifflin Company, 1920 (849 pp.), chap. 2.

Graves, F. P., *A Student's History of Education,* The Macmillan Company, 1936 (rev. ed., 547 pp.), chap. 3; or the corresponding chapters in the separate books in the history of education by the same author: *Before the Middle Ages,* 1909, 304 pp., and *During the Middle Ages, and The Transition to Modern Times,* 1910, 328 pp.

Monroe, P., *A Textbook in the History of Education,* The Macmillan Company, 1930 (772 pp.), chap. 3; or the corresponding chapter in this author's *Brief Course in the History of Education,* The Macmillan Company, 1907, 409 pp.

Moore, E. C., *The Story of Instruction,* The Macmillan Company, 1936–1938 (2 vols.), Vol. I, chap. 3.

C. Secondary Sources

Adams, James, *Religious Teachers of Greece,* University of Aberdeen, 1904–1906 (467 pp.), pp 320–355.

Becker, W. A., *Charicles, or Illustrations of the Private Life of the Ancient Greeks* (translated by F. Metcalfe), Longmans, Green and Co., 1889 (5th ed., 512 pp.), pp. 61–73, 109–129.

Cross, *Socrates: The Man and His Mission,* chaps. 3, 5–7, 12, 13.

Dobson, J. F., *Ancient Education and Its Meaning for Us,* Longmans, Green and Co., 1932 (203 pp.), chaps, 2, 3.

Freeman, *Schools of Hellas,* chaps. 5, 6.

Laurie, S. S., *Historical Survey of Pre-Christian Education,* Longmans, Green and Co., 1895 (426 pp.), pp. 196–300.

Taylor, *Socrates,* chaps. 2, 3.

Tucker, T. G., *Life in Ancient Athens,* The Macmillan Company, 1922 (323 pp.), chap. 9.

van Hook, L. R., *Greek Life and Thought,* Columbia University Press, 1923 (329 pp.), chap. 11.

Wilkins, A. S., *Education in Greece in the Fourth Century before Christ,* G. E. Stechert and Company, 1911 (167 pp.), chap. 2.

D. Translations of Primary Sources

Jowett, *The Dialogues of Plato:* "Lysis" (entire); or "Euthyphro" and "Crito," or the "Apology" or the first half of the "Protagoras." Although Jowett's is the best one, any other translation of Plato may be used.

Marchant, *Xenophon, Memorabilia and Oecomomicus,* book i, chaps. 1–6.

CHAPTER III

QUINTILIAN AND THE SCHOOLS OF ROME

The hero of the present chapter was born after the Roman Empire was firmly established and after the earlier republican institutions of Rome had either fallen into decay or disappeared altogether. The very greatest periods of Roman glory had perhaps gone by, but prestige from the Augustan Age* still lingered on, and Rome remained for nearly two more centuries the ruler of the world. The city must have been an exciting place in which to live and work.

In both his life and his personality Quintilian exemplifies the typical upper-class citizen of the period during which Rome ruled the world. He was by profession a lawyer, orator, senator, and teacher. After some twenty years of public life, Quintilian retired from his professional career and—at the insistence of friends—wrote a sizable book, which, though concerned primarily with the subject of rhetoric, nevertheless gives many sidelights upon general methods of teaching. To be sure, Quintilian is not to be regarded as average or typical, but rather as an example of Roman teaching at its best.

A. QUINTILIAN: HIS LIFE AND WORK

1. Quintilian's Life[1] Quintilian was born in northern Spain, between A.D. 30 and 40. As a boy he went to Rome to study oratory and then returned to Spain, where he remained for less than a decade, working as lawyer and teacher. Of his life up to some age between twenty-eight and thirty-eight little else is known, but in the year A.D. 68 he came again to Rome and remained there the rest of his life. He was a client* of the current emperor at the time of his return to Rome, and a few months later he was appointed as the first public professor of Latin rhetoric in Rome. He was paid from the imperial treas-

[1] Based upon B. Appel, *Das Bildungs-* und *Erziehungs-Ideal Quintilians nach der Institutio Oratoria,* Auer, 1914, 95 pp.; W. Guthrie, *Quintilian's Institutes of Eloquence,* Vol. I, Dewick and Clark, 1905, 448 pp.; A. Gwynn, *Roman Education from Cicero to Quintilian,* Clarendon Press, 1926, 260 pp.; E. Jullien, *Les Professeurs de littérature dans l'ancienne Rome et leur enseignment depuis l'origine jusqu'à la mort d'Auguste,* Leroux, 1885, 378 pp.; J. Loth, "Die Padagogischen Gedanken der Institutio Oratoria Quintilians," Doctor's Thesis, University of Leipzig, 1898; J. Sandys, *A History of Classical Scholarship,* Cambridge University Press, 1906 (2nd ed., 3 vols.), Vol. I; W. M. Smail, *Quintilian on Education,* Clarendon Press, 1938, 143 pp.

ury, and the position was the equivalent of a job for life in the imperial civil service. Quintilian thus became the most outstanding figure among the Roman teachers of his period, especially after his appointment, toward the end of his life, as tutor to the emperor's adopted sons. This appointment seems to have carried with it the rank of consul,* the most sought after honor among Roman citizens.

During the last years of his life, Quintilian wrote a book usually called the *Institutes of Oratory,* although a more expressive and descriptive title would be *The Education of an Orator*. The first section of this work deals with the proper education of a boy before he begins to study rhetoric; the second section discusses the studies that in Quintilian's opinion are proper to a school of rhetoric.[2] The rest of the book, up to the final chapter, is devoted to the theory of rhetoric. At the end, there is a section of advice for the orator who has left school but wishes to improve his standing in his profession. In the course of his writing, Quintilian gives a good deal of information about the current schools at the secondary level. Elementary education was assumed to be given to children by a tutor at home. In reading Quintilian one must remember that he was a distinguished man writing about the education of boys in patrician* families. He is not concerned with the proletariat* but with the training of future leaders for his country.

The importance of the orator in the guidance of the state was a theme that had already been discussed by Cato* and Cicero.* The former had defined an orator as "vir bonus dicendi peritus" (a good man, able to speak). The latter wrote: "In my opinion no one can hope to be an orator in the true sense of the word unless he has acquired knowledge of the sciences and of all the great problems of life." Quintilian merely reiterated these same ideas but in even more forceful form. To quote his own words;

> Now according to my definition no man can be a complete orator unless he is a good man; I therefore require that he should be not only all-accomplished in eloquence but possessed of every moral virtue.[3]
>
> Now I have undertaken to educate a perfect orator, who I insist must be a good man . . . because none but a good man can speak well.[4]
>
> I should prefer the practice of morality to the endowments of eloquence, but in my opinion they are one and the same thing and cannot be separated. For I account no one to be an orator, if he is not an honest man.[5]

There was, however, a vital difference between Quintilian's social and political background and that of the two earlier writers on the value of ora-

[2] See Gwynn, *op. cit.,* pp. 200–218.
[3] Guthrie, *op. cit.,* I, 3.
[4] *Ibid.,* p. 115.
[5] *Ibid.,* p. 18.

tory. In the days of Cicero, Rome was a republic, and orators who could sway the Roman Senate* were leaders in their country. For instance, although a general named Antonius actually put down the serious rebellion led by Catiline,* it was Cicero in the senate who proved Catiline's guilt and so moved his listeners as to wipe out any sympathy for the conspiracy. History has forgotten about Antonius, but Cicero the orator still lives in the minds of men. In the century between Cicero and Quintilian, Rome had become an empire. To be sure, the senate still met, but what was said by its members had little bearing on the practical aspects of government, although some of the emperors paid more attention than others to advice offered them by the senate. The oratory of Cicero's day was developed for the purpose of persuading others into action, but that of Quintilian's had of necessity degenerated because no practical action could result, no matter what was said. The objective of oratory had automatically become to please and to interest an audience, not to convince it. As a result, emphasis was put upon flourishes of style, cleverness in handling of details, and introduction of erudite bits that were often irrelevant. Against this tendency Quintilian fought, but in vain, since degeneration was already begun and the causes that underlay the decay were not such as could be affected by the writings of one earnest schoolteacher.

One has to remember that in ancient days the number of books was limited, and that there were no newspapers or magazines. Opinions were therefore circulated almost wholly by word of mouth. Hence, the man who could speak well had an immense advantage over the one who could not. Almost without exception the famous men of Rome were good speakers who controlled public opinion by the authority, soundness, and brilliance of their oratory.

Quintilian died at some time after A.D. 86—the exact year is not known—full of honors, after a singularly successful life for a schoolteacher.

2. *Quintilian's Character* One can judge of Quintilian's character mainly from his own writings. He is mentioned by contemporaries, to be sure, but for the most part in his public capacities. All agreed that he was a fine orator and a man of blameless character. Even the satirist Juvenal,* who said little that was nice about anyone, describes him as admirable, vigorous, intelligent, well bred, sensible, and noble. Another writer named Martial,* who wrote witty and often unpleasant epigrams* about people, referred to Quintilian as an honor to the Roman toga.* If Juvenal and Martial could find nothing to criticize in Quintilian, there was nothing. Other contemporaries and some of his pupils mention him in much the same terms.

From his own writings one may deduce a bit more about what manner of person he was. In the first place, he was a typical upper-class Roman, with a public-spirited interest in the development of statesmen for the service of the state. In this point of view Quintilian was essentially Roman. No other people have made such a fetish of government, and in no other country have the most educated men so dedicated themselves to public service.

Next to his burning enthusiasm to safeguard the state by the development of virtuous leaders comes Quintilian's sound common sense. The Romans were not, in general, an imaginative people; like other outstanding men of his time, Quintilian was practical, sensible, and shrewd. Such passages as those quoted below, taken at random from a number of different topics, illustrate these characteristics.

There are some who think that a superior teacher will not attend to details in teaching, either because he will not condescend to so inferior a practice or because he is utterly incapable of doing so. For my part I exclude from the rank of professor every man who shall think attention to details beneath his notice, and I affirm that the abler a master is the more capable he is of descending to them. In the first place, we must suppose that the man who excels in eloquence has most accurately attended to all the means of getting it. In the next place, method is of great importance in teaching, and the best master practices the best methods. In the last place, no man who is eminent in great matters can be supposed to be deficient in small ones, unless we can imagine that Phidias*—after finishing a masterly statue of Jupiter*—may find himself outdone by another in the ornaments of the figure, or that a great orator cannot maintain a common conversation, or that an eminent physician cannot cure a stomach ache.[6]

People say that boys have their morals debauched at public schools. I grant this sometimes to be true; but they are likewise sometimes debauched at home. And I am thoroughly convinced that one could find many instances to prove that—both at home and at school—morals have sometimes been ruined and sometimes preserved inviolate. Supposing a youth to have a natural propensity to vice; supposing no care to have been taken in forming and cultivating his morals during the earliest period of his life; supposing this, I say, and he will find opportunities for practicing vice even in solitude.[7]

It might be argued that a great number of pupils prevents a teacher from instructing and inspecting them as he should. Everything has its inconveniences, and I shall admit this to be one, but let me set the advantages against the disadvantages. I am not in favor of sending a boy to a school where he will be neglected. But we cannot suppose that an able master will encumber himself with a greater crowd of scholars that he can manage . . . if a teacher has but a moderate tincture of learning he will, for his own credit, cherish application and genius wherever he finds them. But suppos-

[6] *Ibid.*, p. 86.
[7] *Ibid.*, p. 18.

ing that we were to condemn very large schools (a point to which I cannot agree when the numbers are drawn together by the merits of the teacher) it will not follow that we are to condemn all public schools. To condemn all is one thing; to choose the best is another.[8]

The professor ought not only to inculcate truths, but he ought frequently to examine his pupils and make trial of their capacities. Thus they never will be off guard, nor will his rules slip through their memories, while at the same time they are learning to judge for themselves. For what other purpose has teaching than that a pupil may at last be under no necessity of being taught? [9]

These passages cover a variety of topics, but on all of them Quintilian showed a practical intelligence and an independence of mind. His opinions are not especially dramatic or exciting, but he never wrote nonsense.

Quintilian is sometimes called the first of the classicists; that is, he was the first writer to look back upon the great period of Latin literature in much the same way as today's classical enthusiast, with the difference that he felt himself so immediate a descendant of the classical tradition that he believed a return to the glories of republican Rome still possible. He looked back with special admiration upon Cicero as the personification of perfect oratory. His enthusiasm for the Augustan Age was so great that he concentrated most of his teaching effort upon the Roman authors—Cicero, Virgil,* Livy,* Sallust,* and Horace*—and spent little time upon the great writings of Greece. Perhaps the greatest contrast between him and his idol Cicero was that the latter made history by being a leader among men of affairs while the former only taught about making history by being such a leader. Quintilian wrote his own motto, probably without intention, in the words: *Studendum vero semper et ubique*.[10] This is the sentiment of a schoolteacher.

In only one passage of Quintilian's book does the author become personal. In this instance, however, he is a vividly real human being whose feelings bridge more than eighteen centuries of time. The major part of this passage appears below:

Your commands, my friend, prevailed on me to undertake this work. At the same time, I own I had an eye towards gratifying my own pleasure, in leaving to my son, whose promising genius claimed all the cares of a tender parent, this book, as the most valuable legacy I could bequeath. Thus, if the fates had been so just and so kind as to shorten my days, he still might have had his father for his guide and his instructor.

But, while day and night I was applying myself to finish my book,

[8] *Ibid.*, p. 21.
[9] *Ibid.*, p. 86.
[10] "Indeed, one must study always and everywhere."—*Institutes*, book x, l. 727.

while I was earnestly forwarding it, for fear of being overtaken by death, fortune suddenly laid me so low that all the result of my labours profits no one less than myself. Yes! a repeated blow of fate put out the light of my life by taking from me my darling son, the pride of my hopes, the prop of my bending age. . . . My wife I had lost before she had completed the nineteenth year of her life, after making me the father of two sons. . . . So wretched was I rendered by this single stroke, that it was beyond the power of fortune to restore my happiness. . . . But still the dear pledges she left behind her gave me comfort; as did the reflection, that, unkind and unnatural as it was in her to leave me alive, she had her wish, in escaping by untimely death every pang that can distress nature. While plunged in affliction for her, the loss of my younger son—who was but in the fifth year of his age—took half of all that could make me wish for life.

However, the pride of my wish, the joy of my life, my young son Quintilian, still remained alive, to make amends for all the afflictions I had suffered. . . . By all my woes, by the torture of my soul, by those dear shades which my grief now idolizes, I swear that I had discovered in him such acquirements of learning, such fondness for study, such excellency of genius (I appeal to his teachers), as in the course of my long experience, I never knew excelled. He possessed every virtue of candor, affection, tenderness, and generosity. . . . Even every accidental advantage centered in my boy: his voice was strong and distinct, his aspect lovely; and he spoke the two languages of Greece and Rome with as much propriety as if he had been a native of the one as well as of the other. All these were only promising appearances, but he possessed real virtues. He had resolution, sedateness, and a courage that was proof against pain and fear. With what spirit, even to the astonishment of his physicians, did he bear up against the pains of his disease; how he even endeavored to comfort me amidst his dying agonies! and how, during all his fits and ravings, there still was a meaning in his words, that discovered the love of learning to be uppermost in his mind! . . .

In living I have a purpose which justifies me. For it is not in vain that wise men have observed, that learning alone brings relief to misery. Should the waves of my present affliction subside; should my sorrows admit of other ideas, than those that possess me now; I then shall crave pardon from the public, for so long delaying this work. For, surely, no one will be surprised that a work should be delayed, when it is surprising that it was not completely laid aside. But, if the following books should in their composition bear the marks of the affliction I suffer, let it not be imputed to my negligence, but to my sorrows; which, though they have not extinguished, have damped the vigour of my genius, which never was extraordinary. But let me now make headway against them with the greater resolution. Fortune has done her worst against me; and, amidst all my calamities, I find my work a firm, though an unhappy, security.

Meanwhile, I am in hopes the public will take my labours in good part, because they have been continued for no private or particular purpose of my own. All the pains I have taken have been for the sake of strangers. All my writings, if they contain aught that is instructive, must now instruct strangers; and the fruits of my brain, as well as the acquisitions of my fortune, must go to those who are aliens to my blood.[11]

Behind those sentences one can see a man of at least middle age who was deeply attached to his family, as were most Romans. He lost first his wife, then his younger son, and finally his older son for whom he had originally undertaken the writing of his masterpiece. Now he has nothing left but his work, which he is finishing that other people's children may profit by it.

Quintilian's constant emphasis upon moral character may be attributed to more than one source. As will become clear as this book progresses, all great teachers have been concerned with this same matter. An outstanding teacher often arises at a time when education is at a low ebb and reforms are needed. Most of them are, therefore, vitally interested in character and personality. "Character education" is nothing new, although each reformer seems to think he has invented it. During Quintilian's lifetime some of the influences that led to the eventual downfall of the Roman Empire were already in evidence. On the surface, to be sure, there was wealth and prosperity, but a man of Quintilian's ability could hardly have failed to note the gradual disappearance of the sterling, early Roman character and the insidious replacement of virtue and hardihood by luxury and softness. He wanted virtue partly because all good Romans did, partly because all good teachers do, and partly because he did not see enough of it in the society about him.

From all the above quotations Quintilian emerges as a personality—a man with a clear, sane mind, an excellent understanding of and love for children, a passionate interest in teaching, a deep love for his country, an undaunted courage, and all the instincts of a gentleman. He had, naturally, certain shortcomings, but not many. Perhaps he was too serious, too earnest, and too humorless; in these respects, however, he was only a typical man of his nationality. Educated Romans were not much given to lightness and wit, and in Quintilian's case his personal tragedies had doubtless robbed him of whatever gaiety he might formerly have had. Perhaps the most unusual thing about him was his modernity. One is naturally not to suppose that all Roman schools were managed along the progressive lines laid down by Quintilian. He rather a reflection of Latin education at its best.

3. Quintilian's Methods of Teaching Quintilian's Institutes of Oratory contain twelve sections, each of which is called a "book." In book i Quintilian presents his ideas of what training should be given at home by parents

[11] Condensed from Guthrie, *op. cit.*, pp. 373–379.

or tutor. Book ii treats of the instruction to be given in the school of grammar, the work of which preceded the study of rhetoric. Books iii–xi contain Quintilian's course of study, samples of his exercises, comments on which authors may best be read, analyses of arguments into their constituent parts, advice on style and manner of delivery, and so on. There are occasional side lights and excursions into general methodology, but for the most part these nine books are of relatively little concern to the teacher of today. In book xii, which seems to have been written for the orator already in service, Quintilian expounds his ideas on the characteristics of the perfect orator and the perfect oratory, together with some sage advice about when a man should retire from a public career and what activities are appropriate for one who approaches the end of life. Book xii also contains three chapters on the value of philosophy, jurisprudence,* and history in the training of an orator.

What Quintilian has to say about children, types of discipline, and general methods of teaching is just as valuable for teachers today as it has been for eighteen centuries, for Quintilian showed an especially good understanding of child psychology. One of his ideas was to start training a boy as soon as possible. To quote his own words:

> Some have been of the opinion that a boy's education ought not to commence until a boy is seven years of age, because his mind is neither capable of instruction nor able to stand the strain. They however who think that every moment of the time ought to be usefully employed are more defensible in their opinion. I am however aware that during all the time I speak of (before seven years) a child can hardly make as much progress as he will in a year later on. But how can the time be better employed than in education from the moment a child begins to talk? For it is certain he will constantly be doing something. Or why should we despise the results, be they ever so little, that may be made before the seventh year? And indeed, small as the progress is that a child can make under this age, yet he will be capable later on of greater improvement because during the preceding period he has improved a little. This improvement continued for years becomes considerable in the whole; and every hour saved in early childhood is so much acquired later on.[12]

This passage could be used today as an argument for sending a child to nursery school.

Quintilian noticed that the childish mind differs from an adult mind not only in the amount it can learn but in the way it functions. Thus a good memory, a power of imitation, and a general modifiability provide the mental basis for early teaching. On these points he has the following comments:

> In children the chief symptom of capacity is memory. Its properties are

[12] *Ibid*., p. 11.

two-fold: a ready understanding and a firm retention. The next symptom is imitation. For that too is the property of a docile nature.[13]

Quintilian was quite aware that children cannot apply themselves for long at a time without undue fatigue. He writes: "I am not however so without understanding of childhood as to suggest that children be treated with severity or that a full task be required of them. For we ought to be extremely careful that a boy does not conceive an aversion for learning before he can have a love for it and that he does not preserve in later years a dislike for what once gave him pain." [14] The same point is brought out in another passage that relates to boys of school age:

> Meanwhile, all boys require some relaxation from study; not only because we know nothing that can bear with perpetual application . . . but because application to learning depends upon his inclination, which is a thing that is not to be compelled. For this reason, the minds that generally resist compulsion, when refreshed and repaired, return to study with double vigour and keenness. Neither am I displeased with a boy who is fond of diversion; for even that is a sign of sprightliness; and when I see a boy always sour and always serious, I never can think that he will pursue his studies with any spirit, when at the time of life which nature has chiefly fitted for the love of diversion, he is dull and indifferent about it. A mean, however, is to be observed in this respect; for a total prohibition of diversions may give a boy an aversion to learning, and too frequently exercising them may bring him into a habit of idleness.[15]

These excerpts make clear that Quintilian had no idea of letting children overwork or of treating them as if they were grown people.

On the matter of motivation Quintilian appears to especially good advantage. These passages compare well with what the modern teacher does to stimulate children to their best efforts.

> Let study be made a child's diversion; let him be soothed and caressed into it; and let him sometimes test himself upon his proficiency. Sometimes enter a contest of wits with him, and let him imagine that he comes off the conqueror. Let him even be encouraged by giving him such rewards that are most appropriate to his age.[16]
>
> I remember that my masters observed a custom that had its advantages. For they distributed their pupils into grades. When we repeated our lessons, each boy took his place according to his proficiency. Thus everyone had a chance to advance in proportion to his improvement. Each boy fought hard for the place he took, and his ambition was crowned when he became head of

[13] *Ibid.*, p. 25.
[14] *Ibid.*, p. 13.
[15] *Ibid.*, pp. 26–27.
[16] *Ibid.*, p. 13.

his grade. But he had more than one chance for this, for if he missed it once he had another opportunity a month later. Thus the head boy never grew remiss, and the others eagerly waited for a chance to show themselves. So far as I could judge, this method was a sharper spur to our application than were all the lectures of our teachers, the cares of our tutors, or the wishes of our parents.[17]

The youngest beginners find it more agreeable, because it is easier, to imitate their school-fellows than their masters. For children when in the first rudiments of learning will not aspire to the very limit of it at once. They will rather choose to cling to what is closest. This observation is so true that the teacher who prefers what is serviceable to what is showy will make it his business, while the mind is still unformed, not to overburden the pupil but to accommodate himself to the latter's abilities. It is, therefore, best to associate a pupil with those companions whom he is first to imitate and then to outdo. Thus he will gradually develop hopes of achieving excellence.[18]

Pupils ought sometimes to be allowed to read their own compositions. They will then regard delivering them as a reward for their study and they will take a pride in having deserved this reward.[19]

The emphasis upon encouragement and rewards and the idea of introducing the play spirit into schoolwork sound quite modern. In fact, these passages are reminiscent of many from the pens of the present-day progressives.

Like most of the good teachers who have appeared in the world's history, Quintilian disapproved of corporal punishment. Few people have expressed themselves more forcibly on the matter.

I am by no means in favor of whipping boys, though I know it to be a general practice. In the first place, whipping is unseemly, and if you suppose the boys to be somewhat grown up, it is an affront in the highest degree. In the next place, if a boy's ability is so poor as to be proof against reproach he will, like a worthless slave, become insensible to blows. Lastly, if a teacher is assiduous and careful, there is no need to use force. I shall observe further that while a boy is under the rod he experiences pain and fear. The shame of this experience dejects and discourages many pupils, makes them shun being seen, and may even weary them of their lives.[20]

These are the words of a good teacher who is able through the force of his personality, the excellence of his learning, and the enthusiasm with which he approaches his work so to control and interest his pupils that he does not have to use punishment.

Quintilian gives a good statement of the supposedly modern doctrine of individual differences. Actually, almost every great teacher has emphasized this

[17] *Ibid.*, p. 23. In considering this passage one should remember that in the schools of the period the children came from the upper classes of society and were thus more nearly equal in ability than is the case at present. Such a competitive system would not be satisfactory now.

[19] *Ibid.*, p. 91. [18] *Ibid.*, p. 23. [20] *Ibid.*, p. 27.

point. What is new in recent times is the general acceptance of the doctrine and its wide application—not the concept itself.

> It has generally and deservedly been accounted a great merit in a master to observe the different capacities and disposition of his pupils, and to know what nature has chiefly fitted them for. For in this report, the variety is so incredible, that we meet with as many different kinds of capacities as of persons. . . . Most teachers think that the proper way to educate a youth is to cherish, by instruction, the peculiar talents which nature has given him and to assist his progress in that walk into which his genius leads him. . . . a master of eloquence, after a sagacious inspection, can pronounce that such a boy's genius leads him to a close, polished manner of speaking; and others a keen, a weighty, a smooth, a sharp, a bright, or a witty manner. He will then so adapt himself to everyone, as to improve each in that manner for which nature has chiefly fitted him. For nature may be greatly assisted by art; and a young man who is set upon a study that is disagreeable to his genius, can never make any considerable advance in that study, and by abandoning the path chalked out by nature, he will make a poor figure even in those studies for which she has designed him. It is indeed absolutely necessary to consult a younger genius, and to encourage him to strike into that walk of learning for which nature has fitted him. One may be fit for the study of history, another for poetry, another for the law, and some perhaps may be fit only to follow the plough.[21]

Or, in another short passage:

> When a teacher has observed his scholars well, he can soon judge in what manner each pupil is to be managed. Some are indolent unless they are pushed on; some dislike being commanded; fear awes some and disheartens others; some hammer out their learning; while others strike it out at a heat. Give me a boy who rouses when he is praised, who profits when he is encouraged, and who cries when he is defeated. Such a boy will be fired by ambition; he will be stung by reproach and animated by preference. Never shall I expect any bad consequences from idleness in such a pupil.[22]

In addition to the general concept of individual differences among children it is a common modern idea that pupils should begin a new subject when they have the necessary development to understand it, regardless of chronological age. This point had evidently occurred to Quintilian, for he says: "It is likewise my purpose to inquire into what time a boy is ripe for studying the rules of rhetoric. In this inquiry we are not influenced so much by the consideration of a pupil's age as by his proficiency." [23] Quintilian had no "readiness tests"* on hand, but he did have a keen observation that led him to see the essentials.

In Quintilian's day there was much argument as to whether boys of good family should go to a public school or have a tutor at home. Quintilian

[21] *Ibid.*, pp. 92–93. [22] *Ibid.*, p. 26. [23] *Ibid.*, p. 25.

was decidedly in favor of the public school, on a number of grounds. First, the children are better off together. The "free and open intercourse among pupils" is preferable to the "gloom and solitude" of being instructed at home. Second, the boy who is to become an orator must "from childhood be habituated to company," and this adjustment he cannot make if he remains in isolation from his fellows. Third, schoolboys form friendships that often endure throughout life. Finally, the teaching in public schools is usually better than the teaching at home because only a man of mediocre ability will undergo the drudgery of being a private tutor. And even if a father can afford to hire a competent professor, this man will not do as well with a single pupil as he could with a large number. "Masters when they have only one pupil to instruct do not convey their instructions with that spirit, that efficacy, that energy which characterizes them when they are instructing a number. A man feels a certain secret indignation rise within himself when he uses upon a single auditor those powers which he has so laboriously acquired. . . . Were every audience to consist of a single hearer there would be no such thing as eloquence upon earth."[24] These arguments are certainly sane. If one wants to educate boys to take part in public life and to be leaders, one could hardly devise a poorer method than to keep them at home alone. The value of socialization for normal growth is also intimated.

Quintilian wanted schoolwork to reflect as closely as possible the realities of life outside school. Thus, when a pupil wrote a theme he should write on some subject from his daily life. When he was old enough to practice trying cases before his classmates, he should select a case that—while relatively simple—was of a type such as were actually tried in courts, instead of using purely fanciful situations that had no counterpart in reality. When a student practiced a speech, he should take as his topic some issue of current public interest. The artificialities of his day he heartily deplored, and he fought manfully against the type of eloquence currently prevalent and popular. Three brief quotations from writers a little before, during, or a little after Quintilian's lifetime reveal the decadence* that had already overtaken Roman culture, Roman eloquence, and Roman education:

> A man who composes a declamation does not write to convince but to please. That is why he seeks out tricks of style and leaves the argument alone, because it is troublesome and gives little scope for rhetoric. He is content to beguile his audience with his *sententiae** and digressions; and he wants to be applauded, not to win his case.[25]

[24] *Ibid.*, p. 24.
[25] Seneca the Elder,* *Controversiae,* Vol. IX, preface, §1.

We educate ourselves for the schoolroom, not for life; hence the extravagances with which we are troubled, in literature as everywhere else.[26]

Here I know that I am talking nonsense; but I say many things to please my audience, not to please myself.[27]

In contrast to these apologies for a defense of bad taste, Quintilian's excellent sense stands out, as when he wrote in criticism of the artificial materials used for training pupils in declamation:

What is the use of conciliating a judge when there is no judge, of narrating what is plainly false, of proving a case that will never come up for decision? [28]

Quintilian wanted a return to sanity, to normality, and to practical training for practical ends, but the tide of history was against him.

Quintilian left a considerable heritage for succeeding generations. His rhetoric was used during his lifetime and in the following centuries as a textbook and then—after being lost for a thousand years and found toward the end of the fifteenth century[29]—was again widely used throughout Europe for another five hundred years. Wherever his book went, his ideas about treatment of children, individual differences, and motivation went with it. At intervals ever since, people have "discovered" Quintilian and have found in him much of profit to themselves. Thus, during the Renaissance and Reformation the majority of writers on education borrowed largely from Quintilian's work, without always knowing it. Of Quintilian himself there is a good deal still left in education today, although most people who talk glibly about charac- ter training, education for citizenship, pupil-teacher relationships, the psychology of rewards, the ineffectiveness of corporal punishment, or the need for socialization among children do not know that they are repeating things already well said by a teacher in Rome over eighteen centuries ago.

B. THE SCHOOLS OF ROME

In speaking of Roman education,[30] one needs always to make clear what period is involved, since the nature of the education and the types of schools

[26] Seneca the Younger,* *Letters to Lucilius,* no. 106, l. 12.

[27] The remark of a popular speaker of the day as quoted by Seneca, *Controversiae,* Vol. IX, chap. 6, l. 12.

[28] *Institutes,* Vol. II, chap. 10, § 8.

[29] The manuscript was found in the library of St. Gallen,* Switzerland, in the early years of the Renaissance,* when scholars were hunting all over Europe for lost copies of the classics.

[30] This section is based upon G. Clarke, *Education of Children in Rome,* The Macmillan Company, 1896, 168 pp.; Gwynn, *Roman Education from Cicero to Quintilian;* A. S. Wilkins, *Roman Education,* Cambridge University Press, 1914, 98 pp.; S. G. Williams, *History of Ancient Education,* Bardeen's Inc., 1903, 298 pp.

varied from time to time, as the primitive Roman forms of education were supplanted by or fused with the more advanced Greek ones with which the Romans eventually came in contact. It is therefore desirable to divide this brief presentation into sections upon a chronological basis. The first will deal with the distinctively Roman education of the period from the earliest time up until about 200 B.C. The second will trace in general outline the modifications of this basic Roman model as Greek influences were brought to bear upon it over a period of two centuries and will emphasize the fundamental differences in educational concepts and practices between the two great democracies of the ancient world. The third section will contain a description of what might be called the "school system" of the Roman Empire, a system that emerged as the Greek and Roman cultures, religions, and educational ideas fused to produce a Graeco-Roman civilization. This third period extended roughly from the beginning of the Christian Era until well into the fourth century and gradually crumbled from inner decay, just as the Roman Empire itself disintegrated.

1. Early Roman Education The earliest references to the training of the younger generation make it evident that education was primarily of the spirit, not of the intellect. A boy became subject to silent but powerful forces such as the good examples of his older male relatives, the influence of a close family life, and the national traditions of his people. This indirect sort of control produced high ideals of service to one's family and to one's country. The early Romans emphasized also the utilitarian objectives in education, for they were quite as practical as they were high-minded. The training was intended to produce simultaneously a good man and a skilled man. The usual method for reaching this dual objective was the development of an apprenticeship system within the family and its connections. From his earliest childhood, a boy accompanied his father in the daily round of business and learned how to conduct himself through his father's precept and example. When the time came for a young man to enter a profession, he attached himself to the retinue of some distinguished man, either a relative or a family friend, who taught him, by example rather than by deliberate instruction, and acted as his sponsor. Among the lower classes, the same sort of training led into the trades and various phases of business.

The method outlined above had its weaknesses, among which is the obvious one of its dependence upon the character and ability of a single person, the father of each family. If the father were unwilling or unable to train his sons, they were practically certain to remain uneducated and always to be more or less handicapped. While a father might become the best influence in a boy's life, he might also become the worst. The arrangement also put little faith in formal education. It is likely that boys learned to read, write, and do simple measuring as part of their apprenticeship. The proportion of illiterates among citizens was probably quite low. What paternal education did not often produce, however, was learning. The future citizen was taught to be good and to earn his living, but not to be erudite. "Book learning" was an incidental and accidental feature of education.

It is difficult to find out how far distant in the past there were Roman schools as institutions separate from the home or a class of teachers who were not the parents of those they taught. Certainly, the existence of schools does not reach back into primitive times in Rome as it did in Athens, where one finds mention of them as early as the sixth century B.C., or in Sparta, where schools probably existed even earlier. There were surely schools of some kind in Rome in the third century before Christ, but they did not become common or open to the general public until later.

The early education of boys in the families of Roman citizens had thus its values and its shortcomings. It molded the young through the imitation of its elders, it taught respect for age and tradition, and it gave training in utilitarian skills. Many systems that had more formal organization have accomplished less.

2. *Influence of Greek upon Roman Education* By contrast, the education of the Greek boy was carefully planned by the state and was conceived as the means by which he became acquainted with his literary and cultural heritage, in order that he might ultimately both serve his state and develop his own capacities to their highest level. The Greek ideal of culture thus depended upon deliberate school instruction for the acquisition of knowledge, as the basis of both character and proper civic service. The Greek and Roman ideals in education had much the same objectives in seeking to develop virtue and a desire for public service, but they were at variance as to the means for reaching these ends; moreover, the Greeks stressed the ideals of general culture and of self-development, whereas the Romans preferred the ideal of utilitarian, vocational training by means of apprenticeship. When the two modes of thought came into contact with each other, it was inevitable that conflict should arise.

One cannot date with exactness the beginnings of Greek influences upon the natives of what is now Italy, because the first infiltrations were local, indirect, and relatively minor. Greek colonies were established in Sicily* as early as the sixth century B.C., and goods had been exchanged between Greece and the Italian Peninsula even earlier. With the traders and colonists came the Greek language, culture, and gods. By the first half of the third century B.C. Greek was so commonly known among educated people that an orator could address the Roman Senate in that language and be understood. The lower classes also must have become somewhat familiar with Greek, because the popular dramatists of the time often used jokes which involved a play on Greek words. Hellenic* influence entered Rome also through the ever-increasing number of Greek slaves, especially after the conquest of Greece in the second century. Thus after a single victory, 15,000 Greeks were sold as slaves. Every household among people who were themselves above serfdom contained at least one slave and usually many. These slaves were often more educated than their masters. A conspicuous example was Livius Andronicus, whose translation of Homer into Latin was the main textbook for the lower schools throughout the next two or three centuries. As a reward for his work he was liberated and subsequently exerted great influence upon the use of Greek in the schools. Another man who had been a slave—one Spurius Carvilius—was the first person to conduct what appears to have been a public school to which anyone might come who could pay the fee. Until his time—the last of the third century B.C.—teachers as well as lawyers had given their services free, although they expected gifts in return. By the beginning of the third century Greek had assumed approximately the place in Roman education that Latin still has in some schools today, especially in England. It was the language that educated people learned and was the hallmark of the upper social classes. As soon as this situation developed, the third source of Greek influence appeared—the direct importation of teachers and philosophers from Greece for the purpose of further spreading the culture. Some of these immigrants gave lectures that were tremendously popular, some opened schools, and some became tutors in prominent families. These men were so successful in Hellenizing* certain groups among the Romans that they were more than once expelled from Rome, because the more patriotic citizens thought their own customs and culture were being threatened with extinction.

The antagonism between Roman and Greek educational ideas and the gradual absorption of the former by the latter continued for nearly two centuries. The passage quoted below contains a vigorous summary of the situation in A.D. 75. By this time the Greek influence was predominant, but many a die-hard conservative still thought the old Roman ways were the better. The comparison of the old and the new in educational thought provides, incidentally, a good description of both.

. . . Before I enter on the subject, let me premise a few words on the strict discipline of our ancestors, in educating and training up their children. In the first place the son of every family was the legitimate offspring of a virtuous mother. The infant, as soon as born, was not consigned to the mean dwelling of a hireling nurse, but was reared and cherished in the bosom of its mother, whose highest praise it was to take care of her household affairs, and attend to her children. It was customary likewise for each family to choose some elderly relation of approved conduct, to whose charge the children were committed. In her presence not one indecent word was uttered; nothing was done against propriety and good manners. The hours of study and serious employment were settled by her direction; and not only so, but even the diversions of the children were conducted with modest reserve and sanctity of manners. . . . The consequence of this regular discipline was that the young mind, whole and sound, and unwarped by irregular passions, received the elements of the liberal arts with hearty avidity. Whatever was the peculiar bias, whether to the military art, the study of the laws, or the profession of eloquence, that engrossed the whole attention, that was imbibed thoroughly and totally.

In the present age what is our practice? The infant is committed to a Greek chambermaid, and a slave or two, chosen for the purpose, generally the worst of the whole household train, and unfit for any office of trust. From the idle tales and gross absurdities of these people, the tender and uninstructed mind is suffered to receive its earliest impressions. Throughout the house not one servant cares what he says or does in the presence of his young master; and, indeed, how should it be otherwise? since the parents themselves are so far from training their young families to virtue and modesty, that they set them the first examples of luxury and licentiousness. Thus our youth gradually acquire a confirmed habit of impudence, and a total disregard of that reverence they owe both to themselves and to others. To say truth, it seems as if a fondness for horses, actors, and gladiators, the peculiar and distinguishing folly of this our city, was impressed upon them even in the womb: and when once a passion of this contemptible sort has seized and engaged the mind, what opening is there left for the noble arts? Who talks of anything else in our houses? . . .

[In] the practice of our ancestors . . . the youth who was intended for public declamation, was introduced by his father, or some near relation, with all the advantages of home discipline and a mind furnished with useful knowledge, to the most eminent orator of the time, whom thenceforth he attended upon all occasions; he listened with attention to his patron's pleadings in the tribunals of justice, and his public harangues before the people; he heard him in the warmth of argument; he noted his sudden replies; and thus, in the field of battle, if I may so express myself, he learned the first rudiments of rhetorical warfare. The advantages of this method are obvious: the young candidate gained courage, and improved his judgment; he studied in open day, amidst the heat of the conflict, where nothing weak or idle could be said with impunity; where everything absurd was instantly rebuked by the judge, exposed to ridicule by the adversary, and condemned by the whole body of advocates. In this way they imbibed at once the pure and uncorrupted streams of genuine eloquence. But though they chiefly attached themselves to one particular orator, they heard likewise all the rest of their contemporary pleaders, in many of their respective debates; and they had an opportunity of acquainting themselves with the various sentiments of the people, and of observing what pleased or disgusted them most in the several orators of the forum.* Thus they were supplied with an instructor of the best and most improving kind, exhibiting, not the feigned semblance of Eloquence, but her real and lively manifestation: not a pretended, but a genuine adversary, armed in earnest for the combat; an audience, ever full and ever new, composed of foes as well as friends, and where not a single expression could fall uncensured, or unapplauded. . . .

On the other hand, our modern youth are sent to the mountebank schools of certain declaimers called rhetoricians: a set of men who made their first appearance in Rome a little before the time of Cicero. And that they were by no means approved by our ancestors plainly appears from their being enjoined . . . to shut up their *schools of impudence,* as Cicero expresses it. But I was going to say, our youths are sent to certain academies, where it is hard to determine whether the place, the company, or the method of instruction is most likely to infect the minds of young people, and produce a wrong turn of thought. There can be nothing to inspire respect in a place where all who enter it are of the same low degree of understanding; nor any advantage to be received from their fellow-students, where a parcel of boys and raw youths of unripe judgments harangue before each other, without the least fear or danger of criticism.[31]

In the field of rhetoric especially was the Greek influence dominant. After the middle of the second century B.C. the prominent orators all studied the principles and methods of Greek rhetoric, even though some of the more violently patriotic among them—Cicero, for instance—tried hard not to let anyone know it! As long as the republic was in existence (up until 31 B.C.) a mastery of Greek was still looked upon with a bit of suspicion as being a possibly subversive influence. Indeed, the attitude was not unlike that of many Americans toward Russia at the present time—a fear that foreign influence would undermine national institutions. The transfer of technique in rhetoric from Greece to Rome was, however, quite undeniable. Since Quintilian wrote primarily on this subject he was greatly indebted to Greek influences within the field of his specialty. However, in common with other solid citizens of Rome he would not accept the elegant flourishes with which the later Greeks adorned their speeches. To him, as to other Romans, an oration was a practical means to a practical end—the proper guidance of the state—and not an exercise in verbal ingenuity.

3. The "School System" of Rome It is not to be supposed that the Roman Senate or the early emperors set up a system of schools or even took more than a sporadic interest in such as existed. The schools sprang up spontaneously. It seems reasonable that they were basically a response to the need for a wide and scholarly education for the future citizens of a city that ruled the

[31] Tacitus, *Dialogue concerning Oratory,* condensed from Chaps. 28, 29, 34, and 35.

known world. The later emperors exercised indirect control over schools through the appointment of teachers and some degree of direct control in those schools opened and maintained by imperial decree, but in the century and a half before Christ and for a similar period afterward, the schools of Rome and those of the many cities under Roman influence were independent undertakings.

There appear to have been three types of school. The lowest was the "ludus" or elementary school, in which children learned reading and writing, simple arithmetic and a little history and literature through the medium of

FIG. 10. Styli, Capsa, and Roll. From Th. Schreiber, *Atlas of Classical Antiquities*, Plate IX, No. 7.

The stylus was used by the Romans for writing on wax tablets. The capsa was a round box made of light wood and used for carrying rolls of parchment and papyrus. The rolls were customarily wound up on a stick, to the end of which was attached a label for identification of the contents. The roll in the illustration is not wound on a stick.

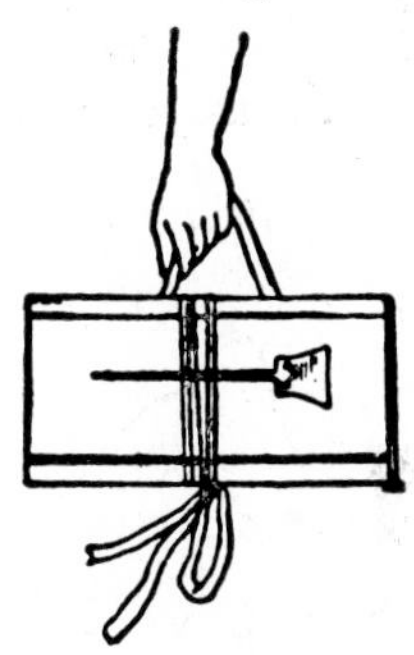

FIG. 11. Writing Materials. From Th. Schreiber, *Atlas of Classical Antiquities*, Plate XC, No. 5.

Wax tablets were fastened together with a cord, having a stylus attached. The wax surface was in a sunken portion of the board, which was scratched by the stylus. When a clean surface was required, the blunt end of the stylus was used to smooth out the wax.

anecdotes and poetry. Children commonly entered this school when they were seven years old. By the beginning of the first century B.C. a Latin translation of Homer's *Odyssey* had been added to the original Roman content of this school's curriculum. The school was commonly held on a veranda. The teacher sat at a desk on a platform, and his assistants—if he had any—on stools placed on the floor. The pupils sat on wooden benches. When they wrote they used wax tablets which they held upon their knees. For equipment they had their wax tablets, a stylus for writing on them, and some manuscript books—large rolls carried in a container. Before the invention of printing, most books were written on long sheets and then rolled up in this fashion. A picture of a young man reading from a wax tablet appears in Figure 12.

The school began very early. Ovid, Martial, and Juvenal all complain in one way or another about the noise children made in going to school before daylight. Martial especially expressed himself in no uncertain manner on this point.

> What right have you to disturb me, abominable schoolmaster, object abhorred alike by boys and girls? Before the crested cocks have broken silence, you begin to roar out your savage scoldings and blows. Not with louder noise does the metal resound on the struck anvil, when the workman is fitting a lawyer on his horse; nor is the noise so great in the large amphitheater, when the conquering gladiator is applauded by his partisans. We, your neighbors, do not ask you to allow us to sleep for the whole night, for it is but a small matter to be occasionally awakened; but to be kept awake all night is a heavy affliction. Dismiss your scholars, brawler, and take as much for keeping quiet as you receive for making a noise.[32]

FIG. 12. Youth Reading a Wax Tablet. From Th. Schreiber, *Atlas of Classical Antiquities,* Plate XC, No. 6.

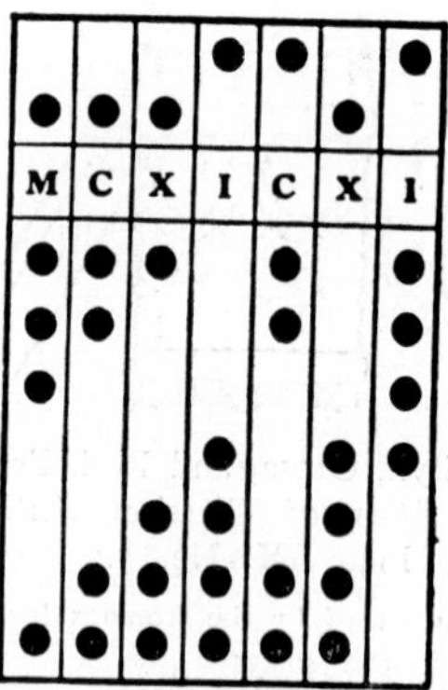

FIG. 13. An Abacus. From E. P. Cubberley, *History of Education,* p. 65. By courtesy of Houghton Mifflin Company, publishers.

Pebbles were used, those nearest the numbered dividing partition being counted. Each pebble above when moved downward counted five of those in the same division below. The board now shows 8,760,254.

The instruction in the ludus was almost certainly poor. Before the children began to read anything, they had to learn by heart the names of the letters and all the possible combinations of syllables. In later years they wrote down from dictation what the teacher said, read it aloud, and memorized it. Writing was taught by guiding the pupil's hand as he scratched the shape of the letters into his wax tablet. The Roman system of writing numbers made arithmetic extremely difficult. As a result the children acquired the fundamentals through elaborate methods of counting on the knuckles, through the use of pebbles as markers, and through the use of the abacus, such as is shown in Figure

[32] Martial. *Epigrams.* Book ix, no. 68.

13. This last device was a complicated board marked out by lines and furnished with knobs that slid in grooves. One could do simple sums upon it, but the labor was great as compared to calculations with Arabic numerals. Let the student compare the same sum in Roman and Arabic numerals and then try to solve the former!

Roman	*Arabic*
XXI + CCCXLIX — CXCIV × XXVIII ÷ XXXIII =	21 + 349 — 194 × 28 ÷ 33 =

The teachers in the elementary schools were not usually educated men; they knew neither how to interest the pupils nor how to teach. The children were therefore restless at best and often rebellious against a training that was

Fig. 14. A Roman School. From a fresco found at Herculaneum.

meaningless and dissociated from daily life. Consequently, it was necessary to employ extremely harsh discipline. The hot temper of the teacher was almost proverbial. Seneca comments upon the inconsistency by which "an excessively angry master argues (the need of) not being angry," Martial mentions the rod as the "sceptre of the school teacher," and Cicero offers the somewhat dubious excuse that "whosoever has an especially quick and fertile mind teaches in an angry and harassed manner; for the person who is quick to learn is tortured when he sees his instruction understood slowly." For minor offenses the teacher used a ferule—or ruler—with which he struck the pupil's hand, but for serious faults he had a whip made from leather thongs with which he beat the boy across the bare back, as depicted in Figure 14. This treatment seems cruel today, but the ancients in general were inclined to the belief that "the man who has not been flogged is not trained." A stern and even cruel discipline was by no means out of keeping with the Roman character, but the practice was doubtless influenced by the beating of slaves. The implements for flogging were therefore at hand. Even if a modern teacher had any desire to thrash a child, he would have a hard time finding any such whip as the Roman master used. All in all, the references to these schools paint a rather gloomy picture. It is probable that for the children of the lower classes among the citizens education in school did not extend beyond the ludus.

Above the ludus were two other types of institution, the grammar school and the school of rhetoric. Both were Greek institutions and were originally conducted only by Greeks. In Quintilian's day, the grammar school had become in the main preparatory to the school of rhetoric, although some masters, in order to hold on to their pupils a few years longer, gave work that paralleled that of the more advanced school.

During the classical period both Greek and Latin grammar schools existed, and some pupils attended both; in this case, they usually went first to the Greek school. The difference between the two appears to have been mainly that in the one they learned Greek only and in the other they studied both languages. The work of the grammar schools centered around Homer and Virgil, with incidental additions from other poets and dramatists. The *Odyssey* and the *Aeneid** were studied intensively not only as literature but as sources of history, geography, religion, customs, and morals. In work of this sort a teacher had a chance to deal with such matters of style and theme as are today discussed by teachers of English literature. The training in these schools included also work in composition, which varied from asking a child to reproduce in his own words the story of a fable, to demanding original compositions on themes derived from the Greek or Roman classics. Most of the work in composition was of necessity oral, since there was no paper to write on. The pupil began his speaking career with simple narration, progressed to the discussion and illustration of maxim and proverbs, and eventually graduated into themes chosen from his reading in the classics. At this point, his oral exercises took a turn toward argumentation. This change was usually coincident with his entrance into the school of rhetoric. Another common exercise was the translation of stories in Greek into Latin, or vice versa.

Boys entered the grammar school at about the age of twelve. Usually, these boys were not graduates of the ludus, but boys who had had tutors at home, where they had acquired the elementary skills in reading, writing, and arithmetic. The length of time the boys remained in school varied with the individual. Some lads seem to have attended two or three grammar schools one after another before entering the school of rhetoric. Others attended several grammar schools without ever going any further, while some lingered on for years in a single school.

The methods of instruction doubtless depended upon the interests and personality of individual teachers, but from the comments one can only assume that the work rested predominantly upon memory and that the same harsh discipline prevailed as in the lower schools. The most common method of instruction seems to have been the lecture, to which the students listened passively while they took down notes. The notebooks must have been much like those of modern students. Quintilian was greatly pleased with the full and accurate notes of some pupils and greatly distressed by others because he found them confused and teeming with mistakes. Sometimes a particularly good set of notes were circulated as a crib, much to the disgust of the master. All of this sounds as if schoolboy psychology were unchanging.

The third type was the school of rhetoric, of which Quintilian in the main wrote. The ages of the boys in this school seem to have varied a good deal. They might enter as early as fourteen years of age and they might remain at least as late as twenty-five years. Probably the majority of the boys were between the ages of sixteen and twenty. In the school of rhetoric they studied debating, oratory, and law; they also read many prose writers in both Greek and Latin. In some cases the curriculum was undoubtedly presented as a narrow, technical training for the future orator and statesman, but in others the linguistic and literary training was of a high order, the quality of each particular school being dependent upon the ability and personality of the master.

The work of the school centered about the training of effective speakers. Continuing with the exercises of the grammar school, the boys began with simple problems in argumentation. For instance, they selected some story or incident, paraphrased it, argued the truth of it, compared and contrasted it with more or less similar stories, reached a conclusion as to its meaning, and usually ended with an exhortation concerning its moral applications. The work included also some consideration of the theory of rhetoric, training in inflection of the voice, in the selection of words, in the development of arguments, and even in where and how to introduce a joke. Along with this work went a good deal of practice in declamation, which consisted of reciting from memory a passage from some author or a production of one's own. It was a common thing for a boy to write a speech, have his master correct it, memorize it, and then declaim it before his parents and friends. While these methods of education should have developed whatever power to think a student had, they easily lent themselves to abuse in that the desire to make a dramatic speech as soon as possible often led to the substitution of ornate phraseology for substantial content. Indeed, the subjects ordinarily chosen for declamation were few in number and hackneyed in character, with the result that the only possible novelty lay in their treatment. While a great writer can develop a common topic in a new way, a schoolboy cannot. Hence the work tended to deteriorate into ornamentation, affectation, formality, and sterility.

Parallel with and subsequent to his practice in declamation a boy began serious work in pleading cases and in oratory. He debated on such common topics as the two given below:

A man had three sons: an orator, a philosopher, and a doctor. He divided his property into four parts, leaving one to each son and the fourth to the one who had proved himself most useful to the state. The sons dispute for the property.[33]

FIG. 15. A School of Oratory. From E. P. Cubberley, *History of Education,* p. 70. Courtesy of Houghton Mifflin Company, publishers.

Three young men who had the habit of dining together arranged for a supper on the seashore. One of them missed the supper, and the others inscribed his name on a tomb, which they had built for him. The young man's father, who had been travelling at sea, happened to land on that part of the coast, and read his son's name on the tomb, and killed himself. The young men are accused of having caused his death.

These topics may seem artificial to the modern mind, but they were simple and practical in comparison with similar training materials of a later day.[34]

Eventually, the boy began to argue cases in a practice court made up of

[33] This and the following example are from Gwynn, *op. cit.*, pp. 213, 208. Reprinted by permission of the publishers, The Clarendon Press.
[34] See pp. 86–87.

his schoolmates. An imaginary scene during such an exercise is depicted in Figure 15. Sometimes he harangued the other pupils as if he were an orator addressing his fellow senators in the forum. Practice of this sort would have been more useful if the arguments in the court and the content of the orations had been based on real cases and real situations, instead of on fanciful and artificial ones. Quintilian apparently did use more sensible training material than most, and he inveighed against the artificialities he saw about him, but he was unable to stop a trend already well advanced.

The work of the school of rhetoric included also some reading of prose in Greek and Latin and the study of famous speeches. The earlier Latin writers were banned because their Latin was archaic and might have a bad influence upon the boys' style. Poets were also banned, unless expurgated. The boys learned a little history, not for its own sake but as a source of timely illustrations for their arguments. They acquired a smattering of geometry and music also, but what they learned was determined by its value for an orator. Music should contribute to the modulation and cadence of his voice and to his ability to quote poetry in correct meter, while geometry should teach him, for instance, how land was measured, so that when he argued in favor of agrarian reform he would not make such factual errors as to arouse derision and thus lose his case.

TABLE 1: TYPES OF SCHOOL IN ROME [a]

Approximate Age of Pupils	Name of School	Teacher	Curriculum	Level as Compared to Schools of Today
6-7 to 11-12	Ludus	Ludi Magister	Reading Writing Arithmetic	Elementary
12-13 to 16-18	Grammar School	Grammaticus	Grammar Literature	Secondary
14-16 to 18-19	School of Rhetoric	Rhetor	Grammar Rhetoric-Dialectic	College
21-25 to 40-45	Greek or Roman University	Professor	Philosophy Law Medicine Architecture Mathematics Rhetoric	University

[a] E. P. Cubberley, *History of Education,* Houghton Mifflin Company, 1920 (849 pp.), p. 72. Used by permission of the publisher.

At the end of his course in rhetoric a young Roman might go to the university at either Athens or Rhodes,[35] where he could study philosophy. Often a student did not arrive at a university until he was a man of thirty-five or forty. Although Greek centers of learning were already past their prime before it became the fashion for young Romans to attend them, many of the most famous Latin writers did at one time or another attend a foreign school—Cicero, Ovid,* and Horace, to mention only a few. In the later days of the empire, students from the provinces came in sizable numbers to the University of Rome, probably for the same reasons that now stimulate a midwestern farm boy to polish off his home-town education in New York City.

The Romans had thus what amounted to a school system, as summarized in Table 1. Each type of school had its own teacher and curriculum. It should be remembered, however, that only a small number of boys ever went through the entire hierarchy* of school. Such training as a boy received was a matter upon which his family made all decisions. Girls apparently received the equivalent of the training given in the ludus; in fact, they sometimes attended the same schools as their brothers, but rarely went further. It should be noted also that while the Romans applied the work in certain of their schools to the training of future leaders for the state, they did not make any effort to develop an education much beyond the level of literacy for the average citizen. To the Latin mind education meant the training of boys from good families along the lines necessary for their future participation in guiding the welfare of the state, but for this one objective they had a school system that was reasonably adequate. One should not, therefore, blame them for not accomplishing what they did not try to do, but should admire them for their clearheadedness in setting up a definite goal and then arranging the work of their schools so that this goal could be reached by an intelligent and industrious boy who really wanted to reach it.

READING REFERENCES

A. General Histories of the Period

Breasted, *Ancient Times,* chaps. 23–28.

Caldwell, *The Ancient World,* chaps. 20, 21.

Cory, M., *History of Rome down to the Reign of Constantine,* The Macmillan Company, 1935 (820 pp.), chaps. 29–34, 39.

Robinson, C. E., *A History of Rome from 735 B.C. to A.D. 410,* Thomas Y Crowell Company, 1935 (456 pp.), sec. i, chaps. 11, 17–19; sec. ii chap. 20.

[35] Later to Rome or Marseilles.*

Rostovtzeff, M. I. *A History of the Ancient World,* Oxford University Press, 1927 (387 pp.), Vol. II, chaps. 8-12, 14-17, 19, 20.
Trevor, A. A., *History of Ancient Civilization,* Harcourt, Brace and Company, 1939 (817 pp.), Vol. II, chaps. 15-28.

B. Other Texts in the History of Education

Boyd, *The History of Western Education,* chap. 3.
Cole, *History of Educational Thought,* book ii, pp. 55–93.
Cubberley, *History of Education,* chap. 3.
Graves, *A Student's History of Education,* chap. 4.
McCormick, P. J., *History of Education,* Catholic Education Press, 1915 (401 pp.), chap. 7.
Monroe, *A Textbook in the History of Education,* pp. 176–207.
Moore, *The Story of Instruction,* Vol. I, chap. 6.
Reisner, *Historical Foundations of Modern Education,* chaps. 5, 6.
Ulich, R., *History of Educational Thought,* American Book Company, 1945 (412 pp.), pp. 51–60.

C. Secondary Sources

Dobson, *Ancient Education and Its Meaning for Us,* chaps. 4, 5.
Gwynn, *Roman Education from Cicero to Quintilian,* chaps. 2–4, 8, 9.
Johnston, H. W., *The Private Life of the Romans,* Scott, Foresman and Company, 1932 (430 pp.), chap. 4.
Laurie, *Pre-Christian Education,* pp. 301–411.
Moore, F. G., *The Roman's World,* Columbia University Press, 1936 (502 pp.), chaps. 8, 9.
Painter, F. V. N., *Great Pedagogical Essays,* American Book Company, 1905 (426 pp.), chap. 5.
Showerman, G., *Rome and the Romans,* The Macmillan Company, 1931 (643 pp.), part ii, chaps. 10, 11; part iii, chaps. 15, 19.
Smail, *Quintilian on Education,* pp. v–xix, xxxix–xlvii.
Tucker, T. G., *Life in the Roman World of Nero and St. Paul,* The Macmillan Company, 1911 (543 pp.), chaps. 17, 20.
Wilkins, *Roman Education,* chaps. 3–5.

D. Translations of Primary Sources

Guthrie, *Quintilian's Institutes of Oratory;* Smail, *Quintilian on Education,* or J. S. Watson, *Quintilian's Institutes of Oratory,* George Bell & Son, Ltd., 1875 (2 vols.), book i, chap. 3; book ii, chaps. 1–5, 8; book xii, chap. 1.
Ulich, R., *Three Thousand Years of Educational Wisdom,* Harvard University Press, 1947 (614 pp.), pp. 102–126.

PART THREE

A PERIOD OF TRANSITION

CHAPTER IV

TWO TEACHERS OF THE LATER ROMAN EMPIRE AND THE SCHOOLS OF THE PERIOD

In considering educational changes during the period of transition between Roman civilization at its height and the beginning of the Middle Ages it is necessary to follow two lines of development, because the imperial schools of the empire gave one type of training and the Christian schools gave another. The educational trends are thus only one phase of the long controversy between Christianity and paganism. The two teachers, Donatus and Ausonius, to be described in this chapter represent the last stages in pagan* education. The next chapter will be devoted to two men—Origen and Jerome—who were teachers in two types of early Christian schools. As the centuries rolled by, the pagan schools dwindled in number and significance, while those of Christendom increased until they dominated European education entirely. During the period under consideration, however, both types have to be described.

For nearly a thousand years after the Roman Empire disintegrated under the attacks of barbarian hordes from without and of increasing poverty and weakness from within, its language continued to be absolutely essential in public life, in education, and in the services of the Christian church. For the first dozen centuries after the birth of Christ it was the language in which every book in Western Europe was written and for even longer it was the language most used by scholars in speaking. A child's first educational task was, therefore, the mastery of Latin. He had to have not merely a reading knowledge of it but the ability to write it easily and to converse in it. Until he reached this level, he was in the situation of the illiterate person of today; that is, he could talk with his neighbors in the local vernacular, but he had not acquired the first skill needed for the most elementary schoolwork.

There were periods during the time from the end of the empire to the beginning of the Renaissance when education consisted of little more than a study of Latin. One reads that in some of the monasteries, where such intellectual life as existed was centered, each monk was given a book on the first day of Lent* and required to read it through in the course of the following year. Evidently even this small amount of mental labor was sometimes too much, because there were penalties for those who had not finished their assignment on time!

Although there were in every generation some individuals who read everything they could get hold of, they were the exceptions. In general, the difference between an educated and an uneducated man lay in the fact that the former knew enough Latin to recite parts of the church service and to plow through an occasional piece of writing. The study of classical Latin literature had its ups and downs throughout the Middle Ages. A few of the classics, especially Virgil and Cicero, were never entirely neglected, even though they were regarded with suspicion because of their pagan authorship. The course of study for a thousand years consisted mainly of Latin grammar and, once this tool was acquired, in a study of the church fathers and of church doctrine. It is because the study of Latin was vital to all academic life that the work of Donatus is included in this history. He contributed the most important of the grammars in wide use during the centuries after his death, and he therefore influenced education far more than did many men whose names are better known.

A. DONATUS: HIS LIFE AND WORK

The biography of the grammarian Donatus is short, since only three facts are actually known about him. He lived in Rome during the middle of the fourth century after the birth of Christ, he was the teacher of Jerome, and he wrote two grammars and two commentaries.* The latter are of no importance in the history of education, but his grammars definitely are.[1]

The "short" grammar—usually called the *Ars Minor*—was every child's first textbook. It was followed by his longer work, or by Priscian's grammar, or by both. The short grammar of Donatus occupies only fourteen printed pages. The excerpt below shows its nature:

> What is a noun? A part of speech, with cases, generally indicating either the essence or the thing itself. How many degrees of comparison are there? Three. What are they? Positive degree, such as "learned"; comparative degree, such as "more learned"; and superlative degree, such as "most

[1] Another famous grammarian, named Priscian, lived in Constantinople,* where one of his pupils in A.D. 526 finished the publishing of Priscian's grammar, which had been written but not yet completely copied for distribution when the writer died. Priscian was a native of Asia Minor,* and there is nothing to suggest that he was ever in Rome. One of his pupils called him the "light of Roman eloquence" and the "universal teacher of men"; of him as a person nothing more is known, but from his principal work one can deduce that he must have been a man of considerable erudition. He shows complete familiarity with both Greek and Latin literature and with the work of earlier grammarians in both languages. His name is usually coupled with that of Donatus, since the two men wrote the most widely used texts of the next 800 years.

learned." The comparative degree governs which case? The ablative without a preposition, for we say "more learned than he." The superlative degree governs which case? The genitive of the plural because we say "the most learned of the poets." How many genders may words have? Four. Which ones? Masculine such as "this teacher"; feminine such as "this muse"; neuter such as "this stool"; or communal such as "this priest or priestess." [2] There are actually, however, only three genders since all are indicated by using "hic, haec, or hoc." How many numbers do nouns have? Two. What are they? Singular, such as "this teacher", and plural, such as "these teachers." In how many ways are words composed? Four: (1) from two whole words such as "suburbanus"; (2) from two corrupted words such as "municeps"; (3) from one whole and one corrupted word such as "insulsus"; (4) from one corrupted and one whole word such as "nugigerulus." [3] How many cases do nouns have? Six. What are they? Nominative, genitive, dative, accusative, vocative, ablative; by them nouns of all genders, pronouns, and participles are declined.[4]

One point about the above passage is of special interest—the use of the question-and-answer method, which was probably introduced as a teaching device in an effort to make the work more interesting and more easily learned. Moreover, the method was used in the church catechism* and had thus become the very latest thing as a teaching method in the early centuries after Christ. The question-and-answer form continued on through the Middle Ages and can still be found once in a while in children's books. At the time of its appearance it had value in reducing the matter to be learned to a familiar form that was well adapted to oral instruction.

Since the *Ars Minor* was taught orally, there was no need of presenting conjugations or declensions in tabular form. Such visual arrangements did not appear until after A.D. 1500, when printed books were read by the students themselves. Scarcity of vellum* or parchment*, plus the labor of writing, plus the custom of oral instruction combined to prevent any tabular arrangements. For many a child this book was both the beginning and the end of education; for those who went further, it was the cornerstone.

The *Ars Minor* was not only the basis of all knowledge for centuries, but it determined the terminology of grammar that is still in use today. The following words were used by Donatus to explain Latin grammar. The student will find most of them so familiar that a translation is hardly needed.

[2] In Latin the word "sacerdos" is masculine if one refers to a man and feminine if one refers to a woman.

[3] These four types are explained as follows: (1) From "sub" and "urbanus" simply combined without alteration; (2) from "munia" and "capio" both of which have been altered; (3) from "in" and "salus", the second of which is changed; (4) from "niger" and "gerulus," of which the former is corrupted. (This last word means a colored porter.)

[4] G. T. H. Keil, *Grammatici Latini,* B. G. Teubner, 1855–1880 (7 vols.), IV, 355. Passages from Keil are quoted by permission of the publisher.

1. *Pars orationis*
(parts of speech)

nomen (noun)
pronomen (pronoun)
verbum (verb)
adverbum (adverb)
participium (participle)
conjunctio (conjunction)
praepositia (preposition)
interjectio (interjection)

2. *Words used in declensions*

casus (case)
nominativus (nominative)
genitivus (genitive)
dativus (dative)
accusativus (accusative)
vocativus (vocative)
ablativus (ablative)
numerus (number)
singularis (singular)
pluralis (plural)
genus (gender)
proprium nomen (proper noun)
masculinus (masculine)
femininus (feminine)
neutrum (neutral)
communis nomen (common noun)
positivus (positive)
comparativus (comparative)
superlativus (superlative)

3. *Verbs*

declinatio (declension)
inflectio (inflection)
indicativus (indicative)
imperativus (imperative)
optativus (optative)
conjunctivus (conjunctive)
passivus (passive)
activus (active)
deponens (deponent)
gerendi (gerundive)
conjugatio (conjugation)
tempus (tense)
praesens (present)
imperfectum (imperfect)
plusquamperfectum (pluperfect)
perfectum (perfect)
futurum (future)
praeteritum (preterit)
modus (mood)
persona (person)
impersonatis (impersonal)
finitus (finite)
infinitus (infinite)

4. *Pronouns*

relativus (relative)
possessivus (possessive)
demonstrativus (demonstrative)
disjunctivus (disjunctive)

5. *Word study*

simplex (simple)
compositus (composite)
terminata (ending)
littera (letter)
syllabus (syllable)
appellativus (apellative)
expletivus (expletive)
copulativus (copulative)[5]

The longer grammar, of which a sample will presently appear, contains not only the definitions and examples of the various inflected* forms but also comments on the common errors students made in writing, and a section on figures of speech. The purely grammatical parts differ from those of the short

[5] Taken from W. J. Chase, "The Ars Minor of Donatus," *University of Wisconsin Studies in the Social Studies and History,* No. 11, 1926 (55 pp.), condensed from pp. 29–32. Used by permission of the publisher.

form by the absence of questions, by the use of longer explanations, and by the inclusion of occasional examples from Virgil or other authors to illustrate some of the points. The additional sections are of some interest in indicating that Donatus, like other ancient grammarians, regarded grammar as covering more than the inflection of words.

He begins the section on errors by deploring the carelessness of many students in their writing, after the manner of almost any modern English teacher. Then he goes on to mention a few common mistakes, the first series of which are errors in spelling. These may occur by the addition, subtraction, substitution, or tranposition of a letter, a syllable, or an accent, as shown below:[6]

Error		Wrong		Right
Addition	of a letter	relliquias	for	reliquias
	of a syllable	abisisse	for	abisse
	of an accent	Itālia	for	Italia
Subtraction	of a letter	infantibu	for	infantibus
	of a syllable	salmentum	for	salsamentum
	of an accent	unus	for	ūnus
Substitution	of a letter	olli	for	illi
	of a syllable	pernities	for	pernicies
Transposition	of a letter	Euandre	for	Euander
	of a syllable	displicina	for	disciplina

This list leads one to think that human nature changes very little. The same types of error could be found in a set of themes today.

Mistakes in expression Donatus called barbarisms. Some of these are due to the character of the Latin language and are not translatable, but others are all too common in any language, as the excerpts on page 77 show.[7] These excerpts have a familiar ring. Their nature suggests that Donatus had been correcting themes!

The last two sections of the grammar deal with figures of speech. Here Donatus becomes more clearly the teacher of rhetoric and literature, although perhaps not on a very high level. He lists and illustrates briefly about thirty constructions such as those shown below.

1. Onomatopoeia: (use of words the sound of which suggests their meaning.)
   The pebble hit the water with a *splash*.
2. Synecdoche: (Use of a part to designate a whole.)
   It was a fleet of a thousand *sails*.

[6] Keil, *op. cit.*, pp. 392–393.
[7] Keil, *op. cit.*, pp. 393–397.

	Wrong		Right
1.	Those who can go will go and those who cannot go will not go.	*instead of*	Those who can, will go; the others will not.
2.	If he speaks by mouth . . .	*instead of*	If he speaks . . .
3.	The delegates returned whence they came; they went home.	*instead of*	The delegates went home.
4.	I see a bronze statue holding a spear.	*instead of*	I see a bronze statue that holds a spear.
5.	The young verse . . .	*instead of*	The new verse . . .
6.	He dashed out sudden and savage.	*instead of*	He dashed out suddenly and savagely.
7.	Into small pieces are the whole divided.	*instead of*	Into small pieces is the whole divided.
8.	They were despoiled and left their nude bodies.	*instead of*	They despoiled the people and left their nude bodies.
9.	Glorious Ilium fell and all Troy smokes from the ground.	*instead of*	Glorious Ilium fell and all Troy smoked from the ground.

3. Simile: (A comparison, in which the words "like" or "as" are used.)
   Life is *like* a lonely road.
4. Metaphor: (A comparison, made by speaking of one thing as if it were another, without the use of such words as "like" or "as".)
   Life *is* a lonely road.
5. Syllepsis: (An application of a word to two others but in different senses.)
   She went home *in* a flood of tears and a Sedan chair.
6. Metonymy: (Use of an attribute or a characteristic for the thing itself.)
   The *Crown* has issued an edict.
7. Anaphora: (Use of excessive repetition.)
   The Lord bless us and keep us. *The Lord* make his face to shine upon us and be gracious unto us. *The Lord* lift up his countenance upon us and give us peace.
8. Hyperbole: (Use of exaggeration.)
   She sent you a *thousand* apologies.

The inclusion of this material had two advantages. It provided a good teacher with an opportunity to talk about literature and—through the examples used—it presented the student with an assortment of quotations from Latin writers.[8]

[8] Priscian's "grammar" was an extremely long and rambling affair, jammed with quotations from classical authors. The excerpts thus used sometimes made up a student's total acquaintance with the great writers of Rome. It has been said that any man who knew Priscian thoroughly already had a fair foundation in classical literature. Indeed, Priscian contributed a good deal toward keeping alive both an interest in and a knowledge of the Latin writers in the centuries during which much of the pagan literature had been temporarily lost, hidden, or forgotten. The book is hardly what a modern student thinks of as

It remains to point out the extent to which Donatus influenced teaching for centuries after his lifetime. For eight hundred years Donatus remained so well known that any elementary grammar was called simply a "Donat." During the Middle Ages there were about twenty revisions and adaptations of his work by as many different writers.[9]

Especially did the *Ars Minor* of Donatus exert a strong influence upon subsequent language teaching. Thus Chrysoloras* during the Renaissance based his Greek grammar upon Donatus; the early French grammars were known as *Donatz Proënsals**; Ben Jonson's* English grammar in 1640 depended upon the *Ars Minor* as its source; it has the same topics, the same five genders, the same arrangement of subject matter, the same eight parts of speech, and even the same peculiarity of considering an adjective as a form of noun rather than as a separate part of speech.

During the twelfth century, when there was a great interest in putting various prose selections into verse, Donatus was turned into rhyme, of no merit either as poetry or as a mnemonic* device. After the fifteenth century the newer grammars of the Renaissance were used in the upper schools, but Donatus still held his place in the lower years. As late as 1496 a picture in a popular encyclopedia of late medieval and early modern times[10] shows a small boy entering the tower of knowledge, inside of which on the lowest floor Donatus, duly labeled, is teaching children.[11] The first handbook put out by one publishing house about a thousand years after the death of Donatus was his short grammar. In one form or another the grammarians were studied by almost every school child for centuries. The men who wrote these grammars were therefore of considerable importance in the history of education.

B. AUSONIUS: HIS LIFE AND WORK

Many Roman schools were still in existence during the third, fourth, and fifth centuries. These schools, their teachers, and their subject matter were just what one would expect from imperial institutions during a period of governmental and economic decadence. An excellent example of late Roman education and its results is found in the work and writings of an elegant gentleman named Ausonius, who flourished in the fourth century. His home was in Bordeaux. There he went to school as a small boy, but at the age of ten he was sent

---

a grammar. It comes closer to being a form of literary criticism, with occasional emphasis upon grammatical constructions, and an admixture of material from the fields of literature, philosophy, geography, astronomy, and history.

[9] Of Priscian there were an equal number of revisions. As late as A.D. 1150 the figure of Priscian was carved into one doorway of the cathedral at Chartres* as the outstanding personification of grammar.

[10] Gregory de Reisch, *Epitome of All Philosophy*. See Figure 24, p. 142.

[11] Priscian occupies a room on the second floor.

to Toulouse,* where his uncle was a professor. He remained in Toulouse for eight years until the uncle was summoned to Constantinople to become tutor to the sons of the emperor, Constantine the Great.* Ausonius then returned home and attended the schools of Bordeaux for another six years. When he was twenty-four he became a teacher of grammar. In due time he was promoted to a professorship and remained in Bordeaux for thirty years, faithfully performing his duties in the classroom.

At this point his life took a sudden change, because he was summoned to Rome to become the tutor of the future emperor, Gratian.* For fifteen years he was away from Bordeaux, first as tutor and later as general adviser and companion to the emperor. He held various political offices and at the age of sixty-nine received the greatest honor of all in being made a consul. Four years later he returned to Bordeaux, expecting to end his life in peace, but he was taken prisoner by rebellious soldiers of the Roman army while he was away from home on a visit, and was held for about five years. Eventually he got back to Bordeaux and stayed there until his death six years later.

From his life history one can see that he was a true Roman who, like many another, came originally from the provinces.* Like most Romans of culture he had a public career. He was indeed as typical an example of the old-style Roman as one could find in the fourth century.

His writings make clear what kind of man he was, what he taught, where he stood on the paganism-versus-Christianity controversy, and what he conceived the ends of education to be. First, as to his personality. He was an elegant courtier, a literary trifler, a flatterer, a person of no sensibility but a great deal of sentimentality, an aristocrat who had little interest in the common people about him, an aesthete,* and a definitely dull person. As compensation for these traits he showed a high degree of loyalty to his friends, his family, his emperor, and his work. Although Ausonius lived in a period of invasions and internal strife, he rarely in his writings mentioned any of the exciting events taking place around him. He wrote eulogies* about Emperor Gratian, but hardly a word about affairs of the empire. To him, education seems to have been remote from life, an attitude that was shared by many men of his time.

Ausonius adorned his writing with all manner of literary affectations. His style is an excellent example of the decadence that had overtaken the literature of antiquity. For instance, he writes in the following manner upon a purely pagan topic of "Cupid Crucified." Only a few of the introductory lines are quoted.

> In the aerial fields, told us in Virgil's verse, where groves of myrtle o'ershade lovers' lorn, the heroines were holding frantic rites, each one of them bearing tokens of the death she died of old, and wandering in a great wood,

lit by a scanty light, 'mid tufted reeds, and full-blown poppies, and still meres without a ripple, and unbabbling streams, along whose banks flowers of woe hung drooping in the murky light, bearing the names of kings and boys of old.[12]

Among other things Ausonius wrote descriptions of the entire faculty of the school of Bordeaux. In spite of the fulsome praise given some and the involved ambiguity with which he describes others, they are recognizable as real people. They still exist upon the faculty of any large university today.

Witty and cheerful, an old man with a heart of youth, whose soul steeped in honey with no drop of gall, never throughout all your life instilled aught of bitterness, balm of my heart, Nepotianus, taking your share in solemn and gay alike: your lips once closed, you could surpass Amyclae in silence; but when once you began to discourse, even Ulysses could not leave you—he who left the tuneful Sirens at their song. Honorable and pure, sparing, frugal, temperate, eloquent, you were second to no orator in style. . . . You were my comrade, companion, and my guest continually: and not my guest alone, but the awakener of my mind. None gave advice out of a heart more sincere, or concealed it when given, with deeper secrecy. When you had been distinguished by your appointment as a governor, and had lived through the changes of ninety years, you met your end, leaving two children, to your kinsfolk's great sorrow as to mine.[13]

Scholarly Victorius, gifted with memory and a quick brain, how patiently you used to pour over books which no one read, and study only abstruse lore! You liked better to unroll worm-eaten and outlandish scrolls than to give yourself to more familiar pursuits. What was the code of the pontifices, what the treaties, what the pedigree of the sacrificial priest at Cures long before Numa's days, what Castor had to say on all the shadowy kings, what Rhodope published out of her husband's books, the code of the priests, what the resolutions of the old Quirites, what the decree of the Senate, what measures Draco, or what Solon passed, and what laws Zaleucus gave the Locrians, what Minos under the reign of Jove's time—all these were better known to you than our Tully or Maro, and all the stories of Roman history.[14]

For Anastasius also shape a mournful lay, my Muse; and you, my dirge recall that poor grammarian. He was born at Bordeaux, but ambition transferred him to Poitiers.* There he lived a poor man stinted alike in food and dress, and in his old age lost the faint glimmer of renown which his country and his chair had shed upon him. Howbeit, I have here paid a tribute to his name, that the tomb should not swallow up his name with his bones.[15]

[12] H. G. Evelyn-White (translator), *Ausonius,* Loeb Classical Library, Harvard University Press, 1921 (2 vols.), I, 209. This excerpt and subsequent ones from this reference are used by permission of the publishers.

[13] *Ibid.,* p. 121.

[14] *Ibid.,* p. 133.

[15] *Ibid.,* p. 117.

> Herculanus, though you came from my bosom and my class, you have repaid your uncle with promise rather than with fruit. You shared in the work of my class, and might have succeeded to my chair had not the swerving steps of slippery youth caused you to fall headlong, through not keeping to the right path traced out by Pythagoras. May you have rest, and your spirit dwell in peace in its last home.[16]

In the entire series of descriptions there are about thirty teachers, all of whom were grammarians, rhetoricians, or orators. There seem to have been no other subjects taught. Probably this overemphasis upon linguistic subjects, however, was the main factor that saved Latin literature from extinction.

Ausonius was quite insensible to the feeling and the human sympathy that should pervade poetry. He apparently believed that poetry was merely a versified exercise in rhetoric. Therefore the harder it was, the more merit accrued to the author. It followed logically that the least promising themes were the best. Ausonius wrote one poem on the topic of the Roman calendar and another that catalogued all the Latin monosyllables. He required 14 lines to say that there were 30 kinds of oysters, a point of questionable value in a lyric. He produced also a poem in which the first word of every line had one syllable, the second two syllables, the third, three, and so on. It does not seem to have occurred to him that verses thus produced contained precious little sense. To be sure, Ausonius wrote one famous descriptive poem about the Moselle River;* some of the lines are very fine, but he could not resist the temptation to catalogue the fishes. The few worth-while things he wrote are snowed under by the avalanche of ornate trifles[17] that flowed from his pen. Among the latter are a host of epigrams, of which the following is a sample:

> As lazy a scribe as a sluggish runner, thou Pergamus, didst run away and wert caught at the first lap. Therefore, thou hast felt letters branded, Pergamus, upon thy face, and those which thy right hand neglected thy brow endures.[18]

The writings of Ausonius have style, polish, grace, and neatness, but they lack life or reality. One writer has said of him:

> He has been at a great feast of language and stolen the scraps and

[16] *Ibid.*

[17] Ausonius was not the only person with this notion of writing elegant and sophisticated nothings. A contemporary, Sidonius,* is famous for having written a Latin sentence that reads the same in both directions: *Roma tibi subito motibus ibit amor.* This sentence is an achievement, but one doubts if it were worth the effort, since the statement makes almost no sense in either direction. The same gentleman prided himself on writing lines of poetry in which each line began with the same syllable that ended the immediately preceding line.

[18] Evelyn-White, *op. cit.*, II, 179.

cooked them into odd little messes of his own, very ingenious but hopelessly trifling.[19]

Fundamentally, Ausonius had nothing to say and said it in infinite detail and with extensive meanderings. He arranged pretty words and phrases—often stolen from classical writers—into complex patchwork designs that sometimes capture the attention but never move the soul or convince the mind. Some of his writings almost prove the existence of form without content.

Ausonius appears to have had a kindly spirit toward his pupils and to have been well regarded by them. Paulinas,* a former pupil, evidently had pleasant memories of his school days, for he later wrote to Ausonius:

> Love joins me to you. In this bond alone
> Dare I to claim equality with you.
> Sweet friendship binds me ever to your heart
> And ever we renew our equal love.[20]

The Romans were by nature a serious-minded people who had little interest in children's games and even less in the nature of the child mind; Ausonius, however, seems to have modified this customary attitude, as is indicated in some paragraphs he wrote to his grandson:

> The . . . stern master does not always drive his pupils; but fixed hours preserve the alternations of recreation and study. It is enough for a boy with memory to have read with a will; then let him rest. . . . Since you are sure that play will come in its turn, learn gladly; for we give intervals to wipe out protracted fatigues. The zeal of a boy is wearied unless joyous holidays relieve his days of severe work.[21]

In this passage Ausonius sounds more like a schoolmaster of the Renaissance* than like a Roman.

Ausonius was nominally a Christian, but his heart and soul were in the ancient world and his whole character was that of an educated pagan. His writing bristles with alluions to Greek and Roman literature, but the early church fathers* might never have existed as far as he was concerned. Not only does he carry on the Roman traditions of writing—albeit in attenuated form—and ignore Christianity whenever he can, but he cannot make head or tail out of the new religion when he is forced by circumstances to consider it.

One of Ausonius's really admirable traits was his devotion to his friends, his family, and his pupils. Among the latter was Paulinas, who later taught with Ausonius for some years, lived near him, and was a dear friend. Eventually

[19] T. R. Glover, *Life and Letters in the Fourth Century,* Cambridge University Press, 1901 (398 pp.), p. 115.
[20] Paulinas, *Eucharisticon,* ll. 55 ff.
[21] Evelyn-White, *op. cit.,* II, 76.

Paulinas was converted to Christianity, went to Spain, gave up his land, and entered upon the life of an ascetic.* In the letters exchanged between the two, one can see, in spite of the florid style, the complete antithesis between the pagan and Christian points of view. On a small scale the letters review the entire struggle; moreover, they show why Christianity was so disrupting. The two men had been close friends for years, but when one of them was converted, the other suffered a deep and permanent personal loss. Thus did Christianity affect the lives of those who literally followed Christ's words to leave all else and follow Him. A few short excerpts from the correspondence appear below:

From Ausonius to Paulinas:

But why weave I such sad refrain in mournful verse, why does my heart not turn to nobler prayers? Sure is my confidence that if the Father and the Son of God accept the reverent words of those who seek, thou canst be restored at my prayer, that I may weep no more for a home scattered and ravaged, for a realm rent in pieces between a hundred owners, once Paulinas's, and for thee that, wandering with a range as wide as the extent of Spain, unmindful of old friends, dost trust in strangers.

Oh hasten hither, my pride, my chiefest care, summoned with vows, good omens, and with prayers speed thee hither, while thou art young and while my old age to win thy favour preserves its vigour unconsumed. Ah, when shall this news break on my ears? "Lo, Paulinas is at hand: now he leaves the snowy towns of Spain, now reaches the field of Tarbellae, now approaches the homesteads of Hebromagus, now enters his brother's domains hard by, now glides downstream and now is in sight: now the prow is being swung out into the stream: now he has passed the thronged entrance of his home-port, outstrips the whole host of folk who hurry to meet him, and passes his own doors now, even now beats at thine."

Do I believe, or do those who love feign dreams for their own selves?[22]

From Paulinas to Ausonius:

. . . But if perchance thou dost likewise hear—and 'tis what I have chosen and what I pursue—that I have vowed my heart to our holy God, following in accord with obedient belief the awful behest of Christ, and that I am convinced by God's words that deathless rewards are laid up for man, purchased by present loss, that methinks, has not so displeased my revered father that he thinks it a perversion of the mind so to live for Christ as Christ appointed. This is my delight, and this "perversion" I regret not. That I am foolish in the eyes of those who follow other aims gives me no pause, if only in sight of the eternal King my opinion be wise. . . .

This is my fear, this my task, that the Last Day overtake me not asleep in the black darkness of profitless pursuits, spending wasted time amid empty cares. For what shall I do if, while I drowse amid sluggish hopes, Christ should

[22] *Ibid.*, p. 87.

flash forth, and I, dazzled by the sudden beams of my Lord's coming from open heaven, should seek the doleful refuge of murky night confounded by the o'erwhelming light?

Wherefore . . . I am resolved to forestall calamity by my plan of life, to end anxieties while life remains, awaiting with untroubled heart fierce Death, the general doom of things for ages yet to come.

If this thou dost approve, rejoice in thy friend's rich hope: if otherwise, leave me to be approved by Christ alone.[23]

The old man cannot be made to understand that his pupil has been seized by a new urge, a new flame that was driving men by the hundred out into places of solitude. Ascetism was as unintelligible to Ausonius as it would be to the sophisticate of today.

Ausonius epitomized the changes that had occurred in Roman education. First it had become wholly verbal. Boys learned only grammar and rhetoric. Second, it had no vitality. For some centuries men had merely imitated the classic writers of Greece and Rome; they wrote grammars, analyzed masterpieces, and made lengthy compilations. They had even gone so far as to make a summary of a transcript of a copy! But of originality, there was almost none. Third, education was artificial and removed from life. The exercises upon which the boys practiced had little relation to the world outside them.[24] A great empire was being broken to bits, and in the midst of it sat Ausonius and others like him, earnestly teaching youngsters to be useless. In the course of time the imperial schools died because, as one writer has said, "All educational institutions must die, which do not directly and conspicuously promote either the spiritual or the material interests of man." [25]

C. SCHOOLS OF THE LATE ROMAN EMPIRE

This chapter and the next cover much the same period of time, roughly from A.D. 200 to 600, but in one case the description covers the state-supported Roman schools and in the other, the new schools established by Christians. Practically all the schools of both types were small and local. By A.D. 600 most, and perhaps all, the Roman schools had disappeared, and what education was given at all was given in Christian schools. Both pagan and Christian writers of the period (from A.D. 200 to 600) exerted a great influence upon the education of the next few centuries. It is therefore necessary to study both types of school and scholar.

[23] *Ibid.*, condensed from pp. 145–147.

[24] See pp. 86–87.

[25] S. S. Laurie, *Survey of Pre-Christian Education,* Longmans Green & Co., 1915 (411 pp.), p 409.

The typical Roman school[26] had been established and was supported by imperial Rome. Originally these schools were numerous in Italy, in Spain, and especially in southern France. It was the imperial intention that the government should maintain a school for grammar and rhetoric in the main city for every province. After the middle of the fifth century all schools were under imperial control, and no private person was supposed to open a school. The government licensed the teachers, either by appointing them directly or by approving a name submitted by local authorities in the provinces. In the first two centuries after the birth of Christ, teachers were sometimes supported by the towns, but thereafter they received money from the emperor. The teachers usually also charged fees for the pupils, and often received gifts from both the emperor and the students' parents as well. The government thus maintained a monopoly on education and tended to interfere a good deal with the work of the schools. From the teachers' point of view, all good things flowed from the emperor, who authorized their appointment, relieved them of certain taxes and of service in the army, paid them, promoted them, and rewarded them by public offices whenever possible. In return, teachers were supposed to write panegyrics* in praise of the emperor. These poems were full of flattery and the abasement of the teacher in hysterical and slavish adoration of the emperor. The whole relationship of the throne to education was abnormal and unhealthy. The same sort of imperial meddling resulted in a warping of history because events from the past were used to glorify the emperor and his ancestors, and if an account of the actual events would not serve this end, the panegyrist rearranged history to suit his purposes. The main result of the imperial policy was an educational system in which naturalness and progress had been sacrificed to uniformity and triviality.

A few fragments still remain of an edict for the organizing of the imperial school in Constantinople. There were to be thirty-one professors in all: one philosopher, two lawyers, five sophists,* ten grammarians for Greek, three orators, and ten grammarians for Latin, plus seven scribes*—not counted on the faculty—for making correct copies of books. The students in the imperial schools had to bring proper certificates with them from the magistrates of their native province, giving their names, addresses, and family connections; the prefect* of the city in which the school was situated was to supervise behavior, expelling those who wasted their time in feasting or at the theater, and was to submit a monthly report concerning the progress of the scholars, so that the more capable might be selected for public service. The students had to return

[26] The material in this section is based upon T. Haarhoff, *Schools of Gaul,* Oxford University Press, 1920, 272 pp., and P. R. Cole, "Later Roman Education," in *Ausonius, Capella, and the Theodosian Code, Teachers College Contributions to Education, No. 27,* 1909, 39 pp.

home when they were twenty years old, because after that age they were taxed. It is probable that this plan was put into effect in its entirety in only a few places. Many imperial schools still existed at the close of the fourth century; those especially well known were at Marseilles, Narbonne,* Bordeaux, Arles,* Toulouse, Poitiers, Besançon,* Vienne,* Autun,* Lyon,* Trèves,* and Clermont*—most of them in southern France.

By the end of the second century the schools of southern France were better than most of those in Rome. Emperors imported teachers from Gaul* to be the tutors of their children, and even Roman writers of the period continually referred to the Gauls as "learned." The curriculum of the school consisted almost wholly of grammar and rhetoric, with the main accent upon the latter. The student was supposed to become an orator, although the complete centralization of the government made oratory quite useless. A pupil read and reread a speech, his own or one from a classic author, trying to give his rendition the precise accent, cadence, and expression with which the words were originally spoken. As Ausonius wrote to his grandson:

Do you with varied intonation read
A host of verse; let your words succeed
Each other with the accent and the stress
Your masters taught you. Slurring will repress
The sense of what you've read; and a pause
Adds vigor to an overburdened clause.[27]

Most of the topics on which the students themselves wrote were artificial and without connection to real life. Their handling of these topics was supposed to be ingenious, but no one seems to have cared whether or not the treatment was truthful or even possible.

The nature of this material can best be indicated by a few samples of the problems about which the boys debated. From them one can see to what extent the vitality of education for public service as it had existed in the Roman classical period had degenerated into formality and artificiality.

A young man is captured by pirates and writes to his father for the ransom. No ransom is sent. The daughter of the pirate-captain makes him swear that he will marry her if he is released. She elopes with him, and they return to the young man's home where they are married. A rich heiress crosses their path. The father bids the young man forsake his wife and marry the heiress. He refuses and is disinherited.[28]

[27] Evelyn-White, *op. cit.*, II, 77.

[28] This item and the following ones are from Seneca, *Controversiae,* Vol. I, § 6; Vol. X, § 3; Vol. I, § 7; Vol. II, § 2, translated in Gwynn. *op. cit., pp.* 159–160. Used by permission of The Clarendon Press, publishers.

During a civil war a woman follows her husband, though her father and brother are on the other side. Her husband's side is defeated and her husband killed. She returns to her father who will not receive her. She asks how she can win his favor, and he replies, "By dying." She hangs herself before his door. The father is accused of madness by his son.

The law requires that children should support their parents or be imprisoned. A man has slain one of his brothers as a tyrant and another because he was taken in adultery, though his father begged for money. The man is captured by pirates, who writes to the father for a ransom. The father answers that he will pay them double if they will cut off his son's hands. The son is released by pirates, and refuses to support his father.

A husband and wife have sworn that neither shall survive the other. The husband goes on a journey, and sends a messenger to his wife with news of his death. The wife leaps from a cliff, but is rescued and restored to health. She is ordered by her father to desert her husband, but refuses. She is disinherited.

These topics are all removed from life situations. They present legal intricacies that are beyond the capacity of the ordinary boy. The only thing a student could do with them was to present a plea that was more dramatic, more intricate, and more elegant than those of other pupils.

Letter writing occupied an important place in the curriculum and was an art sedulously practiced by prominent men. Although the training was careful and the art flourishing, the letters were usually sterile, pretentious, and unreal. Since great men collected and preserved their own letters, the work had at least the value of assembling data for the future historian!

Discipline in the schools was evidently as severe as in those of the classical period, if one may judge from the advice given by Ausonius to his son when the latter entered school:

> Fear you not although the school resound with much thwacking and the old man, your master wear a truculent frown. . . . Prove yourself to be bold and let not the noise and the sounding rods nor the terror in the morning make you afraid. The ferule, the birch, and the tawse* and the nervous fidgeting of the boys on the benches are the show and pomp of the place. All this in their day your father and mother went through. You too will be a man some day and I hope a great man.[29]

The imperial schools were regarded as pagan and therefore enrolled fewer and fewer pupils as Christianity spread. Since they derived their support directly from the emperor, this support was not always forthcoming, because the government was bankrupt. After the fall of Rome the schools were left to the mercy of local patronage, and most of them fell into decay. The families that had been wealthy had often become too impoverished to send their children to

[29] Evelyn-White, *op. cit.*, II, 75.

any school, the teachers were poorly paid if at all, and the Christians were opposed to their very existence. As a result of these various factors, the number of imperial schools dwindled in the fifth century, and by the end of the sixth they had died out altogether, leaving behind them a tradition of elegance in education. During the last two centuries of their existence, the curriculum was restricted chiefly to the elements of grammar and rhetoric, and even these were presented by means of greatly abbreviated texts and epitomes*—a sort of learning-made-easy arrangement that was no more interesting than it was efficient.

The teachers in the imperial schools depended largely upon memory as a method of teaching. Ausonius himself seems to have known all of Virgil's writings by heart. Since books were extremely scarce, a scholar had to carry quotations from many authors in his head. Ausonius expressed the basic idea when he wrote, "A good boy is one with a long memory." [30]

The schools were handicapped not only by the imitativeness and artificiality of their methods but also by the general decay of society about them. If teachers complained that the "pupil material" was not as good as it had been, they were probably correct. Young men of good families had become decadent. They felt little urge for either the active life of the soldier or the intellectual life of the scholar. As early as the second century the elder Seneca, who admittedly took a gloomy view of life, had acid comments to make upon the habits of the rising generation. His remarks were just as true in the next centuries.

> Our young men have grown slothful. Their talents are left idle, and there is not a single honourable occupation for which they will toil day and night. Slumber and languor, and an interest in evil which is worse than slumber and languor, have entered into men's hearts. They sing and dance and grow effeminate, and curl their hair, and learn womanish tricks of speech: they are as languid as women, and deck themselves with unbecoming ornaments. Which of your contemporaries [he is addressing his three sons] has any talent, any industry? Which of them is in any way a man? Without strength, without energy, they add nothing during life to the gifts with which they were born, and then they complain of their lot. God forbid that the gift of eloquence should be given to their like! [31]

If the situation were and continued to be even half as bad as Seneca thought it was, one can see that a sterile education acting upon such decadent youth would have sterile results. Perhaps the most important form of decay in Roman civilization was the decay of the spirit.

[30] *Ibid.*, I, 261.

[31] Seneca, *Controversiae,* Vol. I, §§ 8–9. Translated in Gwynn, *op. cit.*, p. 129.

Only those interested in either the history of grammar or the Middle Ages are likely to have heard of Donatus or Priscian. Yet their influence lives on within their own field, which has with the passage of time become only one subject among many now taught in school. The Latin grammar of today is easy as compared to the *Ars Minor,* and it contains elements introduced for the purpose of interesting the pupils, but it is a lineal descendant from the grammars of the period just discussed. The work of both grammarians was highly instrumental in keeping alive classical Latin through the troubled times of the invasion by and absorption of unlettered people, the disruption of learning, the narrow domination of the church, and the corruption of Latin into the Romance languages. With the first phase of the Renaissance in the fifteenth century, the old grammarians receded into the background. Their work was over, but they had helped materially in keeping alive the thoughts of the best minds in the ancient world.

READING REFERENCES

A. General Histories of the Period

Arragon, R. F., *The Transition from the Ancient to the Medieval World,* Henry Holt and Company, 1936 (134 pp.), part ii, chap. 26; part iii, chaps. 29, 30, 33, 34.

Breasted, *Ancient Times,* chaps. 29, 30.

Burns, C. D., *The First Europe: A Study of the Establishment of Medieval Christendom,* George Allen & Unwin, Ltd., 1947 (684 pp.), chaps. 1–3.

Cory, *History of Rome Down to the Reign of Constantine,* sec. F, chaps. 42, 43.

Moss, H. St. L. B., *The Birth of the Middle Ages,* Oxford University Press, 1935 (291 pp.), part i, chaps. 1–3.

Parker, M. D., *History of the Roman World from A.D. 138–337,* The Macmillan Company, 1939 (402 pp.), part i, chap. 2; part ii, chap. 6; part v, chaps. 1, 4–6.

Robinson, J. H., *An Introduction to the History of Western Europe,* Ginn and Company, 1946 (rev. ed., 1091 pp.), chap. 3.

Rostovtzeff, *A History of the Ancient World,* chap. 21.

Strayer, J. R., and D. C. Munro, *The Middle Ages,* Appleton-Century-Crofts Company, 1942 (568 pp.), chaps. 1, 2.

B. Other Texts in the History of Education

Cole, *History of Educational Thought,* book ii, pp. 93–104.

Cubberley, *History of Education,* chap. 4.

Graves, *A Student's History of Education,* chap. 5.

Monroe, *A Textbook in the History of Education,* pp. 208–212.

Reisner, *Historical Foundations of Modern Education,* chaps. 8, 9.

C. Secondary Sources

Boissonade, P., *Life and Work in Medieval Europe* (translated by E. Power), Routledge and Kegan Paul, Ltd., 1937 (395 pp.), book i, chaps. 1, 2.
Cole, P. R., "Later Roman Education," in *Ausonius, Capella, and the Theodosian Code, Teachers College Contributions to Education*, no. 27, 1909, 39 pp. section on Ausonius.
Dill, *Roman Society in the Last Centuries of the West* (2d ed.), book ii, chap. 3.
Dobson, *Ancient Education and Its Meaning for Us*, chap. 6.
Glover, *Life and Letters in the Fourth Century*, chap. 5.
Haarhoff, *Schools of Gaul*, part ii, pp. 52–118.
Hodgson, *Primitive Christian Education*, chap. 3.

D. Translations of Primary Sources

Chase, "The Ars Minor of Donatus," pp. 29–32.
White, *Ausonius*, any 10 descriptions from pp. 97–140 or 59–67.

CHAPTER V

TWO CHRISTIAN TEACHERS AND THE EARLY SCHOOLS OF CHRISTENDOM

For the purpose of examining Christian education in the first few centuries after Christ, two outstanding teachers have been selected—Origen and Jerome. The former taught in a famous school in Alexandria; the latter established and taught in a monastic school in Bethlehem. Both these schools developed outside the geographical boundaries of Europe, but well within the same cultural sphere, since both places were in countries that were part of the Roman Empire. At the time of their activity there was no such place as "Europe," and the culture of the countries bordering upon the Mediterranean formed a unified whole that was continuous all around the shores of this inland sea. The schools in which Origen and Jerome worked were extensively copied, especcially the monastic* school, all over the Western world. They will therefore serve as typical samples of the better type of Christian schools of the period.

A. ORIGEN: HIS LIFE AND WORK

The name of Origen brings to the minds of those who are acquainted with him the picture of a sincere Christian. He had in a high degree the qualities of meekness, sincerity, asceticism, devotion, single-mindedness, and idealism. In addition, he was a scholar of good standing, well trained in the learning of Greece. In its beginning, Christianity was a religion of the poor and the uneducated. As long as it remained so, it did not come into conflict with pagan philosophies, because the adherents knew little or nothing about them. When it spread to the educated classes, however, the conflict at once arose. Origen was among those who saw that philosophy was an aid to theology and that the ancients had much in their learning that showed no contradiction to the Christian faith. He was, in short, a holy man, a devout Christian, a profound scholar, an inspiring teacher, and a cultured gentleman.[1]

Origen was born in Alexandria before the end of the second century after the birth of Christ and died in the middle of the third. His father was an educated man, probably a teacher of rhetoric in the Hellenized city of Alexandria. Under his guidance Origen was schooled in Greek culture but was also

[1] For an evaluation of this church father, see E. de Faye, *Origen and His Work* (translated by F. Rothwell), George Allen & Unwin, Ltd., 1926, 188 pp.

required daily to learn by heart verses from the Bible. During his early childhood his parents became Christians and apparently embraced the new faith with all the ardor of neophytes.*

At the end of the second century a conversion to Christianity was not a thing to be considered lightly or done casually. Being a Christian meant the likelihood of persecution and the possibility of death, imprisonment, or torture. It meant also a thrill and excitement that is now hard to realize. Among people still alive were some whose great-great-grandfathers had actually known one of the apostles,* and some who knew they were descended from some individual to whom Christ had spoken. The immediate descendants and friends of martyrs and saints existed in numbers. There was already a church, but its doctrines and creed were not yet rigid. Christianity was mainly a spirit that lifted men from the rut of their daily lives, a belief that gave them hope, an inspiration that supplied them with courage and with a promise of beauty in a world to come. In Origen's childhood, Christianity was still spread chiefly by word of mouth, each teacher converting others largely through the contagion of his own enthusiasm and excitement. Origen himself was the child of a martyr and the pupil of saints. One of his teachers was Hippolytus,* who was a disciple of Irenaeus,* who had been a disciple of Polycarp,* who had been trained by the apostle John, who was an immediate follower of Jesus. In the present-day twentieth century, Christ's image is dulled by the passage of time and the addition of intervening interpretations of his message, but in the second and third centuries, Christ was still very near and the magnetism of his personality was still being transmitted in direct succession from those who had actually known him on earth. It was in such an electric atmosphere that Origen grew to maturity.

When he was seventeen years old, a great persecution of the Christians broke out in Alexandria. Origen's father was one of the victims. His death left the young man with a mother and six brothers to support. Since he had had a good education in Greek literature, he sought and found a position as a teacher of grammar. In this work he was, from the first, a great success. His reputation at this time did not depend upon his teaching alone, however. He constantly helped the victims of the persecution, which raged for a long time, and was more than once nearly killed himself. So conspicuous was he in his courage and in his adherence to the faith that he attracted the attention of the bishop of Alexandria, who appointed him head of the catechetical[2] school, although Origen was at the time not yet eighteen.

In this school and in others like it Origen found his lifework, the teaching of young Christians. Indeed, he became so absorbed in the field of educa-

[2] See pp. 106–107.

tion—both teaching and writing—that he felt he must do something to ensure the continuance of his work. He therefore surveyed his worldly possessions and decided he had only one thing of real value—his library. With deep regret he sold it entire to a purchaser who agreed to furnish him an amount equal to twelve cents a day for the rest of his life. On this singular annuity he lived for many years, devoting himself to study and teaching. He remained in Alexandria for the next thirteen years and was then forced to leave because of another terrible persecution. A little later, however, he returned and went on with his work under a sort of "research grant" from a rich patron, who provided him with no less than seven amanuenses* to make copies of his books. These were Origen's happiest years. He was busy with his teaching and his favorite studies; he was able to produce manuscripts as fast as he wished; and he held a place of high honor in the city. After a few years, however, he became involved in some kind of personal trouble with the bishop of Alexandria and was excommunicated.* The matter seems to have been based primarily upon petty jealousy, but the bishop of Alexandria was a powerful person in early church politics. For no apparently adequate reason, he hounded Origen until he forced the latter's departure from Alexandria.

From this time on, Origen lived in Caesarea* in Palestine,* where he soon became a teacher in a school similar to the one he had just left. In the years that followed, he again acquired great fame as a Christian teacher, philosopher, and writer, although he was criticized for certain of his views. One more persecution Origen managed to survive, but in A.D. 249 he was thrown into prison and treated so cruelly that, although released eventually, he was badly weakened and lived only a few months.

The character of Origen was of a remarkable purity and nobility. He saw much unmerited suffering, both in his own life and in the experiences of his Christian friends, but there is among his voluminous writings no word of resentment. Those who mentioned him spoke of him in terms of deepest respect and affection. In his earlier days, Jerome wrote of Origen:

> He was so assiduous in the study of the Holy Scripture that, contrary to the spirit of the times and of the people, he learned the Hebrew language. . . . I do not fail to mention his immortal genius, how he understood dialectics as well as geometry, arithmetic, music, grammar, and rhetoric; and taught all the schools of philosophy in such wise that he had diligent students in secular literature and lectured to them daily; and the crowds which flocked to him were marvellous. These he received in the hope that through the instrumentality of secular literature, he might establish them in the faith of Christ.[3]

[3]Hieronymus (Jerome), *Lives of Illustrious Men* (translated by E. C. Richardson) in *A Select Library of Nicene and Post-Nicene Fathers of the Christian Church,* Second Series. Christian Literature Publishing Company, 1892, III, 349.

A little extreme but typical is the description given of him by one of his students, who related what effect a chance meeting with Origen had had upon him and his brother:

> And thus, like some spark lighting upon our inmost soul, love was kindled and burst in flame within us. And being most mightily smitten by this love, I was persuaded to give up all those objects or pursuits which seem to us befitting, and among others even my boasted jurisprudence,—yea, my very fatherland and friends, both of those who were present and those from whom I had parted. And in my estimation there arose but one object dear and worth desire,—to wit philosophy, and that master of philosophy, this inspired man.[4]

At some time during their long friendship Origen wrote a letter to this same pupil. A few lines from it are worth quoting, both because they indicate his friendliness with his student and because they set forth his ideas about the relationship of pagan and Christian learning.

> Greeting in God, my most excellent sir, and venerable son Gregory, from Origen. . . . I am anxious that you should devote all the strength of your natural good parts to Christianity; and in order to do this, I wish to ask you to extract from the philosophy of the Greeks what there may serve as a course of study or a preparation for Christianity, and from geometry and astronomy what will serve to explain the sacred Scriptures. . . . Do you then, my son, diligently apply yourself to the reading of the sacred Scriptures. Apply yourself, I say. For we who read the things of God need much application, lest we should say or think anything too rashly about them.[5]

Fortunately a good account by one of his students, has been preserved of Origen's methods of teaching. The various excerpts below make quite clear not the details of his technique but the main outline of procedure.

> In suchwise, then, and with such a disposition did he receive us at first; and surveying us, as it were, with a husbandman's skill, and gauging us thoroughly, and not confining his notice to those things only which are patent to the eye of all, but penetrating into us more deeply, and probing what is more inward in us, he put us to the question, and made propositions to us, and listened to our replies; and, whenever he thereby detected anything in us not wholly fruitless and profitless and waste, he set about clearing the soil, and turning it up and irrigating it, and putting all things in movement, and brought his whole skill and care to bear on us, and wrought upon our mind; its uncultured luxuriance and native wildness he thoroughly removed by the processes of refutation and prohibition; sometimes assailing us in the genuine Socratic fashion, and again upsetting us by his argumentation whenever he saw us getting restive under him, like so many unbroken

[4] A. Roberts and J. Donaldson, *The Ante-Nicene Fathers,* Christian Literature Publishing Company, 1886 (570 pp.), VI, 28.
[5] *Ibid.,* IV, 393.

steeds, and springing out of the course and galloping madly about at random, until with a strange kind of persuasiveness and constraint he reduced us to a state of quietude under him by his discourse, which acted like a bridle in our mouth. . . .

And when he had made us adaptable and had prepared us successfully for the reception of the words of truth, then further, as though we were now a soil well wrought and soft, and ready to impart growth to the seeds cast into it, he dealt liberally with us, and sowed the good seed in season. . . . And if there was in us anything of an injudicious and precipitate tendency, whether in the way of assenting to all that came across us, of whatever character the objects might be, even though they proved false, or in the way of often withstanding other things, even though they were spoken truthfully,—that, too, he brought under discipline in us by those delicate reasonings already mentioned, and accustomed us not to throw in all our testimony at one time or to refuse it, just as random, as chance impelled but to give it only after careful examination. . . . In this way, that capacity of our mind which deals critically with words and reasonings, was educated in rational manner. . . .[6]

These quotations show that Origen, like other great teachers, had a sound understanding of human nature and was willing to use time and effort in training a pupil. He guided his students, helped them, inspired them, molded their characters, lived with them, and entered into their thoughts to an extent that is rarely possible for a teacher to do at present—although the serious modern student would like it well enough.

Like many other teachers, Origen had sound ideas about the value of praise and punishment and about individual reactions to these stimuli:

I say then that praise or blame or whatever resembles praise or blame, are medicines most essential of all to men. Some are hard to cure, and, like iron, are wrought into shape with fire, and hammer, and anvil, that is, with threatening and reproof and chastisement; while others . . . grow by praise.[7]

In the first half of the third century the schools with which Origen was connected were the institutions where one could obtain a "liberal" education. His attitude toward the sum total of human knowledge is well expressed in the passage below:

Nor did he [Origen] confine his efforts merely to that form of the mind which it is the lot of the dialectics to regulate . . . he aroused [us] by studies in natural science, illustrating and distinguishing the various divisions of created objects, and with admirable clearness reducing them to their pristine* elements . . . and by those reasonings which he had partly learned from others, and partly found out for himself, he filled our minds with a rational instead of an irrational wonder at the sacred economy of the uni-

[6] *Ibid.*, VI, 29–30.

[7] *Ibid.*, p. 31.

verse [and] he presented geometry lucidly as the immutable groundwork and secure foundation of all; and by . . . astronomy, he lifted us up to the things that are highest above us, while he made heaven possible to us by the help of each of these sciences, as though they were ladders reaching to the skies.[8]

Although Origen's main purpose in education were the development of Christian character and the understanding of the Scriptures, he accepted all secular learning as having its place in a normal life.

The picture of Origen that emerges from the pages of history is that of a man with inexhaustible patience, great gentleness, deep sincerity, a prodigious

FIG. 16. Origen. From S. G. Williams, *History of Medieval Education,* 1903, p. 69. Courtesy of Bardeen's Inc., publishers. This picture is undoubtedly imaginary, since no actual likenesses of Origen are in existence.

learning, and an abiding devotion to his friends and his religion. It is not surprising that one of his pupils, who had to leave him for an indefinite period, ended a eulogy to Origen with these words:

[We] pray, therefore, that some encouragement may be conveyed to us from God when we lose thy presence . . . And [we] entreat Him also to turn our course, for that is the one thing which above all else will effectually comfort us, and bring us back to thee again.[9]

B. JEROME: HIS LIFE AND WORK

In the history of the church there is no more dramatic, exciting, contradictory, and exasperating figure than Jerome. In disposition he was impatient, fanatic, excitable, often unreasonable, intense, imprudent, and highly irasci-

[8] *Ibid.*, p. 30.
[9] *Ibid.*, pp. 38–39.

ble.[10] Throughout his life he got into one emotional episode after another. There is something about Jerome reminiscent of the bull in the china shop. Whenever he became angry—which was often—he lashed out at anyone who happened to be in the way at the moment. The air around him crackled with emotional electricity. He was a natural troublemaker, who was imbued with the most fanatic missionary spirit. As a result he was—according to one excellent description of him—a person who insisted upon doing good to people who did not especially want to be done good to.[11] He had also what amounted to a genius for doing eminently worth-while things in ways that irritated the maximum number of people. Some of his acquaintances quarreled bitterly with him, some detested the flamboyancy of his nature although they admitted his genius, some merely despaired of ever keeping up with such a slave driver, and a few worshiped him. His students clearly felt the vital flame within him and were drawn to his monastery school by the magnetism of a stimulating personality, even though some of them developed feuds with him later on. In the course of his life Jerome did many different things and did none of them by halves. He was equally thorough as a scholar, a hermit, a satirist, a writer, a defender of the faith, and a missionary. Such a man, if he has also real talent, leaves a mark upon his times.

Jerome was born in A.D. 347 in a little town not far from modern Venice.* His parents were Christians, and he was brought up in the faith, although he does not seem to have taken religion any more seriously than did other young men of his acquaintance. Gradually, however, he became interested in theology and joined a group of youthful reformers who thought the church had become too worldly. As a means of reform they wanted to aid in the spread of monasticism* from the East, where it had flourished for centuries. The interest in asceticism* that was to characterize the Middle Ages had already begun before Jerome's birth. The first monastery* in Europe had been founded at Trier* in A.D. 336, and in the following decades others had appeared. By the time Jerome was a grown man, literally thousands of people had embraced the ascetic life and had gone into the mountains and deserts to become hermits. In Egypt alone there were 75,000 men and nearly 30,000 women who had forsaken all their worldly possessions and gone out on the desert to live alone, in prayer and fasting. In his characteristic, headlong way, Jerome threw himself into the reform movements with more fervor than discretion, and got into some kind of trouble so serious that he had to leave the city he was in at the time. Since his heart and soul were at the moment centered

[10] This description is based largely on E. K. Rand, *Founders of the Middle Ages,* Harvard University Press, 1928, 365 pp.; and E. L. Cutts, *Saint Jerome,* E. and J. B. Young and Company, 1897, 230 pp.

[11] Rand, *op. cit.*, p. 105.

upon monasticism, he decided to visit Syria* and obtain a firsthand view of actual hermits. He had hardly more than arrived before he had a serious illness and a terrifying dream. What with weakness from the former and excitement from the latter, Jerome was for some time in a frenzied and overfatigued condition that was—even for him—thoroughly abnormal. He was still determined to sample the hermit's life; so he went out on the nearest desert and at first indulged in many excesses—starving himself until he was emaciated, beating his body, crying for hours, and becoming so exhausted that he could see wondrous visions. This period did not last long, however. Jerome was fundamentally too intelligent to be satisfied with such a life. Although he remained on the desert for five years, his life after the first few months was quiet and regular. He had his library with him and spent much time in study and writing. At times he had scribes to copy new books for him and to write his letters; moreover, he studied Hebrew, having found a Jewish scholar also living as a hermit. By the end of five years his impulse toward asceticism had been satisfied, he was thoroughly bored with the simple life, and he wanted to be in the thick of things again. Jerome was a man of action rather than a reflective thinker, and he was also a fine scholar with a razor-sharp mind. This combination of traits does not lead to a permanent adherence to the life of the hermit, with its autohypnosis,* introversion,* withdrawal from society, and inactivity. Although Jerome approved of asceticism and monasticism throughout his life and was instrumental in developing them in Europe and elsewhere, his absorption in the more extreme forms was short-lived. Like many another he found the monastic solution of life's problems unsatisfactory, presumably because this concept of holy living rested upon a false psychology of human nature.

Upon his return to general circulation Jerome went first to Antioch,* where he was made a priest, and then to Constantinople. There he began the work of translation, Biblical commentary,* letter writing, and heretic baiting that was to continue for the rest of his life. He remained in Constantinople until, at the age of forty-two, he was called to Rome by the pope for the dual purposes of helping to establish monasticism—as a counterbalance against the decadence of the day—and of making an authoritative translation of the Bible. His stay in Rome was, however, short. As usual he plunged into the business of reform with flaming enthusiasm, immense vitality, little discretion, and no discernible tact. A few people—especially a group of wealthy women who had already banded together to live a holy life—were enchanted by him and became his followers, but the majority of prominent people were distressed by his vehemence and annoyed at his importunities. The society of the day certainly needed reform, since most men lived empty lives of frivolity and dissipation, but Jerome was hardly the person to lead such a movement.

Jerome was undoubtedly the best scholar in the church and one of the few men of his generation who were equally at home in Hebrew, Greek, or Latin. On questions of translation he was likely to be right, but his manner of riding roughshod over the opinions of others earned him the antagonism of lesser scholars whose friendship he needed. He brought down upon his head the condemnation of the regular clergy* by criticizing them vehemently for accepting contributions from wealthy patrons instead of going about in poverty as Christ had commanded. At first Jerome was well protected by the pope, to whom he was secretary; if he had been a different kind of man he could even have become pope himself, but gradually he alienated everyone who might have supported him.

At this point the latent antagonism against him was fanned into an outbreak by the death of a young woman, one of the ascetics, ostensibly from the rigors of self-denial. The many people who hated Jerome, primarily because he bothered them continually, used this death as a reason for stirring up the people of Rome against him. A number of charges were leveled simultaneously against Jerome, some of them palpably false and some partly true. All in all, there was a thorough scandal. When the smoke of battle cleared, however, Jerome was no longer in sight. He had had a brand-new idea.

With a small band of faithful followers he journeyed to Bethlehem—after having made a sight-seeing trip to the hermit colonies in Egypt—and there, in the town of Christ's birth, he established a monastery and school. After having been a young revolutionary, a hermit, a brilliant student, a priest, and a papal secretary, Jerome settled down to being a scholar and a teacher. Here, at last, his restless and irritable spirit found an environment in which it could relax. He was surrounded by friends and admirers, he lived a simple and healthy life, and he did primarily what he liked best—teaching, translating, and writing. The monastic atmosphere was soothing without being exhausting. To be sure, he lived in a cave, but from all accounts it was a comfortable one. He assembled a library and a group of scribes for the copying of borrowed books or the writing of letters. In rustic simplicity and in the quiet of his cave, Jerome found contentment for his vexed spirit, work for his active mind, and the emotional satisfaction of being adored by his monks and his students. For thirty-four years he carried on an extensive program of scholarship, the nature of which throws considerable light upon his personality.

First in importance comes his translation of the Bible—from Hebrew and Greek into Latin; his translation is known as the Vulgate,* which was the official version for eight centuries and is at this moment still the accepted version for the greater part of Europe. This translation in itself was a project of sufficient magnitude to give him a rightful reputation as a great man. The Vulgate was a scholarly and workmanlike job in which one sees the saint in his most serious and well-balanced mood. Of similar nature—although of far less volume—are his numerous commentaries upon the Bible.

Second come the histories of three saints. From the titles one might think they should be grouped with the strictly religious writings, but nothing would be less accurate. They are better classified as novels. In writing them, Jerome seems to have had two purposes in mind: to popularize the monastic life, and to give Christians something to read that was as exciting as the pagan mythologies and romances. These latter included tales of Troy* and other Greek legends; of Atlantis* and the lost continents with their idyllic communities; love stories, often concerning Helen of Troy; and the romances of Alexander,* stories of adventure and travel, of which Alexander the Great was the hero. The three productions by Jerome were best sellers of their day. With some basis in fact, the author developed stories that are a combination of *Treasure Island, Robinson Crusoe,* and *Grimms' Fairy Tales,* with a dash of Baron Münchhausen* thrown in for good measure. When it came to a plot, however, Jerome was lamentably weak. The stories give one the impression that he dictated each at one sitting and neglected to proofread the results.

Serious and sound are Jerome's historical contributions, which consisted primarily in bringing up to date the *Lives of Great Men* started by an earlier writer. The saint proved he had a logical mind when he insisted upon including outstanding heretics and prominent pagans on the grounds that they were great men, that a historian's job was to record what happened, and that he had no right to exclude people merely because he did not approve of them.

Finally there are Jerome's many letters, for the saint was an incorrigible letter writer and carried on a lively correspondence from his cave in Bethlehem. Some of his better efforts are thirty printed pages long. To him the reading and writing of letters was a real joy; to quote his own words:

> Now I talk to this letter, I embrace it, it carries on a conversation with me, it is the only thing here that knows Latin. . . . For hereabouts you must either learn a barbarous jargon or else hold your tongue. The handwriting I know so well brings your dear faces before my eyes; and then either I am no longer here or else you are here with me. . . . As I write this letter, I see you here before me.[12]

[12] F. A. Wright (translator) *Selected Letters of Saint Jerome,* Loeb Classical Library, Harvard University Press, 1923 (502 pp.), p. 21. This excerpt and subsequent ones from this reference are used by permission of the publishers.

In another letter Jerome describes the dream that so terrified him during his first months on the desert.

> I could not altogether give up my library, which I had collected at Rome with much zeal and much labor. And so, poor wretch, I would fast, in preparation for reading Tully. After the long vigil of the night, after the tears, which the remembrance of my past sins drew from the depths of my heart, I would take Plautus in hand. If I ever recovered my senses and tried to read the prophets, their uncouth style rubbed me the wrong way; and because with my blind eyes I saw not the light, I deemed it the fault not of my eyes, but of the sun. While thus the old serpent was beguiling me, one day, about the middle of Lent, a fever flooded me to the very marrow and wracked my weary body. Pausing not—incredible as it may sound—it so fed on my hapless limbs that I could scarce cleave to my bones. Meanwhile they made ready for my obsequies. The vital heat of my soul, of my breast, in a tiny spot, was still tepid—when, of a sudden, I was caught up in the spirit and haled before the judgment-seat of God. Blinded by its light and by the brightness of those who stood about it, I fell prostrate to the earth, not daring to look up. When the voice asked me concerning my condition, I replied that I was a Christian. "Thou liest," answered he that sat upon the throne. "Thou are a Ciceronian, not a Christian; for where thy treasure is, there shall thy heart be also." [13]

As a result of the dream Jerome took a vow not to read pagan books. He kept it for about fifteen years, but by that time he had founded his school in Bethlehem, where he taught pagan literature along with religious subjects.

Other letters contained biting satires—often, although not always, of women. There is, for instance, one about a man concerning whom nothing is known except that Jerome saw fit to write a letter about "Onasus, the Windbag," ending with the words: "Let your nose not be seen upon your face and let your tongue never be heard in conversation. Then you may possibly be thought both good-looking and eloquent." [14] The longer satires are often delightful, but there is no room for them here. Throughout his letters Jerome scatters what in the modern vernacular would be termed "wisecracks" such as the following:

> If there is anything holy in a beard, then there is nothing more holy than a goat.

History does not, however, explain why Jerome did not like beards.

Of Jerome's methods of teaching one gets an occasional glimpse through the letters. He wrote, for instance, the following advice on the proper education of a little girl. It should be noted that he leaned heavily upon Quintilian.

[13] *Ibid.*, pp. 125–127.

[14] *Ibid.*, p. 171.

Have letters made for her, of box-wood or ivory, and let them be called by their names. Let her play with them and let the play be part of her instruction. She must not only get the right order of the letters and memorize them in a song, but now and then mix the alphabet, last with middle and middle with first, so that she may tell them by sight as well as hearing. But when she begins with trembling hands to draw the pen through wax, either let her elder's hand guide her tender finger-joints, or let the letters be graven on the slate, that the marks she traces be confined within the edges of these furroughs and not stray outside. Let her learn to join syllable to syllable by the inducement of a prize—something very acceptable to that tender age. She should have companions in her task of learning, whose accomplishments she may envy and whose praises may spur her sense of shame. Don't scold her if she is slow, but arouse her ambition by praise so that she may delight at victory and smart at defeat. Above all, don't allow her to hate her studies, lest the bitterness of them, acquired in childhood, may last to her mature years.[15]

To get her to repeat her lessons in her little shrill voice she must have a prize of honey cake offered to her. She will do her work quickly if she is going to receive as reward some sweetmeat, or bright flower, or glittering bauble, or pretty doll. Let her be rewarded for singing psalms aloud, so that she may love what she is forced to do, and it will not be work but pleasure, not a matter of necessity but one of free-will.[16]

The school Jerome founded was originally for the boys in the village of Bethlehem. The sketch in Figure 17 is presumably intended as a view of Jerome's "school," since the teacher is wearing the saint's halo and is accompanied by a lion—this saint's particular trade-mark.[17] Jerome's school appears to have grown into a typical monastic school, such as will be described in the following section. Young men came from far and near, partly to join the monastic community and partly to attend the school. The comments still extant from Jerome's pupils indicate the existence of a real devotion between him and them. He was evidently an inspiring teacher to whom people flocked, but his success seems due more to his vivid personality than to any specific methodology. If he taught in the way he wrote, it should have been a joy to listen to him. Certainly he had in abundance two of the traits that characterize good teachers—the desire to help others and the ability to explain matters clearly.

For more than thirty years life in Bethlehem flowed on rather quietly, punctuated by enough quarrels with people in distant lands to break the monotony, and occasionally greatly saddened by the death of a favorite disci-

[15] *Ibid.*, pp. 345–347.
[16] *Ibid.*, p. 467.
[17] In later centuries stories grew up to the effect that Jerome shared his cave with a lion.

ple. Jerome outlived both his dearest friends and his most carping critics, and remained a spitfire to the end of his days. It is a revealing evidence of his great fascination that his last years were soothed by the grandchild of his first convert. He died in A.D. 420, when over eighty years old, after having lived for thirty-four years in his cave—writing, teaching, studying, praying, and fasting—a true Christian, and one who never ceased to be delightfully human.

There are innumerable pictures of Jerome, since he was a favorite topic for painters, but all of them are imaginary. The picture in Figure 18 is as good as any. It shows a mature man in a reflective mood.

The fathers of the early Christian church, among whom both Origen and Jerome are to be included, not only formulated doctrines, adopted creeds,

FIG. 17. A Monastic School. From an old wood engraving.

and fought heresies. They also dominated early Christian education and, since they were all more or less deeply stirred by the ascetic ideal, they were the men who turned education away from the practical affairs of the world, away from sense experience, away from physical education, away from normal, healthy growth. The original urge to asceticism had vitality, but even at best its effect on education was to turn it from external reality. The disastrous effects of this change in direction will become more evident in subsequent chapters.

C. EARLY CHRISTIAN SCHOOLS

The third, fourth, and fifth centuries produced most of the church fathers, the men who gave the Christian church its body of doctrine* and interpreted the Bible. Among them were such familiar names as Augustine,* Jerome, Chrysostom,* Ambrose,* Eusebius,* Basil,* Cyril,* and Gregory Nazianzen,* to mention only a few from the third to fifth centuries. In the sixth, seventh, and eighth centuries the procession continued, with such outstanding figures as Benedict,* Gregory,* and Boniface.* Many of these men were teachers as well as writers and missionaries. Thus Augustine in Hippo,* Ambrose in Milan, and Eusebius in Arles all gathered together groups of young students who lived with them and were taught by them—a custom that foreshadowed the cathedral schools of the Middle Ages. As already noted, the concepts of education formulated by the church fathers dominated Christian training for several centures.

FIG. 18. Jerome. From S. G. Williams, *History of Medieval Education,* 1903, p. 75. Courtesy of Bardeen's, Inc., publishers.

1. Attitudes toward Pagan Learning The attitude of churchmen toward Latin and Latin authors was somewhat ambivalent. The Bible and the church services were in Latin; therefore every priest had to learn the language. On the other hand, the literature that then existed in Latin was pagan; therefore the church wanted the language but not the literature. There were some periods of extreme antagonism during which pagan writings were collected and burned, and Christians were forbidden to read them. For instance, the Apostolic Constitutions* say:

Abstain from all the heathen books. For what hast thou to do with such foreign discourses, or laws, or false prophets, which subvert the faith of the unstable? For what defect dost thou find in the law of God, that thou shouldst have recourse to those heathenish fables? For if thou hast a mind to read history, thou hast the books of the Kings; if books of wisdom or poetry, thou hast those of the prophets, of Job* and the Proverbs, in which thou wilt find greater depth of sagacity than in all the heathen poets and sophisters, because these are the words of the Lord, the only wise God. If thou desirest something to sing, thou hast the Psalms; if the origin of things, thou hast Genesis; if laws and statutes, thou hast the glorious law of the Lord God.[18]

A similar attitude was expressed even more vigorously by Gregory the Great,* who said: "Christ cannot be praised by the same mouth that has praised Jove.*" Perhaps these more extreme attitudes might have been milder had the literary products of the third to the sixth centuries after Christ not been so decadent. The noblest of the classics and Christianity fuse rather easily, but one can understand the resistance of Christians toward the writing of the period.

Antagonism toward any pagan writing, however moral, was not without justification, however, if one grant the premises assumed by the early Christians. All the ancient peoples clearly regarded the end of education to be the development of the student into an intelligent citizen. This idea is much the same as the objective of education at present, except that all men are now included, at least in theory, whereas the ancients considered only the upper classes. The Middle Ages constitute a complete break in this train of thought. The church looked upon this life as merely a pilgrimage to an unseen but very real future existence. *The education of antiquity was designed to produce a man of the world; Christian education was designed to produce a man of God.* Since these two concepts are in direct opposition to each other, it is not surprising that the thoughtful members of the early church regarded protection against the classical writings as highly essential.

The two attitudes were not always in violent opposition, however. For instance, Chrysostom has the following comments to offer in regard to the imperial Roman schools:

If you have masters among you who can answer for the virtue of your children, I should be very far from advocating your sending them to a monastery; on the contrary I should insist upon their remaining where they are. But if no one can give such a guarantee, you ought not to send children to schools where they will learn vice before they learn science and where in acquiring learning of relatively small value they will lose what is far more precious—their integrity of soul . . . . The choice lies between two alternatives: a liberal education which you may get by sending your children to the public school; or the salvation of their souls which you secure by

[18] From the *Apostolic Constitutions.*

sending them to the monks. Which is to win the day, science or the soul? If you can unite both advantageously, do so by all means, but if not, choose the more precious.[19]

The more educated men, who had been brought up on the classics, were often more liberal still. They wanted to use the great Greek and Latin writers as models of rhetoric and taste and to preserve the primitive virtues often shown in these writings, but at the same time to create a reformed literature of equal merit based upon Christian ideals. That is, they would salvage whatever was beautiful and good, regardless of its pagan source, thus retaining the culture of the ancients but in a Christian form. This moderate view could be held only by educated men who loved the classics too much to abandon them. It was not widespread, but it did exist and undoubtedly helped to offset the fanatical opposition of certain less educated or less well-balanced individuals. As the church became better established, the ban on classical writings was lifted somewhat, but throughout the earlier part of the Middle Ages the Latin authors were regarded by the majority of people as possible sources of contamination.

2. *Catechetical Schools* The earliest type of school developed by the Christians appeared in the second century after the birth of Christ. It existed originally for the purpose of teaching adult Christian converts to read the Bible and to understand the fundamental doctrines of the church. It was called a "catechetical school" because in the beginning the course of study consisted largely of the church catechism, a set of questions and answers that were learned by heart. The first of these schools appeared in Alexandria in A.D. 180. Within a few years similar schools were opened in many cities of the empire, especially in the eastern half. There were catechetical schools in such ancient centers as Jerusalem, Antioch, Athens, Carthage,* Rome, Edessa,* and Caesarea. It should be noted that most of them are outside the limits of modern Europe, the territory over which hordes of barbarians roamed for several centuries.

For some years after A.D. 180, anyone who wanted any education beyond the elementary level of the catechetical school was still dependent upon the civil schools. As the new faith spread to educated people, however, an extension of the curriculum became necessary because many of the young educated converts had already studied much pagan literature. It was therefore essential to have a few Christian schools of a more advanced character, in which the teachers would be able to discuss ancient philosophies and to relate them to Christian beliefs. Such an advanced school existed in Alexandria, where a

[19] Quoted in G. Hodgson, *Primitive Christian Education,* T. and T. Clark, 1906 (287 pp.), page 223. Used by permission of the publisher.

series of excellent scholars, of whom Clement* and Origen were outstanding, lectured in various fields. These early schools were, however, almost completely dependent upon the individual teacher who gave instruction. When a teacher left his school, his students usually followed him. The life of a school was therefore often short, because it ceased to exist after it lost its outstanding and perhaps only teacher. Thus the catechetical school in Alexandria was practically a university for about fifty years under Clement and Origen, although it had lower classes for beginners, but it sank into obscurity after these famous teachers were no longer there.

In any case, the catechetical school was a transitional institution and adapted to the needs of a growing religion only when that religion was still in its infancy. The school itself had no special building or equipment. The teachers were not paid. The school consisted only of a man who wanted to teach and a small group of young Christians who wanted to learn. They met apparently wherever it was convenient, either at the teacher's house or at that of a friend. There were no regular hours and no fixed curriculum. There is some indication that at least some of the students lived with the teacher. The discussions appear to have started whenever the student asked questions and to have gone on until all concerned wanted to do something else. It is only in the first glow of a great enthusiasm that one finds schools which simply spring up without organization or equipment, with volunteer teachers. Their informality must have been delightful, but their lack of organization and their dependence upon single inspired individuals soon resulted in their complete disappearance.

3. Schools in Monasteries or Cathedrals As the catechetical schools dwindled, two other types made their appearance: the monastery school and the cathedral school. A few isolated examples of each type existed before the sixth century—for instance Jerome's monastic school in Bethlehem—but it was not till the sixth century that these schools appeared in numbers. Even though the following descriptions rather anticipate the next chapter, it seems best to keep together the account of the three main types of Christian school. Beginning in about the middle of the sixth century, boys were educated either in a school attached to a monastery or in one attached to a cathedral.[20] The monks* were responsible for the conduct of the former, and the local bishops for the maintenance of the latter. The majority of the boys in the cathedral schools were presumed to be candidates for the regular clergy, while those in the monastery schools were expected to become monks. In both types of school, however, there were some pupils called "externs" who

[20] For a good description of such a school, see J. M. Clark, *The Abbey of St. Gall*, Cambridge University Press, 1926, 322 pp.

did not intend to become either priests or monks but wanted a general education. Since there were few, if any, secular* schools, they attended those in either a monastery or a cathedral.

Most of the early monasteries were organized under the "Rule of St. Benedict*" devised for the first monastery in Europe, at Monte Cassino,* in A.D. 529. This rule required that the members of holy orders* were dedicated not only to live chaste lives but to carry on work in charity, farming, and teaching. Monastic life in Europe differed from that in the East because the monks were workers; they did not live as hermits nor did they spend their lives in contemplation. Among other activities they taught and made copies of books, thus preserving and passing on much that would otherwise have been lost. Even the classical authors were copied, perhaps on the principle that any book was too valuable to destroy. It is true that the church sometimes repressed the ancient learning, especially in the early years when it was still competing with paganism, but at the same time it was the only agency in Western Europe that tried to carry on, with new materials and objectives, any education at all. It destroyed, but it also preserved and built.

The content of the curriculum was much the same in both monastery and cathedral schools, and consisted of reading, writing, and singing, with sometime a little arithmetic. This material was purely utilitarian. The reading was necessary for studying the Bible, the church fathers, and the church services. The writing was needed for the copying of manuscripts. Since books were so scarce, every monastery had to borrow from others and then make its own copies. Consequently, the ability to form the letters, even though the words might not be understood, was essential. The rudiments of singing were of value because the church services were accompanied by music. Arithmetic was not a universal subject, but a few people had to know how to compute the dates of Easter. Thus the four subjects were all elementary and were conceived along purely practical lines. The academic work in the cathedral schools did not differ sufficiently from that of the monastery schools to make further description necessary.

It was the intention of early teachers in Christian schools to teach without resort to force or threats in the maintenance of discipline. The schools had hardly become going concerns, however, before the wave of asceticism swept over the church, leading men to mortify their bodies in the interests of preserving their souls. The movement was so strong that it tended to drive out the spirit of love in the schools and to substitute for it a severe discipline that was more reminiscent of the Old Testament than the New.

As may be seen at once, these schools represent a retrogression. The schools of antiquity were better taught and included more advanced subject matter. Some of the catechetical schools were also superior, probably because the teachers were men who had obtained their education before the ban on classical learning went into effect. Thus they had a wide culture upon which to base their teaching. By casting aside most of the past, the church inevitably had to begin over with a much lower standard of education until it had created a literature of its own and had trained an adequate supply of Christian teachers.

The church fathers used relatively simple language in their teaching and preaching, because the converts to whom they talked were simple folk who would only be confused by rhetorical flourishes. Their writings were less brilliant than those of many pagan authors, but they had greater vitality and a closer relation to reality. Moreover, these men had something to say. They needed good powers of persuasion in order to preach convincingly, just as the Roman senator had once needed them in order to help govern his country. Rhetoric did not, therefore, become a lost art, although in the earlier centuries of Christianity the leaders favored a direct, forceful style of expression.

During the centuries under consideration, then, the situation may be summed up as follows: there were a few outstanding scholars, most of whom lived rather early in the period before the Dark Ages became as dark as they later were. A small amount of learning was disseminated among members of the priesthood. Noblemen and princes acquired at best only the rudiments of elementary schoolwork. The common people as a whole were taught the dogmas of the church by word of mouth but little more, although individual boys from peasant families did sometimes go as far along the road of learning as anyone else. The minds of people were fixed upon the next world, and education at all could be defended only because reading Christian writings might help the soul on its journey through life.

These centuries bequeathed to posterity two features that remained characteristic of education for a long time. From the Greek and Roman world came the main content of the medieval curriculum and most of the elementary schoolbooks. From the Christian world came the objectives of instruction, the more advanced reading materials, and the new kinds of schools. In the end, Christianity absorbed paganism because it was the more vigorous of the two.

Christianity contributed to education certain basic ideas that have characterized it ever since. Because it stressed the brotherhood and equal rights of all mankind, it laid the foundation for the far-off development of universal education. Because it stressed the power of love instead of force, and of co-operation instead of competition, it created a new kind of society and a new kind of school, in which children were led instead of being driven. Because it valued men above riches, it gave humanity a dignity that made people worth educating, and it stressed the value of ideas and beliefs as sources of power. These basic concepts required centuries of patient effort on the part of many people before they could be even partly realized in the world's schools, but without them education would not have developed in Europe as it did in subsequent centuries.

READING REFERENCES

A. General Histories

Arragon, *The Transition from the Ancient to the Medieval World,* part iii, chaps. 42–44.
Burns, *The First Europe,* chap. 4.
Munro, D. C., and R. J. Sontag, *The Middle Ages, 395–1500,* Appleton-Century-Crofts Company, 1928 (rev. ed., 562 pp.), chaps. 2, 6.
Robinson, *History of Rome from 753 B.C. to A.D. 410,* part ii, chap. 22.
Rostovtzeff, *A History of the Ancient World,* Vol. II, chap. 23.
Seignobos, C., *The Rise of European Civilization,* Alfred Knopf, 1938 (436 pp.), chap. 4.
Trevor, *History of Ancient Civilization,* Vol. II, chap. 30.

B. Other Texts in the History of Education

Cubberley, *History of Education,* chap. 4.
Marique, P. J., *History of Christian Education,* Fordham University Press, 1924–1932 (3 vols.), Vol. I, chaps. 2, 4.
McCormick, *History of Education,* chaps. 8–10.
Monroe, *A Textbook in the History of Education,* pp. 221–273.
Moore, *The Story of Instruction,* Vol. II, chap. 2.
Reisner, *Historical Foundations of Modern Education,* chap. 7.
Ulich, *History of Educational Thought,* pp. 51–60.

C. Secondary Sources

Cadoux, C. J., *The Early Church and the World,* T. and T. Clark, Ltd., 1925 (675 pp.), part iv, chaps. 3, 4; part v, chaps. 3–5; part vi, chaps. 4, 5.
Clark, *The Abbey of St. Gall,* chap. 5.
De Faye, *Origen and His Work,* pp. 11–30.
Dill, *Roman Society in the Last Centuries of the West,* book ii, chap. 1.
Hodgson, *Primitive Christian Education,* chaps. 4, 8.
Laurie, S. S., *The Rise and Early Constitution of Universities,* Appleton-Century-Crofts Company, 1891 (293 pp.), chap. 2.
Magevney, E., *Christian Education in the First Centuries,* Catholic Library Association, 1917, 64 pp.
Nock, A. D., *The Old and the New in Religion from Alexander the Great to Augustine of Hippo,* Oxford University Press, 1933, 309 pp., chaps. 12–14.
Painter, *Great Pedagogical Essays,* chaps. 8, 9.
Rand, *Founders of the Middle Ages,* chaps. 1, 2, 4.

D. Translations of Primary Sources

Roberts and Donaldson, *The Ante-Nicene Fathers,* IV, 223–230, 393–394.
Schaaf and Wace, *The Nicene and Post-Nicene Fathers,* Vol. VI, letters cvii (pp. 189–195) and cxxviii (pp. 258–260).
Ulich, *Three Thousand Years of Educational Wisdom,* pp. 164–173.
Wright, *Collected Letters of St. Jerome,* letters cvii and cxxviii.

PART FOUR

THE MIDDLE AGES

CHAPTER VI

ALCUIN AND THE SCHOOLS OF THE MIDDLE AGES

By A.D. 300 the Roman Empire was beginning to crumble; its classical period was already over, and its literary glory almost a thing of the past. By 1300, the Renaissance, which was to usher in modern civilization, was beginning to stir faintly. Exactly halfway between these two dates stands a historical figure of heroic proportions—Charles the Great, usually known as Charlemagne. Associated with him was a famous teacher by the name of Alcuin. These two men, working together, produced a remarkable revival of learning that began late in the eighth century and continued into the ninth. It did not last long, but before it flickered out it had played a vital role in preserving the ancient learning from complete loss in Western Europe and in laying the foundation for subsequent and more lasting revivals.

The two centuries before and after Charlemagne and Alcuin are often referred to as the Dark Ages during which the people of Europe needed all their energies merely to stay alive. Even the meager education available was a luxury that only a few ever enjoyed. Before relating the story of Alcuin and Charlemagne, it seems best to present a brief summary of the prevailing ideas of the times.

1. *Beliefs of the Dark Ages:** In order to illustrate the appalling intellectual darkness of the period, a few examples will be quoted from an important work produced in the seventh century. Something over a hundred years before Alcuin's birth a certain Spanish bishop, Isidore of Seville,* had produced the world's first encyclopedia. As an effort at collecting and classifying existing knowledge the encyclopedia deserves only praise, but the nature of its content demonstrates well the limitations of knowledge in the early Middle Ages. By the time Alcuin was a grown man the encyclopedia had become a widely used source book for Western scholars. Judged by modern standards much of it is nonsense, but one has no right to judge it by any standards except those of its own period, and by these it was a work of great merit. It was a compendium* of what men knew or believed. The items below have been so selected as to cover a number of different fields. They show the kind of ideas current before and during Alcuin's life.

A. Geography[1]

1. The Tigris, a river of Mesopotamia, rises in Paradise and flows opposite the Assyrians and after many windings flows into the Dead Sea. It is called by this name because of its velocity, like a tiger that runs with great speed.

2. Scotia (Ireland) is an island very near Britain, narrower but more fertile. This reaches from Africa towards Boreas, and Iberia and the Cantabrian Ocean are opposite to the first part of it. Whence it is also called Hibernia. There are no snakes there and no bees. If one scatters among beehives stones brought thence, the swarms desert them.

B. Arithmetic

3. There are 22 sextarii in a bushel because God in the beginning made 22 works; there are 22 generations from Adam to Jacob; and 22 books of the Old Testament as far as Esther and 22 letters of the alphabet out of which the divine law is composed.

4. Number is divided into even and odd. Even number is divided into the following: evenly even, evenly uneven, unevenly even, and unevenly uneven. Odd number is divided into the following: prime and uncompounded, compounded, and a third class that comes between which in a certain way is prime and uncompounded but in another way is secondary and compounded.

5. Some even numbers are excessive, others are defective, others perfect. Excessive are those whose factors being added together exceed its total, as for instance, XII. Defective numbers are those which being reckoned by their factors make a less total as, for example, X. The perfect number is that which is equalled by its factors, as VI (2 plus 3 plus 1). The perfect numbers are VI, XXVIII, CCCCXCVI.

6. A circular number when it is multiplied by itself begins with itself and ends with itself. For example 5 x 5 = 25. A spherical number is that which being multiplied by a circular number ends with itself; for example 5 x 5 are 25 and this circle being multiplied by itself makes a sphere that is 5 x 25 = 125.

C. Language

7. Among the Greeks there were five magic letters. The first is "r" which denotes human life. The second is "o" which denotes death. The third is "t" indicating the shape of the cross of the Lord. The remaining two, the first and the last, Christ claims for himself saying, "I am the alpha and omega."

8. Etymologies are given in accordance with cause or origin, as *homo* because he is from the earth (*humus*), or from contraries, as *lutum* (mud)

[1] These quotations are from E. Brehaut, *An Encyclopedia of the Dark Ages,* No. 120 in *The Columbia Studies in History, Economics, and Public Law,* Columbia University Press, 1912, 275 pp. These excerpts are used by permission of the publisher and the author. The quotations given appear in Brehaut on the following pages in order: 241, 246, 257, 121, 128, 130, 96, 100, 119, 145, 151, 159, 217, 177, 225, 235, 205, 196, 206, 188, 220.

from *lavare* to wash, since mud is not clean—and *lucus* (sacred grove) because being shady it has little light (*lux*).

9. For setting down first the genus, then the species, we subjoin also other things that are possibly related, and by setting aside common qualities we make distinctions—until we arrive at the proper qualities of that which we are examining, its meaning being made definite, as for example: A man is a thinking animal, mortal, terrestrial, a biped, and capable of laughing.

D. Sciences

10. With such swiftness is the sphere of heaven said to run that if the stars would not run against its headlong course in order to delay it, it would destroy the universe.

11. Antegradation is when a star seems to be making its usual course but is really somewhat ahead of it; retrogradation is when a star while moving on its regular orbit seems at the same time to be moving backward; status means that a star while continuing in its proper motion seems in some places to stand still.

12. All diseases arise from four humors, that is from the blood, bile, black bile, and phlegm. Just as there are four elements so also there are four humors and each humor imitates its element: blood, air; bile, fire; black bile, earth; phlegm, water. From blood and bile acute disorders come; from phlegm and black bile, troubles of long standing.

13. The knees (genuae) are so called because in the womb they are opposite to the cheeks (genae). In short, man in his beginning is so folded up that his knees are above, and by these the eyes are so shaped that there are deep hollows. Thence it is that when men fall on their knees they at once begin to weep. For nature has willed it that they remember their mother's womb where they sat in darkness.[2]

14. Night is caused either because the sun is worn out with his long journey and is weary when he comes to the last stretch of heaven and blows out his weakened fires; or because he has driven under the lands with the same force with which he carried his light over them and thus the shadow of the earth makes night.

15. The wolf is a ravenous beast and of it the country people say that a man loses his voice if a wolf sees him first.

16. Atoms exist either in a body or in time or in number or in the letters. In a body as in a stone. You divide it into parts and the parts themselves into grains and the grains into dust until you come to some little particle which cannot be divided. This is an atom in a body. In time you divide years into months, the months into days, the days into hours, and so on, until you come to an instant of time that cannot be divided. This is an atom of time. In numbers, as for example, 8 is divided into 4's, again 4 into 2's, then 2 into 1's. One is an atom because it is indivisible. So also in the case of the letters. For you can divide a speech into words, words into syllables, and syllables into letters. The letter, the smallest part, is an atom and cannot be divided.

[2] This sounds like a forerunner of psychoanalysis!

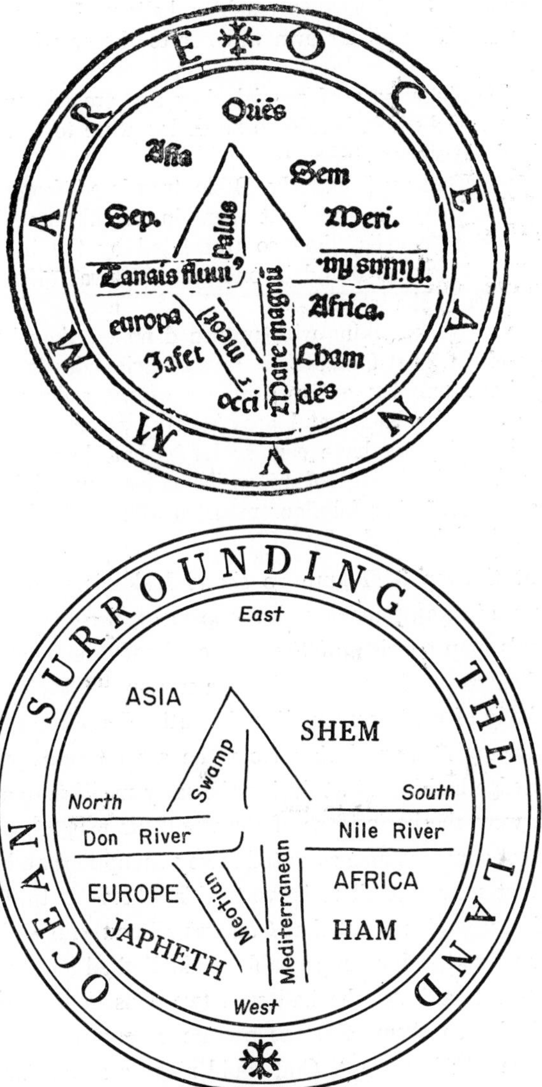

FIG. 19. Isidore's Map of the World. From E. Brehaut, *An Encyclopedist of the Dark Ages,* p. 245. Courtesy of the author and Columbia University Press, publishers.

G. Religion and Magic

17. The demons or bad angels unsettle the senses, stir low passions, disorder life, cause alarms in sleep, bring diseases, fill the mind with terror, distort the limbs, control the way in which lots are cast, make a pretense at oracles by their tricks, arouse the passion of love, create the beast of cupidity, lurk in consecrated images.

18. Heresy is so named from its meaning of choice, since each at his

own will chooses what he pleases to teach or believe. But we are not permitted to believe anything of our own will nor to choose what someone else believed of his.

19. *Larvae* [a minor type of spook] they say are demons made from men who have been wicked. It is said to be their nature to terrify little ones and to gibber in dark corners.

20. This man [Ptolemy] had the Bible translated from Hebrew into Greek by seventy translators and kept them in the library of Alexandria. Being placed in separate cells, they so translated by the influence of the Holy Spirit that nothing was found in one text that was different from the rest, even in the order of the words.

21. The Satyrs are manikins with upturned noses; they have horns on their foreheads and are goat-footed. The race of Sciopodes is said to live in Ethiopia. They have one leg apiece and are of marvellous swiftness. In summer they lie on their backs and are shaded by the greatness of their feet. The Panotii of Scythia have ears so large that they cover the whole body with them. The Antipodes of Libya have feet turned backward and eight toes on each foot. Other fabulous monstrosities of the human race are said to exist, but they do not.[3]

The map at the top of Figure 19 shows Isidore's map of the world. Since the words are in Latin and not clearly printed, there is a translation at the right. Isidore's map consists of the four cardinal directions, three continents, three Biblical races of man, two rivers, a swamp, the Mediterranean sea, and a mythical body of water surrounding the entire flat, circular earth. Comparison with Ptolemy's* map dating from the second century A.D., shows how much knowledge had been lost during the early medieval period.

Such, then, were the basic ideas of the world, its peoples, and its workings. Even the most educated men accepted these assumptions and explanations as true. If any fact seemed a bit resistive to this scheme of things, the average man stood fast upon his belief that God was all-powerful and could bring anything to pass no matter how improbable to the limited mind of man. Thus if Gregory the Great said that he had seen two suns in the heaven at the same time, he had seen them, and the prosaic observation that there was obviously only one was irrelevant. God could make a second sun if He felt like it, and if Gregory saw it where others did not, this fact was proof merely that a saint's mind had less narrow limits than the mind of an ordinary individual. Or if he pursued to its conclusions the logical argument that the less is always derived from the greater and arrived at the belief that rivers always flow out of oceans because they are smaller, he did not allow his conclusion to be upset by the observation that rivers flow into oceans and not out

[3] Apparently there were some things that even Isidore would not believe, but one wonders where they could have been.

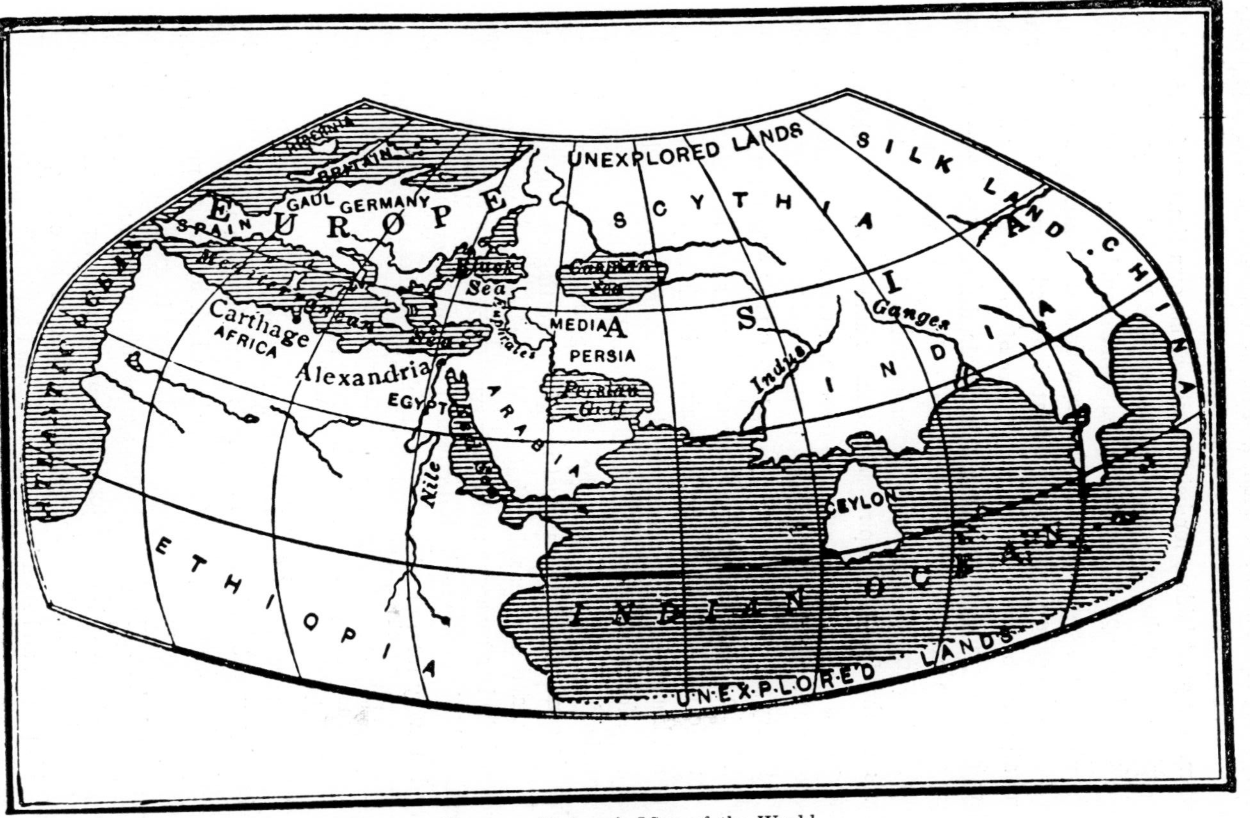

FIG. 20. Ptolemy's Map of the World.

of them. Logic, tradition, religion, and magic were always right; the feeble mind and easily deluded senses of man were always wrong. One must not condemn the good Isidore for being a man of his own times or for accepting the basic attitudes that were prevalent about him. Instead, one should admire his industry in compiling his encyclopedia and should be grateful to him for furnishing such excellent proof of just how dark the Dark Ages were.

2. *Charlemagne* Charles the Great inherited from his father and grandfather a kingdom not far from the size of modern France, in which the rulers had been able to maintain a moderate degree of security for some fifty years. He was himself a "barbarian"; that is, he was descended from leaders of the Franks, one of the barbarian tribes that invaded the northern fringes of the Roman Empire. The tribal name survives in the modern "France." Charlemagne enlarged his domain, increased its security, and did all one man could do to develop its culture.

In every way Charlemagne deserved his title of "the great." As a military leader he fought against the Saracens* on the south and the Saxons* on the north, overcoming both and maintaining in his empire a degree of security not known in Europe since the days of Roman power and not experienced again for several centuries. As a religious leader, he was equally forceful in defending the pope and the church against foes from without and within, in combating heretical doctrines, in converting conquered peoples to Christianity, and in demanding that his bishops* and abbots* reform themselves and the lesser clergy* under their supervision. As an educational leader he exerted his influence by both decree and precept. He made it unmistakably clear that every form of advancement should go to those who were best educated, and he himself laid aside the sword whenever he could and sat humbly in the schoolroom, learning with indefatigable zeal and modest success to write and read.

With the accession of Charlemagne to the throne, in the conveniently remembered year of 800, increased emphasis upon education and culture was at once felt. Even from the first years, during which he had to put his major efforts into military matters, he used his influence to establish schools and to encourage scholars. The cultural odds against him were extremely heavy, but Charlemagne was a vital and determined person. Whatever the cost, he would have peace in his kingdom, decency in the lives of his clergy, Christianity among his people, and such learning as he could get in his schools. After the custom of his time, he was a firm believer in the argumentative power of the sword. He did not hesitate to use this method of persuasion, and it seems probable that few things gave him more genuine pleasure than to subdue a group of stubborn infidels.* By the time he had been king for a few years he had so thoroughly convinced other rulers, the barbarian tribes outside his borders, and the church officials of his readiness and dexterity with three feet of steel that he could turn his attention to other matters, merely rattling the saber from time to time so that people would not forget he had one. Al-

FIG. 21. Charlemagne. From S. G. Williams, *History of Medieval Education,* p. 65. Courtesy of Bardeen's, Inc., publishers.

though he continued to make periodic forays against the Saxons, his main energies were directed to the internal affairs of his kingdom.

Charlemagne was a fine-looking, upstanding man, as may be inferred from the picture shown in Figure 21. One can believe that he had a mind of his own. When he became angry—a fairly common occurrence—his eyes flashed, his great voice boomed out, and he laid about him with great violence, but the storm did not last long and he did not hold grudges. Both his character and his intelligence are reflected in his picture.

Beginning about 775 Charlemagne began to gather together scholars from all over Europe in the hope of finding for his court school a master who could do the things that should be done. The tasks before this teacher were numerous. This man must, first of all, maintain a school at Charlemagne's court for the education of the royal family, the nobles, and the future clergy. Second, he must correct the innumerable errors that had crept into existing books through the frequent and sometimes careless copying of monks. Third, he should collect additional books by having them copied and should build up libraries in the monasteries. Fourth, he must train clerics as teachers to meet the requirement of Charlemagne that education should be available in cathedral and monastery schools throughout his kingdom. Fifth, he should be a distinguished and able theologian, so that he could help Charlemagne defend the church from heresy. Moreover, the man for the position should be a thorough scholar so that he could command the allegiance of churchmen. There are not in any generation many men who have the ability, the education, and the personality for a position of this kind. Such a man the king finally found, however, in Alcuin of York,* who became the foremost teacher of the Middle Ages.

A. ALCUIN: HIS LIFE AND WORK

1. Alcuin's Life Story It is easy to chronicle the objective facts of Alcuin's life.[4] He was born in about 735 in or near London. At an early age he entered the cathedral school of York as a pupil and remained there for over thirty years, during which he was first a student, then a teacher, and—for four years—the headmaster of the school. In 782 he was summoned to France by Charlemagne to the palace school at Aix-la-Chapelle.* After a dozen years as master of the palace school he retired as abbot to a monastery at Tours,* where he remained until his death in 804. No doubt Alcuin found his life exciting, but most of the circumstances that made it so took place inside his head.

Alcuin of York was, by both temperament and training, the right man to meet Charlemagne's needs. As his full name implies, he was an Englishman who had been brought up in English schools, where he had received a better education than he could have gotten on the Continent. In the turbulent centuries just preceding the reign of Charlemagne most European scholars had fled from the Continent and had lit the lamp of learning anew in Ireland

[4] The material in this section is based chiefly upon three biographies of Alcuin: C. J. B. Gaskoin, *Alcuin, His Life and Work,* Cambridge University Press, 1904; 275 pp.; A. F. West, *Alcuin,* Charles Scribner's Sons, 1892, 205 pp.; C. M. Wilmot-Buxton, *Catholic Thought and Thinkers,* Harding and More, 1922, 223 pp.

and northern England;[5] from its light the scholars in English schools received the small amount of education then available. The best scholars and the most active missionaries of the sixth, seventh, and eighth centuries were Irish, or else Englishmen who had been taught in schools founded recently by Irishmen. The cathedral school of York, attended by Alcuin, was such a school.

Because of Alcuin's promise as a future scholar he had been a favorite with his masters and had been taken by them several times through Europe on trips to Rome. He had in this way become acquainted with European affairs and with the theological as well as the practical problems dealt with in Rome. He knew the papal court, and many of the secular* leaders as well were among his friends. There was thus no provincialism about him. Such books as were available he had read; in fact he had practically memorized them, as was usual in that age. He once wrote a poem in which he listed the books, as he remembered them, in the library at York. The total list includes forty-one authors; of the great Greek and Roman writers, the library contained only fragments of Aristotle, Pliny,* Cicero, and Virgil. There were writings by thirteen church fathers, and by several Latin authors of late Roman times, plus two English writers, and a number of grammars. Their content comprised the major part of Alcuin's stock in trade as a teacher and scholar. He was, however, better off than another medieval schoolmaster who made a list of his own books on the flyleaf of one of them. His entire library contained fourteen books—five grammars, three rhetorics, one book from the Bible, one volume of the incomparable Isidore, excerpts from two minor Latin writers, one set of dialogues (unspecified), some notes on Cato, and a lone arithmetic which—from the notation following its name—may or may not have belonged to him.[6] With such meager equipment, he was supposed to shed light in dark places.

Alcuin came to the palace school at Charlemagne's court with a reputation for scholarship, a mastery of such learning as existed, and the eager spirit of a missionary. He had already been headmaster of the famous school at York and had been successful—so much so that young men had flocked to him from many countries. Some of them even followed him to France[7] when he left York. Alcuin wanted to disseminate education just as widely as he could, but he would probably have remained in England had his own country been suf-

[5] For accounts of the Irish and English schools, see H. Graham, *The Early Irish Monastic Schools,* Talbot Press, 1923, 206 pp.; and J. Healy, *Insula Sanctorum et Doctorum: Ireland's Ancient Schools and Scholars,* Talbot Press, 1890, 651 pp.

[6] From A. F. Leach, *The Schools of Medieval England,* Methuen & Co., Ltd., 1915 (349 pp.), p. 95.

[7] For purposes of clarity the modern names of European countries have been used throughout the book.

ficiently peaceful for tranquil study. York lay, however, in the small kingdom of Northumbria* where, during the twenty-five years before Alcuin left England, six consecutive kings had come to violent ends. The court was a center of vice, intrigue, violence, and strife. In such an atmosphere Alcuin could not do good work himself nor could he persuade many young men to forsake the clash of arms or the pagan luxuries and excitements of the court to enter upon the cloistered* life of the scholar. Apparently he felt much like a certain minor poet who lived in Toulouse at a time when the countryside was being periodically laid waste by raiders from the north; this poet was asked why he no longer produced anything of value. He answered, "How can I write six-foot hexameters* when I am surrounded by seven-foot barbarians?"[8] Alcuin also may have believed that in England he could not possibly do the work in which lay his whole heart and soul, and he may have been attracted by the idea of receiving support from a strong ruler in a peaceful country. He therefore, after obtaining the consent both of his king and of his archbishop,* accepted Charlemagne's offer. Thus two men, very different in temperament but alike in ideals, came together. Alcuin contributed learning, balance, methodical persistence, tact, gentleness, and instructional skill; Charlemagne provided imagination, drive, magnetism, authority, and a flaming vitality. Such a combination always produces results.

2. *Alcuin's Character* Through his own writings and through those of his associates and pupils, Alcuin's personality shines forth clearly. Conservatism, simplicity of spirit, absolute dependability, enthusiasm for any task great or small that would promote a pupil's growth, ingenuity in the presentation of material, natural delight in contacts with young people, utter unselfishness, and devoted loyalty were his outstanding characteristics. Excerpts from his own writings reveal him better than the words of another could do.

For instance, Alcuin once dedicated to two friends a treatise on the Gospel according to St. John,* and, in his accompanying letter to them, expressed himself in this manner:

> I have reverently searched the writings of the early church fathers, and whatever I have been able to find there, I have sent for you to read. . . . For I have preferred to borrow their thoughts and words rather than to venture anything of my own, even if the curiosity of my readers were to approve of it, and by a most cautious manner of writing I have been very careful not to set down anything contrary to the thoughts of the fathers.[9]

These words summarize well the conservatism and lack of initiative that char-

[8] See J. Sandys, *A History of Classical Scholarship,* Cambridge University Press, 1903–1908 (3 vols.), I, 246.
[9] West, *op. cit.*, p. 91.

acterized this typical teacher of the Middle Ages. Like many another teacher Alcuin made no attempt to add to the sum total of knowledge or to venture into unexplored fields. He was essentially a "middleman of culture"; that is, he studied what was available in the libraries of his time, assimilated it with patience and diligence, organized and simplified it, and passed it on to his students. He was not a keen thinker nor an original philosopher; he established no school of thought. Although he wrote copiously, he concentrated what originality he possessed upon the manner of presentation and accepted practically without comment the content that had come down to him from earlier times. Like many teachers, he was not even a particularly good writer. He was able, however, to transmit to his pupils not only what learning he possessed but his burning enthusiasm for study and his sterling Christian character. He was, in short, a great teacher and as such he still lives in the minds of those who have an interest in education.

Alcuin's attitude toward secular literature was more tolerant than that of some contemporaries who still clung to the notion that the writings of Greece and Rome, being pagan, were works of the devil. In his youth Alcuin was especially fond of Virgil, and he continued throughout life to quote him, but in his later years he became stricter and reproached some of his own pupils for their attachment to Virgil or other classical authors. Although Alcuin was not entirely blind to the beauty of secular writings from the past, he was skeptical of their moral effect. This attitude led him to prefer inferior literary merit in the works of a saint to literary excellence in a classical author.

To be sure Alcuin and all other educated men of this period actually absorbed a great deal of classical culture without identifying it as such, because they studied and imitated the church fathers, who were for the most part well educated in the literature of Greece and Rome. Although some of them tried to abandon their heritage because it was not Christian, they could no more escape from it than a Protestant minister of the last century could keep Biblical allusions out of his speech. The writings of the church fathers bristle with classical learning. Through them, devout Christians of the Middle Ages learned much of pagan literature, even if they did not realize it.

Alcuin's attitude toward learning in general and the goal of education is wholly typical of his period, as indicated in the passage below:

> Wisdom hath builded her house; she hath hewn out her seven columns . . . . Grammar, rhetoric, dialetic, arithmetic, geometry, music, and astronomy. On these philosophers bestowed their leisure and their study; and by reason of these philosophers the Catholic teachers and defenders of our faith have proved themselves superior to all chief heretics in public controversy. Therefore let your youthful steps, my dearest sons, run daily

along these paths until a riper age and a stronger mind shall bring you to the heights of Holy Scriptures.[10]

Alcuin wanted as much learning as could be gotten, but not for its own sake. The main purposes of secular learning were to act as the basis for philosophy and to contribute to the defense of the church against heresy.

A good evaluation of Alcuin as a person has been given by one of his biographers, who based his opinion upon careful reading of all the sources. It should be noted that there is no effort to gloss over Alcuin's shortcomings or to indulge in unfounded hero-worship. The picture given reveals, however, certain traits of personality that are just as valuable in a teacher today as they were in 800.

> The record of his life is the record of the working of a perfect instrument. Loyalty was perhaps his most striking characteristic. He was loyal to the teaching of his masters and the traditions of the past. He was loyal to the church, even to the point of concealing her weaknesses, to the best of his ability, from all but sympathetic eyes. He was loyal to Charles: reverencing the grandeur of his character, delighting in his friendship, rejoicing to interpret and fulfil his every wish. He was loyal above all to his religion: sparing neither time nor trouble in his zealous defence of its fundamental doctrines, pointing out even to the great king the mischief he was doing by his attempt to force it on the conquered Saxons, warning his pupils against those breaches of its moral precepts which degraded the royal court itself.
>
> His industry was indefatigable; indolence and idleness he held in detestation; he never spared or indulged himself; and against luxury and extravagance he was never weary of inveighing. Yet he was no mere gloomy ascetic: his letters and still more his poems reveal a deep and sympathetic love of nature, and a keen delight in all her varied beauties. . . .
>
> He had indeed the defects of his good qualities. He was lacking in physical courage; he knew nothing of the adventurous spirit of the pioneer; he was totally destitute of originality. He clung timidly to the beaten track, and never in any respect advanced beyond his age.
>
> Nor were his virtues heroic. His career does not challenge comparison with the strenuous, devoted lives of Columcille* and Boniface. But it is easy to belittle his importance overmuch, and perhaps not a few with greater powers of mind and body, and characters cast in a more heroic mould, have done less for their own age and for posterity than he. For through a long and laborious life, though greatly hampered by weakness and ill-health, he remained faithful to ideals unpretentious, doubtless, but not unfruitful, hoarding up for the instruction and edification of future scholars the accumulated wisdom of the past, and fighting error in ritual and doctrine with the weapons of authority and precedent.
>
> He created nothing, he originated nothing, he added nothing to what had gone before. Yet so important, in that epoch, was the work of mere

[10] Wilmot-Buxton, *op. cit.*, p. 191.

conservation, so imperative the need for it, so faithful his performance of the task, that if, as he himself loved to say, the learning of preceding ages was his heritage, the learning of the ages which followed may justly be accounted his memorial.[11]

3. Alcuin as a Teacher Alcuin's reputation as a teacher rests upon five outstanding traits. First, he was a simple, sincere, upright, honest man of learning who aroused admiration and respect by the rectitude of his own daily life during a period when ignorance, cruelty, and vice were accepted as the average for mankind. In the second place, he was to his students an exciting person. His pupils, including Charlemagne, clearly liked to be with him because they had a good time. Although many students—especially among the older people—doubtless came originally as a result of official pressure, there is ample evidence that they remained because Alcuin gave them new things to think about. He excited their curiosity—although he often did not know enough to satisfy it—stimulated their imagination, and led them into the fascinating business of trying to think—along narrow lines, to be sure, but nevertheless to the consideration of something beyond their personal desires.

In the third place, Alcuin treated each pupil differently and individually. For instance, in one letter to Charlemagne he tells how to some of his pupils he "imparted the honey of Holy Scripture," to some the "wine of ancient learning," to others "the apples of grammatical subtlety," and to still others "the knowledge of the stars in their courses." [12] Taken out of metaphor and expressed in simple English, this report to his employer means that Alcuin trained each pupil according to what he could best do.

Fourth, Alcuin adjusted the material to be studied to the capacities of his learners, most of whom knew less of academic matters than does an elementary school child of today. He did not make the mistake of beginning above the intellectual level of the childish and untrained minds with which he had to work. It was a necessary step in the re-establishment of culture that someone should at some time teach the simple rudiments of learning that make the differences between illiteracy and literacy. This work fell to Alcuin. Much of the material he taught was reduced to a point that would bore the modern mind, but this simplification is a tribute to his practical sense and to his realization of the limitations under which he had to operate. Alcuin was not a man of genius or an original thinker, but he was a dynamic teacher who could so clothe the dry bones of grammar and elementary school arithmetic as to interest the vigorous but abysmally ignorant barbarians with whom he worked.

[11] Gaskoin, *op. cit.*, pp. 224–226. This excerpt and subsequent ones from this reference are used by permission of the publisher, Cambridge University Press.

[12] *Ibid.*, p. 190. These subjects were, respectively, theology, rhetoric, grammar, astronomy.

Finally, he had a splendid concept of what a teacher is supposed to do for his students. In one of his many letters to friends who were also schoolmasters, Alcuin explained this concept by saying that he was trying through his instruction to "draw out each pupil's latent powers, just as a man strikes out of a flint the fire that has all the time been hidden in it."[13] From all accounts Alcuin succeeded in this endeavor. Modern teachers are still trying to do the same thing.

4. Alcuin's Methods of Teaching The palace school, which was the center of Alcuin's teaching efforts, was a unique institution. It was more often at Aix-la-Chapelle than anywhere else, but it did travel about, according to where Charlemagne happened to be, except for short and purely military excursions. The king was himself one of the most eager pupils, and he liked to have both his court and his school along with him if he were going to be away from his capital for any considerable length of time. The pupils were of all ages: the king, his family, the nobles, their wives or sisters, and everybody's children. Few of them could read or write. Some of the boys intended to enter the church, but many of the pupils wanted what would now be called a "liberal education."

Day by day, in the midst of this motley group sat Alcuin—patient, indefatigable, stimulating. All work revolved around him, whose meager gleanings from a decayed and fragmentary learning appeared as nothing short of marvelous. Even though some of his more capable pupils—being fundamentally brighter than Alcuin—sooner or later found themselves outgrowing him, there was evidently a time in their lives when he was to them an exciting person who opened the gate into pastures new and lovely.

Alcuin's method of instruction consisted largely of conversations, in part because few of his pupils could read and in part because the supply of books was extremely limited. This question-and-answer technique was a common teaching device in medieval textbooks, but it was not—except in form—a continuation of the Socratic method. Rather, the conversations proceeded mainly by free associations and led from one thing to another without much system. Perhaps Alcuin thought that it mattered little where he began. Perhaps also he could not plan ahead because he never knew when the school would be in session or when Charlemagne would take part in the proceedings, directing the questioning along whatever lines happened to interest him at the moment. In any case, the handling of the group was certainly informal, and the work rested upon personal contact between teacher and pupil. With his younger pupils Alcuin no doubt used a more definite system of instruction than with the older. Since he was not one to introduce innovations, it is

[13] *Ibid.*, p. 197.

more likely than not that he passed on the system in which he had been educated at York to those who were young enough to be in school regularly over a period of time.

Although in general Alcuin was a distinctly serious person, he was not without a certain lightness of touch in the handling of his pupils. While he clearly did not want the boys to waste much time in childish games or in general running about, he often introduced the spirit of play into the work of the schoolroom. He used puzzles, riddles, epigrams, and acrostics,* in part at least because Charlemagne doted upon these forms of intellectual exercise and was constantly begging for more. Alcuin joked, especially with the younger pupils, and led them on to greater effort by talking their language. It is a reflection of his excellence as a teacher that, at a time when flogging was practically universal, there is no mention of it in Alcuin's letters. This omission seems significant; since he wrote freely about whatever struck him as important and was always greatly concerned with the moral development of his pupils he would certainly have mentioned flogging if he were in the habit of using such discipline.[14] His customary attitude is well summed up in a poetical exercise in which he describes himself: "As soon as the charioteer of the dawn floods the world with the new light of day, the old man rubs the sleep of night from his eyes and leaps from his couch, running straightway into the field of the ancients to pluck their flowers of correct speech that he may scatter them in sport before his boys." [15] A teacher who approaches his work in this spirit does not often need to flog his pupils.

Further light upon Alcuin's methods is thrown by a series of exercises he wrote for his students. Many of them were copied from earlier authors, but some of them seem to have been original. They are supposedly exercises in arithmetic and are described by Alcuin himself as being "certain figures of arithmetical subtlety for the sake of amusement." [16] For the most part these exercises are simple enough, but the solutions were all worked out by the primitive method of counting and with the use of cumbersome Roman numerals. No problem calls for more than the four fundamental operations with whole numbers. Several of the problems have no answer and were probably intended as jokes. A few samples appear below:

> If a king were gathering an army and took one man from the first village, two from the second, four from the third, eight from the fourth, and so through thirty towns, how many men would he get in all?

[14] He may have had to—and very probably did—whip a student occasionally, but he certainly made no general practice of it.

[15] West, *op. cit.*, p. 47.

[16] *Ibid.*

There is a ladder with 100 steps. One dove is on the first step, two on the second, three on the third, and so on. How many doves are on the ladder?

After an ox has plowed all day, how many steps does he leave in the last furrow?

When a farmer goes plowing and has turned three times at each end of his field, how many furrows has he made?

There are 300 pigs to be killed on three successive days, an uneven number being killed on each occasion. How can this be done?

How many quadrangular houses [dimensions given in medieval units of measurement] can be built in a triangular city [dimensions also given]? [17]

The first problem requires a geometrical and the second an arithmetical progression.* Alcuin's solutions, however, are given by a laborious technique of counting. Apparently the notion of an underlying principle did not dawn upon him. It is doubtful if, in the first problem, he intended to come out with a billion men in the army, and one wonders what Charlemagne thought about it. The third question is of the purely "catch" variety. An ox does not leave any footsteps in any furrow because the soil covers them; nor does it matter in the least how long the ox has been at the job. The fourth question has a solution, but Alcuin himself gives the wrong answer! [18] The last two problems provide the learner with impossible situations. These exercises represent an effort to introduce an element of lightness into the solemnity of an education dominated by fanatic religious attitudes, and they reveal a desire on the part of the instructor to adjust his materials to the ability of the pupils.

In addition to these problems in arithmetic Alcuin produced a grammar which is a mixture of good judgment and pure fancy. For instance, he defines vowels and consonants as follows: "The vowels are uttered by themselves and of themselves make syllables. The consonants cannot be uttered by themselves, nor can they of themselves make syllables." [19] While this definition does not contain all there is to be said on the subject, still it is entirely sensible and gets at the heart of the matter. But Alcuin, after the fashion of a medieval scholar, was not content with so simple a statement of the case. He went on to say: "The vowels are the souls, and the consonants the bodies of the words. Now the soul moves both itself and the body, but the body is immovable apart from the soul. Such then are the consonants without the vowels. They may be written by themselves, but they cannot be uttered nor have they any power

[17] *Ibid.*, pp. 110–111.
[18] The Venerable Bede,* from whom the problem was borrowed, gave the right one.
[19] *Ibid.*, p. 99.

apart from the vowels.[20] As a simile the above definition is definitely good, but Alcuin undoubtedly intended it to be taken literally. Throughout his grammar he mixed the possible, the improbable, and the completely fanciful, without discernible preference for one over another. Some of his definitions are as amusing as they are childish.[21]

In spite of its defects, Alcuin's grammar in the form of a dialogue between himself and Charlemagne is an interesting educational document. The conversations cover numerous topics of grammar and style, in the manner illustrated below:

CHARLEMAGNE: The plan of our dialogue now leads us to an examination of Style, the principles of which are designed to bestow great charm upon the speaker's subject and great authority upon the speaker himself. And you are not going to be as readily excused from a discussion of this topic as you were when you answered my question in respect to the precepts of Arrangement.

ALCUIN: My Lord King, I do not seek to excuse myself, but you. I may seem indeed to follow your questions with a slow foot, but I shall not follow them with a reluctant will.

CHARLEMAGNE: First, then, pray open the subject as to what quality Style should have.

ALCUIN: Style should be eloquent and open.

CHARLEMAGNE: How is it made open?

ALCUIN: It will be open if you avoid ambiguity and employ words which are concrete, specific, familiar; and if you do not indulge in far-fetched metaphors, nor allow too drastic a transposition of words when hyperbaton* is used.

CHARLEMAGNE: How is Style made eloquent?

ALCUIN: It will be eloquent if it observes the rules of grammar, and is supported by the authority of the ancients.

CHARLEMAGNE: How can our speech attain the authority which that of the ancients had?

ALCUIN: Their books ought to be read, and their words well impressed upon our memory. Whoever has fashioned his style upon theirs cannot consciously express himself in a manner devoid of refinement. Nevertheless, we should not employ antique words that our present usage does not recognize. Of course we may avail ourselves of such words if we do so only now and then, and exercise due thrift in the matter, and omit them except where they are decorative. But true eloquence finds current words more suited to her ends.

CHARLEMAGNE: Is speech more likely to achieve adornment in respect to the separate words of our language, or in respect to words in combination?

[20] *Ibid.*

[21] Many of the very worst ones he got from Isidore, but he apparently copied them because he thought they were good.

ALCUIN: Both are important. That is to say, the adornment of speech depends upon words used severally, and also upon words joined together.

CHARLEMAGNE: If adornment has these two aspects, speak then of both.

ALCUIN: Two kinds of single words add luster to the speech. One kind consists of literal terms; the other, of figurative terms. Excellence is achieved in the use of literal terms when we avoid those which are debased and obsolete, and select those which, being choice and clear, seem to possess the quality of fulness and agreement. The fixed habit of speaking well has the greatest possible influence upon our ability to choose such words. Adornment is attainable everywhere in the realm of figurative terms, which owe their origin to man's need of a language, and to the sterility and poverty of his early speech. More recently, however, his delight and pleasure in the use of figures have given them prestige. As clothing was first devised to protect him from the cold, and in course of time became an ornament of his person and a symbol of his rank, so figurative language was first used to satisfy a need, and later was given new popularity by the pleasure it provided, and by the ornamental effect it produced. Indeed, even farmers speak of "the fingers" of a vine, "bumper crops," and "waving fields." Often a figurative term will on the instant clarify the meaning which a parallel literal term is powerless to convey. Nevertheless, ideas expressed figuratively should always be ideas which achieve greater clarity by that means, as is true when we say that "the sea bristles up, and the waves hotly boil." Sometimes, too, the figurative term is a means of attaining brevity, as in the expression, "The spear escaped from his hand." Here, indeed, literal terms could not possibly convey as briefly the idea that the spear was launched without conscious aim. Thus in general the greatest virtue of figurative terms is that they lay bare the thought.[22]

There is a stilted and artificial quality about this dialogue, but perhaps the fault lies with the subject matter. Even the most skillful modern writer might have difficulty in being spontaneous and witty about the topic discussed.

For drill in penmanhip, it was a common teaching device to have pupils write over and over on their tablets the words: *Ad nexique est globum zephyrique,* a phrase without meaning. The value of this exercise lay in the fact that it contains all the letters of the Latin alphabet. Before one condemns this method, one should pause to remember the modern teacher who, for the same reasons, sometimes has her pupils practice the sentence: *The quick brown fox jumps over the lazy dog.* This statement is not completely devoid of sense, but one could hardly call its meaning especially significant.

5. Alcuin and His Pupils Alcuin's relations with his pupils reveal the true teacher. Of his many letters still in existence,[23] a large proportion were

[22] Alcuin, *The Rhetoric of Alcuin and Charlemagne* (translated by W. S. Howell), Princeton University Press, 1941 (175 pp.), pp. 131–135. Quoted by permission of Princeton University Press, publishers.

[23] Mostly because Alcuin collected and preserved his own letters—like any good humanist* of later times. The letters were also used as models in teaching.

written to former students. The exchange of greetings between him and them continued long after they had left his care. In his letters he showed his concern for their welfare, his enthusiasm for and interest in their work, his patient readiness to answer their many questions—even though some of them were foolish—and his grief when even one of his flock forsook learning for the ways of the flesh. For instance, he wrote in the following manner to a student who was just leaving for a journey:

My dearest Son:
Great is my longing for your health and prosperity. I therefore desire to send you a letter in the place of the spoken word of paternal affection, begging you to keep God before your eyes and in your remembrance with the entire devotion of mind and intention. Let Christ be on your lips and in your heart. Act not childishly and follow not boyish whims, but be upright, content, and moderate that God may be glorified by your work and the father who bore you may not be ashamed. Be temperate in food and drink, regarding rather your own welfare than any carnal delights. Let your feastings be decorous and those who feast with you religious. Be old in morals though young in years.[24]

On another occasion he wrote to the young princes—sons of Charlemagne—a letter full of affection and charm.

To my dearest sons their father wishes eternal welfare. I would write you a great deal if only I had a dove that would carry my letter to you faithfully, but since I have none I will give this sheet to the winds and hope that one of them will bear it to you, so that it may bring you my greeting and my hope for your prosperity and my great desire to see you well and whole, even as any father desires his sons to be. How happy were the days when we played together at the sport of letters! But now all is changed. The old man has been left to concern himself with other sons and to weep for his former children that are gone.[25]

Alcuin wrote more than one letter to a wayward pupil; a good sample appears below:

A troubled father sends a greeting to his prodigal son. Why have you forgotten the father who taught you from early childhood, who fashioned your morals and fortified them with principles? Why do you indulge in the company of loose women and in drunken feasting? Are you not still the boy who was once a praise in our mouths, a delight to our eyes, and a pleasure to our ears? Now you are a reproach in the mouths of all, a curse in their eyes, and a detestation in their ears. What has so changed you but drunkenness and

[24] West, *op. cit.*, p. 114.
[25] *Ibid.*

luxury? What has persuaded you to feed the swine and to eat of their husks? But it is not too late. Arise my son and return to me and to God and say, "Father I have sinned against heaven and in Thy sight." [26]

There is a record of Alcuin's behavior as abbot of Tours when one of his young monks tried to starve himself in order to become a better person. Apparently the young man assumed that, if a little fasting gradually made one more holy, a great deal of fasting would have the same effect much sooner; it appeared, however, to have made him very ill. The incident below is related by a biographer:

So when Father Alcuin came to visit him, he commanded all except the young monk to leave the apartment, and then began: "Why hast thou, without asking counsel of anyone, attempted to practice such extreme austerity? Perceiving that thou hast an inclination to do so, I caused thee to sleep in the same chamber with myself, but as soon as thou supposedst that all were asleep, thou didst kindle a light in thy lantern and watch the whole night." Those things which he had done most secretly, which God only could know, Alcuin discovered to him and added: "When thou camest to me, and I begged thee drink wine, thou didst cunningly reply, 'Father, I have drunk enough at my uncle's.' . . . Thou didst intend to impose upon us and hast deceived thyself. Beware, when thou art cured of this fever, that thou act not so imprudently."

When the monk heard this he was ashamed and frightened at having been detected and finding that he could conceal nothing from Alcuin, he asked him in astonishment how he had become acquainted with this. Even to the present day, he solemnly protests that no man knew it but himself. He repented of his foolish attempt, and never afterwards acted without Alcuin's counsel or command.[27]

In these few excerpts and others of a similar nature, Alcuin has left behind him evidence of the close personal relationship between himself and his students. He regarded himself not only as the master in their studies but as their spiritual father, who watched over their lives and never lost sight of them no matter how many years they had been away from him, or how far short of his expectations they had fallen.

Alcuin's relationship with his imperial pupil is of interest especially in showing what kind of man each was. The king—impetuous, eager, restless, accustomed to having his own way and to the use of force whenever he was balked—could hardly have been an easy person to have in a group. Charlemagne wanted to know everything and he wanted to know it at once, and he did not see any reason why he should not. Alcuin was, on many recorded oc-

[26] *Ibid.*, p. 115.
[27] Wilmot-Buxton, *op. cit.*, pp. 177–178.

casions, quite able to cope with the situation. For instance, after listening to a glowing account of Augustine and Jerome, Charlemagne demanded, "Why can I not have twelve clerks such as these?"—for all the world like an American businessman who wants twelve Edisons. Alcuin answered, "What, the Lord of Heaven and Earth has but two such, and you think you should have twelve?" [28] In his many letters to Charlemagne, Alcuin revealed a deep affection and an intense admiration, but he did not hesitate to remonstrate with the king whenever he thought the latter needed restraint. More than once he condemned Charlemagne's cruelty in killing prisoners, his intemperance, and his general violence. In one of his treatises Alcuin advises his readers "to imitate our monarch's noble traits, to cherish his virtues, but to avoid his vices." [29] In short, while Alcuin had a great respect for his employer and was essentially a timid person, he was ready to chide and was even bold enough to condemn when he felt he had the moral right on his side.

Alcuin was unusually successful in transmitting to his pupils his own love of learning. Among his pupils are to be found most scholars of the next generation upon the continent of Europe. Students came to him from all countries. Indeed during his later years, after he had retired from work in the palace school and had become abbot of Tours, the resident monks complained about the many foreign students who "clustered around the abbot's lodging like bees around a hive." [30] Alcuin's students carried back to their homes such learning as he could give them and—more important—his attitude toward learning. In this ability to inspire, he reveals himself as a natural leader of youth.

6. Alcuin's Work in Preserving and Collecting Manuscripts It remains to say a few words about Alcuin's activities in the cause of education along other lines than direct instruction. One of his tasks was the correction and recopying of manuscripts—especially the books of the Bible and the writings of the early church fathers. The copies that existed in the monastery libraries were so full of errors that the meaning of passages was often completely obscured. Alcuin had first to train a number of monks to work more carefully, not only by admonishing them to greater effort but by teaching them enough Latin so that they could recognize their own errors when through inattention they made them, and by adopting a script instead of a printed alphabet. In this field also one can observe his fund of common sense and his willingness to take human nature as he found it. For the guidance of copyist he produced such rules as the following:

[28] West, *op. cit.*, p. 46.
[29] *Ibid.*, p. 47.
[30] *Ibid.*, p. 192.

If you mean a "vine" write *vinea* with an *i* in the first syllable and an *e* in the second, but if you mean "pardon" write *venia* with an *e* in the first syllable and an *i* in the second.

Write *vacca* with a *v* if you mean a "cow," but write it with a *b* if you mean a "berry." [31]

Write *vellus* with a *v* if you mean "wool" but with a *b* if you mean "pretty."

By no means consider *beneficus*—a man of good deeds—the same as *venificus*—a criminal.

Mālus, "a mast," is to have a long *a*, but *malus homo* (a bad man), ought to have a short *a*.[32]

These excerpts reflect equally the ignorance of the times and the vigorous simplicity with which Alcuin set about making the situation better. He clearly loved every reverent and religious book in the world, he wanted a copy of each in every monastery, and he wanted every copy to be perfect. Such a goal could hardly be reached, but he did all one man could to approach it.

In a letter to the king, Alcuin expresses himself well concerning his efforts to have manuscripts properly copied:

Although the distinctions of punctuation give a fairer aspect to written sentences, their use has almost disappeared because the scribes are so ignorant. But since the glory of learning is by reason of this noble exertion beginning again to be seen, it seems most fitting that the use of punctuation should be resumed by scribes. Accordingly, although I accomplish but little, I contend daily with rusticity at Tours.[33]

For the copying of holy writings Alcuin was not content with any supervision but his own. Every day during the hours devoted to this work he went to the scriptorium, a room where the writing was done, and watched. In the middle of the room a monk read aloud from some book while around him several others sat at desks and wrote what he dictated, thus producing several copies at once. Alcuin evidently hovered over them, passing from one to another, correcting this or that error, showing them how to make their letters more clearly, exhorting them to accuracy, filling them with his own love for the books on which they worked. It is a reflection of Alcuin's simplicity and true humility of spirit that, after many years of being headmaster of the kingdom's leading school and the emperor's teacher, he was willing to apply himself to the daily drudgery of supervising a handwriting and spelling class. Through his incessant labors in the collecting and copying of books Alcuin left

[31] Most of these confusions arose because of similarity in sound. Books were usually written from dictation—hence two similar sounds were easily interchanged.
[32] West, *op. cit.*, p. 103.
[33] *Ibid.*, p. 71.

to coming generations several libraries[34] in which the writings on religious subjects, plus a few books on secular topics, were carefully collected and edited. In this manner he laid the groundwork for the achievements of others. Alcuin evidently believed in the truth of an epigram that was not written until nearly four centuries later—*claustrum sine amario quasi castrum sine armamentario.*[35] A picture of a monk busily employed in copying a book appears in Figure 22.

FIG. 22. A Monk in a Scriptorium. From an illustrated manuscript in the Royal Library in Brussels.

Alcuin's one important innovation was the substitution of script writing—that is, the joining of letters within a word—for the printing of individual letters, in the copying of books. Figure 23 gives a sample of the print used in early manuscripts. These particular lines are from Virgil's *Aeneid,* but even when one knows what they are, one can hardly puzzle them out. The student should try to imagine what reading a page of com-

[34] The palace library was the largest in the kingdom, but some of the monasteries in other countries had libraries containing from 200 to 450 manuscripts.—West, *op. cit.,* p. 189.

[35] A cloister without a library is like a camp without ammunition."—West, *op. cit.,* p. 189

pletely unfamiliar material would be like. Alcuin did not invent the script alphabet, but he did adapt and popularize it by introducing it at Tours, whence it spread to all of Europe. The written alphabet of today is a direct descendant of Alcuin's one innovation. These two contributions, carefully copied books and a script alphabet, are perhaps humble gifts to posterity, but education would be impossible without the one and unnecessarily difficult without the other.

Alcuin's educational contributions were important chiefly to the immediately succeeding generations. The theological problems to which he devoted so much attention have long since passed into the limbo of dead issues, his textbooks are outmoded, and his limited knowledge has been superseded by advances. But he still shines forth in an age when most men were ruthless, ignorant, and venial, as a gentle spirit who led others into better ways of living and thinking, a true Christian who left the world a better place than he found it, a careful scholar who assembled and protected what learning was available, and an inspiring teacher who lived in the hearts of his pupils, stimulating them to carry on the traditions of education through two of the darkest centuries Europe has ever experienced.

FIG. 23. Some Lines from the *Aeneid*. From the Vatican Library in Rome.

B. SCHOOLS OF THE MIDDLE AGES

Throughout Europe, the schools of the sixth through the tenth centuries were of the same types as those already described—in monastery and cathedral

—plus two other types, the parish* and the chantry* school. The former was maintained by the parish priest for such children in each village as cared to come. Some schools of this type had sprung up spontaneously before the time of Charlemagne, because the priest was likely to be the only person in a small community who could read and write. The number increased greatly during and just after Charlemagne's reign, through his vigorous support, as will presently be shown. The parish schools were small and most elementary. The curriculum, if one may apply such a dignified term to the work given, consisted of a little training in copying the letters of the alphabet, a little training in recognizing words, and drill in memorizing the Lord's Prayer and other bits of the church services. It has to be remembered that reading, in the modern sense, was hardly possible, partly because the language read was not the one which the children spoke and heard and partly because the pupils usually had no books. Consequently, it might take a pupil the better part of his brief school career to memorize a psalm,* for instance, since he did not know what the words meant and he might never see them in writing. In the course of time he might come to recognize by ear a particular series of Latin words, or he might be able to pick some of them out of another context, but such skill could hardly be called "reading."

The main purpose of the chantry schools was to train choir boys, but the children who attended them were usually taught to read a little. These boys were, for the most part, orphans or children of very poor people; they lived in or near the church building. The life of these boys was by no means an easy one. They had to sing twelve services in the course of twenty-four hours, including six during the night. In addition they were supposed to attend classes in Latin grammar! From their numbers the monks recruited members for their order. Some boys entered religious orders at an extremely early age; thus Boniface became a monk at five years of age, and the Venerable Bede at the unvenerable age of seven.

1. Education under Charlemagne[36] During the reign of Charlemagne, schools were more numerous and of more varied types than either directly before or in the centuries directly after. Indeed, Charlemagne had what amounted to a school system. At the bottom were the parish schools taught by the parish priests. Next came the small schools in the monasteries and a few larger schools in the cathedrals. The latter were more advanced than most of the former and had a wider curriculum. At the top of the system was the palace school at Charlemagne's court, which differed from the cathedral schools mainly in an emphasis on learning for its own sake and for general culture,

[36] See especially B. Mullinger, *The Schools of Charles the Great,* Longmans, Green and Co., 1877, 193 pp.

as compared to the more specialized training for the priesthood in the schools maintained by the church.

In matters of education Alcuin and Charlemagne saw eye to eye. In one of the most significant state papers of the Middle Ages the two men set forth their intentions. The document appears in its entirety below:

Be it known to your Devotion, pleasing to God, that we and our faithful have judged it well that, in the bishoprics and monasteries committed by Christ's favour to our charge, besides the due observance of a regular and holy life, care shall be had for the study of letters that those to whom God has given the ability to learn may receive instruction, each according to his several capacity. And this, that, just as obedience to the rule gives order and beauty to your acts, so zeal in teaching and learning may impart the like graces to your words, and thus those who seek to please God by living aright may not fail to please Him also by right speaking. For it is written "by thy words shalt thou be justified or condemned"; and though it is indeed better to do the right than to know it, yet it is needful also to know the right before we can do it. Every one, therefore, must learn what it is that he would fain accomplish, and his mind will the more fully grasp the duty which lies before him if his tongue errs not in the service of Almighty God. And, if false speaking should thus be shunned by all men, how much more must those exert themselves to shun it who have been chosen for this very purpose, to be the servants of the truth!

But in many letters received by us in recent years from divers monasteries, informing us of the prayers offered upon our behalf at their sacred services by the brethren there dwelling, we have observed that though the sentiments were good the language was uncouth, the unlettered tongue failing through ignorance to interpret aright the pious devotion of the heart.

And hence we have begun to fear that, if their skill in writing is so small, so also their power of rightly comprehending the Holy Scriptures may be far less than is befitting; and it is known to all that, if verbal errors are dangerous, errors of interpretation are still more so. We exhort you therefore, not only not to neglect the study of letters but to apply yourselves thereto with that humble perseverance which is well-pleasing to God, that so you may be able with the greater ease and accuracy to search into the mysteries of the Holy Scriptures. For, as in the sacred pages there are images and tropes* and other similar figures, no one can doubt that the quickness with which the reader apprehends the spiritual sense will be proportionate to the extent of his previous instruction in letters. But let the men chosen for this task be such as are both themselves able and willing to learn and eager withal to impart their learning to others. And let the zeal with which the work is done equal the earnestness with which we now ordain it. For we desire that you may be marked, as behooves the soldiers of the Church, within by devotion, and without by wisdom—chaste in your life, learned in your speech—so that if any come to you to call upon the Divine Master, or to behold the excellence of the religious life, they may be not only edified by your aspect when they regard you, but instructed by your wisdom when they hear you read or chant, and may return home rejoicing and giving thanks to God Most High.

Fail not, as you would enjoy our favour, to send copies of this letter to all your suffragans* to every monastery. . . . Farewell! [37]

One writer has said of the above document: "The voice is the voice of Charlemagne, but the hand is the hand of Alcuin. The vigorous and commanding tone is the king's own, but he could not have devised the argument and cast it in the mold of the traditions of learning so perfectly unless he had been assisted by his master, and yet throughout the document the influences of Charlemagne and Alcuin on each other are so happily blended that the mind and spirit which dominate them are one." [38]

In the years that followed this communication, local bishops reinforced the order with instructions of their own, for instance:

Let the priests keep schools in the villages and towns and if any of the faithful wish to give his little ones to learning they ought willingly to receive and teach them gratuitously. . . . And let them exact no pay from the children for their teaching nor receive anything from them save what the parents may offer voluntarily and from affection.

It should be noted that instruction was to be free. There was as yet no hint of compulsory education, but the first step toward this final achievement was taken when the doors were opened to all the children whose parents desired to send them to school.

2. *The Curriculum of the Middle Ages* The schools in Charlemagne's reign were more numerous and probably better taught than during either the early or late Middle Ages, but their fundamental nature was much the same. The curriculum consisted of two groups of subjects, an arrangement that had come down from Roman days. The entire field of human learning was divided into the Trivium (the three) and the Quadrivium (the four).[39] The Trivium consisted of grammar, rhetoric, and dialectic. These subjects covered the elements that have developed into the present-day departments of Classical Language and Literature, English Composition, and Debating or Public Speaking. The Quadrivium consisted of geometry, arithmetic, astronomy, and music. A student had to make good progress in the three subjects of the Trivium before he could hope to study the above four, because he had to read Latin fluently in order to pursue them. In fact, a reading knowledge of Latin was a *sine qua non** of any further work in education, until the pressure of mod-

[37] Gaskoin, *op. cit.,* pp. 182–184.

[38] West, *op. cit.,* p. 52.

[39] For a good discussion of the medieval curriculum see Paul Abelson, *The Seven Liberal Arts: A Study of Medieval Culture,* Bureau of Publications. Teachers College, Columbia University, 1906. 151 pp.

ern languages—beginning more than seven hundred years after the time of Charlemagne—squeezed out Latin as the single language of literate people. Commonly quoted lines concerning the function of each subject among these seven were as follows:

FIG. 24. The Seven Liberal Arts. From the Basel Edition of Gregory de Reisch, *Marguerita Philosophica,* 1508.

Grammatica loquitur, Dialectica vera locet, Rhetorica verba colorat; Musica canit, Arithmetica numerat, Geometria ponderat, Astrologia colit astra.[40]

[40] "Grammar speaks, dialectic discovers the truth, rhetoric gives style; music sings, arithmetic counts, geometry considers, astronomy studies the stars."

These seven subjects were known as the Seven Liberal Arts. Their relationship to one another and the end toward which they were directed are shown in Figure 24. Here Wisdom is coaxing a somewhat discouraged, recalcitrant, and adult-appearing child toward the tower of learning. It should be noted that the child has presumably been to the ABC school shown at the lower left of the picture and therefore knows his alphabet. This temple of wisdom shows not only the organization of learning into successive steps and the authors to be read at each level but also the goal of medieval education. Theology, the most important subject of study during the Middle Ages, occupies the top position, and to it all else leads.

The various gentlemen whose faces appear in the windows are labeled by name. Donatus[41] has a room on the first floor and Priscian[41] on the second. In the third floor windows appear Aristotle as the founder of logic, Cicero as the representative of Rhetoric and Poetry, and Boethius* for Arithmetic. In the very cramped quarters on the fourth floor are Pythagoras* for Music, Euclid* for Geometry, and Ptolemy for Astronomy. Above them, from left to right, are an unidentified figure for Physics and Seneca for Morals. From the top of the tower Peter Lombard* emerges, to represent Theology. This picture was taken from a book published early in the sixteenth century, but the arrangement of subjects was the same throughout the Middle Ages, except that Theology could not be identified with Lombard before the eleventh century, since he was not born till then.

There were no additions to or subtractions from the Seven Liberal Arts, because the mystical value of the number seven operated to check any natural growth of the curriculum that might otherwise have occurred. There were seven arts, and there could never be any more, because seven was the perfect number—being compounded of six, the only perfect digit[42] and one, the number that is indivisible. The preservation of the mystical value in the number seven was, to the medieval mind, far more important than additions to human knowledge could have been.[43]

[41] See Chapter IV.

[42] See item 5 in the excerpts from Isidore, p. 115. Many of these concepts about numbers came down from the days of antiquity.

[43] Some further convictions as to the sacredness of numbers are the following: *3* was sacred because it denoted the Trinity;* *7* because God created the world in seven days, and because it denoted the four parts of the body—flesh, blood, bone, and sinew—plus the three spiritual parts—soul, heart, and mind; *12* because there were twelve apostles; *40* because Christ fasted forty days in the wilderness; *4* because there were four seasons, four major directions, and four divisions of the day; *10* because it was the sum of *7* and *3*. As one can readily appreciate, a meaning could be read into almost any number. Before condemning men of the Middle Ages as credulous and silly, one should consider the present-day belief in numerology. As a sham science it still flourishes, as evidenced by the many advertisements in current magazines.

Of the curriculum of the Middle Ages, one writer has expressed himself as follows:

> Up to the end of the eleventh century the instruction was, speaking generally, and allowing for transitory periods of revival, and for a few exceptional schools, a shrunken survival of the old *trivium et quadrivium*. The lessons, when not dictated and learnt by heart from notes, were got up from bald epitomes. All that was taught, moreover, was taught solely with a view to "pious uses." Criticism did not exist; the free spirit of speculation *could* not, of course, exist. The rules of the orders inevitably crippled and confined the minds of the learners, old and young. The independent activity of the human mind, if it could be called independent, showed itself only in chronicles, histories, *acta sanctorum,* and so forth. This was, doubtless, a necessary stage in the historical development of Europe, and it is absurd to talk of these ages as "dark ages," by way of imputing blame or remissness to the Catholic Church. All that could be done was done by the Catholic organizations, and by no other agency. The Catholic Church did not prohibit learning if it subserved the faith. Opinion was watched certainly, but to look with superfluous alarm on possible developments of anti-theological speculation did not occur to the men of that time, and this is conspicuously shown in the attitude which the popes took toward universities when they began to arise (1100–1150). When heresies did show themselves, they were, at least at first, met by laboured argument, and the suppression of them by councils was, in truth, the last act in a series of able disputations—the judicial summing up and sentence, so to speak. In brief, the Christian schools were doing their proper work for Europe. They did not promise learning in any true sense; but they conserved learning, and what was of more importance, they were leavening the life of the people.[44]

3. Teaching Materials Medieval teachers relied for their subject matter, for their texts, and for their classification of knowledge upon the writings of earlier times—the grammars of Donatus and Priscian, the arithmetic, geometry, and music of Boethius, the works on orthography* and the seven liberal arts of Cassiodorus,* the encyclopedia of Isidore, the writings of the Venerable Bede, and the theological writings of Augustine, Jerome, and other church fathers. The contributions of the grammarians and the church fathers to education have been discussed in previous chapters. The three new names mentioned above are Boethius, Cassiodorus, and the Venerable Bede. The first two were born just before the end of the fifth century, during the transition period after the Roman Empire had fallen apart and the new barbarian kingdoms were being set up. They were the last prominent men who had anything approaching a classical education. Boethius even read Greek, but in this he was

[44] S. S. Laurie, *Lectures on the Rise and Early Constitution of Universities,* Routledge and Kegan Paul, Ltd., 1886 (293 pp.), pp. 92–93. Used by permission of the publishers.

unique among his contemporaries. It was his intention to translate all of Aristotle into Latin, but his untimely death prevented him from finishing more than one work of the great philosopher. For the following centuries, however, Aristotle was known to Europe primarily through this one translation. Boethius wrote also the standard textbooks of the period for arithmetic, geometry, and music. Cassiodorus, toward the end of a long and active life, founded a monastery and tried to collect a library. At once he was struck by the many inaccuracies in the copying of books. As a guide to better work he wrote a manual on spelling and penmanship. He produced also a discussion on education, called "On the Seven Liberal Arts." Here he describes the Trivium and the Quadrivium, defining the nature and limits of each subject. Of grammar, he wrote:

> Grammar is the noble foundation of all literature, the glorious mouth of eloquence. The grammarians . . . are the moulders of the style and character of our youth. Let them . . . devote themselves with all their vigour to the teaching of the liberal arts.[45]

This concept of grammar—so unlike modern ideas—was accepted during the Middle Ages and caused grammar to remain for many centuries the basic school subject.

Alcuin's fellow countryman, the Venerable Bede, lived about a century before him. Although he is remembered primarily as a chronicler, or historian, he was also a successful teacher who wrote a number of textbooks which were widely used for many generations. Alcuin also wrote texts, as already discussed.

One other popular medieval text was a fifth-century discussion of the seven liberal arts by Martianus Capella,* entitled "On the Marriage of Philosophy and Mercury." This book was medieval in its content, but pagan in its spirit and its many mythological allusions. Alcuin never mentioned it, although he must have seen it; one may therefore assume that he disapproved of its nature, which was more nearly flippant than reverent. Other teachers, however, used it constantly.

An important characteristic of the medieval heritage of learning was its one-sidedness. Of Greek achievements the teachers knew almost nothing, and of Roman literature the gleanings were but meager. What to the modern mind would seem the outstanding elements in the intellectual and educational heritage of men of the eighth century—namely, direct contact with the classical literature of Greece and Rome—were conspicuously missing. The writings of the early church fathers made up the bulk of the reading matter. These were read and reread, read again, studied, memorized, and quoted. Jerome and

[45] Sandys, *op. cit.*, I, 262.

A

B

FIG. 25. Two Medieval Schools (a). (Left) From the third edition of *Parvus et Magnus Chato,* Library of St. John's College, Oxford. Printed by Caxton in 1481. (Right) From the title page of Anwykyll, *Compendium Grammaticae.*

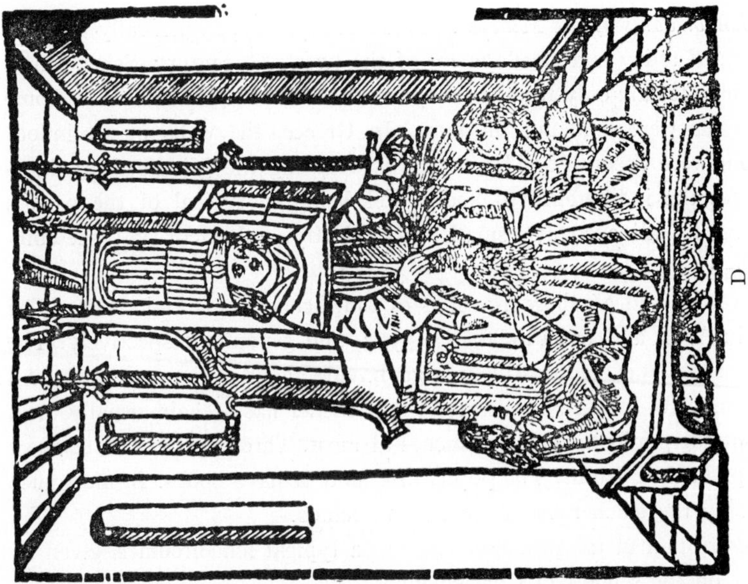

C D

FIG. 26. Two Medieval Schools (b). (Left) Reproduced in Monroe, *A Textbook in the History of Education*, p. 260 (no reference given). (Right) From the *Manuale Scholarium*.

Augustine were as real to the medieval scholar as any living person—and far more important.

4. Schoolrooms of the Middle Ages The light, airy, hygienically planned schoolroom of today is a development of the twentieth century. Schoolrooms that resemble it date only from the Renaissance. In ancient Greece and Rome many schools were held out of doors. In Greece, the walls of an indoor schoolroom were decorated. The rooms used during the Middle Ages, however, reflect the indifference to bodily well-being so typical of the period. They were, by all accounts, small, dark, drafty, unheated, and sketchily furnished—if at all.

Figures 25 and 26 show drawings of four schoolrooms and classes. The teachers in A, B, and D had classes of 5, 3, and 3 pupils, respectively. The class shown in C was comparatively large, having about a dozen externs and a similar number of interns. In all cases, the teacher has a chair, usually most ornate, but the pupils have only benches at most. Three of the four teachers have whips in their hands. The pupils in C and D have books. In most such pictures only the teacher has a book in his hands.

A description of the probable scene in a typical schoolroom is given by one writer on the schools of Charlemagne:

> We may picture to ourselves a group of lads seated on the floor, which was strewn with clean straw, their waxen tablets in their hands, and busily engaged in noting down the words read by the scholasticus from his manuscript volume. So rarely did the pupil in those days gain access to a book that "to read" (legere) became synonymous with "to teach."
>
> The scholars traced the words on their tablets, and afterwards, when their notes had been corrected by the master, transferred them to a little parchment volume, the treasured depository of nearly all the learning they managed to acquire in life.[46]

5. A Medieval Point of View It has been said that the Middle Ages were a period of no progress whatever. This statement is correct only if one defines progress in a modern sense. The leaders of the period had the same urge to make the world a better place that men have always had, but their idea of an ideal world was extremely circumscribed. They believed firmly that the "Golden Age" of humanity lay in the past—in the Garden of Eden or in the age of Augustus, the choice apparently depending upon each thinker's preferences—and that "progress" consisted therefore of a return to what had existed earlier. Added to this idea were the two convictions that the world

[46] Mullinger, *op. cit.,* p. 131. Used by permission of Longmans, Green and Co., publishers. For a good account of other schools, see H. Graham, *The Early Monastic Schools,* Talbot Press, 1923, 206 pp.

would soon come to an end and that one's life on earth was merely a short prelude to eternal life in heaven. Medieval man did not therefore progress in the modern sense because he did not want to, and he retrogressed on purpose.[47] If the world were soon to end, it was hardly worth while to make innovations for such a short time, and if life on earth were unimportant it did not matter how uncomfortable it was. Indeed, the more uncomfortable, the better chance one had for eternal glory. The motives that at present lead to inventions and changes were therefore lacking. Those men with enough education to read were so imbued with the worship of the past that they were unalterably opposed to any innovation, no matter how slight. Even as good a churchman as Cardinal Newman* described the medieval monk as a man who "cared little for knowledge even theological or for success, even though religious. It is the character of such a man to be content, resigned, patient, incurious; to create or originate nothing; to live by tradition."[48]

It would, however, be a mistake to suppose that medieval minds were incapable of thinking or that they did not continually think. They merely started from premises that are totally foreign to a modern mind, they were influenced by considerations now ignored, and they were trying to reach objectives in which men have since lost most of their interest. The net result is a system of thought that seems at present stupid and illogical, although it was neither. A student must keep in mind the basic concepts of the Middle Ages or he is likely to underestimate the intellectual achievements of the period.

READING REFERENCES

A. General Histories of the Period

Boissonade, *Life and Work in Medieval Europe,* book i, chaps. 3, 6.
Burns, *The First Europe,* chap. 9.
Moss, *The Birth of the Middle Ages, 395–814,* part iv, chaps. 11–25.
Munro and Sontag, *The Middle Ages,* chaps. 10, 11, 13.
Robinson, *History of Western Europe,* chaps. 6–8.
Seignobos, *The Rise of European Civilization,* chap. 5.
Strayer and Munro, *The Middle Ages,* chap. 4.
Thompson, J. W. T., *The Middle Ages, 300–1500 A.D.,* 1931 (2 vols.), Vol. 1, chaps. 9–11, 26–28.
Thorndike, L., *Medieval Europe: Its Development and Civilization,* George G. Harrap & Co., Ltd., 1920 (666 pp.), chaps. 11, 15.

[47] For excellent discussions of the basic and somewhat baffling characteristics of medieval thinking, see R. L. Poole, *Illustrations of the History of Medieval Thought and Learning,* The Macmillan Company, 1920, 327 pp.; and H. C. Taylor, *The Medieval Mind,* The Macmillan Company, 1911, 2 vols.

[48] John Henry, Cardinal Newman, *Historical Sketches,* Pickering and Company, 1876–1882 (3 vols.), II, 452.

B. Other Texts in the History of Education

Boyd, *History of Western Education,* chap. 4.
Cole, *History of Educational Thought,* book iii, pp. 105–126.
Cubberley, *History of Education,* chaps. 6, 7.
Graves, *A Student's History of Education,* pp. 274–278.
Marique, *History of Christian Education,* chap. 5.
McCormick, *History of Education,* chap. 11.
Monroe, *A Textbook in the History of Education,* pp. 274–278.
Moore, *The Story of Instruction,* chap. 4.
Reisner, *Historical Foundations of Modern Education,* chap. 12.

C. Secondary Sources

Browne, C. F., *Alcuin of York,* Society for the Promotion of Christian Knowledge, 1908 (329 pp.), chaps. 15–18.
Drane, *Christian Schools and Scholars,* chap. 5.
Farrington, F. E., *French Secondary Education,* Longmans, Green and Co., 1910 (450 pp.), chap. 1.
Gaskoin, *Alcuin: His Life and Work,* chaps. 1–10.
Graham, *The Early Monastic Schools,* chap. 6.
Laurie, *The Rise and Early Constitution of Universities,* chaps. 3, 4.
Lorentz, T., *The Life of Alcuin* (translated by J. M. Slee), T. Hurst & Co., Ltd., 1837 (284 pp.), sec. i; sec. ii, chaps. 2–4; sec. iv, chaps. 3, 4.
Magnevney, E., *Christian Education in the Dark Ages,* Catholic Library Association, 1900, 60 pp.
Mullinger, *Schools of Charles the Great,* chaps. 1, 2.
Page, R. B., *The Letters of Alcuin,* Cambridge University Press, 1909 (102 pp.), introduction and chap. 3.
Painter, *Great Pedagogical Essays,* chap. 10.
Poole, *Illustrations of the History of Medieval Thought and Learning,* chap. 3.
Rand, *Founders of the Middle Ages,* chaps. 5, 6.
West, *Alcuin,* chaps. 1–6.
Wilmot-Buxton, *Catholic Thought and Thinkers,* chaps. 2, 4–6, 10, 11.

D. Translations of Primary Sources

Alcuin, *Rhetoric of Alcuin and Charlemagne,* any 10 pages.
Brehaut, *An Encyclopedist of the Dark Ages,* part ii, any 4 books.

CHAPTER VII

ABÉLARD AND THE MEDIEVAL UNIVERSITY

In the five previous chapters there have been descriptions of teachers and schools at intervals from the Age of Pericles through the Middle Ages. Socrates and Quintilian, the main characters in the second and third chapters, belonged to the world of antiquity. The people described in the fourth and fifth chapters lived while the ancient world was crumbling and the Middle Age were just beginning. Alcuin, the main figure of the last chapter, lived in almost the exact center of the medieval period. Abélard, the main character of this presentation, lived toward the end of the Middle Ages, during an awakening of intellectual life known as the Renaissance or Reawakening of the twelfth century. This period is the last to be discussed before the Renaissance and Reformation of the fifteenth and sixteenth centuries, the two movements that ushered in the modern era. Abélard is a good figure for bridging medieval and modern times, because in some ways he reflected faithfully the attitudes of his contemporaries while in others he struck out boldly along lines of thought that were far in advance of his day, in fact too far in advance for his own safety. Before beginning the story of his life, however, it seems best to present a brief summary of two intellectual movements that greatly influenced him and all scholars of Western Europe: the stream of learning that came from the Arabs and the development of a system of thought known as scholasticism.

1. Arabic Learning and Culture In the eleventh and twelfth centuries two streams of intellectual revival flowed into Europe. Both were from the East; one came directly as a result of the crusades,* and the other indirectly via the Arabs* who had settled in Spain and had developed a culture considerably in advance of the European average. At a time when a European scholar was able to assemble a library of not more than 50 books, educated Arabs had 500 or more; one library was known to have contained 600,000 books.[1] It was during these centuries that scholars went to Arab teachers in Spain or southern Italy in an eager search for knowledge that was not elsewhere available. In medicine, mathematics, and philosophy the Arabs were especially outstanding.

[1] K. Schmidt, *Geschichte der Pädagogik,* P. Schettler, 1873–1876 (4 vols.), II, 111–113.

To some extent they acted merely as disseminators of knowledge from the ancient world and from the Far East,* but in many fields they made original contributions. Among other things they brought to Europe the Hindu notation, which soon supplanted Roman numerals with what are now called Arabic numerals. That is, the figures 1, 2, 5, 10, 20, 50, 100, and so on, took the place of I, II, V, X, XX, L, and C. This change so simplified arithmetic that developments in higher mathematics became possible. In addition, the Arabs had worked out the fundamentals of algebra and trigonometry, and had revived interest in both plane and solid geometry, as developed by Euclid.

In the Arab world the writing of the Greek philosophers had never been banned, as they had been at times throughout Christendom, nor had the invading Germanic hordes penetrated into the eastern portions of the old Roman Empire. The heritage of ancient culture had, therefore, been unbroken. It was through Arab translations that European scholars recovered the writings of Aristotle, upon which the higher education of the period rested.

From the East the Arabs imported also the process of making paper, the formula for gunpowder, the construction of pendulum clocks, and the knowledge of the compass. From the same source they introduced into Europe the use of rice, sugar, cotton, and silk. In the field of science, also, their contributions were significant. They were acquainted with the phenomena* of light refraction,* capillary attraction,* twilight changes,* and specific gravity.* They had determined the height of the atmosphere and the weight of the air. Their astronomical tables and their maps were much better than those in Europe. Their medicine was fairly free of magic and was based upon common-sense observation. The Arabs were thus both transmitters and originators. Although eventually driven out of Europe because they were infidels, their introduction of Aristotle provided the basis for the development of scholasticism,* and their scientific work—both original and borrowed—became the basis for modern science.[2]

Long before the reappearance of Aristotle, however, dialectic had become far more important than literature, and this disbalance had already produced generations of arguers, without much if any knowledge of the ancient philosopher. At this point Aristotle emerged from the fogs of antiquity with a methodology all ready for use, including descriptions of the possible pitfalls in argument. It is no wonder that he became not merely a vogue but practically a god. Only a bold and independent man dared to disagree with the Greek philosopher. Although the slavish devotion of lesser men led to the sterile

[2] For an excellent account, with many examples, see C. H. Haskins, *Studies in the History of Medieval Science,* Harvard University Press, 1924 (411 pp.), especially chap. 1, 8, and 12.

excesses of scholasticism at its worst, the original impact of Aristotle upon the circumscribed outlook of the later Middle Ages produced a renaissance of learning. That Abélard was important in paving the way for the popularity of Aristotle can be deduced from the occasional banning of Aristotle's books on the grounds that they were too much like Abélard's!

2. *Scholasticism*[3] To the modern mind there is nothing in the medieval world more puzzling and generally unappealing than scholasticism. The rediscovery of Aristotle's writings could hardly have been as important as it was in the intellectual life of the times, had Aristotle not exactly fitted a need that already existed. The books of logic appeared at just the time when men were beginning to feel that the church would be strengthened if its beliefs could be proved by reason as well as accepted by faith. As a result of this timeliness, Aristotle became for nearly two centuries the newest thing in education.

The books of Aristotle were written during the fourth century before Christ. They were known to the Romans, but the more philosophical treatises were not especially prized by them, although they used his work on mechanics. With the establishment of Christianity all Greek philosophers were suspect, although many early Christian leaders had read at least some parts of Aristotle. In the fifth century Boethius intended to translate all the great philosopher's books but actually finished only one. At this point the matter rested for eight hundred years. During all the centuries since 400 B.C., no new methods of experimentation had been evolved. Medieval man was still where ancient man had been in his methodology, but he had the new subject matter of the Christian religion.

Because of the disrepute into which scholasticism eventually fell, it is easy to overlook its good points. At its best it represented a great advance over the continual summarizing and compiling of existing knowledge that had characterized the learning, writing, and thinking of the earlier Middle Ages. Scholasticism demanded original thinking and a new approach to problems. There is nothing easy about the thought processes behind a scholastic argument. Even though the field of inquiry was narrow and the approved methods were stereotyped, the thinking was vigorous, independent, and sometimes powerful.

Scholasticism had quite definite objectives. It was designed to give religious doctrines a correct philosophical expression, to reduce the many dogmas*

[3] The presentation of this subject has been simplified and may therefore strike the experienced reader as somewhat naïve. It is admittedly a Protestant rather than a Catholic explanation. It has been written in the way it has in the hope that the simplification may permit students who have little background to grasp some of the essentials of the subject. There is no emphasis upon the present-day discussions of the matter, because the present is no part of this history.

of the church to a harmonious system, to present answers to all possible objections which might be raised to the orthodox view, and to state the proper refutation to all unorthodox interpretations. These objectives required close and careful thinking. They permitted men's minds a considerable degree of independent thought within the confines of religious doctrine. Indeed, scholasticism allowed a man to think without being a heretic. The effort produced one great scholar, Thomas Aquinas,* who was as successful as anyone has ever been in the use of this method. His reconciliation of belief and reason is still accepted by the Catholic Church as the embodiment of authenticity and authority.

A sample of scholastic argument appears below. The subject is the proper treatment of heretics. It should be noted that the author (Thomas Aquinas) first takes the arguments in favor of toleration, then those against toleration, and finally reconciles the two points of view as well as he can.

First. It would appear that heretics are to be tolerated, for the Apostle says (II Tim. 2:24): "The Lord's servant must be gentle, in meekness, correcting them that oppose themselves to the truth; if peradventure God may give them repentance unto the knowledge of the truth, and they may recover themselves out of the snare of the devil." But if heretics are not tolerated but delivered over unto death, they are deprived of the opportunity of repentance. Hence, this would seem contrary to the precept of the Apostle.

Second. Moreover, that which is necessary in the church must be tolerated. But heresies are necessary in the church. For the Apostle says (I Cor. 11:19): "For there must be also heresies among you that they which are approved may be manifest among you." Therefore, it would seem that heresies are to be tolerated.

Third. Moreover, the Lord commands his servants (Matt. 9), that they should let the tares grow until the harvest, which is the end of the world, as explained in the Interliner Glossa. But the tares signify the heretics according to the interpretation of the saints. Therefore heretics are to be tolerated.

But against this is to be urged the saying of the Apostle (Titus 3:10): "A man that is heretical after a first and second admonition, refuse, knowing that such a one is perverted."

I reply that heretics must be considered from two points of view, namely, as regards the heretic himself, and secondly, as regards the church. As for the heretics themselves, there is their sin for which they deserve not only to be separated from the church by excommunication, but to be sent out of the world by death. It is, indeed, a much more serious offence, to corrupt the faith, upon which depends the life of the soul, than to falsify coin, by means of which the temporal life is sustained. Hence, if counterfeiters and other malefactors are justly hurried to death by secular rulers, much the more may those who are convicted of heresy not only be excommunicated but justly put to a speedy death. But on the side of the church, there is mercy looking for the conversion of the erring. She does not therefore condemn immediately, but only after a first and second admonition, as the Apostle teaches. Should the heretic still prove stubborn, the church, no longer hoping for his conversion, shall provide for the safety of others by separating him from herself by a sentence of excommunication. She further relinquishes him to the secular judgment to be put out of the world by death. Jerome also says (on the passage in Galatians 5), "a little leaven"; and as provided in 24, qu. 3, cap. 16 (Canon Law). "Foul flesh must be cut away, and mangy sheep must be kept from the fold lest the whole house be burned, the whole mass corrupted, the whole body be destroyed. Arius* was but a spark in Alexandria but since this spark was not promptly quenched, the whole world has been devastated by the flames."

As to the first argument, namely that which relates to the meekness in which a heretic should be admonished a first and a second time; if after that, he refuses to return he is to be looked upon as perverted, as appears from the authority of the Apostle above cited (in the argument beginning, "But against").

As to the second argument, any advantage which may proceed from heretics, is in no way intentional on their part, as for example, the proof they furnish according to the Apostle, of the constancy of the faithful, or as Augustine says. . . . about the Scriptures. "Their intention is, on the contrary, to corrupt the faith, and this is most harmful." We should, therefore, give more weight to those conscious aims which would cut them off rather than the unintentional good, which would seem to countenance their toleration.

To the third argument we may reply, as it is written in the Decretals* 24, qu. 3, cap. Beginning, "It is to be observed that excommunication is one thing and extirpation another." One is excommunicated with a view, as the Apostle says (I Cor. 5:5), "That the spirit may be saved in the day of the Lord." That heretics shall be totally extirpated by death, is not however, contrary to the command of God, for that command is to be understood as applying only in the case when the tares cannot be destroyed, without destroying the wheat at the same time, as has been said in the preceding question, art. 8, argument 1, when we treated of heretics in common with infidels.[4]

As can be appreciated, logic provides the forms by means of which one can think in an orderly fashion. The assumption underlying it is that a person can reduce any problem to a standardized form, go through the indicated logical steps, and emerge with the right answer in his teeth, provided he has not fallen into one or more of the errors in reasoning that lie in wait for the unwary. This view of things assumes that schematic forms of reasoning can be

[4] J. H. Robinson, "Translations and Reprints from the Original Sources of European History," *University of Pennsylvania Reprints,* Vol. III, No. 6, 1908–1909 (34 pp.), pp. 17–19. Used by permission of the University of Pennsylvania Press, publishers.

applied to all types of content with equal success. The medieval scholar believed that in Aristotle he had found the open-sesame to all wisdom. It is therefore no wonder that other possible subjects were neglected and all effort was put upon mastering this form of magic.

The technique of scholasticism consisted primarily of the disputation. Two or more scholars met at an appointed time and argued about a given topic, usually before an audience. Often one man challenged another to debate. The two pictures in Figures 27 and 28 show disputations. Making allowances for differences in costume and for a certain effect of caricature, intentional or otherwise, the scenes could be reproduced in almost any university today. Scholasticism may be dead, but the arguers are still with us.

FIG. 27. A Disputation (a). After a woodcut from Arnoldus de Villa-nova, *Regimen Sanitatis*. Cologne, 1507.

The faults of scholasticism as a method of approach became clear as time passed. In the first place the data about which the scholars argued were accepted on their face value. No one asked if the beliefs were valid or real. Thus one might discuss the exact position of angels in the heavenly system, but one did not consider the more basic question of whether or not there were any angels. Second, scholasticism tried to settle religious doctrine once and for all, on the assumption that religion was static and that all possible revelation had already occurred. Since religious beliefs grow and develop with fresh insights from one age to another, the assumption that growth stopped at any given time is contrary to evidence. Third, the arguments that originally had much vitality and originality as presented by the leaders soon degenerated into stereotyped forms of logic in the hands of lesser men. Gone was the newness, leaving only sterile formulas behind.

It is hard now to understand why logic should have been of such vital importance during the late Middle Ages, because modern man has developed the controlled experiment as a new approach to problems and uses formal logic only as a secondary check upon the accuracy of his conclusions. Scientific experimentation is, however, barely six hundred years old. Up until then, observation plus logical inference was the standard method of arriving at a conclusion.

FIG. 28. A Disputation (b). From R. Fick, *Auf Deutschlands Hohen Schulen,* 1900.

Logic was, however, a sword that cut in two directions. It gave the pious Christian a means of proving his faith—not in the modern sense of empirical proof but in the same sense as proving a proposition in geometry—but it gave the heretic a means for attacking the church much more effectively than ever before because the weapon was better. The church therefore felt that it must train its defenders so well that they could outargue and outreason the heretics. This desire to train scholars to defend faith with reason and to refute doubt was one basic cause for the development of higher education, especially at the University of Paris.

A. ABELARD: HIS LIFE AND WORK

1. Abélard's Early Life Abélard lived just as the renaissance of the eleventh and twelfth centuries was developing. The period was one of stirring and awakening, during which the content of education increased enormously and intellectual activity was positively hectic. Abélard became a part of this life and made his contribution to its growth, but he died before it reached its height.

Peter Abélard[5] is one of the truly tragic figures of history. Destiny cast him in one dramatic role after another but neglected to give him the right temperament for playing them successfully. He was by turn an expert debater, a profound thinker, an inspired lover, a writer of verse, a great teacher, and a good theologian, but never a hero. His restless and penetrating mind, his uncompromising truthfulness, his personal vanity, and his willingness to offend those who disagreed with him led him time and again into conflict with authority and tradition.

When Abélard first crossed the pages of history he was a gay, debonair, witty, and insolent young scholar. Forty years later he was a prematurely old man, a condemned heretic hemmed in by enemies, a brokenhearted lover who had been separated for years from his wife. In between these two periods lies one of the most exciting lives in the history of education. One can hardly call Abélard an entirely admirable person, but there is certainly nothing boring about him.

Abélard was the oldest son of a provincial nobleman. At an early age he resigned the family property in favor of his younger brother and devoted himself to the life of a scholar. When he was about eighteen he set out as a wandering student, going from one teacher to another as his interests led him. In the course of time they led him to the cathedral school of Notre Dame* in Paris. Here the master, William of Champeaux,* was outstanding in dialectics—Abélard's special field. With youthful exuberance and intolerance of an older person's ideas, Abélard deliberately bedeviled his teacher by outarguing and outmaneuvering him. Other students crowded into class to watch their fellow plague the professor. Day after day the tournament of wits went on until Abélard finally drove the other into a logical corner from which he could not escape. In Abélard's own, far-from-modest words:

[5] This discussion is based upon the following references: G. Compayré, *Abélard and the Origin and Early History of Universities,* Charles Scribner's Sons, 1893, 315 pp.; F. J. C. Hearnshaw (editor), *The Social and Political Ideas of Some Great Medieval Thinkers,* G. G. Harrap and Company, 1923, 233 pp.; R. B. Lloyd, *The Stricken Lute,* Peter Davies, Ltd., 1932, 221 pp.; J. McCabe, *Peter Abélard,* G. P. Putnam's Sons, 1901, 402 pp.; Charles de Remusat, *Abélard,* Paris, 1845; J. C. Sikes, *Peter Abélard,* Cambridge University Press, 1932, 282 pp.

Then, I, returning to him. . . . contrived by the clearest chain of argument to make him alter, nay, to shatter his former opinion with regard to universals*. . . . He now so corrected this opinion that thereafter he proclaimed the thing to be the same not essentially but indiscriminately. And inasmuch as this has always been the main question among dialecticians concerning universals . . . after he had corrected and then perforce abandoned his opinion, with such neglect did his instruction fall that he was scarcely admitted to be a teacher of dialectic at all.[6]

FIG. 29. Peter Abélard. From S. G. Williams, *History of Medieval Education,* p. 81. Courtesy of Bardeen's, Inc., publishers.

Having temporarily put his adversary to rout, Abélard began teaching at other schools near or in Paris and promptly stole most of his former teacher's students, thus making an implacable enemy. The rival schools went on for some time, with the two masters thundering at each other and being most unpleasant and competitive. In a singularly loud-mouthed age Abélard was undoubtedly the loudest of the lot. Challenges to debate flew back and forth between the schools. William fought hard, but the end was a foregone conclusion; daily Abélard gained the students that his opponent lost. Abélard clearly enjoyed

[6] Quoted in Lloyd, *op. cit.,* p. 40. The quotations from *The Stricken Lute* are reprinted by permission of Peter Davies, Ltd., publishers.

this fight, which was of his own provoking. He had announced publicly that he would get the other man's position away from him, and in the course of a few years he did. Teachers could not exist without students any better in the twelfth century than they can now.

This early episode brings out many of Abélard's fundamental traits. He was brilliant, he loved debating, he had supreme self-confidence, he was willing to pick a fight, he was reckless, irreverent, impudent, and clever. In addition, nature had endowed him with good looks, a buoyant disposition, and a magnetic charm. His contemporaries describe him as being intense, lively, and dashing, with great beauty of face and expression, a flexible and melodious voice, and a vibrant gaiety of manner. Something of his intrepid courage and his militancy comes through in his writings, but the other traits that contributed so much to his popularity died with him. The portrait of him in Figure 29 shows a somewhat effeminate-looking but handsome young man.

After his success in dethroning his opponent and taking his place as a teacher in the cathedral school, Abélard became the idol of Paris. Everywhere he went, people, especially women, followed him or ran to the windows merely to see him pass by. Students crowded into his classes. For the first time in the history of the world, students came, not by dozens but by thousands. Everyone connected with the intellectual life of Paris at this period tells the same story, his students by their hero-worship and his foes by their jealous rage. Into Abélard's classes came the young and the old from all parts of Europe. There were so many that the rooms of the school could not hold them. Many were in abject poverty, but they managed somehow to beg, gamble, steal, or borrow the money needed for their fees. The University of Paris was not organized until after Abélard's death, but it was his teaching which first drew so many students to Paris that a university was possible.

Like most teachers who are dear to the hearts of students, Abélard collected an assortment of nicknames. A few of them were "Goliath,"* "Leviathan,"* "Wizard," "Rhinoceros," "Smiter," "Friend of the Devil," "Giant," "Titan,"* "Prometheus,"* "Dragon," "Serpent," and "Hydra."* Perhaps the most frequently used and most descriptive was "Rhinoceros Indomitus," based presumably upon his habit of metaphorically lowering his head and charging at the most powerful opponents, with devastating effect.

2. *Abélard and Héloïse** On the crest of this wave of popularity Abélard met and fell in love with Héloïse. The scholar suddenly turned poet and wrote such charming love songs that soon all Paris was chanting her name. Even his teaching was forgotten. Sometimes he cut his classes, and at others he was obviously unprepared; he continually went about in a fog quite indifferent to his career. Before long Abélard's charm had stirred in Héloïse one of the most

faithful devotions in the annals of history. Thus began an immortal love story, which ended centuries later in Père Lachaise* cemetery in Paris, where the ashes of the two lovers now lie mixed in a single grave. For a while the two young people kept their affair a secret, but soon it came to the ears of the girl's uncle—an abnormal person, who was probably in love with his niece himself. The ensuing difficulties would take too long to relate, but eventually Abélard married Héloïse in secret, sent her temporarily to a convent for protection from her uncle, and returned to Paris himself to go on with his work.

Until this time Abélard had had everything his own way. He had been successful in the long battle with his first rival, he had developed his talent for teaching until he was the center of admiring crowds of students, and he had married the one woman he loved. Along the path to this pinnacle of success and happiness he had, however, made many a bitter and revengeful enemy. Little as he realized it at the time, he had sown the wind—and he was soon to reap the whirlwind. Thus far, only the strong points of his character were in evidence. His youth, his personal charm, his flashing wit, and his phenomenal success had concealed even from himself the essential weaknesses of personality that were to be brought out by adversity.

The first and most shattering blow came from the jealous uncle. This uncle hired some assassins who crept into Abélard's room one night, bound him, and emasculated him. By this violent and bloody deed the uncle intended to separate the two lovers. It is an indication of Abélard's great hold upon the hearts and imaginations of his contemporaries that, while he still lay critically sick from the brutal and unskillful surgery, the people in Paris voluntarily hunted down the assassins and inflicted the same punishment upon them.

To this first and horrible calamity Abélard made a highly characteristic response. He was proud and vain, sensitive to every slur and innuendo, and fearful of those who might ridicule him. In this first emergency of his life he worked himself into what was essentially a state of hysteria. Although Abélard could and did go out of his way to challenge other people intellectually, he wanted to select the nature and place of the quarrel. He was bold and reckless as long as things went to suit him, but when a crisis was forced upon him from without, when he was faced with trouble he had not intentionally precipitated, when life ground him between the upper and the nether millstone, he showed a weakness of purpose, an inability to make up his mind, a deep agitation, and a marked tendency to explode emotionally. In American parlance he could not "hit in the pinches." Strain has different effects upon different people. Some are organized by it and are never so cool and clearheaded as in an emergency; these people are called heroes.

Others are thrown into a state of disorganization by a crisis and cannot think clearly, although they can still feel intensely. If the pressure is sufficient, they go to pieces; these people are called weaklings. Probably neither term is wholly deserved. Abélard, for all his ability and charm, belonged to the latter class.

Worn out from the physical suffering of his injury, appalled at the thought of what effects the situation might have upon his career, furious at the man who had caused the calamity, apprehensive of the probable attitude toward him on the part of his students and friends, and bewildered by this abrupt cancellation of his marriage, he did a somewhat inexcusable thing. He forced his young wife to become a nun so that he might be sure she would never marry again. He knew his Héloïse. If she were a nun, she would never break her vows, and no other man could ever possess her. Héloïse also knew herself. She knew her capacity for devotion, was perfectly sure she would never love another, and was badly hurt by his obvious lack of trust in her. Nevertheless, she saw that only by taking the veil could she help or comfort him. Although she had no desire to lead a conventual* life and although she clearly foresaw the terrible strain such an existence would be to her, she quietly and resolutely did as he wished. Against the advice of all her friends she shut out the remembrance of her husband and her infant son. On the appointed day she went to the church, her family pleading with her up till the last moment, and advanced to the altar. There she stood for a moment before placing the veil upon her head and—instead of saying the usual prayer of thanksgiving to God—she recited a verse from the Latin poet Lucan:*

> O spouse most great,
> O thou whose bed my merit could
> not share! How hath an evil for-
> tune worked this wrong on thy
> Dear head? Why hapless did I
> Wed, if this the fruit that my
> Affection bore? Behold the pen-
> alty I now embrace for thy sweet
> Sake! [7]

Then the convent doors closed upon the one person who, if she had had a chance, might have guided Abélard through the dangers that were soon to beset him. Twenty years later Héloïse wrote to Abélard:

> At thy command I would change, not merely my costume, but my very soul, so entirely art thou the sole possessor of my body and my spirit. Never

[7] Quoted in McCabe, *op. cit.*, p. 141. The quotations from *Peter Abélard* are reprinted by permission of G. P. Putnam's Sons, publishers.

God is my witness, never have I sought anything in thee but thyself; I have sought thee, not thy gifts. I have not looked to the marriage bond or dowry; I have not even yearned to satisfy my own will and pleasure, but thine, as thou well knowest. The name of wife may be the holier and more approved, but the name of friend—nay, mistress, or concubine, if thou wilt suffer it—has always been the sweeter to me. For in thus humbling myself for thee, I should win greater favor from thee, and do less injury to thy greatness. This thou hast thyself not wholly forgotten, in the aforesaid letter thou hast written for the consolation of a friend. Therein also thou hast related some of the arguments with which I essayed to turn thee from the thought of our unhappy wedlock, though thou hast omitted many in which I set forth the advantage of love over matrimony, freedom over bondage. God is my witness that if Augustus, the emperor of the whole world, were to honour me with the thought of wedlock, and yield the empire of the universe, I should deem it more precious and honourable to be thy mistress than to be the queen of a Caesar.[8]

It was not religious fervor that drew me to the rigour of the conventual life, but thy command. How fruitlessly have I obeyed, if this gives me no title to thy gratitude! . . . When thou didst hasten to dedicate thyself to God, I followed thee—nay, I went before thee. For, as if mindful of the looking back of Lot's wife, thou didst devote me to God before thyself, by the sacred habit and vows of the monastery. Indeed, it was in this sole circumstance that I had the sorrow and the shame of noting thy lack of confidence in me. God knows that I should not have hesitated a moment to go before or to follow thee to the very gates of hell, hadst thou commanded it. My soul was not my own but thine. . . . In earlier days, when thou didst seek worldly pleasure with me, thy letters were frequent enough; thy songs put the name of Héloïse on every lip. Every street, every house in the city, echoed with my name. How juster would it be to lead me now to God than thou then didst to pleasure! Think then, I beseech thee, how much thou owest me. With this brief conclusion I terminate my long letter. Farewell, beloved.

It is unfortunate that with all his other talents Abélard could not have had a small share of his wife's loyalty and courage.

3. Abélard as a Monk With Héloïse safely dedicated to God, Abélard himself entered a monastery with the intention of devoting his great gifts to the study and teaching of theology. Almost at once, however, he was in difficulty. He did not like the monastic life, he did not approve of the brethren, and he detested the hypocrisy and venality* of many churchmen about him. It is doubtful if he could have adapted himself to monastery life at any time, but the change in his character as the result of his misfortunes made him even less adaptable than before. Abélard was never one to hold his tongue, and with his new resentment against life he was all too willing to

[8] *Ibid.*, p. 268. The second excerpt is from p. 270. See also *The Love Letters of Abélard and Héloïse*, J. M. Dent & Sons, Ltd., 1904, 132 ff.

criticize literally anyone or anything that did not suit him. He lashed out at his brethren and—as if he did not already have more enemies than he needed—made some more. Finally, to get rid of his nagging criticism, his superiors gave him a small school away from the monastery where he could, within limits, be independent. As soon as word got around that Abélard was again teaching, the students flocked to him in hordes, leaving Paris behind and trudging out into the country where he could be found. For a second time the magic of his teaching assembled a multitude. It was not long before this success stimulated the implacable hatred of those whom he had lightheartedly insulted in the days of his youth and strength. They complained that Abélard was trading upon his recent notoriety; that he was guilty of unprofessional conduct; that to set up a school in opposition to theirs was not consonant with his newly taken vows to follow the professed life of religion; that he was a monk now, not a master; that his proper place was within the confines of his monastery. In order to discredit Abélard with his students and to reduce his popularity in general, his enemies looked about for grounds on which he might be silenced. After some vague charges that he was teaching the classics to the detriment of the church fathers, and that he was teaching without a "licence" from his bishop, they brought forth the really serious accusation of heresy.

In order to understand the grounds for this charge it is necessary to examine briefly Abélard's writings to date. His earliest production seems to have been a purported conversation between a philosopher, a Jew, and a Christian. In it Abélard comes to the impious conclusion that Christianity is the best religion because it is closer to the "natural law" than the others. Its superiority lay, therefore, in its clearer formulation of the law of life, not in the sanctity of its tradition. His second publication was the most famous of his works—his *Sic et Non.*[9] Abélard's object in this book was evidently to provide the reader with such overwhelming evidence of the fallibility of the church fathers as to shatter the reader's illusions about them and his blind allegiance to tradition. For this purpose he first collected some eighteen hundred quotations from the church fathers. Then he listed 158 fundamental questions about church doctrine, such as: Is God one or three? Is God the author of evil, or no? Has God free will, or no? Was or was not Christ part man and part God? Is God all powerful, or no? Is God a substance, or no? Was Adam saved, or no? Should faith be based on reason? Is it worse to sin openly than secretly? Are the flesh and blood of Christ in very truth and essence present in the sacrament of the altar, or no? Finally, he grouped his quotations to show the range of answers to each question. For instance, first

[9] *Yes and No.*

would come an answer quoted perhaps from Augustine and immediately following an exactly contradictory answer from some other church father, possibly Jerome, Chrysostom, or Ambrose. Three samples appear below:

Whether God is one person, or no.

a. And therefore there are not three Gods but one.
b. There is one god, but he is not a single one.
c. But there are three persons, coeternal and coequal.
d. The Father is the Father, the Son is the Son; together they work eternally and never cease to be.
e. Therefore we believe in the father, the son and the holy ghost. These are eternal and unchangeable. God is one substance, but an eternal trinity.
f. The Father is a person, the Son is a person and the Holy Ghost is a person, Father, Son, and Holy Ghost are therefore not one person but three.
g. Three persons but not three gods.
h. What are these three? Father, Son, and Holy Spirit; not three gods, not three powers, not three creators.[10]

Whether Adam was buried in Calvary, or no.

a. In Golgotha, where the grave of Adam is, Christ raised up that mortal man in his own cross.
b. Whence this place in which the Lord was crucified was called Calvary . . . in order that the second Adam . . . might wash away the sins of the first Adam.
c. The three patriarchs, Abraham, Isaac, and Jacob, and Adam are thought to be buried in the place of Calvary, which was formerly Hebron, a city of the Philistines.
d. In the country of Hebron there is a double sepulcre, in the inner part of which Adam is buried and in the outer part, Abraham.

Whether one can resist God's power, or no.

a. Who may stand in thy sight when thou art angry? (Ps. 76: 7)
b. For who hath resisted thy will? (Rom. 9: 19)
c. O Thou that savest by thy right hand them which put their trust in Thee! (Ps. 17: 7)
d. Ye do always resist the Holy Ghost, just as your fathers did before you. (Acts 7: 51)
e. But Jesus said unto them, A prophet is not without honor but in his own country . . . And He could do no mighty work . . . and He marvelled because of their unbelief. (Mark 6: 4–6)[11]

[10] To the Protestant mind, at least, these statements are contradictory. Also apparently to Abélard's.

[11] Translated from Petri Abaelardi, *Sic et Non,* Marburgi Cattorum, Sumptibus et Typis Librariae Academiae Elwertianae, 1851 (444 pp.), pp. 31, 139, 87.

In the last example, all statements were taken from the Bible. The above excerpts are all short, but in some cases the quotations cover several pages. It would be difficult to imagine more damning evidence to show that authority and tradition cannot be regarded as infallible.*

Abélard saw that no one could teach the world to think until the minds of men were free from the shackles of tradition. Scholars were not willing to speculate; they quoted authorities, in the exact manner of the good Alcuin. With his *Sic et Non* Abélard was trying to shatter this excessive dependence upon the saints and church fathers by making a glaring example of their human fallibility. These first two books show the vigor and unconventionality of his mind. Either of them contained matter that was heretical, but actually there had been no trouble up to that time, partly because the books were not widely disseminated and partly because their author was far too popular to be attacked openly.

His third book was of a strictly theological character and concerned the nature of the Trinity.* Even today, any book on this topic is likely to precipitate an argument; in the twelfth century the subject was dynamite. There is no reason to suppose that Abélard produced the book in any but the most reverent spirit, for he had been greatly subdued by his misfortunes and was trying honestly to dedicate his genius to the furtherance of Christianity, but his earlier reputation for arrogance and his earlier antagonisms weighed the scales against him, and he was tried for heresy. At first he was not too greatly concerned because he assumed, with a return of his old self-confidence, that he would be given a chance to defend himself, would of course come off the victor in the ensuing debate, and would emerge the same popular idol he had always been. His opponents evidently had very similar notions about the matter, for they first incited the local townpeople to stone him upon his arrival—before he had a chance to win them over by his charm—and then prevented him from saying a word in his own defense. Actually the council could find nothing that was clearly heretical in the book, and the matter dragged on until the members felt they would lose face if they simply acquitted him. In the end they did not really condemn him, but they forced him to burn his book publicly on the grounds that he had published it without authorization from his bishop! In addition to this humiliation, he was consigned to a monastery that served as a penitentiary for rebellious monks. In short, although Abélard was not legally convicted of heresy, he was treated as if he had been. At the monastery further indignities were heaped upon him by one of his earlier enemies, who had immediate charge of discipline. Of Abélard this man wrote: "The rhinoceros was cowed and became very quiet, more patient under discipline, and of a saner and less raving mind."[12] In simple English, Abélard was beaten until he was docile.

The imprisonment did not last long because throughout France there arose a storm of protest. Presently, by the aid of a little legal chicanery on the part of the church authorities, Abélard was released from the penitentiary and sent back to his own monastery, where he obviously tried hard to be inoffensive. He saw that theology was too dangerous for a man of his clarity of mind and honesty, but he could not be idle. A man of genius has to think about something, and this one turned to history as an interesting and harmless field of endeavor. Quite incidentally, as a result of his reading, he came to the conclusion that the patron* saint of his abbey* was not the person he was supposed to have been. In his pleasure at uncovering what he regarded as an interesting bit of truth, he told his brethren about it. Abélard's simple following of evidence to a logical conclusion again landed him in trouble. The other monks mobbed and nearly killed him for casting aspersions upon their patron saint. While the brethren were in this frame of mind the abbot—an old enemy of Abélard's—called the members together and persuaded them to vote that Abélard be handed over to the king and tried for treason! This injustice was too much to be borne. While waiting for his trial, Abélard's patience gave out, and he ran away from the monastery. His plight was now serious, for he was not only an escaped monk but a fugitive from royal justice. After many weeks of hiding and of a general cat-and-mouse game with the authorities, he, the abbot, and the king finally agreed to a unique arrangement. Abélard was to become a hermit, far away somewhere in the country. In short, he was to stop annoying people by removing himself from human intercourse. By this time Abélard wanted only peace and freedom from injustice. In an effort to appease his superiors, he even recanted his statement about the patron saint; when it came to a choice between more persecution or a recantation, he wrote a letter humbly saying he was mistaken.[13]

4. Abélard's Middle Years Once out of this difficulty Abélard entered into the only years of even moderate contentment left to him. In a lovely valley in Champagne* he settled down with another hermit to live a holy and quiet life. Presumably, he had had more than enough of humanity. Every time he had tried to use his mind for the advancement of knowledge and the glory of God he had been misunderstood and persecuted. To be sure, the ringleaders were all people over whom he had ridden roughshod in his youth,

[12] McCabe, *op. cit.*, p. 189.

[13] As a matter of fact, both he and the brethren were wrong. Subsequent research has shown that the patron saint was someone else altogether.

but this fact did not make the situation easier to bear. For a while all went well in the woodland retreat, but soon he had to do something to earn his daily bread. There was only one thing he knew how to do—he could teach. At first he gave lessons to pupils from a near-by town, but presently the number of pupils increased, and word began to circulate that Abélard was teaching again. For a third time those who hated him watched the miracle of student devotion repeat itself. Out into the country and into the open fields, where there was not even a roof to shelter them, trudged the students. As one authority on Abélard says:

> Week by week the paths that led into the valley by the Arduzon discharged their hundreds of pilgrims. The rough justice of nature offered no advantage to wealth. Rich and poor, noble and peasant, young and old, they raised their mud-cabins or their moss-covered earth-works, each with his own hands. Hundreds of these rude dwellings dotted the meadow and sheltered in the wood. A bundle of straw was the only bed to be found in them. Their tables were primitive mounds of fresh turf; the only food a kind of coarse peasant-bread, with roots and herbs, and a draught of sweet water from the river. The meats and wines and pretty maids and soft beds of the cities were left far away over the hills. For the great magician had extended his wand once more, and the fascination of his lectures was as irresistible as ever.[14]

The students settled down upon him like a cloud of locusts, built him an oratory for his lectures, and by their youth and gaiety raised his spirits to something approaching their old level. It was a curious, isolated colony held together by the personality of one genius. Abélard lectured, the students spent part of their time listening and part in doing the necessary work; in the evening they gathered around a huge fire and sang. This happy state of affairs did not long endure, however. Just as Abélard was reviving under the adoration of his students, the criticisms against him began again. The more popular he was, the more jealous were his enemies. He would willingly have lived out his days in the quiet valley with only youth for company, but he had learned to fear the power of his persecutors. Not only did lesser men criticize and annoy him—them he could have managed—but his popularity with young people and independence of mind had incurred the wrath of the greatest heretic hunter of the century, Bernard of Clairvaux,* a thoroughly pious fanatic who was a power throughout Europe. Bernard had a good mind, but it was as bound by tradition as Abélard's was free.

Bernard and Abélard were natural opponents. For one thing, the former was a leading exponent of the popular doctrine that "faith precedes reason"; that is, in matters of religion, one should put aside all reason and simply

[14] McCabe, *op. cit.*, p. 141.

have faith. This attitude was summed up in the simple statement: "I believe, therefore I know." To reason about divine matters was irreverent and blasphemous, and to seek objective proof of any kind was rank heresy. In this attitude Bernard was typically medieval. For instance, the medieval mind argued that since the smaller always came from the larger, therefore the rivers came from the ocean; the obvious fact that the rivers flowed into the ocean made no difference whatever. The idea of finding objective proof for anything was thus completely foreign to medieval thought. Abélard could not turn his logic on and off as if it were water in a faucet, nor could he believe what did not make sense. He therefore taught his students to believe only what they could verify. Abélard's notion that a human being should scrutinize religious dogmas to see if they made sense was to many people both revolting and shocking. His attitude is summed up in two famous aphorisms:*

> By doubting, we are led to inquire; by inquiring, we perceive the truth.
>
> A doctrine is not to be believed because God has said it, but because we are convinced by reason that it is so.

These remarks were clearly heretical—in fact, to some people today they still are—and they had the further characteristic of being so succinctly phrased [15] that no one hearing them would be likely to forget them. Because Abélard was actually as reverent as he was independent, he could see only service to Christianity in checking its doctrines against his reason and in eliminating those that were demonstrably fallacious; nor could Abélard agree with some medieval scholars that all secular learning was evil and all religious learning good, regardless of its nature. In his own words:

> No scientific reading is improper for any religious person. . . . No one can call any science evil, though it be itself concerned with evil, which an upright man requires. Guilt consists not in the knowledge of a sin, but in its commission. For if any knowledge were sinful, then were it sinful to know anything. So then God, who knoweth all things, could not be held guiltless of sin. For in Him alone is the fulness of all knowledge, whose gift all knowledge is.[16]

These modern sentiments are so unrepresentative of the twelfth century that one can easily believe they were held to be heretical.

As the weeks went by and Abélard continued to teach what he knew would be regarded as heresy, even though he taught in a spirit of complete

[15] The Latin is more condensed than the English translation.

[16] Quoted in Lloyd, *op. cit.*, p. 97. For a modern appraisal of Abélard as a Christian philosopher and theologian, see J. R. McCallum, *Abélard's Christian Theology*, The Macmillan Company, 1949.

devotion to the church, he became more and more uneasy. He had almost decided to leave France and take shelter in Spain when he received an offer from a distant abbey to become the abbot. The net was closing in on him once more and he lacked the courage to face another persecution, so he again ran away, this time by accepting the offer before he had adequately investigated the situation.

The abbey was distant from Bernard of Clairvaux, but it had no other advantages. The monks were a wild lot, who had no intention whatever of leading religious lives. They had wives or mistresses, they drank to excess, and they resented violently the slightest discipline. In fact, the whole association between them and Abélard was undoubtedly based upon a misundertanding. Abélard thought he would find peace and safety in the remote abbey, and the monks—who had evidently heard of Abélard as a freethinker, a man of the world, and a troubadour—thought they were choosing a sophisticate who would let them do as they pleased and would be useful in helping them in the dual task of fleecing the peasants and of preventing the local noblemen from fleecing them first. To their surprise and indignation, this supposed worldling wanted them to live moral lives! When they recovered from their stunned bewilderment they harassed him, threatened him, and in the end tried to kill him.

At about the middle of this period Abélard heard that the nuns in the convent to which Héloïse had gone had been ejected from their house through some political hocus-pocus. He was deeply concerned about her, sought her out, and made over to her and a few nuns who had followed her the ownership of the oratory that his students had built for him. From time to time he visited her there, always remaining distant and impersonal but always helping her insofar as the affairs of the convent were concerned. Either his love for her had really died, leaving only a sense of responsibility, or he used his distant manner as a defense against the possible arousal of an emotion forbidden to both of them, or he feared the calumny and gossip that would inevitably be aroused if he showed the slightest personal interest in her.

5. The Last Years Eventually Abélard was forced to flee for his life from his own monks. For three years he was in hiding. During this time he wrote his autobiography—*The History of My Misfortunes*.[17] One can understand why it is such a gloomy book. A copy of it came, in the course of time, to Héloïse, who was moved to a frenzy of despair at the ignominies that had been heaped upon the man for whom she had sacrificed herself and at her own helplessness to relieve his situation. She wrote him, and there fol-

[17] Peter Abélard, *The History of My Misfortunes* (translated by H. A. Bellows), Th. A. Boyd, 1922, 96 pp.

lowed the correspondence that makes up the *Love Letters of Abélard and Héloïse.*[18] Hers are utterly devoted, with a passion that her years in the convent had not suppressed. His are restrained and formal, except for one or two passages in which his control apparently slipped. Indeed, it seems as if he almost knew he was writing bathos, for his letters have an affectation and artificiality that are quite unlike his usually clear style. Here and there one catches a glimpse of real feeling: in his request that after his death his body be sent to his wife for burial, in his effort to make her position secure, in his willingness to do anything that would not be misconstrued by his many critics, and in his poems, which again appeared for the first time since his youth. Of these the one below is suggestive:

Low in thy grave with thee
Happy to lie
Since there's no greater thing left Love to do:
And to live after thee
Is but to die;
For with but half a soul what can Life do?

To share thy victory,
Or else thy grave,
Either to rescue thee, or with thee lie:
Ending that life for thee,
That thou didst save
So death that sundereth might bring more nigh.

Peace, O my stricken lute:
Thy strings are sleeping.
Would that my heart could still
Its bitter weeping! [19]

In this poem Abélard was supposedly writing a lament for David's son Absalom, but one wonders if he was not lamenting his own loss of Héloïse. At her request he wrote also a number of hymns for her nuns to sing. Among them was the familiar:

Oh what the joy and the glory must be
Those endless Sabbaths the blessed ones see,
Crowns for the valiant, for weary ones rest,
God is in all and in all ever blest.[20]

[18] The excerpts on page 163 are from these letters.
[19] Lloyd, *op. cit.*, p. 153.
[20] *Ibid.*

Perhaps the most beautiful of them all was the simple metrical adaptation of certain verses from the Bible, such as:

Est in Rama
Vox audita
Rachel flentis
Super natos
Interfectos
Eiulantis

Lacerata
Iacent membra
Parvulorum
Et tam lacte
Quan cruore
Rigant humum.[21]

When Abélard came out of his hiding he returned to Paris, where he again began to teach. The inevitable happened: students flocked to him in droves. His many calamities had evidently not robbed him of his ability to attract the young. In this particular group of students were many youths who later became famous: John of Salisbury,* Arnold of Brescia,* Gilbert de la Porrée,* and many others who were to be the bishops and theologians of the next generation. In the course of his life Abélard was the teacher of one future pope, nineteen cardinals, and more than fifty bishops and archbishops. With his scholars Abélard was not long left in peace, for he was now a marked man. Everything he said was noted and reported. At all times Bernard of Clairvaux was watching him and waiting only for a chance to pounce. During these last years Abélard had rewritten, with what he thought were sufficient changes to make it orthodox,* the treatise that he had been forced to burn at his trial for heresy. His judgment on what was orthodox turned out to have been singularly bad. In the revised form the material was still a rationalistic exposition of church dogma. By publishing it he gave Bernard the rope with which to hang him.

By this time it was clear enough to Abélard that another crisis was approaching. He knew the machinery of church politics, and he knew Bernard. He fully realized that he had no chance of an acquittal in the trial which was probably coming if he let Bernard proceed along the somewhat devious lines that gentleman would prefer. Bernard was, however, no debater and would have little chance against the best dialectician of the age, provided the two ever engaged in a verbal contest. Remembering his former trial, during which he had not been allowed to speak a word, Abélard decided upon a bold and shrewd move. He challenged Bernard to a debate on the controversial points of the book. The situation did not appeal to Bernard in the least. In fact, he was so uncertain of the outcome that he "packed" the jury which was to hear the arguments. It is an unwilling testimony to the charm of

[21] *Ibid.*, p. 155. In English the verses are: "In Rama was there a voice heard, lamentation, and weeping and great mourning, Rachel weeping for her children, and would not be comforted because they were not."

Abélard's person and the cogency of his arguments that Bernard should shrink nervously from an oral encounter and should resort to measures that would have been branded dishonorable in any other man. It is probable that Abélard had again dreamed of a real debate, a fair trial, and an eventual acquittal, for he knew he could not be beaten in argument. In fact, it is reported that he entered the cathedral with a smile and a buoyant step; but a moment later, when he came into the room where the trial was to take place and looked about him, he was stunned. In the assemblage before which he was to present his case was every important enemy he had ever made. In the entire gathering he saw only one man who might conceivably give an impartial judgment. As Bernard began his opening remarks, Abélard interrupted with the kind of hysterical outburst that was typical of him in moments of crisis and announced, "I will not be judged like a common criminal. I appeal to Rome." With these words he marched out of the room. This action left Bernard in full control, and the next day he was able to send to the pope a formal notice of Abélard's conviction as a heretic. He then began a course of letter writing to everyone in authority, giving his views on the situation and urging speed in the punishment of the offender. By such means he succeeded in bringing about Abélard's condemnation and excommunication in the record time of seven weeks.

In the meantime Abélard had been making his way slowly southward toward Italy. He was old, very tired, and thoroughly disillusioned. He had done his best to be reverent, and the world had condemned him. At this time he wrote a letter to Héloïse, to justify in her eyes the purity of his faith. Part of it appears below:

> My sister Héloïse, once dear to me in the world, and now most dear in Christ, logic has brought the enmity of men upon me. For there are certain perverse calumniators, whose wisdom leads to perdition, that say I take preeminence in logic but fail egregiously in the interpretation of Paul; commending my ability, they would deny me the purity of Christian faith. . . . I would not rank as a philosopher if it implied any error in faith: I would not be an Aristotle if it kept me away from Christ. For no other name is given to me under heaven in which I may find salvation. I adore Christ, sitting at the right hand of the Father.[22]

In the course of his journey toward Rome, Abélard stopped over night at the monastery of Cluny.* Here he learned from the abbot, who was one of his few friends, that the decree of excommunication had already been proclaimed. This news sapped the last ounce of vitality, and he never again really cared what happened to him. The abbot of Cluny saw that Abélard

[22] Quoted in McCabe, *op. cit.*, p. 365.

was not much longer for this world, and he wanted the harassed man to end his days in peace. He therefore arranged for a meeting between Bernard and Abélard and for a temporary appeasement of the former, enough to keep him from serving the sentence of excommunication until after Abélard was beyond being hurt by it. There was no fight left in Abélard; he went meekly through the necessary forms of apology and retraction, and then retired to Cluny, where he lived in numbed rectitude until he fell sick and died[23]—as much because he did not want to live as from disease.

After his death his body was sent, as he had requested, to his wife for burial. She not only erected a monument to him, but obtained from the pope a revocation of the excommunication and affixed it to his grave, so that all who came there might know that Abélard had been no heretic. There is a legend that when she died twenty years later and her body was put into the same grave, the arms of her beloved opened to receive her.

6. Abélard the Teacher It is not, however, with Abélard the lover that the present chapter deals, but with Abélard the teacher. Like most teachers, he did not write about education, nor did he leave any account of his methodology. It is a fair guess that he thought his teaching skill the natural result of his position as the best educated and most intelligent man of his generation, his own estimate of himself. A more dispassionate judgment would admit his brilliancy but question the depth and breadth of his education. In any case, ability to teach is not an inevitable outgrowth of either intelligence or scholarship. One must therefore discard what Abélard said about himself and rely upon the scattered references made by his students.

The secret of Abélard's success as a teacher seems from all accounts to lie in six elements of teaching skill or personality. In the first place he was facile, spontaneous, and gay. Most teachers of his day, and perhaps of any day, were solemn, dignified, and ponderous; they lectured reverently upon serious topics. Abélard's general impudence was a great and welcome contrast. Not many medieval classrooms rang with merriment, but Abélard's scholars actually laughed in class. One sees today much the same kind of fascination for the student mind in the occasional professor who addresses adolescents in their own language—slang and catch phrases included—draws examples from campus life to illustrate his theories, and jokes pleasantly about important matters. Such teachers are just as much of a trial to the serious-minded among their colleagues as Abélard was to his.

A second element in his teaching success was his skill in using ideas from one field to prove points in another. Thus he would quote Ovid to illuminate the inner meaning of a Biblical quotation, or show the relation of the Song of

[23] Actually not at Cluny but in another establishment owned by the order.

Songs to the ballads of the troubadours, or apply Aristotelian logic to the mystery of the Trinity. This kind of approach is always interesting. It produces sudden insights and appreciations that do not come from intensive study within a single field. Since Aristotle was at the time the very latest thing in education, the use of his methods with materials that had come into being since his death gave much the same effect as was produced in the latter half of the nineteenth century when the biological doctrine of evolution was applied to various nonbiological fields. Thus the teacher of literature in 1890 who could show the evolution of comic characters in English drama stirred up an interest that did not exist in the more conventional analysis of the plays without the developmental angle. Abélard's resourcefulness in relating one field to another was as useful as the same trait is to a teacher of today.

In the third place, Abélard was vivid and dramatic. His classroom was a battlefield. Anyone who wanted to challenge him was welcomed; and, if no one came voluntarily, Abélard issued reverberating challenges to the masters of other schools to come and debate with him. If they came, he slaughtered them unmercifully; if they did not, he was very merry at their expense. His students never knew what the day's work would bring forth, but they were sure it would be exciting. This pugnacity and general baiting of his enemies was the trait that earned for him the nickname of "Rhinoceros Indomitus." Since most people are not especially courageous, they find an outlet for their own repressions in the sight of a person who simply lowers his head and charges into battle, taking rough handling from his opponents and returning still rougher treatment. There was nothing delicate about Abélard's method of attack. He would browbeat, ridicule, and insult those who tried to stand against him. He was not content with a mere defeat but demanded an utter rout. Such an attitude may not contribute to a dispassionate search for truth, but it certainly keeps the class awake. The undergraduate of today, like the student of the twelfth century, also loves a fighter and detests a bore.

A fourth teaching trait was Abélard's definiteness and assurance. He knew perfectly well just what he thought about everything. There were no fuzzy edges to his mind. His opinions were sometimes undoubtedly wrong, but being in error failed to dent his superb aplomb. The authoritativeness that comes from a teacher who knows his own mind is always an element in popularity. Students would rather disagree violently with a professor than find nothing in his remarks to which they can react. Knowing what the teacher thinks gives a student a point of departure from his own cogitations.

In the fifth place, Abélard's presentation of a subject was clear and logical. He proceeded step by step from his beginning to his conclusion, without wandering off on bypaths or becoming confused by complexities. His own mind was crystal clear, keen as a razor, and completely logical. Although Abélard was deeply emotional, his feelings entered remarkably little into his thought processes. Throughout his life he went where his logic led him. Such a method of procedure must have been a fascinating novelty in the twelfth century—and is still a rarity. In contrast to the current tortuous verbiage. Abélard's clarity of thought and expression must have stood out like a beacon.

Finally, Abélard had a passion for telling people what he knew and for shedding upon them what he felt to be a new light. He had that dash of the missionary, that *soupçon* of the social worker, that touch of the fanatic, that nuance of the small-town gossip—who knows all, hears all, and tells all—that go into the psychological make-up of most successful teachers. He really wanted to leave mankind better off than he found it, and he clearly regarded himself as the person best equipped for such a mission. A zeal such as he showed, even though it is overlaid by a surface flippancy, drives any teacher into using whatever abilities he may have—and Abélard had many.

As a summary of Abélard's life and character, one can hardly do better than to quote the following excerpt:

> One is tempted at times to speculate on the probable development of Abélard's thoughts if that great shadow had not fallen on his life at so early a period. There are two Abélards. The older theologian, who is ever watchful to arrest his thoughts when they approach clear, fundamental dogmas, is not the natural development of the free-thinking author of the *Sic et Non.* With the conversion to the ascetic ideal had come a greater awe in approaching truths which were implicitly accepted as divine. Yet we may well doubt if Abélard would ever have advanced much beyond his actual limits. Starting from the world of ideas in which he lived, he would have needed an exceptional strength to proceed to any very defiant and revolutionary conclusions. He was not the stuff of martyrs, of Scotus Erigena* of Arnold of Brescia. He had no particle of the political ability of Luther.* But such as he is, gifted with a penetrating mind, and led by a humanist ideal that touched few of his contemporaries, pathetically irresolute, and failing because the fates had made him the hero of a great drama and ironically denied him the hero's strength, he deserves at least to be drawn forth from the too deep shadow of a crude and unsympathetic tradition.[24]

Abélard was one of the world's great teachers. He was the first to gather together thousands of students, and as such, in spite of his personal defects, he should command respect.

Abélard did not found the University of Paris, but his work paved the way for its development and his popularity helped draw together the hordes of students necessary to maintain a university. Abélard last taught in Paris in

[24] McCabe, *op. cit.*, pp. 395–396.

1136; the university was certainly in existence in 1150, only fourteen years later. Abélard was therefore an immediate forerunner of university education. There had been, in Greece and in other countries bordering on the Mediterranan, schools of sufficiently advanced character to deserve the name of universities, but they did not have the guild* organization that developed in the twelfth century. Since the later years of the Roman Empire, however, the schools of Europe had been largely elementary in their subject matter. The most advanced were no more than secondary schools. The growth of certain cathedral schools into universities marked the emergence of higher education from the decline brought about by the barbarian invasions. In this emergence Abélard has an important part.

Abélard's charm and genius for teaching died with him, but his independent spirit, his following of reason to its logical conclusion, and his insistence upon freedom to think live on, especially in the university which, while most certainly not his creation, may be regarded as his posthumous child.

B. THE MEDIEVAL UNIVERSITY

In the centuries that had elapsed since the spread of Christianity, the church had fostered three types of school, two of which, in cathedral and monastery, still survived into the last centuries of the Middle Ages. The monastery schools existed primarily for the education of future monks, although the schools usually enrolled a few pupils who did not intend to enter the brotherhood. If there were enough rooms and enough teachers, the interns and externs were taught in separate buildings by different people. In general, however, the training in these schools was more professional than cultural. The cathedral schools differed somewhat in this respect. Cathedrals were built in cities, whereas monasteries—being places of refuge from the excitement of life—were erected far out in the country. Within the cities the majority of the pupils wanted a liberal education rather than a technical training for the priesthood. The curriculum of the cathedral schools was therefore more or less modified to meet the needs of these pupils.

In the late eleventh and early twelfth centuries the Mont Ste Geneviève* in Paris was covered with schools, most of which were independent of control by either church or state. A master who wanted to teach simply hung out his shingle and waited for patronage. Students went from one school to another as this or that master attracted them. The work in most of these schools centered upon dialectic.

For several years during the early part of the twelfth century a young Englishman named John of Salisbury was studying in France, going from master to master, as was the custom. He attended schools in both Paris and

Chartres just before universities came into being. In later years he wrote as follows of his experiences there:

When as a lad I first went into Gaul for the cause of study . . . I addressed myself to the Peripatetic* of the Palais [Abélard], who then presided upon Mount Saint Genovefa, an illustrious teacher and admired of all men. There at his feet I acquired the first rudiments of the dialectical art, and snatched according to the scant measure of my wits whatever passed his lips with entire greediness of mind. Then, when he had departed all too hastily, as it seemed to me, I joined myself to master Alberic, who stood forth among the rest as a greatly esteemed dialectician. . . .

With these I applied myself for the full space of two years, to practice in the commonplace and rules and other rudimentary elements, which are instilled into the minds of boys and wherein the aforesaid doctors were most able and ready; so that me-thought I knew all these things as well as my nailes and fingers . . . Then returning unto myself and measuring my powers, I advisedly resorted, by the good favour of my preceptors, to the Grammarian of Conches [William], and heard his teaching by the space of three years. While at Chartres I studied under Richard L'Évêque, a man whose training was deficient almost in no thing, who had more heart even than speech, more knowledge than skill, more truth than vanity, more virtue than show: and the things I had learned from others I collected all again from him, and certain things too I learned which I had not before heard. . . .

And so it seemed pleasant to me to revisit my old companions on the mount* [at Paris], whom I had left and whom dialectic still detained, to confer with them touching old matters of debate; that we might by mutual comparison measure together our several progress. I found them as before, and where they were before; nor did they appear to have reached the goal in unravelling the old questions, nor had they added one jot of a proposition. The aims that once inspired them, inspired them still: they only had progressed in one point, they unlearned moderation, they knew not modesty; in such wise that one might despair of their recovery. And thus experience taught me a manifest conclusion, that, whereas dialectic furthers other studies, so if it remains by itself it lies bloodless and barren, nor does it quicken the soul to yield fruit of philosophy, except the same conceive from elsewhere.[25]

This passage well describes the nature of the schools from which the universities developed. It also illustrates the way in which the students wandered about from place to place.

1. From Cathedral School to University During the first part of the Middle Ages both monastery and cathedral schools were small, but, by the beginning of the twelfth century, some cities had grown so large that the local

[25] J. A. Giles, *Joannis Saresberiensis, Opera Omnia Metalogicus,* 1898 (5 vols.), I, vii–xiii. Used by permission of The Clarendon Press, publishers.

cathedral school enrolled a relatively large number of students. Outstanding teachers might gather together sixty or seventy pupils instead of a dozen. The cathedral school at Chartres was among the best in Europe and illustrates the developments during the eleventh and twelfth centuries that led to the foundation of universities in the thirteenth and fourteenth.[26] The school was probably founded in about the sixth century. For some time it remained small and no more important than many another; it grew somewhat during the relatively peaceful period under Charlemagne, lost ground for a century thereafter, and then developed rapidly for the next hundred years. This growth was accelerated early in the eleventh century by a series of excellent teachers, under whom the school grew from a typical, small cathedral school to an academy. While the studies of the lower years retained their secondary character, the more advanced ones would have overlapped on a university curriculum had there been one. The school of Chartres was far too good to be regarded as typical, but it does show the stages through which many cathedral schools went in becoming universities themselves, or in making universities necessary. On page 180 appears the course of study at Chartres in the first half of the twelfth century.

The list is an interesting combination of the old and the new. The grammars of Donatus and Priscian are familiar. The writings of Cicero are from the classic days of Rome, but the other two writers on rhetoric are early medieval. The list thus far might have been composed by Alcuin. The references for dialectic not only contain new material but are as long as those for the other two linguistic subjects put together. The study of what is now called literature came under the heading of rhetoric. In other schools, in which the literary tradition was less strong than at Chartres, the study of literature practically disappeared, and the time thus gained was devoted to dialectic. Boethius and Porphyry were nothing unusual, but this list marks an early appearance of Aristotle in the schools. Only a few of his works are here, but even so, they take up a third of the list of dialectical references. Within a century Aristotle's books had spread out until in some schools they constituted almost the entire curriculum. Thus in 1240, the courses at the University of Paris required the study of twenty-four references, of which eighteen were books by Aristotle.[27]

The quadrivium was also showing signs of change. The texts for arithmetic were all old, but the work of Adelard had been added in music. In

[26] A. Clerval, "Les Écoles de Chartres au Moyen Age," *Memoire de la Société Archéologique d' Eure-et-Loire,* Vol. XI, 1895, 569 pp. See also M. B. Aspinwall, *Les Écoles Espiscopales et Monastiques,* Oudin et Cie., 1904, 150 pp.

[27] S. J. Paetow, "The Arts Course at Medieval Universities," *University of Illinois Studies,* Vol. III, No. 7, 1910, 96 pp.

TABLE 2: COURSE OF STUDY AT CHARTRES [a]

		Author	Work
The Trivium	Grammar	1. Donatus	Concerning the 8 parts of speech On barbarisms
		2. Priscian	Book 18 on grammatical forms On values and measures On comic poetry On accents On the 12 books of Virgil On declamations
	Rhetoric	3. Cicero	Rhetoric Book 2 Rhetoric Book 4
		4. J. Severianus*	Concerning parts of a dialogue Precepts of the art of rhetoric
		5. Capella	Rhetoric, Book 5
	Dialectic	6. Porphyry*	Interpretation of Boethius
		7. Boethius	Introduction of categorical syllogisms Book on categorical syllogisms Book 2 on the hypothetical syllogisms Topics on the hypothetical syllogism Book 4 on different topics On division On definition
		8. Anonymous	The logic of speech
		9. Aristotle	Categories Peri Hermenias* Analytics Topics Refutations
The Quadrivium	Arithmetic	10. Boethius	Arithmetic, Book 2
		11. Capella	Arithmetic, Book 1
		12. Anonymous	Arithmetic, Book 3
	Music	13. Boethius	Music
		14. Adelard*	Music
	Geometry	15. Isidore	Measurement of fields
		16. Anonymous	Geometric definitions
		17. Anonymous	Measurement of lines, surfaces, solids, liquids, weights, and time
		18. Frontinus*	Measurement of surfaces
		19. Columella*	Measurement of fields
		20. Gerbert*	Measurement among the Romans
		21. Boethius	Arithmetic
		22. Garland*	The abacus
	Astronomy*	23. Hyginus*	Poetry of Astronomy
		24. Ptolemy	Precepts
		25. Ptolemy	Tables

[a] Clerval, *op. cit.*, p. 222–223.

geometry the names of both Gerbert and Garland appear; these men had both had contacts with the Arab scholars in Spain and had learned much about mathematics from them. The inclusion of these two names foreshadows the avalanche of learning from the East that was soon to rush over Europe. Finally, astronomy was escaping from astrology and becoming a true science again.

During the two centuries after this course of study at Chartres was devised, the trivium went on developing in just the way it had started—by the inclusion of more and more Aristotle, with a resulting squeezing out of everything else. The quadrivium was checked in its growth, partly because there was no time left over for it, partly because a sufficient number of ancient scientific writings had not yet been discovered or brought into Europe, and partly because the experimental approach necessary for its further development was not yet in existence. Minor additions to the quadrivium were retained, in case they had been made at all, but the real awakening in science did not come until after the Renaissance. In the meantime, Aristotle and dialectic held the stage. The teaching at Chartres was certainly much better than that in most places—in the twelfth century its masters were the most outstanding in Europe—and its curriculum was therefore presumably more advanced than that of other schools. By comparison with the previous chapter one can see that much progress had been made in the educational field. There were more and better schools, a higher level of educational achievement, and a larger amount of secular learning.

2. *The Growth of Universities* The establishment of universities was the great educational achievement of the Middle Ages, and specifically of the twelfth and thirteenth centuries. An institution of higher learning came into being at this time for a number of reasons. The two quotations below summarize the main causes both general and specific:

> The desire for a higher education, and the impulse to more profound investigation, that characterized the beginning and course of the twelfth century, was only a part of a widespread movement, political and moral, which showed itself in the order of chivalry, Crusades, the rise of free towns, the incorporation of civic life, the organization of industries in the form of guilds, and, we may also add, as another indication of the mental quickening, in the rise of a Provençal modern language and literature and of not a few heresies. The universal domination of the Catholic Church, too, had by this time created a spiritual European commonwealth, and a common language which made communication between the citizens of different countries possible, and secured the safety of travelling clerics*—a word of very wide signification, and gradually extended to all scholars. The abbeys and monasteries had *hospitia,* or hostels, attached to them. and travelers moved from one

to the other. The dress of a monk or the designation of a scholar guaranteed protection wherever the Catholic Church existed, irrespective of nationality. The university movement, accordingly, was not an isolated movement, or due to only one cause. The times were ripe, and the general conditions of life made the new development possible.[28]

The above sources of stimulation were general and affected all phases of life. In addition there were certain specific stimuli within the field of education. The outstanding of these are summarized in the following excerpt:

> Now, looking first to the germ out of which the universities grew, I think we must say that the universities may be regarded as a natural development of the cathedral and monastery schools; but if we seek for an external motive force urging men to undertake the more profound and independent study of the liberal arts, we can find it only in the Saracenic* schools of Bagdad,* Babylon,* Alexandria, and Cordova*. The Saracens came necessarily into contact with Greek literature just when the Western Church was drifting away from it, and by their translations of Hippocrates*, Galen,* Aristotle, and other Greek classics, they restored what may be quite accurately called the "university life" of the Greeks. Many of their teachers were, of course, themselves Greeks, who had conformed to the new faith. To these Arab schools Christians had resorted in considerable numbers, and were cordially welcomed. They brought back, especially to Italy, the knowledge and the impulse they had gained. This will appear more clearly when we come to speak of Salernum,* which unquestionably led the way. We are right then, I think, in connecting the birth of universities, on the one hand, with the cathedral and Benedictine schools, of which they were an evolution, and with the Saracenic impulse on the other,—the latter being, in fact, old Greece at work again through an alien channel. Some influence, also, may have come from the Greeks of Constantinople through Venice, for in the eleventh century there was still a survival of Greek ideas. In the eastern capital Greek literature was still studied, and the Greek tongue written (it is said) with classical purity. But the activity of thought there was as nothing when compared with that of the Arabs.
>
> But the cloister and cathedral schools, and the Saracenic impulse, would not themselves have given rise to universities. There were other actuating causes, and these I consider to have been: (1) The gradual growth of traditionary learning, which accumulated so great a weight on the subjects that most interest the mind of man and are most essential to his welfare as a member of society, as to *demand specialization.* (2) The growth of a lay or anti-

[28] S. S. Laurie, *Lectures on the Rise and Early Constitution of the Universities,* Routledge and Kegan Paul, 1886 (293 pp.), pp. 96–98. This excerpt and subsequent ones from Laurie are quoted by permission of the publishers. See also C. H. Haskins, *The Rise of Universities,* Henry Holt and Company, 1923, 434 pp.; A. O. Norton, *Readings in the History of Education: Medieval Universities,* Harvard University Press, 1909, 155 pp.; F. Paulsen, *The German Universities and University Studies* (translated by F. Thilly), Charles Scribner's Sons, 1906, 451 pp.; H. Rashdall, *Universities of Europe in the Middle Ages,* Oxford University Press, 1936, 3 vols.

monastic feeling in connection with the work of physician, lawyer, and even theologian. (3) The *actual specializing* of the leading studies—medicine at Salernum, law at Bologna,* and theology, with its cognate* philosophy, at Paris. As a matter of course, this specialization drew (as it would today draw) a vast number of students to the noted centres of instruction—both those intended for the religious life, whether as priests or monks, and those who desired as laymen and free from monastic vows and monastic rule, to mix with their fellow-men as professional workers. This, I submit, is the chief key to the explanation of the rise of the higher or university schools. They were specialized schools, as opposed to the schools of Arts, and they were *open to all* without restriction as *studia publica* or *generalia,* as opposed to the more restricted ecclesiastic schools which were under a "Rule." [29]

From a fusion the above causes, plus the concentration of students in various centers, a few of the cathedral schools expanded into universities at some time during the twelfth century. The cathedral school of Notre Dame in Paris developed into the University of Paris at about 1150, but there is no date of foundation. Bologna, Oxford, Montpellier,* and Salerno also just grew, without being definitely founded. The earliest university to have a date of birth is Naples* in 1224.

Most of the universities began from the first to specialize. It is perhaps more accurate to say that the schools out of which they grew had been specializing for a long time, and these interests merely developed further. In Paris there were four courses of study: the arts, canon law,* medicine, and theology. The first and last enrolled by far the largest number of students. The universities of Salerno, Padua,* and Montpellier specialized in medicine. Bologna, on the other hand, was from the first a center for the study of law, especially Roman law.* Almost all the legal lights of the period were at one time or another on its faculty. The other very old university, Oxford, did not specialize; it favored general culture by means of an arts course rather than concentration of any type. In general, however, the universities were specialized—that is, professional—schools. They had practical ends that served society and human needs. As one authority has said:

> It was the needs of the human body which originated Salerno; it was the needs of men as related to each other in a civil organization which originated Bologna; it was the eternal needs of the human spirit in its relation to the unseen that originated Paris.[30]

In the course of time most of the universities established several faculties for instruction in the arts, medicine, law, and theology, but usually one of these faculties was predominant. The modern university continues to have faculties

[29] Laurie, *op. cit.*, pp. 99–101.
[30] *Ibid.*, pp. 109–110.

in several fields—in this respect being different from a college—and it continues to base its activities upon human needs. A consideration of the names given the colleges in an American university of today makes this point clear: agriculture, arts, dentistry, medicine, pharmacy, commerce, engineering, law, and education.

The growth of universities throughout Europe is shown in the table below:

TABLE 3: NUMBER AND DISTRIBUTION OF THE EARLY UNIVERSITIES[a]

Century	Italy	France	Great Britain	Spain and Portugal	Germany and the Low Countries	Other Countries	Total
Twelfth	3	2	1				6
Thirteenth	8	3	1	5			17
Fourteenth	8	4	0	3	5	3	23
Fifteenth	2	9	3	7	11	3	35
Sixteenth	4	1	2	5	12	4	28
							109

[a] Based on a list given in E. P. Cubberley, *Readings in the History of Education*, pp. 154–155.

In Italy and France, universities were founded earlier than in Spain, Germany, or other European countries, except England. The majority of these universities are still in existence, and many new ones have been added.

The location of the 109 universities that were founded before the end of the sixteenth century is shown in Figure 30. The heaviest concentration is in Italy and southern France, the same two areas in which both the Roman imperial schools and the schools of Charlemagne were most numerous in earlier centuries.

Several pictures and descriptions of university classrooms are extant. Figure 31 on page 188 shows a dignified gentleman, complete with beard, addressing a group of students. Teacher and students wear academic robes. The students are portrayed as being well beyond the first flush of youth. Two of them in a corner seem to be having a private argument, and another has evidently gone to sleep! In Figure 32 on page 189, a remarkably young teacher is addressing a class in law.

A good description of medieval classes and students, their behavior in and out of class, appears below:

At five or six o'clock each morning the great cathedral bell would ring out the summons to work. From the neighboring houses of the canons,* from the cottages of the townsfolk, from the taverns and hospices* and boarding-houses, the stream of the industrious would pour into the enclosure beside the cathedral. The master's beadle,* who levied a precarious tax on the mob, would strew the floor of the lecture hall with hay or straw, according to the season, bring the master's text-book, with the notes of the lecture between lines or on the margin, to the solitary desk, and then retire to secure silence in the adjoining street. Sitting on their haunches in the hay, the right knee raised to serve as a desk for the waxed tablets, the scholars would take notes during the long hours of lecture (about six or seven), then hurry home—if

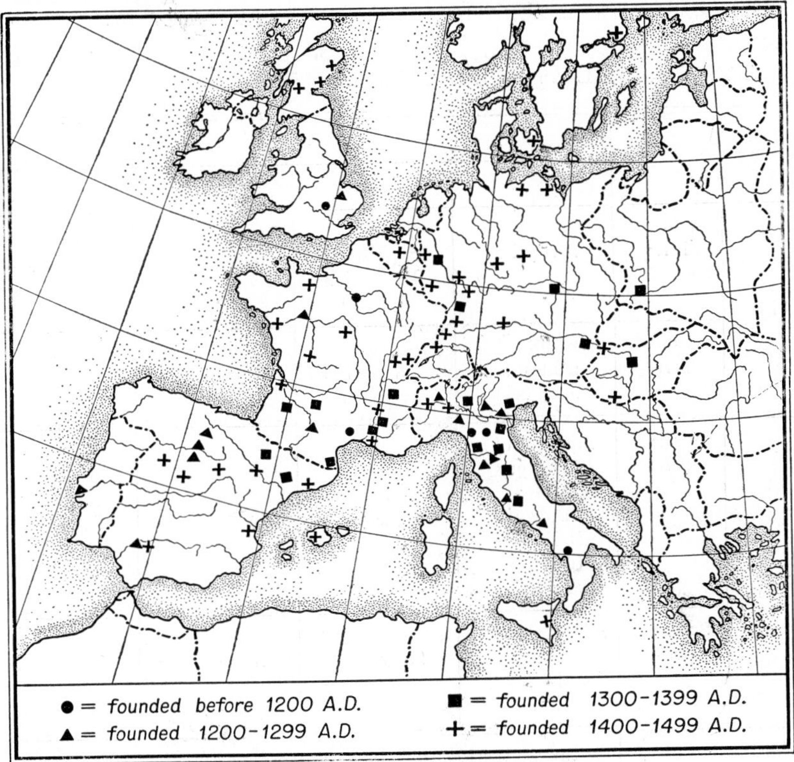

Fig. 30. Map of the Early Universities. Based on a list in H. Rashdall, *Universities of Europe in the Middle Ages,* II, i.

they were industrious—to commit them to parchment while the light lasted. The lecture over, the stream would flow back over the little Bridge, filling the taverns and hospices, and pouring out over the great playing meadow, that stretched from the island to the present Champs de Mars.* All the games of Europe were exhibited on the inter-national playgrounds: running, tossing and thumping the inflated ball,—a game of which some minor poet of the day has left us an enthusiastic lyric,—and especially the great game of war, in its earlier and less civilized form.[31]

[31] McCabe, *op. cit.,* pp. 79–80.

The scene during the long hours of class must have been something like that shown in Figure 33 on page 190. This class seems to have been larger and livelier than those depicted in Figures 31 and 32. These three pictures should be compared with those in Figures 25 and 26.

3. The University Curriculum The nature of the work leading to an arts degree was so different from what it is now that a specific example seems desirable in order to show just what the medieval student studied. In 1309 the schedule of classes at the University of Paris was as shown below:

TABLE 4: A CLASS SCHEDULE IN A MEDIEVAL UNIVERSITY[a]

Periods during the day		Years			
		First	Second	Third	Fourth
First	Winter Term	Aristotle: Analytics	Topics for Sophistical Refutation (Debate)	Same as for first year	Same as for second year
	Summer Term	Aristotle: Ethics, first five books	Aristotle: Ethics, last five books	Aristotle: On the Soul	Same as for first year
Second	Winter Term	Isagoges* of Porphyry Aristotle: Categories Interpretations Priscian Minor	Same	Same	Same
	Summer Term	Gilbert de la Porrée Boethius Priscian	Same	Same	Same
Third		Review period for going over the morning lectures. Two of the bachelors were appointed to take charge of this review, one for each term.			
Fourth		No scheduled work. This period was used for study, sometimes for an extra lecture.			
		Midday Meal			
Fifth		This period was set apart for conferences with the teaching staff or for working on any special assignments the masters might designate.			
Sixth		Topics for sophistical refutation (Debate)	Aristotle: Analytics	Same as for first year	Same as for second year

TABLE 4: A CLASS SCHEDULE IN A MEDIEVAL UNIVERSITY (*Continued*)

PERIODS DURING THE DAY	YEARS			
	First	Second	Third	Fourth
Seventh	Aristotle: Physics	Aristotle: Generation & Degeneration; Sense & Sensible Things; Memory & Recollection; Sleep & Waking; Longevity & Short Life; Life & Death; Respiration & Expiration; Youth & Old Age; Causes of motion in animals; Locomotion of animals	Aristotle: Meteorites; Heaven & Earth	Aristotle: Metaphysics

[a] Paetow, *op. cit.*, p. 96. Used by permission of The University Press, University of Illinois, publishers. See also C. Thurot, *De l'organization de l'enseignement dans l'Université de Paris au moyen âge*, Besançon, 1850, 210 pp

One peculiarity of this schedule is its tendency to repeat in the upper two years the work of the lower two. Indeed, the subject matter for the second period in the day is the same throughout the entire course. The first two and last two periods were used for lectures. In general, the students had work on dialectics during the first and sixth periods, on rhetoric and a little arithmetic during the second, and on science during the seventh. The dependence upon Aristotle is too obvious to need further comment. The method of studying science was characteristically medieval. The students did not do experiments in a laboratory or go out into the world and observe nature; they read what Aristotle had written some seventeen hundred years earlier. This schedule was, for its day, distinctly progressive; however, it contains only a small and restricted amount of subject matter, as judged by modern standards. In fact, there was not yet enough to fill four years without the constant repetition that was necessary as long as books were few and precious.

It should be noted in passing that the curriculum which originally led to the arts degree contained no courses in literature, none in languages beyond the necessary mastery of Latin as a tool, none in mathematics beyond the high school level—even when any was offered—and almost none in any science except astronomy. In short, although subsequent generations have kept the form of university organization, they have changed the content. The literary and linguistic subjects that are now regarded as necessary for a cultural education did not exist in the early days of the university. The collective name of these subjects—the humanities*— shows that they date from the Renaissance, not from the Middle Ages.

FIG. 31. A University Lecture. From an illuminated manuscript, dated 1310, now in the Royal Collection of Copper Engravings, Berlin.

4. University Organization The universities were originally organized just like any other industry of the time. During the late Middle Ages each trade had its own union, which was called a guild. The main purposes of these guilds were, first, to supervise the entire industry; second, to train the proper number of apprentices; and, third, to guarantee the quality of the product. A boy who entered an occupation spent about seven years as apprentice to a master, who taught him the trade. Then he became a journeyman and received wages. After three or more years he might open a shop of his own and advance in rank to being a master. The master was allowed to teach and to take an active part in guild management. The new type of medieval school, the university, imitated this economic organization. Originally, a university was a guild, or rather a union of two guilds, one for students and one for teachers. The commodity dispensed by the teachers' guild was knowledge. It was therefore part of a faculty's business to oversee standards, to determine the nature of the curriculum, and to set its mark of approval upon a student who had completed the work for each degree. The bachelor's degree was the equivalent of the certificate an apprentice got that enabled him to enter the ranks of the journeymen. The work for the master's degree[32] corresponded roughly to that of the journeyman in his early years. At the end of his work, the candidate had to pass a public questioning by which he convinced his faculty that he was

FIG. 32. A Lecture in Law. From a sixteenth-century woodcut now in the National Library in Paris, Cabinet of Designs.

competent. He was then admitted, as a master of learning, to the highest standing in the guild of teachers, formally licensed as a teacher, and granted the privilege of voting at meetings. A sample of the formula used for giving degrees in law is shown below:

Inasmuch as you have been presented to me for examination in both (Civil and Canon) Laws and for the customary approval, by the Most Illustrious and the Most Excellent D. D. [naming the Promoters], Golden Knights, Counts Palatine, Most Celebrated Doctors, and inasmuch as you have since undergone an arduous and rigorous examination, in which you bore yourself with so much learning and distinction that that body of Most Illustrious and Excellent Promoters without one dissenting voice—I repeat, without one dissenting voice—have judged you worthy of the laurel, therefore by the authority which I have as Archdeacon and senior Chancellor, I create, publish and name you, N. N., Doctor in the aforesaid Faculties, giv-

[32] The "master's degree" of the medieval university became the Ph.D. of modern times. The present master's degree is a more recent introduction.

ing to you every privilege of lecturing, of ascending the Master's chair, of writing glosses,* of interpreting, of acting as Advocate, and of exercising also the functions of a Doctor here and everywhere throughout the world; furthermore, of enjoying all those privileges which those happy individuals, who have been so deserving in these fostering colleges, are accustomed to use and enjoy.

And I trust that all these things will forever result in the increase of

FIG. 33. A Medieval Classroom in a University. From a woodcut published in Strasbourg in 1608.

your fame and the honour of our Colleges, to the praise and glory of Almighty God and of the ever blessed Virgin Mary.[33]

The guild organization has almost disappeared from industry, the field in which it developed, but in its borrowed form it still lives in the field of education. Incidentally, the name *university* comes from the old guild name, *Universitas magistrorum et scholarium.*[34]

The guilds into which students and masters in the early universities grouped themselves were called "nations," each of which had a number of subdivisions. The nations were, in theory, merely groups of individuals who came from the same country or spoke the same language. The subdivisions were determined by the locality from which the members came. The masters were also members of these nations, just like the students. As teachers they belonged

[33] Quoted in Rashdall, II, 734. Reprinted by permission of The Clarendon Press, publishers.
[34] The whole body of teachers and students.

also to one or more faculties, and in this capacity they had control over the curriculum, but they were on a par with the students in the affairs of the nation. In Paris there were only four nations, while in Bologna there were thirty-six. The nations were independent bodies which passed their own laws, elected their own officers, kept their own accounts, and exercised supervision over the lodging houses and behavior of the students, whom they both protected and disciplined. Also, they had their own buildings and classrooms. As at once appears, student government is a very old feature of university life. In the southern universities it was developed to an especially high degree. Up until the sixteenth century the head of certain Italian universities was not only elected by the students but often was a student. Presumably the difference in practice between North and South was due to the difference in the age of the students. Boys entered the arts course at Paris and other northern universities at the ages of thirteen, fourteen, or fifteen,[35] whereas grown men who had completed their arts course predominated in the advanced schools of law and medicine at Bologna or Salerno. The students in Italy exercised also more or less control over the curriculum. In Paris, however, the teachers had jurisdiction over whatever affected their work, and the students had similar autonomy* over whatever affected them. The students were organized by 1245 and the faculty by 1260.

There were as many faculties in a university as there were courses of study. Each faculty had its own dean. At the head of the entire university was a rector, who was elected by the students through their proctors. A modern student needs only to look about him on any university campus to find that titles and organization have remained unchanged. Most European universities still use the term "rector" for the university head, although American institutions have substituted the political word "president." The business of university faculties also remains much the same. Teachers are still essentially members of a guild, and the commodity that they handle is knowledge. Where students live on the campus, there is still a student government that is alive and important. The university has thus preserved intact many elements of its medieval organization.

The number of years needed to complete the work for a bachelor's degree, provided a student applied himself, was eventually settled as four. The doctor's (master's) degree required several more years. The degree in theology took twelve or thirteen. The undergraduate of today is so accustomed to the idea of a four-year course in college that he does not stop to wonder where the time limit came from. It came from the University of Paris and dates from about 1250. It is not clear just why the faculties at that time

[35] Laws had to be passed refusing admittance to boys of twelve!

thought four years the proper number; it is to be hoped that they had a reason!

5. Student Life in the Medieval University Once the universities were going concerns and the number of students increased—especially the number of young students—the trade in the neighborhood near the colleges began to depend upon them, and entertainment of all kinds for their benefit soon appeared. The off-campus row of shops, the debts to tradesmen, the letters home for more money are as old as universities themselves. The substance of the following note, which was written about 1220 by a student to his father, might have come from the pen of almost any student since then:

FIG. 34. Begging Students. From a woodcut published in Nuremberg in the fifteenth century.

> B. to his venerable master A., greeting. This is to inform you that I am studying at Oxford with the greatest diligence, but the matter of money stands greatly in the way of my promotion, as it is now two months since I spent the last of what you sent me. The city is expensive and makes many demands; I have to rent lodgings, buy necessaries, and provide for many other things which I cannot now specify. Wherefore I respectfully beg your paternity that by the promptings of divine pity you may assist me, so that I may be able to complete what I have well begun. For you must know that without Ceres and Bacchus, Apollo grows cold.[36]

One of the unique features of student life in these centuries was the wandering scholar. Abélard was for some years one of them, and most of his students were similarly unattached to any one school. These scholars followed a teacher they liked from place to place if he moved about, and they remained with a given teacher only as long as he interested them; then they went on to someone else. Even after the universities were founded, the stu-

[36] Haskins, *The Rise of Universities,* p. 395. Reprinted by permission of Henry Holt and Company, publishers.

dents did not stay long in one school. When one reads the biography of almost any eminent man of the period, one finds that he attended from three to a dozen universities at different times. Many students never took any degree but continued for years to attend first one class and then another. Although boys often left home to study at some university when they were only fourteen or fifteen years of age, they sometimes remained as scholars until they were forty.

Many medieval students became beggars in order to remain at school. Others worked at sundry small jobs, while a few especially fortunate ones were given food left from their professors' tables, and clothing, already well worn, from their professors' backs. A newly arrived freshman at a medieval university did not become a number in the registrar's office as happens much too often now. He was assigned to some one professor who heard his lessons, guarded him, advised him, helped him, and even claimed him from the town authorities in case the latter threw him into jail. Such personal supervision was necessary, since the students arrived at the university at so early an age as fourteen. The communal life resulted in the establishment of lasting friendships in the guidance of new students, and in the responsibility of the entire group for each of its members. In theory this communal life, plus the intellectual freedom of the classroom, leveled all social classes and produced an aristocracy of talent and learning that was independent of social position. To some extent such a leveling really did exist, and many a boy from an obscure and lowly family became educated and famous because of the essential equality of opportunity afforded by university work, but—human nature being what it is—the young noblemen occupied the front seats in the classroom!

There are excellent records of other universities than the University of Paris. Especially interesting is an account of Toulouse, revealing student life as it had developed after a century or two. The University of Toulouse was one of sixteen autonomous universities in France in the early sixteenth century. It was a large institution, with six hundred professors and ten thousand students. One popular professor of law lectured to no less than four thousand young men. The university was founded by the pope, right after the Albigensian Crusade,* with the idea of using the school to increase the authority of the church and to ensure the city against another outbreak of heresy. The students were known throughout Europe as "good" students, in contrast to those in many another university, but this reputation does not seem to have prevented them from getting into continual fights with each other or with the town's police or from developing the usual rich and varied student customs. The serious side of their lives is briefly described in a letter written by a young man to his father in the sixteenth century:

We were in the habit of rising at four o'clock in the morning, and after prayers we would go at five o'clock to the lecture halls, carrying our inkhorns and candlesticks in our hands. We would listen to all the lectures until 10 o'clock without interruption. Then we would go to dinner, after having hastily compared what we had written down. After dinner we were in the habit of reading, as a sort of sport, Sophocles* or Aristophanes or Euripides,* sometimes Demosthenes,* Virgil, Horace, or Cicero.[37]

Fortunately, for a further glimpse into student life, a record book of the Nation of Provence at the University of Toulouse has been preserved. It runs from 1558 to 1630 and was kept by students, the secretaries of the nation. There are records of who entered the group and when, of who was arrested and why, of new rules for conduct or dress, of expenses, and of sundry other matters that the successive secretaries thought worth noting. It is surprising to learn that "crashing" parties was a favorite diversion; a group of students would push their way into a house where a gathering was in progress, help themselves to food and wine, and then dash at top speed for the university grounds when the townspeople called out the guard. In fact, the students carried on a continuous running fight with the police, who were not allowed to enter the school's precincts, and were doubtless greatly annoyed when, after a hot chase, the youngsters escaped and stood just over the boundary, catcalling and making faces at the *gendarmerie*. Students could be punished legally only by college authorities, no matter how much of a nuisance they were to the townspeople, although the latter got in many a sound thrashing when no official eye was upon them. The members of each nation lived, ate, studied, and played together, thus developing a deep loyalty to one another, but they went to the usual adolescent lengths of being intensely jealous of all the other nations. One has only to think of the fraternities on a large campus to see a modern instance of the same situation. The nations were, however, given to direct and violent action. Feuds between them led to fighting and bloodshed, followed by a reconciliation and brief truce—usually after one or more students had been killed in a fight, and the others were sobered by the tragedy. The officers of each nation were elected by the students. The entire group staged a parade in honor of the officers, then attended mass, and ended the celebration with a copious banquet. The head of the nation required feudal homage from all other members; the tale below relates the reaction of a vigorous prior* to a brash freshman who would not salute him.

Upon one occasion when the prior of the nation had assembled his nationaires in one of the lecture halls of the "Estudes" (as the university was

[37] J. C. Dawson, *Toulouse in the Renaissance*, Columbia University Press, 1923 (2 parts), part ii, p. 101. The quotations from this work are reprinted by permission of Columbia University Press, publishers.

called), a certain Gascon* came in and announced to him that a freshman by the name of Crespin from Chambery in Savoy,* accompanied by one Paccot, an old student or "antique," and young Guirod of Annecy,* were going about the city armed, boasting that they would not do homage to the prior. This news, says the chronicle, troubled the assembly, and the prior went away alone to meet them, armed only with his sword. Meeting the aforesaid Crespin and his two companions, the prior hailed the old student and asked if he really meant to refuse the customary act of homage. The "antique" responded that as far as he himself was concerned, he was ready to acknowledge him and had already done so, but that he was in the company of one who was not of the same mind. The prior retorted that he would make him adopt a different tone, at once ordering Crespin to give him the accolade. The latter responded by drawing his sword. The prior drew his, planted the point of it in his enemy's arm, and with a swift upward stroke knocked off Crespin's hat and wig. Crespin, explains the historian, was wearing a wig, because he had recently come out of the monastery of the Chartreux* which he had entered several months previously. In order to gain an advantage, Crespin stepped upon the foot-pavement, but the prior pursued him so hotly that he did not have time to put himself in a defensive attitude, and was compelled to beg for time to get his breath; which the prior very generously granted him. After resting a moment, Crespin rushed suddenly upon the prior, wielding his sword with both hands. The latter, skillful and doughty warrior that he was, struck Crespin's sword up over his shoulder and closed in on him in a bodily embrace. After wrestling thus for some time, Crespin was thrown down, head first, into the mud. The prior followed up his advantage by planting his foot on his adversary's throat with the intention of throttling him; but Crespin used what little strength he had left in begging for mercy and demanding "courtesy." Scarcely could he be heard, his mouth being almost full of mud! The prior granted him "courtesy" on condition that after rising he should give him the accolade in sign of recognition, as was demanded by the good customs of the ancient and honorable nation of Provence. Crespin did not lose any time in extricating himself from his painful situation and in ridding himself of his enemy's body by which he was oppressed. But after standing erect he made so "meager" an accolade that the prior felt impelled to make him repeat the ceremony three times, winding up with an embrace around the thighs. Crespin now became as docile as a lamb and in the end decided that the prior was capable and worthy of his office, agreeing to serve him at all times and in all places.[38]

The new student was hazed in much the same spirit as still exists. He was known as *bejamus* (yellow-bill) or *beanus*. Upon arrival he had to pay an initiation fee—a sum that, incidentally, was sometimes demanded from the innocent traveler in a university town by means of what practically amounted to a hold-up; since the sum was small, most people preferred paying it to becoming the center of a fight. An upperclassman was known as an *antique*. One

[38] *Ibid.*, Part II, pp. 111–112.

form of hazing consisted in a visit to a beanus by several antiques, who announced they were trying to trace a bad smell to its source. They assumed the beanus to be a wild boar, and there was much joking about his eyes, ears, and tusks. Then—to render him fit for human society—the antiques would smear his face with soap, clip his beard, and generally roughhouse him. In some places the freshman was brought before a court of upperclassmen and tried.

One odd custom in the medieval university was the right of the entire group to go on a strike and leave the town. Thus the University of Orleans* in 1320 became vexed at the attitude of the townspeople, so both faculty and students moved in a body to Nevers,* where they remained until they had obtained a satisfactory adjustment—although the town of Nevers seems to have shown a far from welcoming spirit by tossing the rector's chair into the Loire.*

One especially revealing record of student life, called the *Manuale Scholarium* or *Students' Manual,* first appeared in 1481 and may have been intended primarily to show prospective students what kind of Latin they would have to speak. Whatever its purpose, it reveals a good deal about student life. The book consists of several conversations on various topics between two students named Cam and Bart: how to register at the university, what courses and lectures are necessary, attendance, methods of study, the merits of this or that professor, the initiation of new students, how to invite a teacher to a meal, small talk during dinner, quarrels, complaints about the food, bull sessions, and advice to the lovelorn. The *Manuale* is written in barbarous Latin, which suggests that the composer—whoever he was—had a better knowledge of student life than of his studies. The few excerpts that appear below have been translated into modern student slang because the Latin of the original is slangy Latin.[39]

Cam: Bart, do you know how many lectures and exercises we have to complete for the bachelor's degree?

Bart: I know very well; there are nine lecture courses and six exercise courses.

Cam: When do you have to take them?

Bart: The lectures and exercises are in three parts, so it is possible to complete them entirely in three terms, that is in a year and a half.

Cam: How do you know?

Bart: Because I've heard it from students who already have their degrees.

Cam: I intend to go along with you to hear these lectures when you're ready

[39] Reprinted by permission of the publishers from R. F. Seybolt (translator) *The Manuale Scholarium,* Harvard University Press, 1921, 122 pp. The first excerpt is on pp. 34–35, the second on p. 63, and the third on p. 68. See also R. S. Rait, *Life in the Medieval Universities,* G. P. Putnam's Sons, 1912, 164 pp., and C. H. Haskins, *Studies in Medieval Culture,* The Clarendon Press, 1929, 295 pp. This last reference contains, Chapter 1, letters from students; Chapter 2, descriptions of life at the University of Paris; and Chapter 3, manuals for use by students.

to satisfy this requirement. But listen, there's one thing I want to ask. They say that if we are present at the beginning and end of the lectures, it's enough for completion, and we don't have to attend those in the middle.

Bart: Why so? What sort of completion would that be?

Cam: They say that we learn nothing in the lectures, especially in the higher ones on physics and the like, and that when the time comes for promotion, it'll be given to us anyway.

Bart: You're all wet, for the masters of the faculty of arts have decided that it's necessary for each one, before he is admitted, to declare on oath how often he has been present. Previously lots of guys were promoted who had rarely been to a lecture, by paying big money for fines. But our teachers saw that they learned nothing, so now they've decided that one must listen and complete the work, and tell the lecturers to make their lectures useful to us, so that we can get something out of them.

Cam: It's rather dull and tiresome to be present all the time. I'm afraid I'll never do it.

Bart: If you want to be promoted, you can't help it.

Cam: I'll just say I was present.

Bart: Then you'll be a liar. But you have a healthy complexion, and this lie won't show on your face.

Cam: Enough of this. Tell me which teachers shall we hear?

Bart: I saw it announced today that Master Jodocus will read the *libri elenchorum* near the door of the Church of the Holy Ghost at eleven o'clock; and in the morning, I believe, but at twelve o'clock, at the same place, we shall hear the *libri physicorum* from Master Peter; and after noon a lecture will be given by Master James in the school room on the *libri de anima.*

Cam: You seem to know. I'll remember these things, so that when you wish to go, I may be ready. Now what do you know about the exercises?

Bart: My teacher will discuss the *parva logicalia* at his home. I'll be there. And Master John will discuss the *ars vetus,* on which I've got to work hard.

Cam: That's a good idea. And what reviews shall we hear?

Bart: I haven't decided yet, but I'll do some snooping. Lots of us think we get more from the reviews than from either lectures or exercises. If our master should review something, I surely wouldn't neglect it, for he's very eloquent and persuasive; when he explains something, it's just as clear as if it were being done.

Cam: I haven't seen any teacher who can explain so beautifully and clearly a thing hidden and particularly obscure and give the elements of a subject so easily to a beginner. I tell you, Bart, let's always go to his reviews, and with quite a crowd.

Bart: Sure, I'll go; that's what I wanted very much to hear from you.

Cam: Then let's do it. I must go now. Save what you have to say till tomorrow. So long, Bart.

Bart: So long, Cam.

Cam: Do you remember the money I loaned you a while back? You promised to return it right away, but you haven't done it, and I am flat broke.

Bart: Don't get sore, Cam. I meant to give it right back.

Cam: I'm trying to be patient, God help me.

Bart: I'm sunk too right now, but I'm expecting something from home every day. As soon as it gets here, I'll pay up.

Cam: That's the way you always talk. You know I'm poor and need cash the worst way, but you don't even think of that. But if you want to stay pals with me you'd better ante, like you said you would, and not put off paying me any longer.

Bart: All right, all right. I'll do something about it. . . .

Cam: I have a letter from my parents. They say that unless I take the examination, I shan't get any more help from them. I'm worried and scared out of my wits.

Bart: Why?

Cam: I'm afraid I shall flunk.

Bart: Why?

Cam: There are many things. I haven't completed my work satisfactorily, and many masters dislike me; I'm so afraid I'll be kept back. I've accomplished little, and I'm afraid I'll be rejected. So, you see, it's no small matter that upsets me.

Bart: Talk to your teacher. He knows what ought to be done in this matter.

Cam: I have consulted him. He advises against taking the tests now; he says I know too little.

Bart: Oh, he always says that. He's trying to scare you. There's no need of your being so afraid. There'll be others more ignorant than you in the examination; you know you can't win without courage. Put your chin up.

Cam: There's something in what you say, but I may not have any luck. If I flunk, my teacher will just say he's warned me not to take the exam. I should be so terribly disgraced that I couldn't look my father and mother in the face. I should have nothing, and I'd be the laughing stock of the place.

Bart: You'll be able to do it all right, for your master is obliging, and often gives a boost to others when they ask anything of him.

Cam: I hope so.

These selections show that at some time toward the end of the Middle Ages the college student appeared upon the pages of history. He is still with us—grumbling about the courses, discussing his teachers, borrowing money, and shivering over examinations. He does not speak Latin, not even bad Latin, but in most other respects he strongly resembles his early predecessors who attended the universities of medieval Europe.

READING REFERENCES

A. General Histories of the Period

Munro and Sontag, *The Middle Ages,* chaps. 16, 19, 21, 27, 30, 31.
Robinson, *Introduction to the History of Western Europe,* chaps. 10, 17, 19.
Seignobos, *The Rise of European Civilization,* chaps. 7, 8.
Strayer and Munro, *The Middle Ages,* chaps. 8, 10, 11.
Thompson, *The Middle Ages,* Vol. I, chaps. 15, 16, 20.
Thorndike, *Medieval Europe,* chaps. 17–19, 20, 21, 23, 30.

B. Other Texts in the History of Education

Boyd, *History of Western Education,* chap. 5.
Cubberley, *History of Education,* chaps. 8–9.
Cole, *History of Educational Thought,* pp. 127–130.
Marique, *History of Christian Education,* Vol. I, chaps. 8, 9.
McCormick, *History of Education,* chaps. 13, 14, 16.
Monroe, *A Textbook in the History of Education,* pp. 292–340.
Moore, *The Story of Instruction,* Vol. II, chaps. 5, 6.
Reisner, *Historical Foundations of Modern Education,* chap. 11.

C. Secondary Sources

Compayré, *Abélard and the Origin and Early History of Universities,* part i, Chaps. 1–3; part ii, chaps. 1–4.
Coulton, G. G., *Ten Medieval Studies,* Cambridge University Press, 1930 (297 pp.), chap. 7.
Drane, *Christian Schools and Scholars,* chaps. 12, 13.
Farrington, F. E., *French Secondary Education,* chap. 2.
Haskins, C. H., "The Life of Medieval Students as Illustrated by Their Letters," *American Historical Review* (1898), 3:203–224.
———, *The Rise of Universities,* Sec. i, ii, or iii.
———, *Studies in Medieval Culture,* chaps. 1–3.
———, *Studies in Medieval Science,* chaps. 1, 8, 12.
Laurie, *The Rise and Early Constitution of Universities,* chaps. 9–11.
Lloyd, *The Stricken Lute,* entire, if possible.
McCabe, *Peter Abélard,* entire, if possible, or chaps. 2–5, 9, 11, 12.
Paetow, *The Arts Course at Medieval Universities,* chap. 1.
Paulsen, F., *German Education Past and Present,* Charles Scribner's Sons, 1908 (310 pp.), book i, chaps. 2, 3.
Poole, *Illustrations of the History of Medieval Thought and Learning,* chap. 5, pp. 176–189.
Rashdall, *Universities of Europe in the Middle Ages,* Vol. I, part ii, chaps. 6, 7, 8, or 9.
Sikes, J. G., *Peter Abélard,* Cambridge University Press, 1932 (282 pp.), chaps. 1–4, 9.
Townsend, W. J., *Great Schoolmen of the Middle Ages,* Hodder & Stoughton, Ltd., 1881 (361 pp.), chaps. 6, 9, 20.

Waddell, H. J., *The Wandering Scholars,* Constable & Co., Ltd., 1932 (rev. ed., 291 pp.), any 15–20 pages.

D. Translations of Primary Sources

Abélard, *The History of My Misfortunes* (edited by H. A. Bellows), pp. 1–78.

———, *Yes and No,* any six arguments.

Seybolt, *The Manuale Scholarium,* chaps. 1–3.

PART FIVE

RENAISSANCE, REFORMATION, AND COUNTER REFORMATION

CHAPTER VIII

VITTORINO DA FELTRE AND THE SCHOOLS OF THE ITALIAN RENAISSANCE

The written history of mankind is often divided into three major epochs: ancient, medieval, and modern. The first two periods are separated from each other by a period of transition during which the Roman Empire fell to pieces, Christianity developed, and new peoples with new ideas invaded the ancient world. The medieval and modern periods are separated by two great movements, the Renaissance and the Reformation, which put an end to medieval modes of thought and laid the basis for the growth of modern science and culture. The characters in the next four chapters had their part in the great upheaval of thought and belief that came in the fourteenth to sixteeth centuries.

The Renaissance came before the Reformation, developed first in Italy, and subsequently spread to the north. The entire movement included under the name of the Renaissance had three main lines of growth: the intellectual—to which the educational belongs—the aesthetic, and the scientific. For the present text, discussion will be restricted for the most part to the first of these three phases. The revival in science did not develop until two centuries after that in letters and art had already begun.

The intellectual development is usually called *humanism*. The humanist was not merely a man who read Greek and Latin authors; he was a man who tried to introduce into contemporary life the values he had found through his reading. The ideas were often in contrast to accepted medieval tradition. For instance, the writers of antiquity were not especially concerned about a future life and preferred to concentrate upon efforts to make this world one in which men could be moral, cultured, and comfortable. This attitude was in direct opposition to the medieval idea that life on earth was of no importance because it was merely a prelude to life in heaven. The medievalist at best neglected his body because he thought it did not matter and at worst abused it because he thought it to be a source of evil. The humanist [1] cared for and

[1] From the word "humanist" comes the word "humanities," which is now used to indicate certain school subjects. The term originally meant "those activities and pursuits that are proper to mankind." The particular activities then in vogue were mainly linguistic and

developed his body because, like the ancients with whose works he was familiar, he thought a healthy body both necessary and beautiful. Another fundamental concept of antiquity was the idea that each man should develop himself in his own way and to as high a degree as he could, not for the sake of future reward but for the sake of his own personal and immediate satisfaction. The humanist, in accordance with these ideas, was as determined to "be himself" as is the surrealist of today. His objective was the development of a free man with an individuality of his own, who had an understanding of life in the past and an appreciation of life in the present.

Since the humanist was eager to incorporate into the life about him those ideas that he derived from his reading, he sometimes went to extremes and became a bit ridiculous. Thus some men imitated ancient ways with such fidelity that they became atheists and pagans. Others specialized upon being so "individual" as to be merely eccentric. Some cultivated their bodies by exercise, baths, massage, and so on—developing a cult of body-worship, such as existed in ancient Greece and still exists in modern America. These excesses are almost inevitable in any new movement. The better-balanced humanists took what they found in classical literature and tried to use it in modifying their lives according to ancient standards. Most of them remained Christians and worked out some kind of harmony between the basic ideas of the Middle Ages and those of antiquity.

The history of the Renaissance in Italy is concerned with the rebirth of intellectual freedom, not with political or social change. It is a history of the spirit, and it went on inside people. Its main concern was the highest personal development of each individual scholar and with his appreciation of the world he lived in. There was no interest in society, no attempt to reform morals, and no relation to religion, although these elements were added later by the German and Dutch humanists, after the movement had traveled northward from its point of origin.

A. VITTORINO DA FELTRE: HIS LIFE AND WORK

1. Vittorino's Life[2] In the year 1378, in the little Italian town of Feltre, Vittorino was born. Feltre is a picturesque village, which nestles under the

literary. The term "humanities" soon came to mean those subjects in the curriculum that contributed to literary success, namely, languages and literature. At present the word is often used in contrast to scientific or aesthetic subjects. Thus many a college has grouped its offerings into five types: biological sciences, natural sciences, social sciences, appreciation courses in art and music, and the humanities, which include the departments of English, French, German, Spanish, Italian, Latin, Greek, linguistics, and comparative literature, plus numerous individual courses from other departments.

[2] There are few primary sources on the life of Vittorino. He wrote nothing except letters, of which a bare half dozen are still extant. References to him and his work by his col-

southern slopes of the eastern Alps. Vittorino never traveled far from the place of his birth. He spent all his life, with the exception of a few brief visits elsewhere in Feltre, Venice, Padua, and Mantua. These places all fall within a radius of fifty miles, as indicated on the map shown in Figure 35. The story of Vittorino da Feltre proves once more that the world will come to the door of the man who is good enough to attract it.

The objective facts about Vittorino's life are soon told. After a boyhood

FIG. 35. Area in Which Vittorino Lived and Taught.

spent in Feltre, he went, at the age of eighteen, to Padua, where he attended classes at the university. In order to support himself he taught the rudiments of grammar to groups of boys. He remained in Padua for twenty years, during which he was both a teacher and a pupil. In the days of the Renaissance,

---

leagues, friends, and students are numerous but brief. Thus Giovanni Andrea inserts into the preface of his edition of Livy a tribute to his teacher Vittorino; Bartolomeo Sacchi gives several facts about him in his *Historia Urbis Mantuanae;* and Francesco Prendilacqua describes him in his Dialogues (*Intorno alla vita di Vittorino da Feltre,* Coitorchi di Carlo Franch, Como, 1871, 100 pp.). Each such reference adds a few points about Vittorino as a person or relates an incident or two in his life. These numerous but scattered references have been gathered together and woven into a coherent picture by C. Rosmini, *Idea dell' ottinio precettore nella vita e disciplina di Vittorino da Feltre,* Milan, 1845, 302 pp.; by R. Sabbadini, *Il Metodo degli umanisti,* F. le Monier, 1922, 96 pp.; and, in English, by W. H. Woodward, *Vittorino da Feltre and Other Humanist Educators,* Cambridge University Press, 1905 (261 pp), pp. 1–92. There is more or less reference to the work of Vittorino in W. H. Woodward, *Studies in Education during the Age of the Renaissance.* The Macmillan Company, 1906, 336 pp. The discussion in the present chapter is based mainly upon secondary sources since primary ones are few and often not available.

grown men attended classes with boys, even after receiving their doctor's degree. After Vittorino had earned his doctorate from the university, he turned for a time to the study of mathematics with a private tutor. During his last few years in Padua his services as a teacher in both grammar and mathematics were eagerly sought.

For some years while he was in Padua, Vittorino lived in the house of Gasparino da Barzizza,* an outstanding Latin scholar of the early Renaissance. Here lived also several other young men who later became great figures in Renaissance Italy. The daily associations were not only valuable at the time but led to many lasting friendships, notably between Vittorino and Guarino,* the two outstanding teachers of the period. The entire group of men were all fine Latin scholars who were imbued with a love for the classics, an eagerness to learn all they could of the newly found literature, and a desire to pass on their enthusiasm to others.

Vittorino was already thirty-eight years old when he left Padua for Venice, where he began to teach in what was probably the first humanist school to be opened in Italy. During his years in Venice, Vittorino learned Greek by exchanging lessons in Latin with his friend Guarino, who had founded the school. This joint venture in teaching was of short duration, however, and Vittorino was soon back in Padua, where he enjoyed a high reputation as a scholar and a teacher. Following in the steps of his own master, he invited certain of his students to live with him. These young men he not only helped in their studies but also supervised with great care. Life in a university town was beset by dangers for the young. In fact, more than one teacher of the period resigned his university chair because the students were so debauched that they were hardly worth the effort being expended on them. Vittorino therefore took into his house only a few students over whom he watched carefully. If a promising student were too poor to pay his expenses, the master supplied all his needs, but he charged high fees from the sons of wealthy men. Although Vittorino could have had many boys living with him, he firmly refused to take any more than he could look after himself. If a boy did not come up to expectations, Vittorino simply dismissed him, no matter who he was.

Soon after his return to Padua, one of the most important professorships—that formerly held by da Barzizza—became vacant and was offered to Vittorino, who hesitated for a long time before he finally accepted it. From his youth on, he had been highly religious and interested in the monastic life. Now, at the age of forty-four, he felt he must make a definite decision whether to enter a monastery or to spend the rest of his life as a teacher. In the end he accepted the position but did not hold it long. He became greatly concerned about the lax state of morals among the university students, especially as the situation affected those who lived with him. He seems to have felt that he could not guard his charges adequately, no matter how hard he tried, nor could he see any way in which he could remedy the vicious tendencies around him. After only a year as a professor he resigned his chair and went to Venice, where he conducted a school to which pupils came from all over Italy. In this work he was completely content. His reputation as a gifted and reliable teacher increased rapidly, his school prospered, he had in Venice excellent opportunities for continuing his study of Greek with Guarino,[3] and most of his friends were not far away. Here he might have spent his life if a request typical of the times had not been made for his services in connection with a school that eventually became his real lifework.

In the city of Mantua a relatively new ruling family, the Gonzagas,* had been gradually emerging into prominence for nearly a hundred years. The current head of the family had established himself as the ruler of Mantua and had consolidated his position politically through a number of not too obtrusive assassinations. He was now moved by the interests of his times to create an atmosphere of respect for his house by contact with the finer things of life. Having achieved power, he must next have culture. In a different age he might have established a museum, or collected first editions, or built a costly palace, but at the time he could gain the greatest prestige through contact with the exciting new ideas that were developing in Italy. Like a brand-new millionaire, Gonzaga believed that the best was none too good. When he looked for a scholar whose presence would add dignity and luster to his court, he sought out the most distinguished educator he could find. Aside from any prestige that might accrue to him by the presence of a savant in his retinue, he wanted the scholar who could so instruct the Gonzaga children that the next generation of the family might be worthy of its name. The position was first offered to Guarino, who refused it. Gonzaga then sought out Vittorino, who was at first not in the least eager to leave Venice. In fact, he very nearly re-

[3] The revival of interest in Greek was an important element in the Renaissance. All during the Middle Ages the knowledge of Greek authors had been limited for most people to the small amounts of material translated by Boethius. Only a handful of scholars could read the language. During the twelfth and thirteenth centuries, largely through Arab translators, Aristotle had been discovered, read, and discussed. The other philosophers, while known, were not regarded as especially important. With the coming of the Renaissance, many more Greek writers were translated. In 1397 an eminent Greek scholar, Manuel Chrysoloras,* came to Europe and began teaching the language in Florence. The effect upon education was the introduction of a totally new subject into the curriculum and an incidental lengthening of historical vistas.

fused, because he had such an aversion to the customary intrigues of court life and such a deep urge to do really useful work in the world. Moreover, he still had a desire for the monastic life. After much urging from Gonzaga, however, he finally accepted the position, thinking that he could benefit mankind more by teaching the future rulers of a state than by shutting himself up in a monastery. His agreement with his patron well reflects his upright character:

> I accept the post, on this understanding only, that you (i.e., the Marquis Gonzaga) require from me nothing which shall be in any way unworthy of either of us; and I will continue to serve you so long as your own life shall command my respect.[4]

Accordingly he journeyed in 1423 to Mantua, where he remained for twenty-three years until his death in 1446.

2. *Vittorino's School* The school was originally founded for the children of Vittorino's patron. Soon, however, a few other pupils—children of neighboring families—were added, so that the Gonzaga heirs might have comradeship. Later on, as the school developed, Vittorino accepted carefully selected boys from all over Italy and even from foreign countries. At times there were as many as seventy pupils there. The school, like Guarino's in Venice, became a typical school of the new humanistic learning in Europe, and the most outstanding scholars sent their sons to be educated by Vittorino. So also did wealthy men and noblemen, but he accepted only those whom he chose, and he always had room for poor boys of real ability. Like all the humanists, Vittorino believed in the equality of genius and, remembering his own early struggles, he was willing to help those who deserved his aid. The age of the scholars seems to have varied a good deal. Some of them were not more than six years old at the time of their arrival at the school, and some were young men of twenty-five.

From the beginning, Vittorino had a special building set aside for his school because he would not permit contact between his pupils and the courtiers who surrounded his patron. The building was a detached villa standing at some distance from the family residence. Gonzaga had it redecorated and refurnished for its new use. The pupils, their masters, and Vittorino all lived together in a community shut off from the rest of the world. The building was called *La Giocosa* or *The Pleasant House,* a name that reflects the joyousness of Renaissance education. A description of it, pieced together from many brief references, appears below:

[4] Woodward, *Vittorino da Feltre,* p. 24. This excerpt and subsequent ones from Woodward are quoted by permission of Cambridge University Press, publishers.

The house was of stately proportions. The interior was spacious and dignified. Broad corridors, rooms lofty and well lighted, gave to it an air of distinction which suited well Vittorino's idea of what a school-house should be. For, as its name implied, it was to be regarded as a "house of delight." He believed that a certain brightness of surroundings conduced to sound intellectual work. The notion so widely held that the needs of study demanded that a school should be placed in a gloomy, unhealthy situation, was foreign to the true humanist. La Giocosa was, on the contrary, surrounded on three sides by a large enclosed meadow, bordered by the river; this was laid out with broad walks, lined with well-grown trees. The open grass-covered space was highly prized by Vittorino, who made much use of it as playing fields. But whilst he rejoiced in the dignity of proportion which the school house offered, he ruthlessly stripped it of all its luxurious furnishings, its ornaments and plate. The princes received no peculiar consideration in this respect or in any other. Their father trusted entirely in the judgment of the Master and firmly upheld his authority in such wholesome changes as these. For Vittorino had made it clear that, unless temptations to luxury, idleness, or arrogance were once for all removed, and all scholars of whatever rank put upon the same footing of plain and sober living, he could not attempt his task with hope of success.[5]

The work that Vittorino did in his school had five outstanding characteristics. First was the emphasis upon light, pleasant surroundings, fun, and health. The undernourished, precocious, solemn bookworm had no place in this school. The pupils swam, played games, had outings, and took long walks. They were gay, happy, and vigorous. The food given the children was good but simple. No artificial heat was used in the buildings, because the master believed that too much warmth weakened the system. Vittorino watched the health of each lad carefully, built up resistance to disease, encouraged exercise, and took unremitting care of any child who fell ill. This emphasis upon proper care of the body was a continuation of the old Greek concept of a healthy mind in a healthy body. It was in direct opposition to the asceticism, flagellation,* and strain that characterized medievalism. It is told of Vittorino that he once saw two small boys standing apart from others who were playing, and overheard them discussing a point in one of their lessons. "That is not a good sign in a young boy," he exclaimed, and promptly sent them off to join in the games. One cannot imagine a typical medieval schoolmaster doing anything of the kind. Vittorino alternated periods of study and of play; moreover, he changed the subjects of study from hour to hour, so as to introduce variety and combat fatigue, because he believed that the mind needed change in order to remain keen.

[5] *Ibid.*, pp. 32–33.

A second outstanding feature was the community life, with a resulting close personal friendship between Vittorino and his pupils. He loved all of them, watched over them, took great pride in their accomplishment, studied them carefully, adjusted their work to their capacities, talked and laughed with them, played with them, and was at all times ready to help them. There are stories of how he took the children on long walks in the country during the summer and, with the older boys, climbed many of the near-by mountains. He lived the same life as his scholars, not only during class hours but at meals, in games, and in social activities, sharing their interests and their pleasures. To the pupils he was a charming, lovable, intellectual father and friend.

A sample of this relationship is given in the incident told below:

> Vittorino is staying at Gioto in charge of the Gonzaga children. We found him at breakfast with them; he comes out to meet us, greeting us with tears of joy. He entertains us right royally. The children seem to be on the happiest terms with him. We talked together for several hours. Then one of the boys declaims some two hundred lines he had composed upon the state entry of the Emperor Sigismund into Mantua. I was astonished by the taste and scholarship displayed not less than by the grace and propriety of delivery. Two younger brothers and their sister were of the party, all bright and intelligent children. . . . After a morning's most enjoyable intercourse several other youths of distinction were introduced and after courteous greetings escorted us some distance on our way.[6]

A third characteristic of Vittorino's teaching was his discipline. His purpose was so to attract and charm pupils that he would not need to coerce them. The friendship between him and his pupils was so close that the children could not bear to hurt his feelings by being intentionally bad. For small misdemeanors he used merely a word or look of rebuke; for badly done lessons he required a rewriting with more care. It was only moral infractions that drew from him a stern and just wrath. Once in a great while he resorted to corporal punishment, but only after all other methods had failed or when the offense was of a serious moral nature. If a boy tried hard and did his best, but was still unable to do acceptable work, Vittorino would not punish him for what was not his fault but tried to find something that the boy could do with success. Moreover, he encouraged self-government among his boys, partly as a means of education in character and partly as a method of control.

A fourth characteristic was as modern as his discipline. Vittorino kept coming back to the idea that all children were by nature different from one

[6] Quoted in Woodward, *Vittorino da Feltre,* p. 66, from Prendilacqua.

another and should be allowed to develop as nature intended and not forced into a line of study distasteful to them. His method was to study each child over a period of months or even years, giving him what he could learn and insisting only upon Christian behavior, which he regarded as being within the reach of all. In the accounts given of him by his students, this attention to individual differences comes out repeatedly, as in the remarks below:

> He had, as we know, an ample staff, and this enabled him to devote much time to gaining that intimate knowledge of the tastes, capacity and industry of each scholar, which, with his readiness to adapt thereto his choice both of subject and of treatment, secured the unique success for which his school was celebrated. He had an unaffected pride in his work, and a keen interest in the progress of each individual scholar; and with it all an unusual insight into the teaching art itself.[7]

Finally, Vittorino emphasized character first and learning second. He had, throughout his life, two equally passionate interests—his love of religion and his love of the classics. These two devotions fused harmoniously in him into a desire to educate the next generation to be good men and women by means of a thorough understanding of both classic and Christian literature. He saw goodness and purity wherever it existed, equally in Plato and in Augustine, and he saw no difference between the self-indulgence of a pagan and the self-indulgence of a Christian. Bad was bad and good was good, no matter where one found them. In this balanced viewpoint he differed both from those humanists who saw value only in the classics and wanted a return to paganism because they considered the shackles of Christianity too irksome and confining and from the fanatic Christians of the Middle Ages who regarded all classics as sources of evil because the writers were pagan. Vittorino wanted both goodness and erudition in his pupils; he could see no opposition between the two, nor did he believe that the best in Christian and pagan literature was contradictory. The following excerpt shows his attitude:

> But we must remind ourselves of the depth of religious conviction upon which his own educational ideal ultimately rested. Reverence, piety, and religious observance formed the dominant note of Vittorino's personal life. The dignity of humanity was with him based upon its relation to the Divine. Hence the transparent sincerity of his religious teaching; the insistence upon attendance at the ordinances of the Church; the inculcation of forgiveness and humility. He himself accompanied the boys to Mass; he set the example of regular Confession. Part of the religious instruction he himself took every day. Apart from the light that is thus thrown upon his personality, what is of chief interest in this aspect of Vittorino is its relation to his Humanism. This

[7] Woodward, *Vittorino da Feltre,* p. 30.

was with him no nominal reconciliation between the new and the old. Christianity and Humanism were the two coordinate factors necessary to the development of complete manhood. There is no reason to suppose that Vittorino was embarrassed by a sense of contradiction between the classical and the Christian ideals of life. To him, and to men of his temper since, the thought and morals of the ancient world were identified with the ethical precepts of the Stoics and the idealism of Plato: and it was easy for them to point to the consistency of this teaching with the broader aspects of the Christian life.[8]

This stress upon character as the main end of education is highly characteristic of Vittorino. In his school, boys were as safe from temptation as was humanly possible, because their master guarded them from evil with a single-minded zeal. The intellectual education they received was excellent, but the moral training was even better. In this one respect Vittorino's education was not ancient, nor medieval, nor modern—but timeless. All good teachers put character first.

3. Vittorino as a Person The following description of Vittorino's appearance and personality is based upon remarks made about him by his contemporaries and scholars.

In person he was slight and in appearance frail. But by dint of rigorous self-discipline and of active habits he had built up a constitution capable of sustaining the gravest exertions. For the greater part of his life he never admitted a day's illness. The careful practice of gymnastic had given him a peculiar suppleness and grace of movement. His expression was grave though not austere. Sympathy and affection, we are told, readily beamed from his face, though his eye had a penetrative quality before which conscious wrong-doing stood confessed and ashamed. Strong passionate instincts were by constant watchfulness reduced to obedience, and a temper prone to anger became softened and restrained. The simplicity of his nature showed itself in his dress; the long cloak of rough cloth for the summer, with a fur lining for the winter, contrasting with the richness of dress customary in Venetia. He was careless of cold, believing artificial heat to be a source of many humours. We trace something of the old Roman discipline in Vittorino's temper, in his notion of authority, of reverence of elders, of manliness and endurance. But we shall be wrong if we ascribe to the Pagan ideal any other place than this in his view of life. Vittorino was before all also a Christian imbued with the spirit and the doctrine of his faith. This indeed is the dominating note of his personality. It was this which preserved him from exaggerations and moral perversities which disfigured some of his contemporaries and gave an evil name to a certain type of Humanist. It was Vittorino's aim to graft ancient learning upon his stock of Christian training; and we shall see that within the next five-and-twenty years this had become his achievement.[9]

[8] *Ibid.*, p. 67.

[9] *Ibid.*, pp. 20–21.

The only picture of Vittorino was taken from a medal, and presumably gives no better likeness than the profiles on most medals. Moreover, the artist chose to cover much of his head with an extraordinary headgear that makes up in size for what it lacks in chic.

Vittorino was an indefatigable worker. His pupils soon learned to be equally industrious so that he should have no reason to be ashamed of them. A charming and evidently frequent scene is described by an acquaintance:

> I remember that Vittorino, now well advanced in years, would of a winter's morning come early, candle in one hand and book in the other, and rouse a pupil in whose progress he was specially interested; he would leave him time to dress, waiting patiently till he was ready: then he would hand him the book, and encourage him with grave and earnest words to high endeavour.[10]

Fig. 36. Vittorino da Feltre. From a medallion in the British Museum. In E. P. Cubberley, *History of Education,* p. 266. Courtesy of Houghton Mifflin Company, publishers.

Under the stimulus of such care and industry it is not surprising that the school produced many scholars.

The following quotation summarizes Vittorino's character and life:

> Wholly dedicated to the cares of teaching, more anxious to survive in the good fame of his scholars than to secure the immortality of literature, Vittorino bequeathed no writings to posterity. He lived to a hale and healthy old age, and when he died in 1446 it was found that the illustrious scholar, after enjoying for so many years the liberality of his princely patron, had not accumulated enough money to pay for his own funeral. Whatever he possessed he spent in charity during his lifetime, trusting to the kindness of his friends to bury him when dead. Few lives of which there is any record in history are so perfectly praiseworthy as Vittorino's: few men have more nobly realized the ideal of living for the highest objects of their age; few have succeeded in keeping themselves so wholly unspotted by the vices of the world around them.[11]

Although one gets only glimpses of Vittorino through the eyes of associates

[10] *Ibid.,* pp. 62–63. Quoted from Prendilacqua.

[11] A. Symonds, *The Revival of Learning,* Henry Holt and Company, 1881 (549 pp.), p. 297. Reprinted by permission of the publishers.

and pupils, rather than the direct revelation of personality that is shown in a man's own writing, one is left with the impression of a sterling character, whose strictness was softened by a sense of humor, a balanced view of life, an innate gentleness, and a deep love for childhood and youth.

Vittorino and Guarino maintained boarding schools. In earlier times many students had lived away from home in order to attend schools, but generally they lived with some family and went to school only in the daytime. Orphan boys and boys intended for the priesthood had lived in monasteries during their school years, but this arrangement was more for religious than for educational purposes. Vittorino's school was perhaps the world's first secular boarding school. As a model it has been imitated ever since, until it is now familiar. Vittorino wanted to control the entire environment of his pupils so as to protect them from the evils in the world about them. He required, therefore, that the children be turned over to his care during the entire twenty-four hours. His school was in an isolated place amid simple surroundings. Boys and teachers lived together, studied together, had their meals together, and played together. The teachers had authority over both lessons and conduct. His school was called a "sanctuary of manners, deeds, and words." The environment was purposely simplified, and known temptations were, insofar as possible, eliminated. The modern boarding school is run on the same lines.

B. SCHOOLS OF THE ITALIAN RENAISSANCE

The description of subject matter and methods of teaching given in this chapter applies more specifically to the schools maintained by Vittorino da Feltre than to others, although many of the facts were equally true of other good Renaissance schools. All were modeled upon the same basic ideas, and most of those in Italy were copies of either Vittorino's school in Mantua or Guarino's in Venice or later at Ferrara,* but it should be remembered that copies are rarely as good as their models.

1. The Curriculum The typical school of the period was a blend of the old and the new. In general, the subjects taught were those included in the trivium and the quadrivium, but the way in which they were taught differed greatly in spirit and content, although not in the names of the subjects, from the treatment they received during the Middle Ages. The trivium—grammar, rhetoric, and dialectic—was still the basis of all study. Of these, dialectic, which had been the most important subject in the time of Abélard, became relatively insignificant, and the first two subjects had fused to produce a more modern study of letters or, as it is now called, literature. Grammar and rhetoric were still absolutely necessary as the foundation of education, because almost all books were still written in either Latin or Greek. The aim of the humanist educator was, however, to teach pupils to understand the writings of the great men of the past, to develop a critical scholarship toward all writing, and to write good Latin. If one changes the language involved to English, these are the same objectives that the English teacher of today is working toward. They were emphatically not the aims of the medieval scholar, who divided his attention among the formal elements of grammar, sterile commentary, and complex argument.

In the pursuit of a literary education the teacher of the Renaissance be-began his training by teaching good enunciation and pronunciation. In the absence of books, oral instruction, discussion, and oratory were of more importance than they are today, partly from sheer necessity and partly also from a continuance of the old Roman ideal that an educated man must be able to speak well. Good speech was secured by exercises in oral reading, by declamation,* and by recitation. Pupils memorized passages from the classics and recited them aloud as regular school exercises. In Vittorino's school they memorized excerpts from religious writings as well.

Most instruction in language was necessarily oral at this time since the medieval grammars—those of Donatus, Priscian, and their imitators—were deemed old-fashioned, and the newer types of grammar had not yet been written. A pupil first learned words until he had an adequate vocabulary. Then he learned the necessary forms. Since Latin was the spoken as well as the written language of educated people, he had to acquire a correct accent. The usual procedure during these early phases of instruction was for the master to read aloud a passage, dictate it, and comment upon it, as to both grammar and content. The pupils took down the new words and forms, each student thus making his own dictionary and grammar as he went along. Even from the beginning, a good deal of attention was paid to meaning, and important sentences were memorized. If memory seems to play too important a part in the work, it must be remembered that at the time there were few books, and every scholar had to carry most of his learning around in his head. In any case, there is no substitute for constant memorizing when one is learning a language.

After a pupil had built up vocabulary, knowledge of inflection, and skill in speaking, he began to read for himself. The method of approach was not far different from that used today. He first translated a passage into his own language—until he was able to read without translation—then he studied the style, the allusions, the content, and the background. He read poets, orators, dramatists, historians, and philosophers. Greek was also necessary. Sometimes a pupil learned his Latin thoroughly before he began Greek, and sometimes he learned them both together. A true scholar could read either language without the need to translate. One school exercise that would certainly distress the modern student was the translation from Latin directly into Greek, or vice versa!

The quadrivium—arithmetic, astronomy, music, and geometry—also remained practically untouched as far as the subjects were concerned, but again the treatment was more or less different from that given the same topics in the medieval school. In some places a few elements of algebra were added, astronomy was shorn of its accompanying astrology, history entered the curriculum as a separate subject, and some work in natural history was offered, although its nature seems to have been medieval rather than modern. The modernizing of work in science came later. The Renaissance began as a revival of letters, and it did not affect the fields of mathematics and science for about two centuries. What did transfer to all subjects was an attitude of free inquiry, a desire to learn, and a freedom of thought which eventually had their effect in modifying these fields as well.

The great emphasis upon language and literature during the Renaissance has remained in higher education until recently, when the sciences became so important in the modern world that the study of them tended to push the humanities aside. Some college professors still feel, however, that letters and languages are the backbone of culture in any age and should serve as the basis for the bachelor's degree. This attitude, which first became generally accepted during the Renaissance, marks a real change from the attitudes toward the classics up until that time. Latin had been a necessary tool and Greek the language of commerce with the East. It was only after the Renaissance that they became the languages of the cultured man. This heritage is not altogether appropriate to the American spirit and is rapidly becoming less so. The modern world is a world of science. Under these circumstances it seems only sensible that the man of science should be culturally, at least, the equal of the man of letters.

To a select few of his pupils, Vittorino gave an advanced course in philosophy. The position of this course at the end of a pupil's schooling is reminiscent of the Middle Ages, but the content was not. Many of the philosophers studied were not known except by name to many medieval scholars and were not widely read even where they were available. One cannot imagine a flagellant reading Plato! Some of the Renaissance teachers emphasized the differences between the great philosophers of antiquity and the Christian writers, holding the former to be of more value to the educated man than the latter, but others, like Vittorino, saw no fundamental contradiction between the two and tried to bring out the distinctive and educative values of both.

It should be noted that the emphasis shifted from one linguistic subject to another as the centuries went by. Table 5 shows the general development from the early Middle Ages through the seventeenth century. The names of the most important subjects appear in capitals, and the next most important in italics. Those in ordinary print were relatively neglected. The quadrivium grew mainly by differentiation, three of the four original subjects becoming two or more in the later periods covered by the table.

TABLE 5: CHANGES IN THE CURRICULUM[a]

	Early Middle Age	Late Middle Age	Renaissance	Sixteenth and Seventeenth Centuries
Trivium	1. GRAMMAR	Grammar	GRAMMAR	LITERATURE Grammar History
	2. *Rhetoric*	Rhetoric	*Rhetoric*	*Rhetoric*
	3. Dialectic	DIALECTIC	Dialectic	Logic
Quadrivium	4. Arithmetic	Arithmetic	Arithmetic	Arithmetic Algebra
	5. Geometry	Geometry Geography	Geometry Geography	Geometry Trigonometry Geography Zoology, Botany
	6. Astronomy	Astronomy Physics	Astronomy Physics	Astronomy Mechanics Physics Chemistry
	7. MUSIC	8. MUSIC	*Music* (German Schools)	*Music* (German Schools)

[a] Cubberley, *op. cit.*, p. 281. Used by permission of Houghton Mifflin Company, publishers.

The curriculum of Renaissance schools will strike the modern student as narrow. It was. The discoveries of modern science had not yet been made, and the higher mathematics needed by the sciences had not yet been worked out. The nonlinguistic subjects were therefore quite undeveloped. The essential changes between medieval and early Renaissance education were in the content of the linguistic subjects and in the entire spirit of education regardless of subject.

2. *Trends and Attitudes in Renaissance Education* For the first time in a thousand years there was emphasis in education upon the care of the body and the attractiveness of the school environment. The typical schoolroom of the Middle Ages was a small and often dark chapel, a cell, or some other little room in a monastery or cathedral. In general, it was inadequately lighted, uncomfortable, cheerless, and frequently cold. Monks sometimes complained that they did not like to study because they could not keep warm! The typical Renaissance schoolroom was the direct ancestor of those in vogue today. It was

CHAPTER IX

MELANCHTHON AND THE SCHOOLS OF THE GERMAN REFORMATION

In the last chapter the main figure was a teacher who lived during the Italian Renaissance; in this chapter the main character belongs to the Renaissance and Reformation in Germany, about two centuries later. Melanchthon himself was a link between the German Renaissance and the German Reformation, for he began as a humanist and ended as a reformer. In him, the intellectual and religious movements fused into a harmonious whole. Melanchthon was connected with the Reformation from its very beginning and intimately associated with its course of development.

Of the many individuals of importance to education during the period of the German Renaissance and Reformation, three stand out: Martin Luther, Philipp Melanchthon, and Desiderius Erasmus* of Rotterdam.* Two of them, Luther and Melanchthon, were great friends, perhaps because each had in large measure exactly those qualities that the other lacked. Erasmus was a great scholar and an equally great personality, but he could not espouse the Reformation after the movement became violent and after the Protestants broke completely with the Catholic Church. Although the main figure in this chapter will be Melanchthon, one can hardly discuss him without bringing in some mention of the other two. It seems best therefore to describe each briefly.

Luther was a born leader, a magnificent speaker, a dynamic, restless, dominating person given to violent outbursts and opinionated attitudes. He made trouble wherever he went because tact, restraint, refinement, and moderation were all equally foreign to him. Perhaps his most outstanding trait was his flaming courage, which led him to defy anyone and everyone who disagreed with him. One cannot always love Luther, but even those who find his personality distasteful are forced to admire him. He was a tornado that blew across the pages of history, leaving them in a good deal of a mess but making possible an improved rearrangement later on. His picture, shown in Figure 37 suggests a rather coarse, blunt person but does not at all indicate the flame of power and passion within him.

Philipp Melanchthon was as gentle as his friend was violent. His rightful place was within the academic cloisters of a great university. He was in his element as a scholar and a professor of Greek, but through his friendship with Luther he was pushed willy-nilly into a prominent position in the storms of the Reformation. To him fell the task of conciliating those whom Luther had antagonized, of formulating in scholarly form the doctrines of the new church, of devising a school system that would educate children—both boys and girls—equally in humanistic learning and in religion, of teaching advanced students at the University of Wittenberg, of subsequently recommending them to positions as teachers or pastors throughout Germany, and of acting generally as a balance wheel to a revolution. His frail body, his

FIG. 37. Martin Luther and Philipp Melanchthon. From paintings by Lucas Cranach dated 1543, now in the Uffizi Gallery in Florence.

mental sharpness, and his hesitancy are revealed in his portrait, shown in Figure 37. This picture is in contrast to the portrait of Luther and may serve as a basis for comparison with a later picture of Melanchthon.

Desiderius Erasmus was the last of the great humanists. He came originally from Rotterdam, but he traveled about continually. He went everywhere, and he knew everyone. Few people in the world have ever written with more biting wit or more deadly sarcasm. These were his two main weapons in his long and sincere fight to reform the abuses of the Catholic Church—a matter over which he was quite as concerned as Luther—and in his many personal squabbles and feuds. Throughout his life Erasmus was oversensitive, insecure, suspicious, irascible, and critical. The traits in Erasmus that one can admire are his profound scholarship, his love of peace, his devotion to the church, his skill with the pen, and his industry. Less admirable are his excessive caution, his tendency to quarrel, his caustic criticism of people, his conceit, his fawning upon his patrons—although he may have disliked this performance as much as anyone else—and his complete inability to compromise. Erasmus was a typical humanist of the north. He was not interested in aesthetics, in the revival of pagan philosophies, or in self-culture. His burning enthusiasm was for the removal of ignorance and superstition, for the uprooting of evil, for the condemnation of hypocrisy, and for the stimulation of social reform. Indeed, it was a basic tenet* with Erasmus that evil came from ignorance, and would disappear if people were educated.[1]

His relations with both Melanchthon and Luther varied with the years. When Luther first began his protests against the church, Erasmus was greatly pleased because he saw in Luther a courageous man who was as sincere as himself about helping the church to curb excesses. He could not, however, condone an actual separation from the church or any use of violence. It was therefore not long before he and Luther were at swords' points. Both men had violent tempers, and both were about equally skilled in epistolary abuse. Erasmus was determined to work for the church from within, and he never forgave Luther for leading a movement of secession. With Melanchthon he was more moderate. Like many other people, he at first regarded Melanchthon as a young man who had been led astray by Luther. When it became clear that there was no separating the two friends, he and Melanchthon by mutual consent avoided religious issues as much as possible and kept to purely literary matters. In this way a complete break was prevented, but Melanchthon and Erasmus were never the close friends they might easily have become under other circumstances.

Of the three men Melanchthon has been selected as the main character in this chapter because he had more to do directly with schools than did either of the other two. Erasmus was at intervals a university professor and was undoubtedly the man who brought humanism to Oxford and England generally, but he had little contact with the lower schools and he did not teach regularly. Luther was greatly concerned about education because he saw at once that people could hardly be expected to read the Bible for themselves if they were illiterate. He therefore proposed the general principle of universal education. Luther also was a teacher, a professor at the University of Wittenberg. He did not, however, have intimate contact with all kinds of schools or with

[1] For an excellent biography, see P. Smith, *Erasmus,* Harper & Brothers, 1923, 479 pp. For the attitudes of Erasmus toward education, see W. H. Woodward, *Desiderius Erasmus, concerning the Aims and Methods of Education,* Cambridge University Press, 1904, 244 pp.

teaching at all levels, because he left these details to his friend. Melanchthon, like the others, was a university professor, but in addition he had a small preparatory school of his own, he organized dozens of schools throughout Germany, he worked out into practical form Luther's concept of universal education, and in both secondary school and university he set a style that has persisted in Germany up to the present time. In the restricted field of education he was therefore a more commanding figure than either of the other two leaders.

A. MELANCHTHON: HIS LIFE AND WORK

1. Melanchthon's Early Years[2] In 1497, five years after the discovery of America, Philipp Melanchthon was born in a little town near Karlsruhe.* His original family name was Schwarzerd (Black Earth), but during his school years this rather homely name was translated literally into Greek to produce the more euphonious* "Melanchthon." [3] He himself rarely used his changed name, but his students and friends used nothing else; he has therefore come down in history as Philipp Melanchthon. After attending a small local school and then having a tutor for some years, Philipp entered the University of Heidelberg* at the age of thirteen. He received his baccalaureate degree two years later and attempted to enroll for graduate work, but the university refused his application because of his youth. A few months later, however, the University of Tübingen* accepted him, and he received his master's degree at the age of seventeen. He began teaching almost before the ink on his diploma was dry and was from the first extraordinarily successful. It did not take him long to discover that the available textbooks were inappropriate to the humanistic education which was then, two centuries after its development in Italy, just reaching its peak in Germany. He therefore wrote his own textbooks: a Greek grammar when he was only sixteen; a Latin grammar some years later; and at one time or another texts in dialectic, rhetoric, psychology, physics, ethics, history, and religion. The value of his texts is indicated by their long-continued use. His Greek grammar ran through forty-three editions, the last being published a hundred years after the first; the Latin grammar had fifty-one editions over an interval of more than two hundred years.

At the University of Tübingen the humanistic learning had not met with an especially favorable reception, and Melanchthon found himself under fire

[2] The summary of Melanchthon's life is based upon the following references: P. Camerarius, *Life of Melanchthon,* Leipzig, 1566; K. Hartfelder, *Philipp Melanchthon als Praecepter Germaniae,* A. Hofmann, 1889, 687 pp.; J. W. Richard, *Philipp Melanchthon,* G. P. Putnam's Sons, 1902, 399 pp.; C. Schmidt, *Philipp Melanchthon: Leben und Ausgewählte Schriften,* R. L. Frieriche, 1861, 722 pp.

[3] The Greek transliteration of "black earth."

from his older and more conservative colleagues. He was therefore glad when he was called to the University of Wittenberg a year later. He went there originally as a professor of Greek, but within a year he was on the faculties of both arts and theology and busily teaching both linguistic subjects and religion.

2. *Melanchthon and Luther* It was at Wittenberg that Melanchthon met Luther. Their friendship is so important to the history of the entire Reformation that it seems worth while to quote a few of the opinions they expressed about each other and to discuss the relationship between them. Luther contributed to their common enterprises a clear understanding, a deep feeling, a fervently religious spirit, and a heroic courage. Melanchthon contributed a great learning, a fine culture, a grasp of philosophy and theology, a beautiful character, and a loving heart. Luther was in the main a destructive influence, not perhaps by intention but because the destructive work had to be done before anything new could be built, and Luther did not live far beyond this initial period. Melanchthon's work was largely constructive, partly because of his temperament and partly because he lived longer. Both men had courage. Luther's was the heroism of daring and defiance; Melanchthon's was the heroism of endurance and patient suffering. No one can say which man contributed the more to the great friendship between them. Their mutual dependence was demonstrated whenever they were separated.

Of Melanchthon, Luther wrote:

> I am rough, boisterous, stormy, and altogether warlike. I am born to fight against innumerable monsters and devils. I must remove stumps and stones, cut away thistles and thorns, and clear the wild forests; but Master Philipp comes along softly and gently, sowing and watering with joy, according to the gifts which God had abundantly bestowed upon him.[4]
>
> Whoever does not recognize Philipp as his instructor, is a stolid, stupid donkey, carried away by his own vanity and self-conceit. Whatever we know in the arts and in true philosophy, Philipp has taught us. He has only the humble title of Master, but he excels all the Doctors. There is no one living adorned with such gifts. He must be held in honour. Whoever despises this man, him will God despise.[5]
>
> You have seen, or will see, Philipp's theses. They are bold, but they certainly are true. He defended them in such a way that he seemed to us all a veritable wonder, and such he is. Christ willing, he will surpass many Martins and will be a mighty foe of the devil and of the scholastic theology. He knows their tricks and also the Rock Christ. He will powerfully prevail.[6]

[4] Luther's preface to Melanchthon's *Commentary on Colossians.*

[5] *Corpus Reformatorium,* Heinsius, 1834–1936 (98 vols.), X, 302. Hereafter this collection of original data will be abbreviated to *C.R.*

[6] W. M. L. de Wette and J. G. Seidemann, *Briefe, Sendschreiben, und Bedenken,* G. Reimer. 1825–1856 (6 parts), part i, p. 380.

Of Luther, Melanchthon wrote:

> He was the chariot and the charioteer of Israel,* raised up by God to restore and purify the ministry of the Gospel. For we must confess that by him doctrine was revealed which is beyond the range of the human mind.[7]
>
> Some by no means evil-minded persons, however, express a suspicion that Luther manifested too much asperity. I will not affirm the reverse, but only quote the language of Erasmus: God has sent in this latter age a violent physician on account of the magnitude of the existing disorders.[8]
>
> Martin is too great and too wonderful for me to describe in words. . . . the more I regard him the greater I judge him to [be].[9]
>
> Did you ever read anything more bitter than Erasmus's *Hyperaspistes?* It is almost venomous. How Luther takes it, I do not know. But I have again besought him by all that is sacred, if he replies, to do so briefly, simply, and without abuse. At once after Luther published his book, I said this controversy would end in the most cruel alienation. . . . Oh that Luther would keep silent! I did hope that with age, experience, and so many troubles, he would grow more moderate; but I see he becomes the more violent as the contests and the opponents exhibit the same characteristics. This matter grievously vexes my soul.[10]

This mutual love and esteem weathered the storms of the twenty-eight years from the first meeting to Luther's death. When Melanchthon died some years later he was buried beside Luther. It is a fitting tribute to their friendship that they were laid to rest side by side in the college chapel at Wittenberg.

3. The Middle Years Once established at the University of Wittenberg, Melanchthon began intensive work along the two lines of interest that were to continue as his absorbing passions throughout his life—the furthering of humanistic education, and the development of a theology based upon the Bible rather than upon church doctrine. Every day he worked, wrote, and taught from two in the morning until he could no longer keep his eyes open. As the burden of his work increased and his health began to break down under the strain, he voiced his inclination to restrict his labors to the teaching of the classics and to leave theology to others. Luther was not willing, however, to lose his friend's aid. In his usual forthright and determined way he made two changes in Melanchthon's circumstances. First, he found Philipp a wife, so that there might be someone who would care for his health and feed him properly! As it turned out, Luther made an excellent choice. Second, he appealed to the Elector* of Saxony,* who supported the university, to increase Melanchthon's salary and to reduce his teaching schedule. Even with these

[7] *C. R.*, VI, 57.
[8] De Wette and Seidemann, *op. cit.*, part i, p. 312.
[9] *C. R.*, I, 264.
[10] *Ibid.*, I, 688.

changes it was still necessary for Melanchthon to maintain a private school in his own house in order to make ends meet. This small school was a sort of laboratory for working out his ideas about teaching. The boys had a form of self-government and a system of awards for good work. The curriculum was not as narrowly linguistic as one might have expected, probably because Melanchthon did practically all the teaching himself and ranged over the large number of subjects of which he was master.

Melanchthon's theological writings began when he was twenty-one years old and continued throughout his life. They included the Visitation Articles,* upon which the school system of Germany was founded, and the Augsburg Confession,* which contains the fundamental creed of the Lutheran Church. Although his writings in theology were of great importance for church history, they need not be discussed at length here.

In its inception, the Reformation had the same battle cry as the Renaissance: Go back to the original sources! The original source for Christianity was the Bible. In interpreting the meaning of the Scriptures a person should be guided by his conscience, not by the opinions of the church fathers. Before the common people could read the Bible for themselves, however, three situations must be met: there must be enough books, there must be a translation of the Bible into German, and there must be popular education to teach the people to read. The book problem was already on the way to solution through the invention of movable type in about 1450. Luther himself made the translation of the Bible, naturally consulting various friends at different times. When his translation was ready, the printers were ready to print it. No book in the world has ever sold the way the Bible has, once it had been translated out of Latin, the scholar's language, into the many spoken languages of the people. In spite of all the modern skepticism about religion, the Bible is still the world's best seller; in 1940 more copies of it were sold than of any other one book.

To Melanchthon fell the task of formulating the educational plan for eliminating illiteracy and of getting the plan into practice. Early in 1526 he helped in the establishment of new schools in Nuremberg* and two years later wrote his Visitation Articles, after making a survey of conditions in both schools and local churches. The last of the eighteen articles deals with education. In putting this article into practical use Melanchthon had to make a definite plan of work for schools and classes. His final product was a schedule in which there were three levels of work, each of which would require two or more years for its completion. More will be said of this curriculum later, since it furnished the basis for education in the Germanies for the next two centuries and has, in modified form, come down to the present.

In the course of his long years of teaching and of identification with the Reformation, Melanchthon trained most of the next generation of pastors and teachers, either directly or through his students. Whenever a town wanted a teacher or a minister someone wrote to Melanchthon for recommendations. At the time of his death there was hardly a town in all of Germany in which someone approved by Melanchthon was not established.

In his attitude toward education Melanchthon illustrates a complete fusion of two dominant trends. He was a humanist before he turned reformer, and he never lost his great love of the classics. In his zeal to study original sources he learned Latin, Greek, and Hebrew thoroughly. Once he had joined in the religious debates of the period he became devoted with equal passion to the reformed church. In Luther, the reformer outweighed the humanist, and in Erasmus the reverse was true, but in Melanchthon the blend was perfectly balanced. Melanchthon, like other scholars, saw as he grew older that German humanism was dying. He was indeed himself the last of the great ones. What he probably never saw—at least one hopes he did not—was that his friend Luther had started theological disputes which by their intolerant outcomes helped put an end to the composition of Latin poetry or the appreciation of Euripides in the original.

During his lifetime Melanchthon produced no less than 709 publications, not counting his letters. Even in his last year of life he wrote thirteen separate items. In judging of this productivity one must remember that Melanchthon had no typewriter and no stenographer. Moreover, some of his work was of such importance that it had to be written and rewritten many times. In addition to his own work Melanchthon wrote much for his colleagues, especially speeches to be delivered on festive occasions. It was said of him: "Yes, it even happened that the speaker of the day had already begun while Melanchthon still sat at his desk writing down the last part of the speech.[11] Melanchthon wrote day and night. Even when he was eating he had his pen in hand and continued scribbling.

4. Melanchthon's Last Years Until the death of Luther in 1546 the two friends carried on their work, each doing what he could do best. One incident foreshadowed what would happen to Melanchthon without Luther. Three theological troublemakers, styling themselves prophets, descended upon Wittenberg and urged the local pastors into making such radical changes in the church services as to antagonize many people. In the ensuing excitement Melanchthon did his best to restrain everyone concerned from violence, but to no avail. Things went from bad to worse, and serious riots were not far

[11] Camerarius, *op. cit.*

away when Luther heard of the situation. Taking his life in his hands, he crossed territories in which his capture probably meant death at the stake and descended secretly upon Wittenberg. For two days he remained closeted with Melanchthon while he investigated matters. Then for eight consecutive days he mounted a local pulpit and thundered to an audience that jammed the church to capacity. At the end of that time the prophets had disappeared like dew before the sun, and Luther had knocked sense into the heads of all concerned. Then he too disappeared.

After Luther's death Melanchthon no longer had a magnificent orator and magnetic leader to come to his rescue and to hold together the divergent elements within the Protestant church. He did his best—probably he did better than anyone had a right to expect from a man of his temperament—but his last fourteen years were full of controversy and despair. In his own words:

> I could almost believe I was born under an unlucky star. For what distresses me most has come upon me. Poverty, hunger, contempt, and other misfortunes I could easily bear. But what utterly prostrates me is strife and controversy. I had to compose the Confession which was to be given to the Emperor and the Estates.* In spirit I foresaw insults, wars, devastation, battles. And now does it depend upon me to divert such great calamity? . . . Dear brother, I dare not drop the matter so long as I live. But not by my fault shall peace be destroyed. Other theologians wanted to compose the Confession. Would God they had had their way. Perhaps they could have done it better. Now they are dissatisfied with mine, and want it changed. One cries out here, another there. But I must maintain my principle of omitting everything that increases the bitterness. God is my witness that my intentions have been good. My reward is that I shall be hated.[12]

The worst of his troubles came, to be sure, from rival or antagonistic theologians who assailed him on every side. Many of them were men who in earlier years had been silenced by the dominating Luther at various conferences and councils. With Luther gone, they reappeared and pounced upon Melanchthon, causing him much misery and producing schisms* among the Protestants themselves. In spite of his best efforts and in spite of prodigious amounts of work, Melanchthon could not hold the Protestants together. Before the end of his life the Lutheran church had already split in two. Nothing grieved Melanchthon any more than the knowledge that the work to which he and Luther had dedicated their lives was already disintegrating and that he was powerless to stop it.

Melanchthon's life span began before the Reformation started and con-

[12] *Melanchthoniana Paedagogica* (Gesammelt und Erklart Hartfelder), B. G. Tuebner, 1892, p 38.

tinued after its main developments. The central events of the Reformation may be regarded as taking place between 1517 and 1555, although many contributing causes were in operation long before 1517 and many results continued to operate long after 1555. Throughout these years Melanchthon was an important figure. In 1517 he had just received his master's degree from Tübingen; in 1518 he was already in Wittenberg with Luther; for many years he was present at every council to defend the faith; in 1530 he wrote the famous Augsburg Confession; in 1555 he was a tired, embittered old man who had fought a good fight but was too weary to enjoy the victory.

During the last years of his life Melanchthon's work in education went on unabated. It included not only the founding of lower schools but of several universities and the restoration of Wittenberg after a dissension so severe that Melanchthon had to leave the city with his family to avoid actual physical danger to himself and them. Gradually his health broke under the continued strain of work and the ceaseless worry. The last picture made of him is shown in Figure 38. His anxiety and exhaustion are clearly revealed. In 1560 a most welcome death put out the flame that had carried a frail body through sixty-three years of unending labor in the two causes of religion and education, and the Great Preceptor* of Germany was laid to a well-earned rest beside the Great Reformer.

FIG. 38. Melanchthon as an Old Man. From a woodcut by Cranach in the Luther Hall in Wittenberg.

5. *Melanchthon's Relations with His Students* It remains to present in a little more detail what manner of man Philipp Melanchthon was in his capacity as a teacher. First as to his relationship with his students. To them he had not only a warm heart but a sympathetic interest that continued after they had left his tutelage. To be sure, he was sometimes severe with those who were too lazy to exert themselves, but this attitude is understandable. He was such a tireless worker and felt his lack of adequate time so keenly that he quite naturally became irritated at students before whom he spread in vain the treasures of his own mind. He seems to have entered wholeheartedly into general student affairs as is shown by the notices to the entire student body that he posted on his bulletin board. Here they found such items as these:

For the feast of St. John the Baptist* good voices were needed for the church choir. Melanchthon invited the students to a rehearsal because "music is a gift of God granted to men for the maintenance and spread of Christian teaching. . . ." [13]

At the same time the university held itself responsible for warning its members of dangers. Bathing in the torrential Elbe* was dangerous. "We forbid most vigorously, out of fatherly love and with fatherly authority, . . . any bathing in the river on the part of our young people. The parents transferred their burden to us teachers, and God has conferred on the administration its authority. Many a time have tragic instances shown what a treacherous river the Elbe is, of which the students must beware." [14]

In general the young people should behave respectably and modestly in their appearances in public, in their clothes, and in their speech.[15]

Especially should the students practice chastity. As the lyric poet Bacchylides* said: Just as in a painting a well-caught likeness is the greatest ornament so in the character of men is chastity the loveliest jewel. If a man lacks chastity his otherwise good traits are distorted and made of little value.[16]

Immoral dances must be avoided. Many people take indecent liberties on the occasion of a public dance. "Since, however, dances should not be barbaric and ugly pleasures, but are instituted for their training, by which the young men learn to behave themselves decently with the opposite sex, they have respectable grounds for existence." [17]

The students seem to have been particularly rowdy at the time of a carnival. . . . The running about of masked students and the resultant excesses appeared to Melanchthon as survival or imitation of the bacchanalia* upon which even the Roman senate imposed painful punishment. "Such things do harm to morals and increase wantonness and if the administration does not lay a bridle upon youths, the devil will play his little game, by developing anew through heightened audacity the frenzy of the bacchanalian festival. Anyway, we see how vices grow, especially in this latest period of the world." [18]

Also the customary drinking bouts must be stopped, because they rob the parents and increase vice. And it is also completely unpermissible to push one's way into strange houses and bother the residents with dumb gestures. . . . Indeed it is to be feared that God would punish Germany through the Turks if this kind of mischief didn't stop: "Therefore let us improve our morals, so that our prayer and our weapons will be strong." [19]

When in the year 1535 the university was transferred on account of an epidemic from Wittenberg to Jena, the students were informed that the change was suggested more by care for the health of the students than that of the professors. At the same time however they were requested to pay their

[13] *C.R.*, III, 544.
[14] *Ibid.*, p. 512.
[15] *Ibid.*, p. 589.
[16] *Ibid.*, p. 110.
[17] *Ibid.*, X, 80.
[18] *Ibid.*, IV, 99.
[19] *Ibid.*, p. 780.

debts before their departure and not during the last few days to run around the streets armed and rioting. "It is fitting for the students to consider the duties of hospitality," [20] and once arrived in Jena the students would be excellently cared for, and it was announced that the city council had had a lot of cheap beer brought in from outside.[21] When however in spite of this kindness on the part of the magistrate many students invaded the vineyards at the time when the grapes were ripening they were reminded forcibly of the duties of hospitality; "for it is proper for godly and educated people not to transgress the duties of hospitality." [22]

But not only student affairs found their way to the bulletin board. For instance the students were urged to works of Christian charity. A poor man, father of a family, who had through an accident lost his nine-year-old son, should be supported, and Melanchthon reinforced his request with a verse from a Greek tragedian.[23] When in the year 1545 a great part of the small town of Gotha* was burned down, the charity of the students was called upon, "Let us tremble before the thought of God's wrath and let us remember that we also have deserved punishment." [24]

Whenever Melanchthon had to miss class he put up a notice to his students. Thus on his wedding day he posted the couplet below:

> Rest from your studies, Philipp says you may.
> He'll read no lecture on St. Paul today.[25]

He was also in the habit of announcing his courses by a notice sometimes in prose and sometimes in poetry. Like all his other communications with his students these were in Latin. One of them, together with its translation, appears below. Since there was no bulletin of courses, these announcements were the equivalent of a catalogue description. One wonders what a modern student would make out of such a communication from a professor:

Intimatio Philippi
Mel. de Homero
praelegendo 1531

Decrivi aliquot libros Homeri interpretari Deo volente. In eam rem collocabo deinceps horam sextam die Mercurii et praelege, ut soleo, gratis. Quod autem dicunt Homerum mendicasse vivum, id aecidit et etiam

Announcement of Philipp
Melanchthon concerning the
lectures on Homer 1531

I have decided to interpret certain books of Homer, God willing. For this purpose I will set aside six o'clock every Wednesday and I will lecture, as usual, without charge. However they say that because as a

[20] *Ibid.*, II, 890.
[21] *Ibid.*, p. 895.
[22] *Ibid.*, p. 952.
[23] *Ibid.*, IX, 21.
[24] *Ibid.*, V, 890.
[25] Schmidt, *op. cit.*, p. 49. The actual notice was, of course, in Latin, and read:
"A studiis hodie facit otia gratia Philippus
Nec verbis Pauli dogmata sacra leget."

mortuo. Oberrat enim optimus Poeta et rogat, qui se audire velint. Pecuniam polliceri non potest, sed pollicetur magnarum et honestarum rerum doctrinam. Rogat autem non illos banausicous qui quaestuosas artes sectantur, non solum nulla instructi liberali doctrina, sed etiam ex hac una re sapientiae famam captantes, quod magnifice ausint contemnere alias omnes honestas disciplinas. Quodsi casu in horum aliquem inciderit Homerus, est enim caecus, orat se civiliter dimitti, sicut a Platone ex civitate dimittitur. Verum hos ad se vocat audiendum, qui colunt studia liberaliter et virtutis amore. Ego memini quondam non potuisse talium scriptorum copiam fieri studiosis, quamlibet magna mercede proposita; none tantus est contemptus optimarum rerum, ut nisi gratis offerantur et quidem praelegantur a peritis, mendicare Homerus auditores cogatur. Incipiam autem proxime a nono libro Iliadis.[26]

living man Homer went begging, the same thing happens to him in death. For the greatest poet wanders about asking who wants to listen to him. He cannot offer money but he does offer the knowledge of great and good things. However he does not ask those philistines who seek remunerative occupations, who are not only uninstructed in any liberal doctrine but for this very reason desire a reputation for wisdom, who dare to despise haughtily all other good learning. But if Homer met them by chance at any hour, since he is blind, he would ask to be sent away politely just as he was banished from the state by Plato. Truely he calls to attend his classes those who cultivate their studies freely and in the love of virtue. I remember when the most zealous students could not obtain a copy of such writings, no matter how much they were willing to pay; but now there is such contempt for the best things that unless they are offered without cost and are presented by experts Homer is forced to beg for listeners. However, I shall begin tomorrow with the ninth book of the Iliad.

As if Melanchthon did not have enough other things to do, he held for years a special class Saturday afternoon for foreign students who did not understand German well and went over with them the sermon to be delivered by the pastor in church on the morrow, so that these foreigners might get more out of the sermon than they otherwise would.

Many of Philipp's students described him or their feeling toward him. A few of these comments are quoted:

> You love and teach in the most careful way Latin, Greek, and Hebrew; [you present] everything in a way so pleasant, faithful, and upright, as if you wanted that everyone in a single day should be your equal in scholarship.
>
> You love each person according to his deserts. You entrance all people

[26] *Ibid.*, II, 557.

so that they love you; you draw them to you through your wonderful charm and talent.[27]

One man considered it the greatest good fortune of his life to have been a student under Melanchthon, and another explained that Melanchthon's teaching talent revealed itself in the ease with which he adapted himself to the abilities of the learner. A third was certain that the number of grateful students was counted in the thousands and that in Germany all the pulpits and schools echoed his writings.[28]

Popular Melanchthon undeniably was. In his first year he had 120 students in his class; the next four years the enrollment increased successively to 240, 333, and 600. His average number per class over a number of years was between 400 and 500. Since he taught several classes, the personnel of which differed somewhat, he had during some semesters a total enrollment of 2000 students. It was through these tremendous classes that this one frail man was able to leave such a direct personal imprint upon the educational life of his time, wholly aside from the influence he exerted through his writing and organizing. It is a testimony too of Melanchthon's vital power to teach that after his death the university had to hire four different men to carry on his instruction in all its phases.

Melanchthon used chiefly the lecture method for his university classes, but he was quite willing to be interrupted by questions. He was exacting in his demands upon students, especially when it came to examinations. To him the fear of examinations, an emotion that has existed ever since there were any students to have it, was only a spur for the learner and no basis for excuse from a test. Compared to modern standards, Melanchthon favored in principle a rather rigid discipline because he believed one could not train character without it. In actual practice, however, he appears to have been fairly mild, except when students were lazy; then he could, according to Luther, scold like Jeremiah.* His class manner was the exact opposite of that shown by most of the world's popular teachers. His voice was small and weak, he stuttered more or less, his manner was diffident, he used no rhetorical aids, and his speech was dry rather than thrilling. On the positive side, his lectures were models of clarity, his spontaneous choice of words seemed almost inspired, his knowledge was enormous, his memory for the classics excellent, and his devotion to humanism so deep that he communicated his feeling to others. He never used empty words or high-flown phrases, he illumined every topic he touched, and he stuck to whatever matter he was presenting, refusing to be diverted from his objective. Although always rather too much on the serious side for modern

[27] F. von Söden, *Beiträge zur Geschichte der Reformation,* Bauer und Raspe, 1855 (522 pp.), p. 82.

[28] *C. R.,* XIX, 53, 54; XX, 193; X, 301.

student taste, Melanchthon was so simple and direct a person that he presented his subjects by whatever illustrations came first to his mind. He related anecdotes from his own life and the lives of others, he told an occasional joke, he used examples from history and—although in principle he spoke only Latin with his classes—he mixed his languages into a sort of hodgepodge that must have been amusing to his listeners.

6. Melanchthon as an Individual Finally a word about Melanchthon's appearance and character, and his opinion of himself or other people's opinions concerning him. In the first place, he was a small frail man of less than average height, and he carried one shoulder higher than the other, presumably from his interminable hours of writing. His manner was shy, he stammered, and until his last years he always looked absurdly young. As one friend wrote of him:

> In size he is a small, unattractive person. You would think he was only a boy not above eighteen years old, when he walks by the side of Luther. Because of their sincere love for each other they are almost always together. Martin is much taller than he, but in understanding, learning, and culture, Philipp is a great stalwart giant and hero. One wonders that in so small a body there can lie concealed such a great and lofty mountain of wisdom and culture.[29]

As a person, Melanchthon was sensitive to a high degree, a bit effeminate in his softness and dependency upon others, gentle, and lovable. In general, he was lacking in creativeness or originality. His shyness and feeling of inferiority were abnormal and without discernible basis, unless they rested upon physical deficiencies. No man who can write a successful Greek grammar at the age of sixteen needs to distrust his own ability. It is unfortunate from a personal standpoint that such a tender, thin-skinned, pacific person as Melanchthon should have been forced into the fights begun by the thick-skinned, aggressive Luther. Moreover, Melanchthon was a moody person, given to believing that things were much worse than they really were. Periodically he became completely discouraged. On one such occasion he felt that he and Luther had both made a bad mistake in judgment. He became so disturbed over his own error that he made himself ill. After all other efforts to revive him had failed, his wife sent for Luther. The description of the following day is given below:

> When Luther arrived he found Melanchthon apparently dying. His eyes were sunk, his senses gone, his speech stopped, his hearing closed, his face fallen in and hollow . . . He knew nobody, ate and drank nothing. When Luther saw him thus disfigured, he was frightened above measure. He first

[29] F. H. Ch. Schwarz, *Darstellung aus dem Gebiet der Pädagogik,* J. G. Göschen, 1833–1834 (2 vols.), I, 98.

turned forthwith to the window, and prayed fervently to God. . . . Then, said Luther as he grasped Philipp by the hand: "Be of good courage, Philipp; thou shalt not die. . . ." Being thus taken hold of and addressed. Philipp began to draw breath again, but could say nothing for a good while. Then he turned his face straight upon Luther, and began to beg him for God's sake not to detain him any longer,—that he was now on a good journey—that he should let him go—that nothing better could befall him. "By no means, Philipp," said Luther; "thou must serve our Lord God yet longer." Thus Philipp by degrees became more cheerful, and let Luther order him something to eat; and Luther brought it himself to him; but Philipp refused it. Then Luther forced him with these threats, saying: "Hark, Philipp, thou must eat, or I excommunicate thee." With these words he was overcome, so that he ate a very little: and thus by degrees he gained strength again.[30]

In spite of being usually overanxious about personal danger, Melanchthon could be brave enough when necessary. Once when the students had got into a riot with the local authorities and were about to storm the jail to release a comrade, the professors—headed by Melanchthon—bore down upon them and dispersed them. No one laid about him with more determination than he. Not even the roughest student could bring himself to strike the little man, so Melanchthon soon had the situation under control. After persuading the students to go home, Melanchthon turned his attention to the civil authorities and brought about the student's release without violence.

Melanchthon could have had many more honors than he did. For one thing, he was too busy to bother with them, and for another he was too diffident; nothing made him more acutely miserable than to be singled out from others, even for praise. To the day of his death Melanchthon remained unconvinced that he was a person of consequence.

In taking leave of Philipp Melanchthon one can hardly improve upon the words of a friend who read the funeral oration:

> Salve iterum atque iterum. Tua nos immota manebit
> Semper apud memores gloria, nomen, honos.[31]

Melanchthon and Luther together left their imprint upon the schools of their country. Their greatest single contribution was the principle of universal education. The popular educational systems of the world date from the Reformation and are further developments of the basic ideas then presented. The education of girls was a part of the general plan. In Vittorino's school

[30] L. von Seckendorf, *Geschichte des Luthertums,* L. Maimburg, 1692, III, 314.
[31] Camerarius, *op. cit.* "Farewell, again and again! Your glory, your name, your honor will remain unchanged forever in our memories."

there were a few girls whom he taught without discrimination. The barriers against feminine education had therefore been let down a little by humanism, but it took the Reformation to initiate general education for women.

In spite of occasional venerated teachers in earlier times, the respectability of teaching as a profession dates from the Renaissance.[32] The Reformation strengthened the changed attitude toward teaching, but added an aura* of religious fervor that still lingers. Teaching began to be a "career," on a par with medicine, law, or the church. The original Protestant idea was that all these professions should serve both the church and society. The strictly religious connection has disappeared in public schools but the ideal of service to society remains.

It should be noted that Luther and Melanchthon established what has turned out to be the most effective single form of propaganda—the use of the schools for the indoctrination of an entire generation. The reformers wanted to teach the new faith and to combat Catholicism. In recent decades Adolf Hitler wanted to teach National Socialism and to combat both Democracy and Communism, Americans also use their schools for the parallel purpose of teaching democracy, tolerance, and social consciousness. The method is in itself neither good nor bad, only effective, and it can be used equally well for constructive or destructive ends. This deliberate use of the schools for the indoctrination of all the children in a country dates from the Reformation.

B. SCHOOLS OF THE GERMAN REFORMATION

1. Interrelation of Church, State, and School During the entire period of the Middle Ages all schools were mainly creations of the church. It was not until the twelfth century that a few secular schools appeared, and the teachers in even these schools were still sometimes drawn from the priesthood. At the close of the fifteenth century the pressure for secular schools and teachers was increasing. In Germany the nobles already had court schools of their own. According to the Peace of Augsburg,* each prince or nobleman was to decide what the religion of his district was to be. These men were therefore in a strategic position for assuming responsibility for education. This secular control of education was new, and it became a fundamental tenet of the Reformation.[33]

It is not to be supposed that a full-grown educational system sprang into being at once. The first efforts at universal education were on a small and incomplete scale. In 1542 a system of schools appeared in Magdeburg,* and

[32] See pp. 217–218.

[33] For a good account of education after the Reformation see F. Paulsen, *German Education, Past and Present* (translated by T. Lorenz), Charles Scribner's Sons, 1908, 310 pp.

1528 in Saxony. It was not until 1559, however, that the first public schools, open to everyone, came into existence in the small state of Württemberg.* This system provided for instructing the youth of the state from elementary school through whatever grades were necessary for holding office in church or state. It consisted of a vernacular school and a six-year Latin school in every city or town; those pupils of sufficient ability might subsequently enter the University of Tübingen. The Württemberg system was widely copied throughout Germany and became the basis for the German school system of prewar days.

These early systems, though public, were voluntary. The first compulsory system was that of Weimar* in 1619. The compulsion did not at first include girls, but eventually they also were required to attend school. However, the earliest school system that included all the essential modern elements did not appear until 1642, about a century after the Peace of Augsburg. Although the ideas for universal education were already in circulation during the lifetime of Melanchthon and Luther, they did not get into actual practice till long after these leaders were dead.

2. *Melanchthon's Plan for the Schools* As mentioned earlier, Melanchthon devised the basic plan upon which schoolwork in the reformed territories was based. His curriculum is summarized below:

> *The First Group.* The first group shall consist of those children who are learning to read. With these the following method is to be adopted: They are first to be taught the child's-manual, containing the alphabet, the creed, the Lord's Prayer, and other prayers. When they have learned this, Donatus and Cato may both be given them; Donatus for a reading book, and Cato they may explain after the following manner: the schoolmaster must give them the explanation of a verse or two, and then in a few hours call upon them to repeat what he has thus said; and in this way they will learn a great number of Latin words, and lay up a full store of phrases to use in speech. In this they should be exercised until they can read well. Neither do we consider it time lost, if the feebler children, who are not especially quick-witted, should read Cato and Donatus not once only, but a second time. With this they should be taught to write, and be required to show their writing to the schoolmaster every day. Another mode of enlarging their knowledge of Latin words is to give them every afternoon some words to commit to memory, as has been the custom in schools hitherto. These children must likewise be kept at music, and be made to sing with the others, as we shall show, God willing, further on.
>
> *The Second Group.* The second group consists of children who have learned to read, and are now ready to go into grammar. With these the following regulations should be observed: The first hour after noon every day all the children, large and small, should be practiced in music. Then the

schoolmaster must interpret to the second group the *Fables* of Aesop*. After vespers, he should explain to them the *Paedology* of Mosellanus;* and when this is finished, he should select from the *Colloquies* of Erasmus some that may conduce to their improvement and discipline. This should be repeated on the next evening also. When the children are about to go home for the night, some short sentence may be given them, taken perhaps from a poet, which they are to repeat next morning, such as: *Amicus certus in re incerta cernitur.* (A true friend becomes manifest in adversity.) Or *Fortuna, quem nimium fovet, stultum facit.* (Fortune, if she favors a man too much, makes him a fool.) Or this from Ovid, *Vulgus amicitias utilitate probat.* (The rabble value friendships by the profit they yield.)

In the morning the children are again to explain Aesop's fables. With this the teacher should decline some nouns or verbs, many or few, easy or difficult, according to the progress of the children, and then ask them the rules and the reasons for such inflections. And at the same time when they shall have learned the rules of construction, they should be required to construe,* (parse*) as it is called; this is a very useful exercise, and yet there are not many who employ it. After the children have thus learned Aesop, Terence* is to be given to them; and this they must commit to memory, for they will now be older, and able to work harder. Still the master must be cautious, lest he overtask them. Next after Terence, the children may take hold of such of the comedies of Plautus* as are harmless in their tendency, as the *Aulularia,* the *Trinummus,* the *Pseudolus,* etc.

The hour before mid-day must be invariably and exclusively devoted to instruction in grammar; first etymology,* then syntax,* and lastly prosody.* And when the teacher has gone thus far through with the grammar, he should begin it again, and so on continually, that the children may understand it to perfection. For if there is negligence here, there is neither certainty nor stability in whatever is learned beside. And the children should learn by heart and repeat all the rules, so that they may be driven and forced, as it were, to learn the grammar well.

If such labour is irksome to the schoolmaster, as we often see, then we should dismiss him, and get another in his place,—one who will not shrink from the duty of keeping his pupils constantly in the grammar. For no greater injury can befall learning and the arts, than for youth to grow up in ignorance of grammar. . . .

The Third Group. Now, when these children have been well trained in grammar, those among them who have made the greatest proficiency should be taken out, and formed into a third group. The hour after mid-day they, together with the rest, are to devote to music. After this the teacher is to give an explanation of Vergil. When he has finished this, he may take up Ovid's *Metamorphoses,** and the latter part of the afternoon Cicero's [*Duties*], or *Letters to Friends.* In the morning, Vergil may be reviewed, and the teacher, to keep up practice in the grammar, may call for constructions and inflections, and point out the prominent figures of speech.

The hour before mid-day, grammar should still be kept up, that the scholars may be thoroughly versed therein. And when they are perfectly familiar with etymology and syntax, then prosody . . . should be opened to them, so that they can thereby become accustomed to make verses. For this exercise is a very great help toward understanding the writings of others; and it likewise gives the boys a rich fund of words, and renders them accomplished in many ways. In course of time, after they have been sufficiently practiced in the grammar, this same hour is to be given to logic and rhetoric. The boys in the second and third groups are to be required every week to write compositions, either in the form of letters or of verses. They

Das fünfte Gebot.

Du sollst nicht tödten

Was ist das?

Wir sollen Gott fürchten und lieben, daß wir unserm Nächsten an seinem Leibe keinen Schaden noch Leid thun, sondern ihm helfen und fördern in allen Leibes-Nöthen.

Kain tödtet seinen Bruder.

Siehe Geschichte 6. Seite 90.

Leib und Leben deiner Brüder
Schade nie; — Gott straft dich wieder.

FIG. 39. Two pages from Luther's Reader for Children. From Luther's *Kindesbüchlein.* Courtesy of the Teachers College Library, Columbia University.

should also be rigidly confined to Latin conversation, and to this end the teachers themselves must, as far as possible, speak nothing but Latin with the boys; thus they will acquire the practice by use, and the more rapidly for the incentives held out to them.[34]

It should be noted that this plan is highly humanistic. The work consisted of grammar and literature, so selected as to emphasize morality, and instruction in religion.

The emphasis upon religion and morals started as soon as a child entered school, where he at once learned to read by means of such livid reading mat-

[34] From Melanchthon's "Book of Visitation" translated by H. Barnard in "Life and Educational Services of Philipp Melanchthon," *American Journal of Education* (1859), 4: 749–755.

ter as Luther's primer, two pages of which are shown in Figure 39.[35] The strongly religious and moral note is evident.

In the practical application of Melanchthon's general plan of education three types of institutions arose. At the lowest level there was a school in which children were taught to read German. Since the children of wealthy or educated parents usually picked up this skill at home, these schools came to be attended mainly by the children of the common people. In the course of time they developed into the German *Volksschule** of today. From this lowest level children entered the Latin grammar school, the studies of which Melanchthon had outlined. He gave no definite number of years for the completion of the work, but experience soon settled upon six as being about right. This Latin school developed into the modern Gymnasium.* Next came the arts course at the university, and finally the specialization in theology, law, teaching, or medicine. All these schools were important in the growth of the German educational system.

3. The Latin School The curriculum of this school consisted almost exclusively of languages and literature. The old familiar form of the trivium still lingered on, but its content so changed as to be linguistic instead of scholastic. The idea of literature for general culture did not, however, appear. The training had a largely utilitarian objective—in fact, almost the same objective as that of scholasticism, except that the faith to be defended was Protestant instead of Catholic. The dialectic of the twelfth and thirteenth centuries had been developed in the first instance for practical use in defending the church. The languages of the sixteenth were developed for the similar purpose of serving religion. Greek was to Melanchthon the most important of the languages because it was necessary for reading the New Testament in the original, and for history, philosophy, and science. Latin came next, because of its literature and because it was the language of cultured men. Hebrew came last and was regarded as necessary only for students of theology, but to them it was vital because they could not read the Old Testament properly without it. All the works of antiquity, whether read for religious or cultural purpose, could be studied properly only in the original. If this basic contention is granted, then the conclusion that languages are essential immediately follows. Grammar was therefore the basic subject throughout the Latin school.

The other two subjects of the trivium, rhetoric and dialectic, were also in-

[35] *Translation, left-hand page:* The fifth commandment: Thou shalt not kill. What does that mean? We should love and fear God, in order that we should do no damage or harm to our neighbor, but should help and further him in all his bodily needs. *Right-hand page:* Cain killed his brother. Never harm the body or life of thy brothers, or God will punish thee, in return.

cluded in the curriculum. Melanchthon had his own way of expressing the difference between these two subjects. For instance, if a person wanted to discuss virtue as a topic he would choose the art of dialectic because he would want to tell what the concept of virtue was, what its causes and different parts were, and what was the working of each. But if a person wanted to move others to be virtuous, he would use the art of rhetoric. In another place Melanchthon admits that the two subjects have a common content but that rhetoric dresses up an argument, while dialectic presents the same matter but without trimmings.[36] Dialectic therefore appeals to the mind, and rhetoric to the emotions. It is only natural that with Luther moving people by his eloquence, a teacher of the period should be led to give an important place in the curriculum to the art of putting words together so as to influence people.

Of other subjects in the curriculum there is hardly a trace. Melanchthon, to be sure, was such a gifted teacher and generally well-educated man that he gave work in history, geography, philosophy, mathematics, and science, even in the courses that were advertised as grammar or literature, because material from these other subjects was needed in order to understand the masterpieces he discussed. Moreover, he defended their inclusion on the ground of their usefulness. Thus geography was necessary for history, useful for traveling, and of value in locating events described in the Bible. History was not only a great pleasure but a subject by means of which, especially if German history were taught, the patriotism of the young to their country could be aroused. History was useful also in helping one understand the present and as a source of examples, especially moral examples; thus one can illustrate from actual events the general precept that "all they that take the sword shall perish with the sword." One especially valuable type of history was the study of church history. It is, however, an odd feature of education during this period that no mathematics of any kind was taught below the university, with the result that college students had to learn the four fundamental operations now taught in the second and third grades.

In general, the curriculum was narrowly linguistic. The idea was to cover a small area of subject matter, but to cover it thoroughly. The motto was: *Non multa, sed multum* (Not many different things, but much of one thing). Almost the whole curriculum was based upon memory and repetition of grammatical forms, foreign words, and classical phrases. By the end of the Reformation period Melanchthon and his students had succeeded in giving to the classics the position they held till recently in Continental schools, where they

[36] Luther had his own simple definition of rhetoric. Thus "Give me something to drink" was not rhetorical but "Give me from the cellar of the delightful juice that stands with a beady foam and makes people happy" decidedly was!

were regarded for three centuries as the ideal means for the education of youth.

A famous school of a narrowly humanistic type was established in 1537 in Strasbourg* by a teacher named Johannes Sturm.* In this school the pupils spoke not only Latin, but the Latin of Cicero. Sturm's course of study covered ten years, taking the child from the age of seven to some age between sixteen and twenty, depending upon how fast he progressed—and assuming that he was able to graduate at all. The sole concession to the spoken language of the people was the teaching in the first year of the catechism in German. In the fourth and fifth year the pupils had a little instruction in music, in the ninth and tenth some work in logic and mathematics, and in the tenth a bit of astronomy. Otherwise, the pupils studied nothing but Greek, Latin, rhetoric, declamation, prose, and poetry, composition in both languages, drama, and literature. The curriculum for the sixth year, to be studied by twelve and thirteen-year-old boys, consisted of (1) Latin vocabulary, (2) meter, (3) mythology, (4) Cicero's *Orations,* (5) Virgil's *Aeneid,* (6) writing of Latin verse, (7) eloquence and style in Latin, (8) Epistles* of Paul* in Greek, (9) review of Greek and Latin grammars. With such a heavy load in all grades, one does not wonder that an educated man was held in high reverence. The stated aims of Sturm's school were three: piety, knowledge and eloquence. In spite of its difficult curriculum, the school was immensely popular, and there were sometimes a thousand pupils in attendance at once. The school did not last long, but it has its place in the history of education because it provided both the name and the model for the later German Gymnasium—the typical secondary school, in which the curriculum was largely linguistic.

Both Melanchthon and Erasmus may be included in the group of men called "humanistic realists." Another writer of the same generation, Rabelais,* belonged also in the same group, as did the great English poet and writer, John Milton,* over a century later. All these men wanted to use the writings of Greece and Rome as source materials for ideas, not as exercises for training in correct Latin phraseology, whether written or spoken. Drill in language was to them only a means to an end. A pupil should get from the classics an assortment of ideas in history, geography, politics, morals, and science. The "real" thing was the content, not the form. Many leaders in educational thought from the Renaissance to the end of the seventeenth century thus tried to give reality to the study of classics, but most of the schoolteachers during these centuries did not have a sufficiently broad education to put such ideas into effect.

Many of the humanistic schools that began so auspiciously soon became extremely narrow, and limited their main efforts to the formal study of Cicero's writings. The teachers required that pupils use only the phraseology of Cicero for both speaking and writing. This new educational formalism was as narrow and cramping as the older formalism of scholasticism; it differed merely in resting upon linguistic rather than dialectic studies. In fact, in some schools, Cicero was simply substituted for Aristotle without perceptible change in the spirit of slavish imitation. This concentrated linguistic education, which first appeared in the sixteenth century, lingered on until the middle of the nineteenth, gradually losing its original vitality and becoming as profitless as scholasticism had once been.

4. The University Some of the German universities were already in existence before the Reformation, but many more were founded during this period. All were soon reorganized to fall in with the new plans for higher education. These universities differed in certain important respects from the accepted model of earlier centuries. First, perhaps, was the complete abandoning of the scholastic method. When the period of the Reformation began, scholasticism had not only permeated theology but had spread to all the subjects of the university. Thus instead of reading Latin classics, students argued about abstract grammatical principles; instead of observing natural phenomena students argued, on purely logical grounds, about what these phenomena must be and what they meant. This state of affairs infuriated Luther, Erasmus, and Melanchthon about equally, and each after his own fashion tried to improve matters. Luther made open and violent attacks upon a theology based not upon the Bible but upon scholastic logic. In one of his milder moments he wrote: "Our dear theologians have saved themselves trouble and work; they let the Bible rest quietly and just read their silly sentences.*" Erasmus also took up his pen and produced some excellent satire at the schoolmen's expense. A few excerpts appear below:

They [the schoolmen] will cut asunder the toughest argument with as much ease as Alexander did the Gordian* knot; they will thunder out so many rattling terms as shall fright an adversary into conviction. They are exquisitely dexterous in unfolding the most intricate mysteries; they will tell you to a tittle all the successive proceedings of Omnipotence in the creation of the universe; they will explain the precise manner of original sin being derived from our first parents. They will satisfy you in what manner, by what degree, and in how long a time, our Saviour was conceived in the Virgin's womb, and demonstrate in the consecrated wafer how accidents may subsist without a subject. Nay, these are accounted trivial, easy questions; they have yet far greater difficulties, which they notwithstanding solve with as much expedition as the former.

As namely, whether supernatural generation requires any instant of time for its acting? Whether Christ, as a son bears a double specifically distinct relation to God the Father, and his virgin mother? Whether this proposition is possible to be true, that the first person of the Trinity hated the second? Whether God, who took our nature upon him in the form of a man, could as well have become a woman, a devil, a beast, an herb, or a stone? And were it so possible that the Godhead had appeared in any shape of an inanimate substance, how he should then have preached his gospel? Or how have been nailed to the cross? Whether if St. Peter had celebrated the eucharist* at the same time our Saviour was hanging on the cross, the consecrated bread would have been transsubstantiated into the same body that remained on the tree? Whether in Christ's corporal presence in the sacramental wafer, his humanity be not abstracted from his Godhead? Whether after the resurrection we shall carnally eat and drink as we do in this life? [37]

I heard at another time a grave divine, of fourscore years of age at least . . . [who took it] upon him to treat the mysterious name, JESUS, and did subtly pretend that in the very letters was contained all that could be said of it. For first, its being declined only with three cases, did expressly point out the trinity of persons; then that the nominative ended in S, the accusative in M, and the ablative in U, did imply some unspeakable mystery, viz., that in words of those initial letters Christ was the *summus,* or beginning, the *medius,* or middle, and the *ultimus,* or the end of all things. There was yet a more abstruse riddle to be explained, which was by dividing the word JESUS into two parts, and separating the S in the middle from the two extreme syllables, making a kind of pentameter, the word consisting of five letters. And this intermedial S being in the Hebrew alphabet called sin, which in the English language signifies what the Latin term *peccatum,* was urged to imply that the holy Jesus should purify us from all sin and wickedness.[38]

Melanchthon was unable to see anything funny about scholasticism. He hated it as being wicked, because it led to bad thinking. To him all human errors were moral errors and nothing to laugh at. When Melanchthon hated something he could be as full of invective as Erasmus, although his forms of expression were more polite. Borrowing a phrase from another reformer,[39] he proclaimed the German universities to be the *Synagogues of Satin,* the scholastics themselves as *word-slingers* and *hot-air artists;* their theology he declared to be nothing but an "*agrandissement* of trivialities patched together out of Aristotle's philosophy and Law's silliness." Their sentences he called a "forest of countless opinions." And the whole thing he condemned as having nothing whatever to do with Christianity.

The reforms instituted by Melanchthon and Luther required a radical change in the nature and materials of instruction at the university level. There were to be no more sentences, no studying of Thomas Aquinas, and no read-

[37] D. Erasmus, *In Praise of Folly,* Hamilton, Addams and Company, 1887, pp. 131–132.
[38] *Ibid.,* p. 153.
[39] Wyclif.*

ing of any church father except a little from Augustine. All work in theology was to be based directly upon the Bible in its original Greek and Hebrew versions. The scholastic method of approach was to be driven out from all subjects especially from languages, and the humanistic approach substituted. The changes thus far were all for the best. One other improvement, however, did not always have desirable results. The universities, like the lower schools, were closely connected with the reformed church. In fact, their chief business was to train people for service to religion in one capacity or another. Because of this connection all teachers had to take an oath of allegiance to the Lutheran Church. Moreover, since the universities were dependent upon the support of the German princes for their existence, the question of just what teachers could or could not teach was to some extent determined by the local prince's ideas and prejudices. Professors were hence more or less hemmed in by pressure from both church and state. The medieval universities had allowed their teachers a far higher degree of freedom; both faculty and students ruled themselves and were rarely molested by church authorities. To be sure, the joining of church and school in the Reformation was not always as cramping as it might have been, although in specific instances it was undoubtedly severe. The situation has persisted into the present day. In some church schools academic freedom flourishes, but in others it does not. Whenever school and church are joined there is always possibility that religious beliefs, being essentially conservative, will throttle the right and desire of a teacher to pursue his investigations to their true conclusions.

In the middle of the sixteenth century the University of Wittenberg had an arts faculty[40] composed in the following way: There was one professor for Greek, one for Hebrew, two for Latin, one for dialectic, and two for rhetoric. There was also one man who gave a review of Latin grammar. One professor taught arithmetic and another geometry. The remaining two taught physics and botany, both according to Aristotle and without experiments or laboratories. Of these twelve teachers, eight were concerned with linguistic subjects. Because of the intense study of language in the lower schools the students arrived at the university without any mathematics whatever, except such items as they might have picked up by experience in handling money. In addition to knowing practically nothing of the subject, the students were terribly prejudiced against it and certain that they could not learn it. In no field did Melanchthon have to work any harder to get the interest of his students. He pointed out to them how useful arithmetic was in their daily lives, in the sciences, in the various trades, and for building and measuring. He assured

[40] The colleges of theology, law, and medicine had their own faculties that are not included here.

them that addition and subtraction were so easy as to be almost self-evident, although he had to admit that multiplication and division were harder. He tried to convince them that all they needed was good teaching, and they would find great joy in arithmetic. In the end, however, he had to concede that most students had practically no talent in mathematics and could hardly be taught even the fundamentals. Many students are still fearful of subjects that involve numbers.

The methods used in the new universities consisted of lecturing, reading and discussion, disputation, and declamation. The lectures and recitations probably differed little from what the student of today can observe directly in his own classrooms, so there seems little point in describing them, but the other two do not exist as general methods any longer. Melanchthon was quite emphatic about the use of disputations, or formal debates upon a previously announced topic. He wrote, "A school without disputation is of no importance and does not deserve to be called an academy." [41] The debate had already been thoroughly exploited as a method by the scholastics, but the disputations Melanchthon had in mind were to be safeguarded from becoming involved in endless arguments over nothing. The topics were to be such as would be useful in daily life. The head of the university faculty, the dean, was to approve the selection of topics. These could be drawn from problems of the day, from history, or from the classics. In any case they were to be sensible. Each member of the faculty had to take his turn in debating. The students who participated were, in some instances at least, paid. Thus the student who stated the thesis and defended it got two gulden;* his opponent got only one, and each student who contributed a point to either side got five groschen.*[42] The disputations were public and were often held before the local prince as a form of entertainment. The declamation consisted mainly of reciting selected pages in the original from the classics. This form of exercise was common in all humanistic schools and has already been mentioned in the description of Vittorino's school in Mantua. It survived for a number of centuries and could still be found as late as 1910 under the disguise of "elocution."

Although it was the purpose of the Reformation leaders to educate everyone, they realized that there must be a selection of students between each two successive levels of the school system. For university work the selection was especially rigid. Even so, however, the elimination after entrance to the university was somewhat higher than it is today. It is estimated that only about one fourth[43] of the entering students survived to reach the A.B. The course of

[41] *C.R.*, III, 189.
[42] *C.R.*, III, 188; X, 914.
[43] F. Paulsen, *Geschichte des gelehrten Unterrichts auf den deutschen Schulen und Universitäten vom Ausgang des Mittelalters bis zur Gegenwart*, Veit, 1885 (811 pp.), p. 18.

study required many years for its completion, and students showed the same lamentable tendency they do now to cut corners whenever they could, and to take their courses in whatever order was convenient, instead of proceeding logically. Students were supposed to have their A.B. before entering the advanced colleges of medicine, law, or theology, but many of them began their specialized work without the general foundation provided by the arts courses. They managed, in the inimitable fashion of students the world over, to squirm out of examinations that they should have taken, to avoid prerequisites, and to emerge from the university without a balanced training. These complaints in the sixteenth century go to show that no matter how tidy a plan looks on paper, an ingenious student can find a way to keep it from working as it is supposed to.

The affiliation between church and university does not seem to have depressed the spirits of the students to any marked degree. Melanchthon in his anxious and gloomy way stormed at various times against the universities as being swamps of iniquity, in which were bred the sins of hatred, jealousy, pride, and intolerable conceit. He inveighed against the common habit of letting young boys live in a university town and not in dormitories where they could be supervised. Unfortunately the dormitory system of the Middle Ages had fallen into decay, and the students lived wherever they could hire a room.

Melanchthon was also disturbed about the false ideas of freedom that the lads either brought with them or got from older students. In evaluating his complaints, one has to take Melanchthon's own seriousness of mind and strong tendency to worry into consideration, and one has also to deduct something for sheer youthful deviltry, but even so the rules that were in force suggest a degree of license and violence much beyond the modern norm. Thus there were punishments of varying severity for getting into debt, for scorning religious teaching, for patronizing magicians or other exponents of the black arts,* for swearing, for leaving the university without permission, for missing church, for stealing, for damaging property, for rooting up gardens, for breaking in doors, and for carrying weapons. On the last point the directions were explicit. The students were forbidden any "weapon, be it a sword, a knife, a cutlass, a dagger, a sling-shot, a throwing stick, a hatchet, a flail, a hammer, a rifle, or whatever it may be called, that can be used for bodily insult or injury." One can only deduce that students arrived at the university armed to the teeth! In winter, students must be out of the local bars at 9 P.M. and in summer at 10 P.M. On the positive side there are records of aid to students in making a schedule, in planning their work so as to get adequate time for eating and sleeping, and in helping them read the Bible for themselves.

5. The Profession of Teaching Both Luther and Melanchthon worked long and earnestly to raise the profession of teaching from the disrepute into which it had fallen. Melanchthon gives a most melancholy picture of the average teacher's life and work. He complains about the endless task of training children to speak Latin; unless the teacher was very severe, the youngsters just *would* mumble and swallow the endings! He wrote that it was easier to teach a camel to dance or an ass to play the harp than a child to speak good Latin.[44] As soon as pupils began to write, there was the task of correcting papers, on which the same errors were made with nauseous repetition. The pupils hated their teachers, and in spite of the teachers' best efforts, learned little and soon forgot what tag-ends of knowledge they had acquired, whereat the parents blamed the teacher. Since teachers were overworked and underpaid, they soon became exhausted and resorted to disciplinary methods so severe as to alarm even a reformer. Luther testified that during a single forenoon in school he was flogged fifteen times[45] and wrote: "Many unskilled people spoil the fine genius of youth with their noise, disturbances, antics, and beatings." [46] Under such circumstances one can understand that the profession of teaching did not command respect. It does not, however, appear to have crossed anyone's mind that the curriculum was inappropriate to childish abilities. The organization of schoolwork from the pupil's point of view is a wholly modern idea. Up until the last fifty years the matter to be learned was organized logically from an adult angle, and the children could take it with a beating or without.

Melanchthon's ideal for the teacher presents a different picture altogether. He conceived teaching as the best possible life, better by far than the cloistered life of the monk. The *vita scholastica* was no Slough of Despond* but a stirring battleground, and the teacher was a brave fighter who fought to preserve truth and justice. To the reformers generally there was no one more worthy of admiration than a good teacher. Because of the association between church and school, the work of the teacher took on an emotional, mystical significance. The teacher was a man with a mission in life. A tinge of this sense of dedication still lingers on in the minds of those who look upon teaching as a profession and not as a job.

It was quite evident that teaching would not improve much until the teacher was paid a living wage. The table below gives three columns of facts about the wages common at the time. In the first column are listed the annual salaries of twenty-two professors at one university; in the second are Melanchthon's salaries at various times; and in the last are the yearly wages of cer-

[44] *C.R.*, XI, 122.
[45] J. Köstlin, *Life of Martin Luther,* Charles Scribner's Sons, 1883, I, 33.
[46] Martin Luther, *Tischreden,* IV, 130, 542.

tain officials and employees of the local government. The median salary of the twenty-two professors was 117 gulden, and the highest was 200. The average was appreciably below the amount paid the barkeeper, and the top salary did not come up to that of a court secretary. Melanchthon eventually received, partly because Luther insisted upon it, the unheard-of amount of 400 gulden, but even after twenty-five years of active service his income did not overtake that of the rent collector. One point that Melanchthon always made in demanding higher salaries for teachers was the necessity they were under to help poor but worthy students. This point came home with considerable force after

TABLE 6: COMPARATIVE SALARIES OF PROFESSORS AND GOVERNMENT OFFICIALS DURING MELANCHTHON'S LIFETIME[a]

Professors' Salaries	Melanchthon's Salaries (Dates)	Governmental Officials and Employees
3 professors of theology, each 200 gulden	1518: 100 gulden	
1 professor of theology, 60 gulden		
1 professor of law, 200 gulden	1524: 200 gulden	1 Councilor 1190 gulden
1 professor of law, 180 gulden		1 Councilor 771 gulden
1 professor of law, 140 gulden	1536: 300 gulden	1 Rent Collector 640 gulden
1 professor of law, 100 gulden		1 Councilor 639 gulden
1 professor of medicine, 150 gulden	1541: 400 gulden	Court Marshal 513 gulden
1 professor of medicine, 130 gulden		1 Secretary 365 gulden
1 professor of medicine, 80 gulden		
1 professor of Greek, 100 gulden		1 Barkeeper 156 gulden
1 professor of Hebrew, 100 gulden		
9 professors in the arts college, each 80 gulden		1 Wine-master 146 gulden

[a] Based on material in Hartfelder, *op. cit.*, pp. 485–486.

Melanchthon's death, when it was found that he had no money left, in spite of his comparatively large salary, because he had given it all away to help students.

The schools of the Reformation, regardless of their level, were a blend of the old and the new. They kept the medieval organization of subject matter, but in the actual content of their courses they were thoroughly humanistic. The two most important new elements were the responsibility of secular authorities for the maintenance of schools and the demand for universal schooling. It can be seen that the period of the Reformation did a great deal to change medieval into modern education.

READING REFERENCES

A. General Histories of the Period

Ergang, *Europe from the Renaissance to Waterloo,* chaps. 6, 7.
Garrett, M. B., *European History,* 1500–1815, American Book Company, 1940 (715 pp.), chaps. 7, 8.
Hayes, *Political and Cultural History of Modern Europe,* Vol. I, chap. 4.
Robinson, *Introduction to the History of Western Europe,* chaps. 23–26.
Schevill, *A History of Europe from the Reformation to the Present Time,* chaps. 4, 5.
Stearns, *Pageant of History,* part 1, chap. 8.

B. Other Texts in the History of Education

Boyd, *History of Western Education,* chap. 7.
Cole, *History of Educational Thought,* chaps. 2–4, pp. 185–196.
Cubberley, *History of Education,* chaps. 12, 13.
Eby, F., and C. F. Arrowood, *The Development of Modern Education,* Prentice-Hall, Inc., 1934 (922 pp.), chaps. 3–5.
Graves, *A Student's History of Education,* chap. 8.
Marique, *History of Christian Education,* Vol. II, chaps. 4, 5.
McCormick, *History of Education,* pp. 188–194.
Monroe, *A Textbook in the History of Education,* pp. 401–415.
Reisner, *Historical Foundations of Modern Education,* chaps. 15, 16.
Ulich, *History of Educational Thought,* pp. 108–148.

C. Secondary Sources

Barnard, H., "Life and Educational Services of Philip Melanchthon," *American Journal of Education* (1859), 4:741–764.
Eby, F., *Early Protestant Educators,* McGraw-Hill Book Company, 1931 (312 pp.), pp. 177–188.
Magevney, E., *The Reformation and Education (1520–1648),* Catholic Library Association, 1903, 56 pp.
Painter, *Great Pedagogical Essays,* chap. 12.

Richard, *Philipp Melanchthon, The Protestant Preceptor of Germany,* chaps. 2–8, 11–13, 16, 26, 31.

Russell, J. E., *German Higher Education,* Longmans, Green and Co., 1910 (489 pp.), chaps. 1, 2.

Woodward, *Studies in Education during the Age of the Renaissance,* chaps. 6, 11.

D. Translation of Primary Source

Any translation of the Visitation Articles, §18.

CHAPTER X

TWO ENGLISH SCHOOLMASTERS AND THE SCHOOLS OF THE ENGLISH REFORMATION

The last two chapters have dealt with education in Italy and in Germany during the early decades of the Renaissance and the Reformation. In the present chapter the scene shifts to England. The Renaissance began in Italy, spread to France, then moved north to the Low Countries* and Germany, and finally reached England in the sixteenth century, although it did not come into its full flowering until the beginning of the seventeenth. As in other northern countries, the Renaissance fused with the Reformation, both movements together having a marked effect upon the schools of the period.

In contrast to developments elsewhere, in England the Reformation preceded the Renaissance. When the new learning reached England from the Lowlands, being introduced at Oxford by Erasmus, the German Reformation was already in progress. News of its success coincided with a strong desire of the English kings to separate their country, for reasons of their own, from the Catholic Church and from papal supervision and interference in local English affairs. Since Luther had already demonstrated the possibility of withdrawal, the reigning English monarch, Henry VIII,* also withdrew from the Roman Church, set up his own form of worship, the Church of England, which is a sort of hybrid among religious denominations. It is Protestant in the sense that it is independent of Rome, but it has retained many of the Catholic forms and beliefs. From the moment of its birth it has been the official state religion of England, and the religion of most of its rulers. The break with Rome and the pope affected many phases of English life, since it led to the confiscation of land held by the Catholic Church, to the closing of most schools—because they were in cathedrals or monasteries—to the discharge of teachers, and to the diversion of royal favors from Catholic to Protestant individuals and families. The son of Henry VIII, Edward VI,* was a Protestant, and during his brief reign Catholics were persecuted. Henry's oldest daughter, Mary,* was passionately Catholic; under her a counter reformation of such violence developed that she has come down in history as Bloody Mary. The second daughter, Elizabeth,* was more interested in England than she was in religion, and she brought the controversy to a stable and moderately tolerant solution. With the air cleared of strife and persecution, the English Renaissance blossomed.

Until the English Renaissance at the end of the sixteenth century, England had produced only one writer of enduring fame—Chaucer.* Some of the world's most famous men lived and wrote in the days of Elizabeth—Francis Bacon,* Richard Hakluyt,* Edmund Spenser,* Philip Sidney,* Christopher Marlowe,* the incomparable Shakespeare,* Ben Jonson, and a dozen or more lesser lights who might have become more famous had they lived in a less brilliant age. The literature produced by these men is alive and vigorous today. Not even repeated performances of Shakespeare's plays by sweet girl graduates, country bumpkins, high school children, or city sophisticates have dimmed the splendor of his work. Only the Bible and Shakespeare could be as mangled by lesser minds as both have been, and still survive. No such literary outpouring in a single short period had taken place since the fifth and fourth centuries before Christ, when the great writers of ancient Greece were producing their immortal works, nor has there been another comparable literary flowering. The sudden development of art during the Italian Renaissance was a similar phenomenon in another field. Thus far, no satisfactory explanation has been given for these periods of extraordinary intellectual, literary, and artistic activity.

Taken as a whole, Elizabeth's long reign was characterized by peace at home, by the fairly peaceful and permanent establishment of Protestantism, and by an extraordinary output of literature.

Roger Ascham, the first teacher to be described in this chapter, moved in and out of the courts of four monarchs: Henry VIII, Edward VI, Mary, and Elizabeth. He took part in the earlier manifestations of the Renaissance and was caught up in the excitement of the Reformation. The second teacher, Richard Mulcaster, was a contemporary. From Queen Elizabeth both men received pensions. They were part of the stirring life of Elizabethan England.

These two men, both important in the history of English education, represent two quite different trends, both of which have continued in England to the present day. Ascham was the tutor of Queen Elizabeth, Lady Jane Grey,* and other members of noble families. He was therefore an excellent representative of the aristocratic educational tradition in England. Mulcaster, on the other hand, was interested primarily in public education. Of the two, Ascham was more the humanist and Mulcaster more the reformer. Both were somewhat younger than Melanchthon, but they belonged to the same cultural generation. These two men made their contributions to education, each carrying on one or more already familiar concepts to a higher level of development.

A. ASCHAM: HIS LIFE AND WORK

1. Ascham's Early Life Roger Ascham[1] was born in 1515 in a small town in Yorkshire,* early in Henry VIII's reign and two years before Martin Luther nailed his theses* on the church door. At an early age he was practically adopted by a wealthy gentleman, who first kept him at home, where he shared a tutor with his patron's sons, and then sent him to Cambridge University. Ascham arrived in Cambridge just in time to be influenced by the English Renaissance and the wave of Protestantism that was filling all northern nations with controversy. The young man had already shown a great talent for languages, and at the university he centered his attention upon the study of Greek. While still a student he conceived the idea of teaching other young men the language as a means of mastering it himself. Ascham entered the university at the age of fifteen, received his baccalaureate at eighteen, and was almost immediately elected a fellow* of the college. He was popular with the students, who flocked to his room to have him explain Greek authors to them. This situation continued for three years, during which Ascham took his master's degree.

In addition to his excellence as a classical scholar Ascham developed another accomplishment which seems at the present to be quite unimportant but was at that period a skill for which there was a real need—a superior type and style of penmanship. He not merely wrote clearly and neatly, but he also embellished his pages with illuminations of various sorts. He was in great demand, therefore, as a writer of formal letters. Later he became teacher in penmanship to all of Henry VIII's children, and was eventually secretary for two of them. Penmanship was by no means the easy technique it has now become; today a pupil can use either a pencil that has been sharpened mechanically or a fountain pen, he can use paper that is already ruled, and he needs only to make his script passably legible. The directions below give one an idea of what mere writing once involved:

> There must be special care, that every one who is to write, have all necessaries belonging thereunto; as to pen, ink, paper, ruler, plummet, ruling pen, pen-knife, etc.
>
> The like care must be, that their ink be thin, black, clear; which will not

[1] This section on Ascham is based upon the following references in addition to his own writings: C. Benndorf, *Die Englische Pädagogik im Sechzehnten Jahrhundert,* Braümüller, 1905, 84 pp.; A. Katterfeld, *Roger Ascham, sein Leben und seine Werke,* Trübner, 1879, 348 pp.; R. H. Quick, *Essays on Educational Reformers,* E. L. Kellogg and Company (new ed., 335 pp.), pp. 23–27; F. Watson, *Notes on Some Early English Writers in Education,* U. S. Government Printing Office, 1905, 190 pp.; G. Weidemann, *Roger Ascham als Pädagog,* G. Schade, 1900, 77 pp.

run abroad nor blot; their paper good; that is, such as is white, smooth, and which will bear ink, and also that it be made in a book. Their writing books would be kept fair, straight ruled, and each to have a blotting paper to keep their books from soiling, or marring under their hands.

Cause every one of them to make his own pen, otherwise the making and mending of pens will be a very great hindrance, both to the masters and to the scholars. Besides that, when they are away from their masters they will write naught, because they know not how to make their pens themselves.

The best manner of making the pen is thus:

a. Choose the quill of the best and strongest of the wing, which is somewhat harder, and will cleave.

b. Make it clean with the back of the pen-knife.

c. Cleave it straight up the back; first with a cleft made with your pen-knife, after with another quill put into it, rive it further by little and little, till you see the cleft to be very clean . . . [then make] the nib and cleft both about one length, somewhat above a barley-corn breadth, and small, so as it may let down the ink, and write clean. Cut the nib first slant downwards to make it thin, and after straight over thwart. Make both sides of equal bigness, unless you be cunning to cut that side, which lieth upon the long finger, thinner and shorter; yet so little, as the difference can hardly be discerned. But both of equal length is accounted the surest.[2]

It is not surprising that a man who could write not only neatly but elegantly under such difficulties should be highly prized.

Immediately after receiving his degree, Ascham appears to have had two or three years of illness and financial difficulties somewhat relieved by a lectureship in mathematics for one year and a small pension from a certain bishop. When he was twenty-five years old, he was appointed professor of Greek at Cambridge, and five years later he was given a small pension by Henry VIII in recognition of a book, dedicated to the king, on the subject of archery, which was at that time a means of national defense, not a sport. A year later he became the public orator of the University of Cambridge and in this capacity wrote all the official letters. Ascham now had more to live on than had most scholars of his time, but aside from his university salary his money came from uncertain sources. When Henry VIII died, the pension stopped, although it was renewed by Edward VI, and even increased by Mary.

Ascham's connection with court life began when he was asked to come to London for the purpose of tutoring Princess Elizabeth. He remained only a year and then left with such abruptness as to suggest some kind of serious difficulty, although nothing is actually known about his reasons. Back he went to Cambridge, where he found the university in great turmoil over religious

[2] J. Brinsley, *Ludus Literarius, or the Grammar School* (edited by E. R. Campagnac), The University Press of Liverpool, 1917 (363 pp.), pp. 29–30. Used by permission of the publisher.

questions. The Protestant Reformation had already reached its international stage, many of its typical ideas were being discussed in England, and the English king was in the midst of his conflict with the pope. Some of Ascham's letters tell of certain difficulties within the college and of antagonisms among the faculty members, sometimes over religious questions and sometimes over matters of appointment. One short excerpt appears below:

> Certain members of the University took notice of our proceedings in their sermons, and by their means . . . the vice-chancellor, was persuaded to forbid by letter our carrying on the disputation any further. We obeyed, as in duty bound, but we were not content that the right of disputing should be taken from us, whilst the others were allowed the right of saying in their sermons anything they pleased. We heard that the Archbishop of Canterbury was unfavourable to us; nor is this to be wondered at, most discreet sire, for our adversaries (I am compelled unwillingly to use so harsh a name.) used the most tragical language in reporting to him the affair. Whether in doing this they most showed their malice or their ignorance may well be doubted.[3]

The full impact of religious hatred had not yet reached England, but the seeds of war and dissension were already there.

2. *Ascham as Secretary* In the year 1550 Ascham left his university career and entered into public life by becoming secretary to the ambassador from King Edward VI to Charles V,* Emperor of the Holy Roman Empire during Luther's long fight against the Catholic Church. The ambassador made Augsburg his headquarters, from which Ascham seems to have gone here and there in Germany and to have met most of the famous people of the period. He describes vividly and in detail many of the German princes who were powerful forces in the progress of the German Reformation. The trip through Germany lasted for three years but was terminated abruptly with the death of Edward VI. Ascham was again without royal support and retired to Cambridge, where he still held his position as professor and public orator. However, the year at court and the three years abroad had spoiled Ascham for the life academic. He fretted for a while in Cambridge, importuning his friends to help him to another court position. Within a year he had succeeded in becoming secretary to Queen Mary, who was persuaded to increase his pension from ten to twenty pounds by a somewhat shady procedure related by Ascham himself:

> I told an official in the Queen's household that my patent* and living* for my Book of Shooting was lost. "Well," said he, "cause it to be written again, and I will do what I can." I did so; and here I will open to Your Majesty a pretty sublety in doing happily a good turn to myself, whereat per-

[3] J. A. Giles, *The Whole Works of Roger Ascham,* J. A. Smith & Company, Ltd., 1864–1865 (4 vols.), I, 156.

chance your Majesty will smile; for surely I have laughed at it twenty times myself. . . . I caused the same form of the patent to be written out, but I willed a vacant place to be left for the sum. I brought it so written to the bishop; he asked me why the old sum was not put in. "Sir," quoth I, "the fault is in the writer who hath done very ill beside, to leave the vacant place so great, for the old word *ten* will not half fill the room, and therefore surely, except it please your lordship to help to put in twenty pounds, that would both fill up the vacant place well now and also fill my purse the better hereafter, truly I shall be put to new charges in causing the patent to be written again." The bishop fell in a laughter, and forthwith went to Queen Mary and told what I had said, who, without any more speaking, before I had done her any service, of her own bountiful goodness made my patent twenty pounds by year during my life, for her and her successors.[4]

As a secretary to royalty, Ascham was in his element. It is related of him that in the first three days of his new employment he wrote, with no diminution of his customary elegance, forty-seven letters to princes and other personages, of whom the lowest in rank was a cardinal.* For nine years Ascham remained as a court favorite, although it is by no means clear how he managed to do so. Queen Mary was violently Catholic, but she countenanced the presence of Ascham, who was known to be Protestant. To be sure, he was cautious in what he said and wrote, he was very useful as a secretary, and he doubtless avoided religious topics. Still it is a tribute to his unusual abilities that he was a favorite at a Catholic court during a period of persecution. After Queen Mary died, Ascham became secretary to Queen Elizabeth, whom he had tutored some years before. His services as her secretary continued almost until his death at the age of fifty-three.

As noted earlier, Ascham was often ill. Just what kind of persistent fever he had is not known, but it is likely that he made his condition worse by constant worry over money and by the profound depressions into which he fell when he was disappointed. Throughout his life he had great difficulty in sleeping, and for the last few years of his life could do no work in the evening because of resulting insomnia. He seems to have precipitated his final illness characteristically by devoting long hours when he should have been sleeping to the composition of a poem that he intended to dedicate to the queen. This work so exhausted him that he took to his bed and never again left it. He died in 1568.

3. Ascham's Character Ascham was an odd combination of admirable and annoying traits. On the debit side he was vain, he constantly lived beyond his means, he flattered those in high positions, he pestered his acquaintances for aid in all sorts of situations, and he complained a good deal about his own

[4] *Ibid.*, p. 412.

misfortunes. These are characteristics of the courtier rather than of the scholar. On the credit side are his courtesy, his fanatic loyalty to his friends, his scholarship in the field of language, his adaptability, and his willingness to work long and hard. It is probable that his years at court emphasized his least likable traits.

Ascham was constantly writing letters, of which some three hundred are still in existence. About sixty of them were written for Queen Elizabeth in his capacity as her secretary. Most of these are on international matters and reveal little about Ascham except his general grace of style. The remaining letters, while being probably only a sampling of the total number he wrote during his life, reveal clearly what kind of person he was. It seems worth while to analyze the subject matter of these personal letters, especially since certain points keep recurring. There are only eight main topics, although many others naturally appear once or twice. These topics and the proportion that each contributes to the total are listed below:

TABLE 7: ANALYSIS OF ASCHAM'S LETTERS

(*The figures are percentages.*)

Topic	%	Group total
1. Request for favors (for patronage, presentation of gifts, recommendations, intercessions, or apologies)		
a) for himself	13	27
b) for others	14	
2. University business		
a) quarrels among members	5	24
b) quarrels with townspeople	5	
c) support of privileges	4	
d) intercession in Parliament	6	
e) other matters	4	
3. Thanks, congratulations, compliments, letters of introduction	12	41
4. Professional matters (borrowing or returning books, literary topics, professorships)	10	
5. Money	10	
6. Complaints of various kinds (unfair treatment, lack of friends, changes in student abilities, coldness of friends)	9	
7. Illness	5	8
8. Family (parents, wife, children)	3	

The matters about which Ascham wrote indicate that he was not one of the world's strong men. His most common theme is a request that some acquaintance help either himself or one of his protégés. The majority of the letters written on behalf of the university are of the same type: requests for aid against the townspeople, against loss of privilege, against taxation, against demands for military service. These two groups of letters make up 50 per cent of the total. Half of the remaining ones contain complaints about money, unfairness, illness, and so forth. It is only because the collection of letters now extant includes several to the German schoolmaster Johannes Sturm that the summary of topics is not even less imposing; Sturm was not in a position to give favors, and to him Ascham wrote mainly about his literary interests. The one extant letter that he wrote his wife is charming, simple, and entirely without complaints. Most of the other letters are addressed to lords, bishops, earls, dukes, princesses, queens, and kings. From these exalted personages Ascham wanted favors, and the graceful wording of his communications does not conceal their begging nature. He cadged for benefits of various kinds for his friends and himself, he complained when he did not get them, and he was

Fig. 40. Roger Ascham. From S. G. Williams, *History of Medieval Education,* p. 165. Courtesy of Bardeen's, Inc., publishers.

constantly running out of money. A really great man either rises above his poverty or else adjusts himself to it and forgets about it. To be sure, Ascham asked for favors for his friends and his students quite as often as for himself. He obviously believed implicitly in the power of just sheer "pull" and did not hesitate to make use of it whenever he could.

Figure 40 presents a picture of Roger Ascham. His face reveals a rather self-indulgent, sensual,* clever aesthete, just such a person as is indicated by his letters.

4. Ascham's Educational Ideas During Queen Elizabeth's reign, Ascham wrote a treatise on education called the *Scholemaster.* This book was not published until after his death, presumably on account of his limited means, because in those days authors had to pay publishers for accepting a book. In this publication Ascham expressed a number of undoubtedly good ideas concerning education. He had something to say about the relation between teacher and pupil, the nature of children, the selection of those who can best become scholars, the teaching of grammar, the development of morals, the value of exercise, and the characteristics of good discipline. Most of what he says is distinctly modern in tone, even though the language is sometimes old-fashioned.

Like most great teachers, Ascham disapproved of corporal punishment. His attitude is expressed in the passage below:

> I have now wished twice or thrice this gentle nature to be in a schoolmaster. And that I have done so, neither by chance, nor without some reason. I will now declare at large, why in mine opinion love is better than fear, gentleness better than beating. . . . I do gladly agree with all good schoolmasters in these points; to have children brought to good perfitness [perfectness] in learning, to all honesty in manners, to have all faults rightly amended, to have every vice severely corrected; but for the order and way, that leadeth masters, some as I have seen, moe [more] as I have heard tell, be of so crooked a nature, as, when they meet with a hard-witted scholar, they rather break him than bow him, rather mar him than mend him. For when the schoolmaster is angry with some other matter, then will he soonest fall to beat his scholar; and though he himself should be punished for his folly, yet must he beat some scholar for his pleasure, though there be no cause for him to do so, nor yet fault in the scholar to deserve so. These, ye will say, be fond schoolmasters, and few they be that be found to be such. They be fond indeed, but surely over many such be found everywhere. But this will I say, that even the wisest of your great beaters, do as oft punish nature as they do correct faults.[5]

Ascham's whole tone in writing about children indicates a pleasant personal relationship between him and his pupils. In one place he writes:

> Let your scholar be never afraid to ask you any doubt, but use discreetly the best allurements ye can to encourage him to the same; lest his overmuch fearing of you drive him to seek some misorderly shift; as to seek to be helped by some other book, or to be prompted by some other scholar; and so go about to beguile you much and himself more.[6]

On the proper selection of children to become scholars Ascham had several suggestions. It must be remembered that he lived nearly three centuries before the appearance of psychology as a science. His characterizations seem,

[5] *Ibid.*, III, 96.
[6] *Ibid.*, p. 92.

therefore, somewhat naïve, but the experienced teacher can see fairly well what he meant. He separated children into those of "quick wit" and those of "hard wit." Such a dual classification is much too simple to fit the facts about individual differences, but it is a step in the right direction. The quick-witted child Ascham describes in the following words:

> Quick wits commonly be apt to take, unapt to keep; soon hot, and desirous of this and that; as cold, and soon weary of the same again; more quick to enter speedily, than able to pierce far; even like oversharp tools, whose edges be very soon turned. Such wits delight themselves in easy and pleasant studies, and never pass far forward in high and hard sciences. And therefore the quickest wits commonly may prove the best poets, but not the wisest orators; ready of tongue to speak boldly, not deep of judgment, either for good council or wise writing.[7]

In contrast, the hard-witted child is characterized in the following words:

> Contrariwise, a wit in youth that is not overdull, heavy, knotty, and lumpish; but hard, tough, and though somewhat staffish, such a wit, I say, if it be at the first well handled by the school-master, both for learning and whole course of living, proveth always the best. . . . Hard wits be hard to receive, but sure to keep; painful without weariness, heedful without wavering; constant without newfangleness; bearing heavy things, though not lightly, yet willingly; entering hard things, though not easily, yet deeply; and so come to that perfectness of learning in the end, that quick wits seem in hope, but do not indeed, or else very seldom, ever attain unto.
>
> A child that is still, silent, constant, and somewhat hard of wit, is either never chosen by the father to be made a scholar, or else, when he cometh to the school, he is smally regarded, little looked unto; he lacketh teaching, he lacketh encouraging, he lacketh all things, only he never lacketh beating, nor any word that may move him to hate learning, nor any deed that may drive him from learning, to any other kind of living.[8]

The difference that Ascham described is a real one among people; it is the difference between the student who is satisfied with a quick, superficial summary, learned in approximately the words used by someone else, and the student who thinks as he works, puzzles over what he reads, disagrees sometimes, and eventually makes the material an integral part of his own thought. The quick wit is easy to teach. For instance, he reads that a given event had six causes; and the next day in class he can enumerate the six in exactly the order in which he read about them. The hard wit does not rattle off the six and let it go at that; he produces perhaps four but not in the same order as in the book, forgets one, rejects one as being unconvincing, and adds a seventh

[7] *Ibid.*, p. 98.
[8] *Ibid.*, pp. 100–102.

of his own. Moreover, unless he has great ability he is not as fluent as the more quick-witted child, because the intellectual task he has performed is far more difficult.

Ascham goes on to characterize further the nature of the pupil who should be selected for advanced training. He describes seven definite traits: a good appearance, a good memory, a love of learning, a willingness to take pains, a desire to learn from others, an urge to ask questions, and a love of praise. Ascham describes these traits in his own delightful wording:

> (1) He that hath a body . . . not troubled, mangled, and halved, but sound, whole, full. . . . A tongue not stammering . . . but plain and ready to deliver the meaning of the mind; a voice not soft, weak, piping, womanish, but audible, strong, and manlike.
>
> (2) He that hath . . . memory well preserved by use . . . quick in receiving, sure in keeping, and ready in delivering forth again.
>
> (3) He that loves learning: for though a child have all the gifts of nature . . . and perfection of memory . . . yet if he have not a special love to learning, he shall never attain to much learning.
>
> (4) He that hath a lust to labour and will to take pains: for if a child have all the benefits of nature . . . yet if he be not of himself painful [painstaking] he shall never attain unto it.
>
> (5) He that is glad to hear and learn of another: for otherwise he shall . . . catch very little by his own toil, when he might gather quickly a good deal by another man's teaching.
>
> (6) He that is naturally bold to ask any question, desirous to search out any doubt; not ashamed of the meanest nor afraid to go to the greatest until he be perfectly taught and fully satisfied.
>
> (7) He that loveth to be praised for well doing, at his father's or master's hand. And thus . . . a good father, and a wise schoolmaster, should choose a child to make a scholar of, that hath by nature the foresaid perfect qualities.[9]

Ascham was by no means willing to overtax children by giving them too much schoolwork. Like most humanists, he believed thoroughly in physical exercise and diversion. He expresses his views in the following way:

> And I do not mean by all this my talk, that young gentlemen should always be poring on a book, and by using good studies should leese [loose] honest pleasure, and haunt no good pastime: I mean nothing less. For it is well known that I both like and love, and have always, and do yet still use all exercises and pastimes that be fit for my nature and ability: and beside natural disposition, in judgment also I was never either stoic* in doctrine or anabaptist* in religion, to mislike a merry, pleasant, and playful nature, if no outrage be committed against law, measure, and good order.

[9] *Ibid.*, condensed from pp. 106–111.

Therefore to ride comely, to run fair at the tilt or ring; to play at all weapons, to shoot fair in bow, or surely in gun; to vault lustily, to run, to leap, to wrestle, to swim, to dance comely, to sing, and play on instruments cunningly; to hawk, to hunt; to play at tennis, and all pastimes generally, which be joined with labour, used in open place, and on the day-light, containing either some fit exercise for war, or some pleasant pastime for peace, be not only comely and decent, but also very necessary for a courtly gentleman to use.[10]

All generations of teachers, especially all good teachers, are prone to bewail the attitudes and morals of their charges. Teachers are rarely satisfied and seem to think that the "good old days" must have been better, no matter what previous conditions were like. It is a human trait to be emotionally attached to the customs of one's early years and to believe that there was less evil in the world at that time, probably because one did not in one's childhood notice it. Ascham, like all good teachers, was deeply concerned with moral growth and education. It is therefore not surprising that he writes sometimes in a captious and critical vein or that he wants a return to the supposed virtues of former times.

But I marvel the less that these misorders be among some in the court; for commonly in the country also every where, innocency is gone, bashfulness is vanished; much presumption in youth, small authority in age; reverence is neglected, duties be confounded; and to be short, disobedience doth overflow the banks of good order almost in every place, almost in every degree of man.[11]

This last summer I was in a gentleman's house, where a young child, somewhat past four years old, could in no wise manage his tongue to say a little short grace; and yet he could roundly rap out so many ugly oaths, and those of the newest fashion, as some good man of fourscore year old hath never heard named before. And that which was most detestable of all, his father and mother would laugh at it. I much doubt what comfort another day this child shall bring unto them.[12]

In the restricted field of grammar Ascham devised a method that has long been regarded as the best for really mastering a language that is no longer spoken, but it is a method hardly worth using unless the student needs complete mastery, because it requires a great deal of time and effort. The average pupil of today who studies Latin or Greek can learn what he needs by techniques less time-consuming. For the occasional student who has a desire to learn Latin or Greek thoroughly, the method is excellent. The essentials of it are given in the quoted passage:

[10] *Ibid.*, pp. 138–140.
[11] *Ibid.*, p. 128.
[12] *Ibid.*, p. 131.

First let the master teach the child cheerfully and plainly, the cause and matter of the letter [being used as a model]; then let him construe it into English so oft as the child may easily carry away the understanding of it; lastly, parse* it over perfectly. This done thus, let the child, by-and-by, both construe and parse it over again; so that it may appear the child doubteth in nothing that his master taught him before. After this, the child must take a paper book, and sitting in some place where no man shall prompt him, by himself, let him translate into English his former lesson. Then, showing it to his master, let the master take from him his Latin book and pausing an hour at the least, then let the child translate his own English into Latin again in another paper book. When the child brings it, turned into Latin, the master must compare it with Tullie's book, [Tully*] sentence by sentence, and word by word; and where the child doth well, either in choosing or true placing of Tullie's words, let the master praise him and say, "Here do ye well." For I assure you, there is no such whetstone to sharpen a good wit, and encourage a will to learning, as is praise.

In these few lines I have wrapped up the most tedious part of grammar and also the ground of almost all the rules that are so busily taught by the master, and so hardly learned by the scholar in all common schools. . . .

For when the master shall compare Tullie's book with his scholar's translation, let the master at the first lead and teach his scholar to join the rules of his grammar-book with the examples of his present lesson, until the scholar, by himself, be able to fetch out of his grammar every rule for every present use.[13]

As can be seen, the pupil is to have two paper books, one for translation from Latin into English, the other for retranslation from English into Latin.

Finally, Ascham had, in spite of his facile writing of Latin letters, a real love for the English language. He wrote both of his masterpieces in it. His style is excellent, as the above excerpts show. In his devotion to English he is like his compatriot Mulcaster, to be described in the next section, but at that point the resemblance between them stops.

Ascham represents two trends in English education, the aristocratic and the humanistic. He assumes that children have tutors and that they will study Greek and Latin, especially the Latin of Cicero. Ascham's teaching experience was almost wholly tutorial, even in his university work, and his life was spent among aristocrats and royalty. His book gives good advice to teachers within the narrow limits to which the advice is applicable.

B. MULCASTER: HIS LIFE AND WORK

A second teacher of the English Renaissance was Richard Mulcaster, who achieved a reputation as a teacher during his lifetime but was not held in es-

[13] *Ibid.*, pp. 90–91.

teem as a writer, partly because his English had little grace or charm and partly because his ideas were far in advance of his period. With the passage of time, however, he has emerged as a practical and clear thinker in the field of education.

1. Mulcaster's Life and Character[14] Richard Mulcaster was born toward the end of Henry VIII's reign. He was more than fifteen years younger than Ascham. The exact date of his birth is unknown, and of his life only a few facts are recorded. He came of an old and distinguished, but not wealthy, family. As a child he presumably had a tutor, but it is known that at the age of sixteen he entered Eton. After graduating from Eton he entered the University of Cambridge, but remained there only a year, after which he moved to Oxford, where he graduated. He took his degree in four languages: Latin, Greek, Hebrew, and Arabic. Almost at once he began to teach. Five years after his graduation from college he was appointed as director of the Merchant-Taylors' School,[15] which had just been founded by the merchant-taylors' guild in London. Here he remained twenty years, although his salary and conditions of work would discourage a teacher of today. He taught from dawn to dusk every day except Sunday, and he was allowed only twenty free days a year. The governing board could dismiss him at any time without warning, but he had to give a year's notice if he wanted to resign. As headmaster he received the munificent sum of ten pounds a year, or not over fifty dollars in American money. During his years of service, Mulcaster had many pupils who later became famous, among them Edmund Spenser,* writer of the *Faerie Queen.* Presumably he was an excellent teacher, since he built up the enrollment of the school to three hundred pupils—fifty more than he was allowed to have. One of his many rows with the trustees of the school concerned this overlarge enrollment, which he was eventually forced to reduce.

There were sundry complaints about Mulcaster, who was obviously a peppery character, concerning his contempt for orders given him by the guild, his disrespectful attitude toward visitors at the school, and his over strict discipline. One incident told about him appears below:

Every morning Mulcaster was accustomed to explain the reading lesson with painful accuracy to his students. Thereupon he sat at his desk and indulged in his morning nap for precisely one hour (custom made him critical in apportioning it) but woe betide the scholar who also dozed off during this

[14] This section is based chiefly upon the following references: Benndorf, *Die Englische Pädagogik im Sechzehnten Jahrhundert;* Th. Klähr, *Leben und Werke Richard Mulcasters,* Bleyl und Kammerer, 1893, 59 pp.; J. Oliphant, *The Educational Writings of Richard Mulcaster,* Jackson, Sons & Co., Ltd., 1903, 245 pp.; R. H. Quick, *Positions of Richard Mulcaster,* Longmans, Green and Co., 1888, 309 pp.

[15] See p. 277 ff.

time. After awakening Mulcaster took to task each and every one; and Atropos* would have been more merciful than he, if he found a just cause for anger. The pleading of tender hearted mothers moved him as little as the request of indulgent fathers; on the contrary they increased his severity toward the guilty youngsters. In a word, he was *plagosus Orbilibus*;* though it may be truly said (and safely for one outside of his school) that others have taught as much learning with fewer lashes. Yet his sharpness was the better endured because impartial; and many excellent scholars were bred under him.[16]

After twenty years Mulcaster asked to have his salary raised but was refused. In an outburst of annoyance he resigned. Upon being reminded that he should be grateful for his opportunities and loyal to his employers he made the caustic but not altogether uncalled-for remark: *"Servus fidelis perpetuus asinus."* ("The faithful servant is an everlasting fool.") After his resignation he seems to have disappeared for about five years. He then returned to London as teacher in St. Paul's School. Here his salary was not sufficient for his needs, but he managed to persuade Queen Elizabeth to appoint him as rector in a small parish. He also trained his pupils to give plays before the queen. Like other educated men of his time, he found flattery of the ruling monarch necessary. Among his numerous verses—none of them distinguished and many of them awkward—in praise of Queen Elizabeth are the following two:

> Regia majestas, aetatis gloria nostrae
> Hanc in deliciis semper habere solet.[17]

and

> Nec contenta graves aliorum audire labores
> Ipsa etiam egregie voce manuque canit.[18]

Mulcaster remained as master of St. Paul's School for twelve years, during which time he received money for being a rector, although he was certainly not one, except in name. When he resigned from St. Paul's, he was a man of seventy-seven. He then went to the small village, where he was supposed to be the rector and actually worked at the job until his death three years later.

2. *Mulcaster's Ideas on Education* Mulcaster wrote two treatises, one called his *Positions* or fundamental concepts and the other *The First Part of*

[16] Thomas Fuller, *The History of the Worthies of England,* T. Tegg, 1840 (3 vols.), III, 308–309.

[17] These couplets are from George Ballard, *Memoirs of several Ladies of Great Britain, who have been celebrated for their writings, or skill in the learned languages, arts and sciences,* W. Jackson, Oxford, 1752 (472 pp.), XVII, 226.

Translation: Her royal majesty, the glory of our age, is accustomed always to regard this matter [the production of plays] with pleasure.

[18] *Translation:* Not content with listening to the serious work of others, she herself often sings excellently with voice and hand.

Elementarie, in which he set forth his ideas concerning the use and teaching of the English language. He evidently contemplated a second part of this book but never wrote it. Many of his ideas have a decidedly modern ring, as will shortly appear.

Like all good teachers, Mulcaster had an intuitive understanding of at least some phases of child psychology. He had grasped the principle of individual differences, had observed stages of mental growth among children, and had worked out the principle of readiness that is now so popular. The following passages indicate his ideas on these points:

Without making any complete analysis of the mental powers, I would point out some natural inclinations in the soul, which seem to crave the help of education and nurture, and by means of these may be cultivated to advantage. In the little young souls we find first a capacity to perceive what is taught to them, and to imitate those around them. That faculty of learning and following should be well employed by choosing the proper matter to be set before them, by carefully proceeding step by step in a reasonable order, by handling them warily so as to draw them on with encouragement. We find also in them a power of retention; therefore their memories should at once be furnished with the very best, seeing that it is a treasury, and never suffered to be idle, as it loses its power so soon. . . . We find in them further an ability to discern what is good and what is evil, so that they should forthwith be acquainted with what is best, by learning to obey authority, and dissuaded from the worst by the fear of disapproval. These three things, perception, memory, and judgment, ye will find peering out of the little young souls at a time when ye can see what is in them, but they cannot yet see it themselves. Now these natural capacities being once discerned, must as they arise be followed with diligence, increased by good method, and encouraged by sympathy, till they come to their fruition.[19]

In this a special and continual regard should be had to these four points in the child—his *memory,* his *delight,* his *capacity,* and his *advancement.*

As to his *memory,* I would provide that as he must practise it even from the first, so he may also practise it upon the best, both for pleasure in the course of learning, and for profit afterwards. As to his *delight,* which is no mean allurement to his learning well, I would be equally careful that the matter which he shall read may be so fit for his years and so plain to his intelligence, that when he is at school, he may desire to go forward in so interesting a study, and when he comes home, he may take great pleasure in telling his parents what pretty little things he finds in his book. . . . As to his *capacity,* I would so provide, that the matter which he shall learn may be so easy to understand, and the terms which I will use, so simple to follow, that both one and the other shall bring nothing but encouragement. . . . As to his *advancement,* I would be very particular that there may be such consideration and choice in syllables, words, and sentences . . . that there shall

[19] Oliphant, p. 35. This excerpt and subsequent ones from this reference are used by permission of the publishers, Jackson, Son & Co., Ltd.

be nothing wanting which may seem worth the wishing, to help fully either in spelling correctly, or reading easily.[20]

One of the first questions is at what age children should be sent to school, for they should neither be delayed too long, so that time is lost, nor hastened on too soon, at the risk of their health. The rule therefore must be given according to the strength of their bodies and the quickness of their wits jointly. What the age should be I cannot say, for ripeness in children does not always come at the same time. . . . If the child has a weak body, however bright his understanding may be, let him grow on the longer till his strength equals his intelligence. . . . Wherefore I could wish the brighter child to be less upon the spur, and either the longer kept from learning altogether, lest he suffer as the edge of an oversharp knife is turned, or at least be given very little, for fear of his eagerness leading to a surfeit.[21]

The brief excerpt below presents Mulcaster's ideas concerning the length of time a pupil should remain in elementary school:

When the child can read so readily and confidently that the length of his lessons gives him no trouble; when he can write so neatly and so fast that he finds no kind of exercise tedious; when his pen or pencil gives him only pleasure; when his music, both vocal and instrumental, is so far forward that a little voluntary practice may keep it up and even improve it; then the elementary course has lasted long enough.[22]

According to the above passages Mulcaster believed that children were all different from one another and had different growth rates. Because of these differences, progress through school should rest upon readiness and ability, not upon age.

The intimate dependence of education upon child nature was also clear to Mulcaster. Indeed, he emphasizes it over and over again:

The proof of a good Elementary Course is, that it should follow nature in the multitude of its gifts, and that it should proceed in teaching as she does in developing. . . . For the end of education and training is to help nature to her perfection in the complete development of all the various powers. This is what I mean by following nature: after marking with good judgment what are the natural tendencies and inclinations, to frame a scheme of education in consonance with these, and bring to perfection all those powers which nature bestows in frank abundance.[23]

Another fundamental principle in Mulcaster's writings was his firm conviction that education should be public and universal. What he wanted was

[20] *Ibid.*, pp. 35–36.
[21] *Ibid.*, pp. 11–12.
[22] *Ibid.*, pp. 103–104.
[23] *Ibid.*, condensed from pp. 45–47.

education for rich and poor, for boys and girls, for the aristocrat and the common man. A few excerpts show his modernity in this respect:

> How can education be private? It is an abuse of the name as well of the thing. This isolation, for a pretended advantage in education, of those who must afterwards pass on together, is very mischievous, as it allows every parent to follow out his own whims, relying on the privacy of his own house to be free from criticism, and on the subserviency of the teacher whom he may choose to suit his purposes. . . . In public schools such swerving from what is generally approved is impossible. The master is always in the public eye, what he teaches is known to all; the child is not alone, and he learns only what has been submitted to the judgment of the community. Whatever inconveniences may be inseparable from schools, still greater arise in private education.[24]
>
> And to prove that they [girls] ought to receive an education I find four special reasons, any one of which—therefore surely all together—may persuade their greatest adversary, much more than myself who am for them tooth and nail. Then first is the custom of the country, which allows them to learn. The second is the duty we owe, charging us in conscience not to leave them deficient. The third is their own aptness to learn, which God would never have bestowed on them to remain idle or to be used to small purpose. The fourth is the excllent results shown in them when they have had the advantage of good upbringing.
>
> I do not advocate sending young maidens to public Grammar Schools, or to the Universities, as this has never been the custom in this country. I would allow them learning within certain limits, having regard to the difference in their vocation, and in the ends which they should seek in study. We see that young maidens are taught to read and write, and can learn to do well in both; we hear them both sing and play passing well; we know that they learn the best and finest of our learned languages to the admiration of all men. As to the living modern languages of highest reputation in our time, if any one is inclined to deny that in these they can compare with the best of our sex, they will claim no other tests than to talk with such a one in whichever of these tongues she may choose.[25]

Mulcaster's comments about education for girls sound stilted and ultraconservative at the present time. The important thing about them is his underlying contention that girls should be included at all in the educational system.

That Mulcaster was a man of great common sense and of practical insight into everyday matters is shown in a number of passages. He had no fanciful notions or daydreams of an unrealizable future. Always his feet were on the ground, and his interest was in the development of universal education. The

[24] *Ibid.*, p. 62.
[25] *Ibid.*, pp. 51–52.

few excerpts below show his common-sense attitude toward an assortment of problems:

> There is always danger to a State in excess of numbers beyond the opportunities of useful employment, and this is specially true in the case of scholars. . . . because they cannot rest satisfied with little, and by their kind of life they prove too disdainful of labour, unless necessity makes them trot. If that wit fail to preach which were fitter for the plough, and he to climb a pulpit who was made to scale a wall, is not a good carter ill lost, and a good soldier ill placed? [26]
>
> As concerns colleges I do not consider that the scholarships in them are intended only for poor students, for whose needs that small help could never suffice, (though some advantage may be given to them in consideration of special promise which has no other chance of being recognized) but rather that they are simply preferments for learning and advancement for virtue, alike to the wealthy as a reward of well-doing, and to the poorer students as a necessary support. Therefore, as in admission I would give freedom to choose from both sorts, so I would restrict the choice [of scholarships] to those who give genuine promise of usefulness.[27]
>
> Wherefore I make Reading the first foundation on which everything else must rest, and being a thing of such moment, it should be thoroughly learned when it is once begun, as facility will save much trouble both to master and scholar at a later stage. The child should have his reading perfect both in English and in the Latin tongue long before he dreams of studying grammar.[28]
>
> I think it is not good to begin study immediately after rising, or just after meals, or to continue right up to the time of going to bed. From 7 to 10 in the forenoon, and from 2 till almost 5 in the afternoon are the most fitting hours, and are quite enough for children to be learning. The morning hours will serve best for memory work and what requires mental effort; the afternoon for going over again the material that has been already acquired. The other times before meals are for exercise. The hours after meals and before study is resumed, are to be given to resting the body and refreshing the mind, without too much movement.[29]
>
> I should wish parents and teachers should be not only acquainted, but on friendly terms with each other. And though some parents need no counsel, and some teachers can give but little, yet if the wise parent is as well exercised as should follow from the general plan laid down for all young children, they shall have no cause to complain of public education.[30]

It is interesting that Mulcaster foresaw one result of universal education—the overcrowding of the professions. His suggestion of a cordial relationship be-

[26] *Ibid.*, p. 19.
[27] *Ibid.*, pp. 28–29.
[28] *Ibid.*, p. 34.
[29] *Ibid.*, pp. 84–85.
[30] *Ibid.*, p. 119.

tween parents and teachers is an early, faint foreshadowing of the Parent-Teacher Association.

On the subject of discipline Mulcaster agreed to some extent with other famous teachers, but while he recommended the extensive use of persuasion and interest he was too practical and too experienced to overlook the fact that an occasional pupil does not respond to gentleness and consideration. In the first excerpt below he gives his attitude on the punishment of stupidity by whipping; in the second, he goes on to consider what may be done with the child who does not respond to kindness, and probably gives a description of his own behavior.

> The best way to secure good progress . . . is so to ply [pupils] that all may proceed voluntarily, and not with violence, so that they will be ready to do well, and loth to do ill, and all fear of correction may be entirely absent. *Surely to beat for not learning a child that is willing enough to learn, but whose intelligence is defective, is worse than madness.*[31]
>
> A schoolmaster, if he be really wise, will either prevent his pupils from committing faults, or when they are committed, will turn the matter to the best account, but in any case he must have full discretion given to him to use severity or gentleness as he thinks best, without any appeal. But I do think gentleness and courtesy towards children more needful than beating. I have myself had thousands of pupils passing through my hands whom I never beat, because they needed it not; but if the rod had not been in sight to assure them of punishment if they acted amiss, they might have deserved it. Yet in regard to those who came next to the best, I found that I would have done better if I had used more correction and less gentleness, after carelessness had got ahead in them. Wherefore, I must needs say that where numbers have to be dealt with, the rod ought to rule, and even where there are few, it ought to be seen, however hard this may sound.[32]

Actually Mulcaster's reputation as a teacher indicates that he used the rod a good deal, perhaps more than he himself realized.

Most of the teachers who have been described in this book condemned corporal punishment entirely. Mulcaster agreed with them in theory but differed from them in practice. Perhaps he was not as resourceful or talented as some of the others, perhaps his practical turn of mind forced him to subordinate theory to what seemed to him the necessity of the situation in dealing with those to whom an appeal based on reason was not sufficient, perhaps he was strongly influenced by the stern Puritan* atmosphere about him, and almost certainly he was an unhappy man who was easily irritated and angered. Probably he was no more severe than the average teacher of his time; he was merely less opposed to punishment that most good teachers.

[31] *Ibid.*, p. 32.
[32] *Ibid.*, p. 117.

Ascham had a predilection for his national language and used it for his educational writings, but Mulcaster had a crusader's passion for English. A paragraph defending his use of English appears below:

> As for the question whether English or Latin should be learned, hitherto there may seem to have been some reasonable doubt . . . for while our religion was expressed only in Latin, the single rule of learning was to read that language as tending to the knowledge valued by the Church. But now we have returned to our English tongue as being proper to the soil and to our faith, this restraint is removed. And by nature we learn to read first that which we speak first, to take most care over that which we use most, and to begin our studies where we have the best chance of good progress, owing to our natural familiarity with our ordinary language as spoken by those around us in the affairs of everyday life.[33]

Mulcaster shows in this passage and many others the love of Englishmen for England and all things English, a feeling that first arose during the Elizabethan Age. His own writing, however, was plodding, heavy, and awkward. He seems to have realized that his style and his message would not be popular, since he once wrote that his writing "may be without esteem in our age, through the triviality of the time, but may yet win it in another, when its value is appreciated. Some hundred years may pass before . . . books gain their full authority." [34] This prophecy was amply fulfilled. Mulcaster's work lay unread upon library shelves for three centuries before people began to appreciate him. In recent decades his books have been dusted off and his ideas thoroughly considered. After a lapse of three hundred and fifty years he is regarded as perhaps the outstanding writer of English educational theory and practice. The times have finally caught up with him.

The last of Mulcaster's revolutionary but eminently practical ideas was his demand for teaching training. He wanted to make teaching a profession on a par with medicine, divinity, and law. While others—Vittorino and Melanchthon, for example—had had the same notion before him, none of the others, except the Jesuits, had presented any such detailed suggestions as to how the desired training might be brought about. In some passages Mulcaster describes the work and preparation of current teachers; in others, he sets forth his ideals; in still others, he recommends university courses in teacher training. In no other field is he so startlingly modern.

> The elementary school is left to the lowest and the worst class of teacher, because good scholars will not abase themselves to it. The first grounding should be undertaken by the best teachers, and his reward should be the greatest, because his work demands most energy and most judgment,

[33] *Ibid.*, p. 34.
[34] *Ibid.*, p. 191.

and competent men could easily be induced to enter these lower ranks if they found that sufficient reward were offered. It is natural enough for ignorant people to make little of the early training, when they see how little consideration is paid to it, but men of judgment know how important the foundation is, not only as regards the matter that is taught, but the manner of handling the child's intelligence, which is of great moment.[35]

If the master's salary is fixed by agreement at a definite sum, then he should not be given too large numbers to deal with, nor should he be obliged to eke out his income in other ways outside his profession. It is unreasonable to demand a man's whole time, and yet make such scant payment that he has to look elsewhere, outside the school, to add to it. Among many causes that make our schools inefficient, I know none so serious as the weakness of the profession owing to the bareness of the reward. The good that cometh by schools is infinite; the qualities required in the teacher are many and great; the charges which his friends have been at in his bringing up are heavy; yet he has but little to hope for in the way of preferment. Our calling creeps low, and has pain for companion, always thrust to the wall, though always formally admitted to be worthy.[36]

There will be some difficulty in winning a college for those who will afterwards pass to teach in the schools. There is no specializing for any profession till the student leaves the College of Philosophy, from which he will go to Medicine, Law, or Divinity. This is the time also when the intending schoolmaster should begin his special training. In him there is as much learning necessary as, with all deference to their subjects, is required by any of the other three professions, especially if it be considered how much the teacher hath to do in preparing scholars for all other careers. Why should not these men have this competence in learning? . . . Why should not teachers be well provided for, so that they can continue their whole life in the school, as divines, lawyers, and physicians do in their several professions? If this were the case, judgment, knowledge, and discretion would grow in them as they get older, whereas now the school, being used but for a shift, from which they will afterwards pass to some other profession, though it may send out competent men to other careers, remains itself far too bare of talent, considering the importance of the work. I consider therefore that in our universities there should be a special college for the training of teachers, inasmuch as they are the instruments to make or mar the growing generation of the country, and because the material of their studies is comparable to that of the greatest professions wherein the forming of the mind and the exercising of the body require the most careful consideration, to say nothing of the dignity of character which should be expected from them.[37]

Since 1850, almost three hundred years after Mulcaster's time, training courses for teachers have finally begun to appear in sufficient numbers to produce the necessary personnel for public schools.

[35] *Ibid.*, pp. 85–86.
[36] *Ibid.*, pp. 88–89.
[37] *Ibid.*, pp. 97–98.

One would suppose that the writings of an elegant royal tutor, such as Roger Ascham, and of a headmaster of two important London schools, such as Richard Mulcaster, would have been read and heeded, with resulting changes in the methods of teaching. Nothing could be further from the truth. People read Ascham's book on archery more than that on education, and those who attended to the latter publication took from it chiefly his method of double translation. Otherwise, Ascham's influence was slight. Mulcaster's was even less. With the passage of time, however, both have found their niche. The elegant Ascham lives on in the type of education that is aristocratic, tutorial, and cultural. The hard-headed Mulcaster has come into his own since public school systems began to develop. It is only since most of his recommendations have been carried out that his full worth has been appreciated.

C. THE SCHOOLS OF THE ENGLISH REFORMATION

1. Effect of the English Renaissance and Reformation upon the Schools[38] The Renaissance in England dates quite definitely from the visit of Erasmus to Oxford at the end of the fifteen century. At Oxford he found an alert group of scholars who were ready and eager to absorb the new learning. Like humanists elsewhere, the English humanists studied the classics in their original languages. The English Renaissance had hardly gotten under way, however, before it was overtaken by the English Reformation, and it was not until the religious question had reached a temporary settlement under Queen Elizabeth that the full flower of the Renaissance came into bloom. As part of the Reform movement, the schools that had been controlled by the Catholic Church were systematically wiped out. It is estimated that of the three hundred grammar schools which existed before the Reformation, two hundred and fifty-nine[39] were dissolved by Henry VIII and Edward VI. Several plans were proposed for the reopening of some schools and the founding of others, but actually only a few new schools appeared during the reign of Henry VIII.

Further evidence of the effect that the closing of the schools had upon

[38] Material in this section is based upon the following references: Brinsley, *Ludus Literarius, or the Grammar School;* C. M. Clode, *The Early History of the Guild of Merchant-Taylors,* Harrison and Son, 1888, 2 vols.; W. C. Hazlitt, *Schools, School Books, and Schoolmasters,* J. W. Jarvis and Son, 1888, 300 pp.; A. F. Leach, *English Schools of the Reformation,* Constable, 1896, 122 pp.; J. Rodgers, *The Old Public Schools of England,* Charles Scribner's Sons, 1938, 112 pp.; A. M. Stowe, *The English Grammar Schools in the Reign of Elizabeth,* Columbia University Press, 1908, 200 pp.; F. Watson, *The Old Grammar Schools,* Cambridge University Press, 1916, 150 pp., and *The English Grammar Schools to 1660,* Cambridge University Press, 1908, 548 pp.; H. B. Wilson, *History of the Merchant-Taylors' School from Its Foundation to the Present Time,* F. C. and J. Rivington, 1814, 1254 pp., 2 parts.

[39] From Watson, *The Old Grammar Schools,* p. 5. The quotations from this book are reprinted by permission of Cambridge University Press, publishers.

English education generally may be seen in the record of degrees given annually at Oxford. During the first twenty-five years of Henry VIII's reign, the average number was 127. The year after the smaller monasteries were dissolved, the number shrank to 44. Twelve years later, the number was still smaller, only 33. Under Edward VI the number remained small, climbed back to an average of 70 under Queen Mary, and finally recovered the original level under Queen Elizabeth.

This monarch took steps to tighten the hold of the new church upon education by requiring that each bishop visit the schools within his diocese and make inquiries about the teachers. The questions that each bishop was to ask the teachers in his diocese are shown below:

> Who are the teachers? In whose houses do they teach? With licence or without? Do any teach in your Church or Chancel what is to the profanation of that place? Doth any recusant* keep a school? Doth any public schoolmaster teach the children of recusants or sectaries?* Doth the schoolmaster instruct his scholars in the communion book? Doth he orderly bring his scholars upon Sundays and holy-days to prayer and sermons? [40]

All teachers of "unsound opinion" or of "suspected" religious faiths were to be removed from teaching and thereafter banned. All members of the clergy were to teach and were to donate one thirtieth of their salary to the support of poor scholars.[41] After 1581 all teachers had to be licensed by the Anglican* church. This license from the church was needed by every teacher for almost three hundred years, until 1869.

During Elizabeth's reign the number of schools increased greatly. Some were founded by royal decree, some were set up by town councils, a few were endowed by noblemen and some by yeomen.* Many of the best-known and most typical schools were established by guilds of merchants. Among the guilds that founded schools were the tailors, brewers, mercers, drapers, grocers, skinners, and goldsmiths. These new schools were perhaps the most typical of the period.

The effect of the Renaissance upon English education was to give the schools a new content; the effect of the Reformation was to give them a new master. During the Middle Ages the Catholic Church had dominated education in England as elsewhere. Grammar schools had grown up in many places and upon many foundations. Some were founded in connection with colleges, some were originally chantries—or song schools for choir boys—others were founded by guilds, a few grew up as part of a hospital, many were connected

[40] *Ibid.*, p. 79.
[41] In return, they were exempt from certain taxes.

with monasteries or cathedrals, and a small number were secular. In general they taught the old, familiar trivium and quadrivium. In principle they were modeled on the schools of the Roman Empire, but actually they taught mostly the dead shell of grammar without the study of literature with which the shell was supposed to be filled. During the Renaissance the subject matter of classical literature again became important, and the grammar of the classical languages became a means to an end.

The government and the Anglican Church together tried to bring about the same uniformity in education that had been attempted earlier by the Catholic Church. English monarchs were helped in this effort by the invention of printing. As long as books were handwritten, a single teacher had access to only a few and the pupils to even fewer. With the printing of books it became physically possible to have enough copies of a book in existence to require its use in all schools by all students. Thus Henry VIII could require all schools to use a single textbook in grammar and no other. Actually, individual schoolmasters continued, in the inimitable way of teachers in all ages and climes, to use whatever was best adapted to the pupils in their own locality, or whatever they found easiest to teach. But at least some progress was made in the reduction of the indescribable confusion resulting from education based upon the personal whims of each teacher.

Finally the English Reformation introduced into the schools the reading and study of the Bible in its original languages and in English; also there was a small amount of strictly English history. The school boy was to be educated as a Christian, God-fearing Englishman rather than as a spiritual citizen of the world, as had been the case earlier.

2. *Typical Grammar Schools of the period* The two schools in which Mulcaster taught were the Merchant-Taylors' and St. Paul's both of which were typical of the English educational system during the period.

For at least four hundred years before the sixteenth century there had been a school on the location where St. Paul's eventually stood. In 1509 the site was occupied by a school supported by the guild of mercers.[42] Dean Colet,* one of England's greatest humanists and a friend of Erasmus, endowed this school and made it into a typical humanistic institution that was widely copied throughout England. The first headmaster was a layman and married. His salary was set at £35 a year ($175),[43] plus a country house

[42] To this day the chairman of the school's governing board is the master of the Mercers' Company of London.

[43] The American equivalents vary with the exchange rate and are given merely for comparison, since British currency baffles the American mind. The total amounts are not to be thought of in terms of their present purchasing power.

where he could go for a rest when he needed it, plus sick leaves and a pension. Before the Reformation the average teacher had received only 6d 9s[44] (about $30). The headmaster had one assistant and a chaplain as his staff. The number of pupils was restricted to 153, the number of fishes drawn out of the sea by the miraculous draught in the Biblical story.[45] Although this restriction of

FIG. 41. The Merchant-Taylors' School. From J. Rodgers, *The Old Public Schools of England,* p. 57, 1938. Courtesy of Scribner's Sons, publishers.

enrollment no longer exists, there are today 153 holders of scholarships, each of whom wears a silver fish on his watch chain. Education at St. Paul's was free, except for an entrance fee of fourpence (8¢) to be used for "the pore scoler that swepith the scole." Dean Colet spent so much money on the school that he died a poor man, but his spirit lived on in the institution he created.

The Merchant-Taylors' School was founded by the guild of the same name just after the middle of the sixteenth century, over forty years after St. Paul's, upon which it was in large measure modeled. Mulcaster was its head-

[44] Six pounds and 9 shillings.
[45] See John 21:11.

master during the first twenty-five years of its existence. Its enrollment was evidently limited to two hundred and fifty, as may be inferred from the altercation between Mulcaster and the governing board because he had built up the attendance to three hundred. In part the school owed its popularity to Mulcaster's teaching and in part to many fellowships that its graduates might hold at St. John's College, Oxford.

Figures 41 to 44 show, respectively, a view of the Merchant-Taylors' School, one of St. Paul's, and two interior views, one of St. Paul's and one of Eton. The building shown in Figure 42 was not the one built by Colet when the school was founded, but a new building modeled carefully after the

FIG. 42. St. Paul's School in 1670. From F. Watson, *The Old Grammar Schools.* Courtesy of the Cambridge University Press, publishers.

original, which had been destroyed in the Great Fire of London in 1666. A curious point about the rooms in these schools is their size. They are as large as a small church, and one can imagine that teachers might have disciplinary troubles when the rows of benches were filled with a motley assortment of boys of all ages. Often the pupils were not even grouped by grades. Each boy proceeded at his own rate and went to the teacher or an assistant to recite his lessons. There was almost no group instruction. The pupils on one side of the St. Paul's schoolroom would have sat with the light behind them, throwing the shadow of their heads and shoulders across their work, while those on the other side would have faced the windows all day long. The boys in the room at Eton had light both before and behind them, but there does not seem to have been any too much of it. Neither of these interiors looks in the least modern.

Nothing about the grammar schools is more surprising than their hours of work. In the summer, pupils were in school from 6 to 11 A.M and 1 to 6 P.M. In winter the hours were from 7 to 11 and 1 to 5. The shorter hours during the winter were due, not to humanitarian reasons, but to the necessity for artificial light—and candles cost money. In addition to the long school hours, there were usually lessons to be prepared in the evening. A vivid description of a school day appears below:

About a quarter of an hour after 5 in the morning we were called up by one of the Monitors of the chamber; and after Latin prayers we went into

FIG. 43. Classroom in St. Paul's School. From R. Ackermann, *The History of the Colleges of Winchester, Eton, and Westminster,* 1816.

the cloysters to wash, and thence in order, two by two, to the schoole, where we were to be by 6 of the clock at furthest. Between 6 and 8 we repeated our grammar parts (out of Lilie* [Lily] for Latin, out of Cambden* for the Greek); 14 or 15 being selected and called out to stand in a semicircle before the Mr. [Master] and other scholars, and there repeate 4 or 5 leaves, the Mr. appointing who should begin and who should go on with such and such rules. After this we had two exercises that varied every other morning. The first morning we made verses *extempore* Latin and Greek, upon two or three several themes; and they that made the best (two or three of them) had some money given them by the school-Mr.. for the most part. The second morning, one of the form was called out to expound some part of a Latin or Greek author (Cicero, Livie, Isocrates,* Homer, Apollinarius,* Xenophon, &c.), and they of the two next forms were called to give an account of it some other part of the day; or else they were all of them (or such as were picked out, of whom the Mr. made choice by the fear or confidence discovered in their looks) to repeate and pronounce distinctly without book some piece of an author that had been learned the day before. From 8 to 9 we had time for . . . recollection of ourselves, and preparation for future exercises. Betwixt 9 and 11, those exercises were read which had been enjoined us over night (one day in prose, the next day in verse), which were selected by the Mr.; some to be examined and punished, others to be commended and proposed for imitation. Which being done, we had the practice of *Dictamina,** one of the 5th form being called out to translate some sentences out of an

Fig. 44. Classroom at Eton. From H. C. Maxwell-Lyte, *History of Eton College,* 1889.

unexpected author (*extempore*) into good Latin; and then one of the 6th or 7th form to translate the same (*extempore* also) into good Greek. Then the Mr. himself expounded some part of a Latin or Greek author (one day in prose, another in verse) wherein we were to be practised in the afternoon. At dinner and supper times we read some portion of the Latin Bible in a manuscript (to facilitate the reading of such hands): and, the Prebendaries* then having their table commonly in the Hall, some of them had oftentimes good remembrances sent unto them from thence, and withal a theme to make or speak some *extempore* verses upon. Betwixt 1 and 3, that lesson which out of some author appointed for that day had been by the Mr. expounded unto them (out of Cicero, Virgil, Homer, Euripides, Isocrates, Livie, Sallust, &c.) was to be exactly gone through by construing and other grammatical ways, examining all the Rhetorical figures*, and translating it out of verse into prose, or out of prose into verse, out of Greek into Latin, or out of Latin into Greek. Then they were enjoined to commit that to memory against the next morning. Betwixt 3 and 4 we had a little respite: the Mr. walking out and they . . . going in order to the Hall, and then fitting themselves for their next task. Between 4 and 5 they repeated a leaf or two of some book of Rhetorical figures, or choice Proverbs and Sentences, collected by the Mr. for that use. After, they were practised in translating some *Dictamina* out of Latin or Greek, or sometimes turning Latin or Greek verses into English verse. Then a theme was given them, whereupon to make prose of verses, Latin and Greek, against the next morning. After supper (in summer-time) they were three or four times in a week called to the Mr.'s chamber (especially they of the 7th form), and there instructed out of Hunter's Cosmographie,* and practised to describe and find out cities and countries in the maps. Upon Sundays before morning prayers in summer they came commonly into the school (such as were King's scholars), and there construed some part of the gospel in Greek, or repeated part of the Greek catechism. In the afternoon they made verses upon the preacher's sermon, or epistle and gospel. The best scholars in the 7th form were appointed as Tutors to read and expound places of Homer, Virgil, Horace, Euripides, or other Greek and Latin authors, at those times (in the forenoon, or afternoon) . . . wherein the scholars were in the school in expectation of the Mr. The scholars were governed by several *Monitores** (two for the Hall, as many for the Church, the School, the Fields, the cloyster—which last attended them to washing, and were called *Monitores immundorum**). The Captain of the School was over all these, and therefore called *Monitor Monitorum*. These Monitors kept them strictly to speaking of Latin, in their several commands; and withal they presented their complaints or Accusations (as we called them) every Friday morning, when the punishments were often redeemed by exercises, or favours shown to boys of extraordinary merit, who had the honour (by the Monitor Monitorum) many times to beg and prevail for such remissions. And so, at other times, other faults were often punished by scholastical tasks, as repeating whole orations out of Tullie, Isocrates, Demosthenes, or speeches out of Virgil, Thucydides*, Xenophon, Euripides, &c.[46]

It is not surprising that masters had to control their charges by fear of the rod. No normal boy could stand the strain of such long hours and such difficult subject matter. In the schools attended by boys from the upper classes there were three vacations a year, of eighteen, twelve, and nine days respectively; in ordinary schools, however, the boys had only two vacations, one of sixteen and one of twelve days. The school year was approximately forty-eight

[46] The exact wording for this excerpt comes from P. Monroe, *A Text-Book in the History of Education,* pp. 525–527. Since Monroe gives no source for his quotation, it was impossible to trace it further. It is, however, a description of the early curriculum of Westminster College. It may be found in slightly different wording in John Sargeaunt's *Annals of Westminster School,* Methuen & Company, Ltd., 1898, pp. 279–281, or in G. F. R. Barker, *Memoir of Richard Busby, D.D. (1606–1695)*, Lawrence and Bullen, 1895, pp. 77–81.

weeks long, with one half holiday each week. Since boys attended grammar schools for six or seven years, they put in an enormous number of hours. In fact, the total number of class hours in seven years would almost exactly equal the modern total from kindergarten through college. The boy entered grammar school at seven or eight years of age and went on to the university by his sixteenth year. It is not, however, to be supposed that the grammar schools enrolled any considerable proportion of the boys in the country. Many pupils were allowed to enter, but from then on they were selected on the basis of ability. Elimination was high, and not many of the entrants graduated. In a few schools girls were allowed during the early years.

The typical grammar school had six grades. In the first the boys studied Latin grammar and read a collection of moral sayings in simple Latin. In the second they had more grammar and vocabulary drill, and every evening at home they translated a verse from the English Bible into Latin. In the third grade, this assignment was increased to two verses, there was more grammar, and a little rhetoric. If a school had two masters, these lower three grades were taught by the assistant. Theoretically there was no disputation at either St. Paul's or the Merchant-Taylors' School, although actually this practice seems to have lingered on in both places. The founders of both schools wished to get completely away from scholasticism and therefore banned disputation because it had been the technique of the scholastics.

The curriculum was both humanistic and religious. Before a child entered the grammar school itself he attended a primary class in which he learned to read, spell, and write—often through use of the Bible and Psalter* —and to do a little simplified arithmetic; he memorized also some moral precepts, the Lord's Prayer, the Ten Commandments, and the Creed.*

The fourth grade began with a complete review of Latin grammar and an introduction to Greek. Verses from both Latin and Greek Bibles were used as teaching materials. Rhetoric was continued, with the study of Cicero's letters. In many schools Ascham's method of double translation was popular. The boys read and memorized a little Ovid, also. Every night they translated Bible verses or other matter into both Greek and Latin. On Saturdays they studied the church catechism.

In the fifth grade the assignment in Greek increased to twelve verses and the boys began to write Latin themes and short poems. By this time Latin had become a tool, so far as reading was concerned, and the students read the Latin historians, orators, poets, and dramatists. In Greek they were still struggling with grammar and with short translations, such as the fables of Aesop.

The work of the last grade was enough to break the morale and health of all but the most talented. The boys read both Greek and Latin classics, wrote and delivered orations in both languages, wrote not only themes and poems, but also anagrams,* epigrams, and acrostics in both! Moreover, they often began Hebrew, and they studied the catechism as well as the Bible in Greek.

3. Materials of Instruction The small child began his schooling with an ABC book, from which he learned the alphabet and the syllables, the latter in such series as: *ba, be, bi, bo, bu; da, de, di, do, du; fa, fe, fi, fo, fu,* etc.; *ab, eb, ib, ob, ub; ad, ed, id, od, ud; af, ef, if, of, uf.*[47] A common form for introductory material was the hornbook, a sample of which is shown in Figure 45 at the left. A heavy sheet of paper containing the letters and words was attached to a wooden handle and covered with a piece of transparent horn to keep it clean. The hornbook first appeared at the close of the fifteenth century, but it did not come into wide use in England until a century later. Similar materials, usually not mounted in the same manner, existed in France and Germany. A French sample is shown in Figure 46. Work in the alphabet and phonetics preceded any reading. Then the pupil spelled out and pronounced words until he could recognize them by sight. The primers used had a highly religious character. They often contained a simple catechism, graces* to say before and after meals, and a number of moral precepts. Both the method of teaching and the materials used are about as contrary as they could be to the principles of modern child psychology.

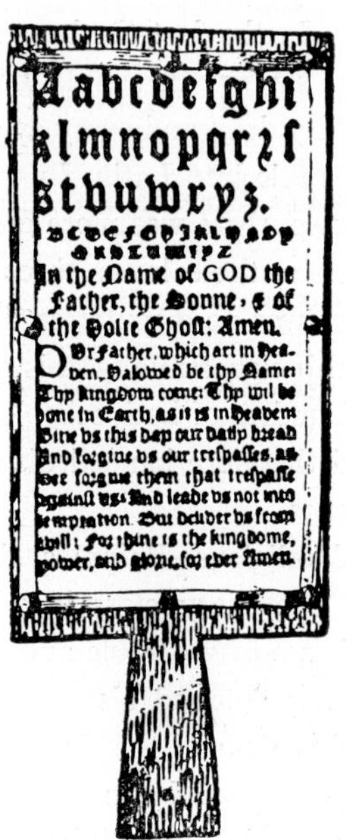

FIG. 45. A Horn Book. From an illustrated manuscript dated 1503.

Until the middle of the seventeenth century children graduated from the alphabet directly into the catechism and Lord's Prayer, but later a primer was introduced, to make the transition a little easier. At first it contained no pictures, but toward the end of the century the illustrated primer made its appearance and immediately achieved a popularity that it has never lost. Figures

[47] Watson, *English Grammar Schools to 1660,* p. 165.

47 and 48 present two examples of early illustrated materials from France. Other textbooks of an elementary character also appeared. The very earliest text of all was a general handbook for all the elementary school sub-

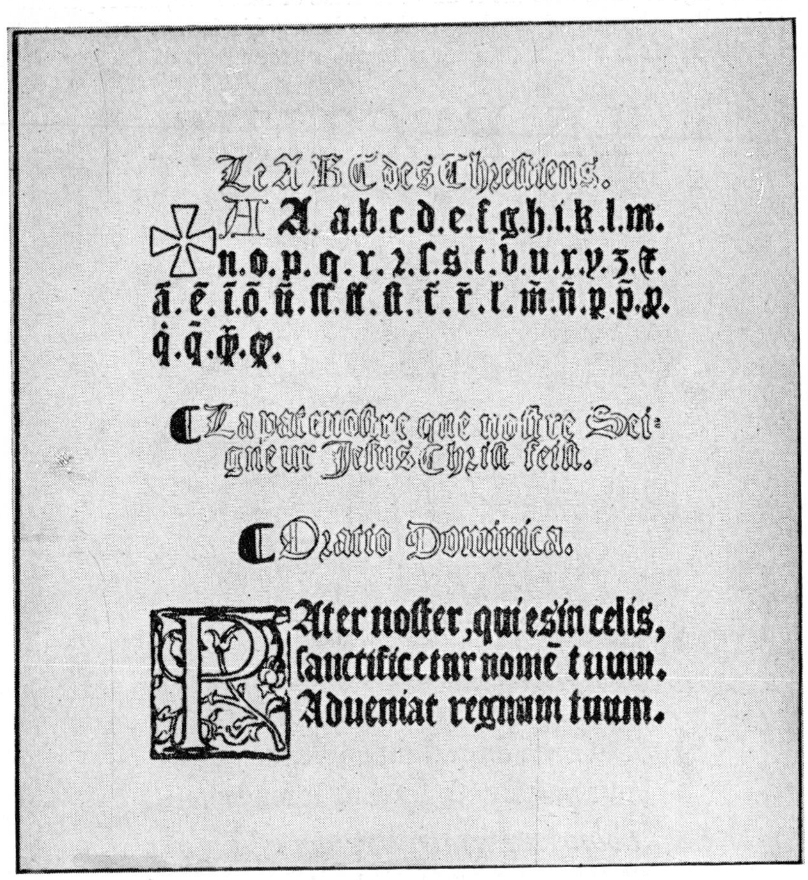
Le A B C des Chrestiens.

A A. a.b.c.d.e.f.g.h.i.k.l.m.
n.o.p.q.r.ꝛ.ſ.s.t.v.u.x.y.z.&.
ā.ē.ī.ō.ū.ſſ.ff.ſt.

La patenostre que nostre Seigneur Jesus Christ feist.

Oratio Dominica.

Pater noster, qui es in celis,
sanctificetur nomē tuum.
Adveniat regnum tuum.

Fig. 46. An A B C and the Lord's Prayer. Facsimile of the first page of the *A B C des Chrétiens,* bound with the *Heures de Notre-Dame* of Jacques Kerver, MDLXXV, in the Bibliothèque Carnavalet Réserve.

Translation: The Lord's Prayer that our Lord Jesus Christ gave us. The Lord's Prayer. Our Father Who art in Heaven, Hallowed by Thy name. Thy kingdom come.

jects. Spellers and arithmetics were used from the very end of the sixteenth century, but did not come into general use for another fifty years.

The lower grades often made use of certain exercises in Latin that were arranged in the form of dialogues. Among the most popular was a book by Vives,* called merely an *Exercitatio,* or set of exercises. A description of this material appears below:

The study of the contents of Vives' *Exercitatio* explains its popularity. It deals with the daily life of the school-boy at school, at home, in the town. It considers his interests minutely. It concerns itself with his work, and still more with his play. It deals with the trifling incidents of the lesson, but it penetrates also into the relations of the boy with his home; his father, mother, sisters and brothers. It is alive with a sense of the surroundings of the boy. It re-

LE RECTEUR.

Mon fils, jusqu'au Cercueil, faut aprendre,
Et tenir pour perdu le jour qui s'est passé,
Si tu n'y a de quelque chose profité,
Pour plus sage & sçavant te rendre.

Commence à faire attention sur ce qui est ici Represénté par les NOMS & FIGURES de Fleurs, d'un Chien, de la Femme, d'un Homme, d'une Maison, d'un Chapeau, du Pain & d'un Coûteau : & continuë d'obser-ver, peu à peu, ce qui suit.

FIG. 47. Page from an Illustrated Reader (a). From the *Very Easy Method of Teaching Children to Read in French and Latin,* published by Claude Michard, printer and music seller at St. John the Evangelist in Dijon (n.d.).

Translation: My son, until the grave, you must learn to regard the day as lost, if you have not gained in it something that will make you wiser and more learned. Begin by paying attention to that which is here shown by the words and the figures of flowers, a dog, a woman, a man, a house, a hat, some bread, and a knife, and continue by observing, little by little, that which follows.

counts the building of a new house, or describes a cookshop and kitchen in the town. It gives the entree to a royal palace and to the education of a prince. And even when Vives goes to far away subjects, he takes his boyish spirit with him. The boy has aspirations in the knowledge of common things, and

Le Maître d'Ecole.

Perd ſouvent ſon tems, d'Enſeigner les Pareſſeux & Néglіgens.

Fig. 48. Page from an Illustrated Reader (b). From *Very Easy Method of Teaching Children to Read in French and Latin,* published by Claude Michard, printer and music seller at St. John the Evangelist in Dijon (n.d.).

Translation:

THE SCHOOLMASTER

The Verb

(French) I love, I am loved, to teach, to read, to hear

(Latin) I love, thou lovest, to love, to teach, to be taught, to read, to be heard

often wastes his time
in teaching lazy and
inattentive pupils

with the true spirit of an educator, Vives recognized that the boy is interested also in uncommon subjects of discourse. The subject matter may be remote, but it is never dull. . . . [Vives] understands that the world of scholarship, of courts, and even intellectual ideals (of fitting kind) are within the boy's mental ken, if they are permeated with what appeals to boyish fancy. . . . But most impressive of the merits of Vives' *Colloquies* is the penetration he shows into the nature of boys. . . . The *Exercitatio* is a clever book because it recognizes that the school is *ludus literarius,** and at the same time it does not degenerate into frivolity. It has considerable dramatic merits. The boys who are introduced as interlocutors have characters of their own.

Subjects that refer to school life in the Dialogues of Vives are: Getting Up in the Morning, Getting Dressed, Morning Greetings, Going to School, Events on the Way to School, Reading, Writing, Return Home, Children's Play, Card Playing of Elder Youths, the Laws of Playing, School Meals, Students' Chatter, Journey on Horseback,[48] a Description of the School and the work there, a student at his study at night.

Dealing with life outside the school are the following: A New House, A Cook and the Kitchen, A Dining Room, A Grand Banquet, Drunkenness, The King's Palace, A Young Prince,[49] The Exterior of Man's Body, and lastly Dialogues on Education, and Precepts of Education.[50]

Three short excerpts from Vives' dialogues are quoted below, to show more precisely their nature. The abbreviations stand for the names of the boys.

Bamb. Listen, there is the nightingale!

Grac. Where is she?

Bamb. Don't you see her there, sitting on that branch? Listen how ardently she sings; and how she goes on and on!

Nugo. (As Martial says) *Flet Philomela nefas.* (The nightingale weeps at injustice.)

Grac. What a wonder she carols so sweetly when she is away from Attica* where the very waves of the sea dash upon the shore not without rhythm.

Nugo. Pliny* observes that they sing with more exactitude when men are near them.

Turd. What is the reason for that?

Nugo. I will declare unto you the reason. The cuckoo and the nightingale sing at the same time, that is, from the middle of April till the end of May or thereabouts. These two birds once met in a contest of sweetness of song, when a judge was sought, and because it was a trial concerning sound, an ass seemed the most suitable for this decision, since he of all the animals had the longest ears. The ass rejected the nightingale, because he could not understand her harmony, and awarded the victory to the cuckoo. The nightingale appealed to men, and when she sees a man she

[48] Which was, apparently, a school or academic journey.

[49] An account of Prince Philip, afterward husband of Queen Mary of England.

[50] Watson, *English Grammar Schools to 1660,* pp. 333–335.

immediately pours forth her song, and sings with zest so as to approve herself to him, so as to avenge the wrong which she received from the ass.

Grac. This is a subject worthy of a poet.

Cels. Don't you study better in the morning? Then it seems to me the season of the time and the condition of the body invite study, since at that time there is the least exhalation from the brain, digestion having been completed.

Plin. But this hour is very quiet, when every one has gone to rest and everything is silent, and for those who eat at mid-day and morning it is not inconvenient. Some follow the old custom and only eat one meal and that in the evening; others merely at mid-day, according to the advice of the new doctors; and again others both mid-day and evening, according to the usage of the Goths.*

Cels. But were there no mid-day meals before the Goths?

Plin. There were, but light meals. The Goths introduced the custom of eating to satiety twice a day.

Cels. On that account Plato condemned the meal-times of the Syracusans,* who had two good meals every day.

Usher. Yesterday I saw committed a crime of deepest dye. The schoolmaster of the Straight Street, who smells worse than a goat, and instructs his threepenny classes in his school, which abounds in dirt and filth, pronounced three or four times *volucres* with the accent on the penultimate.* I indeed was astounded that the earth did not at once gulp him up.

Praec. What otherwise ought one to expect such a schoolmaster to say? He is in other parts of the grammatical rules thoroughly worn out. But you are disturbed over a very small matter and make a tragedy out of a comedy, or still more truly a farce.

Usher. I have finished my task. Now it is your turn. You now keep the conversation going.

Praec. I don't wish to give you the chance to answer me what I don't ask. This broth is getting cold. Bring a table fire-pan. Heat it up a little before you dip your bread in it. This radish is not eatable, it is so tough—and so are the rootlets in the broth.

Usher. They certainly have not brought the toughness from the market, but they have acquired it here in our storeroom in which the pantry is quite unsuited for provisions. I don't know why it is we always have brought to us here bones without marrow in them.

Praec. Bones have but little marrow in them at the new moon.

Usher. What! When it is full moon?

Praec. Then there is plenty.

Usher. But our bones have little, or more truly no, marrow.

Praec. It is not the moon that bereaves us of marrow but our Lamia. She has here put in too much pepper and ginger, and in the soup and particularly in the salad there is also too much mint, rock-parseley, sage, cole-wort, cress, hyssop. Nothing is more harmful to the bodies of boys and youths than foods which make the stomach hot.

Arch. What kinds of herbs then would you wish to be used for food?
Praec. Lettuce, garden-oxtongue, purslain, mixed with some rock-parsley.[51]

Another series of dialogues were those written by Corderius*,[52] a sample page of which is shown in Figure 49. The lefthand column is in French, the righthand in Latin. The end of Colloquy 4 is at the top of the page. The conversation revolves about the lively topic of the past tenses, in indicative* and subjunctive* moods, and the personal endings of each. In Colloquy 5, while the two boys are waiting for dinner, they begin to develop the argument that children should respect their parents. The printing is extremely bad,

8 COLLOQVES

Le Pe. *Ie l'espere aussi auec toy. Il reste maintenant que tu dies le preterit & ce qui descend d'iceluy.* — Pæ. Ego quoque idem tecum spero. Nunc restat vt dicas præteritum cum prole.

P v. Potui, potueram, potuerim, potuero, potuissem, potuisse.

Le Pe. *Di les terminaisons.* — Pæ. Dic terminationes.

P v. i, ram, rim, ro, ssem, sse.

Le Pe. *Di la signification.* — Pæ. Dic significationem

P v. Possum, *ie puis:* Posse, *pouuoir.*

Le Pe. *C'est assez: voila qu'on nous appelle pour disner.* — Pæ. Hactenus: ecce, vocamur ad prandium.

COLLOQVE 5.

ARG. *Du respect d'vn fils bien morigené enuers ses parens, attendant son repas en temps & lieux commandés.*

Claude, Durant.	CLAVDIVS, DVRANDVS
Quand veux-tu disner?	Quando vis prandére?
D. *I'ay desia disné.*	D. Ego iam prandi.
C. *A quelle heure?*	C. Quota hora?
D. *A huict heures & demie.*	D. Sesquioctaua.
C. *Disnez vous donc si matin?*	C. Tam mane igitur prãdetis?
D. *Telle est quasi tousiours nostre coustume en esté: & vous?*	D. Sic feré solemus in æstâte: Vos autem?
C. *Nous ne disnons point deuant dix heures & demie: quelquesfois apres onze.*	C. Non prandêmus ante sesquidécimam: intérdum

FIG. 49. A Sample Colloquy. From the *Colloquies of Corderius,* 1593. Courtesy of the Teachers College Library, Columbia University.

but even so it was clearer than many handwritten books of earlier times. In other colloquies from the same book the two insufferably priggish little boys discuss the sermon, admitting that they deserve a beating because they failed to

[51] F. Watson, *Tudor School Boy Life: The Dialogues of Juan Luis Vives,* J. M. Dent & Sons, Ltd., 1908 (247 pp.), pp. 45–46, 111, and 36–37. Used by permission of J. M. Dent & Sons, publishers.

[52] The schoolmaster of Calvin.* The book came back with the Protestant English exiles when they returned from Geneva,* after fleeing there during the reign of the Catholic Queen Mary.

memorize even a little of it, learn verses from the Bible, or divert themselves while taking walks by "capping" sentences from the New Testament; that is, one boy begins a verse and the second is supposed to complete it. Sometimes they take their Psalter with them and sing psalms under the trees. They pray continually—before and after meals, at night, in the morning, at intervals during the day, in public and in secret. Their speech is heavily interlarded with "God be praised," "Thank God," and "God willing." It is not, however, to be supposed that the Tudor schoolboy scorned this form of intellectual and moral nourishment. There is every evidence that he loved it. Nothing could show more convincingly than this schoolboy approval the extent to which the English Protestants were successful in indoctrinating whole generations.

A form of exercise that somewhat resembles Ascham's double translation was also used for purposes of showing pupils how to get from English into Ciceronian Latin. Cicero actually wrote the two Latin sentences given below:[53]

English	*Grammatical Order*	*Ciceronian Order*
1. No man hath been ever great without some divine inspiration.	Nemo fuit unquam magnus sine afflatu aliquo Divino.	Nemo magnus sine aliquo afflatu divino unquam fuit.
2. God cannot be ignorant of what mind everyone is.	Deus non potest ignorare, qua mente quisque sit.	Ignorare Deus non potest, qua quisque mente sit.

It is hard now to see why a mastery of Ciceronian style should have seemed so important as it obviously was to the humanists.

Only here and there does one read of other occupations that might have relieved the drill on language. In some schools the pupils gave plays. Indeed, the students in both St. Paul's and the Merchant-Taylors' were so good as actors that they gave command performances before the queen. Many schools trained the boys in archery, a combination of physical exercise and preparation for national defense, much like the modern R.O.T.C. There were also a few classes in English history, for the apparent purpose of instilling patriotism. The essential element was, however, grammar, just as it had been for generations before, only now with the addition of literature.

The general atmosphere of the schools is well reflected in the three quotations below. The first incident gives a glimpse into schoolboy psychology and shows how human nature reacts when pupils are faced with a curriculum that is too difficult. The poem and the third excerpt are both about discipline. The

[53] Brinsley, *op. cit.*, p. 148.

master referred to in the poem, Udall,* was Mulcaster's teacher, but the same lines would fit many another teacher about as well. The description of a flogging reveals better than any general statement how brutal school discipline could become.

Upon an accident to me when I was a school-boy

Before Master Downhale came to be our Master in Christ School, an ancient citizen of no great learning was our school-master; whose manner was to give us out several lessons in the evening by construing it to every form, and in the next morning to examine us thereupon; by making all the boys in the first form to come from their seats and stand on the outsides of their desks, towards the middle of the school, and so the second form and the rest in order, whilst himself walked up and down by them and hearing them construe their lesson, one after another; and then giving one of the words to one, and another to another (as he saw fit) for parsing of it. Now when the two highest forms were despatched, some of them whom we called prompters would come and sit in our seats of the lower forms, and so being at our elbows, would put into our mouths answers to our master's questions, as he walked up and down by us: and so by our prompters' help, we made shift to escape correction; but understood little to profit by it, having this circular motion, like the mill-horse that travels all day; yet in the end finds himself not a yard further than when he began.[54]

From Pawles I went, to Eton sent
To learne straightewaies the Latin phraises
Where fifty-three stripes given to me
At once I had,
For fault but small, or none at all,
It came to pass, thus beat I was:
See, Udall, see! the mercie of thee
To me poor lad.[55]

. . . When you are to correct any stubborne or unbroken boy, you [should] make sure with him to hold him fast. . . . To this end to appoint 3 or 4 of your Schollers, whom you know to be honest, and strong inough, or moe if neede be, to lay hands upon him together, to hold him fast, over some fourme, so that he cannot stirre hand nor foot; or else if no other remedy will serve, to hold him to some post (which is farre the safest and free from inconvenience) so as he cannot any way hurt himselfe or others, be he never so peevish. Neither can he hope by any device or turning, or by his apparell, or any other meanes to escape. . . .

To be very wary for smiting them over the backes, in any case, or in such sort as in any way to hurt or indanger them:—And withall, to avoid for these

[54] R. W. Willis, *Mount Tabor,* P. Stephens and C. Meredith, 1639. Quoted in Watson, *The English Grammar Schools to 1660,* p. 410.

[55] From Tusser, *Five Hundred Points of Husbandry* (edited by W. Mavor), Lackington, Allen & Company, 1812, Verse 8 of the "Metrical Autobiography," p. 317.

causes, all smiting them upon the head, with hand, rod, or ferula. . . . That the Master do not in any case abase himselfe to strive or struggle with any boy to take him up; but to appoint other of the strongest to do it, where such need is and the rather for feare of hurting them in his anger, and for the evils which may come there of, and which some schoolemasters have lamented after.

That the Masters and Ushers also do by all means avoid furious anger, threatening, chafing, fretting, reviling: for these things will diminish authoritie and may do much hurt, and much indanger many waies.[56]

This author not only gives cautions about not injuring the boys, but he recommends flogging only for moral offenses and only after milder forms of discipline have failed. He suggests also that the teacher apply encouragement first. Among the forms of motivation he lists frequent promotions from grade to grade, special privileges for all seniors, contests and debates of various kinds, public examinations at the end of each year, elections to various positions of honor, daily arrangement of the class in order of merit, and special rewards for those whose behavior and work are satisfactory. On the negative side he suggests the use of reproofs, demotion in the class order, the posting of a blacklist upon which the names of offenders are written, and "three or four jerkes with the birch, or half a dozen for great fault."[57] Even the best teachers of the period probably used fairly severe measures, but presumably they had sufficient teaching skill to control their pupils without frequent resort to beating. The average and the definitely inferior teacher undoubtedly relied extensively upon beating to atone for their own deficiencies. It is easy to believe that an overworked, underpaid, and ill-prepared teacher who was faced with the task of teaching a too-difficult curriculum to a large group of lively boys for eight to ten hours a day would lean heavily upon the rod as the only means by which he could keep his class in any order at all.

English schools of the Reformation period usually had daily prayers at the opening and closing of school, they gave instruction in the catechism and articles of faith* of the Anglican church, and they required attendance at church—at least on Sundays and often on weekdays—of the entire school, masters and pupils in a body. This connection of religion and education was brought to America by the Puritans and incorporated by them into their schools. The religious atmosphere lingered on in many private schools until after the First World War. For instance, the writer attended a nondenominational private school in which there were morning and evening chapel every day, grace before and after every meal, and moral precepts during the first ten minutes of each eight o'clock class and the last ten minutes of each

[56] Brinsley, *op. cit.*, pp. 188–189.
[57] *Ibid.*, p. 288.

three o'clock class. On Sundays, attendance at church and five-o'clock vespers was required in addition to the two chapel services. Every student in the school took a course in Bible study, a different one each year, for as long as she remained. Fifty years ago there was nothing unique about such arrangements; they presumably represented the tag ends of New England Puritanism. In spite of being only survivals, they imparted to secondary education a flavor that it now lacks.

The grammar schools were at their height between 1600 and 1650. Soon after, they began to decay, partly because of the revolt against Latin as a "useless" subject and partly because of the lack of proper teachers. The Anglican church service was in English, many standard works in Latin had already been translated into the vernacular, and the use of Latin as an international language was declining. As Defoe* said "You may be a gentleman of learning and yet reading in English may do all for you that you need." Similar sentiments were expressed even earlier by both Ascham and Mulcaster. Moreover, the schools lost many of their best teachers and could not replace them because, after 1662, all teachers had to take an oath of conformity to the Anglican church and had to be licensed by an Anglican bishop. Men of spirit would not enter teaching under such strictures, and the quality of the instructional staff declined sharply. As time passed, the grammar school enrolled fewer and fewer students. Other schools arose, notably those of the Dissenters,* in which the curriculum was more liberal and more modern. The resulting competition forced the old grammar schools to go out of business or to modernize also. Many of them still exist, but they have changed out of all recognition. Between 1600 and 1650, however, the humanistic, strongly religious grammar school was the mode in English secondary education.

READING REFERENCES

A. General Histories of the Period

Ergang, *Europe from the Renaissance to Waterloo,* chap. 9.
Garrett, *European History, 1500–1815,* chaps. 11, 16.
Robinson, *Introduction to the History of Western Europe,* chap. 27.
Schevill, *A History of Europe from the Reformation to the Present Day,* chap. 9.
Stearns, *Pageant of History,* part i, chap. 10.
Trevelyan, G. M., *English Social History,* Longmans, Green and Co., 1942 (628 pp.), chaps. 4–7.

B. Other Texts in the History of Education

Cubberley, *History of Education,* pp. 274–282.
McCormick, *History of Education,* pp. 204–209, 260–263.
Reisner, *Historical Foundations of Modern Education,* chap. 17.

C. Secondary Sources

Adamson, *Pioneers of Modern Education,* pp. 20–30.

Barnard, H., *English Pedagogues,* Second Series, J. B. Lippincott Company, 1862 (480 pp.), pp. 177–284.

Bradley, H. C., *Rugby,* George Bell & Sons, Ltd., 1900 (231 pp.), chap. 1.

Brown, J. H., *Elizabethan School Days,* Basil Blackwell, Ltd., 1933 (173 pp.), chaps. 2–6, or entire book if possible.

Carlisle, J. H., *Two Great English Teachers,* Bardeen's, 1890 (252 pp.), pp. 11–33.

Cust, L., *History of Eton College,* Charles Scribner's Sons, 1899 (318 pp.), chaps. 1, 4, 5.

Davis, H. W. C., *Medieval England,* The Clarendon Press, 1924 (632 pp.), chaps. 8, 9, 11.

Drane, *Christian Schools and Scholars,* chaps. 23.

Firth, J. d'E., *Winchester,* Blackie & Son, 1936 (184 pp.), chaps. 1–4.

Leach, *English Schools at the Reformation,* chaps. 7–9.

Painter, *Great Pedagogical Essays,* Chap. 15.

Rodgers, *The old Public Schools of England,* any one of chaps. II–VI.

Stowe, *The English Grammar Schools in the Reign of Elizabeth,* chaps. 1, 3–5.

Watson, *The English Grammar Schools to 1660,* chap. 7.

———, *The Old Grammar Schools,* chaps. 1, 4, 7–9.

———, *Tudor School Boy Life,* any 8–10 dialogues.

Williams, J. F., *Harrow,* George Bell & Sons, 1901 (226 pp.), chaps. 1–3.

Wilson, *History of the Merchant-Taylors' School,* I, 21–85.

Woodward, *Studies in Education during the Age of the Renaissance,* chap. 13.

D. Primary Sources

Ascham, *The School Master,* book i.

Brinsley, *Ludus Literarius,* chaps. 3, 10, 15, 27–29.

Hoole, Ch., *New Discipline in the Old Art of Teaching School* (edited by E. T. Campagnac), University Press, 1913, 357 pp., pp. 129–209.

Mulcaster, *Positions,* chaps. 4, 5, 27–30, 41, 42.

CHAPTER XI

IGNATIUS OF LOYOLA AND THE SCHOOLS OF THE JESUITS

The last two chapters dealt with the period of the Protestant Revolution in Germany and in England. In the present chapter the story of reform continues, but centers around the reformation within the Catholic Church. It concerns the reactions that were made by churchmen to preserve Catholic religion and education. These reactions were precipitated by the Protestant revolt and were a direct answer to it. The resulting movement is sometimes called the Counter Reformation and sometimes the Catholic Reformation, in which the Jesuits, members of the Society of Jesus that was founded by Loyola, played a leading role.

St. Ignatius of Loyola must have been even in life a somewhat baffling and contradictory person. His life divides itself into four rather definite periods, in each of which he shows certain characteristics that appear rarely if at all in the other three. As a result, he impresses one as having been successively four distinct people who were loosely joined together by a few common traits. He was at all times an enthusiast, a Christian, a gentleman, and a sound practical psychologist; but in his different stages of development he was also in turn a successful courtier and soldier, a fanatical hermit, a rather mediocre student, and a superb organizer. Loyola's traits were undoubtedly contradictory enough when he was alive, but further elements of confusion have been added by his biographers, some of whom were determined to prove him a saint and to that end have included in their chronicles a number of miraculous happenings that in the main merely obscure the actual personality of Loyola. The man behind the miracles was a remarkable person, and in the present discussion it is Ignatius the man, not Ignatius the saint, who is important. Similarly, it is his educational system, not his defense of Catholicism, that is of major interest.

A. IGNATIUS: HIS LIFE AND WORK

1. Ignatius the Courtier and Soldier Ignatius of Loyola[1] was born in northern Spain in the year 1491, just as Columbus was gathering his resources for his first voyage, which resulted in the discovery of America. In his boyhood he was sent to court as a page. There he learned to be a gentleman, a courtier, and a soldier. All one can learn of these early days points to uprightness; for instance, he refused to accept his share in the spoils of war, and he had a reputation for truthfulness and reliability. He seems to have been unusually mature for his age, especially in his understanding of people. He often served as an arbitrator of quarrels because he could influence those about him and because they had faith in his judgment and sense of justice. Loyola himself was inclined to disregard these years at court as so much lost time, but actually they were of great value to him in his future work. If he had turned to the solitary life of the hermit much earlier than he did, he could hardly have developed the understanding of human nature that enabled him to found his society upon sound psychological principles.[2] From his early life as a soldier he derived also his notion that the members of his society should be soldiers of Christ and should be organized, disciplined, and controlled after the pattern of an army.

By the age of twenty-nine Ignatius had developed into a man of high morality, loyalty, and dignity, who understood people and was able to influence them. Not that he was without the faults inherent in the life of a courtier; he was vain of his appearance, fastidious in his dress, proud in his bearing, ambitious to succeed in the arts of war. These faults were, however, superficial and were burned out of him by his subsequent religious experiences.

When Ignatius was twenty-nine years old, both his legs were severely injured in a battle. The broken bones were badly set, and, after weeks of suffering, he was dismayed to find that one leg was shorter than the other and that a piece of bone protruded below one knee. He could not face the prospect of being lame or of having a deformity that would show in the kind of clothes he wore at court. With the ruthless determination that in later years was to drive him into accomplishing things far more important, he had

[1] This chapter is based upon the following references: Antonio Astrain, *A Short Life of St. Ignatius of Loyola* (translated by Fr. R. Hull), Burns, Oates & Washbourne, 1928, 116 pp.; T. Hughes, *Loyola and the Educational System of the Jesuits,* Charles Scribner's Sons, 1912, 302 pp.; Henri Joly, *St. Ignatius of Loyola* (translated by Mildred Partridge), Gerald Duckworth & Co., Ltd., 1906, 262 pp.; S. Rose, *St. Ignatius of Loyola and the Early Jesuits,* Burns Oates & Washbourne, Ltd., 1891, 632 pp.; R. Schwickerath, *Jesuit Education,* B. Herder, 1903, 687 pp.; I. Taylor, *Loyola,* R. Carter and Brothers, 1857, 416 pp. The last reference is strongly anti-Jesuit; by itself it is misleading, but it is a good counterbalance for the veneration found in some of the pro-Jesuit references.

[2] Sound, that is, in view of his aims.

the surgeons saw off the offending bone, without the aid of an anaesthetic; then he ordered them to try stretching the shorter leg by tying weights on it. It is easy to criticize Ignatius for his vanity and to overlook the courage, the will power, and the self-control that he exhibited during this episode.

In the months of his long convalescence Ignatius demanded something to read. He would have preferred Spanish romances, but there was none to be had in the neighborhood. However, someone found for him a *Life of Christ* and a *Lives of the Saints.* He read the former carefully and thoroughly, but it was the latter that utterly fascinated him. The book gave him what he had lacked up to that time: a deep-seated, driving motive that gave meaning to his life. It lifted him from the emotional doldrums into which he had fallen when he finally realized that he was always going to limp and could never again cut a gallant figure at court. It opened to him a new way of life. What he did not notice was that the mode of life which so thrilled him belonged to an age already fast disappearing. The secluded, brooding, introverted, abnormal life of the ascetic, with its flagellations, its physical exhaustion, its hysteria, and its mysticism had been tried centuries before and found wanting because it rested upon false premises about human nature. Loyola, however, was not an educated man, and he presumably did not know that, when he decided to atone for his sins by wearing rags, going barefoot all the way to Jerusalem, beating himself several times a day, letting himself become dirty, neglecting to comb his hair or cut his nails, and going for days without food, he was entering a road already found to lead to a physical and emotional exhaustion so profound as to render the would-be worshiper unable to serve God at all. Because he had no historical perspective, Ignatius had to travel the *via dolorosa* himself and learn by experience.

2. Ignatius the Hermit After two years of illness and recovery, he set out upon his travels, determined to become a holy man. He wanted to go directly to Jerusalem, but he felt so weighted down by sin that he thought he should first do penance. After stopping at a shrine to the Virgin, where he hung up his sword and dagger as visible evidence that he was now a soldier of God, he journeyed to the small village of Manresa,* where he settled down to live in a cave, wear a hair shirt—and a dirty one, at that—and pattern himself upon the medieval saints of whom he had read. He went back to the Middle Ages in spirit as well as in practice. His daily schedule in his year at Manresa consisted of three hours spent in church, seven hours of private devotions, and three hours of bodily chastisement. He lived upon whatever food he could beg, went purposely to places where people would laugh at him, and forced his proud spirit to become humble by repeated mortifications. No medieval hermit could have been more thorough.

For a year Ignatius continued to live the life of the anchorite. As time went by, his holy life began to receive much respect from the townspeople, some of whom came to him for help with their spiritual problems. For them he wrote the *Spiritual Exercises,* which are a four-week series of specific exercises in holiness.[3] The idea of writing such a manual is unusual, and the exercises themselves are even more so. The person who takes them first goes to a place where he may be in the dark and alone, except for the daily visit of his adviser; he fasts, prays, and beats his body—although not to excess. It is part of the adviser's business to see to it that the disciple does not exhaust himself. For each day there is a prescribed exercise which, after the first week, consists basically of visualizing a scene over and over again until it becomes clear and real and until the visualizer can feel the appropriate emotions toward what he has created before his mind's eye.[4]

There are definite directions for calling up each scene and making it real and vivid. Two sets of instructions appear below:

1. A Contemplation on the Birth of Christ.

Contemplate the stable which is falling in ruins; the manger where Jesus Christ reposes on a little straw; the coarse swaddling clothes in which He is wrapped; the animals which warm Him with their breath; the Divine Infant Himself, who fixes His eyes on us, and extends His arms to us; Mary and Joseph praying before the manger; the shepherds coming to adore the new-born Child whom the angel has announced to them; all heaven attentive to the great event which is being accomplished at Bethlehem; and, at the same time, the profound indifference of the rest of men to the coming of the Son of God.

Listen to the discourse of the strangers going to Bethlehem; to the conversations of Mary and Joseph during their journey; to the words of the inhabitants of Bethlehem, who repulse them; to Jesus Christ, who speaks to His Heavenly Father, who speaks to us by His cries and His tears; to the angels singing in heaven, "Glory to God in the Highest and on earth peace"; to the shepherds making inquiry from the holy family about the birth of Jesus.

Taste interiorly the bitterness of Mary and Joseph; the peace of their souls; their joy at sight of the new-born God. Unite yourself in spirit to the abasement, the tears, the poverty, the prayer, all the virtues of our Savior at His birth.

Kiss respectfully the walls of the stable, the straw of the manger, the swaddling clothes, the sacred hands and feet of Jesus Christ.[5]

[3] A translation of these exercises may be found in W. H. Longridge, *The Spiritual Exercises of St. Ignatius of Loyola,* A. R. Mowbray & Co., Ltd., 1930, 390 pp.

[4] For a list of scenes to be thus visualized, see E. A. Fitzpatrick, *St. Ignatius and the Ratio Studiorum,* McGraw-Hill Book Company, Inc., 1905 (426 pp.) p. 263 ff.

[5] *Manresa: or the Spiritual Exercises of St. Ignatius* Burns Oates & Washbourne, Ltd., n.d. (new ed., 324 pp.), pp. 129–130. This and the following excerpt are used by permission of the publisher.

2. A Contemplation of the Power of Evil.

Represent to yourself the prince of the reprobates in the vast plains of Babylon, on a throne of fire surrounded by thick smoke, spreading terror around him by the hideous deformity of his features and by his terrible looks. Meditate on the hidden meaning of these figures. These broad plains designate the broad path where sinners walk. Babylon, the city of confusion, signifies the disorder of a guilty conscience. The throne of fire is the symbol of the pride and the passions which devour the soul like a fire. The thick smoke is the image of the blindness of the sinner and of the vanity of his pleasures. The hideous features and terrible look of Lucifer* express the deformity of sin and the operations of the evil spirit in the soul; that is to say, its trouble, its agitation, its depression, its sorrows.

Consider the innumerable crowd of followers and ministers around Lucifer. Here are found united the sinners of all ages;—the spirits who first, even in heaven, raised the standard of revolt against God, degraded beings, with whom evil is become as a nature; all the men who have made themselves the slaves of their passions and sins,—the proud, the impure, robbers, homicides, all the wicked men who at different times have startled the world by their crimes, and of whom there is not a single one who is not, in some way, an object of aversion and disgust. But why does Lucifer convoke these under his standard? For the most perfidious and cruel design that can be imagined; he wishes to seduce the whole human race, and after having seduced it, to drag it down to eternal misery.

Listen, in spirit, to Lucifer addressing his ministers, and ordering them to lay snares on all sides for men: "Come with us, let us lie in wait for blood, let us hide snares for the innocent without cause. Let us swallow him up alive in hell. We shall find all precious substances; we shall fill our houses with spoils." Remark his artifices, and the three ordinary degrees of temptation; how, first, he catches souls by the love of riches; next, how he throws them into the paths of ambition; then, from ambition to pride—a bottomless abyss, from whence all vices rise as from their fountain. See with what patience and creative zeal the ministers of Lucifer execute the task imposed on them by their master, how they make everything conduce to the one end—the ruin of souls; defects of the understanding, inclination of the heart, the character, the habits, the passions, the faults, the virtues even, and the graces of God. Finally, contemplate the success of hell in its enterprise; how many fools are taken in these snares every day; how many blindly throw themselves in; how many who, not content to allow themselves to be seduced, seek also to seduce their brethren. Look on yourself. Be astonished at having given way so often and so easily to temptations of the enemy; weep over your folly and your past weaknesses, and resolve to be wiser and more courageous for the future.[6]

If a person who was already in a depleted physical condition were to remain alone in the dark and were to bring such scenes before him over and

[6] *Ibid.*, pp. 144–146.

over again until they are vivid, one can imagine that a real humility of spirit and a real fear of hell-fire might result.

The exercises are a curious mixture of the miraculous, the sensuous,* the spiritual, the bizarre, and the practical. They have been described in some detail because they were administered to every novice of the Jesuit order, often more than once. Professed Jesuits to this day insist upon the effectiveness of the exercises. Indeed, the claim has been made that any sinner who will take them faithfully will emerge from them a reformed character. Certainly, the twenty-eight days of solitude, restricted nourishment, bodily discomfort, vivid imaginings, and riotous emotional responses would constitute a never-to-be-forgotten experience![7]

After a year in Manresa, Ignatius set out upon his delayed pilgrimage to Jerusalem. He insisted upon walking barefoot, eating only what he could beg, and sleeping wherever he happened to be when night fell. Friends and patrons often sent him money, but he merely gave it away. Only when he had to travel by sea would he accept just enough money to pay for his passage. He went first to Venice and from there to Jerusalem, although his friends begged him not to go because of war with the Turks. Loyola had for a long time been nursing an ambition to settle down in Jerusalem and from there to Christianize the entire Mohammedan world. Much to his dismay, he was allowed to remain only six weeks. The local authorities would not permit a longer visit, because pilgrims tended to linger indefinitely and to overtax the available food supply. Ignatius went about Jerusalem in an ecstasy of devotion and was greatly disappointed when he was forced to leave.

By the time Loyola again reached Venice he had come to certain conclusions. He realized he had been indulging in an orgy of emotion that, while accomplishing certain results, could not be prolonged any further. What he really wanted to do with his life was to fight for God and the church, not to pile up merit for himself in Heaven by acts of devotion that might make him holier but would make the world no better. Nor could he reach his goal through killing himself by slow starvation or through unhinging his mind by emotional overstimulation. The soldier in him told him that he could not fight when he was sick. For some time Ignatius the saint and Ignatius the soldier carried on an inner conflict, with sometimes one and sometimes the other gaining the upper hand, but in the end the soldier triumphed and the saint reduced his physical privations to a level that did not interfere with getting God's work done.

[7] The language of these exercises gives testimony as to Loyola's lack of education. The first form was in ungrammatical Spanish and the second in rather worse Latin. These two forms were presumably Loyola's own work. A third and standard form in good Latin appeared before his death, but he did not prepare it.

3. Ignatius the Student Ignatius realized also that he needed education. He must have sensed his native ability to attract people, to understand them, to influence them, and to guide them, but he could not safely use these powers to the full until he had had adequate intellectual training. Once Ignatius made up his mind, he could not be turned aside by inconveniences or difficulties. He returned to Barcelona,* where he had patrons who might help him, and entered a school, not a university or college but an ordinary grammar school. At this time he was thirty-three years old, but he did not hesitate to go to school with adolescent boys, who doubtless made fun of him. He would not accept money with which to buy food but insisted upon begging from door to door. He was also far more interested in helping his acquaintances with their spiritual development than he was in memorizing conjugations and declensions. So much time was used up every day in begging and advising that he had little left for study. At this time Loyola's mind was untrained and undisciplined. He did not know how to study, how to concentrate, or how to organize his life so that intellectual labor was possible. After two years of intense effort but not much progress in Latin he was encouraged by his teacher to enter upon more advanced studies. Loyola attended two Spanish universities in quick succession, but in each he got into trouble and did not greatly advance his education. His activities in helping people not only took time and energy away from his studies but brought him under suspicion by the Inquisition.* In both places he was tried and acquitted of heresy but was warned not to attempt further religious guidance of others until he had become a priest and had proper authority.

Eventually Ignatius decided to start all over again in Paris, whither he journeyed on foot at the age of thirty-seven. Once there, he spent a year in really learning Latin. For the first time since his conversion he accepted enough money to live on and was thus able to concentrate upon his work. A year later he began his study of philosophy and at the age of forty-three took his master's degree. His work appears to have been good, but not brilliant. It is, however, a tribute to his great will power that he finished his education at all. As one biographer has said of him:

> Already advanced in years, living on alms, harassed by illness, obliged by persecution to change his abode, meeting everywhere with denunciations, processes, beatings, prison, and fetters, he continued calmly with his studies for eleven years, and this not because he experienced any relish in them, but simply because the glory of God required it. Sublime heroism, indeed, which witnesses to a will in Saint Ignatius as resolute and persevering as any which history has recorded.[8]

[8] Astrain, *A Short Life of St. Ignatius of Loyola,* p. 40. The quotations from this book are used by permission of Burns Oates & Washbourne, Ltd., publishers.

In Paris as in other places Ignatius attracted disciples, to whom he administered his Spiritual Exercises. He had decided by the end of his years in Paris just what form his service to God and the church should take. He would found a religious order, members of which should be soldiers who lived only to fight in the cause of religion. In his last year at the university he and four companions met in the Church of the Blessed Virgin of Montmartre* and, after praying and fasting, took an oath of poverty, chastity, and allegiance to the church. Ignatius still had the idea of converting the Mohammeden world, but if this plan proved impossible, the little band was to put its services at the disposal of the pope. The five men agreed to meet in Venice three years later, where they would renew their vows and undertake whatever work seemed best. In the meantime the others were to finish their education while Loyola went to Spain and wound up his own worldly affairs and those of his colleagues.

Three years later the members met as arranged. By this time the little band had grown to include eleven members. Ignatius sent two of them to Rome in order to feel out the pope on the subject of a new order. Upon being assured of the pope's interest, he journeyed to Rome himself, sending the other members into various towns of northern Italy to teach and preach. A year later all of them were called to Rome for final agreement upon the nature of the order, to be called the Society of Jesus. Ignatius had already begun to draft the Constitutions of the society, but he now submitted them to discussion by the members. After some months of weighing every word, all but two members and Ignatius returned to their work in the field while the three left in Rome continued to work upon the organization. Eventually, in 1540, the Society of Jesus was formally established by the pope. Ignatius was by then a man of forty-nine.

4. Ignatius the Jesuit The establishment of religious orders was nothing new, nor was the attention of such orders to education unique. The Benedictines* in the ninth and tenth centuries had built great monasteries in which at least some of the brethren had been scholars and teachers. Their primary aim, however, was to retire from the world and to live simple lives of great purity amidst rural quietude. Their educational and charitable works were secondary. The Franciscans* of the eleventh century also had schools in their monasteries, as did the Dominicans* in the twelfth. In addition, the Dominicans were entrusted with the defense of the church against heresy and therefore became scholars and theologians. Before the sixteenth century the Franciscans and Dominicans had both lost their standing, for the same reason: the orders had become rich. To be sure, the individual members could not own anything, but the orders could and did.

Ignatius was determined that his new order should not make the mistakes of earlier groups. To this end, he ruled that neither the members nor the order could own anything. The members were allowed to accept no more than bare maintenance for their services. No member could hold any position within or without the church. The Society could not inherit property or money, and both it and its members must depend for support upon daily alms, not permanent donations. In common with members of other brotherhoods the Jesuit took a vow of poverty, chastity, and service, but in addition he took an oath of absolute obedience. This is the vow taken by all the professed:*

> I profess and promise to Almighty God, in presence of the Holy Virgin, His Mother, of all the Court of Heaven, and of all persons now present, and to you, Reverend Father General, whom I regard as holding the place of God, and to your successors, perpetual poverty, chastity, and obedience; and in virtue of this obedience, particularly to instruct children, according to the rule of life contained in the Apostolic Letter granted to the Society of Jesus and in the Constitutions.

The fourth vow, taken by some but not all Jesuits, binds the person taking it "to go wherever the Pope should please to send him, whether among the faithful, or the heathen, without offering excuse, or asking money for the journey, and without, either directly or indirectly, seeking to persuade the Pope on the subject of the mission." [9] The last decision of a man's life was thus taken when he became a Jesuit; from that moment on, he was a soldier and obeyed orders.

The work to which a given member might be assigned varied with his capacities. He might be sent out as a foreign missionary, he might be asked to defend the faith against heretics in debates or through writing, he might become the confessor of a ruling monarch, he might be a teacher of boys or a university professor, he might do social work among the poor, he might be an itinerant preacher, he might be sent out into country districts to teach adults and to improve their modes of life, he might be assigned to hear confessions and counsel with perplexed souls, or he might be stationed in a hospital or a prison. Wherever he went, he was to uphold every accepted doctrine of the church; he was to be humble, tolerant, and obedient; he was to fight with all his strength against evil; and he was to follow literally the motto *Omnia ad majorem Dei gloriam* ("Everything to the greater glory of God"). While he should practice self-denial, he was not to starve himself, or to wear sackcloth and ashes, or to go about dirty. He was also not to hear confession from women or to teach women or girls.

[9] Rose, *op. cit.*, pp. 302–303.

Ignatius was most emphatic on the matter of complete obedience. About a year before he died, he one day called an assistant to him and said, "Write my ideas on obedience, which I wish to leave as my will and testament to the Society," and he dictated these sentences:

1. On my first entrance into Religion, and at all times after, I ought to resign entirely myself into the hands of the Lord my God and of him who governs me in His place.

2. I ought to desire to be ruled by a Superior who endeavours to subjugate my judgment and understanding.

3. In all things wherein there is no *sin* I ought to do the will of my Superior, and not my own. . . .

4. In a word, I ought not to be my own, but His who created me and his too who holds the place of God, yielding myself to be moulded in his hands like so much wax. . . .

5. I ought to be like a corpse, which has neither will nor understanding; or like a little crucifix, which can be turned about at the will of him who holds it; or like a staff in the hands of an old man, who uses it where it can best aid him, or puts it where it may best please him. Thus ought I to be ready for anything in which my Order requires my help, and refuse nothing which is ordered.

6. I must not ask, much less beg, the Superior to send me to any place, or appoint me to any office. . . .

7. So, with regard to poverty, I must consider nothing as my own. But as to the things which I use, I must let myself be treated like a statue, which makes no resistance nor opposition to him who takes aught away from it.[10]

The Jesuits were organized as an army. At the head was a General who held his office for life and whose orders were to be obeyed without question. The countries into which members went were divided into large and small governmental units, with an officer for each. Any needed legislation was enacted by a General Congregation made up of these officers and two representatives from each province, but this body met only when called. Within the Society there were various grades of members: the lay* brothers who took no vows and handled the temporal affairs of the group, the scholastics who went to school or taught, the spiritual coadjutors who entered the ministry after at least ten years of training, and the professed members who took all the vows after fifteen to eighteen years of careful training and probation.

The novices were selected with utmost care. At the end of each successive level of work they had to pass more and more rigorous examinations and pass them well. During their school years their lives were strictly supervised. Their health was guarded, they got enough food and sleep, they were not allowed to do remunerative work, everything they needed was given them gratis, they

[10] D. Bartoli, *History of the Life and Institute of St. Ignatius of Loyola* (translated by F. E. Calderon de la Barca), E. Dunigan and Brothers, 1856 (2 vols.), II. 24.

were not permitted to study too long or even to spend too many hours in prayer. They read only the most approved books and were taught only the purest and safest doctrines. After they completed their lower studies they entered a two-year novitiate. They next passed on to some ten years more of study and then a third year of purely religious training within the order. This third year has been called a "training of the heart" and was devoted to educating and conditioning the future Jesuit's emotions. The candidate was constantly studied, analyzed, corrected, watched, supervised, and cared for. When he was considered ready for service he was sent wherever he would be most useful. Throughout his life he worked for nothing beyond this bare maintenance. This uniformity of training tended to result in a uniform product. For this reason, no particular Jesuit teacher has been selected to represent the group, because no one stands out more prominently than many others. This uniformity was at once the strength and the weakness of the order.

The Society of Jesus started with 11 members; sixteen years later there were 1500, and by the middle of the eighteenth century there were over 23,000. In 1939, the Society had 25,954 members, of which 5,440 were in the United States. Jesuit colleges in this same year enrolled over 40,000 students in this country.[11] This powerful order of trained soldiers was primarily the work of Ignatius of Loyola. Others naturally contributed here and there, and Ignatius always submitted every rule to the scrutiny of as many people as were competent to judge its merits. Both the spirit and the form of the order stemmed, however, from one man. Ignatius was the first General of the order and remained during most of the last fifteen years of his life in Rome, carrying on the business of the Society. He died in 1556.

During the last years of Loyola's life, a typical day is reported to have proceeded as follows: The first hour in the morning was spent in meditation and the second in celebrating the Mass. Ignatius then worked, or wrote, or thought by himself for two hours, after which he either went out to visit others or remained at home to receive visitors. He had his dinner at noon. The next hour was devoted to relaxation and conversation. During the rest of the day he wrote or dictated letters, prepared reports, and in general attended to the routine of maintaining the Society. After supper he continued work until late into the night and then ended the day with an hour or more of prayer and meditation. Ignatius required only four hours' sleep each night. His day began about 5 A.M. and lasted until after midnight.

The Society that Ignatius founded lived on for 233 years, during which its members were of great service to the church and to education. Eventually,

[11] The modern figures are taken from M. P. Harvey, *The Jesuits in Education*, American Press, 1941, 531 pp.

however, it was suppressed, whether justly or not is almost impossible to determine. It remained suppressed for only a few years, was then reorganized, and still exists as the most militant Catholic order.

5. His Appearance and Personality Ignatius showed his practical sense and his knowledge of people in some suggestions he once wrote out for three members to follow in dealing with the general public during a rather long absence from Rome. These bits of shrewd advice have been twisted by opponents of the Jesuits into an expression of intentional deviousness and insincerity. It must, however, be remembered that the directions were given by an upright man to other men of presumed equal uprightness. The advice was not being put into the hands of scoundrels! The Jesuits were trained to be unremittingly strict with themselves and with each other, and Ignatius presumably did not want his brethren to carry their habitual directness and bluntness of criticism into their dealings with the general public. It is against such a background that the suggestions below should be interpreted:

(1) When you have to treat on matters of business with any one, particularly with persons who are your equals or inferiors, you should speak but little and slowly, and not till the others have spoken, showing respect to the rank and distinction of everyone; and listen much and readily, until he you converse with has finished. Then answer every point severally; and take leave when you have nothing more to say. If they reply, answer as briefly as possible. Let your leave-taking be concise, but gracious.

(2) In order to make acquaintance with great personages and to gain their affection, for the greater glory of God our Lord, first study their character and act accordingly. If, for example, a man be of a hasty temper, and speaks rapidly and much, then assume with him something of a familiar tone, adopt his way, but let it be about things good and holy, and be not too serious, nor reserved or melancholy. But with those of a more phlegmatic character, who are slow of speech, grave and measured in discourse, adopt a manner similar to theirs; this is sure to propitiate them. *I make myself all things to all men. . . .*

(3) In all conversations, especially those which concern spiritual things, or when trying to reconcile people, be on your guard that everything that is said may be, or really will be, made public.

(4) In expediting business, be liberal as to time; that is to say, give a promise that the thing shall be done soon, the same day if possible.

(5) None of you three should touch any money; let it be rather deposited with someone. Let whoever asks for a dispensation* himself remit the price to this depositary,* and receive from him a regular receipt, after which the dispensation or expedition may be given; or take other means, which you find more suitable; only take care that each of you may be able to say he has not touched any, even the smallest, sum in this mission.

(6) Consult together on all points on which you do not agree; let the advice of two of the three be adopted. Write often to Rome during your

journey, as soon as you arrive in Scotland, and when you have reached Ireland; then every month give an account of your mission.[12]

FIG. 50. Ignatius the Saint. From a document preserved in the printing department. Drawn by Edouard Garnier and engraved by Trichon.

For an unworldly saint, Ignatius had a remarkable amount of worldly wisdom.

[12] From the original Spanish of *Cartas de San Ignacio,* I, 434. Quoted in Rose, *op. cit.,* pp. 309–310.

It is almost impossible to find out what Ignatius really looked like because he is usually represented as a saint, with all the conventional trappings and depersonalization. The man shown in Figure 50 has little individuality, and his face has hardly any expression at all. The second picture gives a better idea of the actual appearance of Ignatius of Loyola, but the artist has seen fit to emphasize his fineness of spirit rather then the ruggedness of his features or the driving intensity that was one of his chief characteristics.

FIG. 51. Ignatius the Man. From a portrait by H. Wierx.

Throughout his years in Rome, Ignatius lived in the house where novices were undergoing their religious training. The personal bond between them and him seems always to have been strong. A few incidents are given below, concerning his handling of the many lively youths who joined the order in high enthusiasm and then became weary of the discipline. Ignatius seems to have preferred young men of spirit to those who were docile by nature; he realized that a vigorous, unruly youth can—if he learns to control himself—become a pillar of strength, whereas a naturally submissive person never will. He was therefore especially concerned about those novices who were full of life, vitality, drive, and general minor naughtiness. One detailed account appears below. It tells how Ignatius dealt with a restless, impudent boy who had got himself into a minor scrape and had taken refuge in the chapter house of the Jesuits.

The Saint received Pedro with the utmost kindness; the other priests were equally paternal. They kept him that night, and next day Ignatius went to Cardinal Farnese, whom he knew well; Farnese only laughed, promised forgiveness, and desired that Pedro should return. But these few hours had produced a wonderful change in the boy's mind. He now wished to remain with the Fathers. He went back to the palace and to some other places only to find friends whom he might consult, as Ignatius bade him, on his choice of life. The step appeared too rapid and extreme to all ordinary judgments; he was hardly fifteen, and the contrast with his former life seemed too great for a boy so young. But Ignatius saw extraordinary promise in [the boy], and thought with a precocious and turbulent nature like his, it was best to begin soon. He kept him in the house; and at last, he received him formally into the novitiate. . . . He was made to retain at first his ordinary dress; it was impossible yet to be quite sure of him; he had not gone through the "Exercises," nor even received his first Communion! And at one time he regretted the splendours and pleasures of the Court; his old impatience and wilfulness seemed to revive. St. Ignatius reproved without the least effect. Pedro was only irritated. Then Ignatius had recourse, as usual with him, to prayer, and earnestly asked that this soul might be given him. He sent for Pedro, who almost as soon as Ignatius began to speak, burst into tears, and said: "Yo los hare, padre, yo los hare—I will take them," meaning the "Exercises." He passed through these, made his Confession, . . . and received the Holy Eucharist at Christmas, the first Christmas after the Society of Jesus had been recognized as an Order.

The two years of his novitiate did not pass without many outbreaks. He disliked early rising, and took to lying down with his clothes on, to save the time appointed for dressing. This was against the rules of the order and cleanliness, and censured accordingly. When he was bidden to sweep the house, he filled it with dust; when he went about, he banged the doors, clattered down the staircase, ran or jumped through the corridors. The grave Fathers began to think Ignatius had introduced a monkey into the house, and one day the Master of the Novices, following the youth into the room when Ignatius sent for him, complained that he was unmanageable, that he disturbed the peace of the house, and that they could do nothing with him. The Saint appeased the Novice-Master, quieted the other Fathers, who urged a dismissal, by assuring them Pedro had made much progress already, and would hereafter be a worthier subject than those who had less effervescence to subdue. The boy really tried, and in part succeeded; he tied something to his legs, that he might remember not to run downstairs; he made less noise and took pains when he was ordered to dress the dinner. . . . Ignatius once asked Pedro "if he knew what it was to be a secretary?" "It is to be faithful in keeping secrets," said Pedro. "Since that is your idea," said Ignatius, "you shall be mine"; and he often gave him letters and other things to transcribe. He wrote badly, and sometimes made mistakes in spelling. Ignatius, fastidious in the matter of neat writing, had much patience, and corrected his copies repeatedly. One day, to give him a stronger lesson, he threw the papers on the floor, and said, "This foolish boy will never do any good!" Pedro wept, and beat his cheeks for grief. Then he infringed the rules of the refectory, and took his breakfast into his own room to save time; then he made grimaces to another novice. He incurred long penances by these transactions, but his courage and desire to join the Order carried him through the two years successfully, though not without many mischances. Less kindness to the boy novice would have caused him to give up hope; less severity would have left him a confirmed trifler.[13]

A few other incidents of Loyola's handling of individual cases are also interesting.

(a) If he perceived a novice inclined to a particular fault, he bade him preach and exhort others to the opposite virtue.

(b) Lorenzo Mazzi, a young nobleman of Brescia, revealed to Ignatius that he was tempted to quit the Society. "If our way of life be too strict for you," said Ignatius, "I will not oppose it." But first, he begged this of him—"When you wake tonight, stretch yourself out as if you were dead, and think to yourself how you will wish to have lived when that time really draws near." The young man remained and became a good priest.

(c) Once, at midnight, Ignatius sent for a young novice who was so displeased at a duty imposed on him that he could not rest, and was thinking of returning to the world. The Saint asked him what advice he would give anyone afflicted by such and such temptations, and so ingeniously depicted the young man's mind to himself, suggesting fit remedies, that the youth, touched and convinced, remained willingly in the house.

(d) Ignatius made another, whose room was disorderly, put all his things into a sack and go through the house with it on his shoulder, telling everyone whom he met of his offense; for the Saint was displeased if, when he visited the room he did not find the bed neatly made, the nightcap, the shoes, the candlestick, in their proper places, the broom put out of sight, and all the small remainder of each one's scanty furniture well arranged.

(e) Sometimes Ignatius caused a circle to be drawn on the floor round an offender, who was not to leave it without permission, but he might sit down if there was room. He would send a culprit to pray before the Blessed Sacrament for a certain time, or till he was sent for; in which case he used to add, "And you had better pray that I may not forget you."[14]

[13] Rose, *op. cit.*, condensed from pp. 268–27[illegible]

[14] *Ibid.*, pp. 338–339.

A good summary of Ignatius as a person is given by one of his biographers:

> There burned in him a zeal, active, ardent, indefatigable, always meditating enterprises, battles, and victories to spread the greater glory of God; . . . he everywhere stood for the cause of his holy Church, and the rebirth of piety and holiness of life, wherever the glory of the Christian name had been tarnished. And all this was united with an unalterable sweetness and gentleness, ennobled by a largeness of heart, which rose above all labors or success, beautified by that noble and delicate urbanity, characteristic of Spanish chivalry of his day, enlightened by the supernatural illumination of heavenly wisdom.[15]

Such then were the life and character of St. Ignatius, the founder of the militant religious order that almost singlehanded checked the further spread of Protestantism and reclaimed many a soul for the Catholic Church.

B. THE SCHOOLS OF THE JESUITS

In the Constitutions, which form the basic law of the Society of Jesus, one chapter is devoted to the activities of the Society in the field of education. The aims, principles, and general organization are there set forth. Ignatius did not himself produce a detailed statement of exactly how each thing was to be done and each problem met, because he wanted such a formulation to rest upon the cumulative experience of many teachers in many places, and Ignatius died before the necessary experience had had time to accumulate. Twenty-eight years after his death, the fourth General of the Society called six schoolmen from different countries to Rome for the purpose of working out a definite plan of education. This committee worked for nine months, using as a basis the relevant chapter in the Constitutions and certain local plans that had already been drawn up by members of the order. The plan or "ratio" that this committee evolved was submitted to Jesuit teachers in all the provinces. Many members had criticisms and suggestions. The plan was first tried out in only a few places, to determine the appropriateness of each detail. Five years after their original meeting the members of the committee again assembled to make such revisions and modifications as seemed desirable. This process of work by a central committee and comments by those who were actually teaching continued for another eight years. No one can say that the Jesuits brought forth their plan of education casually or carelessly; all members had their say, and those most competent in educational matters battled over every word. Eventually, in 1599, forty-three years after the death of Ignatius, the *Ratio Studiorum* or "Plan of Studies" was given to the world.

[15] Astrain, *op. cit.*, p. 115.

In essence it is a set of definite rules for school officials, teachers, and pupils. All Jesuit schools and colleges adopted it; and it, or one of its similarly constructed successors, has been in use ever since as the basis of all Jesuit education.[16]

Although the plan did not come into its final form until decades after the death of Ignatius, it was nevertheless in part his creation. He laid down the principles upon which it was based, and he stamped the entire educational system with his own personality and experience. Many of the provisions show an obvious relationship to incidents in his own life. Thus, his insistence that one level of work be really mastered before another was begun came probably from his own efforts to do university work before he had learned Latin. No student was to be allowed to work while attending school, and poor pupils were to be supplied with whatever they needed. One can believe that this provision rested upon Loyola's sad experiences in trying to work while studying and in using needed study time to beg for food. No excesses of self-mortification were to be allowed. This rule presumably grew out of his own former excesses and his later reaction to them. Many other connections between the rules for Jesuit education and Loyola's experiences could be cited.

1. The General Nature of the Ratio Studiorum[17] The Jesuits showed in the *Ratio* a combination of scholasticism and humanism. The former dominated the work in the higher schools for theologians, but it appeared also in the emphasis upon disputation in all schools. The course of study was, however, humanistic in the extreme. Out of the twenty-five hours a week of teaching in the lower schools, twenty-two were devoted to the study of Latin. For intensive class discussion only Cicero was used, although other authors were read. The plan had only one basic objective: the development of ability to write and speak correct, forceful, and distinguished Latin. A secondary aim was the training and disciplining of the mind that should be brought about by such a program of work. A small amount of Greek was also included, but the main purpose of the Jesuit teacher was to train his pupils to think clearly and to express themselves correctly, using the Roman classics as materials.

The organization of the schools was most precisely described and the

[16] Some minor adaptations were always made to local needs, however.

[17] The material in this section is based upon the following references: T. J. Campbell, *The Jesuits, 1534–1921, A History of the Society of Jesus from Its Foundation to the Present Time,* Encyclopedia Press, 1921, 2 vols.; G. Compayré, *Histoire critique des doctrines de l'éducation en France depuis le seizieme siècle,* Librairie Hachette et Cie., 1879 (487 pp.) Book ii, Chap. 1; F. de Dainville, "L'Éducation des Jesuites," *Ètudes* (1946), 251: 181–201; F. P. Donnelly, *Principles of Jesuit Education in Practice,* P. J. Kenedy & Sons, 1934, 205 pp.; E. A. Fitzpatrick, *St. Ignatius and the Ratio Studiorum,* McGraw-Hill Book Company, 1905 (426 pp.), Chap. 13; Schwickerath, *Jesuit Education.*

duties of each official were clearly delimited. The lower or grammar school was divided into grades. This division has by now become universal in schools, but it was a new idea in the sixteenth century. There were five classes: three in grammar, one in the humanities, and one in rhetoric. The class was, however, a unit of work, not a unit of time. A student might be two or more years in finishing the work of a given grade, and he was almost certain to spend at least seven years in finishing the five classes together. Although the general promotions took place at the end of the school year, a boy might be promoted at any time. To quote the *Ratio:*

> If there are any who greatly excel or seem likely to make more progress in a higher class than their own they should by no means be held back but promoted at any time of the year, after an examination.[18]

The curriculum was entirely prescribed, down to the last detail. An outline of the work to be followed in each class appears below:

> Lower grammar: The aim of this class is a perfect knowledge of the rudiments and elementary knowledge of the syntax. In Greek: reading, writing, and a certain portion of the grammar. The work used for the prelection will be some easy selections from Cicero, besides fables of Phaedrus* and Lives of Nepos.*
>
> Middle grammar: The aim is a knowledge, though not entire, of all grammar; and, for the prelection, only the select epistles, narrations, descriptions, and the like for Cicero, with the Commentaries of Caesar,* and some of the easiest poems of Ovid. In Greek: the fables of Aesop, select dialogues of Lucian,* the Tablet of Cebes.*
>
> Upper grammar: The aim is a complete knowledge of grammar, including all the exceptions and idioms in syntax, figures and rhetoric, and the art of versification. In Greek, the eight parts of speech, or all the rudiments. For the lessons: in prose the most important epistles of Cicero, the books, *De Amicitia,** *De Senectute,** and others of the kind, or even some of the easier orations; in poetry, some select elegies* and epistles of Ovid, also selection from Catullus,* Tibullus,* Propertius,* and the Eclogues* of Virgil, or some of Virgil's easier books, as the fourth book of the Georgics,* or the fifth and seventh books of the Aeneid. In Greek: St. Chrysostom, Aesop, and the like.
>
> Humanities: The aim is to prepare, as it were, the ground for eloquence, which is done in three ways: by a knowledge of the language, some erudition, and a sketch of the precepts pertaining to rhetoric. For a command of the language, which consists chiefly in acquiring propriety of expresson and fluency, the one prose author employed in daily prelections is Cicero; as historical writers, Caesar, Sallust, Livy, and others of the kind; the poets are used, first of all Virgil, also odes of Horace, with the elegies,

[18] Fitzpatrick, *op. cit.,* pp. 181–182.

epigrams and other productions of illustrious poets, expurgated; in like manner orators, historians, and poets, in the vernacular. The erudition conveyed should be slight, and only to stimulate and recreate the mind, not to impede progress in learning the tongue. The precepts will be the general rules of expression and style, and the special rules on the minor kinds of composition, epistles, narrations, descriptions, both in verse and prose. In Greek: the art of versification, and some notions of the dialects; also a clear understanding of authors, and some composition in Greek. The Greek prose authors will be Saints Chrysostom and Basil, epistles of Plato and Synesius,* and some selections from Plutarch*; the poets: Homer, Phocylides,* Theognis,* Saint Gregory Nazianzen, and others like them.

Rhetoric: The grade of this class cannot be easily defined. For it trains to perfect eloquence, which comprises two great faculties, the oratorical and the poetical, the former chiefly being the object of culture; nor does it regard only the practical, but the beautiful also. For the precepts, Cicero may be supplemented with Tertullian* and Aristotle. The style, which may be assisted by drawing on the most approved historians and poets, is to be formed on Cicero; all of his works are most fitted for this purpose, but only his speeches should be made the subject of prelection, that the precepts of the art may be seen in practise.—As to the vernacular, the style should be formed on the best authors. The erudition will be derived from the history and manners of nations, from the authority of writers and all learning, but moderately as befits the capacity of the students.—In Greek; the fuller knowledge of authors and dialects is to be acquired. The Greek authors, whether orators, historians or poets, are to be ancient and classic: Demosthenes, Plato, Thucydides, Homer, Hesiod, Pindar,* and others of the kind, including Saint Nazianzen, Basil, and Chrysostom.[19]

Not only the subject matter but the texts were also prescribed. The Jesuit schools had libraries in which could be found "enough useful books and not too many useless ones." Since the books available at the time of the original *Ratio* were not altogether satisfactory, various members of the Jesuit order were requested to write books that would be more suitable to the plan. These books were compendia, written expressly for students. Thus there appeared a *Precepts of Rhetoric,* an *Art of Composition,* and an *Art of Oratory.* While these were not language textbooks of the modern type because they approached language from an artistic rather than a scientific point of view, they were nevertheless textbooks in that they contained a summary of their respective subjects so arranged as to be digestible by the student mind.

A typical Jesuit school in Upper Germany used the following books as late as the beginning of the eighteenth century.[20]

[19] From T. Hughes, *Loyola and the Educational System of the Jesuits.* Copyright 1912. Reprinted by permission of Charles Scribner's Sons, publishers.

[20] Father F. X. Kropf, *Ratio et Via,* J. J. Vötter, 1736, 288 pp.

1. The Latin Grammar of Alvarez.
2. The *Progymnasmata* of Father Pontanus (a series of easy Latin readings).
3. The Greek Grammar of either Father Gratzer or Father Bayer.
4. The Catechism of Father Peter Canisius.
5. *Rudimenta historica* (a world history).
6. A brief compendium of rhetoric.

These six textbooks, plus numerous readings in the classics of both Greece and Rome, plus selections from the church fathers, the Gospel* in Latin, and the Acts* of the Apostles in Greek made up the basic materials of instruction. It should be noted that a small amount of history was also included in the curriculum.

The pupils in the Jesuit schools had classes for two and a half hours in the morning and two in the afternoon. They had one holiday each week. After school hours they had games and various types of physical exercise. Each day they went to Mass. From the first class on, they had "homework." The daily routine of school life was not much different from that of the average high school of today, except that the modern, pervasive social life did not exist.

At the head of each school was a prefect of studies, who had general charge over the entire school. If he needed an assistant, he could have one. There was also an official who was charged with maintaining discipline. Finally there was the faculty. The prefect was to visit each teacher at least once a month to observe his teaching. He was to approve all theses for disputation. The members of the faculty were to meet at least once every two weeks to exchange ideas and to listen to whatever the prefect had to say to them. This organization is commonplace today. A small school has a "head" with one or two assistants who are in charge of teaching, social life, manners, and morals; there is also a staff of teachers. In the sixteenth and seventeenth centuries, however, such an organization was new.

Perhaps the four most outstanding traits of this plan, insofar as its curricular and administrative organization is concerned, were its continuity, its uniformity, its practicality, and its fixity. The first was a great merit. The work of each teacher was so planned that the student who went through the grades emerged with a coherent and systematic education. All work had the same aim, and each part of the work had its place in reaching that aim. A better coordinated plan of education would be difficult to devise. The second trait, uniformity, was also of value, especially at the time of the *Ratio,* when each schoolmaster in each school in each country was in the habit of teaching whatever suited him. The *Ratio* was extremely practical because it laid down specific rules for teaching, specific methods, and specific cautions. It provided for supervision of all teaching. A man did not have to be a Vittorino da Feltre to be a good Jesuit teacher. He had to be intelligent, educated, interested in youth, able and willing to follow directions, docile in large matters but ingenious in the minutiae of teaching. The last characteristic of the *Ratio,* its fixity, was perhaps the outstanding fault of the system. Every main issue was settled, every procedure was already outlined, and no great initiative was called for. At first, Jesuit education was new and progressive, soon it was the accepted thing, then it became conservative, and in the course of time it was outdated. It should be noted, however, that it was never a decadent education; it did not rot from within. It merely remained the same with only minor alterations from generation to generation, while the world moved on through a series of changes that made obsolete the up-to-date education of 1600.

The Jesuit educational system was an organization of man power on military lines. It was administered and controlled like an army, from the top down. It had all the advantages of cohesion, co-ordination, and unified control, but it had also the weaknesses of any army—overdiscipline, rigidity, and lack of initiative. It exalted authority and subordinated the individual, but for accomplishing the ends for which it was devised, it was an almost perfect organization.

2. *The Training of Jesuit Teachers* It was clear from the beginning that the teacher must be carefully trained if the order were to have the desired influence upon the next generation. The first step was to select as future teachers those youths who were by nature inclined to such work. This selection was based primarily upon the ability of a student to demonstrate in oral, individual examinations his ability to explain clearly what he had learned, to defend his statements, and to convince his hearers. These examinations took place at the end of each grade in school and served both as evidence of sufficient mastery for promotion and as an opportunity for the demonstration of teaching skill. To be selected as a future teacher a student had to pass these examinations not only acceptably but with distinction. After finishing the lower school and passing through the two years of his novitiate,* the young man went to the university and then to an academy for teachers. In the spring of the last year before he was to begin teaching, he was assigned to watch experienced instructors and to confer with them. The prospective teacher also met with the prefect of studies three hours a week and gave practice lessons under his supervision. In this way, according to the *Ratio,* a "class of good professors may be cultivated and propagated like a crop." [21]

Certain of the members taught for only a few years, but many remained

[21] Fitzpatrick, *op. cit.,* p. 132.

teachers all their lives. These latter members were accepted in the order upon condition that they devote themselves to teaching in the lower schools. After a few years of work they might be relieved of their duty for long enough to be ordained as priests, but they were then to return to schoolwork. If their superior decided that they were becoming too fatigued, they might have a change for a year or two, but essentially they belonged to a recognized group of "perpetual teachers."

The prefect of studies visited all classes at least once in two weeks to make sure that each teacher was keeping up to schedule, that he was using proper methodology, that he did not omit the necessary reviews, that he did not introduce extraneous matter, and that he did not express unorthodox views. The prefect was also to commend good work. The new professor was especially supervised to prevent the possible introduction of innovations. The prefect was "to take great care that new teachers retain the method of teaching of predecessors." [22] Even the professors of the higher faculties in the colleges were not to introduce new notions of their own:

> He [the professor] shall obey the Prefect of Studies in all matters which pertain to studies and the discipline of the classes. He shall give him for revision all theses before they are presented. He shall not undertake to explain any books or writings not in the usual course or introduce any new method of teaching or disputation.[23]

The Jesuit teacher was at no time allowed to express before his students opinions of his own. He might have his private views, he might discuss them with other teachers, he might try to have them incorporated officially in the accepted plan, but before his students he must stick to traditional attitudes. The Jesuits were very firm on this point, as may be seen in the passage below:

> If there are any too prone to innovations or too liberal in their views, they shall certainly be removed from the responsibility of teaching.[24]
>
> Let no one defend any opinion which is judged by the generality of learned men to go against the received tenets of philosophy and theology or the common consent of the theological scholars.
>
> Even in matters where there is no risk to faith and devotion no one shall introduce new questions in matters of great moment or any opinion which does not have suitable authority, without first consulting his superiors. He shall not teach anything opposed to the axioms of learned men or the accepted beliefs of scholars.[25]

A teacher was not supposed to use his classwork as a means of self-expression, he was not to use his students as guinea pigs for the trial of his own ideas, he

[22] *Ibid.*, p. 176.
[23] *Ibid.*, p. 151.
[24] *Ibid.*, p. 126.
[25] *Ibid.*, p. 161.

was not to be an original investigator. He was to be an instrument for passing down accepted attitudes and beliefs to the rising generation.[26]

The modern teacher would feel greatly repressed and limited by such rules, although a bit less of unsubstantiated opinion in the classrooms of America might be a good thing. The hedging about of instruction did not, however, apply to the teacher's personal relations with his pupils. The boys had only one teacher for all their work, and this teacher was promoted with them from year to year. He was supposed to study each pupil to determine his capacities. Some boys were to be selected as teachers, some as writers, others as theologians, some as administrators, others as scholars. If a boy showed special ability his teacher was to recommend him for an extra year of study, so that he might have a firmer foundation. The teacher was to be accessible to his pupils, for instance:

> After the lecture let him [the teacher] remain in the classroom or near the classroom for at least a quarter of an hour so that the students may approach him to ask questions, so that he may sometimes give an account of the lectures, and so that the lectures may be repeated.[27]

The teacher was definitely warned against showing favoritism.

> He shall not appear more friendly to one pupil than another, he shall despise no one, he shall attend to the studies of the poor the same as to those of the rich, he shall especially seek the progress of all his students.[28]

From all available evidence, the personal bond between teacher and pupil was unusually close in the Jesuit schools, especially so in the case of those who were being groomed to enter the order. The teachers were men who had a natural interest in youngsters and were able to lead them. They were also men with a burning enthusiasm for and devotion to their work and their religion. Between their natural attraction to their pupils and their desire to indoctrinate their charges with their own sincere attitudes, they were led into close and friendly personal relationships with the boys in their classes.

3. The Students in Jesuit Schools The *Ratio* included various rules as to the conduct of students, their methods of study, and their behavior. Each class was welded into an effective working unit. It had its officers, although these

[26] For the most part the directions in the *Ratio* are straightforward and sincere, but here and there one comes upon an item that shows the sort of casuistry* for which the Jesuits, rightly or wrongly, have become famous. The professor of theology is to avoid even mentioning the Arab philosopher Averroës* whenever he can, and "if anything good is to be cited from him, let him [the professor] bring it out without praise and, if possible, let him show that he has taken it from some other source."—Fitzpatrick, *op. cit.*, p. 168.

[27] *Ibid.*, p. 152.

[28] *Ibid.*, p. 156.

were not elected but appointed by the teacher, who was instructed to choose the boys who wrote the best compositions. These officers were christened with the names of great Greek or Roman leaders. Then there were the decurions,* one for each group of ten pupils. The decurions were assistants to the teacher in the simpler mechanics of class management. In the words of the *Ratio:*

> Let the Decurions be appointed by the Preceptor to hear the memory recitations, to collect the papers for the Preceptor, to note in a little book how many times each failed in memory, who neglected to write or to bring both copies, and to observe anything else the Preceptor may direct.[29]

This arrangement did not automatically make spies out of the decurions, but it certainly gave a boy a chance to be an informer. However, this tendency could be controlled by the teacher, since he appointed the decurions. Aside from the above defect, the idea of having students work in small groups with an appointed leader is a good one.

The class was divided into halves, and each half tried to outdo the other. In addition, individual students were paired with each other and were called "rivals." It was the business of each rival to watch the other, to ask him questions, to correct his work, and to trip him if he could. A modern Jesuit has described a classroom in the following manner: "A class is an armed battalion, always at civil war and ready at all times for special combats." [30] This notion of constant rivalry seems strange to most modern teachers, who are taught to provide an atmosphere in which students can relax, and are warned against allowing rivalry except that of a pupil against his own past record.

The *Ratio* devotes a few rules to conduct, methods of study, and attitudes toward work. For instance:

> Let them [the students] be constant in attending lectures and diligent in studying them beforehand and reviewing them after they have heard, in asking those things they do not understand, in taking notes on those things which are important, to which they can refer later when their memories fail them.[31]
>
> In the hours assigned for private study let those who are working in the higher faculties review at home the things which they have heard or written in class and learn them thoroughly. Let them examine their knowledge by proposing objections to themselves and answering them; if they cannot answer some, let them take note of them for inquiry or disputation.[32]
>
> Let all observe the divisions of time and the method of study prescribed

[29] *Ibid.*, p. 205.
[30] Donnelly, *op. cit.*, p. 44.
[31] Fitzpatrick, *op. cit.*, p. 235.
[32] *Ibid.*, p. 236.

by the prefect or the master and let them not use any other books than those given by the prefect.[33]

Let them not wander about here and there in the classroom but let each study on his own bench and in his own place, quietly and in silence, intent upon himself and his affairs. Let them not leave the classroom except with the consent of the master.[34]

They shall especially apply themselves to anything for which they notice they have natural inclination and shall consult their superiors on the matter. They shall not, however, omit anything which is prescribed.[35]

From these excerpts one can see that the Jesuits were greatly concerned over the behavior and progress of their students. The teacher was to regard his charges with a mixture of paternalism and solicitude. The student was to conduct himself decorously and to study what was given him in the way he was told to study it. A little initiative was allowed, but not much. As Macaulay* once remarked, the Jesuits seemed to have found the exact point to which intellectual development could be carried without becoming intellectual independence!

4. Methods of Instruction Instruction in a Jesuit school was largely oral, and all members of the class took part in most of the work. The education of the schools did not rest upon the written word, as is the case at present, but upon the spoken word. There was much individual tutoring. While other members of a class studied or wrote, the master might call pupils to him one by one and go over each boy's work with him. Remedial work was thus individualized, but teaching was mostly by group instruction.

The Jesuit teacher had several methods of procedure, all prescribed and all good. The first was the *prelection,* which resembled a modern lecture in some respects but differed from it in others. The teacher first read through without interruption the whole passage upon which he based the day's lesson. This passage had to be something from Cicero. Usually the excerpt was not over twenty lines long, and it might be as short as two lines. Next the master went back to the beginning of the passage, explained its meaning, discussed it sentence by sentence, phrase by phrase, and word by word, letting the students take notes. In this analysis the class co-operated as much as possible. The master next gave pertinent illustrations and examples from other passages in Cicero or from other authors, and he might give such further explanations or references to authority as he thought desirable. During the discussion and especially toward the end he was to introduce a few items that might contribute to a historical, geographical, scientific, or literary background. He was not,

[33] *Ibid.,* p. 235.
[34] *Ibid.,* p. 242.
[35] *Ibid.,* p. 239.

however, to forget his main objective of teaching pupils to speak and write Latin. He should not, therefore, be so full of facts about the historical background of Cicero's writings that he neglected Cicero's sentence structure. "Erudition" was to be left in the main to the university; the grammar school was to introduce only such tidbits as might serve either to interest the pupils or to explain the text. For what it was designed to do—namely, to analyze Cicero's style—the prelection is an excellent method. Incidentally, it was described by Quintilian, in almost the identical manner of use by the Jesuits.[36]

A second method was called a *concertatio*. This was a general class discussion in which all members were encouraged to participate. It was somewhat like a modern recitation, but it contained other elements. The rivals could question each other, read each other's papers aloud, and correct each other. The subject matter of the *concertatio* was usually drawn from the prelections or written work of the previous day. It was a combination of oral review, oral examination, and recitation, with a great deal of pupil participation.

A third technique was the *disputation,* a heritage of scholasticism. There was a daily public disputation at which all pupils were present, plus private discussions and others on various important occasions. There were also *declamations,* both private and public.

The Jesuit teachers depended in no small measure for their effectiveness upon constant repetition and review, imitation, thorough examinations, and rewards for success. At the end of each day's work there was an immediate repetition to the decurions and also a daily disputation based on the same material. On Saturday the work of the entire week was reviewed and discussed. There were also monthly repetitions and disputations. At the end of each year the pupils went back over the entire year's work, and at the beginning of each year the teacher gave a brief review of material learned during the previous term. It is difficult to evaluate this great amount of repetition. In the hands of an expert it might be excellent, but in the hands of a mediocre master it would be deadly.

Since the objective of the grammar school was the ability to write and speak Latin with distinction, it is natural that great stress should be placed upon the imitation of famous writers, especially Cicero. The pupils wrote more than they read. In correcting the written work, the master was to analyze the nature of the errors so that each student might know upon what elements to put stress in the future. In addition to the imitations there were sundry other types of composition.

The examinations were oral and were held in the presence of all the

[36] There were also prelections on the "precepts" of rhetoric, but the subject matter is too technical for presentation here. In any case, no new principles are involved.

other students. From these yearly tests no one was exempt. A boy passed with mediocrity if he could give a coherent account of the subject matter covered in the previous year. Those who wished either to go on into theology or to become teachers had to "surpass mediocrity."

There were prizes for good work: eight awards each year in rhetoric, four for Greek and Latin prose and verse, six in the humanities, and four for Latin and Greek prose writing in the grammar classes. These prizes were given at the end of each year at a public ceremony. A herald called out the names of the winners, and a poem might be read in each lad's honor or a verse chanted by the choir. In addition, there were numerous small rewards throughout the year. The master read in class some of the best papers or posted them up on the wall of the classroom. Sometimes he encouraged the pupils to write and act out a short play. Perhaps these types of motivation were inadequate for the average or poor student, but they must at least have affected the work of the most promising pupils.

5. Discipline The Jesuit teacher did not have to handle more than minor problems of discipline, such as arise in any classroom. His function was to teach, not to coerce or to punish. For real infractions of the rules there was a "corrector" who was not a member of the Society. This official had authority to expel from the school any scholar who would not adapt himself to the work of the classroom. Jesuit discipline was undoubtedly strict and repressive, but it does not appear to have been either cruel or unjust. Certainly the instructions in the *Ratio* are wise and tolerant: "Let there be no haste in punishing, nor too much in accusing." [37]

If a boy were clearly unsuited to be a scholar he could be dismissed from the school. If he were in a grade in which the work seemed too difficult for him, he could be demoted. At all levels progress depended upon how much a boy knew, not upon how long he had been in a given grade. Under such circumstances the elimination must have been considerable and the retardation rate* extremely high, but those who survived must have been capable and well educated.

6. The Founding of Colleges and Schools by the Jesuits In the two centuries after the death of Ignatius, the Jesuits founded 612 colleges and 157 normal schools,[38] distributed all over the face of Europe. Figure 52 gives the position of the schools in Northern Europe. The numbers appearing on the map indicate the number of schools in each area. The enrollments were large, even by modern standards. At Utrecht* there were 1000 students; at

[37] *Ibid.*, p. 206.

[38] G. M. Pachtler, "Ratio Studiorum et Institutiones Scholasticae Societatis Jesu," *Monumenta Germaniae Paedagogica,* A. Hofmann, 1887–1894 (4 vols.), Vol. II.

Munich*, 1600; at Rouen, 200; at Louis le Grand in Paris, 300. In all, there were about 210,000 students in Jesuit schools when they were at their height in the late seventeenth century.[39] These schools were all free and public; any boy might attend them without charge, provided he had his parents' permission. No pupil was to be excluded because of lowly social position or poverty. The schools were not, however, charitable or primarily for the poor, as was the case in certain other schools maintained by teaching brotherhoods.[40] The Jesuits established also 59 houses for novices, 340 residences for members, 200 missions in foreign countries, 29 houses for professed members, and 24 universities. The grand total of establishments was 1,421.

Each school was supported by the income from a donation. The Jesuits

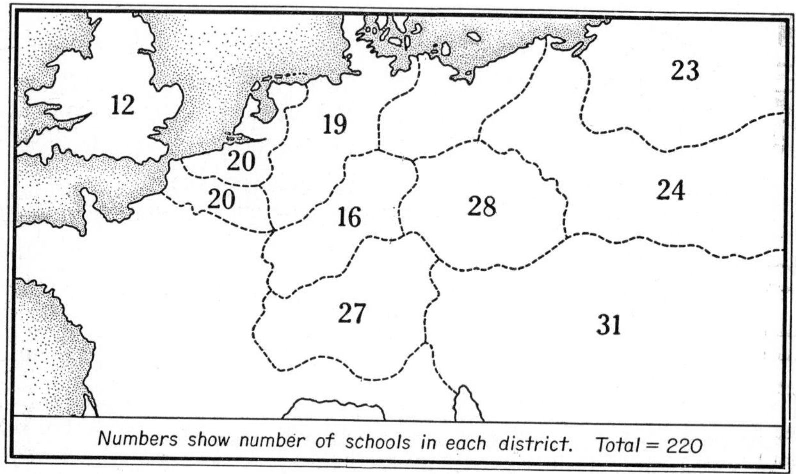

FIG. 52. Distribution of Jesuit Schools in Northern Europe, in 1725. Based on a map in E. P. Cubberley, *History of Education,* Plate 8.

were very careful in their acceptance of a school plant and turned down many offers. A donor had to present an adequate number of buildings and a church, and he had to put aside sufficient revenue for the perpetual maintenance of the faculty and for the support of indigent scholars. For a grammar school there were 20 teachers; for a lyceum or college, 50; for a university, 70. Once the donor had given the necessary buildings, equipment, and funds, he had nothing more to do with the institution, which was then incorporated into the Jesuit system and controlled by the order.

The Jesuit schools had their advantages and their shortcomings, but they

[39] S. J. de Lac, *Les Jesuites,* Plon-Nourrit et Cie., 1901 (488 pp.), p. 297; Hughes, *op. cit.,* pp. 69 ff.
[40] See chap. xiii.

were so superior to other schools of the period that even some Protestants sent their sons to them. Many famous men were educated in Jesuit schools: Corneille,* Molière,* Diderot,* Voltaire,* Descartes,* and Richelieu* to mention only a few. Even Voltaire, who said many harsh things about Jesuits in public life, wrote about their schools:

> The best years of my life have been spent in the schools of the Jesuits, and while there I have never listened to any teaching but what was good nor seen any conduct but what was exemplary.[41]

On the other hand, the schools had the weaknesses of overorganization, rigidity, and prescription. It may be noted that no one Jesuit teacher was selected as a central character for this chapter. The teacher was a cog in a machine and was not allowed individual prominence. Hence it was impossible to select one rather than another.

It is clear that the educational influence of the Jesuits was widespread and, in the main, beneficial. When the order was dissolved, the education of Europe was seriously affected. Because Jesuit teachers received only bare maintenance, several of them could be supported on the salary needed by the average professor in civil life, who had to earn enough for his family, his home, and his own old age. Not everything in Jesuit education was good, but the educational ledger balances in their favor rather than against them.

Jesuit education is still a force, within the Catholic world at least. It now operates under a new *Ratio* that differs from the old in details but not in spirit. The order has preserved remarkably its original character. It is still a militant teaching order, and it still gives a free, prescribed education.

To schools in general the Jesuits bequeathed their division of work into grade levels, their careful training of teachers in special colleges, their practice-teaching and supervision, and their attitude toward teaching as a "calling" and a lifework. Some of these ideas were not unique or new, but they were given widespread publicity because the Jesuits established colleges in so many places and were the teachers of so many people. Like Luther and Melanchthon, they realized the power of education and the necessity for making education universal, even though their reasons for founding schools differed from those advanced by the Protestants.

READING REFERENCES

A. General Histories of the Period

Ergang, *Europe from the Renaissance to Waterloo,* chap. 8.
Garrett, *European History,* 1500–1815, chap. 12.

[41] J. B. Alzog, *Manual of Church History,* M. H. Gill and Son, 1889–1892 (4 vols.), II, 570.

Ogg, D., *Europe in the Seventeenth Century,* A. & C. Black, Ltd., 1925 (579 pp.), chaps. 3, 8.
Robinson, *Introduction to the History of Western Europe,* chap. 28.
Schevill, *A History of Europe from the Reformation to the Present Day,* chaps. 7, 13.
Stearns, *Pageant of History,* part i, chap. 11.

B. Other Texts in the History of Education

Cole, *History of Educational Thought,* pp. 202–207.
Cubberley, *History of Education,* pp. 319–326.
Eby and Arrowood, *The Development of Modern Education,* chap. 6.
Marique, *History of Christian Education,* Vol. II, chap. 6.
McCormick, *History of Education,* chap. 22.
Monroe, *A Textbook in the History of Education,* pp. 420–429.
Moore, *The Story of Instruction,* Vol. II, chap. 9.
Ulich, *History of Educational Thought,* pp. 149–155.

C. Secondary Sources

Donnelly, *Principles of Jesuit Education in Practice,* chaps. 4–7, 11–13.
Fitzpatrick, *St. Ignatius and the Ratio Studiorum,* part i.
Harvey, M. P., *The Jesuits in Education,* American Press, 1941 (513 pp.), chaps. 1–5, 9, 18.
Hughes, *Loyola and the Educational System of the Jesuits,* part i, chaps. 2–4, 6, 8; part ii, chaps. 10–12, 14, 15, 17.
Magevney, E., *The Jesuits as Educators,* Catholic Library Association, 1899, 64 pp.
McGucken, W. J., *The Jesuits and Education,* Bruce Pubiishing Company, 1932 (352 pp.), chaps 2, 3, pp. 271–318.
Painter, *Great Pedagogical Essays,* chap. 13.
Rose, *St. Ignatius of Loyola and the Early Jesuits,* book i, chaps. 1–5, 9, 10; book ii, chaps. 3–5, 9.
Schwickerwath, *Jesuit Education: Its History and Principles,* chaps. 3–6.
van Dyke, P., *Ignatius Loyola,* Charles Scribner's Sons, 1926 (381 pp.), chaps. 2–6, 9, 10, 14–16, 18, 22.

D. Translations of Primary Sources

Fitzpatrick, *St. Ignatius and the Ratio Studiorum,* part ii.
Ulich, *Three Thousand Years of Educational Wisdom,* pp. 272–286.

PART SIX

EARLY MODERN TIMES

CHAPTER XII

COMENIUS AND HIS TEXTBOOKS

The most active years of Comenius's life coincided almost exactly with the duration of the Thirty Years' War,* although he was born twenty-six years before it started and lived for twenty-two years after it stopped. No other such period of destruction ever visited Germany, up until the decade following 1940, and in the earlier instance the quarrels that produced the war were not of the Germans' choosing. Practically all the fighting was done by foreign armies who used the Germanies for a battleground, lived off the country by robbing the natives, inflicted much wanton destruction, depopulated entire districts, and generally demoralized the people. It was in and out of this carnage that Comenius wandered, always an exile, usually alone, and often in danger of imprisonment or death if he were caught. His life was long and unhappy, but it was also useful and highly productive. Since he was the first of Europe's great teachers to reflect the new scientific spirit of the sixteenth and seventeenth centuries, it seems desirable to begin this chapter with a brief statement concerning the various scientific discoveries that were exciting men's minds.

1. The Scientific Renaissance In the chapter on the Renaissance it was pointed out that the stirring of a new life in the sciences came two centuries later than the similar movement in the humanities. The scientific Renaissance began in the fifteenth century, thus paralleling the Reformation in time, although it did not burst into full bloom until the sixteenth and seventeenth centuries. It was stimulated by borrowings from the Arabs[1] and by greater familiarity with ancient Greek scientists. For nearly two thousand years science had almost stood still. When at last activity recommenced it laid the foundations for the modern world, in which science is of predominant importance.

The first developments appeared in the fields of astronomy and geography. The new astronomy led to the voyages of discovery that took place in the fifteenth and early sixteenth century, and the voyages had a retroactive effect by precipitating further developments in astronomy. It was in the fifteenth century that Copernicus* evolved the theory of the universe that is, in its essentials, still accepted today. In the sixteenth century new astronomical instruments were devised and new tables prepared for astronomical

[1] See pp. 151–152.

calculations. Galileo* demonstrated the laws of falling bodies, invented the thermometer, observed through the telescope the irregular surface of the moon and the satellites* of Jupiter, studied the inclined plane, experimented with velocity—analyzing correctly the component motions of a projectile—and used the pendulum as a measure of time. For the first time since ancient days a scientist dissected a human body. There was much study of electrical and magnetic phenomena. Two men independently worked out the theory of perspective, and another pair independently computed logarithms.*[2] Arithmetic was developed and applied to practical problems of military engineering, and the initial work was done in symbolic algebra—such as determining the first six powers* of a binomial,* resolving polynomials* into factors,* and deriving one equation from another. The first tables in trigonometry* appeared. Mercator* designed the first spherical projection for maps, and other scientists demonstrated the parallelogram of forces* and made many careful studies of equilibrium.

The seventeenth century carried on the good work. During it the barometer,* the pendulum clock, and the manometer* were invented. Chemists and physicists studied the production of gases, the rusting of metals, and the phenomena of boiling and freezing; one of them proposed the wave theory of light. A queer old Dutchman named Leeuwenhoek* developed the compound microscope and left drawings of both bacteria and living cells; an English doctor discovered how the blood circulates in the body; and an Italian was the first man to watch blood cells actually passing from arteries into veins. The cellular structure of all living matter was discovered and studied. Descartes invented analytical geometry,* by means of which the facts known about geometry may be translated into algebra and techniques in algebra may be used to solve problems in geometry. Pascal* invented an adding machine and, with other mathematicians, laid the foundation for future applied work in probabilities,* such as have become the basis for the regulation of insurance or annuity premiums. Newton* worked out the binomial theorem,* discovered the laws of gravity, studied reflection and refraction* of light until he solved the problem of the rainbow, established laws of motion, contributed to the theory of equations and analytical geometry, and shared with Leibnitz* the honor of inventing differential calculus.* An astronomer worked out predictions for the future appearance of a certain comet, which crossed the heavens exactly on time in 1759, 1835, and 1911, and is scheduled to return in the year 1987, after a journey of 76 years through illimitable space.

Much of this scientific and mathematical activity took place before the

[2] The first pair were Leonardo da Vinci* and Albrecht Dürer;* the second were Napier* and Bürgi.*

birth of Comenius, and almost all of it before his death. He grew up in the early days of the modern scientific age, at a time when great stress was being put upon observation, experimentation, and inductive reasoning. It is therefore not surprising to find Comenius insisting upon the importance of the senses as a basis for all learning, or stressing the need for accurate observation, or trying to build up a science of education. With Comenius one finally emerges from medieval systems of thought and first breathes the more familiar atmosphere of modern times.

A. COMENIUS: HIS LIFE AND WORK

1. The Life of Comenius[3] Johann Amos Comenius, whose original family name was Komensky, was born in the province of Moravia* in the year 1592, exactly 100 years after the discovery of America and 101 years after the birth of Ignatius. Comenius belonged to the Moravians, a religious sect that took its name from the province. The Moravians were followers of the martyr John Huss,* who had been burned at the stake nearly 200 years before Comenius was born. They were exponents of the simple life based upon a return to the original gospel of Christ, and all they really wanted from the world was to be allowed to live quietly and to read the Bible in peace. In their general pacific attitude they remind one of the modern Quakers. Comenius grew up in a small community and became so imbued with the local religious attitudes that he remained a pious, quiet, simple man all his life. Circumstances took him out of Moravia, but nothing ever took Moravia out of him. His simplicity and naïveté colored all his work and led to misunderstandings among those who were more complex and more sophisticated than he.

During his childhood Comenius attended a small village school, where he presumably learned to read and write Czech, his native language, but not much else. He does not appear ever to have been a brilliant student, but rather one who was thoughtful, painstaking, serious-minded, and observant. Instead of entering secondary school at the uncritical age of seven or eight, he entered at sixteen: and because of his maturity, he saw many faults in the

[3] Based upon J. W. Adamson, *Pioneers of Modern Education, 1600–1700,* Cambridge University Press, 1905 (285 pp.), chaps. 3–5; J. W. Bohlen, *Die Abhängigkeit des Pädogogen Comenius von seinen Vorgängern,* Buchdruch von Junge und Sohn, 1906, 83 pp.; A. Heyberger, *Jean Amos Comenius,* Librairie Ancienne Honoré Champion, 1928, 280 pp.; M. W. Keatinge, *The Great Didactic of John Amos Comenius,* A. & C. Black, Ltd., 1910, 819 pp.; O. H. Lang, *Comenius: His Life and Educational Principles,* E. L. Kellogg and Company, 1895, 26 pp.; S. S. Laurie, *The Life and Educational Writings of J. A. Comenius,* Cambridge University Press, 1887, 3d ed., 240 pp.; W. S. Monroe, *Comenius and the Beginnings of Educational Reform,* Charles Scribner's Sons, 1900, 184 pp.; E. Pappenheim, *Johann Amos Comenius,* F. G. L. Gressler, 1892–1898, 2 vols.; R. H. Quick, *John Amos Comenius,* Bardeen's Inc., 1886, 26 pp., and *Essays on Educational Reformers,* Appleton-Century-Crofts Company, 1896 (568 pp.), chap. 10.

methods of instruction. His descriptions of current schools and methods show that there was great need for reform.[4] The defects of his early education thus provided him with the motives that led him into educational work. After his own torturing experiences of trying to learn Latin by a purely grammatical approach, to translate authors without adequate dictionaries, and to memorize hundreds of rules without first understanding them he wanted nothing so much as to devise easier and better means for teaching children.

From grammar school he went to the universities at Herborn* and Heidelberg, where he completed the theological studies necessary for becoming a Moravian minister. During these same years he read more or less about the newer discoveries in astronomy, and he continued to read about and consider such works on education as he could find.[5] After four years of university life and travel Comenius returned to Moravia. He was then twenty-two years old, too young to be ordained as a minister in his particular sect. During the waiting period he was put in charge of a small local school. Here he came in direct contact for the first time with actual teaching problems and began to devise textbooks, a task that was part of his regular work throughout the rest of his long life. In due course of time he was ordained but continued with his teaching. After four years he was sent to another community as both pastor and superintendent of schools. This year was a memorable one because it marked the beginning of the long, exhausting, dreary Thirty Years' War. For the first three years the struggle did not touch Comenius, but in 1621 Spanish troops burned and plundered the town where he had been living. He lost his library and his manuscripts; in fact, he escaped with only the clothes he had on. For seven years he remained on the estates and under the protection of one or another sympathetic nobleman, but eventually the harboring of Moravians became too dangerous, and most of them left the country. During this period of persecution and hiding, Comenius tutored the children of his protectors, did a little educational writing, tried to comfort his fellow Moravians, and found relief for his own perplexities and uncertainties by an enthusiastic belief in the prophecies made by a pair of visionaries. In his simplicity and honesty he suspected no guile, and—in this particular instance—he was the more ready to believe because the prophets foretold a reunion of the scattered Moravians. One can hardly blame a hounded refuge for believing anything that brings solace to his suffering spirit.

Eventually Comenius escaped to Poland, where he became a master and

[4] See pp. 337–338.

[5] Notably the writings of Ratke,* a slightly earlier educational reformer, from whom Comenius derived some of his basic ideas. Ratke's actual work was restricted to a few small schools and did not last long in these, but some of his ideas were of permanent value.

subsequently the rector of a Gymnasium in the town of Lissa. There he remained thirteen years. It was during this time that he produced the most notable of his educational writings, about which more will be said presently. In his fourth year at Lissa Comenius was elected a bishop of the Moravian church, and from that day on, he had to spend part of his time, thought, and energy in directing church affairs for his widely scattered flock.

It was the original intention of Comenius to write books on teaching methods for local teachers and textbooks for the children in his own and near-by schools, but his writings met with such an enthusiastic reception that he soon began to make plans for work on a larger scale. His most grandiose idea was to publish a series of books that should contain all the knowledge in the world. The idea of an encyclopedia was, of course, not new. Comenius, however wanted to feature the modern scientific discoveries that had taken place during the previous century, he wanted various specialists to write the parts dealing with their particular fields, and he wished the series to be used as the basic text in a special university, which he would later found. The plan was spectacular, and Comenius fell completely in love with it. If he had had his own way, he would have abandoned his other educational writings entirely and devoted himself to the assembling and co-ordinating of "universal knowledge." He made a start in this direction by giving up his school in Lissa and traveling to England, where he had found an enthusiastic but irresponsible supporter. In his innocence Comenius thought he had been summoned by the English Parliament and that he would be paid while he worked out his plan. Actually, England was on the verge of civil war, and the government had no time to bother with the somewhat impractical ideas of a wandering Czech. When funds finally ran low, Comenius had to look elsewhere for assistance.

For some years a Dutch nobleman who had settled in Sweden had been trying to persuade Comenius to write some textbooks for Swedish schools. Upon the collapse of his English venture, Comenius traveled to Sweden, where he hoped to interest his new patron in his plan for universal knowledge. The patron was indifferent to the scheme, however. What he wanted was textbooks of the type that Comenius had already produced. Eventually Comenius put aside his vision and settled down in a little town in northern Germany to compose what was required. He did this work reluctantly, referring to it as *spinosa didactica*[6] of *puerilia illa mihi toties nauseata.*[7] He quite clearly resented the five years thus spent, but since his patron was not only paying his personal expenses but was donating sums of money to other Moravians, Comenius worked, albeit unwillingly, on his schoolbooks.

[6] Keatinge, *op. cit.,* p. 62. The phrase means, "thorny paths of educational writing."
[7] *Ibid.,* p. 97. The phrase means, "those childish things so nauseating to me."

At the end of that period he was elected senior bishop of the Moravians, a position that put him at the head of the church. To be nearer his flock he returned to Lissa. He had hardly entered upon his new duties when the Peace of Westphalia* brought the Thirty Years' War to a close. Comenius had been buoyed up for years by the hope that his beloved brethren could return to their peaceful mode of life in Moravia as soon as the war was over. He was therefore profoundly shocked when he learned that, while tolerance had been granted to many Protestant sects, the Moravians had been definitely excluded. He and his brothers were still exiles. The disappointment to Comenius was tremendous, especially as the Moravians began to leave the communities where they had settled temporarily, seeking shelter and work wherever they could find them. The continued emotional strain seems to have brought out in Comenius his underlying mystical beliefs, and he began again to put faith in prophecies. It is probable that for him prophecy was an escape mechanism. In spite of his best efforts, the Moravian congregation was breaking up, and his great love for his church was powerless to stop the disintegration. It is therefore understandable that he should find release in facile prophecies that all would yet be well. If he had not believed them, he might not have had the courage to carry on his educational work.

In the spring of his fifty-eighth year, he was unexpectedly called to a town in Hungary for the purpose of reforming the schools. His patron, a Hungarian nobleman, agreed to furnish a well-built schoolhouse with seven classrooms and a dormitory near by. He was also to provide seven teachers, some scholarships for poor students, a printing press, and printers to run it. It does not appear that Comenius succeeded in opening more than the lowest three classes. In them he met with much opposition from the teachers, who were accustomed to take their work rather casually and did not like the demands made upon their time by the new methods of instruction. Four years later his patron died, and the patron's mother, although continuing to pay Comenius for his work, made it clear that she would be just as happy without him. He therefore returned to Lissa.

During the next three years the position of the small Moravian group in Lissa changed considerably. They had been, since their arrival in Poland, an insignificant and peaceful gathering of refugees—not popular with their Polish neighbors, but not especially resented. When, however, a Protestant Swedish army invaded Poland, and when Comenius—trusting implicitly to prophecies—allied himself and his fellow Moravians publicly and enthusiastically with the invaders, upon whom he looked as saviors of his faith, the Poles became annoyed at such apparent ingratitude on the part of the refugees whom they had sheltered. An angry mob of Poles presently descended upon Lissa and

The Great Didactic

Setting forth

The whole Art of Teaching
all Things to all Men

or

A certain Inducement to found such Schools in all
the Parishes, Towns, and Villages of every
Christian Kingdom, that the entire
Youth of both Sexes, none
being excepted, shall

Quickly, Pleasantly, & Thoroughly

Become learned in the Sciences, pure in Morals,
trained to Piety, and in this manner
instructed in all things necessary
for the present and for
the future life,

in which, with respect to everything that is suggested,

ITS FUNDAMENTAL PRINCIPLES are set forth from the essential
nature of the matter,
ITS TRUTH is proved by examples from the several
mechanical arts,
ITS ORDER is clearly set forth in years, months, days, and
hours, and, finally,
AN EASY AND SURE METHOD is shown, by which it can
be pleasantly brought into existence.

FIG. 53. Title Page of *The Great Didactic*. Facsimile of the original title page of J. A. Comenius, *The Great Didactic*.

destroyed it. Comenius escaped, but he lost everything he possessed including his library, his manuscripts, his almost-completed grammar of the Bohemian language, his collected sermons of forty years, and the thousands of notes that he had accumulated through the decades to serve as a basis for his *magnum opus* on universal knowledge, a will-o'-the-wisp that he was still pursuing. Comenius was brokenhearted and never really recovered from this devastating blow. He was already sixty-five years old, and he knew that he would not live long enough to assemble such a mass of data again, even assuming that he had the energy.

From burned-out Lissa, Comenius again set forth upon his wanderings, first to Frankfort,* whence he had soon to flee from the plague, and then to Hamburg,* where he fell very ill, probably from sheer exhaustion. At this point, the son of the earlier Dutch-Swedish patron came handsomely to the rescue and insisted that Comenius live under his protection in Amsterdam.* The young man admired Comenius greatly, gave him unlimited credit at the printer's, and encouraged him to write whatever he wanted to. First, Comenius got out an edition of all his previous works, including his *Great Didactic,* the far-from-modest title page of which appears in Figure 53. This book on education was, however, so swamped by the multitude of his schoolbooks that it received little attention and was soon lost sight of. Comenius then turned his major efforts to assembling and publishing material on prophecies. These books were fairly popular, but much murmuring and criticism soon arose, especially as many of the revelations turned out to be false. Things gradually went from bad to worse. The old man's friends died one by one, he spent more and more time writing on metaphysical and mystical topics, his work became vaguer and vaguer, and criticism of him mounted until one of his opponents labeled him as a crazy visionary and a sponger on his patron. The latter accusation was unjustified. Credulous, simple-minded, and fanatic Comenius certainly was, but not dishonest. He was deeply hurt by the attacks upon his character, but he had not the vitality even to answer them. The sands of life ran lower and lower until in 1670, at the age of seventy-eight, the last bishop of the Moravian Brethren died.

To himself Comenius was a failure. He had wanted above all else to see the Moravian congregation re-established in Bohemia, but after wandering as an exile for forty-six years, he lived to see his flock scattered and reduced. He had longed to publish his great encyclopedia and to found his colleges of universal knowledge, but his notes were lost and he could not even find a backer for his scheme until after he was too old to do the work. He had put his faith in revelation, but his beliefs had brought him ridicule and contempt. Every ambition he had ever had seemed doomed to disappointment, and to himself his life was one of futility. He would certainly have been surprised if he had known that he would one day be famous.

In the generations immediately following his death, Comenius had few admirers. The scholars of the period lost no time in attacking his writings on the grounds that his Latin, while usually correct, lacked elegance. In fact, one detractor wrote: "His *Janua* is full of barbarisms, which he tried in vain to defend, for his apology stands itself in need of one." [8] Writers of subsequent generations also belittled his achievements, one even going so far as to say that he "did not believe that there was anything usable in the ideas" [9] of Comenius. A century later his reputation had sunk so low that he was held up to ridicule along with other believers in the occult.[10] Educators took their estimates ready-made from these various popular writers, and Comenius was forgotten until the middle of the nineteenth century. The words of the philosopher Leibnitz concerning Comenius were therefore of greater prophetic value than the revelations in which Comenius put his trust:

> Tempus erit, quo te, Comeni, turba bonorum
> Factaque spesque tuas, vota quoque ipsa colet.[11]

Presumably the picture of Comenius shown in Figure 54 was made after repeated blows and disappointments had given him a morose outlook on life. His whole expression is that of a man who had been intimately acquainted with grief and does not at all understand why he should have been.

2. *The Educational Ideas of Comenius*[12] The main ideas in the writings of Comenius will be summarized under the four headings of his objections to the schools of his period, his plan for schools and basic curricula, his educational principles, and his hints for the conduct of classes. A separate section will be given to his textbooks.

(*a*) *Objections to Existing Schools* Protestant education had deteriorated since the days of Luther and Melanchthon, while Catholic education under the leadership of the Jesuits had improved. Schoolwork consisted in

[8] D. G. Morhof, *Polyhistor literarius, philosophicus, et practicus*, P. Böckmann, 1688 (3 vols.), I, 119–120.

[9] P. Bayle, *Dictionnaire historique et critique*, Desoer, 1820 (16 vols.), II., 559.

[10] J. C. Adelung, *Geschichte der menschlichen Narrheit*, Weygand, 1785–1789, 7 vols.

[11] G. W. Leibnitz, *Gesammelte Werke aus den Handschriften der Katholischen Bibliothek zu Hannover*, herausgegeben von G. H. Pertz. Im Verlag der Hahnschen Buchhandlung, 1846–1863, Vol. IV, 270. "The time will come when the tumult of good people will pay respect to you, Comenius, your deeds, your hopes, and your prayers."

[12] It is not necessary to enumerate all the writings or even all the educational writings of Comenius, because he repeated himself constantly. Nor need one trace the development and varying forms of his schoolbooks. The following discussion of his concepts about education and his materials for instruction will therefore be based upon only a few of his writings, but these excerpts should be sufficient for purpose of illustration. A good modern collection of his writings is J. A. Comenius, *Pädagogische Schriften*, H. Beyer und Sohn, 1904–1907, 3 vols.

the main of meaningless drill in grammar and rhetoric. Against the existing schools Comenius voiced the following complaints:

They are the terror of boys, and the slaughterhouses of minds—places where a hatred of literature and books is contracted, where ten or more years are spent in learning what might be acquired in one, where what ought

FIG. 54. Johann Amos Comenius. From an engraving by Glover, used as the frontispiece of S. Hartlib, *A Reformer of Schools,* 1642.

to be poured in gently is violently forced in and beaten in, where what ought to be put clearly and perspicuously is presented in a confused and intricate way, as if it were a collection of puzzles—places where minds are fed on words.[13]

The study of the Latin language alone (to take this subject as an example), good heavens! How intricate, how complicated, and how prolix it was! Camp followers and military attendants, engaged in the kitchen and in

[13] Keatinge, *The Great Didactic of John Amos Comenius* p. 23. This excerpt and subsequent ones from Keatinge are quoted by permission of A. & C. Black, Ltd., publishers.

other menial occupations, learn a tongue that differs from their own, sometimes two or three, quicker than the children in schools learn Latin, though children have an abundance of time, and devote all their energies to it. And with what unequal progress! The former gabble their language after a few months, while the latter, after fifteen or twenty years, can only put a few sentences into Latin with the aid of grammars and dictionaries, and cannot do even this without mistakes and hesitation. Such a disgraceful waste of time and of labour must assuredly arise from a faulty method.[14]

This description of the schools is gloomy enough, but it is borne out by the comments of others, as will appear in a subsequent chapter.

(*b*) *Proposed Types of School and Curricula* Comenius proposed a definite series of schools that should continue almost from birth and should produce a well-educated man at maturity. He planned also the curriculum to be followed in each class in each school. Both his organization and his plan of studies contain much that is new.

The whole period [of growth], therefore, must be divided into four distinct grades: infancy, childhood, boyhood, and youth, and to each grade six years and a special school should be assigned.

I. For infancy	the	The mother's knee.
II. For childhood	school	The Vernacular-School
III. For boyhood	should	The Latin-School or Gymnasium
IV. For youth	be	The University and Travel.

A Mother-School should exist in every house, a Vernacular School in every hamlet and village, a Gymnasium in every city, and a University in every kingdom or in every province.[15]

The "work" of the Mother-School was concerned primarily with the training of the senses and the mastery of elementary facts and words—much the type of thing now taught in nursery school and kindergarten. This work foreshadows that of both Pestalozzi and Froebel two centuries later.

The objectives and subject matter of the Vernacular-School were—aside from religious topics—those of the primary grades in elementary school today.

The aim and object of the Vernacular-school should be to teach to all the young, between the ages of six and twelve, such things as will be of use to them throughout their whole lives. That is to say:

(i) To read with ease both print and writing in their mother-tongue.

(ii) To write, first with accuracy, then with speed, and finally with confidence, in accordance with the grammatical rules of the mother-tongue. . . .

(iii) To count, with ciphers and with counters, as far as is necessary for practical purposes.

[14] *Ibid.*, p. 79.

[15] *Ibid.*, pp. 256–258.

(iv) To measure spaces, such as length, breadth, and distance, with skill.

(v) To sing well-known melodies, and in the case of those who display especial aptitude, to learn the elements of advanced music.

(vi) To learn by heart the greater number of the psalms and hymns that are used in the country.

(vii) To learn the most important stories and verses in the Bible. . . .

(viii) To learn the principles of morality, which should be drawn up in the shape of rules and accompanied by illustrations suitable to the age and understanding of the pupils. They should also begin to put these principles into practice. . . .

(ix) To learn as much economics and politics as is necessary to enable them to understand what they see daily at home and in the state.

(x) To learn the general history of the world; its creation, its fall, its redemption, and its preservation by God up to the present day.

(xi) To learn the most important facts of cosmography, such as the spherical shape of the heavens, the globular shape of the earth suspended in their midst, the tides of the ocean, the shapes of seas, the courses of rivers, the principal divisions of the earth, and the chief kingdoms of Europe; but, in particular, the cities, mountains, rivers, and other remarkable features of their own country.

(xii) Finally, to learn the most important principles of the mechanical arts, both that they may not be too ignorant of what goes on in the world around them, and that any special inclination toward things of this kind may assert itself with greater ease later on.[16]

In this course of study, geography makes its appearance as a school subject, presumably as the result of the many voyages of discovery in the century after Columbus and before Comenius. This proposed curriculum is remarkably modern.

When it came to the Latin-School, however, Comenius suddenly deserted his own principles and presented a basically humanistic course of study, to which he added work in physics, geography, and history. His outline appears below:

1. In this school the pupils should learn four languages and acquire an encyclopedic knowledge of the arts. Those youths who have completed its whole curriculum should have had a training as:

(i) Grammarians, who are well versed in Latin and in their mother-tongue, and have a sufficient acquaintance with Greek and Hebrew.

(ii) Dialecticians, who are well skilled in making definitions, in drawing distinctions, in arguing a point, and in solving hard questions.

(iii) Rhetoricians or orators, who can talk well on any given subject.

[16] *Ibid.*, pp. 268–269.

(iv) Arithmeticians and (v) geometricians; both on account of the use of these sciences in daily life, and because they sharpen the intellect more than anything else.

(vi) Musicians, both practical and theoretical.

(vii) Astronomers, who have, at any rate, mastered the rudiments. . . .

2. The above are commonly known as the seven liberal arts, a knowledge of which is demanded from a doctor of philosophy. But our pupils must aim higher than this, and in addition must be:

(viii) Physicists, who know the composition of the earth, the force of the elements, the different species of animals, the powers of plants and of minerals, and the structure of the human body. . . .

(ix) Geographers, who are well acquainted with the external features of the earth, and know the seas, the islands that are in them, the rivers, and the various kingdoms.

(x) Chronologers, who can fix periods of time, and trace the course of the centuries from the beginning of the world.

(xi) Historians, who possess a fair knowledge of the history of the human race, of the chief empires, and of the church, and who know the various customs of men.

(xii) Moralists, who can draw fine distinctions between the various kinds of virtue and of vice, and who can follow the one and avoid the other. . . .

(xiii) Finally, we wish them to be theologians, who, besides understanding the principles of their faith, can also prove them from the Scriptures.

3. When this course is finished, the youths, even if they have not a perfect knowledge of all these subjects . . . should, at any rate, have laid a solid foundation for any more advanced instruction that they may receive in the future.[17]

Instead of substituting scientific for linguistic studies, Comenius simply added them to an already too-heavy curriculum. It is doubtful if any but the very best minds of each generation could survive such a burden of work.

At the top of the educational system was the university, but since Comenius had little experience with higher education, his comments are mostly restatements of his scheme for universal knowledge. His real work had no reference to university education, and his somewhat rambling remarks on the matter may as well be omitted.

(*c*) *Educational Principles* A brief summary of the principles and methods recommended by Comenius may be obtained by putting together a number of excerpts from his *Great Didactic*. These quotations cover such diverse points as the fundamental nature of children, the necessity for them to learn through

[17] *Ibid.*, pp. 274–276.

their senses, the need for adaptation of teaching materials to their abilities, the individual differences among them, the types of discipline that are best, the motives that stimulate children, and the desirability of relating schoolwork to life.

Comenius was very sure that children had in them the necessary capacities for becoming educated adults, if they could only receive proper training. For instance:

> The seeds of knowledge, of virtue, and of piety are, as we have seen, naturally implanted in us; but the actual knowledge, . . . virtue, and piety are not so given. These must be acquired by prayer, by education, and by action. He gave no bad definition who said that man was a "teachable animal". . . . For all faculties do but exist potentially and need development.[18]

Comenius was especially emphatic that all learning must come through the senses:

> To the rational soul, that dwells within us, organs of sense have been supplied. . . . These are sight, hearing, smell, sound, and touch, and there is nothing whatever that can escape their notice. For, since there is nothing in the visible universe which cannot be seen, heard, smelt, tasted, or touched, and the kind and quality of which cannot in this way be discerned, it follows that there is nothing in the universe which cannot be compassed by a man endowed with sense and reason.[19]
>
> From this [fact] a golden rule for teachers may be derived. Everything should, as far as is possible, be placed before the senses. Everything visible should be brought before the organ of sight, everything audible before that of hearing. Odours should be placed before the sense of smell, and things that are tastable and tangible before the sense of taste and of touch respectively. If an object can make an impression on several senses at once, it should be brought into contact with several. . . . Surely, then, the beginning of wisdom should consist, not in the mere learning the names of things, but in the actual perception of the things themselves! It is when the thing has been grasped by the senses that language should fulfil its function of explaining it still further . . . .
>
> Since the senses are the most trusty servants of the memory, this method of sensuous perception, if universally applied, will lead to the permanent retention of knowledge that has once been acquired. For instance, if I have once tasted sugar, seen a camel, heard a nightingale sing, or been in Rome and have on each occasion attentively impressed the fact on my memory, the incidents will remain fresh and permanent. We find, accordingly, that children can easily learn Scriptural and secular stories from pictures.[20]
>
> In the same manner, whoever has once seen a dissection of the human body will understand and remember the relative position of its parts with

[18] *Ibid.*, pp. 52–54.
[19] *Ibid.*, p. 43.
[20] *Ibid.*, pp. 184–185.

far greater certainty than if he has read the most exhaustive treatises on anatomy, but had never actually seen a dissection performed. . . .

If the objects themselves cannot be procured, representations of them may be used. Copies or models may be constructed for teaching purposes, and the same principle may be adopted by botanists, geometricians, zoologists, and geographers, who should illustrate their descriptions by engravings of the objects described. The same thing should be done in books on physics and elsewhere . . . . It is true that expense and labour will be necessary to produce models, but the result will amply reward the effort.[21]

Because Comenius was so sure that learning must take place through the senses he was inevitably opposed to both humanism and scholasticism, since both rested upon authority rather than upon observation. He wanted pupils to observe phenomena for themselves, and not to learn by rote what other people had written.

Comenius was one of the first teachers to insist that the materials used in school should be specifically adapted to the abilities and interests of children. The usual practice had been to start children with the writings of Cicero, regardless of the inappropriateness of assigning, for instance, Cicero's essay on old age to a twelve-year-old boy. On the use of properly adapted materials Comenius has the following comments to make:

Care must be taken to suit all these books to the children for whom they are intended; for children like whimsicality and humour, and detest pedantry and severity. Instruction, therefore, should ever be combined with amusement, that they may take pleasure in learning serious things which will be of genuine use to them later on, and that their dispositions may be, as it were, perpetually enticed to develop in the manner desired.[22]

Beginners should at first practice on material that is familiar to them—students should not be overburdened with matters that are unsuitable to their age, comprehension, and present condition, since otherwise they will spend their time in wrestling with shadows. For example, when a Polish boy is learning to read or to write his letters he should not be taught to do so from a book written in Latin, Greek, or Arabic, but from one written in his own language, that he may understand what he is doing. Again, if a boy is to understand the use of the rules of rhetoric, the examples on which he is made to practise them should not be taken from Virgil or from Cicero or from theological, political, or medical writers, but should refer to the objects that surround him, to his books, to his clothes, to trees, houses, and schools.[23]

These suggestions sound commonplace at the present time, but in the seventeenth century they were revolutionary.

Comenius lived about two hundred years before psychology became a

[21] *Ibid.*, pp. 185–186.
[22] *Ibid.*, p. 270.
[23] *Ibid.*, pp. 197–198.

science, so it is not surprising that his treatment of individual differences among children is naïve, but it is a tribute to his powers of observation that he made as good an analysis as he did.

This is a suitable place in which to make a few remarks about differences of character. Some men are sharp, others dull; some soft and yielding, others hard and unbending; some eager after knowledge, others more anxious to acquire mechanical skill. From these three pairs of contradictory characters we get, in all, six distinct divisions.

In the first division must be placed those who are sharp-witted, anxious to learn, and easily influenced. These, more than all others, are suited for instruction. There is no need to provide them with what we may term a nutritive diet of knowledge, for, like goodly trees, they grow in wisdom of themselves. Nothing is needed but foresight; for they should not be allowed to hurry on too fast and thus to tire themselves out and wither away before their time.

Others are sharp-witted, but inclined to be slow and lazy. These must be urged on.

In the third place, we have those who are sharp-witted and anxious to learn, but who at the same time are perverse and refractory. These are usually a great source of difficulty in schools, and for the most part are given up in despair. If treated in the right way, however, they frequently develop into the greatest men. . . .

In the fourth place we have those who are flexible and anxious to learn, but who at the same time are slow and heavy . . . . The teacher must meet their weak natures half-way, must lay no heavy burden on them, must not demand anything excessive, but rather have patience, help them, strengthen them, and set them right, that they may not become disheartened. . . .

The fifth type are those who are weak-minded and at the same time lazy and idle. With these also a great improvement can be made, provided they are not obstinate. But great skill and patience are necessary.

Finally we have those whose intellects are weak and whose dispositions are perverse and wicked as well. These seldom come to any good . . . . But an intellect of this kind, amenable to no treatment, can scarcely be found in a thousand, and this is a great proof of God's goodness.[24]

The above classification, like that given by Ascham in a previous chapter, is much too simple to fit all the facts, but both writers at least made an effort to classify their pupils and to take the differences among them into account in planning schoolwork.

A fifth point to which Comenius gave emphasis was the need for shorter school hours, more play, sounder health, better bodily development, and less strain. In his own words:

We see then that a large portion of the good organization of schools

[24] *Ibid.*, pp. 88–90.

consists of the proper division of work and rest, and depends on the disposition of studies, intervals to relieve the strain, and recreation . . . .

There are twenty-four hours in a day, and if, for the daily uses of life, we divide these into three parts, setting aside eight hours for sleep, and the same number for the external needs of the body (such as care of the health, meals, dressing and undressing, agreeable recreation, friendly converse, etc.), we have eight hours left for the serious work of life. We shall therefore have forty-eight working hours a week (setting aside the seventh day for rest). In one year this will amount to 2945 hours, and in ten, twenty, or thirty years to an immense number.[25]

Comenius planned a school year that should have 42 weeks. Each week was to have two half holidays, and each day was to contain only four hours of schoolwork, with a half hour of play after each hour's work. Three times a year there were to be holidays for a fortnight and in the autumn for a full month.

Moreover, Comenius wanted the spirit of play to permeate the school subjects. He suggested that the children should be given tools and allowed to imitate the different handicrafts

by playing at farming, at politics, at being soldiers or architects, etc. In spring they may be taken into the garden or into the country, and may be taught the various species of plants, vying with one another to see who can recognize the greater number. In this way they will be introduced to the rudiments of medicine, and not only will it be evident which of them has a natural bent towards that science, but in many the inclination will be created. Further, in order to encourage them the mock titles of doctor, licentiate,* or student of medicine may be given to those who make the greatest progress. The same plan may be adopted in other kinds of recreation. In the game of war the scholars may become field-marshals, generals, captains, or standard-bearers. In that of politics they may be kings, ministers, chancellors, secretaries, ambassadors, etc. . . . Thus would be fulfilled Luther's wish that the studies of the young could be so organised that the scholars might take as much pleasure in them as in playing at ball all day, and thus for the first time would schools be a real prelude to practical life.[26]

These excerpts are reminiscent of Vittorino da Feltre and of the ancient world, in which physical and mental growth went hand in hand. They are also prophetic of the modern school.

Comenius was most emphatic about discipline. He believed that punishment was sometimes necessary, but that it should never be associated with schoolwork:

Now no discipline of a severe kind should be exercised in connection with studies or literary exercises, but only where questions of morality are

[25] *Ibid.*, pp. 108–110.
[26] *Ibid.*, pp. 179–180.

at stake. For, as we have already shown, studies, if they are properly organised, form in themselves a sufficient attraction, and entice all (with the exception of monstrosities) by their inherent pleasantness. If this be not the case, the fault lies, not with the pupil, but with the master, and, if our skill is unable to make impression on the understanding, our blows will have no effect. Indeed, by any application of force we are far more likely to produce a distaste for letters than a love for them. Whenever, therefore, we see that a mind is diseased and dislikes studies, we should try to remove its indisposition by gentle remedies, but should on no account employ violent ones. . . .

He [the teacher] may employ advice, exhortation, and sometimes blame, but should take great care to make his motive clear and to show unmistakably that his actions are based on paternal affection, and are destined to build up the characters of his pupils and not to crush them. Unless the pupil understands this and is fully persuaded of it, he will despise all discipline and will deliberately resist it.

The young should never be compelled to do anything, but their tasks should be of such a kind and should be given them in such a way that they will do them of their own accord, and take pleasure in them. I am therefore of opinion that rods and blows, those weapons of slavery, are quite unsuitable to freemen, and should never be used in schools.[27]

This theory of discipline is not far from that generally held at present. Teachers now hope to make schoolwork so interesting, to keep children so relaxed, and to adjust work so well to ability that no discipline need be used in connection with learning. For moral offenses children require punishment as much now as in the seventeenth century.

Comenius had a good deal to say about motivation. Well he knew that a desire for learning could not be forced, but must be kindled. He expressed this thought by first quoting two teachers of antiquity, Isocrates and Quintilian who said, respectively: "He who is anxious to learn will become learned"; and "The acquisition of knowledge depends on the will to learn and cannot be forced." Then Comenius went on to say:

The desire to learn can be excited by teachers, if they are gentle and persuasive and do not alienate their pupils from them by roughness, but attract them by fatherly sentiments and words; if they commend the studies that they take in hand on account of their excellence, pleasantness, and ease; if they praise the industrious ones from time to time. . . . In a word, if they treat their pupils kindly they will easily win their affections, and will bring it about that they prefer going to school to remaining at home. The school itself should be a pleasant place, and attractive to the eye both within and without. Within, the room should be bright and clean, and its walls should be ornamented by pictures . . . without, there should be an open space to walk or play in . . . and there should also be a garden attached, into which the scholars may be allowed to go from time to time and where they may feast

[27] *Ibid.*, pp. 250–254.

their eyes on trees, flowers and plants. If these things are done, boys will, in all probability, go to school with as much pleasure as to fairs, where they always hope to see and hear something new.[28]

A final article in Comenius's educational creed was the necessity for education to be related to the needs of everyday life, instead of being concerned with matters remote from direct experience. Three excerpts express his views on this point:

> What object is there in learning subjects that are of no use to those who know them and the lack of which is not felt by those who do not know them? Subjects that are certain to be forgotten as time passes on and the business of life becomes more engrossing? This short life of ours has more than enough to occupy it, even if we do not waste it on worthless studies. Schools must therefore be organized in such a way that the scholars learn nothing but what is of value.[29]
>
> Truly it has been said, that nothing is more useless than to learn and to know much, if such knowledge be of no avail for practical purposes; and again, that not he who knows much is wise, but he who knows what is useful.[30]
>
> Whatever is taught should be taught as being of practical application in everyday life and of some definite use. That is to say, the pupil should understand that what he learns is not taken out of some Utopia or borrowed from Platonic Ideas,* but is one of the facts which surround us, and that a fitting acquaintance with it will be of great value in life.[31]

No modern advocate of a practical education could put the matter more strongly.

(*d*) *Conduct of Classes* In addition to his general principles, Comenius had certain specific suggestions to make about the conduct of classes. In most of the Protestant schools the children were grouped into grades, but each pupil was still taught separately. The class or grade was a unit of work to be done, not a social unit of scholars. Instruction was therefore individual. Comenius was strongly in favor of group teaching and wrote a rather good defense of the lecture method:

> I maintain that it is not only possible for one teacher to teach several hundred scholars at once, but that it is also essential; since for both the teachers and their pupils it is by far the most advantageous system. The larger the number of pupils that he sees before him the greater the interest the teacher will take in his work; and the keener the teacher himself, the

[28] *Ibid.*, pp. 130–131.
[29] *Ibid.*, p. 144.
[30] *Ibid.*, p. 180.
[31] *Ibid.*, p. 189.

greater the enthusiasm that his pupils will display. To the scholars, in the same way, the presence of a number of companions will be productive not only of utility but of enjoyment (for it gives pleasure to all to have companions in their labours); since they will mutually stimulate and assist one another. Indeed for boys of this age emulation is by far the best stimulus.

If matters be arranged in the following manner, one teacher will easily be able to cope with a very large number of scholars. That is to say:

(i) If he divides the whole body into classes, groups of ten for example, each of which should be controlled by a scholar . . .[32]

(ii) If he never gives individual instruction, either privately out of school or publicly in school, but teaches all the pupils at one and the same time. He should, therefore, never step up to any scholar, or allow any one of them to come to him separately, but should remain in his seat, where he can be seen and heard by all. . . . The scholars, on the other hand, must direct their ears, eyes, and thoughts towards him, and attend to everything that he tells them by word of mouth, or explains by means of his hand or of diagrams.

(iii) If, when he teaches, he take the trouble continually to introduce something that is entertaining as well as of practical use; for in this way the interest of the scholars will be excited and their attention will be arrested.

(iv) If, at the commencement of any new subject, he excite the interest of his pupils, either by placing it before them in an attractive manner or by asking them questions. . . .

(v) If he stand on an elevated platform, and keeping all the scholars in his sight at once, allow none of them to do anything but attend and look at him.

(vi) If he aid their attention by appealing to the senses, especially to that of sight, whenever it is possible.

(vii) If he occasionally interrupt his explanation with the words: Tell me (mentioning some boy), what have I just said? Repeat that sentence! Tell, me; how have I reached this point? and remarks of a similar kind, the exact nature of which must depend on the class that he is teaching. . . .

(viii) If some of the boys cannot answer a question he should ask the whole class, and then, in the presence of the rest, praise those who answer best, that their example may serve to stimulate the others. . . .

(ix) Finally, when the lesson is over, the scholars should be given leave to ask questions on any point that they wish explained, either in the present lesson or in a previous one. Private questioning should not be permitted. . . . If any scholar help to illustrate an important point by the intelligence of his questions, he should be commended, in order that the rest may thereby be incited to industry and keenness.[33]

[32] This arrangement is much like the division of a large lecture class into small sections, each led by an advanced student.

[33] *Ibid.,* condensed from pp. 164–169.

The teaching of groups rather than of individuals is barely three hundred years old. In addition to group instruction Comenius suggested that large classes be broken up into groups of ten pupils, each with a leader. This idea may have been borrowed from the Jesuits, but it is more likely that both he and they got it from the same source—a teaching brotherhood, of whom more will be said in the next chapter.

(4)

Cornix cornicatur. die Krähe krechzet.	*á á*	Aa
Agnus balat. das Schaf blöcket.	*b é é é*	Bb
Cicáda stridet. der Heuschreck zitzschert.	*ci ci*	Cc
Upupa, dicit der Widhopf/ruft	*du du*	Dd
Infans éjulat. das Kind weinert.	*é é é*	Ee
Ventus flat. der Wind wehet.	*fi fi*	Ff
Anser gingrit. die Gans gackert.	*ga ga*	Gg
Os halat. der Mund hauchet.	*háh háh*	Hh
Mus mintrit. die Maus pfipfert.	*i i i*	Ii
Anas tetrinnit. die Ente schnackert.	*kha kha*	Kk
Lupus úlulat. der Wolff heulet.	*lu ulu*	Ll
Ursus múrmurat. der Beer brummet.	*mum mum*	Mm

(5)

Felis, clamat die Katz mautzet.	*nau nau*	Nn
Auriga, clamat der Fuhrmann/rufft	*ó ó ó*	Oo
Pullus pipit. das Küchlein pipet.	*pi pi*	Pp
Cúculus cúculat. der Kukuck kucket.	*kuk ku*	Qq
Canis ríngitur. der Hund marret.	*err*	Rr
Serpens sibilat. die Schlange zischet.	*si*	Ss
Graculus, clamat der Heher/schreyet	*tae tae*	Tt
Bubo ululat. die Eule uhuhet.	*ú ú*	Uu
Lepus vagit. der Hase quäcket.	*vá*	Ww
Rana coaxat. der Frosch quacket.	*coax*	Xx
Asinus rudit. der Esel ygaet.	*y y y*	Yy
Tabanus, dicit die Breme summet.	*ds ds*	Zz

FIG. 55. Two Pages from the *Orbis Pictus* (a). From the first edition of the *Orbis Pictus*, now in the Bibliothèque Nationale.

B. THE TEXTBOOKS OF COMENIUS

Comenius is most renowned for his series of textbooks. In the course of his long life he wrote various forms in sundry languages, but the differences between one form and another of the same book are minor and will be disregarded. In order of difficulty his six books were:

Orbis Pictus	"The World in Pictures"
Vestibulum	"The Courtyard"
Janua	"The Gateway"
Atrium	"The Hall"
Palatium	"The Palace"
Thesaurus	"The Treasury"

Two sample pages from the *Orbis Pictus*[34] are reproduced in Figure 55. The meaning of the object in each picture is given in both Latin and German.

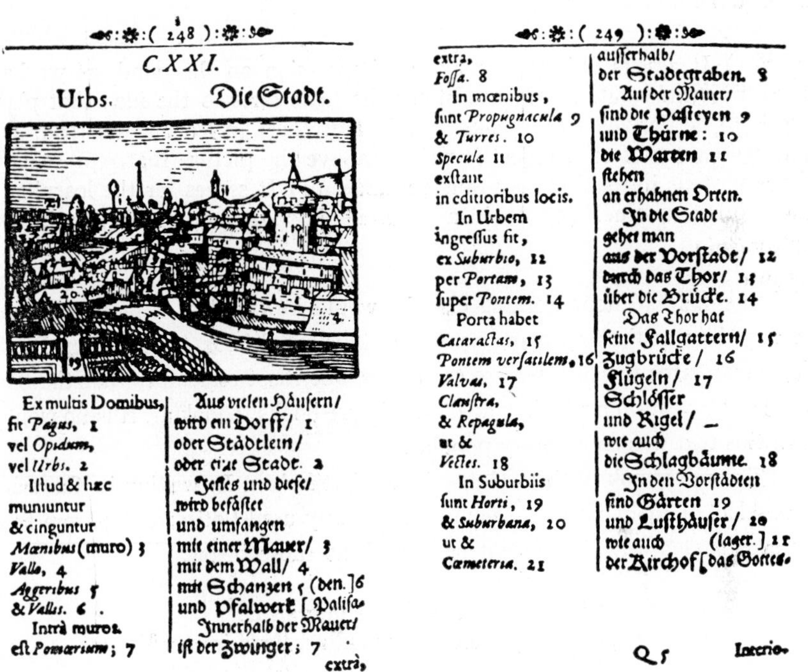

(248)

CXXI.

Urbs. Die Stadt.

Ex multis Domibus,	Aus vielen Häusern/
fit *Pagus*, 1	wird ein Dorff/ 1
vel *Opidum*,	oder Städtlein/
vel *Urbs*. 2	oder eine Stadt. 2
Illud & hæc	Jenes und diese/
muniuntur	wird befästet
& cinguntur	und umfangen
Mœnibus (muro) 3	mit einer Mauer/ 3
Vallo, 4	mit dem Wall/ 4
Aggeribus 5	mit Schanzen 5 (den.] 6
& *Vallis*. 6 .	und Pfalwerk [Palisa-
Intra muros	Innerhalb der Mauer/
est *Pomœrium*; 7	ist der Zwinger; 7

extra,

(249)

extra,	ausserhalb/
Fossa. 8	der Stadtgraben. 8
In mœnibus,	Auf der Mauer/
sunt *Propugnacula* 9	sind die Pasteyen 9
& *Turres*. 10	und Thürne: 10
Speculæ 11	die Warten 11
exstant	stehen
in editioribus locis.	an erhabnen Orten.
In Urbem	In die Stadt
ingressus fit,	gehet man
ex *Suburbio*, 12	aus der Vorstadt/ 12
per *Portam*, 13	durch das Thor/ 13
super *Pontem*. 14	über die Brücke. 14
Porta habet	Das Thor hat
Cataractas, 15	seine Fallgattern/ 15
Pontem versatilem, 16	Zugbrücke/ 16
Valvas, 17	Flügeln/ 17
Claustra,	Schlösser
& *Repagula*,	und Rigel/
ut &	wie auch
Vectes. 18	die Schlagbäume. 18
In Suburbiis	In den Vorstädten
sunt *Horti*, 19	sind Gärten 19
& *Suburbana*, 20	und Lusthäuser/ 20
ut &	wie auch (lager.] 21
Cœmeteria. 21	der Kirchof [das Gottes-

Q 5 Interio-

FIG. 56. Two Pages from the *Orbis Pictus* (b). From the first edition of the *Orbis Pictus*, now in the Bibliothèque Nationale.

It should be noted that in the first series of pictures each view shows something that makes a noise. The alphabetical order applies to the verbs describing the noise, although not as systematically as might be desired. Thus the lamb bleats, the grasshopper grates, the hoopoe calls, the baby cries, the wind whistles, the goose gabbles, and so on. The child's first book today is usually of a similar nature, but with the sounds presented by imitative words: The sheep says, "Baa-baa"; the dog says, "Bow-wow"; and the like.

[34] The entire book, with comments, was reprinted by Bardeen's, Syracuse, 1887, 195 pp.

Some of the pictures were of a more complex nature, such as that given in Figure 56, which shows a walled town. Under it and on the right half of the page are listed the words and phrases in both Latin and German. The numbers after some of the words refer to the numbers on the picture. For instance, in the foreground there is a figure 8 on the ditch and a 4 on the wall above it. In the text the 8 and the 4 appear after the appropriate word in both languages.

According to Comenius the picture book had a number of values, such as are enumerated below:

> (1) It assists objects to make an impression on the mind, as we have already pointed out. (2) It accustoms the little ones to the idea that pleasure is to be derived from books. (3) It aids them in learning to read. For, since the name of each object is written above the picture that represents it, the first steps in reading may thus be made. (4) It serves for the learning of the mother tongue. (5) It is a pleasant introduction to the Latin language.[35]

If Comenius had done nothing else, he would be listed as a famous teacher because he was the first man to write an illustrated book for children. By today's standards the pictures are crude, but one must remember that the book was used by children who had no other picture books to look at. It is no wonder that this text was enormously popular.

The next book in the series was the *Vestibulum.* In writing it, Comenius first selected about 1,000 of the most commonly used Latin words; from these he constructed 427 simple sentences, such as those below.

> Deus est aeternus, mundus temporarius.
> Coelum est supremum, aer medius, terra infima.[36]

The sentences were grouped about topics such as: *Things in the School, Things at Home, Things in the City, Concerning the Qualities of Things, Concerning the Virtues,* and so on. One sample set appears below:

De rebus in Schola:

246. Scholasticus sponte frequentat scholam, quo in artibus erudiatur.
247. Initium est a literis.
248. Ex syllabis voces componuntur, e dictionibus sermo.
249. Ex libro legimus tacite, aut recitamus clare.

[35] Keatinge, *op. cit.,* condensed from pp. 264–265.

[36] *Ibid.,* p. 29. *Translation:* "God is eternal, the earth temporary. The sky is the highest thing, the air is midway, the earth is the lowest."

250. Involvimus eum membranae et ponimus in pulpito.
251. Atramentum est in atramentario.[37]

This book was intended as an introduction to the Latin language, and is certainly more appropriate than Cicero. To accompany it, Comenius wrote a small dictionary containing the 1,000 words, both Latin-vernacular and vernacular-Latin.

Third in the series comes the *Janua*. Comenius used about 8,000 Latin words, with their equivalents in the vernacular, arranged into 1,000 sentences. The two languages were in parallel columns. The sentences he grouped around 100 different topics, each of which dealt with one class of phenomena in art, nature, or society. The topics are diverse: animals, meteors, fruits, houses, diseases, angels, gardens, virtue, creation of the world, water, earth, stone, metal, trees, arithmetic, trade, marriage, the family, ethics, intellect, affections, the will—to mention only a few. The example below gives the material about a garden:

36. De Hortorum Cultura.

379. Hortus, vel pomarium est vel viridarium vel vivarium.
380. Sepitur vel aggere, vel macerie, vel plancis, vel sepe palis (sudibus) longuriis aliisque vitilibus plexa.
381. Hortulanus (olitor) ligone, et rutro, bipalioque fodit, et per pulvinos semina spargit.
382. Arborator seminario vel taleis vel viviradicibus consisto (concinnitas est et elegantia si per quincuncem digerantur) surculos inserit et rigat, scalproque germi germina putat, stolones amputat.
383. Oleum ex olivis exprimitur; subtus amurca fidit, fraces abjicuntur.
384. Aviarius alvearia curat, ceramque liquat.[38]

[37] *Ibid.*, p. 29. The translations are:
Concerning Things in School:
246. "The scholar willingly goes to school where he is educated in the arts."
247. "The beginning is (made) by (learning) the letters of the alphabet."
248. "Words are composed of syllables; a discourse of speaking."
249. "We read silently in the book, or we recite aloud."
250. "We wrap it up in parchment and put it in the desk."
251. "The ink is in the inkwell."

[38] *Ibid.*, p. 22. The translations are: "Concerning the Care of Gardens."
379. "A garden is an orchard, a flower garden, or a park."
380. "It is surrounded by mounds, by a wall, or by a hedge of stakes, bound together by poles or by wicker-work."
381. "The gardener (kitchen-gardener) digs with a hoe, a shovel, and a two-pronged fork, and he scatters seeds in the ground."
382. "In a nursery made up of both slips and cuttings (it is tasteful and elegant if they are grouped into fives) the tree cultivator waters the young plants, prunes the sprouts with a knife and cuts off the extra growths."
383. "The oil is pressed out of the olives; the lees separate out below and the stones are thrown away."
384. "The beekeeper looks after the bees and melts the wax."

Comenius gave explicit directions for the use of this book. It was to be read ten times. First, a child translated from Latin into the vernacular. Then he wrote out every sentence in both languages. On the third trial the teacher read the Latin aloud, and the pupils wrote down the vernacular. Beginning with the fourth repetition the teacher began to add a little grammar each time. One subsequent reading was to emphasize word derivation; another, synonyms; another, analysis of subject matter. By the tenth repetition the children were supposed to know everything by heart.

The *Janua* was the first Latin grammar especially written for children. It was reprinted into every language in Europe and into some in Asia. Its use continued for as long as Latin was a necessary school subject. It is interesting to note that the most modern introductory Latin books have carried on the same tradition as the *Janua*; they treat of everyday subjects in an everyday manner, using easy material especially written for youngsters.

Accompanying the *Janua* was a more advanced dictionary than that which was used with the *Vestibulum*. This lexicon gave not only the translation of the 8,000 words used, but also their etymology, their derivatives, and their compounds. The modern student usually supposes that appropriate dictionaries have always existed. Comenius had to write his own, because there were none that children could possibly use; his were among the first to explain Latin words in the vernacular instead of explaining them in Latin. His were also forerunners of the now familiar "vocabulary" in the back of a text, containing only the words needed for that particular book.

The *Atrium* was in essence a Latin grammar, although it contained 1,000 items grouped into 100 chapters. Instead of being single sentences, however, each item was a short paragraph. The grammatical parts dealt with nouns, adjectives, verbs, and so on, in a simplified approach to grammar. The *Atrium* was written because experience showed Comenius that pupils who had completed the *Janua* were not yet quite ready to begin reading the classics.

The *Palatium* was a collection of excerpts from classical authors, with the emphasis upon rhetoric. The book contained also the rules for altering and paraphrasing sentences in many ways, so as to bring out different elements of style.

The *Thesaurus* was not a book at all but the name given to the entire galaxy of classical writers, or to long quotations from them. For the use of pupils a comprehensive and scholarly lexicon was to be provided, with special emphasis upon the correct translation of phrases and idioms.

One curious point about the texts that Comenius wrote was his concentric arrangement of topics. That is, he presented many of the same topics in all his books, but at each successive level he pursued them in a more advanced way. An example from three books, to be used *seriatim,* illustrates this point:

Example of the Application of the Concentric Method used by Comenius (The Kingdom)

Lowest Book	*Second Book*	*Third Book*
Many cities and many villages make a country and a kingdom. The king or the prince has his residence in the capital.	One calls a kingdom the combination of a certain number of cities and districts under one ruler, constituted so that the moral force thus united will be sufficiently powerful to quell any disorders that may arise. Three things are therefore necessary: (1) a country large enough, (2) appropriate conditions of life, (3) laws, of which the authority will be strongly sanctioned.	The necessity that stimulates a great number of families to assemble themselves into a state binds them together into a sovereign power. It is true that moral force depends upon unity and that plurality is the cause of discord. Nature herself offers examples of this fact in animal societies. Bees have only one king, cattle only one leader. Similarly, it is not useful for men to have many leaders; a single ruler is necessary. The establishment of a kingdom requires first a large country, offering favorable living conditions for a large number of people; next, the possibility of keeping these masses in order; finally, just laws, which permit those thus assembled to live in peace.[39]

This discussion of what constitutes a kingdom begins in a most elementary way and is then developed further in the books used as the children grew older.

The books of Comenius represent a great step forward toward modernity.

[39] Heyberger, *op. cit.,* translated from pp. 168–169. Used by permission of Librairie Ancienne Honoré Champion, publishers.

He substituted teaching through the senses for the memorizing of hardly understood words. He used the vernacular. He selected the words to be taught in terms of their usefulness. He introduced pictures for little children. He wrote about everyday topics in simple phrases, devoid of literary flourishes. He graded his material in terms of difficulty. He wrote dictionaries for children, defining only those words needed for a single book. As a textbook writer, Comenius has rarely been surpassed.

The main contributions of Comenius to education were threefold: He wrote textbooks specially adapted to the needs of children, including the use of pictures to arouse interest and to catch attention. This new idea in textbook writing has persisted and developed until now almost every book for children is illustrated. Second, Comenius taught Latin through the vernacular. To be sure, the vernacular had always been used to some extent in the earliest classes, but it was dispensed with as soon as possible and it had not been given recognition in the textbook. The medieval scholar did not think in the language of his country and then translate into Latin; he thought in Latin as spontaneously as if he had never known anything else. By the end of the seventeenth century, Latin was losing its pre-eminence and the spoken languages were coming to the fore. Comenius reflected this tendency by presenting his texts in both languages, and he dignified the vernacular by printing it. Third, he put emphasis upon the training of the senses. This stress has never been lost. Especially in preschool work one finds many games, exercises, and devices for developing the child's senses of vision, hearing, and touch. Teaching and learning by actual experience rather than by reading a book are commonplace concepts now, and one sometimes forgets that laboratory work, demonstrations, field trips, models, and illustrations as educational aids are less than three centuries old.

Comenius thus still lives in the modern schoolroom with its dozens of illustrated books, its walls covered with pictures, its many objects and models, its use of the vernacular, and its constant dependence upon experience as the best means of learning. Comenius himself was discredited and ridiculed for years before his death, but his textbooks continued to delight successive generations of children, and through them his ideas lived on into modern times.

READING REFERENCES

A. General Histories of the Period

Ergang, *Europe from the Renaissance to Waterloo,* chaps. 13, 14.
Garrett, *European History,* 1500–1815, chap. 18.
Ogg, *Europe in the Seventeenth Century,* chap. 4.
Robinson, *Introduction to the History of Western Europe,* chap. 29.

Schevill, *A History of Europe from the Renaissance to the Present Day,* chap. 12.
Seignobos, *The Rise of European Civilization,* chap. 13.
Stearns, *Pageant of History,* part i, chaps. 5, 6, 14.
Waugh, *A History of Europe from 1378–1494,* chap. 22.

B. Other Texts in the History of Education

Cole, *History of Educational Thought,* pp. 217–221.
Cubberley, *History of Education,* pp. 379–416.
Graves, *A Student's History of Education,* chap. 9.
Marique, *History of Christian Education,* Vol. II, chaps. 8, 9.
McCormick, *History of Education,* pp. 272–282.
Monroe, *A Textbook in the History of Education,* pp. 442–503.
Ulich, *History of Educational Thought,* pp. 188–199.

C. Secondary Sources

Adamson, *Pioneers of Modern Education,* chaps. 3, 4.
Graves, F. P., *Great Educators of Three Centuries,* The Macmillan Company, 1912 (289 pp.), chap. 4.
Keatinge, *The Great Didactic of John Amos Comenius,* pp. 1–102.
Lang, O. H., *Comenius: His Life and Principles of Education,* E. L. Kellogg and Company, 1891, 26 pp.
Laurie, S. S., *Johann Amos Comenius: His Life and Educational Work,* Cambridge University Press, 1887 (2d ed., 240 pp.), pp. 19–70, 174–193.
Monroe, W. S., *Comenius and the Beginnings of Educational Reform,* chaps. 3–5, 6, 7, 9, 10.
Painter, *Great Pedagogical Essays,* chap. 17.
Quick, *Essays on Educational Reformers,* chap. 10.
Spinka, M., *John Amos Comenius: That Incomparable Moravian,* University of Chicago Press, 1943 (177 pp.), chaps. 4–9.

D. Translations of Primary Sources

Comenius, *Orbis Pictus.*
Keatinge, *The Great Didactic of John Amos Comenius,* chaps. 8–10, 14, 26, 27, and any one of chaps. 17–19.
Ulich, *Three Thousand Years of Educational Wisdom,* pp. 339–346.

CHAPTER XIII

DE LA SALLE AND FRANCKE AND THEIR SCHOOLS

This chapter contains the histories of two men whose lives show numerous parallel developments. One was a Catholic, one a Protestant; one worked in France, one in Germany. Both concentrated their attention upon the teaching of primary school children, orphans, and children of the poor. Both made constructive efforts to train teachers. Both founded organizations that carried on their work after their death; in fact, the organizations exist today and still have the same objectives as those laid down by their founders. Jean Baptiste de la Salle, a Frenchman and Catholic, is the first of this pair. His German Protestant parallel, August Hermann Francke, will appear in the next section.

A. DE LA SALLE: HIS LIFE AND WORK

1. De la Salle's Life Story[1] Jean Baptiste de la Salle was born in 1651 in the city of Rheims.* From early childhood he showed a great natural piety and a marked interest in ecclesiastical matters. His superior intelligence is indicated by his entrance at the University of Rheims when he was only eight years old. In spite of his youth he made excellent progress and passed the first ceremonies for becoming a priest at the age of eleven. Five years later he was named a canon in the cathedral at Rheims. He continued to attend the university and took his master's degree when he was eighteen. The next year he entered a seminary to study for the priesthood, but did not remain there long because his parents died and he felt he should return home to care for his younger brothers and sisters. For six years he remained quietly at home, supervising his family and studying at the university whenever he could find the time.

During this period he was thrice asked by friends to help with the organization of groups of teachers for small children. On each occasion he made arrangements of a practical sort, found an adviser, withdrew from further participation in a project that did not excite him particularly, and then retired to the quiet life of study that he enjoyed.

[1] This section is based upon M. J. Heimbrucher, *Die Orden und Kongregationen der katolischen Kirche,* Schöningh, 1908, 3 vols.; Brother Noah, *Life and Work of the Venerable John Baptist de la Salle,* published by the Society, 1883; A. Ravelet, *Le Bienheureux Jean Baptiste de la Salle,* A. Mame et fils, 1888, 686 pp.; J. J. Schuetz, *The Origin of Teaching Brotherhoods,* Catholic University Press, 1918 (104 pp.), pp. 19–35; R. F. Wilson, *The Christian Brothers,* Routledge and Kegan Paul, Ltd., 1883, 203 pp.

No one could accuse De la Salle of making efforts to become an organizer or even of meeting his destiny halfway. Although he had come in contact three times with the establishment of teaching groups and although he had shown his kindly spirit in giving aid, the work had no appeal. He much preferred to continue upon the more orthodox line of Christian endeavor that he had marked out for himself. His studies soon lead him to the priesthood, although his duties to his family prevented him from accepting a parish. He continued, however, to be a canon of the cathedral. In due course he could expect advancement and might hope to become a church dignitary—a bishop, cardinal, or even a pope. In any case, he felt no inner urge to devote his life to teaching.

De la Salle was, however, a man with a painful sense of duty and a degree of efficiency that made bungling seem almost a sin, and he was not long in becoming more involved than he really wished with one group of teachers, who had been assembled by a certain M. Nyel, a layman with vast enthusiasm but little ability to organize or supervise the groups that he had assembled. One such group was composed of earnest young men who were making a commendable effort to carry on their teaching in a worth-while way, but their abilities were inadequate for their task. They lacked experience, training, education, general culture, and even manners. Moreover, their funds were running low, they were discouraged, and they felt that M. Nyel had abandoned them. De la Salle, at the request of M. Nyel, furnished enough money to relieve their immediate difficulties and suggested that they cut down their expenses by living together in a house across the street from his own, where he could have food from his kitchen sent in to them. This much other wealthy and kindly men might have done, but he went on to tasks of supervision that were far more difficult than the making of practical arrangements. Since he soon realized that the young men had no idea of regularity in their life and work, he made out a timetable for their days—hours of rising, eating, retiring, time for study, prayer, and church—and he kept a fatherly eye on the small household to see that the plan was carried out. Moreover, he began to train them. Not that he set out deliberately to do so, but their ignorance and lack of refinement irked him, and they were so delighted with his company that they flocked to him with eager questions. De la Salle, the priest of God, welcomed them, although De la Salle, the aristocrat, must often have cringed. Certainly he had no notion that these young men and others like them were going to be important in his life. As he himself wrote later on, "If I had ever thought that what I did out of pure charity for the poor schoolteachers would make it incumbent upon me to live with them, I would have given it up at once." [2] The teachers re-

[2] *Catholic Encyclopedia,* Encyclopedia Press, 1907–1912. VIII, 444.

mained for two years on the fringe of his attention, absorbing what little time he could give them. De la Salle was continuing with his theological studies at the University of Rheims, where he took his doctorate, he had many duties as canon, and he was still in charge of his household and family.

At the end of two years, after the teachers had come to Rheims, things were going badly, and De la Salle became convinced that the whole project of training teachers and establishing free schools for the poor in Rheims was going to collapse unless someone came to the rescue, and that someone was clearly himself. He was still reluctant to neglect his other work and interests, so he made a compromise by asking the teachers to take their meals with him at his house, and he utilized the time to talk with them and to give them advice. This move on his part aroused the first of many protests that his family and friends were to utter. His brothers and sisters were not unnaturally angry at having their pleasant family dinner table made into a seminar in education for the benefit of some uncouth, uninteresting, and rather dull young men. Being a benevolent patron of a charitable undertaking was one thing, but having the undertaking come to dinner was another! However, De la Salle remained firm, and managed for some months to preserve a sort of armed neutrality between his family and his protégés.

Even this amount of guidance was not enough, however, as De la Salle soon saw. His relation to the teachers was only that of a patron, and he had no authority over them; neither did he have a hand in their selection in the first place, nor could he set up educational or cultural standards for them. The teachers apparently got just enough help from De la Salle to realize how inadequate they were but not enough to remedy their deficiencies. Their work did not go any too well, their funds were inadequate, and many of them were becoming very weary indeed of the hard life they had to lead. They therefore begged their adviser to live with them and to assume full charge of them. De la Salle was unwilling to trust his own judgment in so important a decision, so he journeyed to Paris to consult his spiritual adviser. To him he told the whole story of his connection with the teachers, discussed their prospects with and without his help, and confessed to the development of a real love for these humble men who were trying sincerely but against terrific odds to do some good in the world. The adviser, after considering all the facts, gave De la Salle advice in the following words: "Take your teachers, lodge them in your private residence, provide them with food and clothing; in a word, become their superior and father." [3] This spiritual blessing De la Salle regarded as the voice of God, guiding him into the work he was put

[3] *Annales de l'Institut des Frères des Écoles chrétiennes,* 1679–1719, Paris, 1882 (2 vols.), I, 22.

into the world to do. Having settled matters in his own mind, he hesitated no longer. On the feast day of his patron saint, John the Baptist, a day that was also his own thirtieth birthday, he transferred the entire community of teachers, bag and baggage, to his own house. As he had expected, when the teachers moved in at one door, his family moved out at another. The first sacrifice he was called upon to make was the breaking of family ties with his brothers and sisters, only one of whom remained on friendly terms with him.

De la Salle now went to work in earnest. He required a strict discipline and routine of life from the members of his group, he taught them, and he devoted all the time he could spare from his duties as canon to their cultural and religious development. At first, his sacrifice of his family relationships seemed to have been somewhat premature, because many of the teachers refused to accept the rigorous life demanded of them and left the community. For a year the numbers dwindled, until eventually the wheat had been separated from the chaff. Those who remained were clearly going to stick, and presently new members began to come. In a year's time it became evident that the project would hold together, and De la Salle moved his community to another and more commodious house, where he, too, lived from that time on. He confessed later that he still had no definite plans for either his own life or the development of a teaching brotherhood. He merely went on meeting the problems that arose from day to day and laboring incessantly in the interests of the young men, who had by now become very dear to him. They were equally attached to him and were delighted when their numbers increased and new schools could be opened.

Success of the venture continued to rest upon this purely personal bond for another three years, during which De la Salle made one sacrifice after another. The first was the resignation of his canonry. He found that there were not enough hours in the day to fulfill properly his two jobs, and he was too upright a man to neglect his duty and too efficient a man to be content with anything less than perfection. With his resignation went any hope he might ever have had of ecclesiastical honors. His action was comparable to that of a promising young lawyer who already had been appointed as assistant to the state district attorney and had good prospects for political advancement, but preferred to resign his position to become head of an obscure school for social workers. De la Salle's friends begged him to give up the teachers, but he remained adamant in his decision to remain with them. In his own words:

> In the choice I am about to make, what should determine my resolution? Certainly, the greater glory of God, the service of the Church, my perfection, and the salvation of souls. But if I consult these motives, so befitting a priest of the Lord, I must determine to renounce my canonry, to give myself en-

tirely to the care of the schools, and to form good teachers. Moreover, God, who conducts all things wisely and gently, who forces not the inclinations of men, wishes me to devote myself entirely to the care of these schools. He directs me toward this end in an imperceptible though rapid manner, so that one connection after another has attached me to a vocation that I had not foreseen.[4]

De la Salle was now free to devote his entire attention to his teachers, and they reacted to his devotion by improving both themselves and their work, but there remained still one source of distress among them. They were happy enough at the moment and they were willing to make teaching their lifework, but what would happen to them when they were too old to teach? They could never earn more than a bare maintenance and quite possibly not even that, and would have to depend upon charity to eke out their earnings. While they were young and strong they could stand the hardships, but they were disheartened by the prospect of a penniless old age and the probable dependence upon uncertain charity. As they pointed out, De la Salle did not have to worry because he had plenty of money to fall back on. After much prayer and thought, De la Salle made a final sacrifice: he gave away his entire fortune to the poor. He was then no longer the patron of his teachers but a poor man like themselves, committed to a hard life and to the uncertainties of the future. Having cut his last competing obligation, he could devote his entire time and attention to the development of his lifework.

De la Salle's first step was to organize his companions more closely, so that the group would have a better chance for survival. At this time he gave them only a verbal "rule" to live by. The written one came much later. The name of the group was henceforth to be the Society of the Brothers of the Christian Schools (La Société des Frères des Écoles Chrétiennes). The members were not to take perpetual vows, but were to renew their vows every few years. Each member was to select some name from the Bible and use it, preceded by the title "Brother"; thus, Brother Noah, who wrote an early biography of De la Salle. The brothers were also to wear a distinctive costume, the nature of which is shown in Figure 57. None of them was to become a priest. On this point De la Salle was very definite. He knew that the training necessary for the priesthood would distract attention from teaching, and he feared that some of the brothers would be diverted from teaching altogether, once they were on the road to clerical advancement. At the time of this first organization there were twelve brothers.

De la Salle had his own ideas about the relationship between the individual member and the brotherhood. To quote one of his biographers:

[4] *Ibid.*

His notion was that all the brothers who were sent to teach in schools throughout France, and even all over the Christian world were to form one family, who should have but one father, namely, the Superior: one paternal home, the Novitiate; one law, the Rule. All the Brothers, being called to the same functions, were to be trained by the same method; they were to receive the same teaching, practice the same virtues, imbibe the same spirit, and reproduce, as far as possible, the same type which was that of the founder. In order to realize this unity, they were not only to spend at least one year in the Novitiate, and be there, as it were, cast in the mould of the Institute, but they were to return from time to time and go back into this mould, so that the lines which had been rubbed off by contact with the world, might be renewed, and resume their primitive accuracy. Thus the direction, begun during the first year's training, was continued through life. The Brothers wrote once a month to the Superior general; he answered them, and by this means, as well as through the visitors and his own visitations, he remained in contact with them, and was able to follow all the changes in their souls, to encourage and direct their progress, to prevent or arrest abuses. But for this he was armed with a supreme authority. Every Brother who strayed from the Rule could be called back to the mother house, or sent elsewhere. Every budding evil could consequently be nipped the moment it was perceived. This constitution was simple, wise, and strong. The best proof of its excellence is its duration. It has lasted two centuries, with merely a few changes, which are in reality developments rather than changes, and everywhere the results have been admirable.[5]

The Society of the Brothers of the Christian Schools was not the first of its kind. The earliest of the teaching brotherhoods was founded by a learned and saintly gentleman named Gerhard Groot* in the late fourteenth century.[6] Since De la Salle seems to have been influenced by this early organization it seems well to describe it briefly. The brethren in Groot's communities lived together, owned property in common, maintained their houses by their own labor, voluntarily obeyed their superiors, but did not take religious vows. The members wanted to sanctify their own lives by prayer and good works, but they wished also to bring about a regeneration of society. Among other activities they included teaching, in which they were very successful. Some of the brothers taught in already established schools and others in schools they founded for themselves. Their most famous school was at Deventer* in the Netherlands.* Two graduates from Deventer are well known: Thomas à Kempis* and Erasmus. The school was regarded as a model in its day, and from it the Jesuits as well as De la Salle derived many ideas.

[5] Ravelet, *op. cit.*, pp. 386–387. Passages from this work are reprinted by permission of the Director of the Society of the Christian Brothers.

[6] For accounts of the first teaching brotherhood, see Schuetz, *op. cit.*, and Heimbrucher, *op. cit.;* also K. Grube, *Gerhart Groot und Seine Stiftungen,* J. P. Bachem, 1883, 100 pp.; M. Schoengen, *Die Schule von Zwolle,* Freiburg, 1898, 127 pp.

The Brotherhood of the Common Life, as Groot's followers were called, continued to exist for about 150 years. During this time their chief source of income had been the copying of manuscripts, in which the brothers were highly trained specialists. The invention of printing robbed the order of its livelihood, an early instance of the effect of machines in throwing men out of work. Although the order itself perished from lack of funds, the essentials of its educational work lived on in both the Society of Jesus and the Society of the Brothers of the Christian Schools.

Thus was De la Salle's little community of teachers finally launched. As its reputation grew, adolescent boys who were too young for membership sometimes asked for admission. For them De la Salle organized a novitiate, housing them in a separate building from the older men. For the more adequate training of teachers he opened the world's first normal school [7] (in 1685) in which he himself was most of the faculty. Presently he was training not only the younger brothers of his order but young men sent to him by parish priests. These country schoolteachers-to-be usually remained with him for a year or two and then returned to their homes to open schools. They did not join the brotherhood.

There were thus three separate institutions that grew up together: the house for the brothers, the house for the novices, and the embryo normal school. These three formed the core of De la Salle's organization, although in later years he added an orphanage, a boarding school for boys who were sent to him from a distance, a school for incorrigibles and delinquents, and a Sunday school for young men who were already working at some trade and could attend school only on Sunday. The exact number of these undertakings in operation at any one time depended largely upon the generosity of patrons, since the brotherhood had no money of its own.

After a few years in Rheims, De la Salle had an opportunity to move his communities to Paris, where he had long wanted to go, because he knew that the brotherhood was much more likely to spread over all of France from Paris than from a provincial center. After some moving about, the organization finally settled down in a large house in the country just outside Paris. Here the novices stayed all the time, while the teachers returned for week ends in order to rest and to refresh themselves.

It is not ncessary to go into a detailed description of all the tribulations that De la Salle experienced in establishing his work. His trials arose from five main sources: lack of money, which was sometimes so severe that the

[7] Somewhat earlier there had been some classes for teachers but not a school. See G. Compayré, *Charles Démia* et les origines de l'enseignement primaire,* P. Delaplane, 1905, 118 pp.

brothers were close to starvation; backslidings and bickerings among the teachers; actual betrayal by those he trusted most; friction with ecclesiastical authorities; and, above all, continual accusations and even lawsuits brought forward by local schoolteachers who charged De la Salle with "stealing" their pupils. On various occasions he had to go into either an ecclesiastical or a civil court and prove that the pupils taught by the brotherhood were all so poor that they could not attend schools where the masters charged a fee. In consequence, he was not robbing other teachers of legitimate customers, but was garnering in those children whom they turned away. De la Salle summed up his difficulties in the following words:

> For my part, I own to you that if God had shown me the labors and crosses that were to accompany the good I was to do in founding the Institute, my courage would have failed, and, far from undertaking it, I would not have dared put a finger to the work. I have been persecuted by several prelates,* even by those from whom I had a right to expect help. My own children, those whom I begot in Jesus Christ, and cherished with the utmost tenderness, whom I trained with the greatest care, and from whom I looked for great service rose up against me and added to external trials those inner ones which are so much more acute. In a word, if God had not held out his hand and visibly sustained the edifice, it would long ago have been buried under its own ruins. The magistrates joined with our enemies, and lent them the weight of their authority to overthrow us. As our office offends the schoolmasters, we have in every one of them a declared and inveterate enemy, and all in a body they have often armed the powers of the world to destroy us. Yet, notwithstanding all, the edifice is standing, although it was so often trembling on the brink of ruin. This is what leads me to hope that it will endure, and render to the Church the services she has a right to expect from it.[8]

There came a time when the opposition was so extreme that De la Salle decided he was doing more harm than good by remaining at the helm. He therefore gradually relinquished his authority, trained one of the brothers to carry on his work, and then secretly removed himself to the south of France for several years. By so doing, he allowed the opposition to die down for lack of a victim—since the brothers were inconsequential people, they were not likely to be attacked—and he gave the teachers a chance to direct themselves, as they would be forced to do after his death. During these years he worked at establishing new houses, taught school when occasion demanded, made frequent retreats* to help himself in planning his future action, and tramped about southern France on foot, incognito, and alone. He would willingly have entered a monastery, especially the Grande Chartreuse,* where the monks

[8] Ravelet, *op. cit.*, pp. 399–400.

took vows of silence and spent their lives in prayer, but his work was not yet done. He was in constant correspondence with the acting head of the organization, and he could not feel free to pursue his own desires until the brotherhood was on a surer foundation. Accordingly, after his absence he reappeared and called a general meeting, attended by practically all the brothers, at which he formally laid down all responsibilities and persuaded his followers to elect as formal head of the order the brother who had been acting head for some time. The old man then retired into the community in Rouen, refused gently but firmly to concern himself with affairs of the order, although he still liked to teach the novices, and died two years later, in 1719.

2. *De la Salle's Character* As a summary of De la Salle's personality, the following description is given, although it is perhaps overenthusiastic.

> Blessed [9] De la Salle was rather above the middle height, and well proportioned. His constitution, delicate in childhood, had grown strong from exercise and work, until penances and excessive fatigue weakened his health. His forehead was broad, his nose straight, his eyes large and of bluish grey, his skin was tanned by exposure and travelling, his hair, which curled, and which had been chestnut in his youth, was grey and white in his declining years. His countenance bore the stamp of great sweetness and majesty. His air was modest and serene; his manners simple and gracious. An atmosphere of holiness breathed from his whole person. . . .
>
> His life is the Gospel put into practice. To do penance, to deny oneself, to mortify and crucify the flesh, to pray, to converse with God, to appear amongst men only to labor for their salvation or to receive their contempt, to devote oneself wholly to the poorest and most abandoned, to suffer everything, to give way to everyone, never to complain, never to feel offended . . . to show no aversion towards anything but the world, to hate nothing but sin, to fear nothing but to displease the sovereign majesty, to desire only to imitate Jesus Christ, to be attracted only by the cross, and to love God alone, is this not the epitome of the Gospel and of Blessed de la Salle?
>
> In prayer, he looked like an angel; at the altar, like a seraph; in his conduct he was truly an apostolic man; in tribulation, he was another Job;* in poverty, a Tobias;* in abandonment to Providence, a Francis of Assisi* . . . in the exercises of every virtue, a perfect disciple of Jesus Christ. This is Venerable de la Salle as he really was; this is his true portrait.[10]

In Rouen stands a statue that well reflects the personality of de la Salle and the nature of his work. The sculptor has caught both the gentleness of his spirit and the charming relationship between him and children.

3. *Subsequent History of the Organization* At the time of De la Salle's

[9] "Blessed" is a title given to an individual who has been beatified* but not yet canonized.* For the meaning of these terms, see Glossary C.

[10] Ravelet, *op. cit.*, pp. 426–429.

FIG. 57. Jean Baptiste de la Salle. From the frontispiece of Ravelet, *The Blessed John Baptist de la Salle,* a photograph of the monument by Falquière in Rouen.

death, there were 274 brothers, living in 26 communities, of which 25 were in France. The twenty-sixth chapter house was in Rome. As the brotherhood became larger, it secured both papal approval and secular recognition, and was not therefore subject to the obstructive attacks that had hampered it in its earliest years. On the eve of the French Revolution in 1778, there were 760 brothers who directed 114 houses, and taught 420 schools, in which

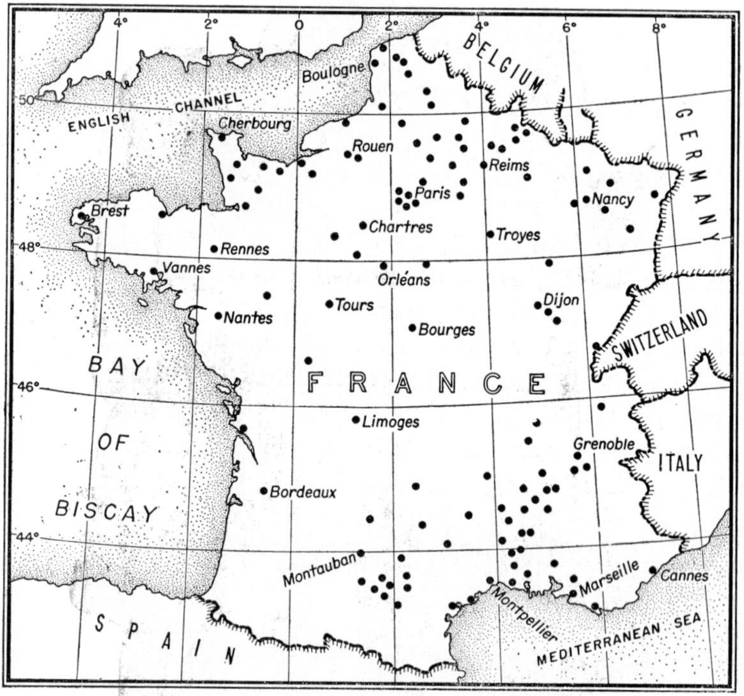

FIG. 58. Distribution of the Schools of the Brothers of the Christian Schools in 1792. Based upon a map in A. Ravelet, *The Blessed John Baptist de la Salle,* p. 621.

were enrolled 31,000 children. The map in Figure 58 shows the location of the schools. The brothers had developed their teaching methods, had written textbooks, and had established normal schools for training new teachers. As soon as the Revolution gathered momentum, the brothers became marked men because of the anticlerical agitations of the period. To be sure, they were not priests, but they did wear a similar habit,* they were ardent Catholics, and they purposely indoctrinated children with Christianity. The brothers refused to recant their religion and were consequently persecuted, driven from their schools, imprisoned, and some of them were killed. By the end of the Revolution some members were dead, others were soldiers, some were working as secular teachers, a few were hiding in remote corners of France, and many had fled the country. Such was their organization, however, that they weathered the storm, reorganized themselves, and continued to develop. A hundred years later, at the time De la Salle was beatified, there were 1896 communities, of which 81 per cent were in Europe, the others being sprinkled all over the world. By 1900 there were 2015 establishments, of which 1741 were schools of some sort. At present there are over 100 schools in the United States.

The Institute was and is a remarkable organization because, while it is strongly Catholic and Christian, its members are not priests. They are a self-perpetuating group of laymen who devote their lives to teaching children. They constitute the largest of the teaching brotherhoods now in existence. This organization from its beginning has emphasized the teaching of elementary school children. Until the end of the seventeenth century the instruction of small children was not regarded as a proper calling for an educated and cultured person. In Catholic communities elementary school work was left to the village priest, and in other places to those who were unable to pursue more lucrative occupations. The teaching personnel, at its best, was composed of just such earnest young incompetents as the original followers of De la Salle; there were also many older men and women who taught school as a side line and were equally incompetent. The notion that an intelligent man should train himself specifically to teach small children and should then devote his life to such elementary work was something new in the educational world.

B. FRANCKE: HIS LIFE AND WORK

In the seventeenth century both German Protestantism and German education were in a bad way. In the century that had elapsed since the days of Luther and Melanchthon many Protestant sects had arisen, and the attacks of the theologians that had so wearied the gentle Melanchthon continued apace. Religion had lost much of its earlier emotional fervor and had deteriorated into an acrimonious battle of dogma and definition. The various Protestant groups had doubtless intended to promote universal education, but they had not had time to establish methods for so doing before their internal squabbles took up all their energy. In the meantime, education suffered from lack of teachers, lack of money, and lack of attention—and elementary education was the most neglected field of all.

As the Protestant faiths overemphasized the intellectual elements in their religion and neglected the emotional side, there developed a desire on the part of many people for a return to the "good old days" when religion had the power to stir its followers. This desire for a reversion to the original church is an old and familiar theme; from the fourth century on, whenever religion became overformalized, there were similar movements. Among Protestants, the return was to the teachings of the Bible rather than to those of the early Christian church, as was the case among Catholics, but the underlying motives were much the same. Those who felt an emptiness of heart, a poverty of spirit, and a decay of fervor bonded together informally to regenerate their faith. They wanted a return to the emotional values of religion, a return to the Scriptures, an end to theological debate, and a resurgence of Christian piety as a way of life. This movement was called Pietism.* It was no new faith, and it presented no new doctrines. It consisted essentially of a desire to live as Christ had lived. An outstanding Pietist, and the main pedagogue of the movement, was August Hermann Francke.

1. Francke's Life Story[11] Francke was born in Lübeck* in 1663, two years after De la Salle's birth in Rheims. His family soon moved to Gotha,* where the boy grew up. Until he was thirteen years old he was taught either at home or in a small group under the care of a private tutor. He seems to have had natural seriousness and piety, even as a child. When he was thirteen, he entered the Gymnasium at Gotha but remained only a year. He was then ready for university work, but on account of his youth, he remained at home for two more years, continuing with his studies by himself. During these early adolescent years his work consisted mainly in reading the classics in both Latin and Greek. He was greatly enchanted by what he read and was suddenly filled with a desire for worldly fame that tended to stifle his earlier zeal for religion. He had always intended to follow his father's wish that he enter the ministry and, at sixteen, he enrolled in the University of Erfurt,* where he studied theology, languages, and philosophy. Later he transferred to the University of Kiel,* since he could there get a scholarship. In both places he seems to have been a good student and to have made progress, but he remained restless and dissatisfied. An inner struggle was developing between his native piety and his more recent scholarly ambitions. In his own words:

> Thus in all my studies I was only a crass hypocrite, who went to church, to confession, and to the holy sacrament, sang and prayed, held also good discourses, and read good books, but actually from all these activities did not derive the strength to forswear the ungodly life and worldly pleasures, and to live disciplined, right, and holy, not only externally but also internally. I grasped my theology in my head, not in my heart, and it was rather a dead

[11] Based upon J. W. Adamson, *Pioneers of Modern Education, 1600–1700,* Cambridge University Press, 1905, 285 pp.; F. A. Eckstein, *A. H. Francke, der Armen und Waisenfreund,* Ferdinand Hirt, 1863, 27 pp. G. Kramer, *August Hermann Francke; Ein Lebensbild,* H. Beyer und Sohn, 1876, 528 pp. A. Otto, *August Hermann Francke,* Verlag des Waisenhauses 1902, 1904, 2 vols.; R. H. Quick, *Essays on Educational Reformers,* E. L. Kellogg and Company, 1890 (335 pp.), chap. 13; K. Richter, *A. H. Francke's Schriften über Erziehung und Unterricht,* M. Hesse, 1882, 758 pp.

science than a living knowledge. I knew very well how to define faith, regeneration, justification, renewal, and so on, and to distinguish one from the other, and to prove each by quotations from the Bible. . . . I put great value upon writing everything down on paper, but I did not attempt, as Paul wished, to write upon the tablet of my heart, through the spirit of God.[12]

In spite of his unrest, however, Francke continued with his academic work, studied Hebrew, Italian, French, and English—in addition to Greek and Latin—and took his doctor's degree at Leipzig* when he was twenty-three years old. He at once began giving lectures and was very successful as a teacher. Certain other instructors who were less learned than he in languages asked him for help in Hebrew and Greek. For this purpose he used chapters out of the Bible as instructional material, and through his intensive study became extremely familiar with the Good Book. This work revived his dissatisfaction because his own interests and attitudes seemed so at variance with scriptural teaching. As he himself said: "My intention was to become a distinguished and learned man, to become rich, and to live in comfort. . . . I was more concerned to please men and to put myself into their good graces than to please the living God in Heaven. Also in externals I imitated the world, in excessive amounts of clothing and other vanities. In short, I was inwardly and outwardly a man of the world." [13] In the decade of his adolescence and early manhood Francke seems to have been on the way to becoming a split personality!

After a year as a university teacher Francke went to Luneberg* to study Biblical analysis with a famous teacher. Here he was away from his friends and from the busy social life of a university. During this time he was asked to deliver a sermon, for which he chose as a text the verse: "These things are written, that you may believe Jesus to be the Christ, the Son of God, and that you have life through belief in His name." [14] As Francke labored over his sermon, he seems to have been afflicted with the most intensive doubts. He discovered that he did not know for sure even if there were a God or, in case one existed, if he really believed in Him. The struggle went on for some days while he made fruitless efforts to compose a sermon that was an honest statement of his views. He had about decided that he would have to decline his chance to preach because he could not come to terms with himself, when he experienced a sudden conversion. It was not accompanied by a bright light or wondrous visions or heavenly music, as is often the case, but its effects seem to have been thorough and permanent. As he describes the experience:

[12] Otto, *op. cit.*, I, 11–12. This excerpt and subsequent ones from Otto are used by permission of the Franckesche Stiftungen.
[13] *Ibid.*, I, 14.
[14] John 20: 31.

One evening, it was a Sunday, I lay listlessly in bed, and thought that I would have to decline the sermon, unless some change occurred, because I could not preach in a state of disbelief and against my own heart, and thus betray the congregation. I did not know either if it would be possible for me to do so. For I felt it too keenly to have no God to whom my heart could turn—and not to know truly if there were a God—to see daily great misery and pain and to know no holy one nor any heaven. In such great anxiety I knelt down, on the before mentioned Sunday evening, and called to the God whom I did not yet really know nor believe in, and prayed for rescue from such a miserable condition—provided there really were a God. Then God heard me, the living God, as I lay on my knees. So great was his paternal love that he did not wish to remove such doubt and disquiet in my heart gradually with which I might well have been satisfied, but in order that I should be the more convinced and would lay a curb upon my straying reason, so that I would not protest against His strength and trustworthiness he heard me suddenly. Then, in a twinkling, all my doubts vanished; I was assured in my heart of the grace of God in Jesus Christ, I knew God not alone as God but as my father; all sadness and unrest in my heart were at once taken away; in their place I was suddenly drenched with a flood of joy, so that I praised God out of the fullness of my heart that he had showed me such grace. I stood up a different man from the one who had laid himself down. It seemed to me as though I had lain in a deep sleep during my whole life up till then and as if I had done everything in a dream from which I had just awakened. It seemed as if I had been dead and were now alive.[15]

This conversion from doubt to implicit belief was a turning point in Francke's life. He was now armored against any worldly trials by a faith that nothing could shake, a faith that gave him inner serenity and strength. The conversion was important also in his later pedagogical work because it influenced him to regard true godliness, faith, and subordination of one's own will to God as the aims of education.

The next year Francke returned to the University of Leipzig, where he threw himself with new vigor into his teaching, especially of the New Testament. He appealed constantly to his students' emotions, encouraging them to feel as well as to think, and trying to awaken in them a living faith like his own. In order to reach his hearers more surely he lectured in German instead of in Latin, thereby arousing criticism among his colleagues, who were not pleased at the sight of his overflowing classrooms while their own were nearly empty. Very evidently he gave the students something of value to them; not only were his classes popular but his followers began to be "different" from other students, by whom they were promptly dubbed "Pietists," a name that stuck. His students talked about him constantly, quoted and doubtless misquoted him, exaggerated what he said, defended him hotly against criticism,

[15] Otto, *op. cit.*, I, 15–17.

and generally behaved like perfectly normal students the world over toward a professor they admire. Although Francke constantly warned them against any separation from the Lutheran Church and was careful not to vary from accepted Lutheran doctrines, he was soon accused of introducing novelties and of misleading youth from pure doctrine by intentional deviousness.

Francke was made so uncomfortable at Leipzig that when opportunity arose he accepted an offer to preach in Erfurt. Here again he was a great success. He preached, he gave lectures both on the Bible and on education, he supervised schools, he taught children their catechism, and he sought continually so to stir the hearts of his parishioners that they would be moved to live better lives. Again he was hounded by enemies, this time by rival clergymen, until he was forced to resign and leave Erfurt. He regretted this necessity, but he was not embittered by it, merely regarding it as the will of God. For some months Francke remained at home in Gotha, but soon after his twenty-ninth birthday he was called as professor of Hebrew to the newly founded University of Halle and simultaneously as pastor in the near-by town of Glaucha,* positions that he continued to hold for many years.

The University of Halle had been in existence only two years before Francke joined its faculty. It was founded specifically to provide an institution in which a free scientific spirit could exist. Many important members of the faculty were Pietists, and others were friendly toward the movement. The teaching at Halle proved immensely popular; from a first-year enrollment of 675, it grew in a decade to 2,000 students. Francke belonged to the philosophical faculty and taught both Greek and Hebrew, using, however, only the Bible as reading matter.

In his small parish of Glaucha he found matters in a very bad way. His immediate predecessor had neglected his duties and had in the end been discharged because of misconduct. In the meanwhile the district had deteriorated. In the entire town there were only two hundred dwelling houses, but there were thirty-seven saloons. Begging, gambling, fighting, and drinking were rife, and the schools were in a state of utter neglect. Francke set to work with a will. He preached, held small meetings at his own house, helped the poor to keep their children in school, preached every Friday about the proper training and discipline of children, sought always to awaken in his flock the spirit of Christianity, and encouraged a more regular attendance of children in the schools. His success in these various undertakings aroused the jealousy and distrust of various clergymen in Halle, who attacked him viciously in writing and tried to influence members of his congregation to turn against him. Francke finally had to request the government to appoint a committee to investigate him and his activities. The committee came, stayed several days, investigated, and gave him a clean bill of health. This report did not entirely quiet his enemies, but at least it kept them from making as open and as disgraceful attacks as they had made in previous years.

From the beginning of his work in Glaucha, Francke had been impressed with the miserable state of the children in the poorest families. They did not go to school, they were wholly illiterate, they were neglected by their parents, they learned early to beg and to steal, they had no training in religion, and they knew nothing of Christian love. In order to obtain a little money with which to help these children, Francke put up alms boxes in the church and in his own study, where people came often to consult him. One day, after he had been three years in Glaucha, a kind lady put four dollars and sixteen groschen in the box at once. While this sum was worth more in 1695 than it is now, it was hardly an amount upon which most people would found a school. Francke, however, decided to use two dollars in buying books and then to hire a young teacher at 6 groschen a week to give two hours' instruction each day; in this way he could stretch the money over eight weeks, and by that time he hoped for further donations. An initial setback in this simple plan came from the children themselves. On the first day of school twenty-seven poverty-stricken children were given books, which they received with great joy and took away from school with them, but only two copies ever came back! Francke was then forced to spend almost another two dollars for books, with the prospect of being forced to close the school within three weeks anyway, for lack of funds. The second set of books was kept safely in the schoolroom, but where the teacher's salary was coming from remained a problem. However, Francke domiciled the school in his own study, invited people to visit it, nailed an alms box on the wall, and put his trust in God. The trust proved adequate, and soon gifts of clothing and food began to flow in. These gifts were distributed from time to time in school, as a means of encouraging the children to come. In the course of a few months, as people saw how well the children were taught, the general public asked leave to send their own children to the school, paying the teacher extra for the additional pupils. Presently there were sixty children altogether, and a large room had to be hired for them; then, as the number still increased, the charity and paying pupils were separated and had separate teachers. Eventually there were two distinct schools, standing side by side, both supported by the townspeople, either directly by fees or indirectly by alms. Thus far, the four dollars had produced two institutions, and they were soon to produce several more.

After the schools had been in existence for a year, a wealthy widow expressed a wish to send her three children from a near-by town to Francke for instruction. He domiciled them in a neighbor's house and saw that they were properly taught and cared for. Rumors of his success brought other boarding students, and presently Francke founded another institution called the *Pädagogium.** It was a boarding school for children from well-to-do people and at the same time a training school for teachers. The scholars—so called, in spite of their tender years, to distinguish them from the pupils of the local schools—were prepared for university entrance and had a more advanced curriculum than was possible in the other schools. The reputation of the school grew apace, and children were sent to it from foreign countries. King Frederick the First* of Prussia* took an interest in it, gave it his patronage, and renamed it *Pädagogium Regium.**

By the time the charity and village schools had been in existence for three years it became clear that certain of the boys in both groups had the ability to go on into secondary education. Because of social conditions, members of neither group could be mixed with the scholars in the *Pädagogium,* so Francke had to found a Latin school for them. In the course of a few years, this school also enrolled many pupils from all over Germany. Each pupil who could afford it paid fifty-six thaler* a year, but there were always some charity pupils and orphans in the group. Those from out of town lived in small groups, each in charge of a student teacher who lived with them. The curriculum of the school was approximately that of the *Pädagogium.*

It presently became necessary to found one more school—this time, an institution for girls of noble birth. Coeducation was virtually unheard of. Even in the elementary school, boys and girls attended separate classes. The girls' school did not prosper and was several times abandoned and again re-established in the years before it vanished altogether.

There was, then, a grand total of five schools: the charity school, the village school, the *Pädagogium* for boys of the upper classes, the Latin school for boys from the middle and lower classes, and the girls' school. The last three were primarily boarding schools, although there were some day pupils. In America, all these schools could have been combined into one elementary and one secondary school, open to boys and girls of all social levels, but not in late seventeenth- or early eighteenth-century Germany.

Francke's trust in God was not misplaced. In the months after the opening of his original school for poor children he received a gift of five hundred dollars that he was asked to use in helping indigent students. He selected about twenty young men of promise as teachers and gave each four, eight, or twelve groschen a week according to his need. Francke was not, however, sure that all the money was properly used, so the next year he decided to give the students free meals instead of money. There were then twenty-four of these special students, but the next year there were forty-two, and the number continued to grow. These students gave some kind of service each day in return for their meals; for some of them, this service consisted in two or three hours a day of teaching. Since Francke came to know these students well, he could select for the teaching those best fitted for it. To help them in their work he gathered them together for conferences, and he appointed an inspector under whose guidance they were to work. In brief, he soon had a normal school, the students of which taught without pay in the charity and town schools. Thus he never lacked for adequate and cheap teaching skill. After the students graduated from the university, many of them went into elementary school teaching throughout Germany and were most influential in raising standards. They had been trained in good methods of teaching, had considered and discussed instructional problems, had had what amounted to practice teaching, and were far superior to the average schoolteacher of the period.

As the teaching seminary developed, certain of the students were selected to form a special group, members of which were to be trained for teaching in the *Pädagogium* and Latin school. These young people had to have a good foundation in the humanities before they were accepted. The course of study in education required five years. During the first two, they devoted themselves to preparation, and then they taught for three years under supervision in one of the above-mentioned schools. These teachers were as well educated as the average college professor. After their training they went forth to teach in the secondary schools of the country.

Francke had hardly got his charity and village schools in running condition, if their somewhat hand-to-mouth existence can be so called, before he started a fresh enterprise that developed out of the charity school. Some of the children were orphans or else came from homes in which parents were depraved and vicious. Francke realized that what good was done these children during school hours was promptly undone by either neglect or corruption at home. So he began to collect orphans, persuading a family here and another there to take them in and feed them. He had no money with which to build a house for orphans, but he followed his usual pattern of behavior, put his trust in the Lord, and went calmly ahead until, in a few months, he had acquired eighteen orphans, a supervisor for them, and a small school. At first, Francke had a difficult time keeping the children under control at all because they were used to poverty, dishonesty, dirt, and idleness, and they did not take kindly to supervision, cleanliness, and discipline. They ran away repeatedly and caused their benefactor all manner of trouble. After three years of makeshift arrangements Francke decided he would have to build an orphanage. He therefore sent his director throughout Germany to solicit sums of money from prominent and wealthy people. Enough money was collected to start the building but by no means enough to finish it. However, Francke laid a cornerstone and began to build. Presently the local nobleman donated 100,000 bricks and 30,000 roof tiles, and other people made other donations of materials, money, or labor. In something less than two years the house stood ready. On this building he caused a motto, subsequently used for all his foundations, to be displayed:

> Those who trust in the Lord obtain new strength, so that they rise high with wings like an eagle's.[16]

In spite of Francke's dependence upon God's bounty he did not neglect appeals for earthly means to forward his work. His financial support came primarily from three sources, aside from such small contributions as filtered in from various friends, well-wishers, and local townspeople. First were the patrons of the undertaking, wealthy men whom Francke managed to interest in his work. Thus he obtained single gifts as large as 7000 thaler, an amount equal to at least $25,000 at present. Francke's friends among the Pietists did not give large sums individually, but *in toto* they contributed a great deal. Second, the numerous rulers, from the King of Prussia to the local noblemen made gifts directly or indirectly. For instance, the foundations paid no taxes, and any materials or foodstuffs they used were duty-free; the employees were excused from all personal taxation, they received their salt as a royal gift, and they were given a fraction of certain moneys collected by the local government. Third, the foundations were allowed to carry on business ventures of their own. Several were tried, of which two were most profitable, the drugstore and the printing press. The former sold what were essentially patent medicines all over Germany and contributed 9000 thaler yearly on the average. The bookshop and printing press yielded about two thirds as much. From all sources combined, Francke got enough support to carry on his numerous foundations.

Francke had come to Halle and Glaucha in 1692. Fifteen years later, he had founded three elementary schools, three secondary schools, an orphanage, a normal school for elementary and another for secondary school teachers, a free table for university students, a home for elderly widows, and a refuge for the many adult beggars who passed through the village. In 1702, he had a total of 125 orphans, his elementary schools enrolled 716 pupils (over 200 from out of town), the Latin school enrolled 55 orphans and 103 boarders; the *Pädagogium,* 70 scholars; and the girls' school, 30 pupils. In addition, 64 university students ate at the free table, and 75 elementary school teachers and

[16] *Ibid.,* I, 53.

about half as many secondary school teachers were being trained in the normal schools.

One other undertaking of importance should be mentioned, although Francke was only one of a group of sponsors and not the main worker. The Pietists based their attitude toward the world upon a thorough reading of the Bible. If people generally were to develop this attitude of mind, Bibles

FIG. 59. Statue of Francke by Rauch, 1829.

must be widely read. Until this time even a printed Bible had been an expensive book, but now a new technique was worked out by which a New Testament could be printed for two groschen. Several million of these cheap Bibles have since been printed at Halle.

Francke remained in or near Halle for the rest of his life. It was not until the last few years that his bitter arguments with the orthodox Lutherans finally died down, partly because Francke had become popular with the King of Prussia and partly because he had received many honors, among them membership in the Scientific Society of Berlin.* The last years of Francke's life were spent in writing and in general supervision of his numerous foundations. He died at the age of sixty-four.

2. Francke's Personality and His Similarity to De la Salle Of Francke as a person, one of his biographers writes as follows:

> "He trusted God!" With these simple words one can best describe the cause of his wonderful success and the fundamental trait of his character. Trust in God and inner faith allowed him to remain steadfast amid the

Fig. 60. August Hermann Francke. Engraving by Büschel.

> storms of life. We have seen how in his parents' house a pious feeling was planted in his heart; but, as every deep spirit must do, he had to fight down serious doubts and to resolve inner struggles; also the splendor and vanity of the earth and the pleasures that it offers tempted him from the right path.[17]

In later years a statue of him was erected at Halle; it makes an interesting comparison with that of De la Salle shown in Figure 57.[18] Francke is shown in his clerical garb, flanked on one side by a boy with a Bible under his arm and on the other by a small girl upon whose head Francke's left hand rests while he points with his right toward heaven. Below the statue is an inscription that well characterizes the founder of so many institutions:

[17] *Ibid.*, I, 54–55.
[18] Also with the statue of Pestalozzi. See Figure 75.

August Hermann Francke: Er vertraute Gott.[19]

The portrait in Figure 60 shows a kindly, simple, unpretentious man.

Francke and De la Salle arrived at their adult personality and their lifework by different routes, but they shared many traits and experiences. Both men had a natural earnestness and a piety that were developed by the religious atmosphere of their homes. De la Salle matured in faith by a continuous and gentle unfolding, while Francke arrived at a similarly deep trust in God by the more devious route of worldly ambition and sudden conversion. Both men were priests and theologians in their respective religions. The modes of expression each used for his religious urge differed, since each fell in with the pattern of his heritage, but the underlying drive seems to have been much the same. The two men both submitted to what they regarded as God's will; they were equally persecuted by enemies, clerical and secular. De la Salle's communities centered about a house for his teachers, a novitiate, and a normal school. Francke's centered about an orphanage, a free school, and a normal school. De la Salle's teachers lived on the premises, but Francke's usually did not. Both men sent out disciples to found new branches. Neither man seems to have set out with an exact notion of what he intended to do. Each was inclined to meet situations as they arose and to systematize his opinions later. Francke arrived at his lifework at the same age as De la Salle, but more directly and with less coercion from circumstances. Both of them knew hunger, privation, and cold, although De la Salle had a more extended knowledge. It was mainly in elementary school that the two men worked, and they restricted themselves for the most part to children who were poor, orphaned, or neglected. Both trained teachers in their own classes, and provided for a long period of practice teaching under supervision. They had remarkably similar goals for their educational efforts: Christian character, faith in God, and mastery of elementary church doctrine. Both men founded institutions that have spread around the world and are still in existence. Although the institutions have been modified somewhat by the passage of time, especially in the elimination of different schools for children from different levels of society, they have remained remarkably constant to the ideals and purposes of the founders.

Naturally, there were differences between the two men in temperament. Francke had a violent temper and was quite lacking in the introverted quality that led De la Salle to desire a secluded life. He was less given to meditation and prayer. De la Salle tended to follow the traditional medieval pattern of austerity and self-immolation; he inflicted pain upon himself in ways that were

[19] *Translation:* "He put his trust in God."

quite outside Francke's tradition. De la Salle began life as a wealthy aristocrat and therefore was called upon to make personal sacrifices that find no parallel in Francke's life.

In spite of these differences, however, both men exerted similar influences in different countries upon the maintenance of schools for poor children and upon the training of teachers for elementary education.

C. SCHOOLS OF DE LA SALLE AND FRANCKE

Both De la Salle and Francke founded elementary schools maintained by charitable contributions, and both wrote manuals to be used by the teachers in their schools. The manuals contained directions on everything from how high the desks ought to be and what kind of stove was best, to suggestions on how to develop harmonious relationships with the home or how to arouse affection in a wronged child. Most of the material in the manuals is highly practical. Since it is a safe assumption that the teachers trained by either of the two gentlemen followed the rules he laid down, one may get a good idea of the procedures in these elementary schools from a reading of the manuals.

1. The Schools of De la Salle[20] The account given below contains material on the daily schedule of work, the curriculum, methods of teaching, conduct of classes, and discipline. These topics will be taken up in order.

The school hours extended from 8:00 till noon and from 1:30 until after 4:30, with a full day's holiday on Thursday.[21] The entire month of September was also free. The children could come to the building at 7:30 A.M. and 1:00 P.M., but if they entered early, it was only to pray. At the opening of school, they were to be in their places awaiting the arrival of the brother who taught them. De la Salle gave specific directions as to the hours for teaching some subjects, but not all; however, the distribution of time could not have been far from that shown in Table 8. It will be noted that the children brought both their breakfast and their lunch with them. The mealtimes were not, however, periods of diversion but periods used for religious training. Some pupil always read or recited while the others ate in silence. The school sessions lasted seven hours each day, of which about half were devoted to religious training or instruction. The four secular subjects of the curriculum were reading, spelling, handwriting, and arithmetic, the same four that still remain the backbone of the first six grades.

The fundamental grouping of the pupils was upon the basis of their

[20] The material about these schools is based upon J. B. de la Salle, *The Conduct of the Schools* (translated by F. de la Fontainerie), McGraw-Hill Book Company, 1935, 242 pp.

[21] Except when there was already a holiday during the week because of a holy day. In all weeks, there was one free day.

TABLE 8: SCHEDULE OF CLASSES IN THE CHRISTIAN SCHOOLS[a]

Hour	Monday	Tuesday	Wednesday	Thursday	Friday	Saturday	Sunday
7:30	Schoolroom open				Schoolroom open		
8:00	Opening prayers, breakfast				Opening prayers, breakfast		
about 8:30–9:00	Writing	Writing	Writing		Writing	Writing	
9:00–10:00	Reading	Reading	Reading		Reading	Reading	
10:00–10:30	Morning Prayers	Morning Prayers			Morning Prayers		Mass
10:30–12:15	Mass	Mass	Mass	FREE	Mass	Mass	
12:15–1:00	Lunch	Lunch	Lunch		Lunch	Lunch	
1:00–1:30	Schoolroom open						Catechism
1:30–2:30	Reading	Arithmetic	Reading		Arithmetic	Reading	
2:30–3:00	Spelling	Spelling	Spelling		Spelling	Spelling	
3:00–4:00	Writing	Writing	Writing		Writing	Writing	Vespers
4:00–4:30	Catechism	Catechism	Catechism		Catechism	Catechism	
4:30	Closing Prayers				Closing Prayers		

[a] De la Salle, *The Conduct of the Schools,* condensed from Chap. III.

ability to read French. As an introduction to reading, the children first learned the alphabet, in large and small letters, from a printed chart that hung in the schoolroom, and a series of syllables from a similar chart. Both are shown in Table 9. The children spelled and pronounced the syllables. The first reading book contained a narrative, but the pupils spelled and pronounced their way through it before they were allowed to read it consecutively. A similar method was used for the second book, which was read aloud by syllables. Continuous reading did not begin until the third book, from which the pupil read aloud by sentences, pausing appropriate lengths of time for commas, semicolons, and periods. The children were considered proficient in French when they reached this point. Since the Psalter was in Latin, the children in later classes began a new language, but they only pronounced it; they did not translate it. Hence, they had no need to study grammar. Finally, after the children had learned to write, they read letters and reports written in script. This course of study in reading is much closer to the needs of the average adult than was the humanistic type of curriculum.

Handwriting came next to reading in importance, but it was not begun until after the pupils could read French well. For equipment they had paper, pens made from quills,[22] penknives for making the pens, models to copy, sheets with heavy guide lines to be placed under the page being written upon, and blotting paper. The pupils who were sufficiently advanced to write at all

TABLE 9: ALPHABETS AND SYLLABLES USED IN THE CHRISTIAN SCHOOL[a]

Part I

a	b	c	d	e
f	g	h	i	y
j	l	m	n	o
p	q	r	s	t
t	u	v	x	z
&	oe	ae	ct	ft

Part II

A	B	C	D	E
F	G	H	I	Y
J	K	L	M	N
P	Q	R	T	U
q	d	h	b	p
A	FF	SST	M	h

Model of Chart of Syllables

me	ca	et	eux	ce	ga	nos
em	gi	je	cho	of	cu	qui
oeu	en	ei	l'hu	vu	go	ont
n'y	ge	in	gue	ha	on	sça
im	eu	xi	cun	ou	he	pei
est	ce	el	gne	gu	j'ai	nez
om	ex	ni	hau	go	ze	moy

[a] De la Salle, *The Conduct of the Schools*, p. 225.

were grouped into six sections. The first learned merely proper position and proper grasp of the pen, without writing anything. The second practiced only five letters, over and over. The third practiced all letters, writing each one enough times to fill a line. The fourth studied the proportions of letters and spaces, and for this purpose practiced the entire alphabet joined together as if it were one word. The fifth section learned a particular alphabet used in commerce, while the sixth wrote sentences in business script on one side of the paper and in an everyday script on the other. At the conclusion of this training, the pupils started all over again and learned a slanting instead of a vertical script! De la Salle gave definite instructions about the position of pen and paper, bodily posture, and grip on the pen. Moreover, he gave some excellent suggestions for the correction of exercises in handwriting.

> When he [the teacher] corrects the writing, he will show the pupils how he forms the syllables or the letters which he wishes to correct for them; and, in order that they may apply themselves afterwards to forming them in the same manner, after having written them at the top or in the margin of their papers, he will make them write a line of each letter or syllable which he has corrected and two lines of each word. If they have not the time to do all this on that day, he will charge them to finish the next day before beginning to copy the model; and if they do not yet succeed even after that, he will oblige

[22] See pp. 255–256.

them to write, during all the time they have for writing, only the letters, syllables, or words which they have written incorrectly, two or three times in succession. When he is correcting the writing of the pupils, the teacher will not write on their papers any lines or words of several syllables. It will suffice that he write the letter which the pupil has written badly; and if the latter has failed in connecting some letters, let the teacher write the two letters joined together, or the syllable at the very most. . . .

The teacher will call the attention of the pupils of the second and third sections—and even of the following ones—to mistakes in the manner of forming letters, for instance whether a B in round hand which a pupil has made is too much inclined to one side or to the other; whether it is curved or humped; whether all its dimensions are correct—that is to say, whether it has the proper height, . . . whether it is too high, whether it has the width that it should at the top and at the bottom, whether it lacks some of its parts; whether the full strokes or the fine ones are where they should be. He will do the same in respect to all the other letters, and he will mark, with a stroke of the pen at each place, all the mistakes that they have made in forming these letters. For example, if the *b* is too much inclined to the right, he will mark it in this manner: b; if too much inclined to the left he will mark it thus: b. He will call the attention of those of the third and of the following sections to all the mistakes which they may have made in respect to connections: whether they have failed to make any where they should have been made; whether they have made any where they should not have been made; whether they have begun them at another point of the letter than at the one where they should start; whether they extend too high or not high enough; whether they are too thin or too thick; whether they are winding when they should be circular; whether they are straight when they should be circular; whether they have held the pen as it should be held. . . .

When the teacher has taught a pupil in the first three sections something or has corrected something for him, he will not leave him at once; but he will make him do in his presence what he has taught him or write the letter which he has corrected. The teacher will watch him, as much to see whether he holds the pen the way that he has shown him as to see whether he begins the letter properly and whether he does well what he has been taught, so that he may tell him in what he fails.[23]

There are equally explicit directions for treating errors in spacing, slant, or alignment. It is especially remarkable that De la Salle should develop a better diagnostic method of teaching penmanship than many schools employ today.

Spelling was begun as a subject separate from reading when the pupils had gained the ability to write the "round" or business script. The method of teaching spelling was to have the children copy letters, receipts, legal con-

[23] From De la Salle, *The Conduct of the Schools,* translated by F. de la Fontainerie. Copyright 1935. This excerpt and subsequent ones from De la Salle are used through the courtesy of McGraw-Hill Book Co.

tracts, leases, deeds, official reports, bills, orders, and so on. After a sufficient amount of copying, the pupils wrote out such documents for themselves. As a method of teaching spelling, this procedure leaves something to be desired, but it had at least an immediate relation to everyday life. The inclusion of business script as a subject in school is further evidence of an effort to adapt schoolwork to reality.

Arithmetic received little stress and seems to have been restricted mainly to the four operations with integers, usually in terms of money. The teacher put only one example on the board each week. Half the time given to arithmetic was used in having this example solved by one child after another, while the others listened. The teacher then assigned some similar examples or asked the pupils to make up some of their own.

De la Salle gave specific directions as to how the children were to be grouped, how the classes were to be conducted, and how each subject was to be taught. The children were grouped for work in each subject and were promoted by subject; a pupil could thus be at different levels in different studies. For moral and religious training, however, the school functioned as a unit. In all instances children were taught as classes, not as individuals; that is, the pupils did not come to the teacher's desk one by one, as was the traditional manner.

The classes were conducted in silence, insofar as possible. De la Salle instructed each teacher thus:

> He will keep a strict watch over himself, so that he may speak only very rarely and in a very low tone—unless it be necessary that all the pupils should hear what he has to say. He will always use a moderate tone when he gives them any instruction, as well as on other occasions when he has need of speaking to all the pupils together. He will never speak, either to any pupil in particular or to all in general, unless he has carefully thought about what he has to say and considers it necessary.[24]

The brothers were trained to use gestures instead of words whenever possible. If a boy mispronounced a word, the teacher rapped twice and pointed to another pupil, who was to correct the error if he could. Punishment was given in silence. This repressive, monastic atmosphere is undoubtedly traceable to De la Salle himself. It will be remembered that he wanted to enter La Grande Chartreuse, taking a vow of eternal silence.

In their behavior generally, the children were cautioned against noise. In De la Salle's instructions:

> The teachers will be attentive and take care that all the pupils walk so lightly and so sedately while entering the school that their steps will not be

[24] *Ibid.*, pp. 147–48.

heard, that they remove their hats before taking holy water, that they make the sign of the cross, and that they go at once directly to their classroom.

It will be instilled into them that they must enter the classroom with profound respect, out of consideration for the presence of God. When they have reached the center of the room, they will make a low bow before the crucifix and will salute the teacher if he is present. Then they will kneel to adore God and to say a short prayer to the Blessed Virgin, after which they will arise, again bow before the crucifix in the same manner, salute the teacher, and go sedately and silently to their regular places.

While the pupils are assembling and entering the classroom, they will maintain such complete silence that not the least noise will be heard—not even of the feet—so that it will not be possible to distinguish those who are entering, nor to notice that the others are studying.

Having reached their seats, they will remain quietly in them, without leaving them for any reason whatsoever until the teacher enters.[25]

FIG. 61. Interior of a Brother's School.

If present-day children are perhaps repressed less than they should be, then the pupils in the Christian Schools were certainly repressed too much.

The brothers were at all times to conduct themselves with dignity and decorum. They were to be friendly with their pupils but never intimate, casual, or undignified. Laughter was regarded as quite regrettable, and the brothers were cautioned never to permit merriment among the children. The schedule of work contained no periods of play, either free or supervised, and the pupils were not allowed to play in the neighborhood of the school. This idea that childish vociferousness and activity were to be suppressed was shared by De la Salle and Francke. Both men considered play a work of the devil, a waste of time, and an affront to God. A sketch of a school, with De la Salle himself in the teacher's chair, appears in Figure 61. The children sat upon benches, while the teacher occupied a chair that was raised considerably above floor level, suggesting that the relationship between teacher and pupil, while friendly, was by no means intimate.

De la Salle's ideas on discipline were colored to some extent by the attitudes of his day, but nevertheless they show that he understood the es-

[25] *Ibid.*, p. 51.

sential psychological principles underlying punishment. He began his discussion as follows:

> To avoid frequent punishments, which are a source of great disorder in a school, it is necessary to note well that it is silence, restraint, and watchfulness on the part of the teacher that establish and maintain good order in a class, and not harshness and blows. A constant effort must be made to act with skill and ingenuity in order to keep the pupils in order while making almost no use of punishments.[26]

Having put his finger upon one main problem, De la Salle goes on to consider what characteristics and actions of teachers make natural firmness degenerate into harshness and what other conditions cause natural gentleness to become weakness. On these two points he itemizes the following characteristics:

Conditions that render the conduct of a teacher unbearable to those in his charge:	*Conditions under which, on the contrary, the conduct of children becomes negligent and lax:*
First, when [the teacher's] penances are too rigorous and the yoke which he imposes on them [the pupils] is too heavy. . . .	First, when care is taken only about things that are important and which cause disorder and when others less important are imperceptibly neglected.
Second, when he enjoins, commands, or exacts something of the children with words too harsh and in a manner too domineering; above all, when this arises from unrestrained movements of impatience and anger.	Second, when not enough insistence is placed upon the performance and observance of school practices and those things which constitute the duties of the children.
Third, when he urges too much upon a child the performance of something which he is not disposed to do. . . .	Third, when what had been enjoined is easily permitted to be neglected.
Fourth, when he exacts with the same ardour little things and big things alike.	Fourth, when, in order to preserve the friendship of the children, too much affection and tenderness are shown them, granting something special to the more intimate or giving them too much liberty which does not edify the others and causes disorder.
Fifth, when he at once rejects the reasons and excuses of the chil-	Fifth, when, on account of natural timidity, the children are ad-

[26] *Ibid.*, p. 161.

dren and is not willing to listen to them at all.

dressed or reprimanded so weakly or so coldly that they do not pay any attention, or it makes no impression upon them.

Sixth, finally, when . . . he does not know how to sympathize with the weaknesses of children, exaggerating too much their faults, and, when he reprimands or punishes them, acts as though he were dealing rather with an insensible instrument than with a creature capable of reason.

Sixth, finally, when the duty of a teacher in respect to his deportment —which consists principally in maintaining a gravity that keeps the children in respect and restraint—is easily forgotten, whether by speaking to them too often and too familiarly or by doing some undignified act.[27]

Actual punishments consisted of reprimands, of blows with a ferule or rod, and of expulsion from school. The ferule consisted of two pieces of leather sewn together; it was about a foot long and terminated in an oval, two inches across. This oval was stuffed with some soft material. Ordinary correction was given with the ferule across the palm of the hand. One blow was generally sufficient, and more than two were strictly prohibited. A teacher might use a rod, but was cautioned against doing so; three blows were regarded as enough and five as the outside limit. Expulsion from school could be resorted to in extreme cases, if the children were of such low moral character that the school was doing them no good and they were doing the school more or less harm.

De la Salle made a list of the characteristics that punishment must have if it is to be effective to the pupils. It must be:

1. Pure and disinterested; without personal vengeance on the part of the teacher.

2. Charitable; that is, both given and received for the salvation of a pupil's soul.

3. Just.

4. Suitable to the fault being punished, both in nature and in degree.

5. Moderate; that is, too lenient rather than too rigorous.

6. Peaceable; so that he who administers it should not be moved to anger, but should be entirely master of himself, and he to whom it is administered should receive it in a peaceable manner, with great tranquility of mind and outward restraint. . . .

7. Prudent; the teacher must be sure that the punishment will have no evil consequences.

8. Voluntary; the pupil must consent to the punishment and regard it as merited.

[27] *Ibid.*, pp. 162–164.

9. Respectful; the punishment is to be received with respect by the pupil.

10. Silent; no words from either child or teacher and no crying.[28]

These principles are as valid today as they were in the late seventeenth and early eighteenth century.

De la Salle gave an especially pertinent list of the faults that teachers were to avoid when they found some punishment of a child to be necessary.

1. No punishment should be given unless it will do some good.
2. No punishment should be given a pupil merely to awe other pupils.
3. No harmful punishment may be used. A pupil may be struck only on the palm of the hand.
4. No punishment should cause disturbance when administered or *should cause the child to detest school.*
5. A pupil should never be punished on account of a feeling of aversion or of annoyance that one has for him, because he causes trouble, or because one has no liking for him.
6. Nor should [a pupil] be punished because of some displeasure caused by him or his parents; and if a pupil should happen to be lacking in respect for his teacher or to commit some fault against him, he should rather be urged by words to recognize his fault and correct it than punished for it.
7. The teacher may never use insulting words when punishing children, nor should he make unseemly motions that are contrary to decorum.
8. The teacher may never punish when he is agitated, angry, or impatient.[29]

De la Salle completed his treatise on discipline in school by pointing out which children should be punished and which emphatically should not be. Pupils who lied, got into fights, stole, told obscene stories, or behaved without reverence in church were to be punished, firmly and at once. The teacher should discipline also those pupils who were bold, insolent, malicious, or stubborn, but different treatment is recommended for the merely heedless:

Their faults do not come from pure malice but from thoughtlessness. They must be treated in such a manner as to prevent them from misbehaving, by showing them affection, without, however, giving them any charge. They should be seated as near the teacher as possible—under pretext of obliging them, and effectively in order to watch over them—and placed between two pupils of a sedate disposition who do not ordinarily commit faults. They should also be given some rewards from time to time, in order to render them assiduous and fond of school—for it is these who absent themselves the most frequently—and to induce them while they are there, to remain still and silent.[30]

[28] *Ibid.*, pp. 170–171.
[29] *Ibid.*, pp. 172–174.
[30] *Ibid.*, p. 179.

The teacher was told to be most chary of punishing a timid child or one whose disposition is gentle and peaceable. Better results may be obtained merely by talking quietly with such pupils, without frightening them. Stupid children should not be punished at all because their defects are not their fault, and they do not usually derive any profit. If a stupid child is also obstreperous he should be dismissed from school. If he is quiet, he had better remain in school, but the teacher should overlook his faults.

De la Salle exempted from punishment also sick children, little children, and newcomers in the school. His remarks about them are of value:

> In respect to those who are sickly, it is of importance that they should not be punished—above all, when the punishment might increase their ailment. Some other means of correction should be used with them, some penance imposed on them.
>
> There are also many little children who likewise must not be punished or who should be punished very seldom, because, not having attained the use of reason, they are not capable of profiting by punishment. It will be necessary to deal with them in much the same manner as with children of a gentle and timid disposition.
>
> Finally, one must abstain from punishing children who are just beginning to come to school. It is necessary, first, to know their minds, their natures, and their inclinations. They should be placed near some pupil who acquits himself well of his duties, in order that they may learn by practice and example. They should ordinarily be left about a fortnight in school before being punished. Punishment of newcomers can only repel them and alienate them from school.[31]

Modern psychology has little to add to the above discussion on discipline, written by a Catholic priest and teacher two and a half centuries ago.

Such, then, were the schools maintained by the brothers. For their period they were excellent, and some of their characteristics are just as superior today as they were then. These schools and the German Protestant counterparts were the first to emphasize elementary education sufficiently to train men for it as a lifework. Although there was much stress upon religion, the teachers were not members of the clergy, but laymen, dedicated to teaching. The schools represent, therefore, a step toward secular education.

2. *The Schools Founded by Francke*[32] In his manual of instructions to his teachers and in his pedagogical writings, Francke expressed himself upon many basic educational matters such as the relation between teacher and

[31] *Ibid.*, p. 182.

[32] Modern and brief accounts of the schools appear in two publications: W. Michaelis, *August Hermann Francke*, Heliand-Verlag, 1947, 16 pp., and *Die Franckeschen Stiftungen zu Halle an der Saale,* Buchhandlung des Waisenhauses, 1926, 48 pp. The latter contains a large number of excellent pictures.

pupil, the goals of education, the training of character, and the nature of discipline. He discussed also such practical matters as the schedule of classes, the curriculum, and the methods of instruction. On some topics he is more modern than on others, but in general he shows an advance over what had formerly existed.

In all his schools Francke insisted upon the maintenance of a pleasant friendly relationship between the teacher and his pupils. He was constantly reminding his teachers that they were inevitably models that the children would imitate, consciously or unconsciously, and that they must conduct themselves accordingly. He expressed his typical attitudes on these points in the passage quoted below:

> Especially must a teacher be careful that his pupils should not notice anything wicked in him. For children notice everything, whether good or bad. . . . Children who see their teachers or fathers drunk, angry, or unchaste and hear them swear and slander and observe through their example the vanity of the world and the pleasures of the flesh and luxurious life will thereafter not easily be brought to a fundamental hatred for these vices.[33]
>
> You should not be sullen, angry, boring, or impatient but must show yourself always full of love and friendliness toward the children, so that you will win their love, upon which so much depends. However, an understanding teacher will see to it that no unrestrained familiarity develops.[34]

Francke's intentions as regards discipline seem to have been unexceptionable, but it is clear from his writings that he found admonition and punishment necessary at times. Since six and a half of the eight school hours daily were devoted to religious and moral training and since little effort was made to adapt the materials of instruction to childish interests, it is not surprising that he could not always live up to his highest principles. The paragraphs below indicate a preference for a discipline based on love but not for an absence of restraint.

> It generally happens that most teachers out of lack of adequate experience and love try to compel goodness through sharp external punishment rather than to enfold those entrusted to their care in a spirit of love and to bring their hearts to goodness with fatherly loyalty, patience, and foresight.
>
> Whoever has such paternal affection . . . will not neglect admonition and punishment; however, insofar as is possible he will not disrupt education by use of physical force and hardness, nor give in in the least to the feeling of anger, but with all kindness and sweetness he will plant in their hearts a childish fear of God and a love toward God and Christ. With friendliness a teacher makes more progress than with everlasting scolding and beating. . . .

[33] Otto, *op. cit.*, I, p. 59.
[34] *Ibid.*, p. 73.

No child should be scolded or punished because he is slow to learn. . . . The teacher should not become impatient and angry if a child, because of limited ability, cannot immediately grasp something, but he should in gentleness and patience that much the more diligently teach. . . . Profane words and ridicule are absolutely not to be used to the children, since they are more hurt than helped thereby. A teacher may not call them, out of impatience, oxen, asses, pigs, dogs, beasts, fools, scoundrels, swineherds, and so on, and still less children of the devil. One shall not swear at them or wish them evil. . . .

No child is to be struck on the head with the hand, with a stick, a ruler, or a book. Still less may one box a child's ears . . . because the children do not profit thereby and much harm may be done to both their spirit and their health. No child should be pulled hither by the arms, yanked by the hair, nor flicked with the stick on the hands or fingers. . . .

In all punishment one must consider the individuality of the child. A teacher should take care to learn the disposition of his children, so that he will not discipline the shy and sensitive spirits as he does the hardened and impudent children; for more children can be won with words than with blows.[35]

In his writings Francke stated the goals of education as being the development of what he called "Christian godliness" and "Christian cleverness"; by these two phrases he seems to have meant a training of the will and a training of the mind. His training for godliness was much like modern character education, except that it contained more specifically religious teaching. His suggestions as to how one can educate a child to be good are as follows: constant good example by the teacher, learning of the catechism, reading in the Bible, demonstration of virtue and vice by numerous examples, warnings and threats to those children who need them, praise for whatever a child does that is right, development of love for truth, obedience, and industry through constant stressing of these virtues in schoolwork, use of prayer, supervision of children at play as well as in school, development of a desire to learn, and the use of proper punishment. With the exception of prayer and the catechism, these suggestions might still be made by an earnest teacher of today. For the education of the mind in "Christian cleverness," Francke recommended training of the attention, supervised experience, elimination of prejudice, application of what is learned, development of a habit of testing principles, and the reading of good books. Although these recommendations do not cover all points about intellectual training, they are sensible as far as they go.

Francke planned the children's day from seven in the morning until six at night for all days, including Sunday. The schedule for the elementary

[35] *Ibid.*, condensed from pp. 108–114.

schools appears in Table 10. One can see at a glance that the school hours were long—from 7 to 11 and from 2 to 6. Religious instruction dominated the plan. The first hour was devoted to prayer; moreover, all periods began and ended with prayer, and after the school day was over, the children went to

TABLE 10: FRANCKE'S PLAN OF TEACHING[a]

Hours	Week Days	Sunday
7–8	Song, prayer, and reading from the Bible; repetition of the catechism	Attendance at the morning service in church
8–9	½ hour reading of Biblical selections; ½ hour catechism with the older pupils	
9–10	½ hour explaining quotations and proverbs to the younger children; ½ hour study of Psalms and the New Testament by the older children	
10–11	Writing hour	
2–3	Prayer and Bible reading. Reading, music, and reading for the smaller children, on different days	Attendance at the afternoon service in church
3–4	½ hour reading by the younger and study of quotations and sayings by the older pupils; ½ hour recitation of the sayings, while the little children listen	
4–5	Catechism	
5–6	Evening prayers in the church	

[a] Otto, *op. cit.*, pp. 92–93. This plan is for the teacher's time. While certain children are being taught, the others are presumably studying, writing, or reading.

church. The first school hour closed with singing and with reading a chapter from the Bible, usually the New Testament. Then the specifically religious instruction began, with a half-hour study of the catechism. The teacher first explained a section, showed its relation to daily conduct, answered questions, and examined the children on previous sections. Unfortunately, few teachers could handle the material properly, and the period tended to degenerate into a dull sort of questioning, or a long sermon on the part of the teacher, or a complete diversion of the period to some other use. After two hours thus filled, the children devoted an hour to learning Biblical matter by heart. The teacher read aloud a quotation to the smaller children, who repeated it after him as many times as necessary to learn it; thereafter it was explained to them. In the meantime, the older pupils learned by heart a psalm, a parable, or some other quotation of moderate length from the Bible.

At ten o'clock the handwriting hour began. The youngest children practiced making individual letters or parts of letters. The next higher group wrote syllables and short words, while the older pupils wrote entire paragraphs. Francke was most emphatic about the development of a good script, and he trained his teachers himself, until their writing was acceptable to him. He even introduced a particular style of script that was used in his foundations into the nineteenth century. It was inevitable that the children should copy selections from the Bible, but other material was also included. The children wrote letters, bills, orders, business communications, and receipts, thus learning to use their skill in practical ways. The teachers were required not only to correct what the children wrote but to produce models for copying, except when the pupils were composing or writing from memory. Since there was no class instruction, a different model had to be written for each child. During the penmanship period the teacher went from one pupil to another giving help where needed.

After a three-hour respite and lunch at home the pupils returned to school. The first half hour was again devoted to prayer and Bible reading, but the second part of the period was used for different subjects on different days. Wednesdays and Saturdays the children sang. They learned to read simple music and to sing both alone and in choruses. The material was mostly hymns, music and words for which were learned by heart. On other days this half hour was spent in arithmetic. The entire course of study in this subject included only writing the numbers, the four fundamental operations with whole numbers, and ratio and proportion. Of fractions the pupils were supposed to get enough understanding to know the value of each but there was no training in manipulation. At the beginning of the period the children recited in chorus a part of the multiplication table. Then each child went on from where he had left off the day before. The teacher called each pupil to the desk singly, corrected his work, and gave him a fresh assignment. The pupils plodded, problem by problem, through a specified arithmetic book, each proceeding at his own rate. When a child emerged from the last problem, his mathematical education was over.

For instruction in reading, the pupils were classified into four groups, although the actual teaching was always individual. The children in the first group learned the alphabet—or rather, the alphabets, since they had to learn German print, in both capitals and small letters, Roman print in both, German script, and Roman script. They had, then, eight alphabets to master. When this Herculean task was finished they moved on to an ABC book, in which they spelled out the words, pronounced the letters by syllables, and finally read the words aloud as units. In the ABC books, the words were already divided into syllables. In the third class the children continued in the same manner as the second, only they "read" from the catechism; the new difficulty lay in the need for each pupil to make his own division of words into syllables. Finally, in the fourth class, the pupils began independent reading in the New Testament. Once this stage was reached, formal instruction in reading ended, since the goal was the ability to read the Bible.

In the early stages of reading, the pupils were likely to show fatigue and to lose interest. Among Francke's directions to his teachers one finds the following bit of good advice:

> You should not give children books that are too long, but those that are as short as possible; for in this way they do not lose their interest so easily, if they soon come to the end and can begin something new. Education must be carried on in the mother tongue; otherwise unrest easily arises and the children pay more attention to the words than to the meaning.[36]

There is little doubt that Francke intended to adjust work to the pupils' capacities or that he did so when possible. The difficulty was that his curriculum contained material that many children could not learn.

The remaining hours of the afternoon were used for the memorizing and recitation of quotations from the Bible, for further study of the catechism, and for a final hour in church. Other subjects than religion, reading, writing, and arithmetic do not appear in the elementary curriculum. It was Francke's idea that such subjects as astronomy, geography, physics, and history should be learned incidentally as forms of diversion outside school hours! Once a week the children were taken, two by two, for a walk, during which they were instructed in science. Play was strictly forbidden; the hours of relaxation were to be used constructively and not to be wasted in running about.

The curriculum of Francke's Latin school and of the *Pädagogium* included the usual courses in Latin and Greek, but with reduced emphasis upon grammar, plus work in geography, history, and natural science. Both in the selection of subjects and in his experimental and observational methods of teaching science, Francke reveals himself as a sense realist. In all classes German was spoken, not Latin. The majority of the orphans and poor children learned a useful trade as a part of their regular schoolwork. In this requirement Francke shows that he was also a social realist. The secondary schools were not perhaps as outstanding as the elementary, but they were appreciably better than most others of the period. In particular, they were much better taught.

The teachers in Francke's schools were without exception the advanced students in his training seminars. He made great demands upon them, trained them well, guided them with exact instructions, supervised their work, and dismissed any who failed to come up to his expectations. First, he required that they be of upright character, that they dress simply, that they abstain from the use of tobacco and alcohol, and that they have a serious interest in teaching. Second, he insisted that each candidate for teaching feel a real affection for children and have the necessary patience for dealing with them. Third,

[36] *Ibid.*, p. 73.

the teacher must stick to the schedule laid out for him, without innovations. If he felt that something needed a change, he should put his suggestion on paper and give it to his inspector for discussion in the next seminar. He had to keep a record for each child, giving his age, date of entrance and leaving, names of parents, marks, types and reasons for discipline, attendance, estimate of ability, and so on. The teacher was required to treat each child individually and to adjust the examinations to the capacity of each by asking less of some than of others. The teacher visited the parents of children in his class and asked them to co-operate by continuing at home the same attitudes that were stressed in class, to send the children regularly to school, and to supervise any homework. Each teacher was to visit the classes of other teachers and to attend regularly the meetings of the seminars, where materials and methods were discussed. He was responsible for the behavior of the children in or near the school or in church when he had escorted them thither. He could not dismiss any pupil from his school, or absent himself from his work. Finally, he was responsible for the cleanliness, attractiveness, and proper heating of his schoolroom. Many of these provisions may seem mere routine to the modern teacher, but most of them were innovations in the late seventeenth and early eighteenth centuries.

Neither Francke nor De la Salle understood the value of play in a child's life. They made few efforts to utilize childish interests and activities to motivate schoolwork. Both men loved children deeply, but the religious fervor in their own natures gave them the urge to use education as a means of building character and saving souls rather than of developing each child according to his natural gifts. Spontaneous play did not seem to fit into such a concept of education. Francke was so much of a fanatic that he regarded with suspicion any form of gaiety or humor. The excerpt below shows the narrowness of his thinking on moral issues and his reluctance to let children find amusement in their work.

> Love of truth can be instilled if (1) you will teach children that all lies are frightful sins and the main characteristic of Satin, who was a liar from the beginning . . . ; (2) if you take care that children do not listen to fairy stories or other tales from old women or from the domestic help, through which the children become accustomed to lie busily; (3) if the children do not observe that their parents consider the so-called "white" lies only minor offenses; (4) if you do not awaken in a child a love for comedies, jokes, novels, or love stories, political nonsense, or other foolishness; (5) if you watch carefully over children's talk and do not let the tiniest lie go unpunished; (6) if you do not repeat children's lies and laugh over them, since the children are likely to hear and to be strengthened in their wickedness.[37]

[37] *Ibid.,* condensed from pp. 66–67.

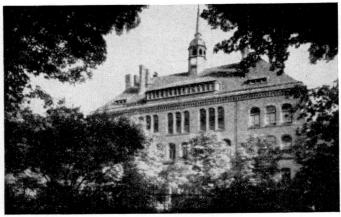

FIG. 62. Modern Views of Francke's Institutions. (*Above*) Main Buildings. (*Top right*) High School. (*Lower right*) Scientific School. Pictures supplied by the Franckesche Stiftungen.

Francke's work had both its strength and its weakness. The curriculum was one-sided and the hours of work were too long. His emphasis upon religious instruction was excessive. He insisted upon the suppression of all that was worldly, including childish play. He did not in the least appreciate art, music, drama, or literature; to his mind, all of them, except church hymns, gave rise to mere pleasure and were therefore to be shunned by Christians. His education was primarily an education of the will and secondarily of the mind; he neglected emotional development, except for religious feelings. Indeed, his idea seems to have been that the only good emotion was a dead one! Moreover, in his zeal for systematizing, he overorganized the children's lives, leaving them little opportunity to develop their individuality. These weaknesses come mostly from an excess of piety, but they show an ignorance of child psychology or an unwillingness to apply such knowledge of child nature as existed. Most of the great teachers in the world have shown a better understanding of children than Francke did and have made better adjustments to their needs.

On the credit side of the ledger one should note Francke's constant emphasis upon the teacher's personality and the important role played by teachers in influencing children. His moral standards for members of the teaching profession were as high as those of today. He sensed the necessity for a harmonious environment, and to this end he brought together the school and the home, the teacher and the parents. He demanded that his teachers pay attention to individual differences and that they adjust work to such differences. He recommended teaching through direct observation, projects, models, and experiments, especially in the sciences that were taught in his Latin school and the *Pädagogium;* in language work he subordinated grammar to correct usage. He related school and adult work by giving training in such trades as flourished in the neighborhood. His ideas about discipline were sound and, for his period, advanced. However, his outstanding abilities were in organizing schools and in training teachers. Each school of his foundation ran like clockwork, and the entire group made a harmonious unit with interlocking parts. The institutions were so well integrated and so well staffed that they continued their work as usual after Francke's death, and are still in existence. A modern picture of his schools at Halle appears in Figure 62.

READING REFERENCES

A. General Histories of the Period

Ergang, *Europe from the Renaissance to Waterloo,* chap. 19.
Garrett, *European History, 1500–1815,* chaps. 20–23.

Ogg, *Europe in the Seventeenth Century,* chap. 7.
Riker, T. W., *A Short History of Modern Europe,* The Macmillan Company, 1935 (890 pp.), chaps. 2, 3, 7.
Robinson, *Introduction to the History of Western Europe,* chap. 31.
Schevill, *A History of Europe from the Reformation to the Present Day,* chap. 15.
Seignobos, *The Rise of European Civilization,* chaps. 14, 15.
Stearns, *Pageant of History,* part ii, chap. 17.

B. Other Texts in the History of Education

Cubberley, *History of Education,* pp. 344–351, 416–419.
Eby and Arrowood, *The Development of Modern Education,* chaps. 9, 10.
Marique, *History of Christian Education,* Vol. II, chap. 10.
McCormick, *History of Education,* pp. 301–310.

C. Secondary Sources

Adamson, *Pioneers of Modern Education,* chaps. 11–13.
Drane, *Christian Schools and Scholars,* pp. 629–636.
Graves, *Great Educators of Three Centuries,* chap. 6.
Quick, *Essays on Educational Reformers,* chap. 13.
Ravelet, *Blessed de la Salle,* any chapters in book ii (pp. 102–431).
Schuetz, *The Origin of Teaching Brotherhoods,* pp. 19–35.
Wilson, *The Christian Brothers: Their Origin and Work,* chaps. 2, 3, 6–11.

D. Translation of Primary Source

De la Salle, *Conduct of Schools,* part i, chaps. 1, 3, 7, 10; part ii. chaps. 2, 5, 7.

CHAPTER XIV

BASEDOW AND HIS PHILANTHROPINUM

With the last two chapters these historical sketches entered modern times. The work of Comenius contained many ideas that mark it off sharply from either medievalism or humanism. By today's standards, both De la Salle and Francke overstressed religion, but their work also showed signs of modernity. Such features become even more obvious in this chapter, which will deal with the further modernizing of educational thought and practice through the influence of of a Swiss named Jean Jacques Rousseau* and the application of Rousseau's ideas by a German named Johann Bernhard Basedow.

By the early years of the eighteenth century, the European world had come to a state of intellectual, moral, religious, and political stagnation. The renewed emotional impetus given to Protestantism by the Pietists and Puritans had in its turn died away into formalism, leaving behind it the gloomy conviction that all pleasure was sinful but offering little other bearing upon daily life. The situation in Catholic countries was no better, because the fervor of the Counter Reformation had dissipated itself, and the church offered the faithful a number of rites and a plethora of miracles but little nourishment for the soul. The artistic and intellectual renaissance, the religious renaissance, and the scientific renaissance had waxed and waned and had become part of modern man's cultural heritage, but these movements had already run their courses. The political and economic situations were nearly static. Absolutism* was the dominant mode of government; inequality of wealth and privilege,* the dominant factor of daily life. In the course of the eighteenth century, two movements developed that brought violent new life into European thoughts and attitudes. The first was the revolt of educated men against religious, intellectual, and political repression. The second was the revolt of the masses against social and economic repression. The former aimed at a freeing of the mind from the shackles of tradition and the substitution of reason for blind acceptance; the latter aimed at the establishment of the rights of the common man. The former was cold, controlled, intellectual, and aristocratic; the latter was warm, emotional, democratic, and difficult to control.

1. The Age of Reason The first of these movements is usually referred to as the Age of Reason or the Age of Enlightenment. The fundamental tenet of the rationalists was a supreme confidence in the power of reason. The leaders of the Enlightenment wanted to combat superstition, terrorism, and the intellectual tyranny of tradition by pouring a mixture of reasonable argument and cold ridicule upon the customs of church, state, and society in general. Of the entire group of men prominent in this movement, none is more outstanding or more typical than François Marie Arouet, better known by his pen name of Voltaire. He was a voluminous, incisive, brilliant, and witty writer, with a vein of cruelty in his wit. Many of the things he said were remembered, not merely because they were trenchant, apposite, and amusing, but because they hurt. There is no space in this text to quote his writings, but it seems appropriate to include a picture of him because it reveals so dramatically the entire nature of the Enlightenment. He is shown as brilliant, keen, hard, and shrewd—a powerful destructive force in a society that needed to be destroyed before something better could arise in its place.

Voltaire and his contemporaries are often called rationalists because they believed that the human reason could solve all human problems. They upheld the right of each individual to his own opinion, to his own liberty of conscience, to his own freedom of thought. Voltaire is credited with the oft-quoted saying: "I disapprove of what you say, but I will defend to the death your right to say it." The rationalists were members of an intellectual aristocracy, the cultured few; it was their intention to establish a new aristocracy of brains to counterbalance that of family or wealth. Because the rationalists had no political authority and no economic hold upon society, the movement, begun with great intellectual vigor, was powerless to bring about the changes it advocated. It presently petered out into skepticism, sophistication, and artificiality. The last of the *illuminati** degenerated into the superficial, cheap cleverness typical of a frustrated, self-centered, polished, refined, but useless society. This movement deliberately eliminated religion as a force in human affairs but provided nothing to replace it. The type of education it produced centered, as shown in the private schools for the nobility, upon the acquisition of worldly wisdom and

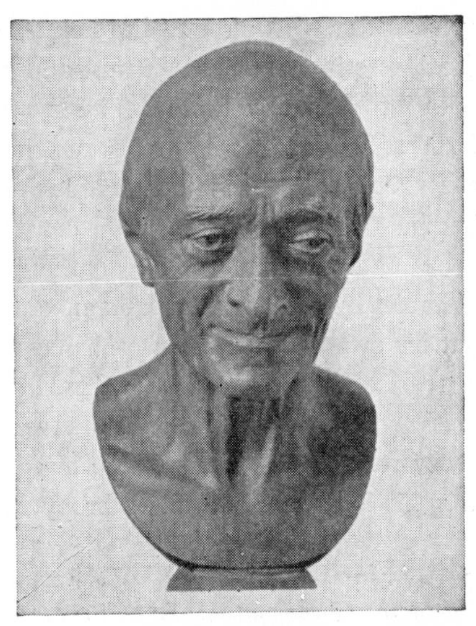

Fig. 63. Voltaire. By Jean-Antoine Houdon, Museum of Fine Arts, Boston.

polished manners.[1] The Enlightenment was nevertheless an important forerunner of later developments, although its main work was destructive and consisted in the tearing down of traditional values.

2. The Emergence of the Common Man The second great movement, the popular revolt, came a little later than the Enlightenment. Its leaders brought to the world a new spirit, a faith in the common man, and a belief in the natural goodness of all nature, including human nature. The appeal was emotional rather than intellectual, and it was made to all the people, not to a small, highly literate group. The resulting emergence of the common man as a force to be reckoned with culminated in the upheavals of the French Revolution. Never since the end of the eighteenth century has he again been forgotten; his rights are established—even though they are sometimes ignored for a while—and governments have learned to tread softly and not provoke him into open rebellion.

The most outstanding writer of this second movement was Jean Jacques Rousseau,[2] one of the most passionate, eloquent, and inspiring writers of modern times. In his own life he had suffered the usual deprivations, prejudices, discrimination, handicaps, and punishments that were the lot of those born into a humble family—plus more of the same at the hands of a brutal father. His was a violent, rebellious, impatient, turbulent nature that resented every slight and every injustice. In his own personal affairs he showed great irresponsibility, however, and he constantly contradicted his own ideals by his behavior. Thus he urged freedom and naturalness for children, personal care of babies by their mothers, and an education based upon child nature—but he put his own children in an orphanage. His writings were presumably a form of release for his pent-up feelings, his misfortunes, and his inferiorities; essentially, he wanted mankind to have everything he had lacked. Although his books reflected his own moods, his contempt for the frivolity of life about him, his loneliness and misanthropy, they also contained revolutionary ideas

[1] For typical expressions of educational ideals during this period see T. Elyot, *The Boke Named the Governour* (H. H. S. Croft, editor), Kegan Paul, Trench, Trubner & Co., 1883, 2 vols, and B. Castiglione, *The Courtier* (Tudor Edition by Sir T. Hoby), 1561, reprinted by E. P. Dutton & Company, 1928, 324 pp.

[2] For accounts of Rousseau's life and work, see W. Boyd, *The Educational Theories of Jean Jacques Rousseau,* Longmans, Green and Co., 1911, 368 pp.; G. Compayré, *Jean Jacques Rousseau et l'éducation de la nature,* P. Delaplane, 1901, 112 pp. (also translated by R. P. Jago, Thomas Y. Crowell Company, 1907, 120 pp.); T. Davidson, *Rousseau and Education according to Nature,* Charles Scribner's Sons, 1898, 253 pp.; O. H. Lang, *Rousseau and His Émile,* E. L. Kellogg and Company, 1893, 36 pp.; J. M. Morley, *Rousseau,* The Macmillan Company, 1915, 2 vols.; A. Pinloche, *La Réforme de l'éducation en Allemagne au dixhuitième siècle et le philantropisme,* Musée Pédagogique et Bibliothèque Centrale de l'Enseignement Primaire, 1889, 597 pp.; R. H. Quick, *Essays on Educational Reformers,* Appleton-Century-Crofts Company, 1896 (568 pp.), pp. 96–138.

as to the nature of man and his social environment. While the rationalists in general made their attacks in a witty, cold, restrained, and logical manner, Rousseau wrote in a fresh and emotional style that charmed his readers and earned for him a place in the world's literature. His *Émile* and his *Social Contract* are the two books by which he is best known.

In the *Social Contract* he formulated his doctrine of popular sovereignty: that the ultimate power of a state rests in its people, not in its rulers. Rousseau did not invent this idea. It had flourished in the republics of Greece and Rome, and had been set forth a century earlier in the writings of John Locke,* but it had been replaced in most of Europe by the doctrine that the power of the state was vested in the monarch, who ruled by divine right.* Rousseau's presentation of popular sovereignty was appealingly written, and it came at a time when France was very tired indeed of absolute monarchs and privileged classes. The country was already seething with discontent, and Rousseau showed his compatriots a way out of their difficulties when he wrote: "The holders of the executive power are not the people's masters, but its officers; it can set them up or pull them down as it likes." A year after Rousseau's death, the delegates of the common people started to "pull them down" and did not stop until they had wiped out the last hereditary privilege through the medium of the French Revolution.

Since so much will be said in the next chapters about Rousseau's educational ideas, it might be well to discuss briefly the nature of *Émile,* the book that did much to revolutionize education. This book is a story of how the boy Émile was properly educated by his tutor.

A few typical passages will do more than a prolonged discussion to show why Rousseau was both popular and revolutionary. His opening paragraph is famous and gives expression to his fundamental ideas that nature is always right and training is usually wrong.

> Everything is good as it comes from the hands of the Author of Things; everything degenerates between the hands of man. He forces one piece of ground to nourish the productions of another, one tree to bear the fruit of another; he mixes and confuses climates, elements, seasons; he mutilates his dog, his horse, his slave; he overturns everything, he disfigures everything; he loves deformity and monsters; he does not want anything as it was made by nature—not even mankind; one has to train him like a circus horse, one has to disfigure him as a tree in the garden.[3]

Nature wants children to be children before they are men. If we try to

[3] J. J. Rousseau, *Émile ou de l'Éducation* (translated by W. H. Payne as *Émile* or *Education According to Nature*) Appleton-Century-Crofts Company, 1908 (363 pp.), p. 5. This and subsequent excerpts are used by permission of Appleton-Century-Crofts Company, publishers.

pervert this order, we shall produce precocious fruits that will have neither maturity nor savor and will not be long in spoiling; we shall have young scholars and old children. Childhood has its ways of seeing, thinking, and feeling that are appropriate to it; nothing is less intelligent than to want to substitute our own ways.[4]

The child who feels the need of help from others, who never ceases to experience their good intentions, has no interest in deceiving them; on the contrary, he has a reasonable interest in their seeing things as they are, for fear that they may deceive themselves to his prejudice. . . . In a natural and free education, why should your child lie to you? What has he to hide from you? You do not rebuke him, you never punish him, you exact nothing from him. Why would he not tell you all that he did as frankly as he would tell a small friend? He cannot see in this confession more danger from one side than from the other.[5]

Now if nature gives to a child's mind this suppleness that renders it capable of receiving all sorts of impressions, it is not for the purpose of engraving upon it the names of kings, dates, terms of heraldry, of the sphere, or of geography and all those words without sense for his age and without utility for any age whatsoever, with which one overwhelms his sad and sterile childhood, but it is for engraving all the ideas that he can understand and that are useful, all those that contribute to his happiness and ought some day to shed light upon his duties; they trace themselves in his mind early in ineffaceable characters and help him to conduct himself during his life in a manner suitable to his nature and his abilities.[6]

Whether he works or plays, both are the same to him; his games are his occupations and he feels no difference between them. He puts into everything he does an interest that makes him laugh and a liberty that pleases, showing at the time the bent of his mind and the range of his knowledge. Is it not a sweet and charming sight at this age to see a handsome child, his eye lively and gay, his manner contented and serene, his face open and smiling—a child who, while amusing himself, does the most serious things or works hard at the most frivolous games? [7]

A sense of duty does not exist at their age [during childhood] and there is not a man in the world who can make it really intelligible to them; but the fear of punishment, the hope of pardon, the importunities, the embarrassment of answering, tear from them all the promises that you demand; and you believe you have convinced them when you have only bored or frightened them. What happens as a result? In the first place, by imposing upon them a duty they do not feel, you prejudice them against your tyranny and turn them aside from loving you; secondly, you teach them to be deceitful,

[4] *Ibid.*, p. 72.
[5] *Ibid.*, pp. 86–87.
[6] *Ibid.*, pp. 100–101.
[7] *Ibid.*, p. 166.

false, untruthful in order to extort rewards or to get out of punishment; finally—accustoming them always to cover over their secret motive with an apparent one—you yourself give them the means for cheating you endlessly, for hiding from you the knowledge of their real character, and of paying you and others with vain words as occasion offers.[8]

If he [Emile] falls, if he bumps his head, if he has a nosebleed, if he cuts his fingers, instead of rushing toward him with an alarmed air, I will remain quiet, at least for a little while. The evil is done, and he will have to endure it. . . . If he sees me running anxiously to console and comfort him, he will think himself lost; if he sees me keeping my composure he will soon regain his own and will believe the evil cured when he no longer feels it. This is the age when one takes the first lessons in courage and when by enduring mild pains without fear one learns by degrees to bear severe ones.[9]

I do not at all like explanations in words; young people give them little attention and hardly retain them. Things! Objects! I cannot ever repeat often enough that we give too much authority to words with our babbling education that produces only babblers.[10]

These few selections contain some of Rousseau's basic ideas on education. Reduced to maxims, the passages could be epitomized thus: go back to nature, let children be children, make games an education and education a game, let nature take its course, teach less from books and more from life, use many objects and few words, let your child be free, win his confidence, protect him from the artificiality of human society, do not coerce him, stimulate his mind with things he can understand, and keep him healthy. In flat contradiction to the doctrine that man is born bad and must be saved by God's grace, Rousseau was emphatic in stating that man was born good and was spoiled by contact with human society and by education. The spirit of severe repression that had dominated the schools for centuries was based upon the supposed need to cure children of their innate badness. Beating the evil out of them in this world was regarded as preferable to letting them continue in sin and suffer hell-fire throughout eternity. If, however, children were by nature good, then all one had to do was to let them stay that way! A school based upon such a theory had no need for harsh discipline. As Rousseau's *Émile* was read from one end of the world to the other, freedom for children became more and more popular until now it is accepted as axiomatic, and harsh discipline has consequently disappeared from the schools.

The movement introduced into education by Rousseau is usually called

[8] *Ibid.*, p. 73.
[9] *Ibid.*, p. 55.
[10] *Ibid.*, pp. 188–189.

naturalism, because the basic tenet was the conviction that the natural growth of children in a natural environment constituted an adequate education. The idea was new at the time of its formulation by Rousseau and was in sharp contrast to both the belief that children were born wicked and the extreme artificiality of the period. Educators who followed Rousseau adopted the same general theory, although they modified it somewhat. Naturalism is still one important element in education today.

A. BASEDOW: HIS LIFE AND WORK

1. The Life Story of Basedow[11] Some teachers of educational history will be surprised to find Johann Bernard Basedow among the world's great teachers. More surprising still is the relegation of Rousseau to a position in the background. The reason for this situation is the author's determination to write a book about teachers, methods of instruction, curricular content, and schools—not a book about educational philosophy. Rousseau was a writer and philosopher, not a schoolteacher. Moreover, his writings were in such a form that they could not be applied directly to schoolwork. Indeed, one of his basic ideas was to dispense with schools altogether. Basedow is included in this book because he combined Rousseau's ideas with some of his own and evolved the first school in which the educational philosophy of Rousseauism found full scope. His school did not last for long, but through the teachers who taught there and the disciples who admired him, he influenced subsequent education in Germany a good deal and that in other countries more or less. Basedow was far from admirable as a person—so was Rousseau, for that matter—and he was more than a little mad, but in the stuffy atmosphere of eighteenth-century schoolrooms he lit a torch that still burns today.

[11] The material in this section is based on the following publications: H. Barnard, "Memoirs of Emminent Teachers and Educators in Germany" (translated from the German of K. von Raumer), *American Journal of Education* (1863) 7:9–153; J. B. Basedow, *Das Elementarwerk* (arranged by Th. Fritzsch), E. Weigand, 1909, 3 vols.; A. J. Becker, *Basedow's Methodenbuch für Väter und Mütter,* F. Schöningh, 1914, 145 pp.; R. Claus, *Basedow's Naturwissenschaftliche Pädagogik im Lichte Naturwissenschaftlicher Forschung,* Thomas und Hubert, 1911, 109 pp.; H. Goring, *J. B. Basedow's Ausgewählte Schriften,* H. Beyer und Sohn, 1880, 519 pp.; G. P. R. Hahn, *Basedow und sein Verhältnis zu Rousseau,* University of Leipzig, 1885, 113 pp.; O. H. Lang, *Basedow: His Educational Work and Principles,* E. L. Kellogg and Company, 1891, 27 pp.; C. Meier, *Basedow's Leben, Character und Schriften unparteiish dargestellt und beurteilt,* B. G. Hoffman, 1891–1892, 2 vols. (In spite of its title, this reference is full of malice, but it does show what those who despised Basedow thought of him.) A. Pinloche, *La Reforme de l'éducation en Allemagne au dixhuitième siècle,* A. Colin et Cie., 1889, 597 pp.; R. H. Quick, *Essays on Educational Reformers,* E. L. Kellogg and Company, 1890 (335 pp.), pp. 139–156; H. Schumann, "Johann Bernhard Basedow: Ein Beitrag zur Kenntniss seiner Schriften und seiner Ansichten über Lehrerbildung," in C. Kehr, *Pädagogische Blätter für Lehrerbildung und Lehrerbildungsanstalten,* E. F. Thienemann, 1877, pp. 1–28; W. Vorbrodt, *Basedow's Leben und Werke,* H. Schroedel, 1920, 2 vols.

Basedow was born in 1723 in Hamburg, of a brutal father and an insane mother. In view of his heredity and early environment, he should never have amounted to anything. As a child he attended school intermittently and most unwillingly, disliking it violently, hating the constant memorizing, and revolting against the harsh discipline. Much of his time was spent doing errands for his father, who was a wigmaker. The young boy ran through the streets making collections and deliveries and, incidentally, picking up the manners of any other rowdy street urchin. He hated the work, and was apparently one of the world's worst errand boys, for which his father beat him cruelly and viciously. One day in his early adolescence, young Basedow ran away from home and, after living for a while as a tramp, found refuge as a servant in a doctor's house. For the first time the boy found kindliness and sympathy, and he developed remarkably during this one year away from home. The doctor saw that his young servant was much too bright to remain in service or to enter a trade, and he eventually persuaded Basedow's father to educate the boy. In the doctor's house Basedow picked up a few bits of surface polish, but his manners, habits, and morals remained throughout his life those of a turbulent gamin from a lower middle-class family devoid of refinement or culture.

Upon his return home, Basedow re-entered the lower class of the Latin school, the work of which he still detested. The humanistic curriculum required a pupil to memorize interminable vocabularies, declensions, and conjugations, without in the least knowing what it was all about. Since Basedow was rebellious, independent, uninhibited, and impudent, he continually brought down upon himself the most extreme school discipline. Flogging did him little good, however, and he continued to stumble along at the bottom of the class, hating the work but determined to become educated. His three years in the upper division of the school went much better, largely because he came in contact with some inspiring teachers who, appreciating the boy's native ability, challenged his imagination with new ideas. Because of their recommendations he was able after graduation to attend the University of Leipzig for two years.

Basedow was already a young man of twenty-one when he went to Leipzig. He had begun his schooling late and had attended to only those portions of it that interested him. His preparation was therefore most uneven; indeed, his main assets for university life were an eager spirit and a lively intelligence. Instead of studying hard to compensate for his inadequate preparation, Basedow devoted his time to tutoring rich students, writing term papers for lazy ones, and spending the money thus earned in riotous living. He attended a few lectures, but he had no notion of self-discipline nor of setting aside regular hours for work. Already Basedow was showing the fundamental instability of his nature. He could never organize himself well enough to complete properly the undertakings suggested by his fertile mind. He was content throughout life to skitter over the surface of things, substituting alertness of mind for thoroughness.

Basedow was supposed to be preparing himself for the ministry and had enrolled as a student of philosophy and religion. Upon his own admission, however, he did not attend more than a few classes and profited mainly from independent reading done in his room. For some reason of his own, he became interested in two contrasting religious philosophies and read voraciously within the narrow limits of his interest. He did not take up with his professors the questions that occupied him, but stubbornly and unsystematically plowed ahead by himself. This performance was characteristic of him: he would not ask for or accept advice from others, and he thought himself perfectly competent to do anything alone. Like many another self-made man, he never found out that, while his achievements were greatly to his credit, he was really not well educated in a balanced and conventional manner. Moreover, his lack of general training prevented him from knowing, until too late, that ideas new and exciting to him were often common intellectual currency among educated people. As a consequence of this ignorance and of his general superficiality, he tended to write boring commonplaces that were new only to him. One of the values of a well-rounded education is to prevent one from regarding as revolutionary a theory that has already been discovered, rediscovered, and exploded three times.

Basedow continued his individualized studies, at Leipzig or at home, with little or no guidance, until he was twenty-six years old. At that time he accepted a position as tutor for a nobleman's son. The appointment gave him a chance to apply some of the pedagogical ideas he had already developed, among them his basic tenet: instruct by means of play. All day every day he was ostensibly playing with his charge, showing him this and that, talking with him, answering his questions, and amusing him, but at the end of three years the boy had made miraculous progress in arithmetic, elementary science, and Latin. Basedow was ingenious in devising games that would be instructive; thus, to teach counting he and the boy played with grains of wheat or green peas, and to teach fractions they divided apples in sundry ways, subsequently eating their fractions! From such elementary matters, Basedow led the boy into more advanced fields, never pushing him but always stimulating him to *want* to learn. The boy, who was ten years old when Basedow left him, is credited with an average adult grasp of religious knowledge, an understanding of world history and geography, an ability to do elementary arithmetic, an extended knowledge of scientific phenomena, and an ability to write and speak both German and Latin. Even assuming that the boy was extraordinarily bright, credit must be given to Basedow for his methods of teaching.

As a result of his success and of the support given him by his noble patron, Basedow obtained a position as professor of "philosophy and eloquence" at the University of Surö* in Denmark. Here he was met at first with great acclaim. His lectures were vivid and stimulating, his assignments had novelty, and his approach to his subject matter was original and interesting. He was hailed as a prophet, and his classes were soon overflowing with eager students. He was so popular that he had to give eight classes a day in order to accommodate his hearers. This situation did not, however, long endure. Other professors became jealous of him, and some quite rightly accused him of superficiality. His boasting and extravagant claims did nothing to help his personal relationships, and the conservative natives of Surö looked askance upon his intemperance. Finally, the theologians were up in arms because of his efforts to substitute a "natural religion" for the dogmas of the orthodox church. Although his students remained enthusiastic about him, Basedow was removed from his position after eight years by order of the government, which, however, offered him a post at the same salary in the Gymnasium at Altona.* This early persecution of Basedow seems to have been without adequate basis, and it earned for him the sympathy and support of many leaders in Germany.

Basedow's personal conduct at Altona remained as unconventional and unacceptable as ever, and his teaching continued in the same vein. The students at Altona were, however, a sophisticated and aristocratic lot, who were offended by Basedow's lack of refinement. In contrast to his previous position, he had only three class hours a week, and after a while he had none at all. Finding himself surrounded by critics, unpopular with the students, and prevented from doing his legitimate work of instruction, he began to publish his religious and philosophical views, in spite of advice from his friends to keep silent. Until that time the charges against him were not well substantiated, but when he put pen to paper he gave his enemies a weapon with which to attack him. Within four years he had produced numerous publications, most of which had better have been left unwritten. In the first place, he condemned himself of heterodoxy;* in the second, he showed that he had no genius whatever for philosophy or theology; in the third, he merely recapitulated in a banal way things that had already been said much better by others; and finally he revealed himself as a common quarreler—noisy, violent, impolite, and often vulgar, but not dangerous. Eventually, even Basedow's pugnacity wore out under the endless attacks of the theologians, and his efforts to cudgel his brain into producing philosophy became increasingly futile. The net result of his literary efforts was a banning of his works, a threat of fine for any printer who worked for him in the future, a general distrust on the part of the public, and a broken heart and a period of deep melancholy for himself.

At this point in his career Basedow read the one book that influenced his subsequent life profoundly, Rousseau's *Émile*. There Basedow found a coherent and artistic expression of views with which he was in sympathy. The relationship of Basedow to Rousseau has been a matter on which investigators differ. Some admirers have credited Basedow with having independently reached most of the same conclusions that Rousseau did, while his detractors have bluntly called him a mere imitator. The truth lies presumably somewhere between these two extremes.[12] Certainly Basedow had already stated in print many of the same ideas that a few years later appeared in *Émile,* although he expressed them incoherently, piecemeal, and without the slightest literary flavor. In particular, the two men shared the principles of back-to-nature, of education-through-play, and of learning-through-experience. Rousseau's ideas therefore fitted in with Basedow's own and soon commingled with them until it is hard to tell which point came from whom. In one respect, however, Basedow was obviously and deeply indebted to Rousseau. *Émile* stands high as literature and was widely read in Europe. Since education became at once very much the center of attention, Basedow profited greatly from the popular interest aroused by Rousseau. Moreover, Rousseau did what Basedow could never have done: he gave in vibrant prose a coherent presentation of the new education, thus ensuring the continuance of his ideas long after his death. Basedow undoubtedly rode into fame on the crest of Rousseau's popularity, but he was not simply an imitator.

In several important respects Basedow contradicted Rousseau completely. In the first place, he believed that schools could be reformed, while Rousseau thought them beyond any hope. *Émile* went to no school; instead, until he reached manhood he was accompanied by a guide, philosopher, and friend. This arrangement was, as Basedow saw, impossible in most families from a financial point of view and undersirable because it isolated a child from his age mates. Basedow wanted a socialized education, while Rousseau threw society to the wolves, along with the schools. In short, Basedow worked out his reforms within the existing social framework, while Rousseau attacked the framework itself.

In other, less fundamental ways Basedow's ideas were in opposition to those of Rousseau. The latter thought children capable only of self-love and wanted no effort made to modify nature; the former believed children had naturally some love for their fellow man and could be educated into having more. Rousseau called childhood the "sleep of reason," and he warned

[12] For an excellent and careful evaluation of the matter, see Hahn, *op. cit.*

adults never to ask children for an opinion or conclusion. Basedow's plans included definite efforts for the use of such reasoning powers as children have at different ages. Rousseau's notion of education in morality consisted in preventing temptation from arising, rather than in helping children to resist it; punishment, except such as was administered by natural consequences, Rousseau banned altogether. Basedow took a more conventional view and approved both punishment and rewards, condemning only the cruel and brutal forms of discipline then common in both school and home. Basedow was not content to leave morality entirely to nature and thought teachers should interest themselves in the proper development of morals. Finally, in the matter of instruction Rousseau and Basedow contradicted each other pointblank. The former wanted no teaching whatever during childhood, except what was provided by the child's own experiences; Émile's business was to grow strong and healthy, and it made no difference if he did not know his right hand from his left. Basedow believed firmly in direct instruction, but he wanted it given through play and without interference with a child's freedom or growth.

It would perhaps be a fair summary of the relationship between the two men to say that both started with the same premises about human beings, that both were flaming revolutionaries against the society of their day, and that both had the same educational objectives, but that they differed in many matters of procedure, in general principles, and in numerous details. Of the two, Basedow had the more immediate effect upon schools because he carried out his reform through existing institutions, but Rousseau had the wider and more permanent influence. As one authority has said: "Basedow succeeded in effecting a complete change in the whole system of education and instruction in Germany—something Rousseau was able to do neither in his native land (Switzerland) nor in France." [13]

Inspired by his new interest in education, Basedow published a monograph, setting forth his plans for educational reform. At this time he was a man of forty-five. His plan—when shorn of its details, digressions, boasts, and promises for the future—contained two main proposals. First, there should be a school that should serve both as a laboratory for the new methods and as a training center for teachers; second, there should be an encyclopedic book on methods of teaching and curricular content, through use of which a teacher could be instructed and guided. By these two means, the grand revolution foreshadowed by *Émile* could be brought into the realm of actuality.

Basedow wanted to put his plan into action by writing his *Elementary*

[13] F. C. Schlosser, *Education in the Eighteenth Century and the Nineteenth to the Overthrow of the French Empire* (translated by D. Davison), Chapman and Hall, 1843–1852, (8 vols.), II, 24.

Book, rather than by founding a school, since he believed that teachers could be quite easily trained, once the proper material on method and content was available. He therefore proposed that the public should subscribe to such a book, and that he should devote as many years as necessary to the writing of it. Such was the enthusiasm already aroused by Rousseau that people were in just the right mood to support Basedow's proposal. The number of subscriptions that poured in was almost unbelievable; in fact, Basedow finally had to set a date after which he would accept no more of them. He worked himself into a frenzy of excitement, forgetting to eat or drink, sleeping only in short snatches when exhaustion overcame him, and renouncing all social intercourse. For some months Basedow worked alone, but eventually he had to admit that even he was not competent to cover all possible fields of human knowledge; he therefore arranged for a colleague named Wolke to write certain sections of the book, to help him with the correction of manuscripts, and subsequently to teach in the school he hoped to found.

The first part of the monumental work appeared in 1770, the second two years later.[14] The first treats of methodology and was intended as much for parents as for teachers. The second and much longer part covered supposedly all the material a teacher would need in all subjects. In selecting what should go into his book, Basedow was guided primarily by what was useful for the needs of everyday life. He gave an important place to both physical exercise and vocational training; restricted languages and sciences to their purely practical aspects—eliminating grammar almost entirely and reducing study of the classics to a considerable degree; presented history as an illustration of moral precepts; and included the arts—drawing, painting, music, and dancing—as having a practical utility for the leisure and personal development of the average citizen. This principle for selecting the materials of instruction has a distinctly modern ring and was diametrically opposed to the humanistic and theological education then in vogue.

Basedow's work was favorably accepted by most people, although, as one might expect, some of the established schoolmasters unleashed upon him their bitterest scorn and most virulent criticism, to which Basedow replied in his worst street-gamin manner. Among the many prominent men impressed by Basedow's book was the prince of Anhalt-Dessau,* who in 1771 invited Basedow to found in Dessau the school that was to give reality to the reform and to act as a training center for future teachers. Basedow therefore went to Dessau, but during his first year there he postponed founding the school because his *Elementary Book* was not yet done. He had already exhausted himself by his immoderate methods of working and had fallen into a mood of melancholy,

[14] *Das Elementarwerk,* published at Dessau.

in which he found application to his *chef-d'oeuvre** quite impossibile, and for nearly a year he found one excuse after another for putting off its completion. In the meantime the enthusiasm of the prince waned, and he did not continue his original gift of funds for the proposed school. After trying in vain to find another patron, Basedow finally decided in 1774 to launch his school himself, depending upon public subscriptions for aid. Almost at once he recovered from his melancholy and entered a manic phase of enthusiasm, again throwing himself recklessly into his work, in spite of his fifty-one years, his already broken health, his seriously impaired eyesight, and his lack of money. He promptly and confidently appealed to the public for funds, publishing combined announcements and advertisements that for incoherency, redundancy, fantastic promises, and solicitations could be equaled only by the appeal of a noisy barker at a sideshow. Money did not, however, roll in as he had expected it would on the basis of his previous experience with subscriptions. He had overlooked an important quirk in human psychology: that people will, in the name of charity, pay too much in order to get some actual object they want, but that they will not contribute as readily to an institution at a distance when they get nothing but God's blessing in return. Basedow was therefore unable at any time to obtain adequate support for his school, a detailed description of which will appear presently.

For two years Basedow struggled on, assisted by excellent teachers, among them Wolke. The number of pupils was always small. Fifteen pupils appeared for the opening of the school, and the enrollment never exceeded sixty pupils at a time. Two years after it opened, the school staged a public examination, to which all the outstanding men in Europe were invited. Many of them came and were greatly impressed by what they saw and heard.[15] The next term of school saw an increase in enrollment and a return of the prince's support. At this moment of apparent success Basedow retired from his headship of the school, partly because he had no ability as an executive, partly because his importunities and quarrels had stirred up too much opposition to himself, and partly because—having got the school started—he had once more run out of energy and enthusiasm. For a year he occupied himself with various publications, with a continuation of an old quarrel, and with starting the first pedagogical journal in Germany. The school prospered, but disagreements among members of the staff soon began to undermine it. After a year, the new director suddenly left, and Basedow returned as head of the institution, but he was in another of his depressed moods and did not apply himself to his work. His chief assistant, the faithful and patient Wolke, taught classes, supervised the staff, handled correspondence, and kept on good terms with the other

[15] See pp. 429–432.

teachers. Gradually, however, matters went from bad to worse. Basedow began to drink more and more heavily, to become jealous of Wolke's deserved popularity, and to be angry because Wolke took to himself a little credit for the success of Basedow's work. The feeling between the two men mounted, Basedow venting his abnormal emotionalism daily upon his subordinate until finally Wolke stopped being patient and sued Basedow for defamation of character. The affair was hushed up and a reconciliation brought about, but the work of the school had been badly disrupted.

Basedow would neither administer the school properly himself nor get out of the way and let someone else do it. The result was profound disorganization and anarchy on the part of the staff. Teachers neglected their work, amused the children instead of teaching them, and dismissed classes for no reason. Each teacher did what he liked, when he liked. The pettiness, laziness, neglect, suspicion, and mistrust shown by Basedow himself spread to the staff, and in a year or two the school was well on its way to decadence. The pupils became restless, unamenable to discipline, disrespectful, and lazy. They not only knew in a general way that Basedow drank to excess, but many of them had seen him stumbling up to his room. Some of the younger teachers tried hard to save the school, but with Basedow in his unhappy, degenerate state, the end was inevitable. As one teacher said, Basedow neglected nothing to ruin an institution that would have prospered without him. Ten years after the foundation of the school, Wolke, its last real prop, left to establish a similar school in St. Petersburg.* The school at Dessau was then reorganized along rather conventional lines under a new and energetic headmaster and staggered along for a few more years, but its fame was already over and in 1793, the same year as the climax of the French Revolution, it closed its doors. It was therefore in existence only nineteen years, but in this short time it influenced education in Germany and elsewhere.

In the meantime, Basedow busied himself with devising a new way of teaching reading to small children. He became so enthusiastic that at the age of sixty-two he began to teach as a volunteer in an obscure school in Magdeburg. The progress of his pupils was phenomenal, and he spent several months each year for the rest of his life in Magdeburg teaching first-graders!

Basedow did not live long, probably because of his immoderate habits. In 1790 he was taken ill with a cerebral hemorrhage and died in a few hours, three years before the school he had founded also passed out of existence.

2. *Basedow's Personality* Basedow was a singular individual. He had clearly inherited both the insanity of his mother and the bad temper of his father. His alternation of moods from hectic excitement to blank despair sug-

gests strongly that he suffered from manic-depressive insanity. When he was excited, he acted as if he were being driven by the Furies; he talked without stopping, not only for hours but for days and nights on end, until he exhausted himself. Subsequently, he was plunged into gloom and did nothing for a period, while his burned-out vitality gradually returned. At all times he was highly irritable and often flared up in pathological rage over nothing. His vanity, conceit, and egotism were also abnormal, as was his alcoholism. The excessive drinking was presumably both a symptom of an unbalanced emotional state and a cause of its continuance. His was a violent and unruly nature that did everything too intensely: he worked to excess, smoked to excess, drank to excess, and bragged to excess. There was nothing wrong with Basedow's mind, except as his judgment was warped at times by his emotional storms, but he never had a normal personality, and his deviations became worse and worse as he grew older.

Fig. 64. Johann Bernard Basedow. After an engraving by D. Chodowiecki.

The picture of Basedow in Figure 64 reflects the man's general bumptiousness and conceit, but does not suggest his more amiable qualities or his fundamental abilities. It is a side light upon his character that, although he advertised himself as an apostle of naturalism, he wore a curly wig when he had his picture drawn.

Basedow has been called everything from a great genius to a complete mountebank. His personality and his glaring faults irritated his contemporaries, while at the same time his ability to talk easily and brilliantly often fascinated them. In his earlier days he was a persuasive salesman of educational reform, but his achievements did not live up to his advance publicity. In general, teachers tend by personality and training to be an introverted, conservative, and well-mannered lot; one does not often find in their ranks a flamboyant, uninhibited person, given to inexcusable language, brawling, gambling, and drinking. Eccentricities many a pedagogue displays, but they are almost never of the extroverted, violent, explosive type shown by Basedow.

One of the best descriptions of this odd personality was written by Goethe,* who is among the world's most famous and brilliant men. Goethe spent some time in the company of Basedow and Lavater,* a gentle, educated person who, in spite of having done many sensible things, has come down in history as the chief defender of phrenology* and other pseudo-psychological ideas. Goethe found Basedow such a fascinating study in contradictions that he simply could not tear himself away. An excerpt from Goethe's account describes both Basedow's personality and his methods of work:

One could not see a greater contrast than that between these two men—Basedow and Lavater. Even a glance at Basedow indicated an antithesis. Whereas Lavater's features were open to the observers, Basedow's were withdrawn and contracted. Lavater's eyes were clear and mild under wide eyelids but Basedow's were small, black, sharp, deeply set in his head, glancing out from under shaggy eyebrows; in contrast Lavater's frontal bones appeared framed by the softest brown eyebrows. Basedow's hoarse, rough voice, his quick and sharp expressions, a certain mocking laugh, a quick change of topic in his conversation, and whatever else might describe him—in fact, everything was diametrically opposed to the characteristics and behavior to which Lavater had accustomed us. However, Basedow was much sought after in Frankfort and admired for his great intellectual gifts; but he was not the man either to edify the spirit or to guide it.

Much more curious and harder to understand than his doctrine was Basedow's behavior. On this journey he had the intention through his personality to win the public for his philanthropic undertaking and, indeed, to open not only their hearts but also their purses. He knew how to talk grandly and convincingly about his project and everyone gladly admitted what he asserted. But in the most incomprehensible manner he wounded the feelings of people from whom he wanted to obtain a donation; in fact he insulted them needlessly through the fact that he could not hold back his opinions and whims about religious matters. Here also Basedow appeared the direct opposite of Lavater. Whereas Lavater accepted as literally true the Bible and all its contents, yes word for word, and valid and applicable for the present day, Basedow felt a most uneasy itch to revise and to remodel according to his own crotchets* both the doctrines of faith and the external clerical acts. . . . In a harsh and irresponsible manner he declared himself before everyone as the most pronounced enemy of the trinity and could never get through arguing against this commonly accepted mystery. Incidentally I had to suffer a good deal from this form of amusement in private conversation. . . . and because Basedow was better read and better adapted to the swordplay of disputation than I as an empiricist* knew how to be, I had to exert myself the more, as we discussed more important points.

I could not forgo such a charming opportunity if not to enlighten myself at least to exercise myself. I induced father and friends to take over my most important business affairs and set out again from Frankfort in the company of Basedow. But what a difference I felt when I considered the graciousness that emanated from Lavater. Cleanly as he was, he created about himself only a cleanly environment. One became virginal at his side so as not to distress him with anything repulsive. Basedow, on the other hand, much too shut in on himself, could not pay attention to his own appearance. The very fact that he smoked bad tobacco uninterruptedly was extremely hard to bear, and all the more so because, after smoking out a pipeful, he immediately struck a dirty piece of tinder that caught fire quickly but gave out noxious fumes; and each time he fouled the air unbearably with the first puff. I called this preparation the *Stinktinder Basedow* and wanted to introduce it under this title into natural history. He had a great joke over this idea and he expounded to me the repulsive preparation circumstantially until I was sick to my stomach, and maliciously gloated over my horror. For this was one of the most deeply rooted bad characteristics of this highly gifted man that he loved to tease and goad mischievously those who were least prejudiced against him. He could never let anyone rest; with grinning mockery and in a raucous voice he irritated you or by asking a surprising question he embarrassed you and laughed scornfully when he had achieved his goal, although he was quite content if you, suddenly regaining your composure, gave him as good as he sent.

I always spent part of the night with Basedow. He never went to bed, but dictated without stopping. Sometimes he threw himself onto his bed and dozed, while his secretary—pen in hand—remained sitting very quietly and was ready immediately to go on writing when the half-awakened Basedow again gave free rein to his thoughts. All this happened in a tightly sealed room that was full of tobacco smoke and fumes from the tinder. As often as I tore myself away from dancing I rushed upstairs to Basedow who was disposed to talk over and dispute every problem; and when, after the passage of some time, I again hurried back to the dance, even before the door closed behind me, he began to dictate and took up the thread of his treatment as if nothing else had been going on. . . .

In view of my overly free convictions and my wholly objectless and planless life and actions I could not hide from myself the fact that Lavater and Basedow used spiritual, indeed ministerial, means for reaching earthly goals. Lavater went at his work softly and cleverly; Basedow, violently, offensively, and even clumsily; however, both were so convinced of the excellence of their hobbies and undertakings that one had to regard them as honest men, to love them, and to respect them.[16]

From the above account, it is evident that Basedow was no poseur, in spite of his many eccentricities; otherwise, Goethe would never have been so attracted to him.

Basedow's school hardly outlived him, and his writings are too prolix, dull, and unorganized for most people to read. His influence was primarily upon other German educators who followed closely upon his heels, but for posterity his chief value lies in his adaptation of Rousseauism to the practical school situation. Rousseau was a revolutionary philosopher and a writer of dynamic prose, not a schoolteacher. He propounded the "natural way" of

[16] Translated from Goethe's *Gesammtliche Werke,* J. G. Cotta, 1857, XXII, 207–213. See also A. Bach, *Goethe's Rheinreise mit Lavater und Basedow, im Sommer 1774,* Seldwyla, 1923, 238 pp.

learning and living and in so doing sowed a seed that is still bearing fruit today. Émile was a single child taught by a tutor; Basedow, with all his faults, was able to take the main ideas of *Émile* and show how education for a group of children could be based upon the same principles. Basedow was perhaps both mad and degenerate—although perhaps no more mad or degenerate than Rousseau—but through his work, brief though it was, teachers with new ideas were sprinkled all over Germany, making ready the ground in which the next of the great teachers, Pestalozzi, was to sow a second and more permanent adaptation of Rousseauism.

B. THE PHILANTHROPINUM: A SCHOOL MODELED ON ROUSSEAU

The school founded by Basedow was extraordinary for its time and would rank in some ways as a progressive school even today. Basedow intended his school to be an embodiment of educational reform and a pattern for all of Germany to copy.

The objectives of the education to be given in the school are stated by Basedow in both generalized and concrete fashion.

> Nature, school, life: if there is friendship among these three, a man becomes what he should become but cannot be immediately: gay in childhood, cheerful and eager to learn during his youth, contented and useful as an adult.
>
> The objective of education must be to educate a European whose life will be as blameless, as generally useful, and as contented as can be brought about through education.[17]

In another place Basedow described the training he gave the children as humanitarian, political, and undenominationally Christian. It will be seen that he had in view both the development of children to their highest capacities and also their adaptation to the society in which they lived; in the second point he differed markedly from Rousseau. The school was called the Philanthropinum.

1. Composition of the School At the time of its opening, the school had a staff of four teachers, of whom the permanent members were Basedow and Wolke. There were two types of pupil in the institution: the *Famulanten* and the *Pensionisten*. The former were children from lower-class families who expected to enter the service of some noble family as tutors. They received a good general education and in addition they had experience in their adult occupation, since each *Famulant* was assigned as a combined personal servant

[17] Göring, *op. cit.*, p. xlvi.

and assistant to one or two *Pensionisten.* Their fees were usually paid either by some charitable person or by the noble family whose service they expected to enter. The *Pensionisten* were children of the upper classes. They received the same education as the *Famulanten.* The distinction between the two classes was thus entirely social and was based partly upon the current stratification of society, partly upon the ability to pay one's own fees, and partly upon future vocational expectations. To the American mind such an arrangement in a boarding school would seem undesirable, but in eighteenth-century Germany there was nothing to be gained by educating a child out of his social class.

In its earlier years, at least, a number of young men who wished to become teachers were working at the school and attending Basedow's seminar in pedagogy. These budding teachers were not required to have a university degree. In fact, Basedow preferred them without university training, before they had had a chance to enter what he called the "thorny path of hair-splitting inquiries." In any case, Basedow was always of the opinion that his own two books could give all the training a teacher needed. These young men were to observe the work of the school and to do more or less practice teaching, usually under Wolke's supervision. Little provision was made for their maintenance, but Basedow promised to give them the highest recommendations and to make every effort to find positions for them. This work with prospective teachers carried out one of Basedow's main purposes in founding the school, since he hoped to make it a center for teacher training and for educational experimentation.

> An examination helps to find good teachers only if they are there, but does not educate a number of them. For this purpose seminaries are necessary. There must therefore be in each country a teacher training school in which are pupils with whom to work and in which young men who desire to enter schoolteaching are under the supervision of experienced professors of education and complete their training years. Toward the end of their training the institution can give a testimonial that gives the choosers more information than an examination. . . .[18]

2. *The Schedule of Work* The pupils were classified into four grades for each of which there was a schedule of classes. These schedules are decidedly more modern than those produced by either Francke or De la Salle. Especially noticeable is the absence of religious teaching. A sample for the highest class is shown on page 418.

The next highest class had a similar schedule, except for the hours from 2 to 3 and from 6 to 7. During the former some of them had drawing, some

[18] *Ibid.*, p. 207

TABLE 11: SCHEDULE FOR BASEDOW'S FOURTH CLASS[a]

Hour	Mon.	Tues.	Wed.	Thurs.	Fri.	Sat.
8–9	German	German	German	Morals	Morals	Morals
9–10	Exercise: dancing or riding					
10–12	Either history or practical philosophy taught in Latin					
12–1	Lunch					
1–2	Handwork: threshing, planing, wood turning					
2–3	Geography	Geography	Physiology	Mathematics	Mathematics	Mathematics
3–5	World history taught in French					Current events
5–6	Mathematics	Mathematics	Mathematics	Physics and Nature Study		
6–7	Twice a week, astronomy; four times, Greek					

[a] This and the next schedule come from Goring, *op. cit.*, pp. lxxxii, lxxxiv.

had arithmetic, and some joined the work of the highest class. From 6 to 7 the pupils in this group studied English—reading, incidentally, the *Vicar of Wakefield*.* The third class from the top had a somewhat different and more informal schedule. The conversation hours centered about the material in specified books, but the talks during the morning and evening strolls might be about anything. The schedule appears below:

TABLE 12: SCHEDULE FOR BASEDOW'S THIRD CLASS

Hour	Activity
8–9	German: both reading and writing
9–10	Sometimes handwriting; sometimes walks, during which there was indirect instruction about what was seen
10–11	Latin conversation
11–12	French conversation
12–1	Lunch
1–2	Music or a free hour
2–3	Drawing
3–4	Dancing
4–5	French conversation
5–6	Latin conversation
6–7	Free hour, for indirect instruction, like 9–10 above

The lowest class had the same general schedule as that just shown, presumably with easier material, except that reading in German was substituted for the second hour of Latin conversation and the last hour was sometimes used for writing letters home.

Several points about these schedules are of particular interest. The first concerns the number of hours devoted to schoolwork of some kind. Work began at 8 A.M. and lasted, with one hour out for lunch, until 7 P.M. A second point is the combination of subjects. Thus history is taught in French or Latin. In languages the emphasis is upon conversation, without grammar until the last year. Two hours during the day were used for nonacademic subjects: one for dancing or riding and one for handwork. Moreover, the Philanthropinum was to maintain a camp for two months in the summer, the children living in tents and incidentally learning a good deal about nature study, geography, farming, hunting, and fishing. Although the schedule is somewhat overweighted with languages, the selection and treatment both show innovations, and the emphasis is much less than it was in the humanistic curriculum. In Basedow's school the ancient languages were no longer dominant, and the modern languages made their appearance as definite school subjects. This use of the vernacular stamps Basedow as a sense realist. Greek was given only in the highest class and did not occupy an important position there; Latin was kept, not as a key to the literature of antiquity but as a language for common speech among all educated men. Both French and German were taught. It will be recalled that the lowest classes in Francke's schools also learned German, but the teaching of French was new with Basedow and was due presumably to the great esteem in which the French writers, the Encyclopedists* and rationalists,* were held throughout Europe. The sciences also gained in number and importance. Finally, the use of schools to indoctrinate children with the dogmas of a given sect was condemned and abandoned; instead there appears a small amount of instruction in a "natural religion" and morals.

The hours of instruction were long, though diversified, but the entire school day was even longer. Basedow considered seven hours a night enough sleep and therefore aroused the pupils at 6 A.M. during the winter or 5 A.M. in the summer. From then until 11 or 10 P.M., according to the season, the time was theoretically divided as follows:

6 hours for eating, dressing, and playing.
1 hour for putting rooms and clothes in order, writing letters, or reading.
5 hours for study.
3 hours for exercise.
2 hours for handwork.

Actually, the schedules do not quite live up to these specifications since there were seven hours of study. The six hours between 6 and 8 A.M. and 7 and 11 P.M. are all that remain unscheduled, and these are not sufficient for the other activities.

In Basedow's *Elementarwerk* the author included a picture of his concept as to what a proper schoolroom should look like. In this picture, reproduced in Figure 65, neither the teacher nor the pupils seem to be dressed in a "natural" fashion, but the walls of the schoolroom surely reflect the new movement in education. There are drawings and charts of animals, of the human body, and of vegetation. These charts show also that Basedow belongs among the sense realists, since he used such materials for demonstration. Although one does not see any windows, the view of the schoolroom suggests light and air.

3. The Selection of Materials for Instruction The subject matter of the curriculum was selected on the basis of its presumed usefulness in the adult life of the pupils. An educated man needed to speak, read, and write both French and Latin, and he obviously needed his mother tongue. Since the dis-

FIG. 65. A "Naturalistic" School. From J. B. Basedow, *Elementarwerk.*

coveries of the fifteenth and sixteenth centuries, geography had become a necessary school subject. History, in Basedow's view, was useful mainly as a source of illustrations of human conduct, moral or otherwise, but in spite of this bias the pupils did presumably learn something of historical movements. The scientific renaissance of the sixteenth and seventeenth centuries had made school instruction in science necessary for an educated man, if he were to understand what was going on around him. In the matter of selecting the subjects that were useful in his day, one can have no quarrel with Basedow.

The selection of material within each subject and the determination of teaching emphasis show both the practical usefulness and the relative modernity of Basedow's ideas. His pupils learned to speak German up until the age of eight; then the emphasis shifted, first to the speaking of French and then to the speaking of Latin. This load seems heavy to the unilingual American, but one should remember that children from good families heard both French and German at home and were more or less bilingual before they entered school. In the highest class of the school, all three languages were to be spoken. Latin grammar was postponed until after the fifteenth year. The reasons for this postponement are given in Basedow's own words:

> If one waits for the right time and then chooses a sensible method, one finds less difficulty in grammatical instruction than he had thought. Postpone it until that age at which the children are able to conceive of the general characteristics and differences of things, of mental operations, and of spiritual conditions in an abstract way outside a particular context. So long as this ability is lacking, both etymology and syntax are a collection of tones without meaning or use. . . . If the pupils, through conversation and reading of their mother tongue, are so competent that they make few errors in speech, a very short grammar should explain matters to them and should be recommended for repeated review. Thereafter one should correct their errors in speech and writing for a while through citation of the appropriate rules. By following this method one can in a half-year bring the pupils to such a degree of grammatical correctness as is necessary for a writer, if one use two hours daily for the purpose. The grammar must, however, contain exclusively those rules through which the use of a great assortment of phrases is determined, but not those rules that apply only to a few cases or which have almost as many exceptions as analogous examples. In this plan, whatever cannot be brought under a rule must be indicated at the end of the grammar in alphabetical order under the individual words. . . . The grammar of the mother tongue must be the first for each person; in dead or foreign languages, one then needs no other rules than those through which one can learn the variations of the new language from that already learned, for one should set aside the agreements as known.[19]

Study of Latin was obviously not intended as a gateway to the knowledge and literature of antiquity, because little attempt was made to read the classical authors. As Basedow wrote: "Learning sufficient wisdom and truth from the old authors themselves is too hard for people and costs an excessive amount of time. They wrote, not for our century but for their own."

Elementary science and mathematics seem to have been taught by means of direct observation, experiments, and illustrative materials. The school had a collection of models and natural objects—such as rocks, birds, metals, bones,

[19] *Ibid.*, condensed from pp. 119–120

and so on. In the sciences the teaching was accompanied by experiments and demonstrations. Whenever possible the teachers took the pupils to the phenomena, conversing with them at length about what they saw. One of the really remarkable things about the science curriculum was the objective discussion of sexual matters. As Basedow wrote: "We tell the children the truth about the procreation of animals and of men. We don't linger over the sexual act itself, but concentrate upon the results thereof, the burdensome pregnancy of the mother." Some of the charts and models dealt with this topic.

On the other hand, the social sciences were probably not well taught, except local geography learned through observation. History was supposed to give "instructive examples of virtues, vices, and the noteworthy fate of mankind," and to develop the ability to read history or to listen intelligently to lectures on historical topics. The number of books selected for the pupils was, however, quite inadequate for even the announced objectives.

Finally, there was the subject of religion. The world had grown very weary indeed of religious quarrels, and many people were already predisposed to substitute morals for dogma. The movement away from bigotry and sectarianism found an expression in Rousseau's "natural religion"; that is, such feelings of awe and reverence as arise in a child through his natural experiences and without adult instruction. Basedow's point of view was similar, insofar as children were concerned. He did not, however, wish to dispense altogether with instruction in morals, as Rousseau recommended, but rather to devise a course of study that would teach the fundamental moral and religious truths common to all faiths and would be without offense to members of the Reformed, Lutheran, Roman Catholic, Greek or Russian Catholic, and Jewish churches. His approach was by means of elements in the child's environment with which he was already familiar. The excerpts quoted below sound commonplace and prosy today, but at the end of the eighteenth century they represented a new approach to religion.

For little children:

My child, if no corn grows, we have no bread; if no grass grows, we have no meat and no milk, . . . if no plants grew any more from the earth, all men and all animals would die of hunger, we would have no flax for linen, no wool, no cotton, silk, or leather for other pieces of clothing. . . .

Listen, my child, you cannot yourself make bread from grain, nor meat from animals, nor cloths from wool and flax. But your father who loves you sees to it that these things are brought and made for you. . . .

All men have an unseen father whom they call God or Jehovah. He is, to be sure, invisible and untouchable . . . . but you know that he is there by what he does. He brings it about that the sun shines or does not shine at the right time, that it rains or does not rain at the right time, that it becomes cold or warm at the right time, so that at the right time fodder grows for cattle and food for humans, of which they save something until again the new crop grows—as it certainly will grow.[20]

For older children:

A father who truly loves his children forbids what will harm them even if they do not understand it; he commands what is useful for them, even if they do not understand it. God, our unseeable father, also gives laws to men as his children. . . .

I know many things that God has forbidden me and commanded me and I am very glad of such laws, for I know it is good for me to obey them. Therefore, when I have something to do or want to leave something undone I say often to myself: What has God ordered or forbidden about this matter? And then I direct myself according to his command and after my knowledge of what he wishes, that is, after my conscience. I am, however, a weak man who must become better. Sometimes I do not think at the right time of this or that commandment of God's and I incautiously break it. That is known as a sin. If I later become aware of my transgression, I am sorry and fearful, and would gladly undo what is done, but I must bear the evil that my disobedience has produced. But God punishes the errors of men with a wise moderation and is gentle, if they will only seek daily to better themselves.[21]

For adolescents:

Because men are spoiled they call many circumstances evil that are only less good than the situation they wish or which is the most common among men of their kind. He who loses an eye or a foot has merely one member less than other men and has retained many valued limbs. Is his condition bad or only less good? Precisely this question . . . one can ask of all those who complain about an evil condition when their parents, brothers, or friends have died and when they still have enough people left of whom they can make friends to a certain extent; when a fire destroys their house and when another house that is somewhat less comfortable becomes theirs; or when they lose two children out of the three they love; or when through accident they lose a part of their fortune but still retain a part, besides the hope of daily gain. . . .

. . . Nature mixes good with evil, evil with good, but not in equal measure; far more of the good, far less of the evil; and even the evil comes from causes that are good and produce much that is good.[22]

The above material has been quoted at some length to show the change in the teaching of religion. As will be remembered, the children in Francke's schools spent half their school time memorizing the church catechism and selections from the Bible. In Basedow's school the religious teaching was reduced to three hours a week and was of a totally different type: no cate-

[20] *Ibid.,* condensed from pp. 379–380.

[21] *Ibid.,* pp. 381–382.

[22] *Ibid.,* selected paragraphs from pp. 385–391.

chism, no dogma, no indoctrination. Indeed, the approach was about what it is today among those who teach religion at all, with the exception of definitely church schools. Although Basedow went on to discuss such matters as the immortality of the soul, consequences of virtue and vice, and the nature of God, prayer, and providence, he continued to use simple examples from everyday life and simple, nontheological reasoning. The latter part of the course dealt exclusively with morals. Basedow began his discussion with the presentation of twenty-seven "commandments" about behavior, such as: "You should not slander nor speak slightingly of anyone, and you should not make known their faults and sins unless it is your special duty to do so." One may feel that all such instruction is rather useless, but at least Basedow's materials and methods of instruction were in advance of those previously used.

4. Methods of Instruction Perhaps the most outstanding features of the Philanthropinum were the methods. It was a basic principle that all education should be by means of pleasant and entertaining play. No child was to be forced in any way. Because play was the child's natural behavior, Basedow and Wolke devised games with words through which language could be learned. Some of these games taught merely the names of objects or of their parts; another required a pupil either to classify an object or to give an example of an indicated classification. That is, one child said "chair" and the correct solution was "furniture"; or else the child gave "furniture" as a class of objects and the second responded with "chair" as an example. Further games consisted in making as many words as possible out of a selected series of letters, naming all the objects of a given classification in a room, or finding an adequate class name for a series of objects. Another type of game taught individual sounds by imitation, and later syllables and words. Alphabet blocks were also used, the pupil sometimes selecting letters to form words that were dictated to him and sometimes copying words from a model. Memory games consisted in having the children observe some phenomenon and report to the teacher what they had seen. A guessing game and a hidden-answer game, which will shortly be described, were also frequently used.[23]

Still other games were intended to develop motor control. One of these was a variation of the still familiar "going to Jerusalem." When the game started, one child with a sack on his shoulders stood in front of a row of chairs, the number of which just equaled the number of other children. The participants had to keep changing chairs. The sack-carrier tried to throw his sack onto a momentarily empty chair. If he succeeded, the players scrambled for seats, and whoever was left became the sack-carrier. If, however, the child threw the sack and missed the chair, he remained "it" and in addition got a

[23] See p. 430.

second sack. Then, in order to get rid of his burden, he had to land both sacks on a chair at once.

Basedow observed that children like certain definite features in their games. They want a game to be noisy and to require great activity. The winner should earn some advantage, usually only temporary and incidental, over the losers. Games should require little or no supervision after they are first presented, since they should be so well within the children's capacity and so interesting that no supervision is needed. Preferably they should imitate some activity with which the children are already familiar. Basedow tried to introduce these elements of play into schoolwork. He made education pleasant and amusing; he presented work in game form; he let the children move about freely, except during the handwriting and reading periods.

Basedow banned all memory work during childhood except by means of games, and wanted teachers never to require memorizing at any stage—only to encourage memory work on the part of pupils who voluntarily learned by heart such things as were appropriate to their stage of development. He expressed himself as follows:

> Never pester your children with the command to busy themselves with memorizing. For if one is once willing to use the right methods in languages or history, then no child will need more practice in them than he gives himself with perfect willingness. . . . Words are easily memorized if the mind at the time thinks of their meaning, or if the heart feels them. Therefore all words that you require your children to memorize must be understood beforehand by them and where possible their content should be made pleasant. But practice in the memory for things is far more important; one can call this an exercise in proper attentiveness and in recollection of one's thoughts. At first accustom your children to be able to note so exactly everything they see and hear in certain places or under certain circumstances and can observe anew as they wish, that no circumstance of any importance is omitted and the order of things or of events is correctly kept. . . . If they are exercised somewhat in this attentiveness and in the art of keeping the order of presentation for a while in their memory, then try how much of a verbal or written report they can observe for a certain purpose and retain, at least as regards things. Let them recount after some time what has been told and again what has been described. If a lecture consists of main theses and their explanations, proofs and reasons, teach them to note the essentials while listening and reading and to retain for a short or long time. This is the memorizing of things, from the very name of which it follows that everything must be comprehensible to the children.[24]

The particular procedure against which Basedow was protesting was the memorizing of paradigms,* word forms, and vocabularies—that is, series of items

[24] Göring, *op. cit.*, condensed from pp. 98–99.

that make no coherent whole. Such memorizing had formed the backbone of the Latin curriculum.

Instead of requiring children to sit quietly and learn material that was unintelligible to them, the teachers of the Philanthropinum constantly took their pupils for walks, during which they examined some object with care, visited some place, or discussed some topic. Spontaneous conversation was so guided to yield educational results. Basedow had the following suggestions about the proper use of natural human loquacity:

> 1. If a natural phenomenon appears, or if one is mentioned, consider if you can tell the children something useful about it. . . .
>
> 2. Should words or idioms appear to which your children do not yet attach such meanings as are so right, so exact, or so vivid as you could wish, improve their knowledge of both words and things through many examples of things that bear the same common name or of which these same phrases can be used.
>
> 3. An adult can tell the children what he has done, what he plans, what his purpose is, what aims he seeks, what obstacles he fears, what contrary measures he has in mind, and how he would conduct himself, as much when his intent is unsuccessful as when it is successful. In the evening he can tell the children the story of the day; at the end of the month or year, he can go look back briefly over everything; he can mix fictional with true stories, provided they are instructive. . . . All are opportunities for incidental conversation and exercises in understanding that, if one knows how to select them properly, can become harmless and instructive.[25]

Basedow believed also in teaching by object lessons, but he warned his teachers to be very certain that they did not merely substitute words for things:

> I insist so often upon knowledge of things and one begins more and more to grasp its necessity, but what one presents under this guise must be actual knowledge of things. If a child names all parts of a watch and all the instruments of a watchmaker and images their outlines without having a concept of the strength and effects of the parts that are in this mechanism, then the child has no knowledge of a watch but only perhaps of a cogwheel. He has approached the knowledge of a watch, but he does not yet actually have it. If he knows the parts and tools only by name but not according to their form amd efficacy, he has in this respect no knowledge of things at all. If schools or teachers have the reputation of leading youth to an understanding of things, and if they still do not occupy themselves with the familiarization and promotion of useful insights, then all is idle boasting. The instruction about things must really give new ideas to the understanding, and not merely fill up the memory with words. But schools and teachers can be just as guilty of a very harmful pedantry if they substitute word knowledge for object knowledge as when they burden youth with the knowledge of things, so

[25] *Ibid.*, condensed from pp. 97–98.

many and such things that they are either of no use to youth or in the case of necessities can be learned later and better through inquiry and experience or through books. A small measure of useful and complete knowledge is better than a potpourri of numerous informational bits that appear to have been thrown together by chance and to no item of which it has been possible to devote the necessary attention for lack of time.[26]

This warning is still pertinent. Many a modern teacher turns an inherently educational project into mere busywork by just such means.

It should be noted that the work of the Philantropinum was highly socialized. The children and their teachers worked and played together from morning till night. Every activity was necessarily a joint undertaking. In most instances, learning was a part of doing something. Moreover, the children were definitely encouraged to help each other. Basedow had evidently noticed that children were remarkably good at teaching each other.

"Helpers" are older children who take pleasure sometimes in playing with the youngest children. They have been according to their age most carefully educated and reared, and they have the gift, knowledge, and disposition to make themselves much loved by the youngest children. They all play, mainly for the sake of the younger pupils, instructive games desired by their friends; they make movements and gestures, they undertake actions, they exchange questions and answers, they receive apparent praise and reproach, they tell apparently new things, they pretend error or doubt or let themselves be instructed, they make apparently unsuccessful experiments which give the younger children an example of the virtues appropriate for their age. . . . Such are the helpers or models of whom I often speak, with whom one cannot dispense at home or in school.[27]

Basedow had, incidentally, a few remarks to make about the recognition of and adjustment to individual differences. Especially good are his comments on the proper treatment for brilliant children, who were customarily stuffed with knowledge and advanced through school at an exceedingly rapid rate.

You say perhaps: "My child has an extraordinary genius, why should I curb him in his natural course?" "With what then," you ask, "should I keep him busy if he grasps and learns everything so much faster than the others?" I answer: "Well, let him do everything to as many degrees more perfectly as the exercise is made easier by his genius. Do not lead him from field to field earlier than the others, but let him harvest in each field more carefully and let him repeat the aftermath; and finally give him more time for manual work and for physical exercise." [28]

[26] *Ibid.*, p. 99.
[27] *Ibid.*, pp. 265–266.
[28] *Ibid.*, p. 95.

This solution of the problem presented by the brilliant child is not far from that most widely accepted at present.

5. Teacher-Pupil Relationship The relationship of teachers and pupils was apparently close and friendly. As one of the teachers in later years expressed himself to the children in his class: "My dear children, we are creating here a little republic, in which each one among us is a free member; you are my young friends and I am your older and more experienced friend." [29]

To some extent this relationship rested upon the informality of the lessons, the small size of the classes, and the methods for making work interesting, but it stemmed also from Basedow's clear idea of just what he wanted in his teachers. In commenting upon the use of examinations for selecting teachers he wrote:

> If I wanted to summon anyone to the position of teacher, I should consider especially good morals, love for youth on the right grounds, inclination towards his work, natural ability to learn quickly what he does not know, gift of quick, sensible deliberation, readiness to express his thoughts quickly and well, health, customary cheerfulness, and such training of the body as arouses esteem, and only then the least point—namely, to what degree he already knows what he is to teach others.
>
> I call it in comparison to the foregoing the least important point if a teacher must begin a science along with his students and not at once continue in the middle: for whoever can, and will, and is allowed to begin with the fundamentals learns a science best at the time when he needs to learn it. And although he who begins later never achieves the highest level in a science, nevertheless this impossibility will not prevent a man who possesses the above-mentioned gifts from guiding pupils to all useful levels (I do not speak of university professors who must, in their science, be oracles of an entire country).[30]

The picture of a friendly, intelligent, flexible, healthy teacher coincides with present-day demands in the best schools.

6. Motivation and Punishment Like most outstanding teachers, Basedow abhorred punishment and greatly preferred praising children to blaming them. Vividly did he remember the many and futile beatings of his own school days. In his school at Dessau no child was to be coerced into learning and no child was to be punished for poor work. Whatever a pupil could not learn joyously he could omit, but it was the responsibility of the teachers to present material in such a form that children wanted to learn.

In addition to making the work exciting, Basedow used a system of merits and privileges as further stimulation, not only for schoolwork but for

[29] *Ibid.*, p. lxxix.
[30] *Ibid.*, p. 206.

behavior. He stressed also the avoidance of disciplinary crises by allowing the children great freedom of movement about the rooms and grounds, by using guided conversation as a basic teaching method, by interspersing hours of physical exercise throughout the day, and by encouraging a maximum of participation by the children in their own education. Probably these measures were more effective than the system of merits, especially since Basedow's system was too complex for children and quite ridiculous for adolescents. A brief statement of Basedow's upon the prevention of laziness in school summarizes his attitude:

> If one makes instruction as pleasant as in its nature it can be, if one refuses to lead children before it is time to a height that will make them dizzy, if one through imperceptible instruction lightens as much as possible the difficulties of application to schoolwork . . . I am entirely certain that no child who is capable of becoming valuable to the community through schoolwork would be guilty of laziness in school for any length of time.[31]

While Basedow would not allow punishment for failure to learn, he realized that some children have to be restrained from forming personal habits that are dangerous to themselves or to others. He therefore used punishment for moral offenses, but he did not permit flogging upon any grounds. Nor was schoolwork ever to be used as punishment. A disobedient child might lose his previously acquired merits and his privileges, he might be sent for a while to a completely empty small room and left to think, he might have to eat alone at mealtimes, or he might be deprived of attendance in classes and kept all day at some simple form of handwork. If children did not respond to such treatment within a year of their entrance into the school, parents were asked to remove them. Basedow knew well enough that intractable children existed, but he did not make the mistake of thinking they could be beaten out of their intractability.

After Basedow's school had been functioning for two or three years, he held a public examination to which he invited all the notables in Germany and other countries. A number of people came and stayed for several days, while the children were put through their paces. One of the observers wrote a description of certain phases of the examination. Part of his letter is quoted below, since it gives more vividly than a summary could do the essential character of the work done in the Philanthropinum.

> The youngsters prepared an amusing thing. First they played the "Command" game. You see, it is this way: first they all stand in a row like soldiers, and Herr Wolke is the officer who commands in Latin, and they must do everything that he orders. For instance, when he say *claudite oculos,* they

[31] *Ibid.,* pp. 95–96.

close their eyes tightly; or, *circumspicite,* they peer around in all directions; or, *imitamini sartorem,* every mother's son of them sew together as tailors; or, *imitamini sutorem,* they pull the tarred thread as shoemakers. Herr Wolke commanded a thousand different amusing things.

Another game, a sort of hide and seek, I will tell you about also. Someone writes a name behind the blackboard in such a way that the children cannot see it—say, some part of the human body, a plant, an animal, or a metal—and then they guess until someone gets it right, and he wins an apple or a piece of cake as a reward. One of the visitors wrote on the back of the blackboard the word *intestina* (the intestines) and then told the children it was part of the human body. Then it started: one guessed *caput,* the others *nasus, os, manus, pes, digiti, pectus, collum, labium, genu, aures, oculi, crines, dorsum,* and so on for quite a while, until at last one pupil cried out: *It is the intestines!* Then Herr Wolke wrote the name of an animal . . . and the guessing continued: *leo, ursus, camelus, elephas*—you understand, it was a four-footed animal—*equus, bos, asinus, vacca, sus, canis,* and so on. At last, one child stepped up and said *mus* (mouse). He had won and got a small piece of cake. Then the name of a city was written, and the guessing went on: Lisbon, Madrid, Paris, London, Stockholm, Copenhagen, until one child said St. Petersburg—the name that stood on the back side of the blackboard.

They played still another game. Here Wolke commanded in Latin and the children imitated the voices of animals. One could have laughed himself weak. Now they roared like lions, now they crowed like roosters, now they miaowed like cats; then they imitated donkeys, dogs, ravens, in short every animal they were told to imitate.

Then Herr Wolke brought a picture, hung it up, and said: "Dear children, I bring you here a picture which you have not yet seen, but I tell you beforehand that it concerns the most serious thing in the world, so you be serious too." The children were. Now I must tell you what was in the picture. A pregnant woman sat sadly in an armchair and near her stood her husband and held her hand. On the other side of the picture was a table on which lay two tiny caps, one for a girl, the other for a boy, and under the table stood a tub with water and a sponge in it. Then Herr Wolke began to ask what kind of a woman it was, and why she seemed so sad, and why her husband had seized her by the hand. Then the children said it was a pregnant woman, the man was her husband who wanted to comfort her because she was in great danger and she well might die. Whereupon Herr Wolke questioned further, what the two little caps might mean. Then certain of the onlookers began to laugh; but you should have seen Herr Wolke, how earnest he became and with what bearing he suddenly turned upon us. He requested us kindly not to laugh at so serious a matter; otherwise he would prefer not to teach at all. For an instant it was so still you could hear a pin drop. Then he continued at once and asked again about the two caps. Then the children said that one could not know whether a boy or a girl would come; therefore the parents had provided both caps. There were a host of other things that Herr Wolke said and asked: for example, about the tub with water he said that when a child came into the world it would at once strangle in its own blood if the good parents did not take care of it, wash it, and clean it. . . . Herr Wolke asked little Fabreau where the babies came from. The child began to grin and said parents told different stories. There were sensible parents and silly parents. The sensible ones said: Mother has borne a child. But the silly ones would say: The stork brought it. Thereupon he questioned further: "If then your mother bore you, to whom do you owe it that you are in the world?" The child answered: "I owe it to my mother." "But what if the stork brought you?" "Then I owe it to the stork," said the boy, and laughed heartily. Oh that I had been so understanding as Fabreau when I was six years old! . . .

First Herr Wolke dictated a number as long as my arm; it was hardly on the blackboard before Emilie began: 149,532 quadrillion, so many trillion, so many billion, and then the millions, then the thousands, hundreds, until the numbers were all read. Then they went on to addition. Herr Wolke wrote a long column of figures, easily ten. None of the little children had a piece of chalk in his hand; they added everything in their heads or counted sometimes on their fingers. They did everything on the dot and sometimes even corrected Herr Wolke when he did not add correctly—but he did that only in fun. So it went on for a while and all the onlookers were greatly pleased that the children had so much dash and could add up a problem in the twinkling of an eye.

When this exercise was over, Wolke . . . took the chalk and asked the pupils what they wanted to have drawn: *Leonem, leonem,* they all shouted together. Now Herr Wolke started off as if he was going to draw a lion, but instead he drew a quite dangerous-looking beak. Then the children cried: *Non est leo, non est leo.* Why not? *Quia habet rostrum,* they answered, *leones non habent rostrum.* Whereupon Herr Wolke drew the ears, but extremely long. Then the children cried out again that it was not right, that they were donkey's ears. In short, they prescribed for Herr Wolke what he should draw from head to tail, and even then they had not had enough. They demanded also that a boy should be standing on top of the animal. Herr Wolke purposely drew the boy incorrectly; now he lacked an eye, now an ear, now a nose; but the children saw each error in an instant and had it corrected. Still it was not enough! The animal must have a bit in his mouth and the boy must have the reins in his hand; it was certainly a figure at which one could shake with laughter. When that was done, Herr Wolke said he would draw them something else; then they all cried out again, *domum, domum.* "Good," said Herr Wolke, "what is the first thing for a house?" *Fundamentum, fundamentum.* In a moment he drew the foundation. Then they told him to draw the first story, the second story, and then the roof—which he did. What next? *Januam, januam.* Where should the door be put? *In medio, in medio.* "But I don't want to put one door in the middle," said Herr Wolke, "here's where it will be," and he drew it somewhat to one side. "All right," said the children, "but then you must draw another door on the other side." Why then? *Propter symmetriam.* When the doors were finished they went on to the windows. Herr Wolke again purposely drew them incorrectly; but the children told him at once how it must be and which were too big or too small. Then came the chimneys, and then Emilie had him draw a chimney sweep with a broom on one of them.[32]

It is easy to believe that such an exhibition greatly impressed its audience.

Perhaps the one most important thing to remember about the Philanthropinum was that within its walls *education was fun.* From all accounts the children were not aware that their school days stretched from dawn to eve because they were constantly going somewhere to see or do something interesting, and their learning was so incidental that they hardly noticed it. In its essentials, then, the Philanthropinum was a distant forerunner of the modern activities curriculum.

READING REFERENCES

A. General Histories of the Period

Garrett, *European History, 1500–1815,* chaps. 27, 31.
Grant, A. J., and H. Temperly, *Europe in the Nineteenth and Twentieth Centuries,* Longmans, Green and Co., 1939 (716 pp.), chap. 1.
Hayes, *Political and Cultural History of Modern Europe,* Vol. I, chap. 11.
Schevill, *A History of Europe from the Reformation to the Present Day,* chap. 19.
Stearns, *Pageant of History,* part ii, chap. 21.
Turner, E. R., *Europe since 1789,* Doubleday & Company, 1924 (846 pp.), chap. 1.

B. Other Texts in the History of Education

Cole, *History of Educational Thought,* pp. 233–243.
Cubberley, *History of Education,* pp. 530–538.
Eby and Arrowood, *The Development of Modern Education,* chaps. 13, 14.
Graves, *A Student's History of Education,* chap. 11.
Marique, *History of Christian Education,* Vol. III, chap. 3.
McCormick, *History of Education,* pp. 312–321.
Monroe, *A Textbook in the History of Education,* pp. 533–585.
Ulich, *History of Educational Thought,* pp. 211–224.

C. Secondary Sources

Boyd, W., *The Educational Theory of Rousseau,* Longmans, Green and Co., 1911, (368 pp.), chap. 7.
Graves, *Great Educators of Three Centuries,* chaps. 7, 8.
Painter, *Great Pedagogical Essays,* chap. 21.
Quick, *Essays on Educational Reformers,* pp. 96–156.

[32] *Ibid.,* pp. lxxi–lxxv.

D. Translations of Primary Sources

Elyot, T., *The Boke Named the Governour,* parts iv–vi, xvi, xvii.
Rousseau, *Émile,* or Education according to Nature, book i or half of book ii, or book iii, any translation of *Émile.*
Ulich, *Three Thousand Years of Educational Wisdom,* pp. 383–425.

CHAPTER XV

TYPICAL SCHOOLS OF THE SEVENTEENTH AND EIGHTEENTH CENTURIES

The lifetimes of Comenius, De la Salle, Francke, and Basedow extend from 1592 to 1790, a period of approximately two hundred years. All four men founded schools which had some influence upon contemporary education. These men were, however, in the vanguard. While they lived and worked and experimented, a number of more conventional and conservative schools went their own way, picking up an idea here and there from others, but changing remarkably little during the period under consideration.[1]

The first point to note is the variety in types of elementary and secondary school that existed in one or more of the countries of Europe. The methods of teaching in these schools and the characteristics of the teaching personnel will also be discussed. Another section of the chapter contains a brief statement concerning the movement toward realism in education, since it began to influence schoolwork during the seventeenth and eighteenth centuries.

A. TYPES OF ELEMENTARY SCHOOL

1. The Parish School In Catholic countries the usual elementary school was the parish* school, taught by the village priest or by a member of a teaching brotherhood or sisterhood. These schools were numerous. For instance, between 1710 and 1717, the archbishop of Rouen visited the 1159 rural parishes in his diocese, in which he found 855 parish schools for boys and 306 for girls; only 304 parishes had no school at all.[2] Some of these schools were supported by the community, some by the church, and some by charity. It was a fairly common practice for wealthy people to give donations to schools, either out of spontaneous generosity or as penance* for their sins.[3]

[1] After a good deal of thought and a number of false starts, the descriptions of the schools for these centuries—the end of the sixteenth to the middle of the nineteenth—have been combined. Many of the schools continued on into the early nineteenth century, with little change in their organization or methods. It was not until governments began to control schools, to set up requirements for teachers, and to supervise the work in the classroom that modifications slowly began to appear in the work of the average school.
[2] Ravelet, *op. cit.*, Chap. 1.
[3] For educational conditions within France before the French Revolution, see L'Abbé Allain, *L'Instruction primaire en France avant la Revolution,* La Société Bibliographique,

In England and Germany also there were many parish schools maintained by the local pastor. Records of these schools show them to have been small, usually enrolling from 12 to 30 children, although a few of them enrolled as many as 250. Instruction was given in the three R's as well as in religion, and the girls were taught to sew and knit. The conviction that education was the business of the minister was strong in seventeenth- and eighteenth-century Europe. These small parish schools are easy to overlook in a summary of European education. They were humble and unostentatious, but they did much to reduce illiteracy and to spread elementary skills and culture among the common people.

2. The Vernacular School In Germany as in France, secular elementary schools were in existence before the days of Francke and De la Salle, and wealthy patrons often made contributions to education.[4] In the German states the commonest elementary schools were the vernacular schools, so called because all work was given in German, not in Latin. The work of these schools consisted of reading, writing, very simple arithmetic, and singing, the total being roughly the equivalent of the work now covered in the first three or four grades of elementary school.

3. The Village School The pictures shown in Figure 66 (a) & (b) were drawn to represent typical village schools, one in England and one in Switzerland. Both are imaginative and both illustrate school life of the middle nineteenth century. However, from such verbal descriptions as exist of these schools there seems no reason to suppose that the town-supported schools were appreciably different in earlier centuries. One school is represented as being held in a pleasant room, but there is a good deal of disorder, and the teacher appears to be taking no active steps toward either control or instruction. In the second picture, the pupils appear to be quieter, although a few are carrying on conversations in little knots. One boy, presumably being punished, is kneeling in front of the teacher, a grim-looking man who seems to have reduced a

---

1881, 304 pp.; Alfred Babeau, *L'Instruction primaire dans les campagnes avant 1789,* Didier et Cie., 1875; F. Buisson, *Dictionnaire de pédagogie et d'instruction primaire,* Hachette et Cie., 1882–1887, 4 vols.; G. Compayré, *Histoire critique des doctrines de l'éducation en France depuis le seizième siècle,* Hachette et Cie., 1880, 2 vols.; A. de Foulques de Villaret, *L'Enseignment des lettres et des sciences dans l'Orléanais depuis les premiers siècles du Christianisme jusqu'à la fondation de l'Université d'Orléans,* 1785, 145 pp.; A. F. Théry, *History of Education in France from the Fifth Century to Our Times,* C. Délagrave, 1861, 2 vols.

[4] For the development of schools in Germany, see F. Paulsen, *German Education: Past and Present;* S. Lorenz (pseudonym, Lorenz Schmitt), *Volkserziehung und Volksunterricht im späteren Mittelalter,* F. Schöningh, 1887, 132 pp.; Karl von Raumer, *Geschichte der Pädagogik,* D. C. Bertelsmann, 1877–1897, 5 vols.; G. W. Rein, *Encyklopädisches Handbuch der Pädagogik,* H. Beyer und Sohn, 1899, 7 vols.; K. Schmidt, *Geschichte der Pädagogik,* P. Schettler, 1861–1868, 4 vols.

small girl to tears. Some pupils have books, but the majority do not. The small village school that enrolled a dozen to twenty pupils of sundry ages was a typical institution, from the sixteenth through the nineteenth centuries.

Fig. 66. Two Village Schools. (*Top*) An English school, from an old woodcut. (*Bottom*) A Swiss school, from a painting by Albert Anker, now in the Kunstmuseum in Berne.

The main differences among the parish, the vernacular, and the village schools lay in the sources of the funds for their support and in the degree to which some church participated in their control, either directly through the use of clergymen as teachers or indirectly through supervision. The curriculum and methods of teaching differed little from type to type, except as some schools included more religious instruction than others.

4. The Charity Schools During the closing decades of the seventeenth century and the early part of the eighteenth, a wave of philanthropy swept over Europe. In France and Germany charitable people supported the work of De la Salle and of Francke, as well as that of less conspicuous teachers. In England many charity schools were founded at the beginning of the eighteenth century. By 1714 their number had grown to 4818. These schools were under the control of philanthropic societies, notably the Society for the Promotion of Christian Knowledge, founded in 1699, which furnished the funds. A picture of such a school appears in Figure 67. The children who attended the charity schools[5] were mostly those who would go to work by the time they were eight years old, so the curriculum was naturally quite elementary and consisted of a little reading, writing, counting, some training in handwork, and instruction in religion and morals. Probably a second-grade pupil of today has already had more educational advantages than the children who attended the charity schools.

FIG. 67. A Charity School. From the *Londina Illustrata* of 1819.

5. Vocational Schools England had other schools that were similar in nature to the charity school but were supported either by grants from Parliament or by local taxes. The former were called schools of industry; the latter, workhouse schools. The main objective of both these institutions was the training of boys to enter trades and of girls to enter domestic service. Most of the

[5] See J. H. Cardwell, *History of a Charity School (1699–1899),* Truslove, Hanson, and Comba, 1899, 126 pp.

work was therefore vocational, but the elements of reading, writing, and counting were included. The schools of industry were usually held in the shops or industrial plants in which the children would presently go to work. Such a school in a tailor's shop is shown in Figure 68. As one can easily imagine, the amount of formal education in such a school would be meager indeed, but for most of these children the tiny bit of reading and writing thus secured constituted an entire educational equipment for life.

FIG. 68. A School for Apprentices. From a drawing in the German School Museum in Berlin.

6. The Hedge School These schools, which existed on the Continent as well as in England and Ireland, were originally so called because they were taught by men who for some reason were not supposed to be teaching at all and were therefore forced to hold their schools behind a hedge or in some other place where they felt freer from detection than they would have been had the place of meeting been more public. The name subsequently spread to any school that was held in an irregular manner. The hedge school was taught by itinerant teachers, artisans, tutors who were temporarily out of a job, unfrocked* priests, or anyone else who wanted to earn a few pennies. Because of their informal nature it is impossible to determine how many there were, but from all accounts England was full of them, and they were frequent enough in Germany to precipitate decrees against their existence. The amount of training was certainly small and must have varied greatly from teacher to teacher. Nothing reflects the dearth of educational institutions more clearly than the widespread popularity of this "bootlegged" schooling.

7. The Dame School This type was a thoroughly British institution and did not have its counterpart in other European countries. The pupils in the dame schools gathered in some woman's living room or kitchen, where they were given such education as the "dame" was able and willing to impart. The schools were small and were attended usually by boys and girls too young for

FIG. 69. A Dame School. From a drawing by Barclay of a school in the heart of London.

the parish or village school, although in some cases they were simply the feminine equivalent of the others. Reading and manners were the basis of instruction, but the curriculum—if it could be called that—varied with the resources of each woman. Presumably a few were fairly competent, as judged by the standards of the time, but most of these teachers had a poor reputation. The view of the dame school in Figure 69 certainly does not arouse confidence, but it probably exaggerates the situation somewhat for purposes of caricature.

As may readily be appreciated, the schools enumerated above were mostly of inferior quality, although they were the best that sincere, well-meaning people could produce. There was not much to choose among the parish schools, the charity schools, the schools of industry, the workhouse schools, the dame schools, and the hedge schools, except that two of them added vocational training to their teaching of the three R's and some of them were under direct religious control.

B. CONVENTIONAL TYPES OF SECONDARY SCHOOL

The commonest type of secondary school was the traditional Latin school. In most cases the curriculum was humanistic and represented a formalized survival of an earlier movement that originally had great vitality. The Italian humanists had concentrated upon literature and languages as the best means for self-culture and individual development, and the German humanists had concentrated upon the same subjects as the best means for moral and religious growth and for preparation for useful service to the state. From the early sixteenth century in Southern Europe and from the early seventeenth in Northern Europe, the secondary schools began to degenerate, largely because the classical languages were no longer taught with the aim of furnishing a liberal education but to train the mind. The languages became ends in themselves, and the teaching was concentrated upon mastery of detail rather than upon the growth of the inner man. Cicero ceased to be a fine human being with something worth while to say on a number of subjects and became merely a model for style, with emphasis upon the exact arrangement of words.

The Latin-dominated secondary school did not participate in the great educational progress of the eighteenth century shown by the elementary schools. Its curriculum was formalized, its teaching lifeless, and its development stationary. In England and France its life was further stifled by legislation that required uniformity of religious affiliation among the teachers. In England, for two centuries—from 1662 when the Act of Conformity* was passed till about 1870—the pressure on teachers was especially severe, since each teacher was investigated by church authorities in such a searching and degrading way that men of ability and character would not submit to it. The Jesuit schools, which had been of superior quality for two centuries, had deteriorated and were eventually legislated out of existence.

Only in Germany were there efforts to revive the Latin school, with the aim of returning to a cultural education. Frederick the Great* became king of Prussia in 1740 and at once began to reorganize the schools. He frowned upon the court schools as inadequate and upon the old Latin schools as definitely out of date. The curriculum that resulted from his reforms included work in German, French, mathematics, and elementary science. On the other hand, the emphasis upon Greek as the language to be known by the cultured man was greatly increased. Courses in Greek language, literature, and history became immensely popular, and the idea that a study of such material would both lead to a high cultural development and train the mind continued to dominate the German Latin school from the last decades of the eighteenth century till the close of the nineteenth. Because of Prussia's prestige among the German states, the Prussian models were widely copied. There was thus a revival of interest in education throughout Germany and new subjects did creep into the curriculum, but the major emphasis was upon a return to the Renaissance rather than upon an advance into modernity.

In general, however, secondary schools in Europe failed to show marked changes of any kind during the seventeenth and early eighteenth centuries. With each passing decade, the work became perhaps a bit more formalized, a bit more remote from daily life, and a bit less adapted to the inquiring mind of youth. The teaching was of inferior quality, the subject matter tedious, and the discipline severe. In Germany and France two despots—Frederick the Great and Napoleon*—issued a series of orders for changes in the organization and content in secondary schools during the half century from 1750 to 1800 (approximate dates only) and thus led the way for new developments during the nineteenth century. The English model of the Latin school persisted essentially unchanged, perhaps because the English lacked a proper kind of despot! The traditional classical school during the centuries under consideration is an uninteresting topic for discussion and will therefore be abandoned in favor of a new type of school that was developing alongside it during the eighteenth century.

C. REALISM AND THE SCHOOLS OF THE REALISTS

The word "real" as applied to schools in the late sixteenth and early seventeenth centuries refers to the substitution of "reality" for verbalism.* Thus Comenius broke away from the humanistic preoccupation with classical languages and from the scholastic quoting of authority. In the place of both he substituted an observation of the world through the senses. These are "realities." The word "real" is best pronounced in the German fashion "re-äl," partly to distinguish it from the commoner meanings of the English word "real," partly because the German word has a more specialized meaning,[6] and partly because the modern school system of Germany uses the word to designate those schools in which the sciences, applied mathematics, and such technical subjects as engineering have been substituted for some or all of the linguistic studies.

The movement was initiated and popularized by a group of outstanding

[6] "Realien," for instance, are useful, practical, technical facts. A "Realencyclopädie" contains scientific and technological matter. A "Realschule" is a school in which scientific subjects are substituted for linguistic ones.

writers on education in the late sixteenth and early seventeenth centuries. These men had an assortment of good ideas that, if put into execution, would have improved the work of the schools; unfortunately, the writers were not teachers and had little if any connection with the schools of the period. Their influence was indirect and in some cases was not felt for several decades after the publication of their writings. The most prominent individuals in the group were Montaigne* in France and John Locke and Francis Bacon in England. The first two are usually referred to as "social realists," while the last was a "sense realist." [7] The difference lies in what aspects of reality were considered most important. The social realists wanted to change the content of the curriculum so as to adapt it better to the needs of society, or rather to the needs of the upper classes. The sense realists wanted to change both curriculum and methodology by the substitution of sciences for languages and by the use of experimentation, observation, laboratories, demonstrations, and pictures. They advocated also the replacement of Latin by the vernacular. Sense realism in education was a natural result of interest in and study of science. Hence the study of any and all sciences, of mathematics, and of the vernacular, since it was more practical than Latin and better adapted for the discussion of scientific topics because of its more modern vocabulary. Both groups of realists were alike in demanding that life in school bear a closer relation than it then did to life outside school. In general, the changes brought about by these writers on education are to be found in the secondary rather than in the elementary schools.

1. Schools of the Social Realists The advocates of social realism influenced chiefly the boarding schools maintained at various European courts[8] for the children of the nobility. These boys were supposed to be in training for public life at court, a type of existence for which a concentrated study of Latin syntax did not seem especially appropriate. In the new court schools they were, instead, taught history, geography, politics, and such mathematics and physics as would be of value to them as future officers in the army. In addition, they learned to fence, to ride, and to be proficient in many sports. In France and Germany especially, a considerable number of court schools were founded during the seventeenth century. They introduced modifications into the traditional curriculum in order to produce a rationalistic, realistic, practical education for the future courtier, soldier, and man of affairs, as opposed to the formal, linguistic studies of the Gymnasium. Because the sons of gentlemen and noblemen attended them, the court schools had through their prestige an influence quite out of proportion to their actual numbers.

[7] These were also humanistic realists. See Chapter IX.
[8] For earlier court schools, see Chapter VIII.

2. *Schools of the Sense Realists* In England, the modifications of the curriculum to conform with the new ideas of the sense and social realists occurred first in the schools of the Dissenters, those who refused to join the Church of England or who left it after having been members. The ministers among the Dissenters were dismissed from their parishes in 1662, and a little later Dissenting students were expelled from the universities. As a result, a large number of teachers and students were without school affiliation and promptly banded together to form their own schools. Some twenty-five years later the government finally decided upon a policy of toleration, and gradually the privately supported academies of the Nonconformists lost their individuality and were absorbed into the school system. For more than half a century, however, these schools were outstanding as examples of realism. In them a boy could obtain the best education in England. Since they were created at just the time when realism was the last word in education and since they wished to differ clearly from the traditional schools, from which both faculty and students were barred, they espoused the new movement and included a wide variety of subjects among their offerings. Not all the subjects listed were taught in any one school, but in the entire group one finds geography, anatomy, celestial mechanics, natural philosophy, logic, French, Italian, Hebrew, history, economics, arithmetic, algebra, geometry, trigonometry, surveying, and shorthand. Some of the schools specified that the students were to learn to dissect animals, to make almanacs, and to run boundary lines. All work was given in English. These schools show a definite break with tradition and a concentration upon such realistic studies as the sciences or mathematics, and such practical subjects as the modern languages, surveying, and shorthand.

It was not until the middle of the eighteenth century, however, that the new ideas found their most permanent expression in Germany in the Realgymnasium* and the Realschule.* After much agitation and publication of articles in favor of a more practical education, the first Realgymnasium was opened in Berlin in 1747. These schools were supposedly parallel to the Gymnasien, but their work was more scientific, more technical, and less linguistic, although Latin was still included. A typical curriculum of these schools in about the middle of the eighteenth century contained, besides Latin, writing, drawing, history, geography, arithmetic, mechanics, surveying, natural history, religion, and ethics. All classes were taught in German. These schools were for a long time considered newfangled and of considerably lower merit than the traditional Latin school. In 1859 they were reorganized and incorporated into the system of German schools. Their number has continued to increase till the present day. In the two hundred years since their appearance they have become more and more scientific and practical. In 1900 there were made equal to their more "cultured" rival, the classical Gymnasium. The Realschulen have an even greater concentration upon scientific subjects and do not include either Greek or Latin in their curriculum, although there is work in modern languages. They are much like the American technical high school.

D. TEACHING METHODS AND DISCIPLINE

In the three quotations below, the conditions in the majority of schools during the late sixteenth, seventeenth, and early eighteenth centuries are described. The first passage stresses the discipline and the artificiality of the schools; the second rails against the dullness, monotony, and meaninglessness of education; and the third, againt the inefficiency of the teaching in most schools.

Grammar was flogged into the memory, as well as sayings from the Holy Writ and verses of songs. A common school punishment was the memorizing of the 119th psalm. The schoolrooms were gloomy to the point of melancholy. It never occurred to anyone that young people could learn anything at all with love, as little as that they had eyes for anything but writing and reading. The unhealthy age of Louis XIV* brought, besides, to the poor children of the higher social classes curled, powdered, pomaded hair, coats trimmed with braid, short pants, silk stockings, a dagger at their sides; all this was for active, healthy youngsters the most intense torture.[9]

The school dust has been lying for centuries. Young and old, whoever must wander there and breathe it, become sick in the brain; this tough covering, through which truth and goodness can hardly penetrate, is deposited in the workshop of reason. . . . Most of my weaknesses, which I cannot now conceal, I owe to the breathing in of this dust or to the cure which likewise—although in another way—weakened my nature . . . The vaulted roofs [of schools] echo daily from the cries of those who are thrashed; here, of a creature who is supposed to use more comprehension and memory than God gave him, there perhaps of a future Newton who forgets the case ending of a never-understood word, there again of a spirit that was created for something better who unwittingly and erroneously interchanges words and phrases of Rome and the Fatherland—words that are empty of content for him.[10]

Each child read by himself; the simultaneous method was not known. One after another stepped up to the table where the master sat. The teacher pointed out one letter at a time, and named it; the child named it after him; he drilled him in recognizing and remembering each. They then took the words, letter by letter, and by getting acquainted with them in this way, the child gradually learned to read. This was a difficult method for him, a very difficult one. Years usually passed before any facility had been acquired; many did not

[9] Von Raumer, *op. cit.*, II, 296.
[10] Göring, *J. B. Basedow's Ausgewählte Schriften,* p. lxvii.

learn in four years. It was imitative and purely mechanical labor on both sides. To understand what was read was seldom even thought of. The syllables were pronounced with equal force, and the reading was without grace or expression. Where it was possible, but unnaturally and mechanically, learning by heart was practiced. The children drawled out texts of Scripture, Psalms, and the contents of the catechism from the beginning to end; short questions and long answers alike, all in the same monotonous manner. Anybody with delicate ears who heard the sound once would remember it all his life long. There are people yet living who were taught in that unintelligent

FIG. 70. A Typical Sixteenth-Century Schoolroom. From a woodcut by Burgkmeier in Rhyn's *Kulturegeschischte des deutschen Volkes.*

way, who can corroborate these statements. Of the actual contents of the words whose sounds they had thus barely committed to memory little by little, the children knew absolutely nothing. They learned superficially and understood superficially. Nothing really passed into their minds; at least nothing during their school years. The instruction in singing was no better. The master sang to them the psalm tunes over and over, until they could sing them, or rather screech them, after him. Such was the condition of instruction in our schools during the sixteenth, seventeenth, and two thirds of the eighteenth centuries; confined to one or two studies, and those taught in the most imperfect and mechanical way.[11]

With the exception of the Jesuit schools, the method of instruction used

[11] F. A. W. Diesterweg (H. Barnard, editor), *German Educational Reformers,* American Journal of Education, 1863 (586 pp.), p. 576.

FIG. 71. An Eighteenth-Century German School (a). From a picture in the German School Museum in Berlin.

FIG. 72. An Eighteenth-Century German School (b). From an engraving by J. Mettenleiter now in the Kupferstichkabinet in Munich and printed in F. J. Schlez, *Dorfschulen zu Langenhausen,* Nuremberg, 1795.

in the eighteenth century was still individual, just as it had been for many centuries. Even a good teacher spent almost all his time listening to one child after another, as each came to his desk. It is not surprising that children profited little by such training.

The discipline in the schools was almost everywhere severe. In drawings of schoolrooms, the teacher is always equipped with a switch and is frequently portrayed in the act of using it. The pictures in Figures 70 and 71 show schoolrooms, in which one or two of the pupils are holding a classmate so that the teacher can whip him. In the first picture, some educational activity is also in progress and the room is reasonably quiet. The second, however, shows a scene of cruelty and complete confusion. Two children are being beaten with sadistic fury, two are wearing dunce caps, two are standing with their legs tied together, and no one is pursuing an education. In a third picture, Figure 72, one boy is being ridiculed by being made to wear a dunce cap, while another is kneeling on a triangular-shaped piece of wood, a punishment that must have been acutely painful. Although two of the pictures show German schools, it should not be inferred that those in other European countries had a discipline that was much, if any, less severe.

The employment of untrained and low-grade teachers always results in constant disorder in the schoolroom, basically because the teacher has no idea what to do with the children or how to interest them enough to keep them under control. The only method known to the harassed inadequates who tried to teach the ordinary sixteenth- and seventeenth-century school was corporal punishment, often of a severe sort. Since the teacher did not know how to charm his pupils, he avoided absolute chaos by beating them into a semblance of docility. One German schoolmaster, with a Teutonic* exactitude worthy of a better cause, kept a record of what punishments he had used during his fifty-one years of teaching. The totals were:

blows with a cane	911,527
blows with a rod	124,010
blows with a ruler	20,989
blows with the hand	136,715
blows with a book	22,763
blows over the mouth	10,235
blows over the ears	7,905
raps on the head	1,115,800

The same man had punished pupils 777 times by making them kneel on peas and 613 times on small triangles of wood. On 3001 occasions he had made a pupil put on the fool's cap, and in addition he had invented a few tortures of his own. Even his scoldings were carefully recorded in a list of some 3000 abusive words or phrases that he used for minor offenses.[12] Nothing shows the condition of elementary teaching any more clearly than the fact that such a man could hold a job for fifty-one years. Altogether, the picture of schools during the seventeenth and eighteenth centuries indicates that their reputation as being poor places for children is completely justified.

E. TEACHING PERSONNEL IN THE ELEMENTARY SCHOOLS

Until the sixteenth century there were almost no elementary schools, but under the stimulus given by the Reformation to educate all children, they began to appear. By the end of the century there were vernacular schools all over Germany and in the seventeenth century over most of Europe, although more of them were in predominantly Protestant than in predominantly Catholic countries. It proved, however, much easier to open the schools than to find teachers to teach in them.

At first, the church sexton was pressed into service and told to add the teaching of the catechism to his regular duties of cleaning the church and burying the dead, but it soon became evident that he was incompetent to deal with the living. In other schools, the teachers were bellringers, shoemakers, pensioners, invalids, or destitute widows. Frederick the Great, in the eighteenth century, used the position of schoolteacher as a form of pension for his crippled soldiers. The pay was so low that no one could live on it. Teachers were therefore forced to have two jobs, unless they had a pension, and in their minds the less important of the two seems to have been the teaching. With such a personnel it is not surprising that the elementary school teacher was looked down upon.

The descriptions of and references to the teachers of vernacular schools in the sixteenth, seventeenth, and eighteenth centuries fail to excite admiration. They were reported to the authorities for being drunk over the week end, for immorality, for gambling, for living beyond their means, for laziness, for neglect of duty. One town council passed the curious regulation that in schools having two teachers only one might go to a wedding celebration at once, presumably leaving the other to carry on while the celebrant became sober. The complaints against the teachers seem rarely to have concerned their inefficiency in instruction or even the harshness of their discipline, but were centered upon their lack of sterling moral character. However, it is probable that in this respect they were superior to the general level about them;

[12] H. Barnard (editor), *Memoirs of Eminent Teachers and Educators in Germany*, American Journal of Education, 1863 (586 pp.), pp. 509–510. (Translated from Karl von Raumer.)

and they should be judged against their own background, not against present-day conditions. Considering the insecurity of their positions and the lowness of their pay, it is surprising that they were as good as they were. They could be dismissed at any time by those who hired them, and they were dependent for their salary upon gifts, fees from their pupils, and sums paid by the town council or by the church. Usually the teacher was given living quarters in the schoolhouse, but the rest of his support was irregular in the extreme. Despite the insecurity of the work, however, a definite class of professional teachers for small children had made its appearance by the opening decades of the seventeenth century.[13]

Most of the teachers in the centuries under consideration undoubtedly meant well, but they were themselves too poorly educated to teach others effectively. Many of them were themselves graduates of only the vernacular school. They could read, write, and do simple arithmetic—and that was about all. Few of them had ever attended a Latin school, and university training for them was unheard of. The average education would be about equal to that of a fourth- or fifth-grade child today. Toward the close of the eighteenth century one finds reports of such incidents as the following: there was a schoolmaster who claimed that the school district owed him 200,705 thalers; upon investigation, however, it appeared that the debt was 275 thalers but that the teacher had not known how to write the numbers properly and had simply written down 200, then 70, and then 5 instead of combining them.[14] Since he could not read the resulting figure, he did not find his error. Others are reported who could not write and spell well enough to compose a letter or read more than the most elementary material.

Although the general picture of the schools was gloomy, there was here and there a man of high ideals, good intelligence, and general competence. Such a one was Dinter,* who was a teacher and supervisor in the Prussian schools during the late eighteenth and early nineteenth centuries. He expresses well the attitude of the best teachers of the time when he writes: "I promised God that I would regard each Prussian peasant child as an individual who could complain to God about me, if I did not provide for him the best education that I could possibly give him." [15]

Dinter goes into the minutiae of daily life in the schoolroom, telling one incident after another about himself or others. He shows an excellent degree of rapport between himself and the pupils, and seems to have maintained in-

[13] For an excellent discussion, see C. L. Robbins, "Teachers in Germany in the Sixteenth Century," *Teachers College Contributions to Education,* No. 52, 1912, 126 pp.
[14] For numerous examples of incompetence, see G. F. Dinter, *Dinter's Leben von ihm selbst beschrieben,* A. Pichler's Witve und Söhne, 1879, 474 pp.
[15] *Ibid.,* p. 219.

terest so well that severe punishments were not necessary. In between his accounts of episodes in the schoolroom he sandwiches a number of shrewd observation about education in general. He objected to the curriculum of the Gymnasium because he thought it ridiculous to give the same classical training to all boys, regardless of their future occupations. He wanted future businessmen excused from Latin and given training in French or English that would be of some use to them. He thought the uniform and rigid course ineffective because it took no account of the differences among the pupils.[16] Dinter was especially emphatic that the purpose of education was to show pupils how to help themselves, not to pour facts into them. He constantly besought the teachers under his care to stop teaching details and to concentrate upon training in how to think and how to study. Dinter undoubtedly did much to help raise the standard of teaching in the districts under his supervision, and there were presumably other equally thoughtful though less vocal teachers, but these few were not enough for the needs of the schools.

The typical schools of the seventeenth and eighteenth century present a melancholy picture. Perhaps it was for the best that many children never attended them at all and that most of those who did were generally in them for only two or three years.

READING REFERENCES

Adamson, *Pioneers of Modern Education,* chaps. 5, 8–10.

Birchenough, C., *History of Elementary Education in England and Wales from 1800 to the Present Time,* University of London Press, 1930 (2d ed., 514 pp.), chaps. 1, 8.

Boyd, *The History of Western Education,* chaps. 8–10.

Cubberley, *History of Education,* pp. 420–425, 437–461.

De Montmorency, J. E. G., *The Progress of Education in England,* Knight & Co., Ltd., 1905 (366 pp.), chap. 4.

———, *State Intervention in English Education,* Cambridge University Press, 1902 (366 pp.), chap. 5.

Dowling, P. J., *The Hedge Schools of Ireland,* Longmans, Green and Co., 1935 (182 pp.), chaps. 2, 5–8.

Eby and Arrowood, *The Development of Modern Education,* chaps. 7, 8.

Magevney, E., *Systems and Counter-Systems of Education (1648–1800),* Catholic Library Association, 1903, 53 pp.

Marique, *History of Christian Education,* Vol. III, chap. 2.

Monroe, *Comenius and the Beginnings of Educational Reform,* chap. 1.

[16] As he wrote, "Man will aus Allen Alles machen, und weil das nicht gelingt, ist man oft unzufrieden." ("They want to make the same thing out of everyone, and because they are not successful, they are often unhappy.")—Dinter, *op. cit.,* p. 258.

Parker, I., *Dissenting Academies in England,* Cambridge University Press, 1914 (168 pp.), chaps. 1, 2.
Paulsen, *German Education: Past and Present,* book iii, chaps. 1–3.
Reisner, *Historical Foundations of Modern Education,* chap. 17.
Robbins, *Teachers in Germany in the Sixteenth Century,* chaps. 2, 3, 5, 7.
Woodward, *Studies in Education during the Age of the Renaissance, 1400–1600,* chap. 13.

PART SEVEN

THE NINETEENTH CENTURY

CHAPTER XVI

PESTALOZZI AND HIS SCHOOLS

The main characters of the next three chapters—Pestalozzi, Herbart, and Froebel—were all in the same generation of educators. Their lifetimes stretch over a century; all three were alive between 1782 and 1828, a period of forty-six years. Both the younger men visited Pestalozzi, studied his methods, and were much influenced by him. With the work of these three men, one enters upon modern times.

A. PESTALOZZI: HIS LIFE AND WORK

1. Pestalozzi's Early Life[1] Henry Pestalozzi was born in Zurich,* Switzerland, in the year 1746. When he was five years old, his father died, leaving his mother and a faithful servant to bring up the children. During Pestalozzi's early years, the family consisted of two grown women and an older sister. There was not much money, but there was an abundance of love, generosity, devotion, peace, and harmony. The boy did not attend school until he was nine years old. In fact, he hardly left the house at all. Instead of playing rough-and-tumble games with boys of his own age, he sat at home, listening to stories and daydreaming. It is not strange that this child—undersized and underdeveloped, always indoors, deprived of masculine society, continually dominated by women, and kept from a comprehension of reality outside his home—should grow up into a small, weak man, shy and awkward, absent-minded, emotional, impressionable, impractical, and intuitive. His character

[1] Based upon H. Barnard, *Pestalozzi and Pestalozzianism,* F. C. Brownell, 1859, 2 vols.; G. Compayré, *Pestalozzi and Elementary Education* (translated by R. P. Jago), Thomas Y. Crowell Company, 1907, 139 pp.; F. Delekat, *Johann Heinrich Pestalozzi: der Mensch, der Philosoph, und der Erzieher,* Quelle und Meyer, 1926, 362 pp.; R. de Guimps, *Pestalozzi: His Life and Work,* Appleton-Century-Crofts Inc., 1892, 438 pp.; F. Herisson, *Pestalozzi, Élève de Jean-Jacques Rousseau,* C. Delagrave, 1886, 246 pp.; A. M. Kellogg, "Life of Pestalozzi: His Educational Work and Principles," *Pamphlets on Education,* Vol. 16, No. 15, 1891; H. Krüsi, *Pestalozzi: His Life and Work,* Wilson und Meyer, 1927, 220 pp.; H. Morf, *Erziehungs-und Unterrichtsplan der ersten Lehranstalt im Schlosse zu Münchenbuchsee,* Bleuler-Hausheer, Winterthur, 1868–1889, 4 vols; A. Pinloche, *Pestalozzi and the Foundation of the Modern Elementary School,* Charles Scribner's Sons, 1901, 306 pp.; R. H. Quick, *Essays on Educational Reformers,* E. L. Kellogg and Company, 1890 (335 pp.), pp. 157–197; J. Ramsauer, *Kurze Skizze meines pädagogischen Lebens,* Schulzes Buchhandlung, 1838, 103 pp.; A. Steffen, *Lebenbildness Pestalozzi,* Verlag für schöne Wissenschaften, 1939, 68 pp.; *Pestalozzi and His Times: A Pictorial Record,* Zentral Bibliotek, 1928, 63 pp.

seems to have been formed during these early years of home education, because the Pestalozzi who entered school as a child of nine already showed the traits and the maladjustments that were to characterize him as long as he lived. He recalls this period of his life in the following manner:

From my childhood I have been everybody's plaything. My education, which gave food to all the dreams of my fancy, left me alike incapable of doing what everybody does, and of enjoying what everybody enjoys. From the very first, little children, my schoolfellows, sent me where they would rather not go, and I went; in short I did all they wanted. . . . But, in spite of all this, there was no intimacy between my companions and myself. Although I worked hard and learned some things well, I had none of their ability for the ordinary lessons, and so I could not take it amiss that they dubbed me Harry Oddity of Foolborough.

More than any other child, I was always running my head against the wall for mere trifles; but it did not trouble me. I measured the whole world by my mother's house and my schoolroom, and the ordinary life of men was almost as unknown to me as if I had lived in another world.[2]

In spite of his general meekness and gullibility Pestalozzi had courage and drive upon occasion. Once when a teacher was unjust and cruel, small and inoffensive Henry Pestalozzi became an avenging fury, filled with the wrath of God and with a courage that knew no limits. He not merely arraigned the teacher but set about getting him removed. This queer, brooding child who went right on trusting even those who treated him with contempt was capable of becoming a crusader and champion of the underdog whenever his horror of injustice and oppression was aroused, nor did he pause to consider the cost to himself.

Pestalozzi was hardly a passable elementary school pupil, presumably because he paid too little attention to what was said to him and refused to memorize half-understood words as the other children did. Eventually, however, he struggled through the lower schools and reached the University of Zurich. Here he came under the influence of teachers who were able but as visionary as himself. As Pestalozzi wrote in later years:

The spirit of the public teaching in my native town, though eminently scientific, was calculated to make us lose sight of the realities of life, and lead us into the land of dreams. We had decided to live for nothing but independence, well-doing, sacrifice, and love of country, but we were without the practical knowledge necessary for reaching these ends. We were taught to despise the external advantages of wealth, honour, and consideration, and to believe that by economy and moderation, it is possible to do without most of the things considered essential by ordinary middle-class people. We were be-

[2] De Guimps, *op. cit.*, pp. 5–6.

guiled by a dream, to wit, the possibility of enjoying independence and domestic happiness without having either the power or the means of acquiring that position which alone can give them.[3]

Before he ever entered the university the young man was already a dreamer; what he found there was a particular dream that was to be his as long as he lived—the vision of regenerating and dignifying the common man through the power of education.

At first, Pestalozzi had intended to be a minister, but his shyness, uncertainty, awkwardness, self-consciousness, and rather thick speech made preaching impossible. He therefore turned to the study of law, hoping to become a crusader in that field. It was at this time that he first read Rousseau. The revolutionary ideas of Rousseau, especially those of a political nature, were spreading across the face of Europe, in spite of efforts by sundry officials to stop them. Switzerland, though in theory a democracy, was by no means so democratic as to welcome such revolutionary doctrines. The authorities in Zurich therefore banned *Émile* and the *Social Contract*. A group of the more liberal students, among them Pestalozzi, became indignant and undertook a general crusade against local abuses and injustices. They caused the dismissal of certain dishonest officials, they published a liberal paper, they founded a Helvetian* Society, and on local issues they sided openly and vocally with the people against the magistrates. It was not long before they were accused of trying to undermine the government, put into jail, condemned as revolutionaries, warned that they would lose their citizenship if they did not stop their activities, and forbidden to meet for purposes of political discussion. This outcome ruined any chance Pestalozzi might have had of raising the level of the people by bringing about a change of existing laws, because the public appointments necessary to such reform would be closed to him. He consequently entered another field of action altogether—agriculture. It may seem as if Pestalozzi swung about with every gust of wind, but actually he seems to have been motivated by one underlying idea: he wanted to devote his life to curing the intellectual and moral degradation of the poor people he saw on all sides, to improving their material condition, and to helping them help themselves. At first, he thought he could best accomplish his purpose as a village pastor, then as a reformer of the law, then as a leader in scientific agriculture, then as a writer, then as a philanthropist, and only finally as a teacher. His reigning principle thus remained stable, although its modes of expression varied.

At the beginning of his period of agricultural experiment Pestalozzi married a childhood friend who was to remain his staunch helper throughout her

[3] *Ibid.*, pp. 10–11.

life. In many ways she guarded and guided her impractical husband, thus fulfilling a need recognized by a friend who died just before Pestalozzi's marriage:

> I am going, and you will be left alone. Avoid any career in which you might become the victim of your own goodness and trust, and choose some quiet life in which you will run no risk. Above all, do not take part in any important undertaking without having at your side a man who, by his cool judgment, knowledge of men and things, and unshakable fidelity, may be able to protect you from the dangers to which you will be exposed.[4]

2. *His Agricultural and Social Experiments* As a model farmer Pestalozzi was not successful, although he worked hard and faithfully. He never realized his dream of making his farm the "center of a large sphere of benevolent activity" as he had hoped. Many of his ideas were excellent and have since been carried out by others on the same land, but Pestalozzi himself was so intoxicated by his enthusiasm for his project that he overlooked certain practical details necessary for success. He was always of the opinion that interest, enthusiasm, and an inner conviction of being right would compensate for omissions and shortcomings, and he showed throughout his life a marked tendency to rush into an activity upon a wave of fervor and excitement before making sure he was ready to begin it. His failure to prepare adequately for his farming venture, except for making excellent plans on paper, led to the collapse of his entire undertaking. He thus found himself, at the age of twenty-nine, badly in debt and with no visible assets. In fact, he and his wife and child were not far from starvation.

During the years of the agricultural interlude Pestalozzi began his first experiment in education through his efforts to bring up his own son, little Jacobi, who became the experimental rabbit for the educational method that his father would some day give the world. Influenced by Rousseau, Pestalozzi set out to bring up Jacobi in the manner of Émile, but he soon began to make modifications of his own. A few excerpts from his diary at this time seem worth quoting because of their relevance to Pestalozzi's future methods:

> February 2nd.—I tried to make him understand the meaning of numbers. At present he only knows their names, which he says by heart without attaching any precise meaning to them. To have a knowledge of words with no distinct idea of the things they represent enormously increases the difficulty of getting at the truth. . . . Why have I been so foolish as to let him pronounce important words without taking care at the same time to give him a clear idea of their meaning? Would it not have been more natural not to

[4] *Ibid.*, p. 23.

teach him to say "three" till he thoroughly understood the meaning of "two" and is it not in this way that children should be taught to count? [5]

I would say to the teacher: be thoroughly convinced of the immense value of liberty; do not let vanity make you anxious to see your efforts producing premature fruit; let your child be as free as possible, and seek diligently for every means of ensuring his liberty, peace of mind, and good humour. Teach him absolutely nothing by words that you can teach him by the things themselves; let him see for himself, hear, find out, fall, pick himself up, make mistakes; no word, in short, when action is possible. What he can do for himself, let him do; let him be always occupied, always active, and let the time you leave him to himself represent by far the greatest part of his childhood. You will then see that Nature teaches him better than men.

But when you see the necessity of accustoming him to obedience, prepare yourself with the greatest care for this duty, the most difficult of all in such an education as we are considering. Remember that if restraint robs you of your pupil's confidence, all your labour is lost. . . .

He must trust you. If he asks for something you do not think good, tell him what the consequences will be, and leave him his liberty. But you must take care that the consequences are such that he will not easily forget. Always show him the right way. Should he leave it and fall into the mire, go to his rescue, but do not shield him from the unpleasant results of having enjoyed complete liberty, and of not having listened to your warnings. In this way his trust in you will be so great that it will not be shaken even when you have to thwart him. He must obey the wise teacher or the father he has learned to respect; but only in cases of necessity must an order be given.[6]

The little experimental rabbit did not profit too well in some respects by being on the receiving end of so much attention. His education was "progressive," to be sure, but it left him somewhat maladjusted to the ordinary life of his time.

With the failure of Pestalozzi's agricultural undertaking, it became evident that he must turn his attention to something else. Only a thoroughly idealistic and impractical man would, however, have made Pestalozzi's selection of something to do. He had lost what little money he had ever had, plus what he could borrow, he had no lucrative work in sight, and he had never completed the training necessary to enter any profession. So he turned his farmhouse into a refuge for destitute children! It had occurred to him that the natural need for children to be active and the natural versatility of their inborn powers could, if properly guided, lead to self-support at an early age and also be the means for the development of their intellectual and moral natures. He conceived, therefore, a project for combining education, moral regeneration, and practical training in both agriculture and handicrafts. The

[5] *Ibid.*, pp. 41–42.
[6] *Ibid.*, pp. 46–48.

experiment began with several children, some of whom were vagrants picked up from the wayside. The children lived with Pestalozzi, who clothed, fed, and taught them. On pleasant days they worked beside him in the fields, and on rainy days they spun cotton indoors. Of formal schooling there was little, but Pestalozzi was always with them and always teaching them by means of conversations on all kinds of topics. At first there were about twenty children. Within a few months these waifs had changed from undernourished, disheartened, demoralized, bewildered little creatures into sturdy, competent, cheerful, devoted workers. Many more children were anxious to come to Pestalozzi, but the number he already had under his care was larger than he could support, since their labor by no means sufficed for proper cultivation of the land. Since many people had become interested in the undertaking, Pestalozzi published an appeal for funds and received a number of donations that permitted him to continue and enlarge the work.

For the next two years the experiment ran along successfully. Pestalozzi published an account of his work, in which he noted down a few items about each of the thirty-seven children at that time living with him. A few of his characterizations appear below:

1. Barbara Brunner, of Esch (Zurich), 17; admitted three years ago in a state of utter ignorance, but very intelligent. Now she spins, reads and writes fairly well, likes singing, is principally engaged in the kitchen. . . .

6. Henri Vogt, of Mandach, 11; has been here three years; can weave, is beginning to write, works hard at French and arithmetic, is exact and careful in all he does; but he seems cunning and deceitful, suspicious and greedy; has good health. . . .

10. Lisbeth Renold, of Brunegg, 10; when admitted a year and a half ago she was so weak from want of proper food that she could hardly walk; has made great progress; enjoys good health now, and is very intelligent, but there is little hope of her ever being strong enough to work in the fields. She spins well and diligently. . . .

12. Leonzi Hediger, of Endingen, near Baden (Aargau), 14; has been here three years. He is a healthy boy, strong and accustomed to working in the fields; the best weaver in the house; is beginning to write a little, and likes French. He is quick at everything, but ill-mannered and uncouth. . . .

16. Friedly Mynth, of Bussy, near Aubonne, lived afterwards at Worblauffen, 10; has been here six months; she is very weak, and incapable of real work, but clever in drawing, and has very artistic tastes. Inclined to fun; does nothing but draw. . . .

19. Babeli Baechli, 17; has been here three years; she is very inattentive and thoughtless, and only useful for running errands; of very little intelligence, but strong and healthy.

20. Jacob Baechli, her brother, 15; here three years; is also inattentive and thoughtless; spent his childhood in begging and idleness; weaves

fairly well, and is beginning to write, but has no taste for French; discontented and hard to satisfy. . . .

23. George Vogt, of Mandach, 11; here two years; a very promising boy; takes pains with everything; kind, intelligent, lively, healthy, and useful in the fields and in the house.

31. Suzanne Dattwyler, of Elfingen, 10; her unfortunate father is in prison; she came to me half dead from want and trouble, but her bodily strength is returning in a surprising manner. She spins well; is very quick, especially at singing.[7]

Soon after this report was published, Pestalozzi increased the number of children to about eighty, in the hope that the combined efforts of a larger community would result in self-support. In this assumption he was quite wrong. Moreover, by increasing the number of children, he automatically decreased the number of personal contacts between each of them and himself. His entire system of education and training rested upon his ability to make youngsters love him, but he could not reach the hearts of so many neglected children all at once. Progress became slower and regenerations fewer. Some of the children ran away and continued their vagrant lives, while others returned to degraded and vicious parents. Pestalozzi had no ability to organize a large institution or to control a large number of children. After five years of social experiment, in Pestalozzi's thirty-fifth year, the heroic struggle against poverty, degradation, and misery came to an end, and he was reduced to a state of poverty no better than that of the children whom he had hoped to benefit. He and his wife had both exhausted their strength in their work, and they were now bankrupt in health and purse. Some kind friends sent them a little help, and Pestalozzi's creditors, while taking over his farmlands, permitted him to remain in his house. The little family was, however, soon without food or fuel and was actually suffering from illness, cold, and want when their good deeds in the community began to pay unexpected dividends.

In the neighborhood there lived a woman named Elizabeth Naef, an uneducated servant, who had heard of Pestalozzi's work through her master. Upon learning of his distressed condition, this good woman hastened to offer him her services, even though he and his wife were strangers to her. At first Pestalozzi tried to refuse her aid, since he hesitated to involve an innocent bystander in his troubles, but she was quite determined to carry out her intention, even more so after she had seen the disorder and confusion to which Pestalozzi's awkward efforts at housekeeping during his wife's illness had reduced the premises. She restored cleanliness and order, and then proceeded to plant a small plot of land beside the house in so successful a manner that the family soon had food again. Elizabeth had no education, but she had a

[7] *Ibid.*, condensed from pp. 63–66.

heart of gold and a practical intelligence that supplemented the weaknesses of Pestalozzi's idealism. From that time on, the family rested upon Elizabeth's capable shoulders, and though often poor, was never again reduced to destitution.

3. Pestalozzi's Writings Elizabeth's labors maintained the small family, but she unconsciously did more than that. In the months that followed her arrival, Pestalozzi tried his hand at writing, but with only modest success. Finally, it occurred to him, as it has to most successful authors, to write of what he really knew instead of what he could only imagine or imitate from others. What Pestalozzi knew was the life of Swiss peasants, and of them he wrote, using Elizabeth as the model for his heroine in *Leonard and Gertrude.* He intended to preach a sermon on uplift by means of this story, but the reading public saw only the simple story of peasant life and loved it. For the first time in his life Pestalozzi had actually succeeded in something! Inspired by the reception of *Leonard and Gertrude,* he wrote three more volumes, continuing the story begun in the first; he also edited a newspaper, and wrote a number of short articles on a variety of subjects. Although he earned little, he managed to keep his family from actual want, and he slowly regained his self-respect, which had been badly dented by previous failures. His first period of literary effort was about seven years long. It served to restore Pestalozzi's health as well as his self-confidence, but it did not suffice to maintain him. He therefore returned to farming, but on a less ambitious scale than formerly. For ten years he wrote nothing more. These were years of hard work and grinding poverty, but through them Pestalozzi kept up his correspondence with many distinguished men in Switzerland and abroad. Two excerpts from letters of this period appear below:

> My agriculture swallows up all my time. I am longing for winter, with its leisure. My time passes like a shadow, and though my experience may be ripening, I am prematurely losing the power of expressing my ideas. I impatiently long for rest, and a cell where I should be free from cares. Here I am never free from weariness and disturbance. . . .
>
> Ah, my friend, I have lived many years in a state of indescribable misery, and my experience has taught me much; amongst other things, that Nature, herself, bids a man look to his own interests and those of his family. My own early education, unfortunately, did not in any way prepare me for this duty, and the harm is irreparable.[8]

After ten years of silence Pestalozzi published his *Fables,* short animal stories with a moral. These he presumably wrote in what little leisure time he had. Two of them will serve to show the style:

[8] *Ibid.,* condensed from pp. 101–102.

92. The Lime-Tree and the King.

A King, who was standing alone under a lime-tree, was struck by the beauty of its foliage, and exclaimed: "Would that my subjects held to me as these leaves hold to thy branches!"

The Tree answered him: "I am forever carrying the sap of my roots to each of my leaves."

116. The Feeling of Equality.

A shepherd, who fed his sheep rather poorly but all alike, found that, as a rule, they were satisfied. But one day he picked out a dozen for better treatment, and from that moment there was discontent in the flock, and many ewes died of vexation.[9]

At about the same time, he brought forth what he intended to be a systematic, philosophical exposition of his views about the development of human nature. Pestalozzi lacked the patience, coherence, and logical thought necessary for philosophical writing, and the resulting book—while perhaps the most important he ever wrote—is repetitious, obscure, and tedious. However, it contains a number of fine passages and presents many fundamentally sound ideas. This book over which Pestalozzi labored long and earnestly brought him no returns. As he himself said:

For three years I took immense pains with my *Inquiry,* my chief object being to co-ordinate my favourite ideas, and bring my natural sentiments into harmony with my view on civil law and morality. But my work was but another proof of my incapacity. . . .

And so I reaped no more than I had sown. My book had no more effect than my previous labours, nobody understood me, and there was not a man who did not give me to understand that he considered the whole work a jumble of nonsense.[10]

The book is not nonsense, and it would be of considerable value if some sympathetic person would rewrite it, extricating the author's sound ideas from his digressions.

*4. The Experiment at Stanz** Between Pestalozzi's failure in his first home for destitute children and his second attempt stretches a period of eighteen years during which he wrote, or devoted himself to agriculture, or both. In this long interval the French Revolution began, developed, went out of control, and subsided. Pestalozzi watched these changes with great interest. At first he hailed the Revolution as a movement to relieve the misery of the poor; but before long, its violence and terror revolted his gentle nature. He soon became worried that the principles of the Revolution would be accepted in the Swiss Republic* and would result in similar outbursts there. Actually, a Swiss Revolution* did take place, although it was not especially

[9] *Ibid.,* pp. 107–108.
[10] *Ibid.,* p. 111.

violent. In the course of the upheaval the government had to contend with the obdurate inhabitants of three small districts who were unwilling to give up their age-long habits of local government and to become a part of the new Swiss Union. The authorities therefore borrowed an army corps from the French and sent them into the districts. The soldiers expected no trouble and became greatly exasperated by the stout resistance put up by every man, woman, and child. They vented their annoyance by a terrible slaughter in the small village of Stanz. In the official report, one finds the following figures:

> Dead: 259 men, 102 women, 25 children.
>
> Buildings burnt: 340 dwelling-houses, 28 barns, 144 small outhouses.
>
> Approximate value of buildings and furniture destroyed: £85,000.
>
> Of the 350 people whose homes have been burnt, only 50 are in a position to rebuild with their own money; 97 others require more or less help; 203 have absolutely no means of building again.
>
> The most unfortunate, however, are the very large number who had no houses of their own, and have lost everything they possessed. Amongst these are 111 infirm old men; 169 orphans, not counting 77 who have been provided for by private charity in other cantons*; and lastly, 237 other children who, without being orphans, are still practically homeless on account of the utter destitution of their families.[11]

This catastrophe stirred Pestalozzi into a frenzied longing to go at once to Stanz and become a teacher and friend of the many orphaned children. He applied to the government for both permission and funds, and for the first time in his life he undertook a piece of work with adequate backing.

The Swiss Revolution forms a dividing line in Pestalozzi's life, cutting it into contrasting halves. In the first half, he worked alone, he lived in an obscure retreat, his undertakings failed, he was terribly poor, he was regarded as being an impractical visionary by the most generous estimate—and many people despised him as a fool. At the time he went to Stanz, he was fifty-two years old and considered himself an old man whose useful span of life was already over. In point of fact, his chief service to humanity had not yet begun. Financial support, disciples, success, and fame awaited him in the second half of his life.

After some weeks spent in making necessary repairs to buildings, Pestalozzi opened his orphanage with about fifty ragged waifs, who brought with them not only their diseases and vermin but also their bad habits and vices. To look after the cleanliness, health, and education of these children there were only Pestalozzi and one woman servant. He worked incessantly and was, at first, extraordinarily successful, as indicated by official reports:

> The poor-house is doing well. Pestalozzi works night and day. There are

[11] *Ibid.*, p. 132.

now seventy-two children in the establishment, though not more than fifty can stay all night, as there are not enough beds. It is astonishing to see how active this indefatigable man is, and how much progress his pupils have made in so short a time. They are now eager for instruction. In a few years the State will certainly be more than repaid for the sacrifices it is making for this useful institution.[12]

The enterprise did not, however, continue to prosper, for two reasons. One was the hostility of the citizens. Stanz was in a solidly, fanatically Catholic district, and the good burghers resented Pestalozzi, whom they regarded as no better than an arrant heretic. The good he might do for children's minds and bodies was, in their opinion, as nothing compared to the damage he could do their immortal souls. In the second place, Pestalozzi was not willing to proceed according to the accepted teaching methods of the day. At first he had neither books nor other school materials, he held no classes, he gave no formal instruction; he merely kept the horde of children with him, gave them his affection, talked with them, and waited for them to manifest their faculties and impulses. Whatever powers the children showed, he tried to guide, but he was careful to force nothing upon them from without. Inspectors from the government and other visitors saw only confusion, disorder, noise, and an apparent absence of any effort at instruction.

The scene shown in Figure 73 was probably typical. The children are certainly not regimented, but they are busy, and the disorder is mainly on the surface. Only one child in the room seems idle. Complaints were made to officials that Pestalozzi was not capable of so much as controlling the children, the complainants having entirely missed the point that he did not intend to control them but to lead them to control themselves. The critics admitted that children who came to the orphanage sick, dirty, and distrustful soon became healthy, active, eager, and joyful; but they lamented the absence of instruction, of discipline, and of training in manual skills. To be sure, Pestalozzi eventually settled upon a vague plan of having lessons from 6 A.M. to 8 A.M., vocational training from 8A.M. to 4 P.M., and lessons again from 4 P.M. to 8 P.M., but it is doubtful if he stuck to even this generalized routine.

Under more or less criticism, the institution was proceeding rather well when a fresh outburst of war again brought troops into the district and caused the orphanage to be closed because the building was needed as a military hospital. A few of the children remained, but most of them were sent away to private homes. By the time he had done what he could to protect his charges from the results of war, Pestalozzi was exhausted and had to go to a health resort. The orphanage lasted only five months, but it had given Pestalozzi a chance to work out some of the ideas he had had in mind for thirty years.

Pestalozzi hoped to return to Stanz as soon as the troops left, reassemble

[12] *Ibid.*, p. 137.

FIG. 73. Pestalozzi at Stanz. After a picture in H. Barnard, *Pestalozzi and His Educational System*. Syracuse: C. W. Bardeen, 1906.

the children, and start anew, but the authorities turned over what remained of the orphanage to a native of the district. Pestalozzi was therefore again deprived of a chance to try to raise the level of humanity by education.

5. Pestalozzi the Teacher Bitterly disappointed, he at last turned to schoolteaching as a method for gaining his ends, and offered his services without pay to the small village of Burgdorf. The local authorities were reluctant to let him try teaching, but eventually gave him the lowest class in a small school maintained for the children of noncitizens. Even this humble post he could not keep because his methods of instruction, sans books and especially sans catechism, aroused too much suspicion. Hurt by the lack of trust in him on the part of those whom he wished to serve, Pestalozzi managed to get himself transferred to one of the schools for citizens' children, where he was allowed to teach a preparatory class of pupils who were below the school entrance age of eight. With this group he was left in peace for eight whole months, at the end of which the annual school examinations were given by the school commissioners. The examiners sent Pestalozzi a letter of appreciation, parts of which seem worth quoting:

Citizen—

You have given us great pleasure in submitting to our examination the children you have been teaching for the past eight months, and we feel it to be our duty, not so much for your sake as for the sake of your work, to put before you in writing the opinions we have formed concerning them.

So far as we are able to judge, all that you yourself hoped from your method of teaching has been realized. You have shown what powers already exist in even the youngest child, in what way these powers are to be developed, and how each talent must be sought out and exercised in such a way as to bring it to maturity. The astonishing progress made by all your young pupils, in spite of their many differences in character and disposition, clearly shows that every child is good for something, when the master knows how to find out his talents, and cultivate them in a truly psychological manner. Your teaching has brought to light the foundations on which all instruction must be based, if it is ever to be of any real use; it also shows that from the tenderest age, and in a very short time, a child's mind can attain a wonderful breadth of development which must make its influence felt, not only during his few years of study, but throughout his whole life.

Whereas by the difficult method hitherto in vogue, children from five to eight years old learnt nothing but letters, spelling, and reading, your pupils have not only succeeded in these things to a degree which is altogether unprecedented, but the cleverest among them are also distinguished for their good writing, and their talent for drawing and arithmetic. In all of them you have aroused and cultivated such a taste for history, natural history, geography, measuring, etc., that their future masters will find their task incredibly lightened.[13]

[13] De Guimps, *op. cit.*, pp. 177–178.

Pestalozzi's many personal and professional friends were greatly cheered by his progress at Burgdorf, but they felt he was not in a position to disseminate his ideas sufficiently. They therefore founded a Society of the Friends of Education, specifically for the purpose of making these views more generally known. For this group Pestalozzi wrote out the first systematic statement of his "method." This summary began with the sentence, "I want to psychologize human education." He then went on to present his basic ideas: adaptation of learning to mental development, simplification of knowledge, drawing out of the individual, following of nature, and use of sense impressions. Pestalozzi's friends presently interested the national authorities in the foundation of an institute at Burgdorf, in which Pestalozzi could work out his ideas. Especially was it necessary for him to have some assistance. His untiring efforts to evolve new methods, to write new texts, and to teach intensively for several hours a day were ruining his health, and his inability to provide even the necessities of life for his family was ruining his courage. He revived somewhat under the promise of an institute, but there were many delays, only a little money actually reached him, and the next opening of school found him still struggling on alone. His discouragement is reflected in a letter he wrote at this time.

For thirty years my life has been a well-nigh hopeless struggle against the most frightful poverty. . . . For thirty years I have had to forgo many of the barest necessities of life, and have had to shun the society of my fellowmen from sheer lack of decent clothes. Many and many a time have I gone without a dinner, and eaten in bitterness a dry crust of bread on the road, at a time when even the poorest were seated around a table. All this I have suffered, and am still suffering to-day, and with no other object than the realization of my plans for helping the poor.[14]

Assistance was, however, at hand, and again from an unexpected source. In one of the small villages in another Swiss canton* there was a young man named Krüsi* who had opened a school in his room, although his own education was less than that of the elementary school graduate of today. The way in which he had been chosen schoolmaster for the village reflects well the ignorance of the general public.

The day of examination arrived. One candidate, older than myself, exhibited his learning. He was ordered to read the first chapter of the New Testament and write some lines, a task which took him half an hour to perform. I was called in. The examiner placed before me a genealogical table from Adam to Abraham, as a reading exercise. He then handed me an unmended quill pen, desiring me to write something. "But what shall I write?" said I. "Write the Lord's Prayer, or whatever you like," was the reply. As I

[14] *Ibid.*, p. 189.

had no knowledge, either of parts of speech or orthography, or of punctuation [he explained elsewhere that he scattered capital letters at equal distances thinking they were for ornament] the result of my scribbling may be imagined. This was all the examination, and after it we retired. When we were recalled, the chairman informed us that neither had been found overburdened with learning; that one of us was better in reading, the other in writing; but, that since my rival was already forty years old, while I was only eighteen, they thought I would sooner acquire the necessary knowledge. Moreover, since my dwelling (the town had no schoolhouse) was better adapted for a school than that of my competitor, they had appointed me schoolmaster. No doubt I felt happy at this unexpected decision, though I had no reason to be very proud of my salary, which was only one dollar per week, while my vanquished opponent was appointed policeman, with one and a half dollars per week.[15]

Perhaps because Krüsi had had so little formal schooling himself, he was not dominated by traditional methods of instruction, about which he knew practically nothing. He had been doing the best he could for a few years and had independently hit upon some of the same principles as Pestalozzi, when the French armies pillaged the district in which he worked. The children were gathered together and sent out of the canton, to be housed with loyal citizens in other parts of the country. One group of children came to Burgdorf with Krüsi, who was to remain there to teach them. Other refugees followed presently, until Krüsi had a good-sized school. He and Pestalozzi got along together from the first. They shared the same ideals and ideas, and presently they were living together and discussing education interminably; after a few weeks they combined their schools. Krüsi was still young, and he learned Pestalozzi's methods so thoroughly that they became a part of him; in addition, he was strong, practical, and well acquainted with the world. Since the combined schools needed more room than was available, Pestalozzi obtained gratis the use of the old castle of Burgdorf and its surrounding gardens. His practical young assistant augmented the staff of the school by recruiting two more teachers. These four men formed a highly unusual group. As described by one of them:

Our society thus consisted of four very different men, brought together by a strange combination of circumstances: the founder, whose chief literary reputation was that of a dreamer, incapable of practical life; and three young men, one a private tutor, whose youth had been much neglected, who had begun to study late, and whose pedagogical efforts had never produced the results that his character and talents seemed to promise; another a bookbinder, who devoted his leisure to singing and drawing; and the third a village schoolmaster, who carried out the duties of his office as best he could without having been in any way prepared for them. Those who looked on

[15] Krüsi, *op. cit.*, pp. 68–69.

this group of men, scarce one of them with a home of his own, naturally formed but a small opinion of their capabilities. And yet our work succeeded, and won the public confidence beyond the expectation of those who knew us, and even beyond our own.[16]

Added to these four a bit later was a retired soldier who taught gymnastics and a little elementary work. None of the men had had much formal education, but all were free of tradition, and all loved children. With this odd assortment of helpers Pestalozzi achieved his first general success.

The school at Burgdorf was soon running well and harmoniously. Visitors came to it from various parts of Europe and were impressed by the progress the children made and by the natural and relaxed emotional atmosphere. Because of his success and his growing reputation Pestalozzi was assured financial support by the government, but no sooner had the funds actually begun to arrive than the Swiss cantons started to fight among themselves, and the government was overthrown. The disturbance did not last long, because Napoleon—then First Consul of France—took a hand in it. As a means of restoring peace he asked that each canton send a representative to Paris for a conference. Pestalozzi was among those chosen, but he did not linger long in Paris. He was more eager to get a hearing on his educational methods than he was to discuss politics, but Napoleon refused to see him, saying he had no time to "consider questions of ABC." Pestalozzi therefore returned home. The reorganized government, set up as a result of the Paris conference, was willing to give him some support, but the officials wanted to use the castle of Burgdorf for other purposes, and Pestalozzi had to move his school. For two or three years he had a temporary school in a small town near by, but in 1805 he moved his institution to Yverdon, where he lodged it in an old castle, which seems to have been a pleasant and commodious place.

Pestalozzi remained at Yverdon for twenty years. For the first few years his school was a wonderful success; scholars came to it from all over Europe, and visitors appeared almost daily. The procedures used were so unlike those of the traditional school that they made an impression, favorable or otherwise, upon the visitors, many of whom remained for weeks to study the "method," which was later carried to France, Germany, Denmark, Holland, and the United States by enthusiastic admirers of Pestalozzi. In Germany the method was introduced widely, since it had the backing of the king of Prussia.

As pupils from many lands poured into the school and necessitated the hiring of more and more teachers, the institution became so large and so complex that its nature inevitably changed. Although Pestalozzi could weld twenty Swiss children and five Swiss teachers into a harmonious family, he could not

[16] *Ibid.*, p. 204.

do as much for two hundred children of various nationalities, forty teachers, and twenty assistants, some of whom had not been thoroughly grounded in his methodology. No one was more aware than Pestalozzi himself that his school was changing; indeed, when it was at the height of its popularity, he foresaw that it would not long endure. As the years rolled by, the teachers began to quarrel among themselves and to modify Pestalozzi's principles. Some of them left Yverdon to set up competing schools of their own. Gradually the prestige of the institution diminished, its funds gave out, and it closed. Pestalozzi stuck to it till the end, working day and night to save it, but characteristically putting his faith in the wrong man and backing the wrong

FIG. 74. The Castle at Yverdon. From H. Krüsi, *Pestalozzi: His Life and Work,* Van Antwerp, Bragg, and Company, 1875, 248 pp., p. 46.

policies. When the school finally closed, Pestalozzi was eighty years old.

With the failure of his last hopes, Pestalozzi retired to his farm. He did not, however, escape from the domination of a former teacher, a man named Schmidt, who had helped ruin the school at Yverdon and had antagonized many of Pestalozzi's friends. The old man continued to publish articles justifying Schmidt and blaming himself for the school's failure. In his effort to protect Schmidt from condemnation he was unfair to some of his former teachers, who had left him largely because of Schmidt.

One of Pestalozzi's articles was answered by an outsider to the whole group, a man with a poison pen and little common decency, who attacked the old man vehemently and insultingly. The publication was a terrible blow to Pestalozzi. Against his doctor's advice, he insisted upon trying to answer it. In his last notes were the following paragraphs:

Fig. 75. Pestalozzi Monument at Yverdon, by Alfred Lanz.

My sufferings are inexpressible; no man could understand the sorrow of my soul. People despise me as a feeble, infirm, old man; they no longer think me good for anything; I do but excite their derision. It is not, however, for myself that I am troubled, but for my idea, which shares my fate. My most sacred possession, the belief that has inspired the whole of my long and painful life, is scornfully trodden under foot. To die is nothing; I even welcome death, for I am weary, and would fain be at rest; but to have lived a life of sacrifice and to have failed, to see my work destroyed and go down with it to the grave, this is frightful, more frightful than I can express. Would that I could weep, but my tears refuse to flow.

And you, my poor ones, the oppressed, despised and rejected of this world; you too, alas! will be forsaken and ridiculed, even as I am. The rich, in their abundance, care nothing for you; they may, indeed, cast you a morsel of bread, but nothing more, since they too are poor, having nothing but their gold. As for inviting you to the spiritual banquet, and making men of you, the world has not yet thought of it, nor will it for a long time. But God who is in heaven, God who cares even for His sparrows, God will not forget you, but will comfort you, even as He will comfort and not forget me.[17]

A few days after writing these words Pestalozzi became much weaker and died, in the year 1827, at the age of eighty-one. He was buried in a simple country churchyard, as he had requested, under a "rough, unhewn stone, such as I myself have always been." However, on the hundredth anniversary of his birth, his remains were moved to a more suitable place. The monument shown in Figure 75 was erected and the memorial below engraved upon a bust of Pestalozzi, which stands in a niche near the tomb:

Here Rests

HENRY PESTALOZZI

Born in Zurich, the 12th of January, 1746
Died at Brugg, the 17th of February, 1827

Saviour of the poor at Neuhof and Stanz, father of orphans at Burgdorf and München-buchsee,* founder of the popular school at Yverdon. The educator of humanity; man, Christian, and citizen. All for others, nothing for himself. Peace to his ashes.

TO OUR FATHER PESTALOZZI

Grateful Aargau [18]

6. *Pestalozzi's Work with Preschool Children* About a hundred years before Pestalozzi's birth, Comenius was engaged in writing picture books for

[17] De Guimps, *op. cit.*, p. 364.
[18] *Ibid.*, p. 367. "Aargau" is the name of the district. The Aar is a river; "Gau" is a district. The same word appears in the term "Gauleiter," or district leader.

school children. In the course of his work, it occurred to him that the task of educating a child inevitably began with the mother, who could use the preschool years to better purpose than was often the case, so that children might arrive at school age already in possession of simple facts and skills. The time thus saved would permit teachers to give a more advanced education during the school years than was possible when the children had had no training before entrance in the lowest class. Comenius therefore wrote out a number of suggestions for use by mothers, but his work was only a tentative beginning and was lost in the profusion of his writings and in the disrepute into which he fell in his later years. Pestalozzi developed the same idea, whether independently or as a result of influence by Comenius cannot be said with certainty. In any case, he wrote a sort of manual for mothers, with the title, *How Gertrude Teaches Her Children.*[19]

In this book he set forth a number of exercises, some of which are certainly too hard for preschool children. The book was widely read and had some influence upon many people, but the greatest effect of Pestalozzi's work in this field was upon an idealistic young man by the name of Friedrich Froebel, who took up the work and, nearly a half century later, developed it further. Of him, more anon.

7. *Pestalozzi's Appearance and Personality* There is no question that the valuable work done by Pestalozzi was constantly hindered and handicapped by his appearance and behavior. Nor is it surprising that many people thought him quite mad. A few anecdotes about him and descriptions of him bring out his grotesqueness and at the same time his great goodness of heart.

A. What Pestalozzi said of himself:

I hope to remain innocent to the grave; it is so pleasant to be still a child, to believe, to trust, to love, to be sorry for your mistakes and folly, to be better and simpler than knaves and rogues, and at last, by their very wickedness, wiser. It is pleasant to think nothing but good of men, in spite of all you see and hear, to still believe in the human heart, even though you may be deceived every day, and to forgive the wise as well as the foolish of this world, when each, in his own way, would lead you astray.[20]

B. What his pupils and colleagues said of him:

At that time the Burgdorf authorities would not have dared to entrust Pestalozzi with a primary school; this man, since so celebrated, would have had no chance whatever against even the most ordinary candidates. He had everything against him; thick, indistinct speech, bad writing, ignorance of drawing, scorn of grammatical learning. He had studied various branches of natural history, but without any particular attention either to classification or terminology. He was conversant with the ordinary numerical opera-

[19] J. H. Pestalozzi, *How Gertrude Teaches Her Children* (translated by L. E. Holland and F. C. Swan) Bardeen's, Inc., 1874, 256 pp.

[20] De Guimps, *op. cit.*, p. 94.

tions, but he would have had difficulty to get through a really long sum in multiplication or division, and had probably never tried to work out a problem in geometry. For years this dreamer had read no books. . . .

But instead of the usual knowledge that any young man of ordinary talent can acquire in two years, he understood thoroughly what most masters were entirely ignorant of—the mind of man and the laws of its development, human affections, and the art of arousing and ennobling them. He seemed to have almost an intuitive insight into the development of human nature, which indeed he was never tired of contemplating.[21]

Imagine, my children, a very ugly man, with rough, bristling hair, his face scarred with smallpox and covered with freckles, a pointed, untidy beard, no necktie, ill-fitting trousers, stockings down, and enormous shoes; add to this a breathless, shuffling gait, eyes either large and flashing, or half-closed as though turned within, features expressing either a profound sadness or the most peaceful happiness, speech now slow and musical, now thundering and hurried, and you will have some idea of the man we called "Father Pestalozzi."

Such as I have described him to you, we loved him; yes, we all loved him, for he loved us all; we loved him so much that when we lost sight of him for a time we felt sad and lonely and when he came back to us again we could not turn our eyes away from him.[22]

C. What visitors said of him:

I have seen more than the paradise of Switzerland, for I have seen Pestalozzi, and recognized how great his heart is, and how great his genius; never have I been so filled with a sense of the sacredness of my vocation, and the dignity of human nature, as in the days that I spent with this noble man. I cannot think without emotion of this little company of brave men, struggling with the present that the future may be better, and finding alike their joy and their reward in the hope they have of raising children to the true dignity of humanity. I have watched the growth of this precious plant, I have even drunk of the waters and breathed the air that gives it life. I have learned to understand this "method," which, based upon the nature of the child, develops so naturally and so freely.[23]

I had not seen him for thirteen years, and found him looking older certainly, but on the whole very little changed. He was still active and strong, simple and open; his face still wore the same kindly, plaintive expression; his zeal for human happiness, and especially for the education of poor and little children, was as keen as thirteen years ago. . . . The vivacity of his speech and the vigour of all his movements inspired me with the hope that the term of his earthly existence was still far off. My heart was full when I took leave of the kind old man. I shall never forget the time that it was my good fortune to spend with him.[24]

[21] *Ibid.*, p. 174.
[22] *Ibid.*, p. 253.
[23] *Ibid.*, p. 263.
[24] *Ibid.*, p. 263.

D. A few typical anecdotes about him:

There was a famous criminal called Bernhard, big and strong as a giant, who had several times escaped from prison, and each time had been brought back to the Castle and confined in a still deeper dungeon. On these occasions Pestalozzi would slip a piece of money into his hands, saying: "If you had received a good education, and learned to use your powers to good ends, you would now be a useful member of society, and instead of being obliged to put you in a hole and chain you up like a dog, people would honour and respect you."

One day, when [Pestalozzi] was confined to his bed by a sharp attack of rheumatism, the French ambassador, Reinhardt, came to the Castle to visit the institute. In spite of doctor and friends, Pestalozzi insisted on getting up. As he could scarcely stand, and could only be dressed with extreme difficulty, everybody implored him to go to bed again, pointing out how little fit he was to do what he wanted; but he turned a deaf ear to all their entreaties, and, supported by friendly arms, painfully dragged himself out of his room. As soon as he saw the ambassador, however, he shook himself free, and began eagerly to expound his doctrine. The more he talked, the more he seemed to regain strength and brightness, and when at last he ceased, his rheumatism had disappeared.

At the time of which we are speaking, Fellenberg* and Pestalozzi had been friends for twenty years . . . . Now it happened one day that some of Fellenberg's workmen brought him a poorly dressed man, whom they had found, they said, in the fields, half dead with hunger and fatigue. This man turned out to be no other than Pestalozzi, who, carried away by his passion for minerals, had wandered such a long distance filling his handkerchief and pockets with them, that he had lost his way, and, at last, fallen down dead-tired beside a ditch. It was about the same time, too, that Pestalozzi, dragging wearily along one evening near the gates of Soleure, with his handkerchief full of stones, was arrested by the police as a beggar and suspicious character, and taken before the judge. The judge was out, and the old man had to wait a long time in the antechamber with his custodian. Great was the latter's astonishment when the judge, on his return, recognized Pestalozzi, and, after greeting him warmly, invited him to supper.[25]

There are several portraits of Pestalozzi, among them the picture shown in Figure 76. Care, work, and anxiety had worn deep furrows in his face, but his gentleness and lovableness show in his really beautiful eyes.

Such, then, was Pestalozzi, a man in whom the sublime merged with the grotesque. Pupils, friends, and visitors agreed on two essential characteristics: he had many ideas—even though his expression of them was sometimes incoherent—and he loved humanity with an utterly selfless devotion.

The greatest immediate results from Pestalozzi's work were to be found in Germany, partly because both Herbart and Froebel—two subsequent leaders

[25] *Ibid.,* condensed from pp. 222–223.

of educational thought—had direct personal contact with him and partly because the German officials, especially those from Prussia, made definite efforts to learn of his methods and to apply them to their own schools. Thus, during the Napoleonic era, after Germany had suffered the appalling defeat at Jena and throughout the country a sullen feeling of hopelessness had arisen, the great philosopher Fichte pointed out that the type of education developed

FIG. 76. Johann Heinrich Pestalozzi. From a painting by F. G. A. Schöner, 1811, now in the Pestalozzianum in Zürich.

by Pestalozzi would regenerate the nation in twenty-five years if the children just entering school could have the advantage of it. Young teachers were therefore sent from Germany in numbers to Yverdon to study Pestalozzi's methods and to transplant them to Germany, where they took deep root.

What Pestalozzi contributed to education throughout the world was a basic idea that education consists of guiding children into a natural and orderly unfolding of their innate capacities, plus several brief experiments to show how his idea of a "child-centered" school would work. The torch that eventually fell altogether from his feeble hand was caught by a dozen other men with less genius but more sense of the practical and was by them carried throughout Europe and the United States. The modern school is a Pestalozzian school because its work centers upon the children, is adapted to them, and encourages them to grow. If the ghost of Henry Pestalozzi still roams the earth, nothing could more delight it than the busy and orderly disorder of a truly progressive elementary school.

B. PESTALOZZI'S SCHOOLS AT BURGDORF AND YVERDON

Pestalozzi's educational work started from his desire to rescue the common people from their poverty and degradation. He had seen the failure of the most generous charity to accomplish this end, because it did not teach people to help themselves; it merely relieved the physical conditions for a while without effecting changes in the character of those who received alms. Indeed, it sometimes degraded the recipient still further. Nor was Pestalozzi any better pleased with current education than he was with charity as a means of improving the human lot. The schools of his day put before a child a logical summary of the thoughts of others, asked him to memorize this knowledge, and then expected him to act in accordance with it. The object of schooling was assumed to be the training of children in their intellectual heritage, without much thought as to their development during the process. Education was imposed upon the learner from without, and he was supposed to fit himself to the needs of the situation.

1. Basic Principles of Pestalozzi's Method Pestalozzi believed that in every child there lay dormant a wealth of abilities, feelings, tastes, and sentiments, waiting to be evoked by the proper environment. The whole problem of education must therefore be seen from the developing mind of the child, not from the already developed mind of the educated adult. Education was to be from within, not from without; and the child, not the subject matter, should be the center of the educational system. Instead of stifling a child's individuality under a mass of borrowed ideas, a teacher should encourage every pupil to develop himself in whatever way was most suited to his talents. Growth was more important than achievement, and reaching an incorrect conclusion by one's own mental effort was preferable to memorizing the right answer given in a book. The objective of education was thus the harmonious development of all the powers—moral, intellectual, and physical—of each individual child. In short, Pestalozzi was practically the progressive movement of today, all by himself.

Because he thought of children as growing organisms, he conceived of education as a means for guiding growth, by following the laws of nature and working with them. In its practical applications, this principle meant the use of materials appropriate to each successive stage of development and the arrangement of all school activities to conform with the basic laws of growth. Pestalozzi believed that all the knowledge, useful powers, and noble sentiments shown by mankind are but extensions and developments of the traits and abilities implanted by nature in every newborn child. Education should supply merely guidance and stimulation, and should never interfere with the natural and orderly development from within. Pestalozzi expressed these basic ideas in several places; a few of his best formulations are presented below.

1. All the pure and beneficent powers of humanity are neither the products of art nor the results of chance. They are really a natural possession of every man. Their development is a universal human need.

2. The exercise of a man's faculties and talents, to be profitable, must follow the course laid down by Nature for the education of humanity.

3. Each branch of instruction must start from a point which is within reach of the child's earliest powers. From this point he must be led forward by a chain of ideas so carefully graduated, that he is able to reach each successive link by his own strength.

4. In each branch the child must be exercised in the simplest elements till he is entirely master of them, and it must be the same for every step that adds anything new to what is already known. Wherever this principle is not faithfully observed, there can be no true intellectual culture, but merely a confused knowledge, which must remain barren.

5. The schools hastily substitute an artificial method of words for the truer method of Nature, which knows no hurry and is content to wait. In this way a specious form of development is produced, hiding the want of real inward strength, but satisfying times like our own.[26]

Pestalozzi's "method," which he never succeeded in expounding clearly or succinctly in any one place, seems to have had a number of important characteristics, most of which are still regarded as basic to good teaching. His contributions to school procedures were of two types, one concerning methodology and the other concerning the attitudes and spirit of the schoolroom. The main elements of both types are listed below.

Method	*Spirit*
1. Use of sense perception as the basis of instruction.	1. Effort to develop children along all lines.
2. Constant connecting of words and objects.	2. Respect for each child's individuality.

[26] *Ibid.*, condensed from pp. 122–123 and 171–172.

3. Use of exercises from simple to complex, from the child's point of view.	3. Increase of each child's natural powers.
4. Insistence upon complete mastery.	4. Use of discipline based upon love.
5. Development of the object lesson.	5. Study of the child mind.

This twofold attack upon the traditional schoolroom was important not only in itself but in its effects upon two outstanding followers, Herbart and Froebel. The former, a highly intellectual man, emphasized and systematized the methodological elements in the program, while Froebel, an extremely emotional person, followed the spirit of Pestalozzi and his interest in the nature of children.

Pestalozzi's method rested, then, upon belief in the innate abilities of each child, a conviction that education should merely guide normal growth, a dependence upon sense impression for all learning, and a deep love for all the children of all the people.

2. *Materials of Instruction* For carrying out his method Pestalozzi devised various materials, some good and some only mediocre. He made great use of the object lesson, which was designed to teach children to observe and to express their observations in correct language. This basic method was simply to put an object before the children and then let them tell what they saw.

Like Comenius, Pestalozzi was a great believer in the value of sense impressions for learning. He contended that there was too much teaching of words without an adequate basis in experience; hence his emphasis upon the object lesson as the main means of instruction. The pupils began with familiar objects and words and gradually deduced the general principles, instead of learning the rules first and then perhaps applying them and perhaps not. In one place Pestalozzi wrote: "Man's knowledge must be founded on sense impression. Without this basis, it is but empty verbiage, fraught with more danger even than ignorance for the future happiness of men."[27]

Pestalozzi put much faith in graphic exercises which consisted of the most elementary type of drawing, mostly of lines, angles, and forms. As the children talked their way through an object lesson they kept their slates on their knees and drew constantly. This practice supposedly taught them the eye-hand control that would be needed later on in learning to write. Incidentally, it doubtless simplified the disciplinary problem, since the pupils could always draw in case the lesson bored them.

[27] *Ibid.*, p. 171.

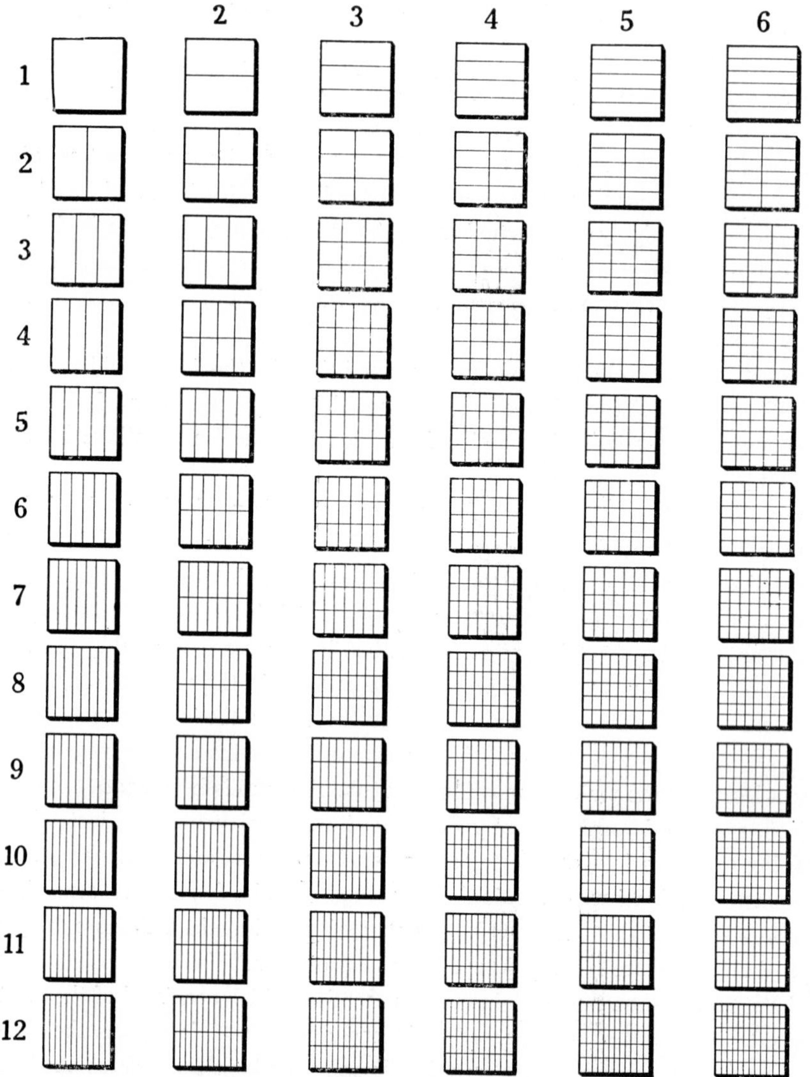

FIG. 77. Part of a Chart for Teaching Fractions. From H. Pestalozzi, *How Gertrude Teaches Her Children,* p. 239.

For instruction in arithmetic Pestalozzi worked out tables of units and tables of fractions to help the children in visualizing the relationships between numbers. A sample of one such diagrammatic table is reproduced in Figure 77. This table can be used in a number of ways, for either whole numbers or fractions. First, the children can learn to count small numbers in a series and larger numbers up to 50. Later, they can learn multiplication of the numbers from 1 x 1 to 12 x 6; thus the solution to the problem 2 x 4 is to be found by following the column headed "2" until it intersects with row "4," and then counting the number of spaces. A pupil could thus discover for himself the answer to the simple combinations or could check an answer of which he was not sure. Moreover, any column or row yields the multiples of a single number; thus either the third column from the left or the third row gives the multiples of 3. The children can see that the divisions in any column or row are produced by superimposing each horizontal division upon each vertical one. Division may also be taught from this table. The child counts the total number of small divisions within a square and divides it by the number of vertical spaces; he checks his answer by counting the horizontal ones. The table can be used also to teach common fractions. The relative size of the fractions 1/2, 1/3, 1/4, 3/4, 1/5, 2/5, 1/6, 5/6, etc., is clearly represented and also the interrelations; thus, three sixths occupy the same space as two fourths or one half and are therefore equal to each of the others; similarly, one third occupies the same space as two sixths. It is clear also that fifths will not combine directly with halves or thirds with fourths, for instance; the need for tenths or twelfths as common denominators is thus demonstrated graphically. Multiplication of 1/2, 1/3, 1/4, 1/5, or 1/6 by each other can also be shown; for example, if the pupil wants the answer to 1/2 times 1/6, he follows the column under 6 and the row across from 2 to their point of intersection, where he finds a square with twelve divisions; his answer is therefore 1/12. He can also see that 1/12 divided by 1/2 will be 1/6 even before he discovers the method of computation. Pestalozzi constantly used such visual aids in the teaching of arithmetic.

The lowest classes in the school worked chiefly with object lessons and graphic exercises. To obtain a basis for future reading they played with movable letter blocks, learning the letters and later on arranging the blocks into words. Elementary work with small numbers was also included. The pupils learned the number names by counting objects and gradually worked their way into addition and the other operations by counting objects in groups. They also sang simple melodies. When this fundamental work was completed, the children could speak with fair correctness, they had learned much about number and form, they knew their letters thoroughly, they could sing, and they had had a wealth of experience.

In the upper classes the pupils went on with arithmetic and added plane geometry, which grew out of the graphic lessons. They learned reading and writing together, but it does not seem that either field was especially stressed. Geography and natural history were, however, important subjects, both of which were taught by direct observation. The children worked out the geography of their own district, to start with, by the simple method of tramping through it, observing it, measuring it, and making their own maps. For their work in natural history they collected minerals, plants, and animals. Naturally, the teachers added much to what the pupils could discover for themselves, but the discussions were always based upon the children's actual experiences.

Pestalozzi was especially interested in both singing and gymnastics, because the children participated in them willingly and because the effect upon their growth was beneficial. The emphasis upon games as a means of education was similar to the work of the Philanthropinum. Pestalozzi never tired of watching children express their natural drives through the medium of play.

Pestalozzi wrote a number of textbooks for use in his schools, but he was not especially successful in his formulations. Where Comenius was at his best, Pestalozzi was at his worst. His books were rather uninteresting, crammed with details and numerous digressions, and generally unsuited to either the children or the methodology. Pestalozzi had a quick intuition which prevented him from trying to teach children what they could not learn, as long as he was face to face with them, but in the quiet of his study, he lost his touch; moreover, he had neither the system nor the patience to write a good textbook.

3. Descriptions of Pestalozzi's Schools Some of the descriptions to be quoted presently refer to the school at Burgdorf and some to the school at Yverdon during its early years. The general life and atmosphere of both schools were much the same, although Burgdorf was smaller, more intimate, and less influenced by outsiders. Yverdon was managed with more system, partly because the methods were in a less experimental stage and partly because the many teachers there contributed the elements of order that Pestalozzi lacked. In all, six descriptions, some by visitors and some by former students will be presented.

The thirty or forty children of both sexes of Pestalozzi's old school came from the town to the Castle to take part in the singing lessons. Buss made his pupils sing as they walked up and down the big corridors of the castle, two and two, and holding each other's hands. That was our greatest pleasure; but our joy reached its height when our gymnastic master Naef, who was a most original man, joined us. He was an old soldier, who had seen service in nearly every part of the world. He looked a rough, bearded, surly giant enough, but as a matter of fact he was kindness itself. When he marched with a military air at the head of some sixty or eighty children, loudly singing a Swiss song as he went, nobody could help following him.

Indeed, singing was one of our chief sources of pleasure in the institute. We sang everywhere—out of doors, on our walks, and, in the evenings, in the court of the Castle; and this singing together contributed in no small measure to the harmony and good feeling which prevailed amongst us. I must add that in spite of his rough exterior, Naef was the chief favorite with the children, for the simple reason that, as he was never so happy as in their society, he was always with them. He used to play, drill, walk, bathe, climb, throw stones with them, just like a big child, and in this way gained almost unlimited authority over them. And yet he had nothing of the pedagogue about him but the heart . . . .

I must further say that in the first years of the Burgdorf institute, nothing like a systematic plan of lessons was followed, and that the whole life of the place was so simple and home-like, that in the half-hour's recreation which followed breakfast, Pestalozzi would often become so interested in the spirited games of the children in the playground as to allow them to go undisturbed till ten o'clock. And on summer evenings, after bathing in the Emme, instead of beginning work again, we often stayed out till eight or nine o'clock looking for plants and minerals.[28]

If the Burgdorf school thus presented the picture of a great family, it was only because Pestalozzi was a father for everybody, and lived but for others. His activity and love inspired the whole household. His assistants, who had a profound affection and veneration for him, were Krüsi for language and arithmetic, Tobler for geography and history, Buss for geometry, drawing, and singing, and Naef for gymnastics and one or two elementary subjects.

Even the financial difficulty which weighed upon the establishment exercised a wholesome moral influence. The masters had refused good offers to remain with Pestalozzi, and went so far as to give up a portion of their salary, small as it was, to make up for his want of means. The pupils, on their side, contented themselves with little, and did all they could to keep down the expenses. It was indeed a practical school of sacrifice and renunciation.

The children's trust in their masters, their love and gratitude for them, took the place of rules and discipline; there were no rewards, and, except in very exceptional cases, no punishments; obedience was perfect because it was spontaneous. The children were lively and happy, they liked their lessons almost as well as their games, and it was not rare to see some of them stop in the middle of their play to go and work together before a blackboard or a map.[29]

My fellow-citizens of Yverdon, my native town, had generously placed at [Pestalozzi's] disposal the old Castle. It was built in the shape of a huge

[28] *Ibid.*, pp. 209–210.
[29] *Ibid.*, pp. 210–211.

square, and its great rooms and courts were admirably adapted for the games as well as the studies of a large school. Within its walls were assembled from a hundred and fifty to two hundred children of all nations, who divided their time between lessons and happy play. It often happened that a game of prisoner's base, begun in the Castle court, would be finished in the grass near the lake. In winter we used to make a mighty snow-fortress, which was attacked and defended with equal heroism. Sickness was hardly known among us. . . .

Our masters are for the most part young men, and nearly all children of the revolutionary period, who had grown up round Pestalozzi, their father and ours. They were, indeed, a few educated men and scholars who had come to share his task; but, taken altogether, there was not much learning. I myself have heard Pestalozzi boast, when an old man, of not having read anything for forty years. Nor did our masters, his first pupils, read much more than Pestalozzi himself. Their teaching was addressed to the understanding rather than the memory, and had for its aim the harmonious cultivation of the germs implanted in us by Providence. . . .

The first elements of geography were taught us from the land itself. We were first taken to a narrow valley not far from Yverdon, where the river Buron runs. After taking a general view of the valley, we were made to examine the details, until we had obtained an exact and complete idea of it. We were then told to take some of the clay which lay in beds on one side of the valley, and fill the baskets which we had brought for the purpose. On our return to the Castle, we took our places at the long tables, and reproduced in relief the valley we had just studied, each one doing the part which had been allotted to him. During the next days we took more walks and made more explorations each day on higher ground and each time with a further extension of our work. Only when our relief was finished were we shown the map, which by this means we did not see till we were in a position to understand it.

We had to discover the truths of geometry for ourselves. After being once put in the way of it, the end to be reached was pointed out to us, and we were left to work alone. It was the same with arithmetic, which we did aloud, without paper. Some of us became wonderfully quick at this, and as charlatanism penetrates everywhere, these only were brought before the numerous strangers that the name of Pestalozzi daily attracted to Yverdon. We were told over and over again that a great work was going on in our midst, that the eyes of the world were upon us, and we readily believed it.

The Pestalozzian Method, as it was somewhat ostentatiously called, was, it is true, an enigma, not only to us but to our teachers, who, like the disciples of Socrates, each interpreted the master's doctrine in his own way. But we were still far from the time when these divergences resulted in discord, and when the chief masters, after each claiming to be the only one who had understood Pestalozzi, ended by declaring that Pestalozzi had not understood himself.[30]

[30] *Ibid.*, condensed from pp. 254–256.

When the weather was favourable, some hours in the afternoon were given every week to military exercises. The pupils formed a little regiment of their own, for which neither flag, drums, band, nor armour was wanting; they soon learned to go through the most complicated manoeuvres with wonderful precision. When there was any shooting to be done, the noncommissioned officers had to make the cartridges under the direction of an instructing officer. From time to time they had a sham-fight in some suitable spot a few miles from the town. They used then to start very early in the morning with a waggon for the provisions and ammunition. Many parents and sightseers often joined the party, so that it was a great day for the pupils. Sometimes there was target-shooting, the prize for which was a ewe with its lamb, and the use of a small shed in the garden. . . .

The end of the year was devoted to making New Year albums to send the parents, containing drawings, maps, mathematical problems, fragments of history, descriptions of natural objects, and literary compositions. On New Year's day there was a religious service, with a discourse by Pestalozzi; a distribution of presents from the parents; a grand dinner; and in the evening, a torch-light procession through the town (each pupil made his own torch), followed by a ball, to which the girls of the neighboring institute were invited, together with a certain number of guests from the town. For the next few days very lttle work was done, everybody being occupied in preparing for Pestalozzi's birthday, the 12th of January. The pupils of each class decorated their room, transforming it into a woodland scene, with cottage, chapel, ruins, and sometimes a fountain, which was so arranged as to play on Pestalozzi's entrance. Fir-branches, ivy, and moss were fetched in large quantities from the neighboring forests, and transparencies, with emblems and inscriptions, were secretly prepared; for the decoration of each room was to be a surprise, not only to Pestalozzi, but to all the other pupils. Songs were also learnt in Pestalozzi's honour. . . . Often, too, on that day, the pupils gave a dramatic performance, the subject of which was generally chosen from among the great episodes of Swiss history in the middle ages. On these occasions the actors made their own dresses and armour from cardboard and coloured paper.[31]

At seven o'clock, after the first lesson, the pupils washed in the courtyard. The water, pumped from the well, ran through a long pipe with holes on both sides, from which each child received a pure, fresh stream, jugs and basins being unknown. After this came breakfast consisting of soup. Lessons began again at eight. At ten came an interval, when any one who was hungry could get dried fruit and bread from the housekeeper. At mid-day there was an hour's recreation for bathing or prisoner's base on the grass behind the lake. At one o'clock dinner of soup, meat, and vegetables. Lessons again from half-past one till half-past four. Then the afternoon meal, either of cheese and fruit or bread and butter. Each could take his share away with him and eat it where he liked during the play-hour, which lasted till six o'clock, and which was passed, when the weather was fine, either behind the lake or

[31] *Ibid.*, condensed from pp. 271–27[illegible]

in the large garden adjoining the Castle, where every child had his own little plot. From six to eight, more lessons; and then supper, which was the same as dinner.[32]

Pestalozzi took a singular pleasure in watching the games of his pupils, which he considered of very great importance, his idea being that children when not at work ought to enjoy themselves, and that a state of total inactivity is bad, both physically and morally. If he noticed a child taking no part in the games during playtime, he could seldom rest till he had tried to find him some other amusement.

In this connection an incident comes back to my memory which did not strike me particularly at the time, but which I now feel to have been exceedingly characteristic. One day, when a fire of sticks had been lighted in the garden, the elder pupils amused themselves by leaping over the flames through the smoke, Pestalozzi eagerly encouraging them. When the flames had died down, and little but hot embers and smoke remained, the little ones leaped in their turn. But the scene had other witnesses, for the little girls of the Niederer institute, the garden of which joined that of the Castle, were looking through the palings at the beautiful flames and happy leapers. No sooner did Pestalozzi see them than he went and fetched them, and they too were soon jumping over the remains of the fire. Never was delight so cheaply purchased! [33]

These descriptions reveal the fine spirit of the schools, but they contain little in regard to academic achievements. One more series of excerpts covers this point. These remarks were written by four unprejudiced observers.

I was amazed when I saw these children treating the most complicated calculations of fractions as the simplest thing in the world. Problems which I myself could not solve without careful work on paper, they did easily in their heads, giving the correct answer in a few moments, and explaining the process with ease and readiness. They seemed to have no idea that they were doing anything extraordinary.

At the Burgdorf institute children of from six to eight drew difficult geometrical figures without rule or compass so correctly that no one would believe it who had not seen it.

I have seen a child of ten, who had only been a pupil of Pestalozzi's for ten months, reduce a map of Scandinavia to a smaller scale in an hour with such exactness as to defy the most searching examination.[34]

Children of five and six years joyfully spent hours together at exercises in number and form, and even still younger children learned something from merely being present at the lessons. Some were so zealous that they needed restraining rather than encouraging. The best scholars were soon set to teach

[32] *Ibid.*, p. 269.
[33] *Ibid.*, p. 391.
[34] *Ibid.*, p. 215.

others, which they did well and gladly. Winter and summer, day and night, they would run off to Grandson, a village in the neighborhood of Yverdon, to give lessons to people older than themselves, often sitting up a part of the night. At Yverdon, their teaching was preferred to that of some of the masters.[35]

As is clear from the above quotations, Pestalozzi was the forerunner of modern progressive education. His schools were based upon child nature and the spontaneous activity of children.

READING REFERENCES

A. General Histories of the Period

Ergang, *Europe from the Renaissance to Waterloo,* chaps. 23–25.
Garrett, *European History, 1500–1815,* chaps. 32–39.
Grant and Temperly, *Europe in the Nineteenth and Twentieth Centuries,* chaps. 2, 3.
Hayes, *Political and Cultural History of Modern Europe,* Vol. I, chap. 12.
Riker, *A Short History of Modern Europe,* chaps. 8, 9.
Robinson, *Introduction to the History of Western Europe,* chaps. 34–36.
Schevill, *A History of Europe from the Reformation to the Present Day,* chap. 20.
Seignobos, *The Rise of European Civilization,* chap. 16.
Stearns, *Pageant of History,* part II, chap. 22.
Turner, *Europe since 1789,* chap. 2.

B. Other Texts in the History of Education

Cole, *History of Educational Thought,* pp. 253–257.
Cubberley, *History of Education,* pp. 539–549.
Eby and Arrowood, *The Development of Modern Education,* chap. 17.
Graves, *A Student's History of Education,* chap. 14.
Marique, *History of Christian Education,* III, 107–116.
McCormick, *History of Education,* pp. 326–337.
Monroe, *A Textbook in the History of Education,* pp. 597–622.
Ulich, *History of Educational Thought,* pp. 258–270.

C. Secondary Sources

Compayré, *Pestalozzi and Elementary Education,* chaps. 3–8.
De Guimps, *Pestalozzi: His Life and Work,* any 3 chapters selected from chaps. 3–5, 9, 11–13.
Graves, *Great Educators of Three Centuries,* chap. 9.
Green, J. A., *The Educational Ideas of Pestalozzi,* W. B. Clive, Ltd., 1911 (3d ed., 22 pp.), chaps. 2–6.
———, *Life and Work of Pestalozzi,* W. B. Clive, Ltd., 1913 (393 pp.), part I, chaps. 1–6; part II, chaps. 7–10, 15.

[35] *Ibid.,* p. 340.

Krüsi, *Pestalozzi: His Life and Work,* chaps. 1–6.
Painter, *Great Pedagogical Essays,* chap. 23.
Pinloche, *Pestalozzi,* part I, chaps. 1–6; part II, book II, chaps. 1–5.
Quick, *Essays on Educational Reformers,* pp. 157–197.

D. Translations of Primary Sources

Green, J. A., *Pestalozzi's Educational Writings,* Longmans, Green and Co., 1912 (328 pp.), any 20–25 pages.
Pestalozzi, *How Gertrude Teaches Her Children,* letters iii–vi.
Ulich, *Three Thousand Years of Educational Wisdom,* pp. 480–507.

CHAPTER XVII

HERBART AND HIS PEDAGOGY

Johann Friedrich Herbart was as much a philosopher as a teacher. Of the teachers described in this book, he and Socrates were the ones with the most strongly philosophical turn of mind. Both, however, contributed specific methods of instruction that are still in use today. In accordance with the general principles of this text, little mention will be made of Herbart's philosophy. In a history of educational thought Herbart would have an appreciably larger place than he holds in a history of schools, methods of teaching, and teachers. This chapter will therefore be relatively brief.

A. HERBART: HIS LIFE AND WORK

1. His Life Story Herbart [1] was born in 1776 in Oldenburg,* a city in northwest Germany, some ten years before the beginning of the French Revolution. He was a lad while it was in progress, and he grew to maturity in the postrevolutionary period when Napoleon was coming into power. He had just entered his teaching career at the University of Göttingen when Napoleon became emperor. Herbart's father was a lawyer of some local prominence, who seems to have been a man of moderate ability and complete trustworthiness, but rather staid and conventional. His mother, however, made up for the father's lack of color; she was energetic, ambitious, intelligent, dominating, and so unconventional as to be eccentric. She kept her son at home until he was twelve years old, hiring private tutors to instruct him. These lessons she

[1] Based upon J. Adams, *The Herbartian Psychology Applied to Education*, D. C. Heath and Company, 1910, 284 pp.; G. Compayré, *Herbart and Education by Instruction* (translated by M. E. Findley), Thomas Y. Crowell Company, 1907, 142 pp.; A. Darroch, *Herbart and the Herbartian Theory of Education,* Longmans, Green and Co., 1903, 148 pp.; M. de Garmo, *Herbart and the Herbartians,* Charles Scribner's Sons, 1896, 268 pp.; W. J. Eckhoff, *Herbart's ABC of Sense Perception,* Appleton-Century-Crofts Inc., 1896, 288 pp.; H. M. Felkin and E. Felkin, *Introduction to Herbart's Science and Practice of Education,* D. C. Heath and Company, 1895, 193 pp.; J. F. Herbart, *Pädagogische Schriften,* Siegismund und Volkeng, 1876–1878, 2 vols.; O. H. Lang, *Outlines of Herbart's Pedagogics,* E. L. Kellogg and Company, 1894, 72 pp.; E. F. Lange and C. de Garmo, *Herbart's Outlines of Pedagogical Doctrine,* The Macmillan Company, 1901, 334 pp.; P. Leach, *Johann Friedrich Herbart,* Herman Schroedel, 1903, 70 pp.; C. A. McMurray, *The Elements of General Method Based on the Principles of Herbart,* Public School Publishing Company, 1895, 224 pp.; A. Pinloche, "Johann Friedrich Herbart: principales ouevres pédagogiques," *Traveaux et Mémoires des Facultés de Lille,* Vol. IV, No. 15, 1894, 400 pp.; C. Ufer, *Introduction to the Pedagogy of Herbart* (translated by J. C. Zinser), D. C. Heath and Company, 1894, 123 pp., and *Vorschule der Pädagogik Herbart,* Bleyl und Kammerer, 1893, 116 pp.; E. Wagner, *Vollständige Darstellung der Lehre Herbarts,* Julius Beltz, 1890, 398 pp.; T. Wiget, *Die Formalen Stufen des Unterrichts,* J. Rich, 1911, 119 pp.

also attended, partly to learn the material so that she could help her son and partly to prevent any untoward influences or ideas from touching him. The boy was not entirely cut off from others of his own age, but he was with adults more constantly than most children are, and he developed adult ideas and attitudes while he was still a child. When he finally entered the Gymnasium he had already covered so much of the material that he was advanced rapidly and was soon among boys three or four years older than himself. With two of his fellow students he entered into a lifelong friendship, but he was too restrained and distant to be popular with his other classmates, although they seem to have respected his ability and never to have actually disliked him. His interests were not, however, their interests; any boy who, as Herbart did, writes voluntarily at the age of fourteen an essay entitled "Concerning the Doctrine of Human Freedom," and at seventeen delivers a speech "Concerning the Commonest Causes that Affect the Growth and Decay of Morality in Various States" is not likely to be a popular leader also. A year later Herbart impressed his teachers by comparing, in a Latin oration, the thoughts on the "greatest good" as given by Cicero and the German philosopher, Immanuel Kant.* A similar performance would impress modern teachers even more!

At the age of eighteen, Herbart entered the University of Jena, where he dedicated himself to an intensive study of philosophy. Here he became a member of a group of serious students who met once a week for reading and discussion of their own papers. To gain admission to this group a student had to be free of membership in various social and political clubs and to present and defend an original piece of writing as a sort of trial flight. Herbart was an active and popular member of this small and select group, but he did not enter into the ordinary activities and amusements of student life.

After three years in Jena, Herbart accepted a position as tutor for three small boys in a Swiss family. He interrupted his own education partly because he wanted to consolidate his knowledge by teaching, partly because he thought he would profit more by the remaining years of study for his doctorate if he waited until he was older, and partly because he wanted to establish himself early in some type of work that would support him in later years, while still leaving him free to follow his first love, philosophy.

Herbart's sojourn in Switzerland did not make him any less of a philosopher, but it had a great influence upon his subsequent career because it made him pay attention to educational problems. Up until this period he had had no training that would specifically help him in dealing with three small boys, and it is likely that they taught him more than he taught them! He was, however, a serious-minded and responsible young man, and he applied himself to the problems presented by his job. Knowing little of traditional lore about teaching, he was reduced to studying his small charges and simply using his head. As a result he developed a lifelong interest in education and laid the basis for his subsequent methodology. By the end of his tutoring days he was already convinced that a truly educational type of instruction required a foundation in philosophy, a careful selection of subject matter, a scientific methodology, an adaptation to individual differences, and a proper guidance of interests and inclinations. Even this early in his career, Herbart did not favor education-made-easy procedures, and he frowned upon any artificial lightening of difficulties or any method that went around the hard points instead of mastering them.

In Switzerland Herbart met Pestalozzi, then approaching the height of his fame, and visited the school at Burgdorf. Pestalozzi's methods interested Herbart but puzzled him greatly; he could not see *why* the children learned so much and so willingly. But Herbart was not one to disregard a fact merely because he did not understand it. He therefore kept on studying Pestalozzi as a man and a teacher, until he could explain what made the methods work. The two men were a rather oddly assorted pair—one emotional and impulsive, the other reserved and intellectual—but even Herbart's reserve was thawed by Pestalozzi's enthusiasm and charm. He described the latter as a man who was kindly, human, friendly, and loveworthy. Herbart obtained much stimulation from the older man and conceived an admiration that led him later to formulate a synthesized philosophical and psychological basis for Pestalozzi's work —something Pestalozzi himself was never able to do.

After three years as tutor in Switzerland, Herbart returned home in the year 1800. He did not, however, remain long in Oldenburg because his parents were in the midst of arranging a separation and the emotional atmosphere was too highly charged to suit Herbart. His next stop was in Bremen,* where he remained for two years to tutor and to complete the work for his doctor's degree. Then he went to the University of Göttingen as a teacher, and finally, seven years later, settled in Königsberg, where he remained for almost a quarter of a century. At the University of Königsberg he held the professorship of philosophy and pedagogy last occupied by the philosopher Immanuel Kant. Here Herbart built up a great reputation as a teacher, especially as a lecturer. After twenty-five years in Königsberg, he returned to Göttingen, where he remained for another eight years until 1841, when he died of a stroke shortly after delivering a lecture. His adult life thus centers around two places—Königsberg and Göttingen.

Herbart's life was quiet and uneventful; like those of most college professors, his journeys consisted mainly of short daily trips from his study to his classroom, and the real events of his life took place in his mind. Aside from his three years in Switzerland, he spent his days in academic retreats devoting his abilities to establishing education as a science based upon psychology, and to instructing generations of students in the fundamentals of his pedagogy.

2. *His Personality* Herbart's ideas about learning and teaching show clearly the impress of his own personality, both his faults and his virtues. It is therefore desirable to consider what the inner Herbart was like, in order to view his methods with more understanding. Excerpts from two descriptions of him appear below:

> His outward appearance was, as has been quite correctly described, that of a distinguished man: dignified, reserved toward strangers, commanding respect by accommodating politeness, plus a uniform, calm seriousness. He never let himself go, either in his outward bearing, nor in his conduct toward others, nor in his speech or conversation. He spoke naturally, with excellent choice of words, in the way he wrote; he spoke little or not at all if the subject did not interest him, but one then saw that more thoughts flowed through his mind than he cared to express. His large, deep-blue eyes gleamed with an enhanced brilliancy and moved with a greater liveliness; and he devoted himself to the subject of conversation with the entire, undivided energy of his mind, until he broke off abruptly, either because he discovered a contradiction in principles or because the subject seemed to have been exhausted. Merely individual opinions, half-developed ideas, fragmentary inspirations he himself almost never expressed; just as little did he listen willingly to them from others—for which reason he did not enter into mere doubts, misgivings, general and vague objections against the principles of his system, while, on the other hand, the attempt to refute him in a close sequence of thought was always able to arouse his interest. As a result he may have appeared harsh and unadaptable to many people. . . . he had too often in his life experienced how little is to be done with subjective opinions, so-called views, standpoints, and so on, that one could easily forgive him if he was not inclined to answer everyone.

> The most outstanding trait in his character as a scientist was his deep respect for the truth, which penetrated his mental life to its deepest roots. His love of truth made him despise all false appearances, all dictatorial utterances, all empty, high-flown phraseology, all scientific boasting and bombast. But truth could not have been regarded as a character trait if he had not manifested this respect for truth in his volition and especially in the rigor and conscientiousness of his own investigations. . . . But his character was not merely the expression of a natural disposition; it was the result of self-cultivation, of self-control. Moreover, forced to rely at an early age upon his own efforts he was obliged to find the support for his will only in himself and, lacking as he was by nature in any kind of play instinct, which to be sure cannot guide life but can make it more beautiful and easier in many ways, he would not allow anything in his own action and thought to

depend upon chance. Therefore he deliberately deprived himself of the gay volatility that allows a man to be carried without care through the vicissitudes of life. The seclusion in which he devoted most of his life to research made him for the most part unfamiliar with external circumstances, and accordingly a superficial observer might see him as a strange phenomenon that was easily misunderstood. . . . When he recognized something as clearly his duty he was conscientious to the point of anxiety and precisely because he was, he was accustomed to act in complex circumstances less rapidly and decisively than one would have expected from a man of similar decisiveness of character but of less caution. His conduct toward others was considerate in the highest degree but to the casual observer he might appear as cold and formal. Nevertheless in the depth of his soul there lay buried a treasure of benevolence, sympathy, and kindness that betrayed itself often in the most insignificant actions in a surprising way. Whoever was able to look through the pattern of his feelings, as his writings let one observe the pattern of his thought, soon recognized in him the softest, mildest, and friendliest spirit; much that was harsh and even repulsive was then understood as a product of circumstances and external pressures which had established a distance between the expression of his character at a particular time and his true essence.[2]

From the funeral oration delivered by one of Herbart's colleagues comes the excerpt below. Like all such orations it is expressed in rather flowery language, but it adds certain points not included in the first quotation.

His name is written into the annals of our university, his fame is ours, his picture lives in our memory; the noble forehead, the clear glance, the irridescence of his speech—always in choice and often surprising expressions—and, in harmony with these outward traits of a fine personality, the nobility and dignity of his spirit as it revealed itself in word and deed before friends and strangers alike. Was it principally acquired self-control or inborn delicacy—whoever heard from his lips an offensive word or an ill-considered jest, even in a circle of intimates or under the influence of Bacchus? . . . Certainly he demonstrated the old saying about the refining and ennobling power of learning . . . . His entire cycle of studies Herbart covered not merely in summary survey but for the most part as an expert. He was never superficial, and preferably cultivated that field that we now call classical literature. He knew the ancient languages as did very few of his profession—Latin with complete perfection, both orally and in writing; he was at home in the domain of Greek poetry, at home among the philosophical authors, most intimately acquainted with Plato and the sages of Elia.* And many a trait of the ancient spirit bore witness to his intercourse with the classical world of antiquity. Hellenic was the euphemy of his expression and judgment; his sense of beauty, the elegance with which he expressed

[2] Wagner, *op. cit.,* condensed from pp. 16–19.This excerpt and subsequent ones from Wagner are quoted by permission of the publisher, Julius Beltz.

the outward forms, remind one of the old academicians;* and Socratic seemed often to us his ignorance of the sophistications of life, his harmless belief in the power of right, and the justice of power.[3]

Herbart emerges from these descriptions as a man of unusual intellectual power, of brilliant speech, of sterling character. His colleagues and students liked him, but they were not intimate with him. Herbart had a coldness, a measured restraint, a cast-iron self-control, and an inability to relax socially that kept others at arm's length. He enjoyed long talks or debates upon philo-

FIG. 78. Johann Friedrich Herbart. Drawn by C. H. Steffens and engraved by C. Geyer.

sophical or other impersonal and generalized matters, but at the first hint of personal intimacy, he retreated into his shell and stayed there. He distrusted emotion; to be sure, he understood in an intellectual way the role of the emotions in human life, but he did not care to experience any that he could avoid. No doubt his students, even those most fascinated by the brilliant play of Herbart's mind, described him to each other as a "cold fish." After the profound emotionalism of both Pestalozzi and Basedow, Herbart provides a cold shower of intellectualism. He was a man of great natural rectitude, and he had an

[3] *Ibid.*, condensed from pp. 19–20.

earnest desire to improve the human race through education, but his approach was intellectual and philosophical. One can respect him as an impersonal logic-machine, but it is hard to feel a deep affection for him. The incoherent and blundering Pestalozzi appeals to the heart; the precise and didactic Herbart, to the head—and most people prefer Pestalozzi. Herbart's portrait reflects well his personal traits.

In view of Herbart's personality it is not surprising that his educational theories and techniques are overintellectualized, oversystematized, and dehumanized. They have educative worth, although they provide little nourishment for the teacher's spirit. One must be careful, however, not to underestimate Herbart merely because he lacked the lovableness and spontaneous charm of most great teachers.

B. HERBART'S PEDAGOGY

Herbart developed what Pestalozzi, Basedow, and Comenius were unable to produce, a systematized theory of education. Moreover, he was the first of the great teachers intentionally to base education upon the budding science of psychology, and it was not his fault that psychology had at that time not budded sufficiently to be adequate for the purpose. He expressed his conviction as to the need for psychology in no uncertain terms:

> I have for twenty years employed metaphysics* and mathematics, and side by side with them self-observation, experience, and experiments, merely to find the foundations of true psychological insight. And the motive for these not exactly toilless investigations has been and is, in the main, my conviction that a large part of the enormous gaps in our pedagogical knowledge results from lack of psychology, and that we must first have this science—nay, that we must first of all remove the mirage which to-day goes by the name of psychology—before we shall be able to determine with some certainty concerning even a single instruction period what in it was done aright and what amiss.[4]

Since Herbart, it has become an educational commonplace that teachers should study and apply psychological principles, but in his day the idea was a new and fruitful one.

Herbart's pedagogy contained certain basic ideas of great importance, which led to definite instructional procedures by which the teacher of today can profit. Although the intricacies of Herbart's psychology and philosophy are sometimes difficult to grasp, the essence of his argument is not. He believed that the mind at birth was a blank and possessed innately only one power, that of entering into relation with its environment by means of sense perception

[4] J. F. Herbart, *The Science of Education* (translated by H. M. and E. Felkin), Routledge and Kegan Paul, Ltd., 1924 (286 pp.), p. 141. Used by permission of the publishers.

through the workings of the nervous system. The mind was therefore built up through the presentation of ideas from the external world, not through the development of its own innate faculties, of which it has none. This extreme position was doubtless a reaction against the metaphysical notions of his time that the mind had inborn capacities and even already formed inborn ideas. A mind is thus neither good nor bad of itself, but may become either, according to its experiences. The main business of education is therefore the imparting of the most useful knowledge in such a way that it can be most easily grasped and most completely retained by children. One must know what a pupil's interests are and how his mind is developing, but only for the purpose of providing the necessary stimulation to lead him from where he is to where he ought to be.

In Herbart's view, the presentations will through interaction with one another lead to generalized concepts and eventually to reasoning and morality. All spiritual qualities are thus dependent upon knowledge. Both conduct and character grow out of ideas acquired by the mind and the interaction of these ideas upon one another. Thus instruction alone is enough to produce good conduct and ideals. Herbart's system has at least the value of being coherent, even though subsequent investigation has proved some portions of it to be in error.

Certain educational implications grow logically out of this psychological basis. The position of the teacher is of paramount importance because he or she literally makes the minds of children. To *in*struct a mind was, actually, to *con*struct it. The teacher's main business is to furnish the right ideas, to determine the relation of these ideas to one another, and thus to form the child's character and to control his conduct. Since a teacher's principal concern was the actual creation of minds, his task was a sacred one and should be undertaken only by the best of men.

1. The Doctrine of Apperception If a mind is an aggregation of ideas, it seems reasonable that the ideas already ensconced there will select, from the total number offered by the environment, those that fit in with themselves and will reject those that do not. Apperception is, then, the assimilation of new ideas by means of ideas already acquired. This well-known psychological principle of today was an innovation in the educational thought of the early nineteenth century. Ideas facilitate the acceptance of some stimuli and inhibit the acceptance of others; therefore, the same idea presented to three people may be accepted *in toto* by one, partially accepted by another, and rejected by a third. For instance, according to popular legend Newton discovered the law of gravity because an apple fell on his head, and Maxim* invented the Maxim silencer because he saw water running out of a bath tub. The falling apple and the swirling water presented valuable ideas to these two men because of the thoughts already in their minds, not because the phenomena themselves were startling nor because these experiences had never happened to anyone before. According to this theory of apperception, the teacher is to impart knowledge in the way that it can be most rapidly and profitably assimilated. The teacher should know the children's interests, not for the purpose of developing them but in order to use them for better assimilation of ideas. He should select the materials of instruction with respect to the ultimate aims of education and to the pupil's level of development and should so arrange these materials as to promote the maximum degree of learning in the shortest time. To Herbart, education consisted in careful instruction, not in mere guidance of nature.

2. *Lesson Plans* By means of his lesson plans, Herbart applied his ideas on the proper methods of instruction. These plans constitute the chief device for teaching introduced by Herbart. Even though they were perhaps too rigid, too systematized, and too complicated, the idea of having a logical lesson plan at all was both new and excellent, and the plans themselves have merit after they have been "humanized." According to Herbart, the act of instruction consists of four stages or parts: first showing, then associating, then teaching, then philosophizing.[5] When decoded from Herbart's phraseology, these successive steps mean that a teacher should go through a definite routine in the presentation of new material. His first step in starting a new topic is to recall to the children's minds any relevant facts they already know, by stirring their interest in the matter to be presented, and by showing them numerous objects, pictures, or other representations. That is, there should first be a period of preparation of the pupils' minds to receive new matter, so that the already established ideas may facilitate the new ones as much as possible. A teacher should thus "begin where the child lives," using what he knows to teach him more. This first stage requires no formal instruction and is carried on by conversation with the children and voluntary remarks by them.

In the second stage, the pupils and teacher are together to proceed by association from the specific bits of knowledge furnished by observation or memory to the level of general ideas. Thus, for instance, one small child sees that 2 pennies and 2 pennies make 4 pennies, another that 2 apples plus 2 apples make 4 apples, and a third that 2 boys plus 2 boys make 4 boys; by comparing these specific instances with each other, the pupils can deduce the concept that 2 plus 2 make 4, regardless of 2 and 4 of what. Concrete realities furnish the raw material, but the abstract notions buried therein have to be dug out before one can indulge in much thinking; otherwise the

[5] In other passages, Herbart uses the words "clearness," "association," "systematization," "method" to indicate the four stages. Another parallel series is "intuition," "comparison," "generalization," "application."

thinker would be too weighted down with irrelevancies and incidental features to proceed far. During this second stage the teacher guides the children's efforts to separate the general from the specific, but he does not instruct. He talks with and interrogates the children.

Up to this point, the teacher has let the children do the contributing, drawing out from them the needed facts and observations. During the third stage, the teacher begins to expound at greater length, to add what the pupils could not find out for themselves, to point out additional relationships, and to systematize and synthesize the data previously offered by the children. Herbart carefully warns the teacher not to let his contribution get separated from the pupils' knowledge, not to indulge in dogmatism, and not to neglect a frequent return to perception and experience.

The fourth stage, in spite of its various somewhat misleading names, consists merely in an application, by means of definite exercises, of the knowledge acquired through the first three stages. The pupil is supposed to give proof through his personal work that he has profited by the instruction and can use the concepts developed in the lesson. He may be asked to work out problems, to give definitions, to write a summary of main points, and so on.

In addition to analyzing these four steps in instruction, Herbart, with his love for classification, grouped lesson plans as being either inductive or deductive. An inductive lesson plan begins with specific instances from which general principles are developed; the deductive lesson plan begins with a statement of general principles and ends with illustrations thereof. Suppose a science teacher wants to teach a group of children that materials lighter than water will float, while those that are heavier will sink. If he proceeds inductively, he lets the children drop each of many collected objects into a tank of water and note its behavior. Then he shows them a table giving the comparative weights of water and of the materials used in the experiment. The children list everything in order of weight and then look at their notes on how each object behaved in the water. Presently some child sees that objects lighter than water floated, those of about the same weight submerged, those slightly heavier sank slowly to a point somewhat above the bottom of the tank, and that the much-heavier things sank at once to the bottom. By this procedure the children have induced a principle from raw data. Undeniably a scientist proceeds inductively when he first discovers a general principle, like Galileo dropping stones of different sizes from different heights to determine the laws of falling bodies, but a teacher may follow this method or he may teach deductively. In a deductive lesson on the topic of weights the science teacher begins by telling the children the principle of floating bodies and then showing them the table of weights. Next he recalls to their minds facts that they already know about the weight of various objects and their behavior in water, and finally he tells the children to find a dozen objects apiece, bring them to class, and be prepared to explain their behavior.

That is, the pupils deduce the illustrations from the principle. Most people cannot or do not stick to one or the other type of plan, but prefer to combine them; all teachers, of course, use both at one time or another. Of the two, deductive teaching covers ground faster and is therefore used more and more as children grow older and have more material to cover. Thus, the first-grade teacher uses inductive teaching most of the time, and the college professor uses deductive. The type of subject matter also influences the selection of one or the other approach, or some fusion of the two.

Herbart's lesson plan was his basic method for achieving the most efficient comprehension of new ideas and the best integration of them with previous knowledge. By means of it each successive series of new presentations is deliberately set in a matrix of connected ideas and is therefore more readily learned and retained.

3. Development of Moral Character In addition to the lesson plans, Herbart contributed some characteristic ideas about moral education and discipline. Like Basedow, he separated religion and ethics, leaving the former to the separate churches and assigning the latter to teachers. Like Socrates, he tended toward the naïve idea that correct instruction in morals would automatically produce good behavior. Herbart believed that the human will developed on the basis of the ideas presented to the mind by experience and instruction and that its nature depended upon the kind of ideas already acquired by the mind. Conduct and character were therefore direct outcomes of instruction; for their development mere teaching was sufficient. Morality was evidently supposed to follow enlightenment as the day follows the night. Herbart summarized his theory of the relationship between ideas and morality in the following words: "Instruction creates the content of the mind, and education creates character. The last is nothing without the first. Herein lies the main principle of my pedagogy." [6] Appeal to or guidance of emotional life is conspicuously lacking in Herbart's conception of education.

In spite of his theories, however, it would seem that Herbart had some doubts about instruction alone being sufficient, because he proposed the use of rewards for good behavior and punishment for bad as further incentives to morality—thus, for once, contradicting himself. He doubtless wanted to believe that good teaching would automatically produce morality, but his keen observation told him that human beings were not always governed by what they knew was right, and he was too honest to disregard truth, even when it upset his theories, so he included the modern notions of praise and blame as forms of moral guidance. The subject matter selected by Herbart as being most likely to lead to the desired moral ends consisted chiefly of literature and history.

[6] Compayré, *op. cit.*, p. 46. The quotations from this book are used by permission of Thomas Y. Crowell Company, publishers.

He began with the Homeric* poems and arranged subsequent literary productions according to the "culture epochs" of the human race. It was his assumption that the psychological development of each individual paralleled that of the race;[7] thus, since the earliest folk tales were epics,* he began schoolwork with epics and proceeded by historically verifiable steps from simple and primitive literature to that which was complex and modern. Herbart was by no means unique in this misapplication of evolutionary doctrine.

Discipline, according to Herbart, was the means of training the child's will to desire what is good. The objective of all discipline was therefore strength of moral character. To make discipline effective, it was always essential to have the child's co-operation, because he would not grow in moral stature under punishment that he resented; all harshness and cruelty were therefore completely banned, because they inevitably produced antagonism. As Herbart wrote: "All is lost if from the beginning we have been clumsy enough to make study a source of misery and torment." [8] Character, as Herbart saw, depended upon one's will and one's desires; discipline became, then, a training of the will to desire what was right. The methods suggested by Herbart may be too intellectual, but his concept of discipline was far removed from the repressive theories generally current in previous centuries.

Since small children cannot be reasoned with, Herbart thought a direct appeal to their feelings was the best procedure, but with older children he favored an approach through the mind. That is, one should make clear to an older child what the discipline is for, what results it may be expected to have, why it is desirable, and so on, until he sees for himself that he needs guidance or merits punishment. Discipline should be just as educational as any other school procedure and it should rest upon direct instruction, like learning in any other field. Since discipline is to be educational, a teacher cannot simply deal out punishment to offenders and then forget all about it; he must work slowly, continually, and thoughtfully as he educates his pupils' wills. In Herbart's own words:

> Discipline is not short and sharp, but drawn out, continuing, slowly penetrating and gradually ceasing. For discipline must be felt as education. . . . Discipline must not strike the spirit obliquely, must not be felt contrary to its purpose, must not antagonize the child inwardly in any way, must not drive him by two forces to pursue a diagonal. . . . Moreover, dis-

[7] The so-called "theory of recapitulation." Because the human foetus* in its growth from a one-celled organism to a baby goes through a series of stages that roughly parallel those of the human race, it was once assumed the mind also went through a similar series of stages. Each individual thus "recapitulated" or lived through the same periods by which the race had slowly evolved.

[8] Compayré *op. cit.*, p. 48.

cipline occurs only in proportion as an inner experience persuades the pupil to subject himself and to accept discipline willingly; the power of discipline reaches only so far as the pupil's agreement.[9]

The younger child is not yet ready to value the objective of education. The twelve-year-old boy who has been properly guided from an early age prizes it above everything, out of his inner feeling for the need of guidance. The sixteen-year-old youth begins to take upon himself the business of the teacher; he has grasped in part his teacher's point of view, plans his own way and conducts himself accordingly, and this conduct is similar to that which his teacher has continually exacted from him.[10]

Most of Herbart's discussion of discipline, its relation to character building and to one's already existing system of ideas is highly theoretical, but he sometimes descends from the realms of philosophical reflection to the level of practical suggestion. He speaks little of punishments, but notes that a mere expression of pleasure or displeasure is often all that is needed to guide children. Deprivation of free time is also mentioned as an effective punishment, but in general Herbart pins his hopes upon the use of reasoning and upon the additional motivations of the teacher's praise. On certain matters, however, he warns the teacher. He must not use even slight punishment or rebuke too often, or it will lose its effectiveness. "There is a host of details in daily life into which order must be brought, but rebukes must not be squandered on slight negligences because you will need them for important things." [11] Herbart suggests routine in small matters as the best technique for avoiding constant bickering. The teacher must also avoid exaggeration of minor misdemeanors. Children rarely do anything seriously wrong or bad; they are only ignorant, careless, and lighthearted. What they need, therefore, is a kindly guidance that will minimize their undesirable reactions, not severe blame that will magnify them out of all proportion to their importance. The teacher must also avoid overworking the children by assignments that are too long or too hard, or that prevent them from getting adequate exercise and recreation.. Much childish misconduct arises from the strain involved in schoolwork that exerts too much pressure.

Herbart stresses four conditions that help punishment to be effective. First, it should be the logical result of the misbehavior, thus imitating nature in so far as possible. "Any pupil who misses time, loses his enjoyment; he who has spoiled his belongings, must do without them; he who has chattered, is sent away." [12] Second, punishment should be uniform. In no case should it depend

[9] Wagner, *op. cit.,* condensed from pp. 317–318.
[10] *Ibid.,* p. 48.
[11] *Ibid.,* p. 354.
[12] *Ibid.,* p. 355.

upon the whims of the teacher. "The teacher's mood of the moment—like the weather—is the first thing that pupils observe and tell each other about. A bad mood is feared, and a good one is used to obtain permissions otherwise unobtainable. Pupils thus seek to move the fixed point that should be holding them, and the slightest success nourishes disproportionate hopes." [13] Third, punishment should be certain; and, finally, it should be administered in a quiet, self-controlled way. A teacher cannot discipline a child educatively when he is himself in an emotional state. Such comments and suggestions as the above indicate that, although Herbart's main interests were theoretical, he based his theories upon actual observation of teachers and pupils.

4. Doctrine of Interest Under Pestalozzi and the various followers of Rousseau, the child's interests were of paramount importance because the teacher took whatever the child had to offer and merely guided it. Under Herbart, interest is a motive power to be used in attaining some worth-while end, rather than a spontaneous outpouring of childish enthusiasm. Herbart analyzed interest and found it to be of two kinds—indirect interest which arose when a child worked from fear of punishment or under some other emotional pressure, and direct interest that sprang naturally from the material being studied. The former type he would eliminate entirely because it was inefficient. The latter he would cultivate because it leads to an intense voluntary attention that makes learning easy, to pleasure in work, and to continued effort. Interest becomes thus a valuable tool rather than an end in itself. Herbart did not approve of giving interest its head and following where it led. He had no notion of making education into a game or of amusing the children. Nevertheless, he made interest a keynote in his pedagogy because he thought it an essential condition of mental effort. He considered it the first business of a schoolteacher to be interesting to the pupils, and he regarded dullness and repression as inexcusable. As he once wrote: "To be dull is the worst sin of teaching." [14]

Herbart did not mean by "interest" the same natural outpouring of childish enthusiasm that was the basis of Pestalozzi's methodology. Interest did not boil up from within but was manufactured from without by the teacher. It was therefore a result of instruction, not a prelude to it. The interest thus aroused should be many-sided. The growth of an active attitude of mind toward many things was, to him, inevitable if instruction was good. A narrow mind was thus merely the result of bad teaching. Herbart wanted pupils to be so taught that their minds would have many facets, would be alert in many directions, and would be awake to all kinds of stimuli. He abhorred narrow-

[13] *Ibid.*, p. 360.
[14] *Ibid.*, p. 205.

ness, exclusiveness, and specialization. He believed that an educated man should have an empirical interest in concrete objects, a speculative interest in natural phenomena, an aesthetic interest in all beautiful things, a sympathetic interest in people, a social interest in humanity, and a religious interest in morals and beliefs. The school subjects should arouse one or more of these interests, which, once stimulated, should become the motive power that brings about mastery of relevant material.

Interest was useful not only in producing mastery of subject matter but in leading to the growth of character. In Herbart's own words:

> The ultimate purpose of instruction is contained in the notion, virtue, But in order to realize the final aim another and nearer one must be set up. We may term it *many-sidedness of interest*. The word *interest* stands in general for that kind of mental activity which it is the business of instruction to incite. Mere information does not suffice; for this we think of as a supply or store of facts, which a person might possess or lack and still remain the same being. But he who lays hold of this information and reaches out for more takes an interest in it. Since, however, this mental activity is varied, we need to add the further determination supplied by the term *many-sided*.[15]
>
> Every man must have a love for all activity, each must be a virtuoso in one. But the particular virtuosoship is a matter of choice; on the contrary, the manifold receptivity, which can only grow out of manifold beginnings of one's own individual efforts, is a matter of education. Therefore we call the first part of the educational aim *many-sidedness of interest*, which must be distinguished from its exaggeration—dabbling in many things. And since no one object of will, or its individual direction, interests us more than any other, we add to this, lest weakness may offend us by appearing on the side of strength, the predicate—proportionate many-sidedness.[16]

Herbart's doctrine of interest as a reaction developed in children by the teacher has in recent decades been pushed into the background by the Pestalozzian principle of interest as a function of normal growth. Perhaps both types exist. Surely, a student can recall instances in his own school experiences in which an interest has been created in him by the skillful instruction of a teacher.

5. Position of the Teacher Herbart's concept of the teacher's duties and position was very high. To him a teacher was not only a leader and inspirer of youth but also a leader in the intellectual life of his community. Only constant study would, in his opinion, fit a person to occupy such a position of trust. In his own words: "It is by meditation, it is by reflection and research, it is through scientific study that the educator must prepare his mind and

[15] *Ibid.*, pp. 181–182.
[16] Herbart, *Science of Education*, pp. 110–111.

heart to fit himself to conceive, feel, and judge rightly the particular incidents, the special cases which he must meet in his career as a teacher." [17] To Herbart, the educator was the main hope for the progress of mankind. He was himself too inhibited a person to show much emotion toward people, but toward education he had a great depth of feeling. As one of his interpreters has said:

> He had faith in education, and this well-considered and philosophic faith was an active faith, which he testified and proclaimed by fifty years of reflection. Not in vain did he devote a long life to the study of pedagogical problems, bringing to it not only the resources of a free and profound intellect, but also all the warmth of his heart. He was, before all else, skilled in reasoning, but the abstractions with which his volumes are replete are based on observation and experience. Reflective and scrupulous to excess, in both his writings and his actions, he took up his pen only when he believed he had reached the truth. And just as under the stiff formulae in which he enclosed his thoughts there moves a spirit that is very supple and resourceful, so under an appearance of coldness there is hidden a generous soul, which at times reveals itself. . . . Education, in the opinion of Herbart, is not a trade like other trades, it is a sacred mission. All who engage in the education of their kind, if ever so little fitted to their task, believe themselves below its claims; and when they think of the difficulties of the work which they undertake, of the responsibilities which they incur, they experience, as it were, a shudder of emotion. Herbart had known this shudder. He placed all his hopes of a better humanity in education; and that is why he expressed the wish that in each society, in the most secluded village, just as there is a doctor for the health of the body, there should be also an accredited teacher for the health of the soul. He should pay visits to the families and give them advice, and act as consulting educator, watching over the intellectual and moral progress of the younger generation.[18]

The teacher occupies the central position in Herbart's system, not the child, although the teacher's activities are all directed toward the best development of his pupils.

Herbart, in common with other educators, established a seminar in pedagogy and a practice school in which teachers could work under his supervision. During his lifetime he indoctrinated a considerable number of teachers with his theories of education. Herbart's students carried his ideas all over Germany. Some of them preached Herbartianism *in toto,* others made sundry modifications, while a few eventually revolted against the master. Some of his more ardent disciples have followed each other, generation after generation, in the chairs of pedagogy at German universities, until the Herbartian school of thought has permeated German education. A statement made forty years ago is

[17] Compayré, *op. cit.,* p. 43.
[18] *Ibid.,* pp. 135–136.

still true today: "In Germany, Pestalozzi was the founder, but his successor—the philosopher Herbart—has been the logician and organizer of modern pedagogy; and his methodical work, having rendered service to first one and then another distinguished man, still maintains its place intact and full of energy, sanctioned by one hundred years of experience and success." [19] The journals of the middle nineteenth century are full of arguments for or against his theories, and many Herbartian societies were formed for the spread of his ideas.

Some of Herbart's basic principles have become educational commonplaces, even though their phraseology has altered, and some have been discarded. One does not have to defend the principle of apperception any more, because no one challenges it. Whenever a teacher brings out the association of a new point to ideas already acquired, he is proceeding in a correct Herbartian manner. Herbart's theory that morality develops from training of the intellect has, however, been superseded by the theory that the springs of action are emotional.

The Herbartian remnants in modern education are usually so much a part of what to Americans is traditional school procedure as to be almost unnoticed. A young teacher learns to make lesson plans, perhaps both inductive and deductive, without knowing of her debt to Herbart. Many teachers of today are convinced that they can make or remake their pupils according to the nature of their instruction, and they are quite sure that they can create interest where none grew before. Although the progressive movement of recent decades had tended to alter the relation of the teacher to the class, the teacher still remains the font of knowledge in most schoolrooms. Most teachers believe in using childish interests for the purpose of better adapting a child to his present environment. The mother who says that her child was a good boy under Miss X's teaching but has become a bad boy since being exposed to Miss Y's instruction is also being Herbartian without knowing it. Perhaps the greatest significance of Herbart's work, however, was his insistence upon pedagogy as a science, based upon application of psychology to the procedures within the classroom. If this idea were not generally believed at the present time, the complex program of teacher training would hardly be necessary.

READING REFERENCES

A. General Histories of the Period

Artz, F. B., *Reaction and Revolution, 1814–1832,* Harper & Brothers, 1939 (317 pp.), chaps. 1, 2.

[19] M. F. Guex, in *L'Éducateur,* Organ of the Pedagogical Society of Switzerland, February 28, 1903.

Ergang, *Europe from the Renaissance to Waterloo,* chap. 26.
Garrett, M. B., and J. H. Godfrey, *Europe since 1815,* Appleton-Century-Crofts Company, 1947 (763pp.), chaps. 2–4.
Grant and Temperly, *Europe in the Nineteenth and Twentieth Centuries,* chaps. 4, 5, 8, 10.
Hayes, *Political and Cultural History of Modern Europe,* Vol. I, chaps. 13,14.
Riker, *A Short History of Modern Europe,* chaps. 10,11.
Robinson, *Introduction to the History of Western Europe,* chaps. 37, 38.
Schapiro, J. S., *Modern and Contemporary European History, 1815–1941,* Houghton Mifflin Company, 1942 (rev. ed., 909 pp.), chaps. 1, 2.
Schevill, *A History of Europe from the Reformation to the Present Day,* chaps. 21, 22.
Seignobos, *The Rise of European Civilization,* chap. 17.
Stearns, *Pageant of History,* part II, chap. 23; part III, chap. 25.
Turner, *Europe since 1789,* chaps. 3, 4.

B. Other Texts in the History of Education

Boyd, *The History of Western Education,* chap. 11.
Cole, *History of Educational Thought,* pp. 258–261.
Cubberley, *History of Education,* pp. 759–764.
Eby and Arrowood, *The Development of Modern Education,* chap. 20.
Graves, *A Student's History of Education,* pp. 376–390.
Marique, *History of Christian Education,* III, 117–127.
McCormick, *History of Education,* chap. 27.
Monroe, *A Textbook in the History of Education,* pp. 622–638.
Ulich, *History of Educational Thought,* pp. 271–283.

C. Secondary Sources

Cole, P. R., *Herbart and Froebel,* Columbia University Press, 1907 (117 pp.), chap. 2.
Compayré, *Herbart and Education by Instruction,* chaps. 1–3.
Darroch, A., *Herbart and the Herbartian Theory of Education,* Longmans, Green and Co., 1903 (148 pp.), lectures 2, 4.
De Garmo, *Herbart and the Herbartians,* chaps. 1–7.
Graves, *Great Educators of Three Centuries,* chap. 10.
Herbart, *The Science of Education,* translator's introduction, pp. 1–56.

D. Translations of Primary Sources

Herbart, *The Science of Education,* book i, chap. 2; book ii, chaps. 1, 5; book ii, chaps, 5, 6.
Ulich, *Three Thousand Years of Educational Wisdom,* pp. 508–522.

CHAPTER XVIII

FROEBEL AND THE KINDERGARTEN

The violence of the French Revolution plus the aggressiveness of Napoleon* combined to scare the rest of Europe into a strong reaction against liberalism* in any form in any field. Some of the gains made for the common man during the early days of the Revolution were, to be sure, preserved by Napoleon, not presumably because he was concerned about Jacques Bonhomme* but because certain of the reforms were useful in producing the kind of France he wanted. Other advances were, however, completely offset by reaction.

The main character of this chapter, Friedrich Wilhelm August Froebel, was a young man at the time of the Congress of Vienna.* In 1813 he volunteered as a soldier in the War of Liberation* against Napoleon. The excitement of 1830 led local police to suspect his first school apparently because the boys wore their hair long, and in 1848 he was openly condemned. At no time in his life was Froebel in the least concerned with politics, but the spirit of the spy hunt was so strong that he was involved more than once, in spite of his palpable and childlike innocence. The times in which he lived helped to give Froebel his intense love of freedom, but they operated also to check those manifestations of freedom which Froebel introduced into the practice of education.

A. FROEBEL: HIS LIFE AND WORK

1. His Early Years Friedrich Wilhelm August Froebel[1] was born in 1782 in a small Thuringian* village called Oberweissbach.* His father was a

[1] Based upon H. C. Bowen, *Froebel and Education for Self-Activity,* Charles Scribner's Sons, 1893, 209 pp.; G. Compayré, *Froebel et les jardins d'enfants,* P. Delaplane, 1912, 86 pp.; F. W. Froebel, *Autobiography* (translated by E. Michaelis and H. K. Moore), Bardeen's, Inc., 1889, 167 pp., *Education of Man* (translated by J. Jarvis), Appleton-Century-Crofts, Inc., 1886, 273 pp., and *Education and Development* (translated by J. Jarvis), Appleton-Century-Crofts Company, 1899, 347 pp.; W. H. Herford, *The Student's Froebel,* D. C. Heath and Company, 1906, 112 pp.; J. L. Hughes, *Froebel's Educational Laws for All Teachers,* Appleton-Century-Crofts Company, 1903, 296 pp.; M. A. Kuntze, *Friedrich Froebel: sein Weg und sein Werk,* Quelle und Meyer, 1930, 129 pp.; E. R. Murray, *Froebel as a Pioneer in Modern Psychology,* Warwick and York, 1914, 230 pp.; E. Sheriff, *A Short Sketch of the Life of Friedrich Froebel and His Kindergarten System,* Chapman and Hall, 1887, 134 pp.; D. J. Snider, *The Life of Friedrich Froebel,* Sigma Publishing Company, 1900, 470 pp., and *Froebel's Play Gifts,* Sigma Publishing Company, 1900, 384 pp.; B. von Marenholtz-Bülow, *Reminiscences of Friedrich Froebel* (translated by Mrs. Horace

country clergyman for a district that spread over several villages. Froebel's mother died when he was a baby, and his father soon married again. In his earliest recollections, Froebel was a lonely and unhappy boy; his older brothers were all away from home at school, his father was overworked by the demands of his 5000 scattered parishioners, and his stepmother had a son of her own in whom she was greatly interested. It does not appear that she was actually cruel to Froebel, but she evidently regarded him as a stupid and trying child. At school he trailed along at the bottom of the class, largely because he had great difficulty in learning to read. The chief attention paid to him at home seems to have been in the form of pressure to make him conform to his father's stern and orthodox views on morals and manners. Rejected at home, scorned at school, and represssed by a narrow religion, the boy was in a continual state of moody revolt against life; he was disobedient, untruthful, insolent, and lazy. In modern parlance, he was a problem child, created by neglect and misunderstanding. By the time Froebel was ten years old, he and his stepmother could no longer get along together, and every day the child seemed to be getting more and more out of hand. It was a relief for all concerned when an uncle in Switzerland agreed to have young Friedrich come and live with him for a while.

For the first time the boy experienced trust instead of suspicion, kindness instead of severity, and freedom instead of restriction. As he later wrote in his autobiography, "I could go into my uncle's gardens if I liked, and I was also at liberty to roam all over the neighborhood." [2] He was sent to a school in which there were some forty other boys of his own age, where he encountered for the first time the rough-and-tumble life of normal boyhood. The uncle was also a minister, but his tolerance and liberality of thought were far different from the narrow and gloomy orthodoxy of Froebel's father. Froebel remained five years with his uncle and seems to have made a quite good recovery from his earlier maladjustments. He was happy in his new home relationships, he met with some really good teaching at school, he learned to get along passably well with his age mates, and he so overcame his childhood prejudice against religion as to be confirmed.

After five years, the boy returned home, with his education supposedly finished. His brothers had all gone to a university, but he was regarded as being far too stupid; moreover, his young half brother was a precociously bright child, for whose higher education the parents were already saving

---

Mann), Lathrop, Lee & Shepard Co., 1897, 359 pp., and *The Child and Child Nature,* Bardeen's, Inc., 1889, 207 pp.

[2] Froebel, *Autobiography,* p. 18. The quotations from this reference are used by permission of the publishers, Bardeen's, Inc.

money. It was essential for Froebel to become self-supporting as soon as possible, so he was soon apprenticed to a forester. For some time things went well, but at the end of two years there was some kind of dispute and Froebel left his position. At home he got no comfort. His stepmother was sure Froebel had been in the wrong, and his father lived up to a statement he had made two years earlier, when Froebel went to the forester's to live: "Never come back to me with any complaint, for I shall not listen to you, but shall consider you wrong beforehand." [3]

Froebel was thoroughly gloomy and disillusioned, and he did not know what to do next. He stayed at home for a few weeks, becoming steadily more and more despondent and surly. At this time an older brother who was attending the University of Jena* needed more money, and Friedrich, being unoccupied, was sent on the errand of transporting the funds. At Jena, the center of his dreams, he found so much to awaken him from his lethargy that he obtained permission to remain with his brother until the end of the term, only eight weeks away. This short taste of Jena, however, made him more determined than ever to enter the university. The next year he received a small inheritance from his mother that became available to him on his eighteenth birthday, and with this money, against family advice, he became a regularly enrolled student.

In the early years of the nineteenth century Jena was a center of philosophy and literature. It was under the personal supervision of Goethe, who constantly sought out for it the most stimulating professors he could find. The philosophical blaze had already been started by a dynamic professor named Fichte* who came to Jena in 1793, the same year as the Reign of Terror* in Paris. This fiery gentleman put extreme emphasis upon the individual ego,* considering it a creator of the universe; he taught that the ego builds its own environment and is the only real thing in the world. This philosophy came into popularity at just the time when the Germans were thoroughly under Napoleon's heel and was an important intellectual element in the revolt that finally drove foreign influence out of the Germanies. Following Fichte came Schelling,* who, incidentally, had considerable influence upon Froebel. Schelling accepted the importance of the ego, but he did not attribute to it the power of creation; rather he regarded it as an inner force that observes, understands, and recognizes Nature in all its phases. That is, Nature exists of itself, but it is the human ego that has the power to interpret, organize, and unify Nature. Froebel's interest in an "inner unity" of life seems to have dated from his contacts with Schelling. Hegel,* perhaps the greatest of the German philosophers, was also at Jena, although he does not appear to have had an in-

[3] *Ibid.*, p. 27.

fluence upon Froebel. The philosophy of Fichte and Schelling laid the groundwork for a movement called romanticism* that reached into the fields of literature, art, religion, and education. The romanticist looked within himself to find the materials for his writing; he turned his back upon the world about him and tried to create an ideal world of his own. The resulting product was not supposed to reflect reality, but to interpret Nature in terms of his own inner unity. Perhaps because romanticism offered an escape from the current dissatisfaction with church, state, and the entire social order, it was tremendously popular. The center of this movement was Jena during the years that Froebel attended it, and there he acquired the current attitudes of his time. He was by nature and early experiences already turned in upon himself and given to escaping from reality, and he was therefore ready to react strongly to an innoculation of romantic ideas.

In addition to philosophical and literary developments at Jena, there was much creative work in the field of drama. In all probability Froebel saw Schiller's* greatest plays when they were first produced at Weimar. Students from Jena were accustomed to walk to and from Weimar to attend the theater, and Froebel mentions frequent attendance. His reactions must have been deep, for years later in his schools he always made provision for little theaters, puppet shows, and play acting generally.

So far as actual class enrollment was concerned, Froebel's work at Jena was restricted to mathematics, physics, architecture, surveying, and chemistry, but on his own statement he constantly visited other classes and learned much of current philosophies. He was, however, expected to become a forester, farmer, or builder, and not a professional man. His family's low opinion of his abilities seems to have influenced his own thinking, and he intended entering some practical type of work. In the meantime, however, he was roaming about the university, sampling whatever intellectual nourishment was offered.

In his second year, he got into serious difficulties with the authorities because he ran into debt. He had loaned some of his scanty funds to an older brother who did not repay him as agreed, and he had been unable to persuade his father to advance the small sum needed to tide him over until the brother could return the loan. A less obstinate young man or one less thirsty for knowledge would have given up the uneven struggle, but Froebel was determined to remain in his paradise, come what may. What actually came was a sojourn for nonpayment of debts in the prison maintained by the university for its recalcitrant students. Here he became despondent and reverted to his earlier patterns of frustration and revolt. Finally, his father agreed to pay off the debts, provided his son would renounce all claims to the paternal inheritance he might otherwise have expected. It is true that the young man received somewhat harsh treatment in this whole episode, but his own behavior was not blameless. When he found himself getting into debt, he should have left the university. His stubborn clinging to a course of action and his willingness to let others foot the bill were traits that he carried with him into adult life. He did not especially want or need money for himself, but once he became hypnotized by an idea or purpose he was willing to sacrifice himself or others to its fulfillment. The Jena interlude that began so auspiciously ended in shame, humiliation, and a dejected return to his father's house, where he was not wanted at any time and where at the moment there was more tension than usual because of the endless recriminations on both sides about the debts and the manner of their settlement.

For some weeks he remained at home, trying to do some reading in lieu of his interrupted university work and even writing out summaries of what he read, but his father had no use for such a "foolish waste of time and paper." Froebel, now nineteen years old, was not trained for any type of work, but he saw it was necessary for him to get away from home and learn to support himself. First he was sent to a near-by farmer for whom he worked a while. Then he was called home by his father's last illness, during which father and son seem to have become reconciled. After his father's death, Froebel was a clerk in a bishopric, but he got tired of the "everlasting scribbling" and resigned. On the rebound from too much confinement indoors, he went into surveying. Tiring of this, he became in turn a private secretary and a bookkeeper. To give some nourishment to his spirit in these days of rather dull routine, he read the romantic novels popular at the time and further developed the idealism that had begun to blossom at Jena.

Still dissatisfied with his work, Froebel decided that he wanted to study architecture. For this purpose he persuaded an older brother to advance him some money, and with funds in his pocket he set off for Frankfort, where he applied himself with almost frantic zeal to his studies. He was not, however, happy, and he was soon plagued by doubts as to his new choice of vocation. Throughout this four-year period of vacillation Froebel seems to have had no feeling of "inner unity," a feeling apparently necessary to his contentment with life. During this period of great perplexity he chanced one day to visit an experimental school maintained by a former pupil of Pestalozzi's. Here Froebel met several members of the teaching staff and observed the work with the children. As he became better acquainted with the group, he began to discuss aims and philosophies of life and education with them, incidentally revealing his own interests and motivations. The head of the school, after studying his visitor for a while, one day spoke a few words that changed Froebel's life. "Be a teacher," said he, "give up architecture. It is not your vocation."

Up till that moment teaching had apparently never occurred to Froebel as a possibility for himself, and he was by no means sure now that it was practicable. He had had no training, knew nothing about teaching, and had no money for more schooling. Still, the older man's words had rung a bell inside him, and for the first time he seemed to be choosing a vocation with his heart rather than with his head. While he hesitated, not seeing his way through the various practical difficulties involved, a teacher at the model school resigned and he was offered the job with a promise of guidance from the head of the school. The final straw that tipped the balance toward teaching was the loss of certain papers of recommendation that Froebel considered necessary for getting a job in architecture. As Froebel said in his autobiography, "I interpreted this mishap to signify that Providence Himself had broken down the bridge behind me and cut off my retreat. Willingly, joyfully, I seized the proffered hand and soon was a teacher in the Model School at Frankfort-on-the-Main." [4] At last he had arrived at work that really satisfied him.

At the time of his entrance into the teaching profession, Froebel was twenty-three years old. He was a somewhat introverted young man whose mild manner covered a driving determination, a settled obstinacy, and an inflexible will. He was already a man with an Idea, although this controlling concept was still hazy even to himself. As he grew older, his Idea grew ever clearer, and he was more and more dominated by it. Many elements entered into this dominance. Froebel's repressed and frustrated childhood had given him no sense of security in his home or family, and his university experiences had produced further frustration. Always he was forced back upon himself, and he had found security in his dreams, his ideals, and his purposes in life. In his childhood he was not only neglected but ridiculed for his supposed stupidity. The only way for him to obtain the education that he craved was to develop enough obstinacy and inflexibility of purpose to overcome the obstacles in his path. His intense ambition to make something of himself was also presumably due to the constant reflections upon his ability. There is evidence that Froebel had none of the quick verbalism that distinguishes most brilliant students. He absorbed what he heard, turned it over and over in his mind, chewed on it, related it to pre-existing ideas, and finally accepted or rejected it on the basis of its value to him. His mind was deliberate and of a philosophical bent, but it was independent, and an idea once accepted could not be dislodged from it. To such a mind and personality, harmony of thought and purpose of the inner and the outer man, of the real and the ideal, is essential. In teaching, Froebel found the harmony he sought, and thus came to an end of his prolonged adolescent struggles and wanderings.

[4] *Ibid.*, p. 52.

From the first day in the model school Froebel was a success as a teacher. Without an hour of intentional preparation for this work, he walked into his first class of some thirty-five small boys between the ages of nine and eleven, and started to teach as if he had been doing it all his life. In his own words:

> From the first hour my occupation did not appear in the least strange to me; on the contrary, I seemed to myself to have been a teacher already for a long while, and in fact to have been born for the business. I cannot tell you in words sufficiently striking how peculiar was this experience of mine. It seemed to me as if I had never been willing to live in any other condition but this, and yet I confess that not the least idea of becoming a teacher in a public school had ever entered my mind. I find myself, when I am occupied with instruction, just in my element. You cannot believe how delightfully the hours glide away. I love the children from the bottom of my heart, and when I am out of class I long to get back to their instruction.[5]

In spite of his natural talent for teaching, however, Froebel felt a need for some degree of guidance and soon made a trip into Switzerland to observe Pestalozzi's school at Yverdon. What he saw there thrilled and inspired him, but he was by no means satisfied with Pestalozzi's explanation of teaching and learning exclusively by sense perception. This theory left out the inner values so important to all romanticists. At this time Froebel does not seem to have formulated in his own mind just what was lacking in Pestalozzi's work, but he was aware of dissatisfaction. However, his observation of the children and of the general Yverdon atmosphere filled him with new eagerness to get back to his own schoolroom.

Things went well with Froebel for about a year. He was especially successful in his teaching of geography, but in all fields he was more than adequate. He loved the children, but he chafed under the necessary routine of a large school. Actually, the model school had far less routine than most schools of the period, but it had more than Froebel could stand. He had spent his life in a continual revolt against authority, and he could not now alter his behavior pattern. When he was told to take the children out for recess from 10:10 to 10:50, he reacted with the same evidences of frustration and impotence that he had shown as a child when his stepmother ordered him to do this or that. Now that he was at last free from home domination, he could not bear the slightest curb. Therefore, in spite of his great promise as a schoolteacher, Froebel left his position.

During the next few months Froebel made one of his numerous efforts to master a language—in this case French, which was then greatly in vogue—but he was incapable of learning grammar. Aside from having little verbal facility

[5] *Ibid.*, p. 109.

of any kind, Froebel always revolted against rules and regulations—and grammar is largely rules. Instead of accepting the fact that the French put most adjectives after their nouns, Froebel spent his energy in arguing the premises. From the point of view of a beginner in a language, grammar has no sense; one simply takes it on faith. This was precisely what Froebel would not do. Coupled with his limited verbal ability, his attitude of revolt against formalism of all kinds, and his tendency to argue about basic concepts resulted in failure whenever he tried to learn a language for practical purposes.

After a few months of struggle with French, Froebel accepted a position as tutor, upon the condition that he and the three boys should live by themselves in the country and that he should have complete control over them. Accordingly he went into a sylvan retreat where he was free of all institutional life. The boys lived a normal, healthy existence, raised their own vegetables and other necessities, learned to do simple manual work, and spent a little time each day in formal schooling. For city-spoiled youngsters, the change was probably a good thing, but Froebel was not happy. He felt that his life and the lives of the boys lacked any guiding principle or inner unity. During this period Froebel wrote: "All is unity, all rests in unity, proceeds from unity, leads to unity, and returns to unity." [6] Although he felt the need of a central principle, he could not decide exactly what it should be. After a year of wrestling alone with this problem and of living with three small boys, he decided he had had enough of rural simplicity for a while and insisted upon making another trip to Pestalozzi, taking the boys with him. Thus ended Froebel's first attempt to follow Rousseau and to educate little Émiles.

At the time of his second trip in Yverdon, there were some two hundred pupils in Pestalozzi's school, located in the old castle. The building was more than half ruin, but within it there was a bustling, creative life, produced by a group of strongly individual, independent, sturdy teachers and pupils. In this environment of spontaneous activity Froebel and the three boys remained for two years, they as pupils and he as a teacher-pupil. That is, he attended classes with the children, sometimes helped one of the teachers, and tried to master the method of instruction as both a teacher and a learner. There were many of these teacher-pupils in the school, men of mature minds who spent long periods at the school studying the New Education. With them Froebel fraternized, and from them he learned much concerning his own defects of training and culture. Froebel was enormously attracted to Pestalozzi, although he saw the latter's shortcomings and noted how these were contributing to the disintegration of the famous school. From these two years at Yverdon, Froebel derived much that was to help him in later years. Among other things, he be-

[6] *Ibid.*, p. 69.

came interested for the first time in very small children and in preschool education through his perusal of Pestalozzi's *Mother's Book.* This germ of Froebel's greatest achievement—the kindergarten—did not grow for many years, but it was doubtless implanted at this time.

After his return to Germany, Froebel continued as tutor for one more year and then, the boys being now too old for tutoring, he resigned and at once enrolled in the University of Göttingen. Here he tried a new attack upon his old enemy, language, partly because he did not enjoy being defeated, partly because he had been made aware of his defects by his experiences at Yverdon, and partly because he saw that language study made up a major part of elementary school work and that mastery was necessary on purely practical grounds. This time he tried to master what he regarded as two "primitive" languages, with the idea of proceeding from them to other ancient tongues, then to modern languages; eventually he intended to find a unifying principle for all languages and to vivify them for the learner. The two languages he selected for the initiation of this great scheme were Hebrew and Arabic! He could hardly have chosen a worse combination. One semester of effort finally convinced Froebel that he was not the man to bring order out of linguistic chaos and thereafter he concentrated his attention upon other and more congenial fields.

Determined to find an inner unity somewhere, Froebel turned to the sciences and studied physics, chemistry, mineralogy, and natural history, thus continuing the line of work begun a decade earlier at Jena. For these subjects he had real ability. Gradually he concentrated upon one narrow field, the study of crystallography. To Froebel the crystal was an expression of natural orderliness and unification; to his romantic mind it was not so much an object as a symbol. If he could solve the mystery of the crystal, he was sure he could solve the essential mysteries of nature and thus find his unifying principle of life. He often called his crystals "voiceless witnesses to the silent, thousandfold creative activity of Nature." At about this time, the people of the Germanies were suffering under the burden of Napoleonism and were determined to become their own masters. Froebel heard much patriotic talk, but at first he was not interested in it. By the spring of 1813, however, he had been caught up into the fiery spirit that was sweeping across Germany, inspiring every man to rise up and throw off the yoke of the foreigner. He therefore left his quiet room, forsook his books and crystals, and volunteered in the service of his country. At this time Froebel was thirty-one years old. He had gone from one job and interest to another, never satisfied and always revolting against something. It did not yet appear that he was ever going to render any remarkable service to the world.

Froebel's year as a soldier was of great educational value to him in two ways. First, it broke into his seclusiveness and forced him to be constantly among people. Second, it furnished him with two helping friends who loved him devotedly and furnished him the elements that he conspicuously lacked. One of them, Heinrich Langenthal, was twenty-one years old, and the other, Wilhelm Middendorf, only twenty. The differences in age led to a decided hero-worship on the part of the two younger men, both of whom had recently been students of theology at Berlin. They were drawn to Froebel because of his intellectual superiority, but it was their youthful society that finally brought the older man out of his hermitlike existence and socialized him. They were Froebel's first intimates and to them he imparted his ideas about education. Middendorf, especially, drank in Froebel's conversation with an emotion bordering upon ecstasy. Middendorf was a handsome youth who attracted both men and women, but from his twentieth year until his death he concentrated his main attention upon his friend and became an apostle of Froebelianism.

2. *The School at Keilhau* By the year 1816, eleven years after his initial teaching experience, Froebel deemed himself ready to become an educator; he was through with learning, either of subject matter or of method. He therefore took temporary leave of his two friends, whom he had been seeing at intervals in Berlin, and set off on foot to a small village in Thuringia, whither he had been summoned by a letter from the widow of an elder brother. Presently Froebel opened his experimental school in the near-by village of Keilhau. For the first year the enrollment consisted of five boys. Three of them were sons of the dead brother, while two were sons of another brother; that is, all the pupils were Froebel's nephews! The school, nevertheless, had a high-sounding name—The Universal German Institute. At first it was financed mainly by the widowed sister-in-law, who clearly expected Froebel to marry her after a suitable period of mourning had elapsed. In the meantime she sent her three sons to the school, sold some of her property to buy the school grounds at Keilhau, and was most enthusiastic about Froebel's ideas. During the second year, Middendorf arrived at the school, bringing with him a younger brother of Langenthal; from this time on, Middendorf never left Froebel, never questioned him, never criticized him.

The school at Keilhau was based upon the principle of natural development through freedom. It rested squarely upon Rousseau, but—as usual—Rousseauism as it appeared after being filtered through another person's mind. The boys wore few and simple clothes, ate simple food, did a good deal of work outdoors, and roamed the countryside, but they also studied arithmetic, geometry, geography, and German. Little discipline was needed, because of the close personal bonds between teachers and pupils. Everything was on the same informal and homelike basis as in Pestalozzi's schools. The main differences were a lessened dependence upon sense perception, an increase in the emphasis upon the integration of experience from within, and a greater fluidity in the curriculum.

During the second year of the school Langenthal arrived for a visit. He had completed his training in theology, had accepted a parish, and had come to the school partly to visit his two friends and partly to take his brother home with him. The prospective loss of the only non-Froebel was serious, but not as serious as the prospective loss of Langenthal to the educational project. During his visit, Langenthal was constantly subjected to pressure and persuasion, for he had qualities the other two completely lacked, qualities essential for the school's success. He had a far better classical education than they and could consequently teach older children, he was perhaps less inspired than Froebel as a teacher but clearer and more logical, he had a markedly practical mind, he was a cultured gentleman, he could get along with other people, and he had an imposing, handsome, and dignified presence. As a representative of the school to the outside world he could hardly have been improved upon. Middendorf had an almost effeminate beauty, but was dreamy, impractical, and docile. Froebel himself was a man of the people and homely besides, a solitary genius who was so dominated by his ideas as to be often regarded as a crackpot. His notion of proper social contact with an outsider was to buttonhole him firmly and to lecture him unintelligibly and rather incoherently for hours. In the end, Langenthal resigned his new position, forsook the ministry, and remained at Keilhau.

The three friends and their little flock spent a glorious year together. To be sure, food was scarce, the dormitory was cold, and furnishings were inadequate, but all of them lived in a world of ideas and ideals and hardly noticed the inconveniences. When actual starvation was not far away, Froebel's sister-in-law sold her silverware to get money for food during the remaining winter and spring months until the school's gardens could begin to yield adequate supplies. She had furnished most of the financial support thus far and had lived for a year at the school as cook, housekeeper, and general manager. Froebel was certainly indebted to her enormously for both real and spiritual support. To what extent there was ever an agreement between them is not known, although the widow certainly expected marriage and a permanent connection with the school.

Froebel, however, had other ideas. He had met in Berlin an attractive young woman. She was well born, well educated, held a high position in Berlin society, came of a wealthy family, and was a charming and alert conversationalist. To be sure, she knew little of housekeeping and nothing of managing supplies for a school community. Froebel had been attracted to her, and Langenthal had been even more attracted to her adopted daughter. Both the latter and Middendorf kept urging Froebel to marry the lady from Berlin, ostensibly on the grounds that he needed just such a woman to give his school the prestige it needed. If Froebel had originally intended to marry his sister-in-law, he was argued out of it. He consequently ignored her and married the high-born lady from Berlin.

His act was incautious, to say the least, because he was indebted to his brother's wife for the land and buildings of his school, for the money raised by her sale of silverware, and for half of his enrollment. Moreover, after the arrival of Madame Froebel and her adopted daughter, it developed that the boys did not like either her or her high-toned ways. Langenthal, Middendorf, and Froebel were very happy to have two cultured ladies in their midst, but the country boys resented them. Also, in their youthful way, they resented the rejection of a woman—the mother of three of them—to whom they were all accustomed. The close association of teachers and pupils was interrupted, the bachelors' paradise no longer existed, and the teaching staff divided its attention between its charges and the newly arrived womenfolk. Naturally the sister-in-law left Keilhau in a rage, withdrew all support, and settled down in an adjacent village, where she remained, embittered and resentful.

It soon became evident that the school was on the brink of ruin. Madame Froebel was a bad manager, and Froebel was an equally bad administrator. He was also extremely stubborn and would not take advice, even from his best friends. In his little circle he was almost tyrannical in his insistence upon being the sole and unquestioned authority. By 1820 the school was saved from bankruptcy by the arrival of another family of Froebels. Christian Froebel, with his wife and three daughters, joined the two boys of the family who were already in school at Keilhau. Christian had been a successful merchant and was now a man of moderate wealth, but he retired from business and devoted himself for the rest of his life to the school. His three daughters all married into the instructional staff, the oldest marrying Middendorf. The character of the school naturally changed after this addition, for it was now a family affair in which a number of women had an influence. Soon the school began to prosper, and its enrollment increased in three years from six to sixty.

This state of affairs was, however, short-lived, largely because of Froebel's bad management and his belief in his own infallibility. He demanded absolute obedience from his staff, he would not allow the least independence on the part of his teachers, he regarded a dissenting opinion as a sign of disloyalty, he dictated even in subjects of which he was densely ignorant, and he would listen to no advice on money matters. Not even his friends and relatives could put up with him. They still loved him, but they banded together to save the school from his exaggerated ideas of his own importance. A second source of difficulty came from Froebel's nephews, the sons of the sister-in-law he had been expected to marry. They had remained in the school, but as they grew older and understood more of the circumstances, they became his enemies, hating him, stirring up trouble among the pupils, and eventually leaving the school. In addition to these sources of dissension within the school, there were accusations from without that the school was a center of radicalism and sedition. The government made investigations that were very trying, even though the reports officially cleared the school of the charges against it. The school was in debt, the enrollment had shrunk to only five pupils, Froebel had spent not only the fees from previous years but also the fortune of his brother Christian, and Middendorf's small savings. In the interests of the school, he had to be expelled as the head; he was still at liberty to live there, but from this time on he had no voice in the management. Christian Froebel, his daughters, and their husbands took over the school and made a success of it.

Froebel now had to face the results of his own foolishness. He tried to interest various local governments in educational schemes, but his reputation as a troublemaker was against him. It seemed as if his lifework would all come to naught. In a mood of deep despair he went on a visit to Frankfort, apparently in an effort to recapture the youthful enthusiasm of his first teaching days. Here he met a young Swiss nobleman who became so thrilled over Froebel's ideas as to invite him into Switzerland. The young man offered the older one his castle as a site for a school. The offer was accepted, and within two weeks Froebel was ensconced in a Swiss castle and heralded as a successor to Switzerland's own great educator, Pestalozzi.

3. Swiss Interlude Froebel was in Switzerland for over five years, during which he was connected with three different schools. The first one he left because he and the Swiss nobleman found upon further acquaintance that they could not get on together; the second, he left in charge of Middendorf, who had followed him to Switzerland, because the canton was torn by religious strife and the school had become a target for Catholic criticism. In both places he was subjected to attack from his embittered nephews, who were also living in Switzerland at the time. They even printed newspaper articles assailing his character as a citizen, a teacher, an administrator, and a debtor. Many points in these attacks were of course true, and Froebel could not publicly refute them. He had never paid back either his sister-in-law or his brother, both of whom had entrusted him with money for the school at Keilhau; he had been under suspicion of treason; his administration had been demonstrably bad, and his school had been taken away from him. He was thus in no position to answer these attacks or others of similar nature that were made by his nephews throughout his remaining years. In his third Swiss school, located at Burgdorf where Pestalozzi's first school had been, Froebel was somewhat protected by a strong local government, but even so there was muttered criticism of him as a person. The autocrat of the Keilhau school had to learn in a hard way that he was by no means infallible.

At Burgdorf, Froebel spent part of his time at an orphanage where, for the first time, he came in contact with children of preschool age. Two lines of thought about them occupied his mind. It seemed to him that these children needed to be presented with an orderly series of phenomena that would call forth their abilities, stimulate their mental activity, and produce an inner organization and integration. Thus arose the idea of the Play-Gifts, of which more will be said anon. The second line of thought concerned the position of the mother in preschool education and the need for educating both her and her child together. For this purpose he devised the first of the Mother's Play-Songs.[7] His new enthusiasm for very young children soon smothered his interest in older pupils and thus helped to heal the wounds inflicted by his enforced separation from Keilhau. Froebel did not yet know just what he did want, but he was tired of his present duties, so he resigned and returned to Germany, with ideas of play-songs and play-gifts simmering in his mind.

4. The Development of the Kindergarten and the Training of Teachers: For a few weeks he stayed in Berlin, where he studied the day nurseries that had recently developed in cities throughout Europe. These nurseries did not, however, appeal to him as a formulation of his ideas, and he soon returned to Keilhau, hoping to get money for a new venture. He found the atmosphere there distinctly hostile, but he did succeed in persuading the new head of the school, his youngest niece's husband, to advance him a small sum. With it he rented an abandoned powder mill in the neighboring village of Blankenburg* and there opened his first kindergarten. It was strictly pioneer work, because Froebel wanted to develop a school that was not merely custodial and charitable, but educational. The natives of the village regarded him as more than a little crazy, although they admitted he did have a way with small children. During his first two or three years at Blankenburg he worked out more of his gifts and songs. He had to hire someone to make the illustrations and print the material, and, since there was as yet no commercial value in his work, he had to set up a small printing press of his own in one part of the old mill. Froebel worked tirelessly, in a glow of almost fanatic

[7] See pp. 535–538.

enthusiasm about his new undertaking. At the time of his arrival in Blankenburg he was already a man of fifty-five, and he had already passed through a series of vicissitudes that would have discouraged a man of less native buoyancy and less determined stubbornness. Even the death of his wife, although a great blow to him, did not prevent him from developing his first little group of children into a school of some fifty preschool youngsters who ranged in age from one to seven. He now felt himself ready to advertise his new type of school, but he wanted a really good name for it. Up to this point he had used the descriptive but clumsy title, *Kleinkinderbeschäftigungsanstalt*—literally, an institution where small children are occupied—but this name was apparently too much even for a German. One day as he was taking a walk with Middendorf, the right word came to him. "Eureka," he cried, "I have found it! *KINDERGARTEN* it shall be called."

For seven years Froebel continued to labor at Blankenburg, working with the children and preparing his kindergarten materials. Finally, in his sixty-second year, he was ready to propagate the kindergarten all over Germany. His play-gifts were prepared, packed in boxes with printed directions for use, and his play-songs were written, illustrated, and printed.

During the remaining eight years of his life Froebel traveled about Germany, stirring up interest in his ideas, inspiring disciples, founding kindertens, and training teachers for them. For some months Middendorf accompanied him on his journeyings, but thereafter for a while Froebel went on alone. He visited city after city, town after town, village after village, first explaining his ideas to the people, then finding a proper teacher, and finally helping with the actual setting up of a kindergarten. During the winter months he returned to Keilhau, where he was most unhappy, and maintained a small training school for teachers. He could not persuade the head of the school to advance him enough money to have his school anywhere else, for his relatives well knew how his schemes always ate up funds. In the summer months, however, they let him have a sufficient sum for going about the country, perhaps to relieve themselves of his presence. The training school at first enrolled only four pupils, all men. In fact, Froebel had tried to direct his appeal chiefly to men, insofar as teacher training was concerned; married women had no time to teach, and such work was not then regarded as proper for young girls before marriage. Small children do not, however, appeal to most men. In the school's second year, three young women enrolled. All three of them soon became ardent disciples and remained Froebel's enthusiastic followers during his remaining years. Their work gave him his last great inspiration, the training of women as teachers of young children. There had been, to be sure, a few women who had taught school, but mostly they were deserving widows who taught from stern necessity and without training. The present preponderance of young women in elementary education was unheard of and unthought of. The first step toward that development was Froebel's deliberate selection and training of women for his kindergartens, a step he was led to take by the success of the three strong-minded damsels who enrolled for his school's second year.

The following winter, instead of returning to Keilhau, where he felt he was not wanted, he remained in Dresden,* teaching a group of prospective kindergartners. As the winter progressed, he became determined to establish a permanent training school of his own, but not at Keilhau. The situation there was especially difficult at this time. Aside from Froebel's usual protests at the tight financial rein kept upon him and his usual chafing at being only a hanger-on where he was once an autocratic ruler, he now stirred up a new tempest by deciding to marry one of the three kindergartners. This young woman was a country girl, a childhood friend of Froebel's youngest niece, who had come to Keilhau as a superior sort of kitchen help. The various nieces, who by now formed the feminine background of the school, were horrified and indignant. Not only was the girl more than thirty years younger than Froebel, but she was an ignorant country girl, quite unsuitable as the wife of a prominent man. In this girl—Luise Levin—Froebel found affection, understanding, and devotion instead of the constant opposition and criticism to which he was accustomed at Keilhau. During the years she attended the kindergarten school, the situation became so critical that she gave up her position at the school and went to live with one of the other students. At the end of the school year she traveled about Germany with Froebel, demonstrating the games and songs to groups of parents who were interested in opening a kindergarten. This journey was regarded as scandalous by Froebel's family, and he could not any longer return to Keilhau even for the winters.

He therefore selected a well-known watering place called Bad Liebenstein. Here Froebel opened his school for kindergartners in a big farmhouse, assembled some peasant children for a practice school, and sent for Luise Levin to join him. The peasant folk of Bad Liebenstein thought Froebel slightly insane because he spent his days apparently playing and dancing with children, and they nicknamed him "The Old Fool." The wealthy people, distinguished men and court followers who came to the baths, lived, for the most part, in a world quite apart from the peasants, but even they heard rumors about the strange old man. One of the visitors, the Baroness von Marenholtz-Bülow,* one day saw Froebel playing with a group of peasant children and was intrigued by the charm and patience with which he managed the little ones and by their obvious devotion to him. They were barely old enough to toddle about, while his flowing locks were gray, but in spirit he and they were alike. She was greatly impressed and called Froebel to her. After a short conversation he invited her to the farmhouse to see his play-gifts. Of all Froebel's converts and disciples, the baroness was perhaps the most extraordinary. She was a woman of forty-two, of aristocratic birth, wealth, position, and education; like other women of her period and class, she lived a rather idle life; but unlike many others, she was far from satisfied with it. After her first visit to Froebel's farmhouse, she announced, "I wish to become one of your pupils," and a pupil she became, taking lessons with the other kindergartners—young country girls for the most part—playing with barefoot, dirty, little children, and absorbing Froebel's spirit and doctrines. To her, the work brought interest instead of boredom, joy instead of sadness, and a goal instead of aimlessness; to it she brought her aristocratic presence, her acquaintance with all the great personages of her time, her driving energy, and her ability to philosophize and organize. She was to Froebel's doctrines what Paul was to the Christian religion. She recommended and explained them to the ruling powers, to the lesser nobility, to ministers and other governmental officers, to university professors, to authors, and to wealthy patrons of education. She had the entrée to social and educational levels that Froebel alone could never have reached. Moreover, the baroness wrote well and was able to publish articles in newspapers and magazines, interpreting Froebel's ideas and expressing them a great deal better than he could. Thus the convert of his old age was perhaps his most valuable one.

5. The Last Years This spring and summer of his sixty-seventh year Froebel spent in Bad Liebenstein. The following winter he received a call to come to Hamburg, where he was to be paid 100 thalers a month plus expenses. Such a remuneration—one suspects the baroness behind the offer—was unheard of heretofore, and the aging but inspired Froebel set out for Hamburg, where there was already much interest in his kindergarten, largely because one of Middendorf's daughters, whom he had earlier trained as a kindergartner, had been working there. Moreover, Middendorf himself was in Hamburg also, partly to see his daughter and partly to make the opening addresses for Froebel. He had performed this John the Baptist* role many times, for he was handsome, silver-tongued, magnetic, and persuasive, while Froebel was uncouth, incoherent, unimpressive, and homely. With such adherents to right and left, and with the fresh impetus given to his work by the admiration of the baroness and the devotion of Luise Levin, Froebel advanced upon Hamburg, sure of success and fame, at last. But once again, the hatred that had been generated years before by his failure to marry his brother's wife reached out of the past and dealt him a terrific blow.

One of Froebel's nephews had gone into educational work, having been trained for it by Froebel himself, had worked near his uncle in Switzerland, and had attacked him virulently both in speech and in print. This nephew, Carl Froebel, was in Hamburg trying to interest the people in the establishment of a Female University for the training of teachers and the higher education of women generally. Moreover, he had appropriated his uncle's latest brain child, the kindergarten, and had added it to his plans for a training school. There were thus two Froebels in Hamburg, both concerned with the education of women, both talking about kindergartens, both supported by the same class of people, and both having many ideas in common. Carl Froebel hated his uncle violently and passionately for what he regarded as a betrayal of his mother, while Friedrich Froebel hated his nephew for what he regarded as the latter's ingratitude toward him. Each Froebel reviled the other, and each had his disciples and adherents. In spite of this tense situation, however, Froebel's winter in Hamburg began well enough. Middendorf's lectures aroused great interest, and his daughter's fiancé, a young author began a series of articles on Froebel's doctrines in one of the local papers. This initial success Carl Froebel tried to counterbalance by publishing a pamphlet entitled *High Schools for Young Ladies and Kindergartens.* Since his uncle's interest in female education and schools for young children was well known, it is not surprising that most people should have supposed Froebel to be the author. The quarrel between the Froebels waxed hot and heavy—being, incidentally, the beginning of the various schools of Froebelianism in subsequent years—until at last the older man was exhausted and fled from Hamburg, leaving the field to his nephew.

Back at Bad Liebenstein, Froebel found Luise Levin and the baroness waiting for him, the latter occupied with the social stratagems necessary for obtaining the use of a near-by hunting lodge for Froebel's school. In the early spring the school moved into its new and pleasant quarters, and Froebel entered into the last happy year of his life. He had more kindergartners in training than ever before, and the stream of visitors to his school grew daily in volume. He put out on a long table sample sets of his materials, samples of things made by the children, and copies of his two main writings: *The Education of Man* and *The Mother Play-Songs.*[8] At certain hours he was present to explain his objectives and methods. During the summer, Froebel staged a great kindergarten festival on the grounds of the ducal castle. Over three hundred children from five towns, led by twenty-five trained kindger-

[8] *Education of Man* (translated by W. N. Hailmann). Appleton-Century-Crofts Company, 1910, 340 pp.; and *Mother-Play and Nursery Songs,* Lothrop, Lee & Shepard Co., 1906. 192 pp.

gartners, took part in the celebration. The play festival began with singing, marching, and folk dancing by the children, while the parents and the many guests at Bad Liebenstein watched. The entire affair went off very well and advertised Froebel's work still further.

Later on in the same summer, Froebel married Luise Levin, by this act breaking finally with his entire family. The only people present at his wedding were the faithful Middendorf and the baroness. These three disciples—Luise Levin, the baroness, and his old friend Middendorf—were the ones through whom his ideas were to be propagated and popularized after his death. Froebel now, however, experienced a period of youthful vigor and happiness, but not for long. His nemesis, the old quarrel with his nephews, again smote him, and this time very badly indeed.

As already mentioned earlier in this chapter, the people of Europe broke out in 1848 in widespread opposition to the reactionary* governments that had followed upon the French Revolution and the Napoleonic Wars. Most young men of the time were revolutionists, and it is not surprising that Carl Froebel, an unhappy and discontented person, should have been among the more extreme group. Froebel himself had always steered clear of all political involvement, mostly because he had no interest in such matters. To be sure, he was by nature a rebel, and he thought the governments of Europe tolerably bad when he thought about them at all, but he was too wrapped up in his own ideas to pay much attention to outside situations. Carl Froebel had, however, already come to official Prussian attention as a young revolutionary. In the autumn of 1851, the Prussian Minister of Education issued the following announcement:

> Whereas it appears by a pamphlet written by Carl Froebel, entitled, *High Schools for Young Ladies and Kindergartens*, that kindergartens form a part of the Froebelian socialistic system which is calculated to train the youth of the country to atheism, such schools and kindergartens cannot be suffered to exist.[9]

Both the publication and the participation in politics were the work of the nephew, but the blow fell mainly on the uncle. Prussia was the leading German state, and it had great influence upon the others. Froebel thus saw his lifework in danger of being throttled by administrative decree. The confusion of the two Froebels was clear enough in the wording of the decree, and the old man at first thought he could clear up the matter by submitting proofs of his continued and violent opposition to his nephew. The Prussian minister merely reaffirmed the interdict,* adding the untrue comment that the systems of both Froebels, whatever their other differences, were alike in being hostile to Christianity. At this rebuff to Froebel, the baroness promptly went

[9] From a decree issued on August 7, 1851, by the Prussian minister of education.

into action. She buttonholed every important figure in Berlin and even had an audience with the king of Prussia, but she could not get the decision rescinded. She therefore set about circumventing it by forming parents into kindergarten associations and using the Froebelian gifts with groups of children gathered together in someone's home. She kept working away at the situation, however, and finally, in 1860, succeeded in getting the ruling annulled.

FIG. 79. Friedrich Froebel. From R. Werkmeister, *Das neunzehnten Jahrhundert in Bildnissen.*

In a way, all the excitement about the kindergarten was probably helpful in the end, because the attempted suppression stirred up all Froebel's followers to greater efforts and gave his kindergartens more publicity than they would otherwise have received.

The effect of the blow upon Froebel was immediate and marked. The vigor that had always characterized him began to wane, and suddenly he was an old man. Throughout the winter of 1851–1852 Froebel became steadily weaker. His seventieth birthday was celebrated in the spring of 1852 by a children's festival, and a month later he roused himself sufficiently to attend a national convention of German teachers, where his work was praised and where his mere entrance into the assembly hall brought the applauding audience to its feet. Back in Bad Liebenstein after this excursion he became so weak that he had to stay in bed, and on the first day of summer in 1852, he died peacefully and quietly, surrounded by the three people who loved him best. Over his grave Middendorf caused to be erected a monument of his own design, based upon the ball, cylinder, and cube of the second Froebelian gift, and inscribed with the words of the great poet Schiller: "Come, let us live for our children."

The portrait of Froebel, reproduced in Figure 79, shows him to have been an individual of unusual appearance. Even when carefully combed and dressed he was far from handsome. His face was not that of a contented, well-balanced, and happy man.

After Froebel's death his work was carried forward by his many former pupils and especially by his three dearest friends. The baroness spent her life and fortune spreading Froebel's doctrines and methods throughout Europe. Middendorf intended to join in this work, but after Froebel's death he drooped and grew tired; within a year he, too, had died. Luise Levin Froebel continued in charge of her husband's training school, which she moved after some years to Hamburg, the city that became the center of her activities. She was so much younger than her husband that she outlived him by nearly fifty years. It was not until 1900 that her death broke the last personal bond with Froebel, the original kindergartener.

B. THE KINDERGARTEN

Froebel's permanent influence upon education is confined mainly to the preschool level and to the introduction of young, unmarried women as teachers for children. Even today, an observer can hardly help seeing strong traces of Froebel's work and materials in his main creation, the kindergarten. The present account will therefore be restricted to a statement of Froebel's basic tenets and a description of the materials devised by him for putting his theories in effect.

1. Froebel's Basic Point of View Froebel held views in basic contradiction to those of Herbart. Whereas Herbart exalted the function of the teacher, Froebel exalted the interests and spontaneous activities of the child. In fact, he was lyrical, mystic, sentimental, and ecstatic over the nature of little children. To him the child was the sole source of educational principles, and the teacher merely followed where the pupils led. The child thus becomes educated by developing himself through his own creative activities. Education, according to Froebel, is the constant progressive adjustment of an individual to the world around him by which he discovers his true self; it is thus only one phase of the general process of evolution. It is therefore not the teacher's business to teach but to keep out of the way and let the child grow. Two quotations from Froebel's writings express his basic point of view:

> It is not the educator who puts new powers and faculties into man, and imparts to him breath and life. He only takes care that no untoward influence shall disturb nature's march of development. The moral, intellectual, and practical powers of man must be nurtured within himself and not from artificial substitutes. Thus, faith must be cultivated by our own act of believing, not by reasoning about faith; love, by our own act of loving, not by fine words about love; thought, by our own act of thinking, not by merely appropriating the thoughts of other men; and knowledge, by our own investigation, not by endless talk about the results of art and science.[10]

> For the purpose of instruction is to bring ever more *out* of man rather than to put more and more *into* him; for that which can get *into* man we already know and possess as the property of mankind, and every one, simply because he is a human being, will unfold and develop it out of himself in accordance with the laws of mankind. On the other hand, what yet is to come *out* of mankind, what human nature is yet to develop, that we do not yet know, that is not yet the property of mankind; and still human nature, like the spirit of God, is ever unfolding its inner essence.[11]

Self-activity is a second principle of Froebel's approach to education. His concept of self-activity may be defined as an activity determined by one's own interests, sustained by one's own power, and carried to conclusion in an atmosphere of freedom from interference by others. Because he was willing to leave children free and to take his cue from them, Froebel discovered the great educational value of play, of handwork, and of spontaneous co-operation among children. He did not, however, leave children without guidance. Like many other people with a quick intuitive understanding of human nature, he saw what each child was like and what he needed, just as clearly as he saw the color of the child's eyes, and he adapted himself automatically to his intuitive grasp of another's inner life. What he could not do—perhaps no one can—was to tell other people how he proceeded. Froebel's own kindergarten was a little world in which everyone shared the responsibilities, enjoyed the rights, and contributed his share.

Another cardinal point was his insistence upon the necessity of a unified

[10] Froebel, *Education of Man,* p. 4. Excerpts from this work are used by permission of the publishers, Appleton-Century-Crofts, Inc.
[11] *Ibid.,* p. 279.

inner life. It is not always quite clear what he meant, but he left no doubt as to the importance of inner unity and peace. The selections below give an illustration of his attitudes on these points:

Play is the purest, most spiritual activity of man at this stage [childhood] and, at the same time, typical of human life as a whole—of the inner hidden natural life in man and all things. It gives, therefore, joy, freedom, contentment, inner and outer rest, peace with the world. It holds the sources of all that is good. A child that plays thoroughly, with self-active determination, perseveringly until physical fatigue forbids, will surely be a thorough, determined man, capable of self-sacrifice for the promotion of the welfare of himself and others. . . . The plays of childhood are the germinal leaves of all later life; for the whole man is developed and shown in these, his tenderest dispositions, in his innermost tendencies. The whole later life of man, even to the moment when he shall leave it again, has its source in the period of childhood. . . . If the child is injured at this period, if the germinal leaves of the future tree of his life are marred at this time, he will only with the greatest difficulty and the utmost effort grow into strong manhood; he will only with the greatest difficulty escape in his further development the stunting effects of the injury or the one-sidedness it entails.[12]

It is the spirit alone, then, that makes the school and the school-room; not the increasing analysis and isolation of what is already isolated—a process that has no limits and supplies ever-new data for further analysis and reduction—but the unification of that which is isolated and separate by attention to the uniting spirit that lives in all isolation and diversity. This is that which makes the school.[13]

Therefore at an early period, even in boyhood, man seeks unity and union for this externally separate diversity and individuality among objects; seeks unity and union in a separation which in obedience to a necessary law of inner development presents things outwardly in apparently confused heaps. His mind is contented when he begins to apprehend this unity and union, but only later on, when he has found it, is his spirit fully satisfied.[14]

The [boy's mind] thus steadily grows in clearness and purity, his powers are ever enhanced and increased, his courage and perseverance strengthened by thus finding the confirmations of these truths in his own life and in that of others, in individual and common life, in experience and revelation; by thus finding the harmony and unity of revelation in scripture, nature, and life; by thus seeing himself the member of a whole unfolding from the small domestic circle into ever wider and higher realms, of a whole whose common purpose he recognizes, amid the most positive evidences of divine guidance and care, in the representation of the spiritual in and by the corporeal, of the divine in and by the human.[15]

[12] *Ibid.*, pp. 55–56.
[13] *Ibid.*, p. 134.
[14] *Ibid.*, p. 166.
[15] *Ibid.*, p. 237.

These passages are crystal-clear in comparison to many others, although Froebel's mysticism permeates all his writing, opening vistas to those of similar disposition, but leading to confusion in more practical minds.[16]

2. *Froebel's Materials and Procedures* Undoubtedly, it was the materials[17] that made the kindergarten what it was. Most of these are by now so familiar, in either their original or their many derived forms, as to seem commonplace, but in 1830 none of them existed. Their appropriateness to the mentality of little children is shown by their continued use and popularity. Although few children of today are presented with Froebel's "gifts" just as he designed them, most small children are provided with closely related materials, generally purchased at the five-and-ten-cent store. Froebel's influence is thus likely to continue as a vital factor in the lives of preschool youngsters, wholly aside from his direct influence upon kindergartens and nursery schools.

Froebel's kindergarten centered around three procedures—the use of his gifts, the singing of his songs, and the playing of various educational games in the play-circle. These three features will be considered in order.

Froebel's gifts consisted of blocks or other materials arranged as a unit in a box, from which the child removed them to play with and to which he returned them. The manipulations with each gift, the study of it, and the conclusions drawn from it required weeks for their completion. In addition to certain prescribed handling and discussion of each gift, there was a great deal of free play, with each child following where his fancy led him. The materials were of two types: geometrical patterns, and the essentials for such activi-

[16] Anyone who wishes to read a passage from Froebel at his most mystical might try the following, written in 1821: "The spherical is the symbol of diversity in unity and of unity in diversity. The spherical is the representation of diversity developed from the unity on which it depends, as well as the representation of the reference of all diversity to its unity. The spherical is the general and particular, the universal and the individual, unity and individuality at the same time. It is the finite development and absolute limitation; it connects perfection and imperfection. All things unfold their spherical nature perfectly only by representing their nature in their unity—in some, individuality; and in some, diversity. The law of the spherical is the fundamental law of all true and adequate human culture."—*Education of Man,* p. 169.

[17] Descriptions of Froebel's materials and methods may be found in the following references: F. W. Froebel, *Mother-Play and Nursery Songs* (translation of Mutter and Koselieder), Lothrop, Lee & Shepard Co., 1906, 192 pp. (two other translations and adaptations of the same book are J. L. Hughes, *Froebel's Educational Games and Stories,* Appleton-Century-Crofts Company, 1885, 289 pp., and D. J. Snider, *Froebel's Mother-Play Songs,* Sigma Publishing Company, 1895, 394 pp.); H. Goldammer, *The Kindergarten Handbook of Froebel's Methods of Educational Gifts and Occupations* (translated by W. Wright), E. Steiger and Company, 1892, 2 vols.; W. H. Herford, *The Student's Froebel,* D. C. Heath and Company, 1906, 112 pp.; D. J. Snider, *The Psychology of Froebel's Gifts,* Sigma Publishing Company, 1900, 384 pp.; K. D. Wiggin and N. A. Smith, *Froebel's Gifts,* Houghton Mifflin Company, 1897, 202 pp., and *Kindergarten Principles and Practice,* Houghton Mifflin Company, 1896, 205 pp.

ties as modeling, drawing, sewing, coloring, and so on. The latter were referred to as the "occupations" and the former as the "gifts."

A few comments should be made upon the nature and inner connections between these gifts and the use made of them. The first gift consists of six soft, colored balls; the second includes a cube, a cylinder, and a sphere. The later gifts in the series are derived from the second. Gifts 3, 4, 5, and 6 result from various dissections of the cube, as shown in Figure 80 on page 532. Gift 7 consists of two cylinders that are divided in different ways. Gifts 8, 9, and 10 are designed to represent, in turn, planes, lines, and points. The last four gifts appear in Fig. 81 on p. 533. The tablets in the eighth gift are made by cutting a thin piece off the end of a shape formerly met. The sticks of the ninth are the lines, and the small objects of the tenth are the points. The same geometrical motifs are thus repeated over and over. The gifts are not, therefore, merely building blocks cut at random, but blocks so made as to illustrate certain relationships and to form a unified whole.

The materials are used in sundry ways in the teaching of form, number, and measurement. The child learns to count, to combine and divide, to make fractions out of wholes. The fundamental concepts grow naturally out of the materials; thus the third gift provides the child with the means of discovering halves, fourths, and eighths—also for counting up to eight or backward from 8 to 1, or dividing 8 by either 2 or 4, or squaring or cubing 2. The fifth gift gives similar opportunities to manipulate 3, 6, 9, 12, 15, . . . or 1/3, 1/6, 1/9, 1/12, 1/15 . . . or squaring or cubing 3. By arranging the pieces side by side, one can demonstrate the basic geometrical concepts underlying all square measure and by arranging them in solid form, those underlying all cubic measure. Even the simplest of the gifts, the six balls, permits counting and combining. The whirling of the cube, cylinder, and sphere of the second gift demonstrates the interrelation of forms, because one form can be so whirled as to turn into another. The gifts therefore lead children to examine, compare, arrange in order, measure, count, and analyze because the pupils see for themselves that two blocks are the same shape but of different size or the same size but different shape, or that two smaller blocks just equal a larger one, and so on. Many kindergarten teachers personify the forms. Thus the cubes in the third gift may be thought of as a family of eight children all just like each other; in the fifth, there are three generations. The brick-shaped pieces can be, in successive positions, a man standing on his feet or his head, lying on his back, his stomach, his right or his left side.

Naturally, the children use the blocks in free play. They build houses, barns, autos, airplanes, schools, and so on. They also make patterns of various kinds, some geometrical, others not, some copied, others invented. Sample designs are given in Figure 82. A great deal of both sensory and muscular education is inherent in the mere playing with these materials.

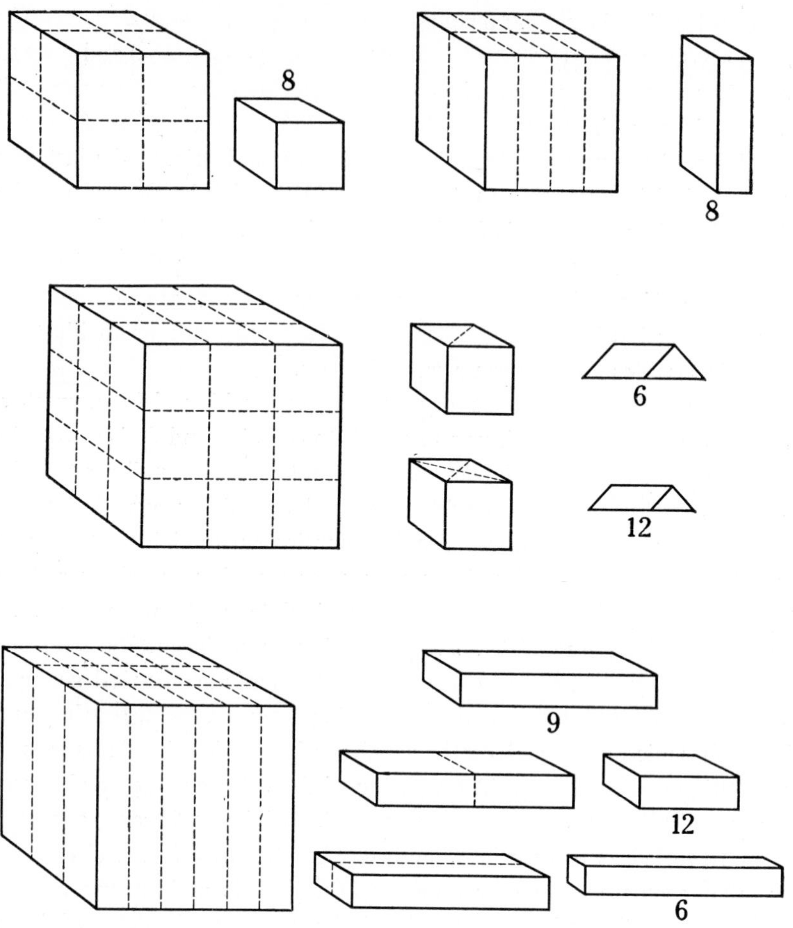

FIG. 80. Materials for Gifts 3, 4, 5, and 6.

The second series of gifts are called "occupations." Their order is not as well established as that of the geometric series, upon which they are in considerable measure dependent. That is, a child would make slow progress with the occupations if he had not been given the gifts first. Usually, however, the first occupation is clay modeling, perhaps because it does not require any implement except the child's two hands. One of the simpler occupations is the production of patterns by dots with colored pencils or by perforating a paper with some pointed instrument. Cutting is also simple so far as concepts are concerned, although some small children have trouble making the scissors work. As the children develop more and more muscular control, they proceed to such occupations as bead stringing, sewing in outlines on a perforated card, paper weaving, paper folding, the making of cardboard de-

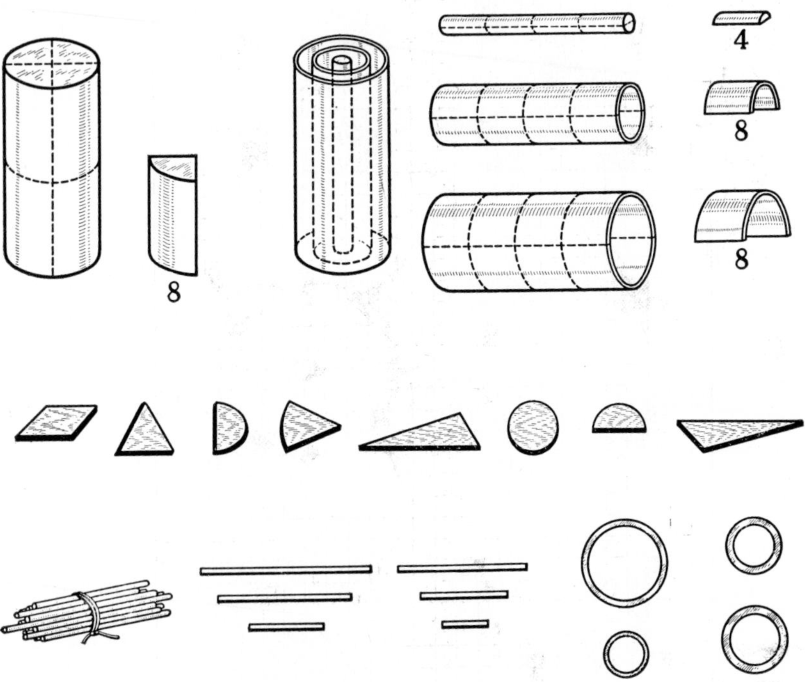

FIG. 81. Materials for Gifts 7, 8, 9, and 10.

signs, freehand drawing, coloring, tracing, and pasting. All of these activities call forth a child's creative activity and are therefore of interest to him. Two samples of work done by the author at the age of four during a year in what must have been a Froebelian kindergarten are shown in Figure 83.

3. Other Features of the Kindergarten Two other elements of Froebel's kindergarten were the play-circle and the play-song. Froebel was struck by the fact that children spontaneously play games in which they join hands to make a circle, and he adapted this procedure to his work. To this day, the chairs in a kindergarten are almost always arranged in a circle. Froebel had a complicated symbolic interpretation about the circle, most of which is by now forgotten, but the arrangement has remained largely because of its convenience, its elimination of distance between teacher and pupils, and its sociability. The educational and purely recreational games that are played in a circle are legion; some of them have come down from antiquity, while others were invented by Froebel or his followers.

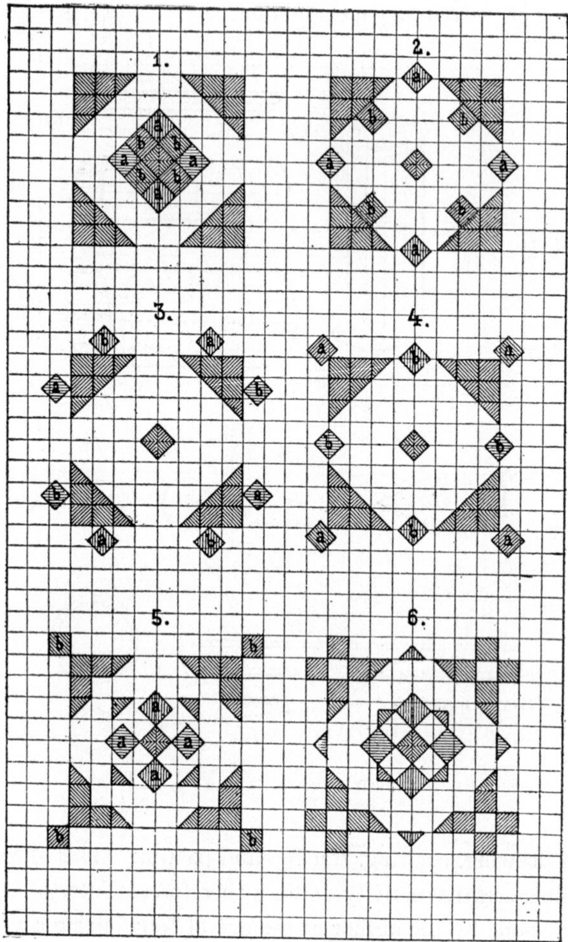

Fig. 82. Diagrams and Objects Made from Geometrical Forms. From F. Froebel, *Kindergartenwesen,* 1883; (a) *Schönheitsformen,* p. 260.

Finally, there were the Froebelian play-songs. Originally these were for use by the mother, and some of them could be used only by her, but others are equally valuable in the kindergarten. The book of play-songs is unique in a number of ways. It consists of inferior verse, worse music, and pictures that, while competently drawn, are odd and stiff—the whole production being wrapped in a sticky sentimentality and mysticism. One would hardly expect it to be a best seller, but actually its sale has been wide and continuous, and its imitators are legion. In composing this masterpiece Froebel had a good deal of help. Middendorf wrote many of the verses, another man contributed the music, and a third made the cuts, while Froebel seems to have furnished

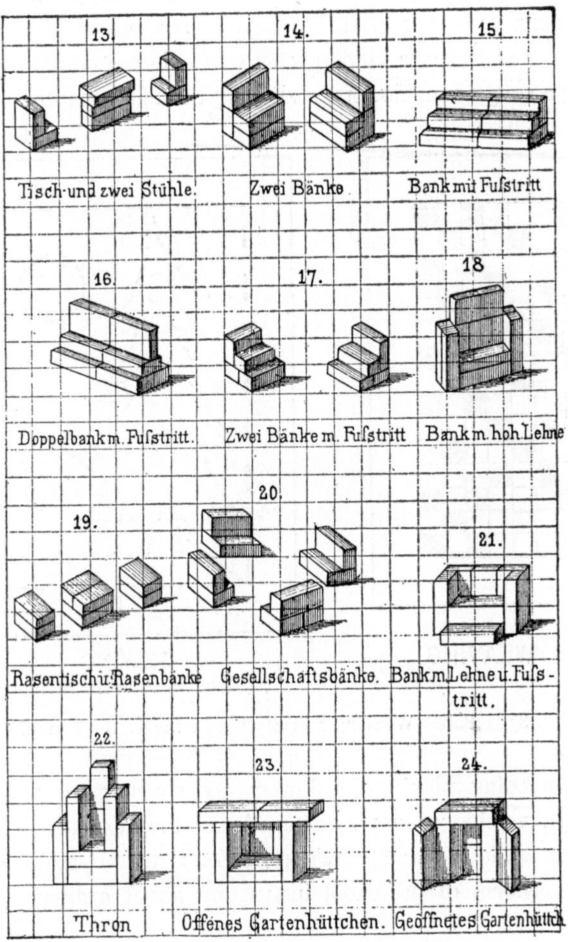

FIG. 82 (b) *Lebensformen,* p. 225.

Translation: Table and two chairs (13). Two seats (14). Seat with steps (15). Double seat with steps (16). Two seats with steps (17). Seat with a high back (18). Lawn table and seats (19). Party seats (20). Armchair with footstool (21). Throne (22). Open bower (23). Open bower (24).

the general idea, some of the verses, the arrangement of the material, and the driving power. Four sample pages appear in Figures 84 and 85.

The first one shows the common game of pat-a-cake that mothers play with their children, but it also links up the game with activities in the home.

The second starts as a shadow game but goes on to be a study of rabbits and hunting; using the pictures as a basis, the mother weaves a story for her child. The third page presents a number of activities connected with building. The teacher or mother explains the pictures and encourages questions from the child. The last picture is only incidental to a story about the knights and a good little boy, the picture being largely a focus for attention. Many kindergarten songs, plays, and stories have grown out of Froebel's original material. When a visitor to a kindergarten sees a dozen toddlers standing in a circle, singing a song about flowers, and going through a pantomime of plant-

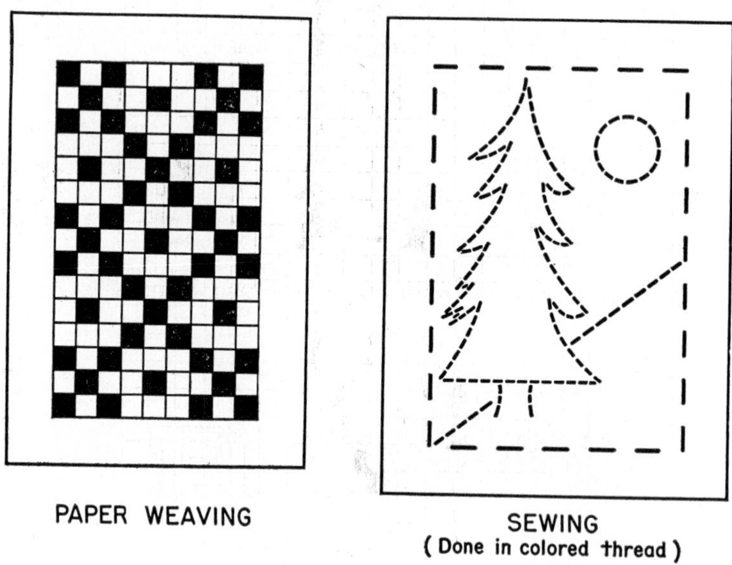

FIG. 83. Paper Weaving and Sewing in the Kindergarten.

ing, watering, weeding, picking the flowers, and smelling them, he is observing the modern version of a play-song. As in the case of the play-circle, Froebel took his model from children's spontaneous actions, added refinements, and evolved a system of preschool instruction about ordinary objects and activities.

The gifts, the occupations, the play-circle, the play-songs, and the woman teacher made Froebel's kindergarten what it was—something new in education. In the kindergarten the modern idea of an education adapted to childish needs, interests, and abilities rather than one arranged for adult activities from an adult point of view was clearly demonstrated. In spirit, Froebel was a descendant of Rousseau in his insistence upon letting children develop natu-

FIG. 84. Illustrations from the Mother-Play Songs (a). From F. Froebel, *Mutter- und Koselieder*, pp. 124, 194.

FIG. 85. Illustrations from the Mother-Play Songs (b). From F. Froebel, *Mutter- und Koselieder,* pp. 216, 240.

rally, and at the same time he was a follower of Pestalozzi in both his emphasis upon the education of the mother and his use of sensory stimulation as a means of promoting growth. In his belief that children develop best through guided self-activity rather than through instruction he was himself—Froebel, the first kindergartner.

Froebel conceived the kindergarten as an educative institution, determined its basic principles, and designed its first materials. With the passage of a century it has become, if anything, rather more Froebelian in spirit. Its modern descendant, the nursery school, is more nearly Froebel's idea of a proper environment for small children than his own kindergartens were. His gifts have been modified and made more flexible, and other materials have been added. The gifts still fascinate the small child, the occupations still stimulate him, the socialized games continue to enchant him, the songs, dramatizations, and stories are as bewitching as ever. Froebel thus continues to live in the happy self-activity of kindergarten children the world over.

READING REFERENCES

A. General Histories of the Period

Artz, *Reaction and Revolution,* chaps. 4, 7.
Garrett and Godfrey, *Europe since 1815,* chaps. 6–8.
Grant and Temperly, *Europe in the Nineteenth and Twentieth Centuries,* chaps. 11, 12, 15.
Hayes, *Political and Cultural History of Modern Europe,* Vol. II, chaps. 16, 17.
Hazen, C. D., *Europe since 1815,* Henry Holt and Company, 1910 (829 pp.), chaps. 7, 8.
Schapiro, *Modern and Contemporary European History,* chaps. 4–7, 12.
Schevill, *A History of Europe from the Reformation to the Present Day,* chaps. 23–25.
Stearns, *Pageant of History,* part ii, chaps. 26–29.

B. Other Texts in the History of Education

Boyd, *The History of Western Education,* chap. 12.
Cole, *The History of Educational Thought,* pp. 262–273.
Cubberley, *History of Education,* pp. 764–772.
Eby and Arrowood, *The Development of Modern Education,* chap. 21.
Graves, *A Student's History of Education,* pp. 390–409.
Marique, *History of Christian Education,* III, 128–234.
McCormick, *History of Education,* pp. 349–357.
Monroe, *A Textbook in the History of Education,* pp. 639–666.
Ulich, *History of Educational Thought,* pp. 284–291.

C. Secondary Sources

Bowen, *Froebel and Education by Self-Activity,* chaps. 1, 2, 5, 7.
Claxton, P. P., *Sketches of Froebel's Life and Times,* Milton Bradley Company, 1914 (194 pp.), pp. 28–123, 147–194.
Cole, *Herbart and Froebel,* chap. 1.
Graves, *Great Educators of Three Centuries,* chap. 11.
Herford, *The Student's Froebel,* pp. 68–97.
Kraus-Bölte, M., and J. Kraus, *The Kindergarten Guide,* E. Steiger and Company, 1906, Vol. I, *Gifts*; Vol. II, *Occupations.* (For descriptions of materials.)
Marenholtz-Bülow, B. von, *Reminiscences of Friedrich Froebel,* chaps. 1, 2, 4, 5, 13, 18, 19.
Painter, *Great Pedagogical Essays,* chap. 24.
Snider, *The Life of Friedrich Froebel,* book i, chaps. 1–3; book ii, chaps. 1–4.: book iii, chaps. 1–3.

D. Translations of Primary Sources

Fletcher, S. S. F., and J. Welton, *Froebel's Chief Writings,* Longmans, Green and Co., 1912, (246 pp.), part i, chaps. 4, 5, 12; part ii, chaps. 1–6.
Froebel, *Autobiography,* any 25 pages.
———, *Education of Man,* chap. 1, nos. 1–9; chap. 2, nos. 24–30; chap. 3, nos. 45–55; chap. 4, no. 56.
———, *Mother-Play Songs,* any 8–10 songs.
Ulich, *Three Thousand Years of Educational Wisdom,* pp. 523–576.

CHAPTER XIX

SEGUIN AND BINET: WORK WITH HANDICAPPED CHILDREN

Since the beginning of the nineteenth century two interrelated educational movements have traveled from Europe, and especially from France, to America. The first of these contributions concerned the proper teaching of handicapped children, especially the blind, the deaf, and the defective. It is easy enough to recognize which children are blind or deaf, but in order to determine which were defective it was necessary to devise some means of measurement. Under this stimulus, tests of intelligence were invented and the "testing movement" was thus begun. In both of these movements Èdouard Seguin, the main character of the first section in this chapter, played a prominent role. His methods of training are still used every day by those who teach low-grade defectives. Teachers of special classes in the public schools also use his materials for giving sensory training to their pupils. Some of the tests he devised were taken over by others and incorporated into scales for measuring intelligence. Two educators who followed him, Binet and Montessori, carried on his work. The former, who appears in the second section of this chapter, developed the first scale for measuring intelligence, while the latter followed Seguin's work with defectives and then went on to apply similar methods to the early education of normal children.

Children who are deaf or blind have always presented an educational problem. Until a century or so ago the best they could hope for was kindness and charity. Education was closed to the blind because they could not read, and to the deaf because they could not profit by oral classroom instruction. In the early half of the nineteenth century the Abbé de l'Epée* and Braille,* both of them Frenchmen, revolutionized the teaching of deaf and blind children, with the result that these handicapped pupils could go as far in school and do as well as anyone else. The last section of this chapter will contain a brief description of their work.

A. SEGUIN: HIS LIFE AND WORK

1. Seguin's Life story[1] Édouard Seguin was born in a little town in France in the year 1812. After a normal and well-adjusted boyhood he

[1] This account is based upon William Boyd, *From Locke to Montessori*, Henry Holt and Company, 1914 (272 pp.), pp. 88–129.

went to Paris to obtain his degree in medicine. While there, he studied in an institution for deaf-mutes and in a hospital for the insane, thus having opportunity to observe many types of defective intelligence.

As an adolescent Seguin came under the spell of a leader by the name of Saint-Simon,* the originator of a social theory that ultimately developed into socialism. Saint-Simon advocated a social reconstruction that would ameliorate the physical, intellectual, and moral lot of mankind, especially of the lowest classes. Some of his followers overlaid with a coating of mysticism and symbolism, his simple thoughts of a society based on the "love-one-another" theme, but others took his ideas literally and sought to regenerate humanity through love and kindness. Seguin became a follower of Saint-Simon and was inspired by him to love all human beings, even those who seemed most degraded and least worth saving. Even in his youth, Seguin did not subscribe to the accepted opinions concerning the educability of idiots. Contemporaries wrote such statements as this:

> Idiots are what they must remain for the rest of their lives. Everything in them betrays an organization imperfect or arrested in its development. No means are known by which a larger amount of reason or intelligence can be bestowed upon the unhappy idiot, even for the briefest period. . . .

or:

> It is useless to combat idiocy. In order to establish intellectual activity it would be necessary to change the conformation of organs which are beyond the reach of all modification.[2]

Seguin, although he followed in the footsteps of earlier French physicians and alienists, was saved from their doctrine of fatalism by the influence of Saint-Simon.

Seguin's main concern was with those sad creatures at the bottom of the human scale, the idiots. These forlorn and neglected children he loved with a gentle, Christian devotion. He thus approached the problem of idiocy from two directions: on the one hand, he was a well-trained physician and had had adequate opportunity to learn what was then known about the causes of and treatments for defectives, while on the other hand, he had a deep emotional attachment to the poor unfortunates and showered upon them an affection that most of them had never known. His work was possible because he blended the best features of medicine and philanthropy by having a scientist's sound knowledge and an idealist's boundless enthusiasm.

By the time he was twenty-five, Seguin thought he was ready to begin his

[2] The first was the opinion of the great alienist* Esquirol* and the second appeared in the *Dictionnaire de médicine* published in 1837. Both are quoted on p. 91 of Boyd, *op. cit.*

lifework, on a small scale. He therefore undertook the education of an idiot child, with whom he worked for eighteen months, developing the fundamentals of his method. At the end of this time the idiot could look after his bodily needs, use his five senses, speak intelligibly, write a little, and count. Encouraged by this success Seguin opened a small school for idiots. Five years later he requested that a commission be appointed by the Parisian Academy of Sciences to examine ten of his pupils. The commission's report was most favorable, even stating flatly that Seguin had solved the problem of educating idiots. This commendation stirred up great interest, and soon doctors, alienists, and teachers began to visit Seguin's school in Paris, some of them remaining to be trained by him as teachers for defectives. From his embryo training school he sent out a number of graduates who founded schools in Europe and America. The idiot child is always such a pressing problem that news of a solution spread quickly, and classes modeled upon Seguin's sprang up everywhere.

The work was thus well under way, but in a few years it came to an abrupt end, so far as the school in Paris was concerned. The Revolution of 1848, with its aftermath of reaction, discontent, and oppression, disgusted and infuriated Seguin. He had no particular interest in politics, but he felt a burning devotion to his fellow man, and he did not believe that human beings could work effectively in an environment of suspicion and discontent. He therefore closed his school in Paris and emigrated to the United States. For some time he worked as a practicing physician in Ohio, but he soon became again identified officially with the education of defectives by accepting an appointment as head of the Pennsylvania Training School for Idiots. Here he remained for several years, but he did not like administrative details and routine. He loved to teach idiots, but such chores as signing requisitions, dealing with tradesmen, supervising buildings, and so on, only annoyed him; so he resigned his post and went to New York City, where he lived for the rest of his life. He was constantly consulted by those in charge of institutions for the feeble-minded, he gave lectures, he devised new methods or materials, and he wrote. By the time of his death in 1880 he had seen the fulfillment of his youthful dreams in the widespread use of his methods in both his native and his adopted country for the education of idiots, and the further adaptation of his methods to the instruction of normal children.

2. *His Methods:* Seguin's methods can be described in their essentials in a few paragraphs, but even the best teacher must expect to apply them over a period of years in order to educate an idiot. The extreme defective does not react to stimulation from his environment, not only because his mind is subnormal but also because both his sensory equipment and his muscular control are deficient. A stimulus cannot, therefore, "get through" to the brain. Nor can

the idiot carry out an intention, assuming he has one, because he cannot direct his muscular responses. Seguin's technique begins, therefore, with motor education, so that the disordered and un-co-ordinated movements may be brought under control.

To teach an idiot to stand up the trainer holds the child upright upon two flat pieces of wood, the same size as the child's feet and then releases him. The idiot promptly falls down, but enough repetitions will teach him to stand. Some defectives begin to walk of their own accord as soon as they can hold themselves upright, but most of them do not. Seguin devised a walking machine that gave the idiot some support and automatically pushed his legs forward for each step.[3] Once walking is achieved, the idiot becomes less of a problem because he can be out of bed, he can stay with other children whose presence will help stimulate him into taking an interest in life, and he will soon learn such group actvities as marching to music, especially to heavily accented drumming. The motor education continues with exercises in climbing over boxes, in going up and down stairs, in following a series of footprints that wind about in unexpected directions; in swinging Indian clubs, in throwing a ball, in carrying objects from one table to another. Often an idiot cannot grasp anything in his hands; before the above exercises can even be started he must develop a power of prehension* that a normal child has naturally. To obtain this, the teacher lifts the child a few inches off the floor and presses his hands under her own around a rung of an inclined ladder; then she releases her own hand, and the idiot falls because his hands will not grasp the rung alone; just before he hits the floor she catches him, thus avoiding injury but not preventing altogether the fright that comes even to an idiot when he falls. She then puts the child's hands back on the ladder and repeats the whole performance again and again until the child learns that only by hanging on can he prevent an unpleasant result. Once he can support his own weight, such exercises as traveling from rung to rung, swinging on rings, or clambering over a jungle-gym can be introduced.

When the idiot has gained voluntary control over his larger muscles it is time to eliminate most of the artificial aids to learning and to apply the skills already gained to such activities as digging a hole in the ground, sweeping a floor, pushing a lawnroller, and—a little later—getting dressed or undressed, eating properly, washing, and going to the toilet. The cost of caring for an idiot is enormously reduced when he reaches this stage, and he begins to get some pleasure out of life and to be of slight value in the world.

The education thus far has awakened the idiot to a consciousness of the world about him, and he now begins to imitate. The teacher first teaches him to imitate such large movements as sitting or kneeling, then smaller movements such as waving an arm, then finer and more complex actions such as standing a book upright on a table or balancing a larger block on a smaller one. At first, the imitation lesson has to be given individually because the idiot's at-

[3] Such machines are now in use to re-educate wounded soldiers, infantile paralysis victims, and spastic children.

tention wanders easily, but after he has begun to get enjoyment out of imitating the teacher, several children can be trained at once, especially if the exercises are carried out to drum beats. With the habit of imitation well established the child can be taught all manner of simple, useful tasks.

In the course of this training the idiot's mind has slowly awakened. To be sure, his intellectual capacities are of a low order, but he is by no means entirely without them. The motor education has also trained the mind, for, as Seguin correctly said, "The act of directing each foot on each form [of a series of prepared forms] is one of the best exercises for limbs which have previously escaped all control; but what a superior exercise it is for the head above, which has never suspected its regulating power. To walk among so many difficulties is to think." [4] With muscular control sufficiently developed to permit voluntary attention and voluntary reaction, the training takes a new turn and begins to stress sensory education, by means of which the meager mental equipment can be more directly stimulated. The first problem is purely medical, that of putting the child's sensory apparatus into as good condition as possible, but from there on the problem is one of education.

A normal child learns by himself to distinguish heat from cold, softness from hardness, roughness from smoothness, rigidity from suppleness, and so on, but the idiot has to be taught. Thus the teacher plunges the child's hands alternating into hot and cold water, gives him alternately a soft cushion and a stone, runs his hands over sandpaper and glass, lets him break a twig and then try to break an elastic band. The idiot is given a series of objects, similar in size and shape, to arrange in order of their smoothness, or a series of similar size and appearance to arrange in order of weight, and so on. Similar stimulation has to be given the senses of taste and smell; otherwise the idiot will continue to eat anything and to be dirty in his personal habits.

The three senses of touch, taste, and smell are the first to receive training because they are the simplest; next comes hearing, and finally sight. The sense of hearing is trained primarily through music, to which idiots are extraordinarily sensitive. Even their wildest outbreaks can usually be quieted by music that is loud and accentuated, these features being necessary to catch their wandering attention and to stimulate their dull ears. Music is also used as a transition to speech. The idiot does not spontaneously "pick up" words as a normal child does, although he has the fundamental equipment of sounds, but, like his muscular reactions, his sounds are un-co-ordinated. Imitation of musical notes changes the animal cries to properly articulated vowels. The child has to learn the consonants also by a combination of imitating both the sounds and the position of the speech organs. Some idiots who can produce every necessary sound or combination of sounds never speak. Others can imitate words and phrases but never use them spontaneously;

[4] Quoted in Boyd, *op. cit.*, p. 101.

when asked a question they repeat the question instead of giving an answer At most, an idiot develops a speaking vocabulary of perhaps two-hundred words, although he may be able to understand more.

The last sense to be trained is the sense of sight. Instead of beginning with what seems simple enough to the uninitiated, the distinguishing of colors, for instance, the teacher begins by training a child merely to fixate his eyes. While a flash of light or a sudden sweeping gesture will catch his eye for a second or two, he has no power of looking intentionally at anything. The most effective exercise is very simple, although rather nerve-wracking for all

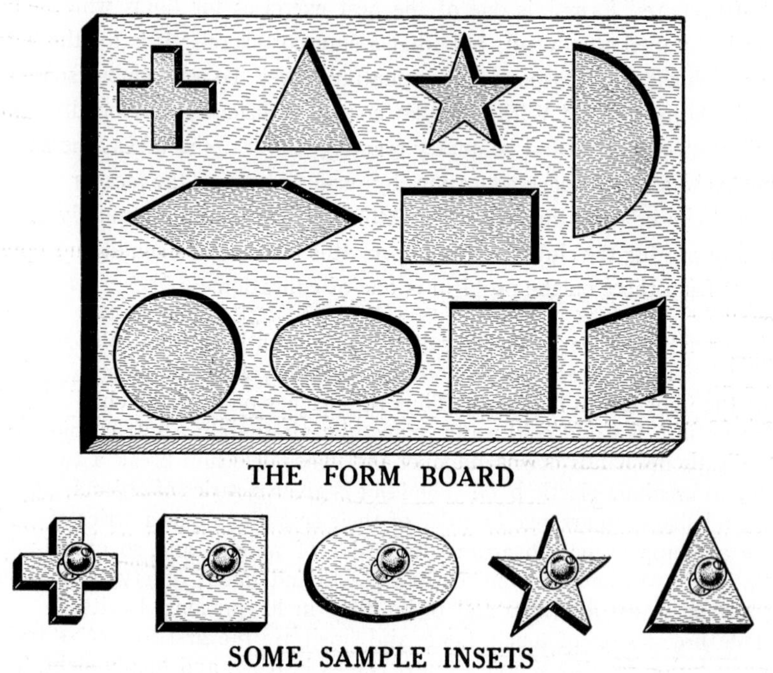

Fig. 86. A Séguin Form Board.

concerned. The teacher stands the child before her, in a quiet room, holds his body immobile, and stares into his eyes. The child invariably tries every means in his power to twist away from the steady glance, but the teacher outwits every reaction and goes right on staring. This exercise may have to be repeated three or four times a day for weeks or even months, but in the end the idiot can look at the teacher almost as steadily as she can look at him; having learned how to fixate his eyes, he is now ready to use them to apprehend color, shape, size, and distance. At first he merely adds vision to touch and smell, but gradually he substitutes it for them; thus, at first he distinguishes different colors by the odor of the dyes, and for a long time he may use smell to check his vision. Colors are taught by means of cards or other small objects, but not so small that the idiot can eat them, that can be sorted by color or put into containers of matching hues. Shape is taught by means of blocks; especially useful is the form board which consists of a small board into which shapes such as squares, circles, triangles or stars have been cut, with cut-out pieces that fit these openings. The child has to learn to recognize the shapes by sight, instead of fitting them into the right holes by touch. A picture of such a board appears in Figure 86. The dimensions of objects are taught by having the child arrange a series of sticks in order of their length, a series of cubes in order of their size, a series of discs in order of their diameters, and so on.

Through months and sometimes years of such elementary exercises the inaccessible and uncontrollable idiot can be changed into an oversized child with a mentality of about two years, but the difference in the ease and expense of caring for him is worth the trouble. The gains made through the entire training are usually consolidated by teaching idiots some simple routine tasks by means of which, under supervision, they can at least partially support themselves, or if incapable of so doing can contribute something to the upkeep of the institution where they live. They polish floors, wipe dishes, dig up potatoes, water the garden, feed the chickens, and so on. In addition, the idiot can usually be trained to obedience and good behavior within his greatly simplified environment. The basic procedure is the same as with all human beings: a desirable reaction is met by praise and rewards, while an undesirable one leads to pain and punishment. It may take hundreds of repetitions, but eventually the idiot learns what he may and may not do.

Seguin's training of defectives has been described in some detail partly because it is so different from what one ordinarily thinks of as education, partly because similar training was later used for normal children, and partly because the education of defectives still rests upon the same principles—and idiots, like the poor, are always with us. Since society recoils from euthanasia,* the only solution for the problem of idiocy lies in the slow, painstaking muscular and sensory education first devised by Édouard Seguin.

Seguin is one of the forgotten men of education, but his direct influence upon the training and testing of children of low ability was very great, and his indirect influence upon sensory education in the schools was even greater. One finds evidence of his work in kindergartens and first-grade rooms. Children who are developing slowly are often not yet ready to begin reading at their entrance to school and are therefore given exercises of a kind similar to those used with defectives. Although Seguin did not organize his tests into a scale, as Binet later did, his were the first modern tests for the measurement of intelligence. The student of today meets his name mainly in reference to the "Seguin Form Board," which is one of the tests in the third year of the Binet Scale.

B. BINET: HIS LIFE AND WORK

The main character of this section was only incidentally a teacher, but his influence upon American educational procedures was so great that he cannot be omitted from this history if one is trying to show what ideas in current schoolwork represent our European heritage in education. Binet was one of the early school psychologists, he was the inspiration for much of the movement to substitute scientific fact for tradition as a basis for teaching, and he constructed the first scale for measuring intelligence. Since many procedures in American schools rest upon a basis of objective measurement, one cannot ignore the man who gave the testing movement its first great impetus.

1. His Life Story Alfred Binet [5] was born in Nice* in 1857. He began his schooling there, but a few years later he went to Paris, where he attended the Lycée Saint Louis and then entered the university, first taking a course in law and then completing his doctorate in physiological psychology. In fact, after the first year he took the two courses simultaneously. While still a student he became interested in hypnotism and worked for many months at La Salpêtrière, the great hospital for the insane in Paris. He graduated in law at the age of twenty-one and then continued his medical and psychological studies. He spread his activities over so many fields, however, that he did not graduate in science until he was a man of thirty-three, and it was four years more before he took his Ph.D., writing his thesis upon the subject of the nervous system in insects, a curious theme for a future psychologist.

His entrance into his lifework was quite accidental. At the end of a summer spent in the country he happened to be waiting on a station platform when he recognized a gentleman, also waiting, as the director of the Laboratory of Physiological Psychology at the Sorbonne* that had just been founded. He got into conversation with the director, argued a while, and agreed to visit the laboratory to see what experiments were in progress. Presently he was added to the staff of the laboratory and in a few years became the head of it. This position he still held at his death in 1911. Binet was never a teacher at the Sorbonne, but many students from there came to his laboratory and worked sometimes for years, under his supervision. These students must have profited greatly by the progressive methodology of their teacher, who expressed him-

[5] Based upon F. L. Bertrand, *Alfred Binet et son oeuvre,* Presses Universitaires de France, 1930, 355 pp.; A. Binet and Th. Simon, *The Development of Intelligence in Children,* (translated by E. S. Kite), Publications of the Training School at Vineland, N. J., 1916, 336 pp.; E. Claparède, "Alfred Binet," *Archives de psychologie,* (1912), 11:376–388; J. L. des Bancels, "L'oeuvre de Alfred Binet," *L'Anée psychologique,* (1912), 18:15–32; G. Dwelshauvers, "Alfred Binet," *Psychologie et vie* (1927), 1:61–64; E. J. Varon, "The Development of Alfred Binet's Psychology," *Psychological Monographs,* Vol. XLVI, No. 3, 1935, 129 pp.

self as follows: "All pedagogy in advanced teaching consists in the example of the teacher working before the eyes of his pupils and introducing them to the efforts of his creative thought, without hiding from them his guesses, his doubts, and even his errors.[6]

On two occasions Binet had direct instructional contact with schools and teachers, once when he went to Bucharest* to help the minister of instruction in planning work for teachers and later when he worked out similar plans for the superior normal school in Paris. In Bucharest he held a seminar for teachers for about six months. He was once recommended as a professor at the Sorbonne, but he did not push his candidacy, preferring to remain free to follow whatever paths intrigued him. He had all the contact he needed with schools and children, and it is probably well that he did not actively seek a teaching position, for he would never have been able to turn out his enormous volume of work, had he been forced to divide his attention between teaching and his research: experiments with young children, methods of experimental psychology, classification of subnormal children, psychology of testimony, and measurement of intelligence.

Binet was a prodigious worker and a facile writer. His productions cover not only psychological topics, but various side lines that one would not expect. Among other things, he wrote several fairly successful plays, each with a plot revolving about an abnormal person, and he worked out a psychological criticism of artists and dramatists. He published his experimental results in psychology in a journal that he founded the year after he got his Ph.D. and became director of the laboratory—*L'Année psychologique.* Many issues consist entirely of articles by himself or his students, and there is hardly an issue without at least one article by him. Indeed, the first fifteen volumes are a record of his intellectual life. All told, Binet produced 11 books and 256 articles in psychology and pedagogy.

Binet's days were spent in the laboratory, the hospitals, and the schools, or in writing at his desk. For months at a time he spent two or three days a week at La Salpétrière, where from 8 A.M. to 7 P.M. he observed the mental changes in insane people. At other times he was in the elementary schools all day, testing the memory, suggestibility, or attentiveness of children. He always insisted upon collecting his own data, talking directly with patients or children, carrying on his own experiments, and discovering facts for himself. Very early he developed the habit of writing down verbatim what patients or children said, because in this way he ran no danger of losing any part of his record. Naturally, his notes grew to imposing numbers, and over them he poured until late into the night, wringing from them the last drop of meaning. He thought

[6] Des Bancels, *op. cit.,* p. 19.

over his thousands of items on a given subject, reflected upon them, talked about them, compared each with the other, and finally summarized the gist of the matter in "dix lignes précises." [7] When Binet had started an experiment in the schools or the laboratory he usually sat at his desk writing all morning and then spent the afternoon giving individual examinations and tests of whatever kind was indicated. During the last ten years of his life he spent more and more time in the schools and less and less in his laboratory. In this quiet and busy way, life flowed on for two decades of great productivity.

In 1904, Binet was asked to give what help he could to a commission that had been appointed to investigate and improve the teaching of defective children and deaf-mutes. The members of the committee could recognize a deaf-mute, but they were baffled as to how to decide whether or not a given child were defective and, if so, how defective. For assistance in this situation, the members turned to Binet as the man who knew about the minds of children. In response, he devised the first "ladder for the measurement of intelligence," the Binet Scale. Binet was already a distinguished psychologist, but his test of intelligence was the achievement that made him famous. Its extensive use precipitated the entire testing movement that has had a profound effect upon schools, especially in America. The scale will be described later.

Binet first published his scale in 1905, but continued for another six years to work out tests that could be added to his original series. He was busy almost to the moment of his death in 1911 from a heart attack, brought on by his years of overwork. By that time his scale had traveled to America and had been revised for use with American children. At the present time it has been translated into fifty languages, not by a mere translation of the original tests but by experimentation and adaptation of them to rate the growth among normal children who speak each language.

2. *His Personality* Most of Binet's outstanding personal traits were intellectual rather than emotional. First was his love of working and thinking. He enjoyed cerebral activity above all else and remained at work for long hours with all the *joie de vivre* of a man doing the thing he likes best. As his daughter wrote of him: "He could not desist from making investigations. He spent his entire life in a task joyously chosen as the very best, not from necessity, but from preference." [8] A second trait was the great fertility of his mind. He constantly thought up new ideas or new modifications of old ones. When another person asked his opinion upon a subject, Binet's quick and facile mind pro-

[7] "Ten concise lines."

[8] Bertrand, *Alfred Binet et son oeuvre,* Presses Universitaires de France, 1930, p. 295. The excerpts from this reference are quoted by permission of the publisher. In another place Binet wrote: "One of my greatest pleasures in life is to have before me a white sheet of paper to be filled."—Claparède, *op. cit.,* p. 386

duced an answer that enriched and illumined the topic. He was so full of ideas and so spontaneously generous with them that he gave them away with a prodigal hand. He wrote *de nouveau* or rewrote dozens of articles for other people, refusing to sign them or take any credit, and anxious only for the "little idea that ought to be expressed or the little fact that should be made known." A third trait was his absolute independence of thought. He went where truth led him, regardless of whether or not he had company. Before he began a piece of work he usually collected many references, but he then put them aside and did not read them until *after* he had finished his own experiments and had come to his own conclusions. Binet's restless, inquiring mind urged him into investigating one field after another, and his apparently inexhaustible ingenuity contributed to whatever subject he investigated.

Binet had an extraordinary sense for methodical experimentation along realistic and practical lines, and he was a remarkably accurate and scrupulously honest observer. When he gathered information from a defective child or a lunatic he concentrated upon what he was doing to the absolute exclusion of all else, noticing every flicker of expression, every gesture, every unconscious movement, every word, every intonation. His accuracy was phenomenal. Moreover, he recorded everything, whether or not relevant to the particular problem on which he was working at the moment, on the principle that "un fait est toujours un fait" [9] and ought to be preserved. He was especially successful in catching facts "on the wing." In order to keep items from getting lost he developed the habit of writing down an informant's exact words as part of a permanent record that could be studied, reviewed, and analyzed at leisure.

Binet was at all times the experimentalist, intolerant of unsubstantiated opinion and determined to believe only what had been proved. In his devotion to the truth, he was sometimes so frankly critical of less objectively minded men as to make enemies. His solution to each problem that arose was to set up an experiment. If a student or acquaintance asked him for his opinion as to whether or not some point were true, the reply was always the same, in case he did not actually *know* the answer from his own investigations: "It remains to be seen [if the point is true]. You could have there a new and interesting idea. But have you made any experiments?" [10] No investigator was ever more careful in safeguarding his experiments from error or more scrupulously fair in the interpretation of his results. Nor could anyone be more patient than he in adding detail to detail for months and even years on end, until he could see a sensible whole emerging from the assembly of specific data.

[9] "A fact is always a fact."
[10] Bertrand, *op. cit.*, p. 3[illegible]

Two quotations below reveal the impression he made as a person upon two people, his daughter and a close colleague. His daughter wrote of him:

> My father was above all else a gay, smiling, often ironic person, gentle in manner, wise in judgment, a little bit skeptic, well-balanced, resourceful, witty, and imaginative. No phrase-monger, but a simple person; underneath his very good-nature, he had a very real disdain also for mediocrity in all its forms. Pleasant and co-operative with all men of science, he was merciless toward an importunate fool who made him waste time and thus threaten his work. The expression of his face was by turn meditative or smiling. He seemed always to be thinking.[11]

His teacher and colleague, Claparède,* wrote:

> He had the most curious, most investigating, and finest mind that one could imagine. He showed in his work an astonishing knack for seizing on the spur of the moment the living mind that thinks, the thought that flits by, or the most subtle manifestations of mental activity. . . . No one had a greater sense for or devotion to experimentation. . . . He was a personification of loyalty to science. . . . In his hands studies and experiments yielded all the information they were capable of giving. Another characteristic was his absolute independence of character.[12]

Binet's picture, shown in Figure 87 shows a scholarly, alert, shrewd face, the face of just such a man as the quotations above would indicate.

3. His Work Although the titles of Binet's psychological writings cover a variety of topics, his investigations center around a relatively few themes: the refinement of methods for investigating mental phenomena; the study of memory, suggestibility, and attention; the investigation of all possible individual differences; the classification of human types; the development of tests; the nature of abnormal states; and the creation of a new pedagogy based upon accurate, scientific observation of children. For purposes of the present text, the discussion of Binet's work will be restricted to four topics only: his point of view about a proper pedagogy, his study of individuals, his method of test construction, and his scale of intelligence.

Binet was of the opinion that current teaching in the schools was all wrong, partly because it employed rule-of-thumb methods that had their basis in tradition rather than in scientific experiment and partly because it was too static, too mechanical, and too artificial. The passages below give his opinion of teaching in the decades from 1890 to 1910.

> General experience does not prevent teaching from having its theory or its doctrine, but it is a vague and purely literary doctrine, a combination of

[11] *Ibid.*, p. 63.
[12] Claparède, *op. cit.*, p. 376.

Fig. 87. Alfred Binet. Courtesy of the C. H. Stoelting Company.

hollow phrases that cannot be criticized because the thought is too vacillating. It is not even sufficiently precise to be wrong.[13]

Teaching is bad if it allows the pupil to be inactive and inert. It is essential that teaching be a series of intelligent acts on the part of the teacher. . . . It is also necessary that teaching be a stimulus causing the pupil to move, to create for himself an intelligent activity.[14]

Binet had his own ideas as to the proper foundation for pedagogy, as expressed in the following passages:

After experimenting already for a long time—for twenty-five years I have been making experiments in the schools—I believe that the determination of aptitudes of children is the greatest business of instruction and education. It is according to their aptitudes that one must teach them and guide them to a profession. The teacher ought to have as a preliminary a study of individual psychology.[15]

The new pedagogy ought to be founded on observation and experiment. It ought to be wholly experimental.[16]

Teaching is idea, thought, life—not a dead letter or an empty formula.[17]

Binet sometimes referred to books on pedagogy as "manuals of recipes" because of the underlying assumption that one had only to follow instructions, use the right ingredients, mix them properly, and presto! one could teach. Pedagogy was not, in his opinion, anything so simple. Its proper scientific basis should be built up by having a laboratory in every school for the investigation of each child's capacities. He recommended repeated examination of each child each semester, in order to supply teachers with necessary information about the children's abilities and also to accumulate data of scientific value concerning the growth rates of the higher mental functions. With his usual penetration, Binet saw that such work could not involve complex experimental apparatus, because teachers could not use it intelligently. He was therefore careful to restrict his own testing to what could be done with "a pen, a bit of paper, and a great deal of patience." He summarized his point of view as follows: "What is needed from modern psychology is not at all theories or poems but some clear little facts very accurately determined in conditions that are easy to reproduce and control." [18]

Binet's main objective in his work was to determine individual differences of all kinds. The studies for which he is best known, those that led to his scale of intelligence, were offshoots of his main purpose. He began by measuring everything he could think of about an individual: size and shape of head,

[13] Bertrand, *op. cit.,* p. 288.
[14] *Ibid.,* p. 59.
[15] *Ibid.,* p. 57.
[16] Des Bancels, *op. cit.,* p. 29.
[17] Bertrand, *op. cit.,* p. 269.
[18] *Ibid.,* p. 84.

size of each facial feature and of the face as a whole; height, weight, lung capacity, strength, size and shape of hands; reaction time, motor co-ordination, attentiveness, suggestibility, memory, aesthetic reactions; rate of learning, ability to discriminate among small differences, ability to solve puzzles, and so on. In addition, he collected many facts about each child's medical and educational history. Since Binet was precise and scrupulous, he insisted upon making each measurement repeatedly on each pupil, and then taking an average. When he had finally finished with the examination of a single child he had a complete case history, with special emphasis upon medical history, and a great deal of data about intellectual and physical abilities. Incidental to these studies was his discovery that children who are defective mentally are also defective physically. In his first group of thirty known defectives, he found twenty-four who were smaller than other children of their own age. This fact has since been verified for many other groups by other investigators. Binet noted also that certain "stigmata of degeneracy" [19] appeared among defectives more often than among normal children; he was too cautious an observer, however, to conclude that these malformations were the exclusive possession of the feeble-minded and the criminal. He found them oftener among defectives than among normal children, but further than that neither he nor other accurate observers have been able to go. When Binet assembled all his measurements of children at various age levels he found that he had established a veritable anthropology of childhood.

Binet's methodology for giving tests was his own invention. When he studied an individual child, he took the pupil into a room alone, talked to him, became friendly before any test was given, presented the tests as if they were amusing games, wrote down verbatim what the pupil said, and watched carefully for signs of fatigue. The examination of one child was continued over many days, sometimes many weeks, in order that fatigue might not invalidate the results. Moreover, he insisted upon great flexibility in the manner of the examination. What must be kept the same from child to child was the *degree of comprehension,* not the exact wording of the questions. He believed that the examiner must always make sure that the pupil knew exactly what was to be done, and if one child needed more explanation that another, then he should get it. The procedure may seem vague and unreliable, but the experienced tester knows its value. Unless the method of approach is adapted to each individual, the results are not reliable. The student of today who learns

[19] Misshapen ears, crossed eyes, thick tongue, bad teeth, deformed palate, excessive or irregular reflexes, disbalance in the two halves of face or body, gross abnormalities of bone structure, misshapen head, enlarged adenoids, speech defects, defects of hearing or vision, malnutrition, and so on.

to give the Binet Scale is told that he must establish rapport* before he gives any tests, that he must stop if the child becomes tired, that he must present the tests as games in which the pupil seems always to be successful, that he must write down the child's answers, and that he must be flexible in his procedure—keeping the degree of comprehension constant from child to child but varying the words as needed to get this result. For instance, if a child is nervous and inattentive, the examiner may require three or four half-hour periods and a great deal of incidental conversation before he can determine the child's mental age, because he has to discard results of a test if the pupil's attention lapses, repeating the test at a later time. No test should be counted unless the pupil is paying attention and really doing his best. This methodology, which always seems vague to the inexperienced, comes down from Binet himself. It is because of this flexibility that individual testing is more reliable than group testing.

The writing down of answers has a further advantage, namely, that one can thus take account of the child's maturity of expression or of other indications of growth that cannot be recorded as numerical values. As Binet wrote:

> It is well understood that these questions of measurement are not the only objective of individual psychology, which does not limit itself to determining the degree of different processes but also their qualities. In any group whatever of individuals there are qualitative differences that it is no less important to know than the quantitative differences.[20]

For instance, if two children are asked, "How are wood and coal alike?" they may both answer correctly, but there may still be a qualitative difference between the two correct answers. One may say, "You can burn them both," while the other replies, "Both wood and coal are forms of fuel and may therefore be used, more or less interchangeably, as sources of heat." The former answer is ordinary, while the latter is unusual; but the difference is lost unless the exact answers are recorded.

In order to trace the development of a single trait, such as memory or judgment, Binet proceeded in the following way, as described by himself:

> It is enough for us to put into a series, in order of their intellectual development, a given number of defectives and then to study throughout the series a particular phenomenon such as pain or attention, in order to see what necessary levels of development are presented by the phenomenon and how it is evolved. Seen from this point of view of psychology, the study of the defective approaches that of the normal child at one end and that of animals at the other.
>
> Thanks to these studies of imbeciles by this new method one can trace the mental evolution of attention, effort, movements in writing, perception,

[20] *Ibid.*, p. 131.

pain, association of ideas, intellectual activity in general, ability in arithmetic, reason or suggestibilty.[21]

By application of this method, once he had arranged a number of children by extensive individual study in order of their abilities, Binet was able to standardize his tests and to determine which would best differentiate various levels of intellectual development.

Binet experimented with a large number of tests of various types. The list below contains those that he found to be more or less diagnostic of intellectual level.

1. Visual acuity.
2. Grasp of an object, placed in the hand.
3. Grasp of an object when only seen.
4. Knowledge of food.
5. Quest for food when complicated by a mechanical difficulty.
6. Execution of simple orders and imitation of simple gestures.
7. Verbal recognition of objects.
8. Verbal recognition of images.
9. Naming of designated objects.
10. Comparison of two weights.
11. Repetition of three numbers.
12. Comparison of two pictures.
13. Taking of suggestions.
14. Verbal definitions of known objects.
15. Repetition of a sentence composed of 15 words.
16. Differences between known objects, from memory of the objects.
17. Memory for images.
18. Drawing a design from memory.
19. Immediate recall of numbers in a series.
20. Resemblances among known objects, from memory.
21. Comparison of lengths.
22. Putting in order different weights.
23. Filling in a missing weight in a series.
24. Thinking up rhymes for a given word.
25. Filling in missing words in a sentence.
26. Making a sentence from words in random order.
27. Response to an abstract question.
28. Reversing mentally the hands of a watch.
29. Tests of induction (paper-folding).
30. Definition of abstract terms.[22]

Many of these tests were Binet's own invention, although he derived some of them from laboratory experiments, especially those carried out in German laboratories of psychology. He eliminated at once, however, all tests that required apparatus, because teachers would not have easy access to laboratories. He borrowed a few tests from Seguin, sometimes using them as they were and sometimes modifying them for work with normal children.

It was Binet's intention to measure innate ability, not knowledge. He tried,

[21] *Ibid.*, p. 94.
[22] *Ibid.*, pp. 88–89.

therefore, to avoid tests that depended upon schoolwork, insofar as possible. He did not ask children to read the directions for a test but gave his instructions aloud. He did not call for knowledge of arithmetic, but asked about making change—a skill that may be learned outside school. Moreover, he tested both city and country children in order to eliminate any tests that required a background of urban life for their solution. Binet's efforts to disengage intelligence from achievement were not entirely successful, but he came as near to achieving this end as anyone has come since.

One other point about testing should be mentioned, partly because of

TABLE 13: BINET'S CLASSIFICATION OF VARIOUS INTELLECTUAL LEVELS[a]

Different degrees of mental defect	Intellectual development compared with that of a normal child	Social relations with other persons	Nature of the work that these individuals are capable of doing
Idiot	Development of 0 to 2 years	By gesture only	Pick up an object; walk, sit down, get up, etc.
Imbecile	Development of 2 to 7 years	By speaking	Eat alone, get dressed, wash the hands, be clean, sweep, make beds, polish boots, etc.
Moron	Development of 7 to 12 years	By writing	Comb the hair, garden, wash and iron clothing, do simple cooking, etc.

[a] Bertrand, *op. cit.*, p. 248.

Binet's emphasis upon it and partly because his wise insistence has been disregarded by many people who have since used tests of intelligence. Binet asserted that no test could take the place of accurate individual observation. A test can be used to make observation more complete, to check it, to control it, to make possible the further examination of some characteristic that might not otherwise be elicited, but *never to replace it.* Observation of a child is thus the main method, tests being of great value in helping the observer to see more than he otherwise would. It should be noted in passing that when an investigator gives group tests to children whom he does not know he is flouting Binet's advice and is substituting tests for observation. A teacher who knows pupils already through observation can get a good deal that is valuable from group tests, although he would get more aid from individual examinations because of the increased opportunities for observation.

Binet hoped that eventually the testing of higher mental processes would become so precise and so controlled as to have scientific value, but the most he claimed for his own scale of intelligence was sufficient accuracy for classification. It was for purposes of classifying children as brilliant, normal, or defective, and if defective to what degree, that the scale was constructed. Binet did not think it adequate for individual diagnosis.

Since the scale was originally constructed to aid a committee in determining what children were defective, Binet's first effort at classification was to define the various levels of deficiency. The result appears in Table 13. Binet intended to establish similar classifications for the normal and superior levels of intelligence, but he died before he could do so. It should be noted that the levels of defect are described in terms of objective, observable behavior.

Binet's original scale consisted of fifty-five tests arranged according to the year in which the majority of normal children acquired each skill or ability. It began with tests for age 3 and went up, one year at a time to the ten-year level, and then by longer jumps to the few adult tests that he devised. The scale appears below:

Age 3: Can (1) point to features of face, (2) repeat two digits, (3) enumerate objects in a picture, (4) give his last name, (5) repeat a sentence of six syllables.

Age 4: Can (1) tell his sex, (2) name a key, knife, and penny, (3) repeat three digits, (4) compare two lines of slightly unequal length.

Age 5: Can (1) compare two weights, (2) copy a square, (3) repeat a sentence having ten syllables, (4) count four pennies, (5) play a game of patience with two pieces.

Age 6: Can (1) tell if it is morning or afternoon, (2) define familiar nouns by use, (3) copy a diamond, (4) count thirteen pennies, (5) make an aesthetic comparison as to which of two faces is the prettier.

Age 7: Can (1) tell left from right, (2) describe a picture, (3) execute three simple commissions, (4) count nine single and nine double pennies, [23] (5) name the four primary colors.

Age 8: Can (1) compare two objects from memory, (2) count from 20 to 0, (3) indicate what is missing from incomplete figures, (4) give the date, (5) repeat 5 digits.

Age 9: Can (1) make change with sums under 20 sous, (2) give definitions superior to use, (3) recognize value of coins in common use, (4) give the months in order, (5) understand easy questions.

[23] French coins.

Age 10: Can (1) arrange 5 weights in the correct order, (2) copy a design from memory, (3) "see through" absurd statements, (4) understand more difficult questions, (5) place 3 missing words into two sentences.

Age 12: Can (1) resist suggestions concerning the length of pairs of lines, (2) place 3 missing words in one sentence, (3) give 60 or more words per minute spontaneously and without prompting, (4) define abstract words, (5) arrange a disjointed sentence in its correct order.[24]

There were only two groups of tests for levels above age twelve, one at fifteen years and one for adults, but neither series was adequately established. They are therefore omitted. The above scale was published in 1905. Three years later it was established on American children for use in the United States. Since then there have been several revisions, with some additional tests for the lower years and many more at the upper end. The tests for ages 3 through 12 are, however, still fundamentally as Binet left them. The scale has long since proved its value and has become a fixture in schools, institutions, clinics, hospitals, and courts. It has also served as the model for other individual tests of intelligence and for many group tests.

C. WORK WITH HANDICAPPED CHILDREN

Deaf children were the first handicapped group to receive attention. There is a record of a Spanish monk who worked with deaf pupils during the sixteenth century, but his efforts did not produce lasting results. The first classes for the deaf were opened in Paris in the year 1770 by the Abbé de l'Epée, who had been forced to retire from his church position because of heresy. He became interested in the education of two deaf children and from this experience went on to develop his school. He was the inventor of the sign language, which, with a few modifications, is still taught. In the United States, work with the deaf was begun about 1820 by Thomas Gallaudet,* who studied in the school in Paris. He, and later on his son, developed the first school for deaf-mutes in America in Hartford, Connecticut. About twenty years later a teacher in Germany began trying to teach deaf children to read lips and to speak. His efforts were not altogether satisfactory, but his basic ideas were taken over by others and worked out more adequately. For half a century a heated debate went on between those who advocated sign language only for the deaf and those who wanted to add lip reading and speech. In recent decades the latter group has succeeded in establishing its methods. Deaf children still learn sign language and use it among themselves, but most of them now learn also to speak passably well and to read lips expertly. They are thus able

[24] Bertrand, *op. cit.*, pp. 125–126.

to make and maintain a better adjustment to society than had ever been the case when they were isolated by lack of communication with others.

As long ago as 1784 there was a school for blind children in Paris, the first school of its type in the world.[25] Within the next twenty years similar schools appeared in other European countries, and were supported for decades by philanthropy. The main problem in dealing with the blind lay in teaching them to read, so that the world of books might be open to them. The founder of the school in Paris tried for years to reproduce books by means of raised letters, but the resulting "books" were enormous, and the time needed to read one of them was very long indeed. It was not until 1825 that Louis Braille, himself a blind pupil and later a teacher at the school in Paris, invented the system that still bears his name.[26] The reading is done by feeling with the fingers over a series of tiny raised dots that form different patterns for the different letters. Since the invention of this alphabet the blind child could become literate, a privilege previously denied him, and his curriculum could include the same material as that in curricula for normal children. Insofar as mere reading was concerned, blind children could go as far along the road to learning as their abilities and interests urged them to go.

The defectives were the next group to receive special attention. In 1811, four years before his downfall, Napoleon ordered a survey to be made to determine how many feeble-minded people there were in France, but nothing came of this work because of subsequent disturbances. A few years later, however, a school for defectives was opened in Vienna. It remained in existence for almost twenty years, but the results were not satisfactory. During this period a similar class was tried with not much success by Gallaudet in the United States. It was not until 1837, when Seguin began his work, that progress was made. The first institution for the feeble-minded in the United States was opened in 1851 in Massachusetts. Before that time adult defectives had been kept in jails, workhouses, and insane asylums when they could not be cared for by family or friends, and defective children had attended the regular schools if they went anywhere. About 1850 the lower schools in Germany began to provide special classes, but the practice did not become general in other countries until the end of the nineteenth century.

The needs of the cripples were the last to receive special attention. Many of these children had gone to the regular schools, where the course of study above the first few grades was not adapted to their needs. In European countries, as in the United States, the first schools were private enterprises that

[25] *L'Institution nationale des jeunes aveugles.*

[26] For a good, brief article, see J. A. Kugelmass, "He Gave Windows to the Blind," *Christian Herald,* November, 1948, or a summary in the *Reader's Digest* for December, 1948.

were gradually taken over first by philanthropy and then by the state. The first such school opened its doors in Munich, in 1832. The special problem of the crippled child is his preparation to earn a living. Since he cannot compete with normal people except in certain lines, he needs such good training in these fields that he can at least keep up with his normal competitors. Most cripples, unless they are also defective mentally, can learn to support themselves, provided they attend the special schools now open to them. Some of the schools for cripples are still private, but since the beginning of the twentieth century, most of them have become a part of the public school system in various countries.

It should be noted that the French contributed more to the education of handicapped children than any other country. One Frenchman invented the sign language, another the raised alphabet; a third devised the only successful method for training extreme defectives, and a fourth constructed the first scale of intelligence by which mental defect could be proved and its degree measured. The first successful schools for deaf, blind, and defective children were all opened in Paris.

READING REFERENCES

A. General Histories of the Period

Garrett and Godfrey, *Europe since 1815,* chaps. 1, 9.
Hayes, *Political and Cultural History of Modern Europe,* chap. 15.
Hazen, *Europe since 1815,* chap. 15.
Riker, *A Short History of Modern Europe,* chap. 12.
Schapiro, *Modern and Contemporary European History,* chap. 13.
Schevill, *A History of Europe from the Reformation to the Present Day,* chaps. 26–28.
Seignobos, *The Rise of European Civlization,* chap. 18.
Stearns, *Pageant of History,* part iii, chaps. 26, 27.
Turner, *Europe since 1789,* chaps 5, 8.

B. Other Texts in the History of Education

Cubberley, *History of Education,* pp. 818–821.
Marique, *History of Christian Education,* III, 140–142.

C. Secondary Sources

Boyd, *From Locke to Montessori,* pp. 88–129.
Culverwell, E. P., *The Montessori Principles and Practice,* George Bell & Sons, Ltd., 1913 (309 pp.), chap. 2.

D. Translation of Primary Source

Binet, *The Development of Intelligence in Children,* chap. 2, pp. 184–239.

CHAPTER XX

MONTESSORI

AND HER SCHOOLS

The central figure of this chapter was born a year before Italy finally became a single nation. She grew up in the stirring times that followed upon the establishment of Italian unity and independence. She became famous through her work in schools that were located in the model apartments built by the new government for industrial workers in the cities. She was therefore identified with Italy as a young nation trying to organize itself.

Mme. Maria Montessori is the only feminine figure in the present text, and there are people who might challenge her right to be regarded as a great teacher. One difficulty in estimating the value of her work is its recency, but a still greater difficulty lies in the fact that Americans are accustomed to think of their own version of the so-called "Montessori method" rather than of what she herself did or said. To be sure, the lady has been a popularizer as well as a teacher. If, however, one rejected teachers upon such grounds, one would have to eliminate Roger Ascham, Peter Abélard, and a number of others whose faults have been buried under the snows of yesteryear, snows that have not yet had enough time to fall over Mme. Montessori's work. Because of her real contributions, however, she will be included as one of the world's outstanding teachers.

A. MME. MONTESSORI: HER LIFE AND WORK

1. Her Life Story Maria Montessori[1] was born in 1870. She came of a good family and was given a sound education. Her training, however, was scientific rather than classical. In defiance of feminine tradition in Italy, she entered the University of Rome as a medical student and received the first degree of Doctor of Medicine ever given there to a woman. After her graduation she began working among insane and defective people, who at that time were usually still housed together. Gradually she became more and more

[1] Based upon Boyd, *From Locke to Montessori,* pp. 130–268; Culverwell, *The Montessori Principles;* D. C. Fisher, *The Montessori Manual,* W. E. Richardson, 1913, 126 pp.; M. Montessori, *The Montessori Method* (translated by A. E. George); J. B. Lippincott Company, 1912, 377 pp.; H. Hecker and M. Muchow, *Friedrich Froebel and Maria Montessori,* Quelle and Meyer, 1927, 214 pp.; T. L. Smith, *The Montessori System in Theory and Practice,* Harper & Brothers, 1912, 77 pp.; E. Y. Stevens, *A Guide to the Montessori Method,* J. B. Lippincott Company, 1913, 240 pp.

interested in defective children and began searching the literature for suggestions on how to train them. She soon found Seguin's writings and started to apply his principles of education. She was even more convinced than he that the proper treatment of mental deficiency in children was more an educational than a medical problem.

Mme. Montessori was a person of great determination, vigor, and driving power. She made up her mind quickly, acted with speed and decision, talked willingly about her ideas, and worked incessantly to put them into effect. As a result of her constant advocacy of education for defectives, she was asked by the minister of education to deliver a series of lectures before the teachers in Rome, in the year 1898. These lectures aroused so much interest that a school for defectives was founded, and for two years Mme. Montessori not only trained the teachers for this school and supervised their work but also taught the children herself. Her day began at 8 A.M. and lasted till 8 P.M. The children who attended the school were remarkably successful in learning the usual school subjects. Mme. Montessori was constantly devising new methods, adapting old ones, studying each child, analyzing subject matter, and investigating the techniques used by other workers in the field. Her combination of careful study, teaching skill, vitality, and ingenious resourcefulness resulted in the development of the defective children so that they could read and write as well as ordinary children could. Those concerned with education in Italy were most enthusiastic about the results, but Mme. Montessori's restless mind was already seeking new problems to conquer. As she wrote: "While everyone was admiring the progress of my idiots, I was searching for the reasons which could keep the happy, healthy children of the common schools on so low a plane that they could be equalled . . . by my unfortunate pupils." [2] The conclusion she came to was that the training of defectives stimulated them to the best possible use of their powers, while that currently given children in public schools so inhibited their development that they were unable to use more than a small proportion of their native capacity.

Up to this point, Mme. Montessori's work had dealt only with defectives, but in 1900 she decided to devote herself to educational work with normal children. She therefore resigned her position and re-entered the University of Rome to take courses in experimental psychology and anthropology, in order to obtain a scientific foundation for the pedagogy she hoped to develop. At this time she was already sure that she wanted to introduce into the common schools some of the techniques she had found so successful with defectives, but she had by no means worked out her entire method. She continued with

[2] Montessori, *op. cit.*, p. 132. This excerpt and subsequent ones from this reference are quoted by permission of Mme. Montessori.

her studies, carried on independent investigations with small groups of school children, and read constantly for a period of seven years, in preparation for the main work of her life.

By 1907 she had formulated her plans for a rejuvenation of education. In this year, it happened that a number of new tenement buildings were constructed under the supervision of a philanthropic organization, the director of which advocated the establishment of a small school in each tenement, to be attended by all children between the ages of three and seven who lived in the building. In each school there was to be a teacher who was also a resident in the tenement. Mme. Montessori was asked to take charge of training the teachers, selecting the materials, and devising the methods for use in these schools. For four years, until 1911, she continued with this work, in which she was extraordinarily successful. Her methods, as will appear shortly, were derived partly from Seguin, partly from Froebel, partly from her own experience with defectives, and partly from experimental psychology. Her organization of the work was flawless and her supervision excellent if sometimes a bit imperious. She sometimes wore her subordinates out by her tireless energy, but she developed the tenement schools into a semblance of what she thought schools for small children ought to be.

By 1911, however, she had again succeeded so well in an undertaking that she had worked herself out of a job! She had little taste for the routine of running a well-established school and greatly preferred to attack some fresh problem. She therefore withdrew from association with the Children's Houses and applied herself to two new lines of activity. The first was to acquaint the educational leaders of other countries with her methods, and the other was to work out an application of them to older children. To reach her first objective she published books and articles, visited numerous countries, gave lectures, taught groups of teachers, supervised the introduction of her materials into various schools, and encouraged the establishment of Montessori Societies. So successful was she that she caused a veritable furor in educational circles. In the United States she had a tremendous vogue, in England there were many devoted disciples, in Switzerland public Montessori schools were established by law, and throughout the world private schools adopted her methods. Although the Montessori school is no longer the last word in American education, her work has left behind it a permanent impress. She was not as successful in her efforts to apply her principles to the upper years of school, and her main contribution continues to be on the preschool and elementary levels.

The picture of Mme. Montessori in Figure 88 shows a fine-looking woman whose face reflects intelligence, competency, strength, and determination. She is shown in a characteristic pose of waiting and watching while a small child gives herself training in the recognition of geometrical forms. The rapport between teacher and child appears excellent. One doubts that the little girl will make a motion or have a thought that is not observed, remembered, and interpreted by the keen analytical eye of Madame.

2. *Basic Ideas of the Montessori Method* The so-called Montessori method has three main characteristics. First is the adaptation of schoolwork to the individuality of each child. This principle is not, of course, new in the

Fig. 88. Mme. Montessori and Pupil. From the frontispiece of *The Montessori Method*. Courtesy of the Author.

history of education. No teacher, however, has put more stress upon it than Mme. Montessori, and she has been more successful than most in selling the idea to the rank and file of the teaching profession. Mme. Montessori believed firmly that the first duty of each human being was to be himself and that anything which checked this development did him a serious injury. She therefore encouraged pupils to work at their own rate, to concentrate upon what interested them, and to use school materials in whatever way would serve to develop their latent* abilities and to solve their current problems. In her teaching she made every effort to adapt what she had to say to each child, often teaching pupils individually so as to get the greatest possible adaptation. Moreover, she studied and tested and observed each pupil until she felt she had an understanding of him as a growing, developing individual before she tried to teach him at all.

A second feature of her method was her insistence upon freedom, which she considered an essential requirement for any true education. Both the teacher and the pupil must be free; the former should not dominate the latter, nor should the latter depend more than absolutely necessary upon the former. As she said. "No one can be free unless he is independent; therefore the first active manifestations of the child's individual liberty must be so guided that through this activity he may arrive at independence." [3] And in another place: "My method is established upon one fundamental base—the liberty of the pupils in their spontaneous manifestations." [4] Or again: "We cannot know the consequences of stifling a spontaneous action when the child is just beginning to be active; perhaps we stifle life itself." [5]

The meaning of the above statements is perhaps best revealed by presenting an incident related by Mme. Montessori:

> One day, the children had gathered themselves, laughing and talking, into a circle about a basin of water containing some floating toys. We had in the school a little boy barely two and a half years old. He had been left outside the circle, alone, and it was easy to see that he was filled with intense curiosity. I watched him from a distance with great interest; he first drew near to the other children and tried to force his way among them, but he was not strong enough to do this, and he then stood looking about him. The expression of thought on his little face was intensely interesting. I wish that I had had a camera so that I might have photographed him. His eye lighted upon a little chair, and evidently he made up his mind to place it behind the group of children and then to climb up on it. He began to move toward the chair, his face illuminated with hope, but at that moment the teacher seized him brutally (or, perhaps, she would have said, gently) in her arms, and lifting him up above the heads of the other children showed him the basin of water, saying, "Come, poor little one, you shall see too!"
>
> Undoubtedly the child, seeing the floating toys, did not experience the joy that he was about to feel through conquering the obstacle with his own force. The sight of those objects could be of no advantage to him, while his intelligent efforts would have developed his inner powers. The teacher *hindered* the child, in this case, from educating himself, without giving him any compensating good in return. The little fellow had been about to feel himself a conqueror, and he found himself held within two imprisoning arms,

[3] Montessori, *op. cit.*, p. 95.
[4] *Ibid.*, p. 80.
[5] *Ibid.*, p. 87.

impotent. The expression of joy, anxiety, and hope, which had interested me so much, faded from his face and left on it the stupid expression of the child who knows that others will act for him.[6]

From some of Mme. Montessori's statements one might assume that she meant to give children perfect freedom and let them grow up à la Émile. Such was, however, not the case. She knew very well that life in a schoolroom makes "complete freedom" impossible. Moreover, Mme. Montessori is a wellborn, cultivated Italian lady who would be most unwilling to let children dash about a schoolroom whooping like Indians because at the moment that was what they felt like doing. She tells in her own words her reactions to scenes of unrestricted freedom in certain schools that had taken her principles too literally: "I saw children with their feet on the tables and with their fingers in their noses, and no intervention was made to correct them. I saw others push their companions and I saw dawn in the faces of these an expression of violence, and not the slightest attention on the part of the teacher. Then I had to intervene to show with what almost rigor it is necessary to hinder and little by little suppress all those things which one must not do." [7] These are not the words of an apostle of freedom, but those of a sensible woman who shares the world's disapproval of hoodlums. Her theory and her practice do not agree.

In a true Montessori school the teachers give no commands to the pupils, nor are there either punishments or rewards. The burden of control is thus put upon the children themselves, and they respond by learning to direct their own activity. Mme. Montessori expressed her basic idea about the control of children as follows: "The liberty of children should have as its limit the collective interest [of the group]; as its form, whatever we universally consider good breeding. We must therefore check in the children whatever offends or annoys others, or whatever tends to rough or ill-bred acts." [8] In short, when Mme. Montessori was confronted by actual children she did what was sensible, practical, and possible—and did it superlatively well.

There were small, light chairs and tables that the children could move around at will. Each pupil selected from the available materials in the room whatever he wanted to work on, took them to a place that suited him, and went to work in his own way. There was no group instruction, although the children sometimes played group games or spontaneously did their work together. There was always a teacher present, but her function was to observe and guide. She helped each child when and if he needed it, suggested a better procedure if she saw him getting into difficulty, and gave him encourage-

[6] *Ibid.*, pp. 91–92.
[7] *Ibid.*, pp. 92–93.
[8] *Ibid.*, p. 92.

ment, but otherwise left him alone. If a pupil failed to complete an exercise he received no penalty; his failure was taken merely as an indication that he was not yet ready for the work, and the teacher suggested something else for him to do. Whenever possible the materials with which the children worked were self-corrective, so that pupils could find their own mistakes and thus become even more independent of the teacher.

Naturally, such an arrangement called for a new concept of discipline.[9] The child who moves about the room as he needs to, intent upon carrying out his own purposes and indifferent to what the teacher is doing, is a "good" child, even if he is sometimes noisy. Under a repressive discipline, immobility is often confused with goodness and spontaneity with mischievousness. For forced immobility Mme. Montessori would substitute the quietness that comes from concentration upon a fascinating problem; for pressure from the teacher she would substitute the pressure of the children upon each other; for forced learning she proposed spontaneous interest. The pupils would thus learn to control themselves because they would find out that only by so doing could they accomplish the things their interest was urging them to accomplish.

Since freedom implies independence from the services of other people, it is natural that small children in the Montessori schools should be given "practical exercises in daily life," as they are called. The pupils learn in school to dress themselves, keep themselves clean, to dust the room, to care for school equipment, to help serve lunch, to attend to their own toilet needs. The youngest children begin with exercises in buttoning, hooking, and lacing pieces of cloth together. Later they learn, as a regular part of their schoolwork, to walk about quietly, to move their chairs without noise, to handle more and more delicate objects. At first they are helped by the older children, but such great prestige is associated with independence that new pupils dispense with aid as soon as they can. This practical training is especially characteristic of Mme. Montessori's attitudes and interests.

Finally, the Montessori system gives an important role to the training of the senses. Indeed, this emphasis upon sensory education is perhaps the most distinguishing mark of the system. The training is used not only as a means of development but as an introduction to reading, writing, and arithmetic, as will presently be shown. Training in sensory discrimination was given so prominent a place because Mme. Montessori believed that there was a close relationship between the senses and the intellect and that if the senses were neglected during the early years, the intellect would not develop as it should. She was so emphatic about this point as to state that a man whose sense training was inadequate might in later life learn all there is to be known about his profession

[9] See *ibid.*, chaps. 5, 21.

and yet remain inefficient by reason of his sensory obtuseness. Thus a doctor might be well informed about diseases of the heart but be unable to apply his knowledge because his ears could not discriminate sounds sufficiently well.

Mme. Montessori's own statement of the objective in sense education was as follows: "The education of the senses has as its aim the refinement of the differential perception of stimuli by means of repeated exercises." [10] These exercises are necessarily self-educative, since no teacher can do a pupil's seeing, hearing, and touching for him. Most of Mme. Montessori's exercises are also self-corrective. For example, the first in the series consists of a block of wood with ten holes of different diameters bored into it and ten little wooden cylinders that just fit the holes; obviously, a child cannot put a cylinder into a hole too small for it, and if he puts one into too large a hole he will have at the end of the exercise a cylinder left that will not go into the only remaining hole. When he makes an error, the materials automatically inform him of it. The exercises are so designed as to train all the senses and thus offset the predominance of vision, the one sense ordinarily so highly trained that many people depend upon it almost exclusively. It may not be true that a child adds a cubit* to his mental stature by means of sensory training, but he certainly does develop finer powers of discrimination in many fields and thus lays the basis for a greater variety of experience than he might otherwise have.

It was not originally Mme. Montessori's idea to teach reading and writing or arithmetic to small children, but gradually she modified this view because she found so many children voluntarily trying to teach themselves the rudiments of these skills.[11] She therefore added some further exercises that should furnish a transfer from purely sensory training to the school subjects. Children who can already recognize and sort figures begin to count them, forward and backward, to group them by twos and threes, to dissect them into halves, thirds, and quarters, thus laying the immediate foundation for arithmetic.

The transition from sense training to writing is especially good. After the children have had a good deal of experience in tracing contours made from sandpaper they are given cards, each containing a letter of the alphabet in sandpaper against a smooth background. The children learn to recognize the letters, but they also practice running their forefingers over each letter, again and again, often with their eyes closed; the object of this game is to see if they can follow the sandpaper quickly, lightly, and surely, from memory. In this way they practice the alphabet. To get proper control over a pencil they merely color in the outlines of pictures. They are soon familiar with the muscular-tactical sensations of writing and have a visual perception of each letter. They then learn the sounds of the letters. The pupil is provided

[10] *Ibid.*, p. 173.
[11] See *ibid.*, chap. 16.

with a box of letters identical in size and form with the sandpaper models but cut in cardboard and unmounted; there are three or four copies of each letter, which are kept in a fixed compartment. The teacher pronounces a short word, enunciating each component sound carefully, while the pupil selects from his letters the ones that the teacher is sounding.[12] When he has laid out several words he reads them back to the teacher. In this way he builds up a small vocabulary of words he can both spell and read. He is now all ready to begin writing, since he has all the necessary skills. However, no one does anything about teaching him further except to provide some large sheets of paper and some soft pencils. He continues to play with the sandpaper letters, to make words from dictation, and to color pictures, until some day, when he spontaneously gets a paper and pencil and begins to write.

There is no question in the mind of one who has watched a child's natural burgeoning into penmanship that the Montessori method is the best possible introduction to the subject. Moreover, the time needed is very short; even four-year-olds require only about six weeks from the initial preparatory exercise to the spontaneous writing of words in better script than the average child twice their age.

Usually the transfer from sensory training to reading comes later than in the case of writing. When the children can produce written words and can read their own writing, the teacher gives them little packages of cards on each of which is the name of some object in the room. The pupil then scampers around the room putting the cards on the appropriate objects. After a while he gets cards with phrases such as "stand up," "jump three times," or "open the door"; he looks at the cards and shows his comprehension by carrying out the command. Although there is no pressure whatever upon the children, most of them learn the elements of arithmetic, reading, and writing before they enter the regular schools, and all of them have acquired the sensory discriminations upon which such achievements are based.

The Montessori system is, then, a fusion of somewhat divergent elements, of which three are outstanding. Two of these basic principles—respect for the child's individuality and encouragement of his personal freedom—compose what might be called the Montessori point of view. They determine not only the atmosphere of the schoolroom but the relation of teacher and pupil, the arrangement of the schoolroom, and the nature of the instructional procedures. The sense education, together with its transfer to the elementary school subjects, is better referred to as the Montessori technique. The two fundamental educational tenets and the specific methodology together give the Montessori method its distinctive character.

[12] Since Italian is a completely phonetic language, each letter has only one sound and the spelling presents no great problem.

3. Shortcomings of the System Before one can fairly criticize the Montessori system one has to realize that there is often a marked divergence between what Mme. Montessori wrote and what she did, between her philosophy and her pedagogy, between her theory and her practice. In general she seems to have gotten her theory out of a book and her practice from a shrewd observation of human beings. As a result, her teaching procedures may either contradict her general principles or else have no discernible relation to them. And it is her reactions to children, her grasp of their needs, her handling of them, and her methods of teaching that are right. As a clinician and a teacher she is magnificent, but like many other great teachers she is an indifferent philosopher. As a result, Mme. Montessori sometimes seems to do the right things for the wrong reasons.

A second point to consider skeptically is the claim that the Montessori system is rigidly scientific. No one could be any surer of its firm foundation in science than Mme. Montessori herself, but to the observer it seems that the essence of her method is highly intuitive. It is probable that Mme. Montessori's long training in science was invaluable to her in her work, but the main elements in her method of teaching are intuition, shrewdness, hard common sense, knowledge of the world, keen observation, and the same controlled guesswork that characterizes the conclusions of any other expert diagnostician. Mme. Montessori's work needs neither theoretical nor scientific justification—and in the writer's opinion it would be better off without them.

It seems quite clear that Mme. Montessori was in error in certain of her concepts about personality. One's personality is a fusion of biologically and socially determined elements, but Mme. Montessori so greatly overstressed the former as to regard personality as an inheritance through the germ cells. By overemphasizing biological inheritance and understressing social forces Mme. Montessori has produced a concept of personality and individuality that is at present untenable—in case it ever were defensible. An especially striking feature of her system is the absence of training for the emotions. Everything is intellectual. To be sure, the child is never forced, but the schoolwork makes little demand upon his spontaneous desire to play. There are almost no games, and what do occur seem to be tacked on as a sop to immaturity; little constructive use is made of them, and they are not regarded as educational. The children do not act out plays, nor does the teacher tell them stories. While spontaneous flights of imagination are not repressed, they are certainly not stimulated. Little provision is made for aesthetic interests. The pupils rarely sing, or play singing games, or play Victrola records, or look at pictures, or model with clay, or draw pictures, or mess about with paints—all activities dear to the childish heart. It is typical that when a child does color pictures, it is to learn how to control a pencil, not to create something he thinks is beautiful. Naturally, such activities are not forbidden—on her own principle of freedom Mme. Montessori cannot reject anything a child does, provided it is not actually harmful or indecent—but there is little in the training to give nourishment to aesthetic sensibilities.

The method is deficient also in social training because the work is almost all individual. The children indulge in more or less free play together, but they fail to get the social training that comes from joint undertakings and group instruction. While the pupils inevitably educate each other socially to some extent in Montessori schools as elsewhere, the system itself does not arrange for and encourage the social growth that is now regarded as a chief result of schooling at all levels.

Even within its relatively narrow intellectual limits, the method shows other defects. The sensory education rests directly upon the laboratory psychology of the late nineteenth century. In the psychology of that day, mental life was conceived of as being built up out of elements which combine in thousands of different ways, just as chemical elements combine to produce the varied forms of matter. The experimental work of the period was one-sided because it dealt primarily with sensory discrimination and other simple phenomena in a laboratory atmosphere of artificial detachment and purposely suspended animation. Naturally, sensations are important, but they do not constitute the whole of one's mental life. Moreover, on the assumption that sensations are an early and simple form of mental activity, Mme. Montessori defended sense education as peculiarly appropriate for early childhood. The more modern view is that proper training of the emotions should come first. What might be called the subject matter of the Montessori method is, therefore, distinctly one-sided and based upon a type of psychology that has been outgrown.

Some critics have raised the objection that enough training of the senses for any ordinary purpose is automatically given by the processes of growing up and achieving an ordinary education, and that additional training, if needed for a particular job, can be acquired at any period of life up to senescence. Whether or not the average person gets "enough" sensory education by ordinary means is still an open question because no one can say with exactness how much is enough or even how much children usually get. In any case, the whole matter of sensory training has to be considered in the light of a child's total needs and such time assigned to it as will not interfere with the development of other and equally important abilities.

Finally, there is one defective point in the general procedure for building a curriculum. Mme. Montessori wanted everything in her school to spring from the nature of small children. Like everyone else who has based school work upon what came spontaneously from children, she is confronted with the problem of what fails to come. Mme. Montessori herself was greatly concerned because her system included no training in religion. Since she is committed to a learning that is free and unforced, she has automatically excluded didactic* instruction of any kind, and cannot introduce what the children do not voluntarily show a desire for. She is not alone in this dilemma of curriculum building. Since 1900 many people in many places have tried to make a course of study out of childish activities and have all found the same difficulty: that the work is one-sided and does not contribute enough in the way of preparation for later stages of development. It has by now been demonstrated that while children's interests and spontaneous activities can and should be used to motivate schoolwork, they cannot be used as the sole basis for determining its content.

The Montessori system has, then, its virtues and its faults. As in the case of other systems that have come from the thinking of a single individual, it has the same strong points and the same shortcomings as its author. Mme. Montessori's outstanding virtues are her sturdy independence, her insistence upon being herself, her willingness to let other people be themselves, her devotion to science, her deep love of learning, and her intuitive understanding of children. Her shortcomings are her overintellectualized interests, her dogmatized science, and her lack of provisions for the emotions.

To a considerable degree Madame's great skill in teaching offset the weaknesses of her system, whenever she was doing the actual teaching. In her hands an exercise in walking on a chalk line became an exercise in manners and morals; a test for visual acuity was transformed into training in systematic observation; a drill in putting buttons through buttonholes developed into an exercise in independence. It has been said that a child who was exposed to nothing but the Montessori method during his preschool and school years would emerge as an individual cast in the same mold as Mme. Montessori herself: scientific, precise, objective, accurate, unemotional, independent, vigorously individual. Education has often fared worse than this, but certain modifications could eliminate the defects of the Montessori system and make it approach more nearly to the educational ideal.

At the moment, in America, the influence of Mme. Montessori is somewhat in abeyance, largely because teachers are now concentrating upon the training of the emotions and the development of personality. For these objectives sensory training is largely irrelevant. The progressive movement has caught up and incorporated as a basic tenet the concept of the child's freedom to be and to become himself, but not many teachers associate that doctrine with the name of Montessori, although they should.

There is, as yet, no end to this life story, since Mme. Montessori is alive. She disapproved violently of Mussolini's repressive effects upon the schools and protested that he was training children merely to be slaves. She was so outspoken that she had to leave Italy. When last heard from[13] she had returned to Amsterdam from India, where she was maintaining a school and experimenting with the teaching of school subjects to very young children. As

FIG. 89. Maria Montessori in 1948. From a photograph by *Life* published in *Time*, October 20, 1948. Courtesy of *Time*, Inc.

indomitable as ever, she recently said, "Work is necessary. It can be nothing less than a passion. A person is happy only in accomplishment." A recent picture of her appears in Figure 89. Mme. Montessori is the one living[14] link with the great teachers of yesterday, the last member in a remarkable procession of teaching talent.

B. MONTESSORI MATERIALS AND SCHOOLS

1. Materials for Training Mme. Montessori developed her own materials, borrowing much from both Froebel and Seguin, as she readily admits. These materials are mainly of three types: those that are designed to train the senses, those that teach practical skills, and those that help children to adapt themselves to the needs of schoolroom life.

[13] August 12, 1949.
[14] At the time of publication. Mme. Montessori died on May 6, 1952.

The exercises are arranged in series from easy to difficult. Thus an easy exercises consists of putting into their appropriate holes some cylindrical pieces that are all of the same length but of different diameters, as shown in Figure 90. In another exercise in the same series the pieces differ in both dimensions, while in a third they are of identical diameter but of different

FIG. 90. Montessori Solid Insets. From *The Montessori Method,* p. 190. Courtesy of the author.

length. This last is quite difficult because the openings into which the cylinders fit are of the same diameter, and the child has to estimate the depth of each, since some of the pieces will sink into some holes farther than others.

Experience with building blocks of sundry shapes and sizes gives training in perceiving length, breadth, and thickness. The children build such complex figures as the Long Stair, the Broad Stair, and the Tower, shown in

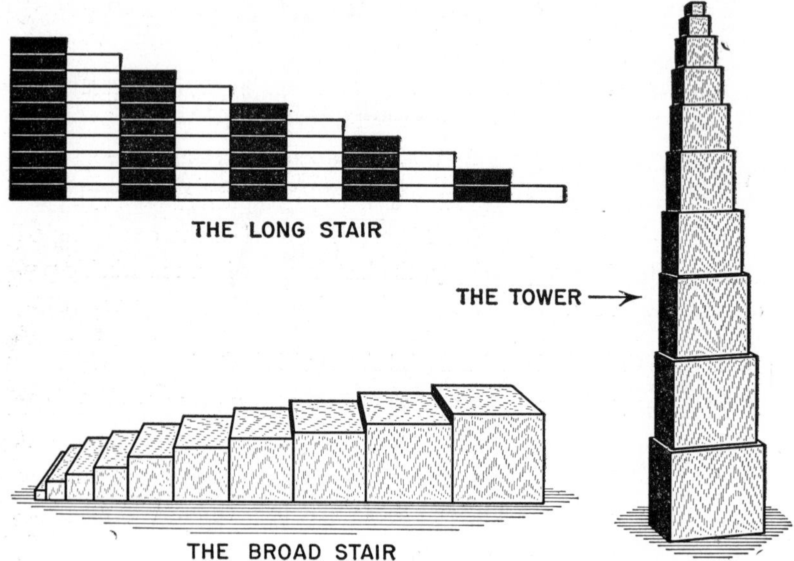

FIG. 91. Montessori Stairs and Tower. From *The Montessori Method,* p. 191. Courtesy of the author.

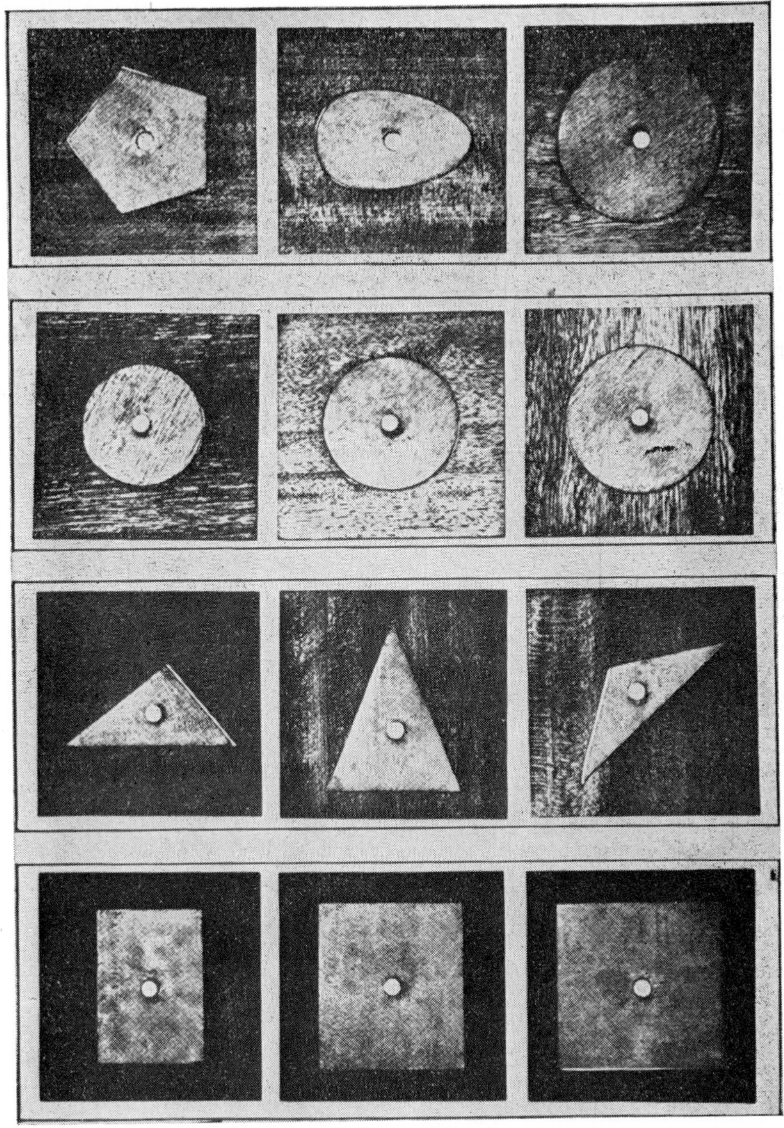

FIG. 92. Montessori Series of Wooden Insets. From *The Montessori Method,* p. 194. Courtesy of the author.

Figure 91. These materials show an obvious relation to those of Froebel.

In another set of exercises the children are presented with a series of wooden forms and insets.[15] At first they use their fingers to feel along the edge.[16] When they can put the pieces in place quickly and accurately, they are given cards upon which the silhouettes of the same forms appear; then comes a series in which only the contours of the forms are drawn in heavy blue lines, and finally a set of cards that contain the same figure bounded by simple, thin lines. The pupil is to place the wooden insets first over the corresponding silhouettes, then over the heavily drawn outlines, and finally over the line drawings. He knows when he is right because the wooden inset just covers the blue figure or lines; if any bit of blue still shows, he has made a mistake.

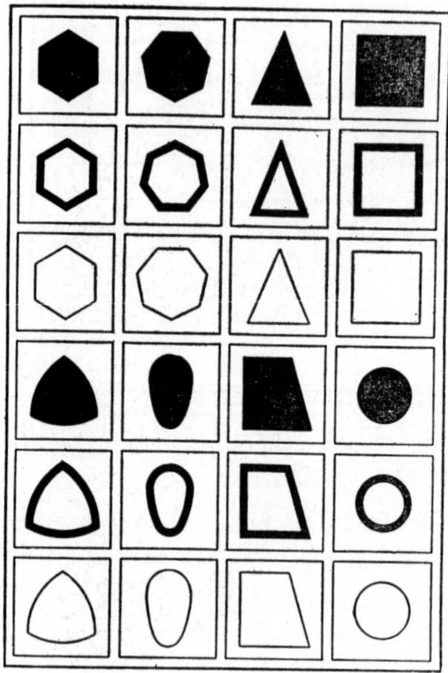

FIG. 93. Montessori Cardboard Forms. From *The Montessori Method,* p. 196. Courtesy of the author.

At first the children do not necessarily associate words with their sensory experiences, but gradually they acquire a descriptive vocabulary. Gradually, also, they discover in their surroundings the same qualities that they have been experiencing in the exercises; they find out for themselves that their shoes feel smooth, that the soup is hot, that the rose is red; and they get great pleasure from these simple discoveries.

The exercises in practical skills consist in fastening and unfastening buttons, hooks, laces, and so on. Sample frames for developing these skills are shown in Figure 94.

The third type of exercise gives the children experience in such simple tasks as moving chairs about quietly, setting a table, putting the room in order, and the like. In actual school use, these three types of exercise are parallel rather than consecutive, as appears from the following sequence of exercises suggested by Mme. Montessori:

First Grade

As soon as the child comes to the school he may be given the following exercises:

[15] Compare Figure 92 with Figure 86, which shows the Seguin Form Board.
[16] See Figure 88.

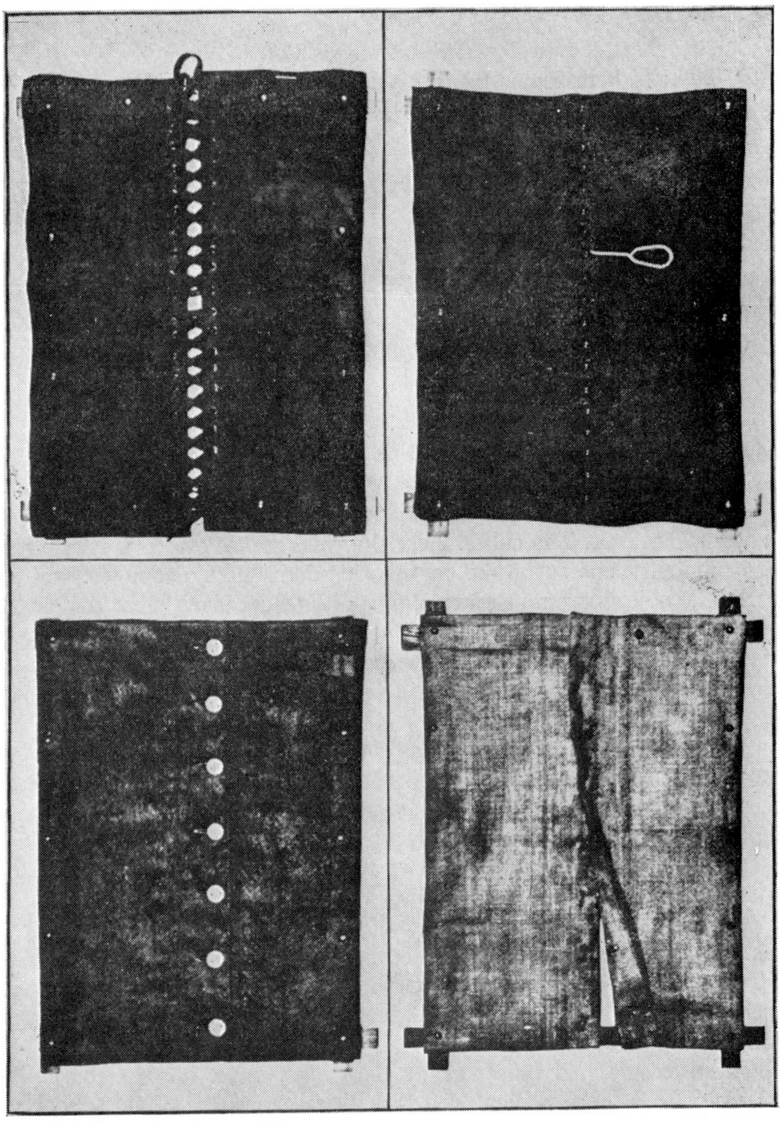

FIG. 94. Montessori Frames for Lacing, Buttoning, and Hooking. From *The Montessori Method,* p. 200. Courtesy of the author.

Moving the seats, in silence (practical life).
Lacing, buttoning, hooking, etc. (skills).
The cylinders (sense exercises).

Among these the most useful exercise is that of the cylinders (solid insets). The child here begins to *fix his attention*. He makes his first comparison, his first selection, in which he exercises judgment. Therefore he exercises his intelligence.

Among these exercises with the solid insets, there exists the following progression from easy to difficult:

(a) The cylinders in which the pieces are of the same height and of decreasing diameter.

(b) The cylinders decreasing in all dimensions.

(c) Those decreasing only in height.

Second Grade

Exercises of Practical Life. To rise and be seated in silence. To walk on the line.

Sense Exercises. Material dealing with dimensions. The Long Stair. The prisms, or Big Stair. The cubes. Here the child makes exercises in the recognition of dimensions as he did in the cylinders but under a very different aspect. The objects are much larger. The differences much more evident than they were in the preceding exercises, but here, only the eye of the child recognizes the differences and controls the errors. In the preceding exercises, the errors were mechanically revealed to the child by the didactic material itself. The impossibility of placing the objects in order in the block in any other than their respective spaces gives this control. Finally, while in the preceding exercises the child makes much more simple movements (being seated he places little objects in order with his hands), in these new exercises he accomplishes movements which are decidedly more complex and difficult and makes small muscular efforts. He does this by moving from the table to the carpet, rises, kneels, carries heavy objects. . . .

Arrived at this point in his education, the child is capable of fixing his attention, with interest, upon the thermic* and tactile* stimuli. . . . Therefore, when the education of the attention has been begun, we may present to the child the rough and smooth surfaces (following certain thermic exercises described elsewhere in the book).

These exercises, if presented at the proper time, interest the children immensely. It is to be remembered that these games are of the greatest importance in the method, because upon them, in union with the exercises for the movement of the hand, which we introduce later, we base the acquisition of writing.

Together with the two series of sense exercises described above, we may begin what we call the "pairing of the colours," that is, the recognition of the identity of two colours. This is the first exercise of the chromatic* sense. . . .

Meanwhile, the child has heard music; has walked on the line, while the directress played a rhythmic march. Little by little he has learned to accompany the music spontaneously with certain movements. This of course necessitates the repetition of the same music. (To acquire the sense of rhythm the repetition of the same exercise is necessary, as in all forms of education dealing with spontaneous activity.)

The exercises in silence are also repeated.

Third Grade

Exercises of Practical Life. The children wash themselves, dress and undress themselves, dust the tables, learn to handle various objects, etc.

Sense Exercises. We now introduce the child to the recognition of gradations of stimuli (tactile gradations, chromatic, etc.), allowing him to exercise himself freely.

We begin to present the stimuli for the sense of hearing (sounds, noises), and also the baric* stimuli (the little tablets differing in weight).

Contemporaneously with the gradations we may present the plane geometric insets. Here begins the education of the movement of the hand in following the contours of the insets, an exercise which, together with the other and contemporaneous one of the recognition of tactile stimuli in gradation, prepares for writing.

The series of cards bearing the geometric forms, we give after the child recognizes perfectly the same forms in the wooden insets. These cards serve to prepare for the abstract signs of which writing consist. The child learns to recognize a delineated form, and after all the preceding exercises have formed within him an ordered and intelligent personality, they may be considered the bridge by which he passes from the sense exercises to writing, from the preparation, to the actual entrance into instruction.

Fourth Grade

Exercises of Practical Life. The children set and clear the table for luncheon. They learn to put a room in order. They are now taught the most minute care of their persons in the making of the toilet. (How to brush their teeth, to clean their nails, etc.)

They have learned, through the rhythmic exercises on the line, to walk with perfect freedom and balance.

They know how to control and direct their own movements (how to make the silence,—how to move various objects without dropping or breaking them and without making a noise).

Sense Exercises. In this stage we repeat all the sense exercises. In addition we introduce the recognition of musical notes by the help of the series of duplicate bells.[17]

2. *A Montessori School* In the spring of 1913 an English woman, vice-president of The Home and Colonial Kindergarten Training School, visited

[17] Montessori, *op. cit.*, pp. 338–343.

several schools in different Italian cities, remaining some weeks in each place and spending every day at the school. She had already read Mme. Montessori's books and had heard lectures on the method, but she still found herself unable to visualize an actual school or to make up her own mind as to the practicability of the method. She therefore went to see for herself. She was an excellent observer—unprejudiced, accurate, and thoughtful—and she had the requisite preparation for sound observational work: acquaintance with many other kindergartens, knowledge of what results are usually expected from small children, and a wide observation of kindergarten teachers. Her report, an excerpt from which appears below, is therefore especially valuable.

The Casa dei Bambini* in the Via Solari in Milan is on the outskirts of the town in one direction, beyond the cattle market and shambles and near big engineering works. The workmen's flats are built round wide open courtyards in which are grass plants, small trees, and palms. A porter's lodge in both cases guards the entrance to the courtyard, which is open only to the inhabitants of the flats and those who have business with them.

There is a middle block of flats with a courtyard back and front, and it is in this that rooms on the ground floor are given up to the Casa dei Bambini. This contains two good-sized working-rooms, both of which open out by a short flight of steps into the garden. Between these is a small room with hand basins. Beyond is the room of the directrice, in which she keeps her weighing and measuring machines, her medicine chest, and the biographical charts which she and the visiting doctor fill in for each child. Next to this there is a bathroom, with a bath supplied with hot and cold water; and the offices, which are divided from the workingrooms by a passage.

The garden is a piece of the courtyard which has been railed in. All that goes on there is open to the observation of people in the courtyard and at the many windows overlooking the garden. A flower bed runs within the railing, and this is divided up into little oblong plots which belong to the different children. There are also several round beds, one of which has been converted into a fountain. This is much appreciated by the children. Against the wall is a fowl-pen in which are fowls which the children feed, and on the wall is a pigeon-house from which pigeons come fluttering down into the garden. The ground between the beds is covered with loose grey pebbles which serve as gravel.

The steps which lead down from the windows to the garden are flanked by sloping walls. It does not take the visitor to the Casa long to discover what an inexhaustible source of exercise these sloping walls are to the children. Again and again they slide down them without any of the danger risked by adventurous children when they slide down the banisters. It did not seem to me that their clothes suffered appreciably. . . .

The working-rooms are simply furnished. On the walls are a few pictures, one a photograph of the Madonna della Sedia, which Montessorians have adopted as their picture. In the one room is a piano, seldom used now, unfortunately, as the present directrice cannot play. In the other are the cabinets which contain the Montessorian material and children's drawings and writingbooks, which the children themselves keep in a state of neatness and order. The tables for the children, though not made for one child only as in some of the Case, are light and can be carried by two children. All the time I was there they were placed two or more together, so that a group of children could gather round one table as they would in an ordinary nursery. . . . The chairs were light, as are the chairs used in many English kindergartens. But practice in carrying them had given even the smallest children an agility and ease in doing this such as I have not seen in English schools.[18]

The school hours were long, from 8:30 to 12, and from 1:30 to 5, making a seven-hour day, whether the children were three, four, five, or six years of age. The Casa thus relieved the mothers of the children from all anxiety about them during the greater part of the day. Punctuality in arrival, though desired, was not enforced. Often the children were, perhaps necessarily, taken out by their parents in the evening, and made up in the morning for the sleep that they lost at night. The close touch between directrice and parents, made possible by the position of the school in the midst of the homes and by the simplicity of the organization, enabled the directrice to dispense with a hard and fast rule in regard to punctuality of arrival.

Before the end of May, when the weather grew very hot, the children had no sleep in school. Then when some of the children began to lose weight owing to the heat, the doctor ordered them to sleep or rest in darkened rooms for two hours in the early afternoon. Previously, among the thirty-five children I saw none who appeared to need more sleep than they were getting, or who showed signs of fatigue at the end of the long school day. Their freshness at five o'clock never failed to excite my surprise, accustomed as I was to children tired out at the end of a shorter school day. I attribute this to two factors. First, the wisdom of trusting the children to choose for themselves when and for how long they will work, and, secondly, to the meal which they had, usually in the open, between four and five o'clock.

The food for this meal they brought with them from home in baskets, which were put away in an airy cupboard on their arrival. Although there was no time-table, yet certain events repeated themselves daily with uniformity. One of these was assembling in the room with the piano about four o'clock. The children carried their chairs and formed a big circle round the room. The cleanliness of their hands was examined. Then they either listened to the directrice, played the Silence Game devised by Dr. Montessori, or, what they liked better, played one of the singing games which they knew—one, for instance, about the spring, in which one of the children personating a butterfly moved round the room waving her arms to the music and approaching the children who represented flowers, or one of a didactic nature which described how they kept faces, ears, and hands clean. Then the baskets were brought out by one or two of the children and distributed. The whole party, carrying chairs, trooped down the steps into the garden, there to enjoy the

[18] Condensed from Jessie White, *Montessori Schools as Seen in the Early Summer of 1913*, Oxford University Press, 1914, 185 pp. This excerpt and the following ones from this reference are used by permission of the publisher.

good things contained in the baskets. Some brought eggs, some salad, some chocolate or apples, together with big pieces of bread. There was no attempt in connexion with this informal meal at anything but picnic manners. . . . One thing, however, was strictly observed, no rubbish of any kind was left. Even the smallest pieces of paper were carefully gathered up and put by the children into the waste-paper basket.[19] After this *al fresco* meal they usually washed their hands, and some occupied themselves in arranging the chairs in the working-rooms. All was left neat, and the children departed from school as clean as, or in some few cases cleaner than, when they came. They had charming little hands with well-kept nails. Their clothes were neat, and their hair clean and well brushed. They all had pocket-handkerchiefs, and learnt to use them. Before going they shook hands with all the grown-up people present. They did not tear out of school in an unmannerly way. To reach their homes they had only to cross the courtyard, and even the youngest could safely do this alone. They did so in a sober, well-behaved manner. Having been free all day to move about or sit as they pleased, they felt none of that rough exuberance which marks the exit from school of those who have been for hours deprived of their natural right to spontaneous movement.[20]

The atmosphere was one of freedom, for the directrice took Dr. Montessori's principle of liberty seriously, yet not, I think, with the unwisdom of exaggeration. It was spring weather, and it was natural for the children to wish to be much in the open air. There was plenty to be done in their little gardens, and tools and watering-cans were ready for their use. Usually when I was there a great deal of watering went on in the early morning. Needless to say the children were proud of their gardens. Some of them showed their love of flowers in a touching way. They lay down on the loose grey pebbles and gazed at the growing blossoms in the beds[21] . . .

The only way to gain a true idea of the work of such a school is to stay among the children long enough to know them, with some small part of the knowledge possessed by the directrice. It is astonishing how interesting it is just to be an observer hour after hour among little creatures who are free to manifest their individual bents, and who make one feel part of the school with touching friendliness. There is no showing off in this Casa of the clever children; it is only gradually, for instance, that one finds out that a certain sedate little maiden of five can write with considerable facility on the blackboard, or in an exercise book, any sentence which she takes it into her head that she wants to write, though since there are no miracles here, this is sometimes with faults of grammar or spelling. If she is writing on one of the many blackboards, these mistakes soon get corrected. It is one of the virtues of the blackboard writing that several children can write at once what they want to write, and all be under the observation of the directrice. . . .

One could not watch the children without being struck by the different amounts of energy they showed. Some of the younger children were quite astonishing. There was one little girl, Bruna by name, almost or just four

[19] *Ibid.*, condensed from pp. 13–15.
[20] *Ibid.*, pp. 16–17.
[21] *Ibid.*, p. 18.

years of age—I forget which—fair-haired, blue-eyed, with a command of language surprising for her years. She was one of those children who are demonstratively affectionate, but ready to transfer this affection to the latest comer. Probably spoilt at home, she liked to be the centre of attention. If there was any visitor present whom she could induce to occupy the little chair which she placed beside her own and to watch her work, she would always do so. During the time that I spent in the school I had ample opportunity of observing the strong appeal which the Montessorian material made to her. Very often, it is true, she built with the Froebelian bricks. These were kept in two large boxes in that state of confusion loved neither by Froebel nor by Dr. Montessori. The neat little Froebelian boxes, one for each child, had been discarded. As I sat at the table with Bruna, watching her as she tried to cover the large brick-box with her small chubby arms, to prevent the other children from sharing the bricks, I realized the advantage of Froebel's plan from the point of view of order. The intervention of the directrice was constantly required when Bruna had the bricks and other children wanted them, but she was usually speedily won over to share them. She was learning to keep calm when one or other of the children came and overthrew the castle she had built. They certainly loved, though not unkindly, to tease her, and she was receiving a training from their hands which she could not possibly have received in an atmosphere of less freedom.

It was curious that the altercations that arose over the building bricks never, as far as my experience went, arose over the Montessori material proper. The colour tablets were great favorites, and several times a day Bruna would arrange the pairs of different shades of some one colour, yellow, perhaps, or red, in descending order. The doing of this requires the closest attention, for there is so little difference between some of the shades that a very careful scrutiny is necessary in order to be able to do it successfully. If Bruna made mistakes, she did not necessarily correct them herself, as she was obliged to do with the solid insets, where the putting of one inset into a wrong hole leaves one which will not go into any hole. I found that if I pointed out mistakes while she was arranging the shades, her interest in doing so diminished. The plan of the directrice was to let her finish, and then, without saying anything, to exchange any two shades which were wrongly placed. Very often Bruna would arrange the series correctly, but not even an adult could do so without fully concentrated attention. It seemed to me that these colour tablets were doing a good deal for Bruna with her boundless energy and quickly diverted attention. They set her a task which was not too long to get finished, but which could not be done even imperfectly without a high degree of concentrated discriminative attention. Further, the exercise was not complete until the tablets had been replaced in their proper compartment in the box and the box in the cabinet, unless wanted by other children. With little new-comers this habit of orderliness had to be inculcated. The vigilance of the directrice herself and of the elder children was required. But the strong imitative faculty of little children came into play. Example achieved what, no doubt, precept alone would have failed in doing.

Not only were the buttoning frames great favourites of the children, but the cylindrical and the geometrical insets also. The directrice needed no special vigilance when the children were occupied with these. An English professor of education, referring to the Montessori material, spoke as though the children would succeed with and exhaust the interest of this fitting in of cylinders in a very short space of time. This, however, was not the case. Watching the children at work, one perceived great differences in their modes of procedure. With some children the method semed to be one of fortuitous trying. Having selected one hole to fill, the child would take up the insets one after another, until at last one was taken up that fitted. I was many times astonished by seeing children trying to fit one of the largest cylinders into one of the smallest holes. The children who made most use of their sense of touch in measuring the span or depth of the hole succeeded best.[22]

One of the most popular occupations here, as elsewhere, was the filling in of outlines with coloured crayons. There was no giving out of the coloured pencils, which would have savoured too much of ordinary school practice. When the children wanted them, one of them or the directrice set the box with compartments in which the different colours were kept on the table, and the children helped themselves from the box. One heard even the little ones calling the colours by name. If they wanted yellow they took yellow, and when they had finished with the yellow pencil they put it back. This, of course, afforded great opportunity for the exercise of good manners. Further, it taught them that sometimes one has to go without what one wants or to wait for it, surely a valuable lesson. It is quite a mistake to interpret the principle of liberty as meaning that the children get all they want at the moment of wanting it. This is far from being the case. The conditions in the Casa dei Bambini approximate much more to those of real life than do those of an ordinary school, where everything required is passed round, and where the children have very little responsibility as to the care of the material used . . .

[Bruna] had seen the elder children using coloured pencils to fill in outlines, and she was quite satisfied to make her outline with the metal frame. Then having chosen a pencil from the box, she proceeded to fill in the circle with colour, just as a little child scribbles. At first the lines often went beyond the outline and patches were left uncovered. These patches the directrice would point out to her, saying "not coloured." Gradually the colouring grew more uniform and was kept better within the outline. From day to day, for she spontaneously returned to this exercise at some time or other every day, her hand gained mastery over the pencil, and she was being prepared to write, though of course she was unaware of this. It was her progress in the actual operation of colouring which gave her satisfaction. . . .

In Via Solari each child had an exercise book for his coloured outlines. These were kept in a drawer in one of the cabinets. Each piece of work was dated by the directrice, and one could follow by means of the dates the rate of progress of any particular child. This keeping and dating of the coloured outlines gives them importance and value, and helps to arouse in the child a sense of his progress and to develop his power of self-criticism. It is a de-

[22] *Ibid.*, pp. 20–24.

veloped self-criticism and not emulation which is the lever used in these schools to secure improvement. The competitive spirit is wholly absent. In all the time I spent in the Via Solari I never heard there, any more than I did in any of the other schools, one child pitted against another. There is a recognition of difference of gifts. The work of each child is praised, not because it excels that of other children, but because it is an advance on what he has done before. The growth of each child is watched for and recognized. Since originally children are no more mentally facsimilies of one another than they are physically, there are differences in their ways of growth. The atmosphere which favours their growth is happy and moral on account of this absence of emulation and this appreciation of individuality.[23]

Further preparation for writing involved several lines of activity. The speech training was of the greatest importance. This the directrice was continually giving the children in the informal conversations which she had with them. They talked constantly, both among themselves and with her, and they learnt to pronounce properly and clearly. She noted babyish lisps which had to be cured, and she practised the children in giving the full value to the sounds and the correct accent in the words which they used. This was easy in the short individual lessons, in which such words as circle, cylinder &c., were learnt, or the names of the colours, stuffs, &c., easier than in connexion with the words which were part of their home vocabulary. This practice in careful pronunciation taught them to appreciate letter-sounds in the words, and they were consequently ready to associate the letter-sound with the form of the letter when they began to use the sand-paper letters.

When I was there, Bruna had just reached this stage. She had, as I have said, a great command of language, and her interest was directed towards the letters, though the only one of which she was certain was an *r*. At the sight and feel of this letter, she trilled it out with a facility which I, who had never been able to produce the trilled *r* sound, envied. She liked going round the letters with her first and second fingers. Very frequently she seized my finger and dragged it round. The sensations which I received from this contact with the roughened surface were not, I must confess, pleasurable; but this only shows with what caution one must infer from one's own feelings those of a child. If, as Dr. Montessori does, one takes as a reliable test of a child's feelings the readiness and frequency with which he performs a certain operation when quite free to carry it on or not as he pleases, then certainly these sand-paper letters are acceptable to children.

It is customary to begin with some of the vowels, and then being guided by the child's liking to choose a few consonants, but each consonant is at once joined with the vowels to form syllables, though the consonant sound is repeated separately so as to isolate it from the syllable.

Then the boxes of pink and blue paper letters are used when the child can recognize the letters learnt with certainty and can pick them out on hearing the sound. The directrice says a word, then gives the sounds of the letters separately, and the child picks out from the box the letter corresponding to each sound. The letters are put together to form the word, which child and

[23] *Ibid.*, condensed from pp. 25–30.

directrice read. It adds to the child's interest if the word is read by an older child or another grown-up person.

In this way, first by means of the sand-paper letters and then by means of the blue and pink movable letters all the letters are mastered, and from words the composition extends to phrases. Some children will write for themselves when only a few of the letters have been learnt and when consequently only a few words can be written. Others prefer to master all the letters first.

Very often this composition with the movable letters would be done out of doors. A table and chairs were carried out, and then the big boxes containing the paper letters. By watching these being taken from their compartments in the boxes and by seeing them replaced, the younger children as mere spectators often advance far on the path of letter-sound knowledge.[24]

The children learn to write when they are ready to write and want to do so. The rates at which the children learn writing differ greatly. Some children learn in a very short time, and their writing is excellent from the first. In some cases children who have learnt how to write do not derive much pleasure from doing so. I was speaking about writing one day with the directrice in the Via Solari, and she said, pointing out one little girl, "Marta can write, but she never does." Only a few minutes later Marta, who had heard this, came up to the blackboard, together with another little girl, whom I had never seen write. Dividing the board between them, both began to write and continued doing so for some time. Marta could indeed write quite well. The reason for her disinclination I did not discover. She formed a great contrast to such a child as Antoinetta, who wrote something every day.

It is the study of these personal differences which makes the work so interesting for the directrice. What we want are records which relate to such points as this. Was the difference between Marta and Antoinetta one which depended on home environment, or did it depend on a difference of nature? There are some children who take up interests which they rapidly drop, there are others who persist in their interests and tend to form spontaneously habits of daily repetition. It might be that in this case Marta's distaste for writing arose from inability to spell, perhaps due to defective pronunciation or hearing, or it might have arisen from lack of sufficient initiative to frame sentences.[25]

The altered relation of the teacher to the children was, of course, indicated by the choice of the title directrice, instead of the more familiar one of head mistress. The directrice guides the children; she does not seek to coerce any more than she seeks to bribe to good conduct. During the time I spent in the Via Solari I never saw any child whose will came into conflict with that of the directrice. The relations between the adults and children were entirely trustful and loving. There were occasional collisions between the children themselves when two or more of them wanted the same thing, but when the directrice intervened they never seemed to doubt the justice of her ruling. The atmosphere was one of real courtesy, and the directrice in the Via

[24] *Ibid.*, pp. 33–35.
[25] *Ibid.*, p. 37.

Solari could be her natural self, cheerful, alert, composed, and enjoying the children as one can only enjoy them when they are free to reveal themselves, and when one is conscious that one need not drag them to a certain level of achievement to meet the requirements of others, whether it is good for them to be so dragged or not.

If the children did not learn to write and read there, they learnt in the lowest class of the Municipal School. There was consequently no attempt to force growth. Some of the children, both directrices said, left them without being able to write and read. But they did not regard the learning of writing and reading as the all-important thing. The growth of graces of character occupied the centre of their field of vision. Such graces showed themselves in neatness and order, in cleanliness, in deftness, in courtesy, in helpfulness, in kindness, in reliability. I do not remember asking about truthfulness and honesty. Where children are not cowed, there seems no occasion for untruthfulness. The work with the material conduced to accuracy and clearness of statement. Confusion was prevented by the brief, simple teaching and by banishing the adventitious wrappings in which the instruction given to the children is so often enveloped from a mistaken idea of what constitutes interest. As for honesty, the material in the cupboards was open to all, but it did not disappear, and I never saw anything that looked like an attempt to preserve the school property from the depredations of the children. When we know that it has been found necessary, even in a respectable working-class neighborhood in London, to make the children give up at the door of the feeding centre the fork and spoon which they have been using in order to avoid disappearances, I think we may well ask whence comes this difference, and regard it as an ethical problem which needs elucidating. Can the changed attitude of the children to the school account for this desirable moral elevation?[26]

Such a description not only gives a good idea of what a Montessori school is like but also indicates the extent to which the modern progressive movement, with its emphasis upon freedom in the schoolroom, the natural development of children, and self-instructional materials, is indebted to the work of Mme. Montessori.

READING REFERENCES

A. General Histories of the Period

Benns, F. L., *European History since 1870,* Appleton-Century-Crofts Company, 1943 (1061 pp.), chap. 5.

Garrett and Godfrey, *Europe since 1815,* chap. 10.

Grant and Temperly, *Europe in the Nineteenth and Twentieth Centuries,* chaps. 14, 16.

Hayes, C. J. H., *Generation of Materialism, 1781–1900,* Harper & Brothers, 1941 (390 pp.), chaps. 1, 2.

[26] *Ibid.,* condensed from pp. 39–43.

Riker, *A Short History of Modern Europe,* chap. 13, part ii.
Robinson, *Introduction to the History of Western Europe,* chap. 40.
Schapiro, *Modern and Contemporary European History,* chap. 14.
Schevill, *A History of Europe from the Reformation to the Present Day,* chap. 29.
Stearns, *Pageant of History,* part iii, chap. 29.
Turner, *Europe since 1789,* chap. 10.

B. Secondary Sources

Bailey, C. S., *Montessori Children,* Henry Holt and Company, 1915. (188 pp.), any 4 descriptions of children.
Boyd, *From Locke to Montessori,* pp. 172–268.
Culverwell, *The Montessori Principles and Practice,* chaps. 4, 5, 7.
Fisher, *The Montessori Manual,* pp. 16–29, 107–123.
Smith, A. T., *The Montessori System in Education,* U. S. Government Printing Office, 1912, no. 17 (30 pp.), pp. 5–25.
Stevens, *A Guide to the Montessori System,* chaps. 1–3, 6, 8, 10.
White, *Montessori Schools as Seen in the Early Summer of 1913,* chap. 1, chaps. 10 and 11, or chaps. 2, 7, 13.

C. Translation of Primary Source

Montessori, *The Montessori System,* chaps. 5–7, 10–13, 16, 17, 19, 20.

CHAPTER XXI

DEVELOPMENT OF MODERN SCHOOL SYSTEMS

The present chapter will deal with the national school systems in three European countries as samples of similar development in practically all Occidental countries and states. A school system appeared in Germany at an early date and became the world's first public, state-supported, compulsory system. That of France emerged much more slowly, and that of England more slowly still. The educational systems of each country developed in response to the particular requirements of its citizens and reflected both the attitudes of society and the growth of the intense national spirit, which characterized European countries during the eighteenth and nineteenth centuries. The differences from country to country will be illustrated by a series of descriptions, diagrams, and quotations from writers in Germany, France, and England.

A. GERMANY[1]

The ideal of schooling for every child was nearly four hundred years old before it was put into effect on a national scale. The beginnings, however, were made during and following the Protestant Reformation. In 1559, the southwest German duchy of Württemberg organized the first complete school system, with elementary schools in every village. During the next decades, two other German states made similar provisions. In 1619 the duchy of Weimar set up a school system in which attendance was compulsory between the ages of six and twelve, and some twenty years later the duke of tiny Saxe-Gotha* established the first modern school system with compulsory education, well-paid teachers, free schoolbooks, a system of grading, and even pensions for retired teachers or for their widows and children. These schools were controlled jointly by state and church. The religious wars that followed the period of the Reformation halted the growth of universal education, but by the middle of the seventeenth century most of the German states had a system

[1] F. Paulsen, *Geschichte des Gelehrten Unterrichtes auf den deutschen Schulen und Universitäten vom Ausgang des Mittelalters bis zur Gegenwart,* Veit, 1885, 811 pp. (in translation by T. Lorenz, *German Education: Past and Present,* T. F. Unwin, 1908, 310 pp.); J. E. Russell, *German Higher Schools,* Longmans, Green and Co., 1899, 455 pp.; K. G. von Raumer, *Geschichte der Pädagogik vom Wiederaufblühen klassischer Studien bis auf unsere Zeit,* Bertelsmann, 1877–1897, 5 vols.; K. Schmidt, *Geschichte der Erziehung und des Unterrichtes,* P. Schettler, 1876, 551 pp.

of schools, in many of which attendance was compulsory. The joint control by church and state continued to the end of the eighteenth century, but at some time between 1750 and 1800 the various state governments throughout Germany took over complete responsibility for education.

The final stimulus toward making education a function of government grew in large measure out of the intelligence and forcefulness of Emperor Frederick William* and of his son, Frederick the Great, of Prussia. Before the former had been king for a year he had issued his first school code, to be followed four years later by an "advisory order" in which he urged parents under threat of "rigorous punishment" to send their children to school. He instructed communities to pay the tuition of destitute children out of the poor box,* he interested himself in getting better teachers, he personally founded over one thousand elementary schools by means of endowments, and he prescribed conditions for the maintenance of teachers, the collection and size of fees, and the degree of aid that might be expected from the central government. Even though some of the king's rulings were so advanced that his people were unable to carry them out, he nevertheless laid the foundation upon which his son was to build the first large, state-controlled, compulsory school system in the world.

Frederick the Great began his work of organizing education by centralizing control of the churches in 1750. A little over a decade later he initiated a series of decrees that culminated in the Prussian School Codes of 1763 and 1765. By these decrees the king ordered compulsory education for all children between the ages of five and thirteen or fourteen. The decrees also regulated school hours, vacations, fees, fines for parents who would not send their children to school, standards to be met by teachers, licensing of teachers, selection of textbooks, nature of the discipline, and the content of the curriculum. They ordered also the taking of a school census and the payment from public money of fees for poor children. To be sure, these sweeping decrees could not be put into effect immediately because there were not enough teachers nor enough public funds, but at least the necessary laws were enacted, and it remained only for practice to overtake principle. By the end of the eighteenth century, most of the other German states had followed the Prussian example. Germany was thus about a century ahead of other countries in forcing its children into the schoolroom.

The centering of authority in the state applied at first only to the elementary schools, but it was extended later to both secondary schools and universities. To be sure, the church shared in the control of the schools, but the rules were laid down by the state. This fact is well demonstrated in the following law enacted in 1794:

Schools and universities are state institutions, charged with the instruction of youth in useful information and scientific knowledge. Such institutions may be founded only with the knowledge and consent of the state. All public schools and educational institutions are under the supervision of the state, and are at all times subject to its examination and inspection.[2]

The high aspirations of Frederick the Great did not come into the desired fruition during his lifetime, partly from lack of funds, partly from lack of co-operation by the general public, and partly from the diversion of attention by the outbreak of a disastrous war. During the first decade of the nineteenth century, Napoleon dealt the country a devastating blow, humiliated Prussia upon the field of battle, and reduced the country to barely half its former size. The schools naturally suffered in consequence, but not for long, because the king, his ministers, the leaders of the people, and the people themselves united in a burst of patriotism and effort to throw off the yoke of the "foreigner." In the revival of Prussia and other German states nothing was considered more vital than the reorganization of the schools. Writers and orators pointed out that only by educating everyone could Prussia develop the necessary will to survive and conquer.

The government promptly established the first State Department of Public Instruction and appointed an efficient and intelligent man as its head. He at once sent a group of seventeen teachers at government expense to spend three years with Pestalozzi. They were to study his methods, but even more important, they were to absorb his spirit and his attitudes toward education. Upon their return to Germany, the seventeen were made directors of normal schools to train teachers in Pestalozzi's methods, aims, and ideas. Prussian teachers caught the spirit of reform at once and began to teach with a devotion to children that has rarely been equaled.

In order to provide enough teachers of high caliber, the state established normal schools in large numbers. Within a single decade the fervor of the people and the wise leadership of the government had transformed the purposes and methods of the elementary schools. Before the middle of the century, there were in Prussia alone thirty-eight normal schools for training elementary teachers, and one sixth of Prussia's inhabitants of all ages were attending some kind of school.

This extensive education for the masses was given a strong national flavor from the first and was deliberately used as a means of inculcating what the Prussian leaders regarded as necessary learning and desirable attitudes. In addition to the three R's, the schools taught German geography, history, and language, and they put great stress upon singing as a preparation for the

[2] German Civil Code, State Law of 1794.

martial songs of the period and upon physical exercise as a means of building strong soldiers and healthy mothers for the future. The narrow religious instruction of former days was abandoned, but in its place the teachers did all they could to instill into the children an obedience to authority and a willingness to sacrifice themselves for their country's welfare. The educational leaders of the German people thus realized, far ahead of other nations, that education had the power to mold each generation of children into whatever the state wanted them to become.

One effect of the great attention paid to the proper training of teachers was the increase in their social standing. Not only were they better paid, but they now had professional training. Since teachers in the Gymnasium had to be university graduates, teaching was soon bracketed with other professions and accorded a similar respect. University professors became the most revered individuals in Germany. Up until the beginning of Nazi domination, respect for professors was so great that a foreigner traveling in Germany could get better hotel rooms, better seats in a train, and better service in restaurants if he were known to be "Professor Smith" rather than just "Mr. Smith"; and the difference in treatment was even more pronounced if he were called "University-Professor" Smith. Even the relatively lowly elementary school teacher profited by the general reverence of the German public toward learning.

The secondary schools needed less reorganization as far as content and teaching methods were concerned, but the state took over in 1810 the tasks of examining and certifying teachers for them, of opening university seminars in pedagogy, and of providing for each new teacher a trial year of teaching under supervision. To standardize the work of secondary schools, the state revived a former plan of examining all graduates, and made the passing of these examinations necessary for obtaining any kind of civil service position. Those schools that could not provide the required nine-year course as a Gymnasium were permitted to have only six years, but they were called Progymnasien. The Gymnasien were required to have a uniform course of study consisting of Latin, Greek, German, mathematics, history, geography, and science. The Realgymnasium also had its place in the system. With true German passion for details, the state prescribed the amount of time to be devoted to each subject.

The resulting system of education had two parallel lines, which did not meet much more frequently than those in the geometry textbooks. Figure 95 shows the general plan. The children of the lower and middle classes, about 92 per cent of the entire number, entered the Volksschule and then, as the opportunity arose, went on into a continuation school that fitted them to become artisans, businessmen, or technicians. The children of the upper classes were, in theory, to become the leaders of the next generation. To be sure, pupils from the Volksschule could transfer to the Gymnasium, and a few especially able pupils did so, but the number was not large enough to offset the dual character of the system. The 8 per cent of the children who were to become future leaders received their preparatory training at home or in a private school and entered the Gymnasium at the age of nine. Upon graduation they could go into the university to be trained in one of the professions.

The basic objectives and means for achieving these aims were therefore determined before or during the first two decades of the nineteenth century. German teachers were to produce a literate, patriotic, docile citizenry in the

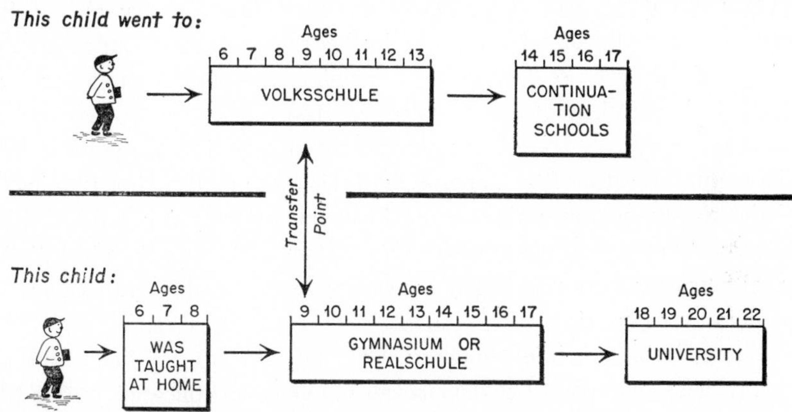

FIG. 95. Diagram of the German School System.

Volksschule and a small, socially secure, carefully selected band of leaders in the Gymnasium. The original intention was the freeing of Prussia from foreign domination, but once this was accomplished, the system was not abandoned but was used for other ends, first by the German emperors and militarists to bring Germany into the rank of European powers and then to pursue a course of aggrandizement. As one writer on German education has said:

> In a state such as the Germans proposed building there were to be leaders and followers. The followers were to be trained for a docile efficient German citizenship. That is, the lower classes were to be made into God-fearing, patriotic, economically independent Germans. This was the task of the Volksschule, and it has been wonderfully accomplished. This type of German is created to do the manual work of the state.
>
> The leaders were to be trained in middle and higher schools and in the universities. There were to be different grades of leaders: leaders in the lower walks of life, leaders in the middle walks of life, and leaders of the

nation. . . . The leaders think and do; the followers merely do. The schools were organized for the express purpose of producing just these types.[3]

If one has ever wondered why the average German is docile and obedient, one can here find the answer.

The German elementary schools that became imbued with Pestalozzian ideas early in the nineteenth century did not continue in this spirit, once Prussia had achieved its immediate goal of independence from France. The spirit of free inquiry was discouraged at elementary levels, the normal schools gave less and poorer training than they had given when first established, the curriculum was restricted, and the lower schools gradually became institutions for developing what was regarded as the "good" citizen. The Revolution of 1848 was laid at the door of too liberal an education of the masses, and for a time the elementary schools were even further restricted. The instruction was good enough of its type, but the old principle of pouring proper ideas into children took the place of the Pestalozzian theory of drawing ideas out of them. The secondary schools became somewhat more varied, in the latter half of the century, because of the importance of scientific and technical training in an industrialized nation, although the Realgymnasium[4] did not receive the same respect as the more conservative Gymnasium, until after the First World War, although its work was legally equivalent to that of the Gymnasium for some decades before then.

Before leaving this brief summary of the national pattern of education in Germany one should point out the changes in university education during the nineteenth century. The new developments were precipitated by the loss of many universities after Prussia was reduced in size by the Napoleonic Wars. To offset this loss, the University of Berlin was founded in 1810; in subsequent years other universities appeared. Although the government regulated elementary and secondary education, it left the new universities to the professors. For the University of Berlin only those men were appointed who were eminent scholars in their own field and had proved themselves to have a flair for research. These professors taught their students as they saw fit and were especially concerned with developing for the next generation scholars who were capable of advancing knowledge by research. Their ideal of university work was the discovery of truth, without reference to where the truth led them, and they insisted upon having freedom to pursue any subject in whatever way seemed best to them. Modern academic freedom thus came into existence and exerted a profound influence upon all collegiate and university

[3] From T. Alexander, *The Prussian Elementary Schools,* pp. 537–538. Copyright 1918 by The Macmillan Company. Used by permission of The Macmillan Company, publishers.

[4] See pp. 443 444.

life. Nowhere was this freedom so guarded as in Germany, and nowhere did it bear more distinguished fruit. The emphasis upon research in a student's undergraduate[5] days was also new. The usual procedure was for a professor to lecture for a while upon a topic and then to let his students verify in library or laboratory the truth of what he had told them. As students advanced, they selected unsolved problems and worked on them, under the guidance of their teachers. Such methods are now familiar enough to the college undergraduate, but they were new and revolutionary in the early decades of the nineteenth century. American scholars went to Germany to study and brought back with them the combination of lecture, seminar, and laboratory as a means of instruction to be used for the development of research in an environment of free academic inquiry into the truth. As a result of their new concept of university education, the Germans led the world during the latter half of the nineteenth century. There is no greater educational tragedy than the recent throttling of academic freedom in the land of its birth.

B. FRANCE[6]

The early rumblings of discontent with church-dominated schools in France and the first suggestion of state control of an education suitable for the needs of society came in the middle and later part of the eighteenth century. Plans for a "new" education for the common man, to uplift him and to give him the knowledge he needed to govern himself, were formulated during the first years of the French Revolution, but the ink on the plans was hardly dry before the destructive phases of the Revolution set in and aroused such distrust that any plans made by the revolutionists were regarded with suspicion if not with abhorrence. The Revolution further disrupted education in France by putting to an end, temporarily, the work of the teaching brotherhoods, by whom the best schools had been maintained, and by failing to set up nonreligious schools to take their places. For a decade French children of the lower classes got little schooling. When Napoleon came to power, however, he promptly set about organizing existing schools and founding new ones, until he had brought order out of chaos. He returned elementary education, in which he had little interest, to the brotherhoods but enacted a law re-

[5] German students entered the university at about the third-year level of American colleges, but they were somewhat older, more mature, and much better prepared.

[6] See M. Arnold, *Popular Education in France,* Longmans, Green and Co., 1861, 294 pp.; F. E. Farrington, *Public Primary School System of France,* Columbia University Press, 1906, 305 pp., and *French Secondary Schools,* Longmans, Green and Co., 1915, 454 pp.; F. P. G. Guizot, *Mémoires pour servir à l'histoire de mon temps,* Michel Levy frères, 1858–1867, 3 vols.; F. C. Schosser, *Education in the Eighteenth Century and the Nineteenth Till the Overthrow of the French Empire* (translated by D. Davison), Chapman and Hall, 1843–1852, 8 vols.

quiring each commune to furnish a school house and a home for the teacher, who was to be paid by tuition fees, although as many as one fifth of the pupils might be given training gratis. The schools were under state supervision but received no state funds. Napoleon's main concern was for the secondary and technical schools that would produce the trained men whom he needed to administer his empire and to lead his armies. He therefore established lycées and several special schools of a more advanced nature. The lycée* was a boarding school in which the pupils studied the ancient languages, literature, logic, mathematics, science, and a little modern language. The students paid tuition, but the state provided over six thousand scholarships for promising students who could not afford the fees. All other existing schools, whether public or private, in which Latin, French, history, geography, and mathematics were taught were also classed as secondary, but were regarded as inferior. Within two years there were 46 lycées in France and 739 other secondary schools. By 1850 there were over 50 lycées and in 1870 about 75. Napoleon also established 3 medical schools, 12 law schools, 4 schools of natural history, 2 of mechanics, 1 of history and political science, 1 of arts and trades, and a Superior Normal School to train teachers for the lycée. All were of university level. To control this motley assortment, Napoleon created the University of France, which was not to be a teaching university but a body of men who were to supervise education, examine students, inspect schools, disburse funds, and exercise jurisdiction over both teachers and pupils in all schools.

In the years following Napoleon's exile the situation remained much the same except that more attention was given to elementary schools, the members of the teaching brotherhoods were made to submit to the state examination that the other teachers took, and 30 new normal schools were founded for the training of teachers in the lower schools. In 1831 the French government sent a careful and unprejudiced observer[7] to study the Prussian school system. Two years later, on the basis of the report submitted by this observer, France enacted the School Law of 1833, which concerned elementary schools chiefly. This law required each commune to support primary schools, it created a new level called the "higher primary school," it established more normal schools, and it provided for state inspection of schools and state certification of teachers. The bill did not require compulsory attendance nor did it provide for free instruction except for those who could not afford the small tuition. The school Law of 1833 furnished the basis for French elementary education, just as the Napoleonic decrees had done at the secondary level.

The primary schools were to give instruction in reading, writing, arith-

[7] Guizot.*

metic, French, and religion. The higher primary school continued these subjects and added geometry, drawing, surveying, physical science, geography, history, and music. These schools were specifically ordered to emphasize the "history and geography of France, and the elements of science, as applied every day in the office, the workshop, and the field." This statement reveals a new and practical trend in education.

The nineteenth-century school system of France really took form in 1833, although there were some further developments and even a few retrogressions, especially in and after the disturbances of 1848. The next period of real growth occurred after the downfall of the second Napoleon* and the establishment of the Third Republic.* After nearly a century of experimentation the French finally committed themselves to a republic and at once set about making the schools into instruments for developing a national spirit and a national educational level that would give Frenchmen both devotion to their country and the knowledge to govern it. The government ordered new schoolhouses, new normal schools—especially those for prospective women teachers—substituted lay teachers for clerical, eliminated the teaching of religion in the schools, increased the available amount of technical and scientific education, gave state financial aid, modernized the curriculum of the lycées, reorganized or established state universities, and eventually suppressed all the teaching congregations. By the opening years of the twentieth century all elementary education in France was free, public, secular, and compulsory, and all education was under state control. Thus, about 125 years after the early leaders of the French Revolution had written down their ideas about education, their plans finally came into being.

The basic plan of nineteenth-century French schools is given in Figure 96. It will be seen at once that it also is a dual system, based largely upon social stratification, as was the case in Germany. The children of the lower and middle classes went through the infant, primary, and superior primary schools, after which some of them stopped and those who wished to do so went on into schools in which they received training in commerce, agriculture, manufacture, or the trades. Children were required to attend school only till the age of twelve or till they finished primary school. Those who intended to enter the army or elementary school teaching omitted most of the superior primary school and entered the continuation schools, from which they went into military or lower normal schools. Children of the upper social classes ascended a different educational ladder. After tutoring at home and spending two years in primary school, some went to the nine-year lycée, from which they continued into law, medicine, dentistry, or theology, or into the training

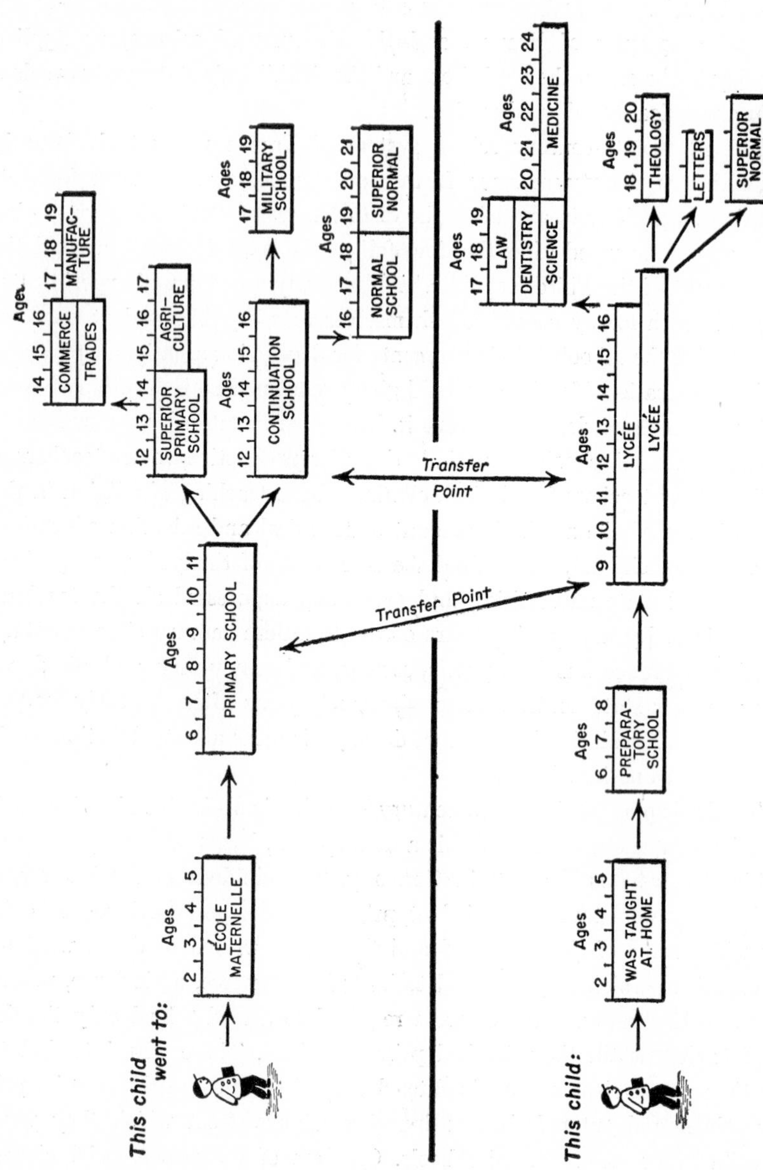

FIG. 96. Diagram of the French School System.

schools for prospective lycée teachers; others attended the eleven-year lycée, after which they took a university course with a "major" in either the sciences or the humanities.

For a democratic country, this plan looks remarkably undemocratic. It seems, however, to have been satisfactory, probably because it reflected existing society. There were, as can be seen in the diagram, two points at which transfer from one series of schools to the other could be made. The best time was when the pupil was ready to enter primary school, but a second chance was given when a child was ten or eleven years old.

C. ENGLAND [8]

From the time that ideas for national control of schools were first introduced, England showed a deep-seated disinclination to centralize authority in the hands of the government. Most Englishmen felt that the state should not assume responsibility for the instruction of its individual citizens. This attitude seems to have been based upon a fear that state-controlled education would eventually destroy civil and religious liberty. During the entire eighteenth century, Parliament enacted no legislation concerning elementary education, except for rescinding previous laws against Dissenters and Catholics and making available a minimum of schooling for pauper children in London. In 1833 an effort was made to pass a resolution requiring parents to send their children to school, but the measure was defeated by a large majority. As the chancellor of the exchequer summed up the matter, the government "might give a father the means of educating his children and put it in the power of a man who could not afford the expense to do so without expense; but the actual punishing of a man for not having his child properly educated would . . . be going further than they ought." [9] Although funds were voted for the erection of schoolhouses, so as to help provide education for those who wanted it, the government took no responsibility for the training of teachers, the attendance of pupils, or the inspection of work. One must remember that England already had a state-supported church, the fundamental doctrines of which were taught in all schools that wished to remain open. It was felt that further national control of education would give too much power to the central

[8] Based upon J. W. Adamson, *English Education, 1789–1902,* Cambridge University Press, 1930, 519 pp.; W. O. B. Allen and E. McClure, *Two Hundred Years: The History of The Society for the Promotion of Christian Knowledge,* published by the Society, 1898, 551 pp.; H. B. Binns, *A Century of Education,* J. M. Dent and Company, 1908, 330 pp.; C. Birchenough, *History of Elementary Education in England and Wales from 1800 to the Present Day,* Tutorial Press, 1938, 572 pp.; J. E. G. de Montmorency, *The Progress of Education in England,* Knight & Co., Ltd., 1904, 207 pp.; H. Holman, *English National Education,* Blackie & Son, Ltd., 1898, 256 pp.

[9] Adamson, *op. cit.,* p. 33.

government. The English therefore voted to continue the decentralization and local independence that had characterized education in previous centuries. England thus continued to depend upon philanthropy for the main support of schools and teachers and upon parental initiative in the matter of attendance.

Parliament did not approve a bill to use funds for support of elementary schools until 1833, and at that time the sum granted was very small. The amounts increased during the next four decades, but up until the establishment

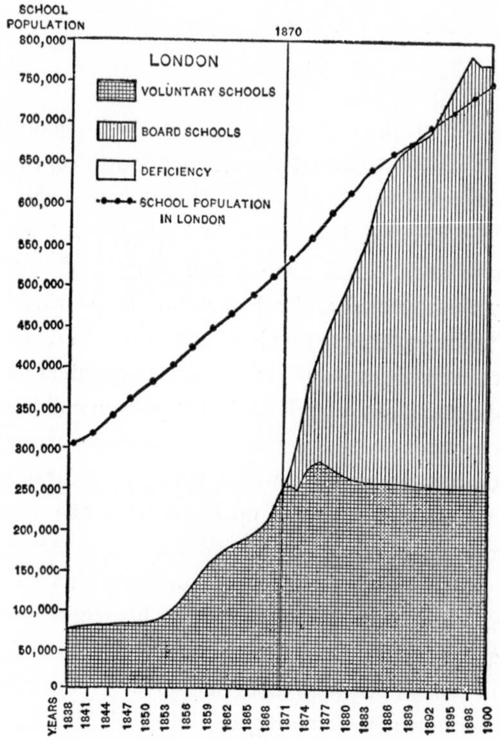

FIG. 97. School Needs versus School Accommodations in London. From E. P. Cubberley, *History of Education,* p. 643. Courtesy of Houghton Mifflin Company, publishers.

of a state-controlled system in 1870 the funds were most inadequate and were still dispersed through sundry philanthropic and religious societies. In the middle of the century, grants were made for the erection of more normal schools, although the number of these schools long remained insufficient to meet the demand for teachers. The English attitude that education should be voluntary, private, and no concern of the state resulted in totally inadequate educational facilities, as shown in statistics for the city of London in Figure 97. Voluntary efforts never at any time succeeded in supplying elementary schooling for as

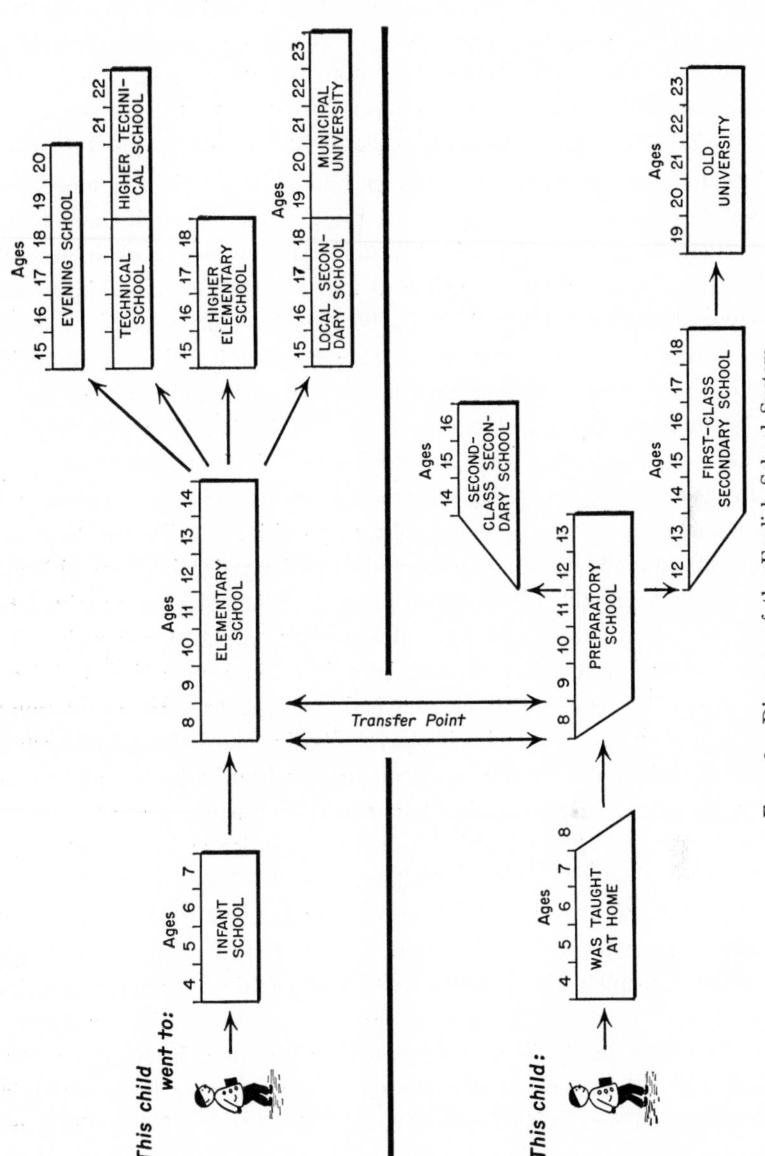

Fig. 98. Diagram of the English School System.

many as half the children of school age. When eventually it became evident that the state must supplement private efforts, Parliament in 1870 divided the country into school districts and authorized the creation of board schools wherever they were needed. The voluntary schools continued to exist as before. Even the board schools were not free, but the fees of poor children were paid from local funds. Within each district the school board might, if it wished, compel attendance between the ages of five and twelve, but it did not have to do so. The central government limited its functions to supervision by means of examinations, to grants on the basis of the results, and to the certification of teachers. The school examinations covered work in reading, writing, and arithmetic, and were given at four consecutive levels. This system of "payment by results," by which a school received funds according to the scores made by its pupils, proved thoroughly bad; it led to a cramming technique, since school support depended upon how many children passed their examinations. Nevertheless, the system remained in force until 1890. In 1880 elementary education became compulsory and in 1891 it became free.

In their curiously muddling way, the English let the situation develop as it would until 1902 when, against bitter opposition, Parliament took full responsibility for all secular education and created a national system, although many details were still left to local option. The Act of 1902 provided for unified control of both elementary and secondary education, although it left private schools free to reject government aid and inspection if they did not want them; but if they wanted one they had to accept the other. In the course of years most of the endowed schools voluntarily joined the school system, most of the voluntary elementary schools became board schools, and in 1918 the English quietly enacted the last laws needed to produce the system shown by the diagram in Figure 98. It has a dual organization as had all schools of Europe in the nineteenth century. Children from the lower or middle classes could, however, get a college education by attending first the high school and then the municipal university. In both France and Germany a child who started in the people's school had to transfer at a fairly early age to a higher class system or be denied a college degree, because he could enter the university only from the lycée or the Gymnasium. Because the English system did not "jell" till the end of the nineteenth century, after the demand for higher education for middle-class children had made itself felt, the worst features of the dual system were avoided.

What are perhaps the most distinguishing characteristics of the system do not, however, show up in a diagram. Although the system has order and organization, it is not a bureaucracy. Local initiative and independence, variations from school to school—provided minimum standards are met—and freedom for each school to develop as it will are outstanding values that the British have achieved in their slow process from chaos to system.

1. Types of School The English did not lack for variety in their elementary schools. Some types had persisted from earlier centuries: charity schools, parish schools, village schools, dame schools, apprentice schools, workhouse schools, and schools in industry,[10] plus a motley assortment of small classes taught by private tutors. To these were added, during the late eighteenth and early nineteenth centuries still more types: Sunday schools, "ragged" schools, infant schools, and monitorial schools, all of which will be described shortly. There were also a few special schools for blind, deaf, and delinquent children. If to the reader this array of institutions seems confusing, the impression is entirely correct. The situation continued to baffle the English for several decades.

Toward the end of the eighteenth century two movements developed, both of which resulted in the establishment of new types of school and in an increased attendance at the elementary level. The first of these movements was a fresh outburst of philanthropic activity;[11] the second was the development of the monitorial system of instruction. Both movements were strong while they lasted, but both were transitory.

The Sunday schools made their appearance about 1790. By 1800 these schools were everywhere. At first the instruction was entirely religious, but very early secular subjects were included, especially reading and writing. The classes were held for four or five hours on Sunday. The demand for education was so great that some of the Sunday schools were open on weekdays as well, and many of them offered evening classes for adults. It has been estimated that the attendance in the English Sunday schools grew from 234,000 in 1790 to 1,548,890 forty-five years later. Almost all the teachers in these schools gave their services. The Sunday school that in America was an adjunct to other schools provided, in early nineteenth-century England, the nearest existing approach to universal education.[12]

Most of the charity schools of various kinds were supported by relatively wealthy people, but humbler citizens also did their part toward relieving the

[10] See chapter XV.

[11] For a description of a similar period of philanthropy, see chap. xv.

[12] The voluntary philanthropic and educational societies in England during the decades under consideration were numerous and did a remarkable amount of work in founding schools and training teachers. By 1850, the church societies alone had opened 10,595 schools. Almost all funds for education came either from philanthropy or from local taxes, and what little money the government granted was usually dispersed through one or more of the societies. The method by which the funds were collected by the organizations is interesting as a sample of ingenuity. The societies were in effect joint-stock companies, in which people of means bought stock—not for profit, but for investment in humanity.

ignorance of those poorer than themselves. In about 1800 a type of school called the "ragged school" came into being through the activity of a kind-hearted cobbler named John Pounds,* who gathered destitute children off the streets into his six-by-eighteen foot cobbler's shop, where he cared for them, loved them, played with them, and taught them as he worked. His instruction included reading, writing, counting, cooking, and cobbling, although he did not apprentice the children. He made no charge for his services. A picture of his school appears in Figure 99. Other men of equally humble position opened similar schools, sometimes charging a few pennies a month, but in most cases giving their instruction free. From its small beginning

Fig. 99. A Ragged School. From H. Birchenough, *History of Education in England and Wales from 1800 to the Present Day,* London University Tutorial Press Ltd., 1930.

the movement slowly grew. The schools sprang up in a sporadic manner, and it was not until the middle of the nineteenth century that the Ragged School Union was formed. The schools evidently met a need because, without much organization and with almost no funds, they continued to exist until they were absorbed into the English school system in 1870. At that date there were still 200 ragged schools in London alone, with a total enrollment of 23,000 pupils.

Froebel was not the first man to have the idea of collecting preschool children into some kind of school, where they could be given both care and training. By the beginning of the nineteenth century there were numerous day nurseries and infant schools in England. In France also the infant school idea took root, but a little bit later; in 1850 there were 2000 of the "écoles maternelles" as they were called, and in 1880 there were 6500. The best known of the infant schools in England was founded at New Lanark* by a young millowner named Robert Owen,* who took over management of his father's mills in 1800. Some five hundred children were employed there. Owen established an infant school for children under six years of age and an elementary school for pupils from six to twelve. The infant school was patterned after the work of Pestalozzi, and a spirit of joyousness seems to have characterized all its classes. The building in which the school was housed was used in the evening for teaching adult mill hands and as a social center for them. Owen was about eight years in developing his system, which he maintained in good working order for another eight years, during which thousands of visitors came to see his work. The experiment did not long endure, however, probably because its socialistic principles were not in tune with the dominant capitalism of the age. So popular was Owen's work that the London Infant School Society was founded in 1824 to foster the establishment of similar classes. It and its successor, the Home and Colonial Infant School Society, trained teachers and in a few years opened 150 new schools. One of the leaders in this movement had worked with Pestalozzi; through him the Swiss reformer's ideas filtered into England and were applied to the work done in the schools for very young and very poor children.[13]

England, in common with other countries, had great difficulty in finding enough teachers for its elementary schools. This lack of competent teachers was so acute that a curious type of school, called the monitorial school, was devised for the dual purpose of making such skilled teaching as was available go as far as possible and of training teachers for the next generation. The method used seems to have been invented twice, once by a good churchman named Bell* and once by a Dissenter named Lancaster.* The distinguishing characteristics of the Bell and the Lancaster systems were (a) that a single teacher controlled a class of several hundred pupils, (b) that the brighter pupils were used as monitors for small groups of their fellows, and (c) that the teacher gave instruction *to the monitors only,* although some general directions were given to the class as a whole. The monitors passed on to their schoolmates the instruction they had received and did most of the actual teaching. The use of bright pupils as monitors was not a new idea. The Jesuits had a similar arrangement, and long before them it was used by the Brothers of the Common Life.[14] The systems of Bell and Lancaster put a greater responsibility upon the monitors, however. They were not merely "teacher's helpers," but more nearly apprentice teachers who were beginning their practice teaching at an

[13] For further information concerning infant schools, see D. Salmon and W. Hindshaw, *Infant Schools, Their History and Theory,* Longmans, Green and Co., 1904, 324 pp.

[14] See chaps. xi and xiii.

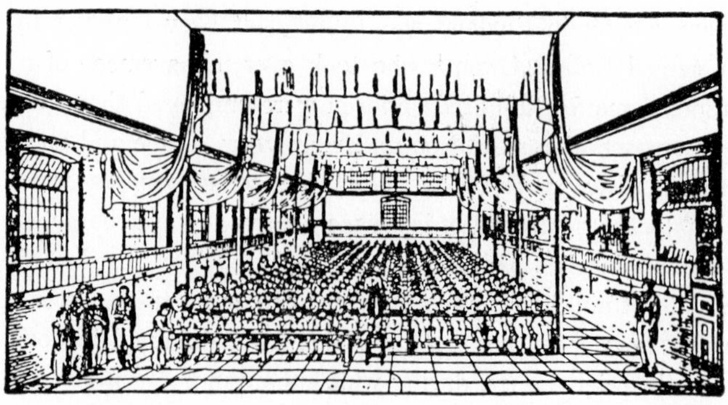

FIG. 100. A Monitorial School. From F. P. Graves, *A Student's History of Education*, Figs. 39, 40, 41. Courtesy of The Macmillan Company, publishers.

early age. The three parts of Figure 100 illustrate the stages of instruction. In the first view, the entire class is assembled; in the second, each monitor is teaching his small group; and in the third, the monitors are inspecting their pupils' work.

In spite of its obvious defects, the monitorial technique achieved some valuable results. Because it was extremely cheap, it made education on a large scale possible. Even children of very poor people could attend a class in which each child had to contribute only one five-hundredth of the single teacher's salary.[15] The number of children enrolled in these schools far exceeded any previous totals. The system also bridged over the drastic shortage of competent teachers and the almost complete lack of normal schools, because the monitors were deliberately recruited for the profession. The monitorial school did not last long, but it did give an added impetus to the idea of popular education.[16]

2. *Surveys of Educational Facilities* From time to time during the nineteenth century the government appointed a commission to study conditions in the schools of England. The first of these reported in 1818 that 130,000 children in London alone were without school accommodations of any kind. The numerous subsequent reports stressed four points: the shortness of the period during which pupils attended school, the irregularity of attendance, the lack of sufficient schools for all the children, and the incompetence of the teachers. Children went to school, if at all, between the ages of six or seven and eleven; attendance diminished rapidly after eleven, and only 5 per cent of thirteen-year-old children were still in school.[17] The average school life was thus about four years and rarely exceeded six. The typical school of the middle nineteenth century had one certified teacher and a number of apprentices, although some schools were unable to get even one teacher who had proper training. The situation called aloud for compulsory education and a generous support of normal schools, but the English showed a prolonged resistance to compulsion and a desire to keep down the national expense of education, leaving both the responsibility and the cost of schooling to the parents, the general public, and the philanthropic societies.

With such a great assortment of schools as the English possessed, one might suppose that most English children were getting at least the rudiments of an education, but such was not the case. A government committee in 1816 reported that of the 12,000 parishes in England and Wales, 3500 had no school at all. Since one ninth of the population at that time was between the ages of seven and thirteen, this proportion should have been in school, but the total enrollment was only one sixteenth for England and one twentieth for Wales. Nor was mere insufficiency of institutions the only difficulty. Such schools as existed were badly distributed. Thus, in the city of Carlyle,* with a school population of 2680, only 13 per cent of the total—or 348 children—was in school. The city had an impressive array of schools, however; one infant school, nine private schools "for the upper classes," forty private schools—

[15] Societies for the spread of monitorial schools defrayed even this small expense in some instances.

[16] For an evaluation of monitorial schools see, D. Salmon, *The Practical Parts of Lancaster's Improvements and Bell's Experiments,* Longmans, Green and Co., 1904, 112 pp.

[17] As late as 1847.

mostly dame schools—"for the lower classes," one school of industry, one national school, one Roman Catholic school, and twelve Sunday schools. The average enrollment per school, not per class, was 5.3 children. Another investigation in 1833 revealed that throughout the country at least two fifths of the children from workingmen's homes were without education; two out of every five grew into adulthood still illiterate. Moreover, there was no established relationship among the numerous schools. Although England made some provision for all grades of education, there was no school system and few regulations of any kind. The average length of attendance was from two to three years. The curriculum consisted of reading, writing, simple arithmetic, and religious teaching, with sometimes a little geography, surveying, or handwork. Reading was the basic subject, but even it was not brought to a high enough level to enable most pupils to read with pleasure.

3. Control of Secondary Schools The secondary schools that existed in England in the middle of the nineteenth century were in the main private, endowed institutions, many of which had for centuries been training the children of a small ruling class. These schools gave a classical education, a relic that had come down almost intact from the days of the Renaissance. In the intervening centuries it had lost its original vitality, but it remained as the aristocratic model, upon the debatable theory that a large dose of Latin in the classroom would train the mind to think,[18] just as a large dose of competitive games would train the body and develop a sense of sportsmanship, or a similar application of religious doctrines would train the soul. To this type of education for its future rulers the British clung obstinately, despite such blasts of criticism as that given in 1893 and quoted below:

> Modern geography, modern history, modern literature; the English language as a language; the whole circle of the sciences, physical, moral and social, are even more completely ignored in the higher than in the lower schools. Up till within a few years back, a boy might have passed through any one of the great public schools with the greatest distinction and credit, and might never so much as heard of one of the subjects I have just mentioned. He might never have heard that the earth goes around the sun; that England underwent a great revolution in 1688, and France another in 1789; that there once lived certain notable men called Chaucer, Shakespeare, Milton, Voltaire, Goethe, Schiller. The first might be a German and the last an Englishman for anything he could tell you to the contrary. . . .
>
> Now let us pause to consider this wonderful state of affairs; for the time will come when Englishmen will quote it as the stock example of the stolid stupidity of their ancestors in the nineteenth century. The most thoroughly commercial people, the greatest voluntary wanderers and colonists the world has ever seen, are precisely the middle classes of this country. If there be a

[18] More will be said about this theory in chap. xiv.

people which has been busy making history on a great scale for the last three hundred years—and the most profoundly interesting history, history which, if it had happened to be that of Greece or Rome, we should study with avidity—it is the English. If there be a nation whose prosperity depends absolutely and wholly upon their mastery over the forces of Nature, upon their intelligent apprehension of and obedience to the laws of creation and distribution of wealth, and the stable equilibrium of the forces of society, it is precisely this nation. And yet this is what these wonderful people tell their sons:

"At the cost of one to two thousand pounds of our hard-earned money, we devote twelve of the most precious years of your lives to school. There you shall toil, or be supposed to toil; but there you shall not learn one single thing of all those you will most want to know directly you leave school and enter upon the practical business of life. You will in all probability go into business, but you shall not know where, or how, any article of commerce is produced, or the difference between an export and an import, or the meaning of the word 'capital.' You will very likely settle in a colony, but you shall not know whether Tasmania* is a part of New South Wales, or *vice versa*.

"Very probably you may become a manufacturer, but you shall not be provided with the means of understanding the working of one of your own steam-engines; and, when you are asked to buy a patent, you shall not have the slightest means of judging whether the inventor is an imposter who is contravening the elementary principles of science, or a man who will make you as rich as Croesus.*

"You will very likely get into the House of Commons. You will have to take your share in making laws which may prove a blessing or a curse to millions of men. But you shall not hear one word respecting the political organisation of your country; the meaning of the controversy between free-traders and protectionists shall never have been mentioned to you; you shall not so much as know that there are such things as economical laws. . . ."

Said I not rightly that we are a wonderful people? I am quite prepared to allow, that education entirely devoted to these omitted subjects might not be a completely liberal education. But is an education which ignores them all a liberal education? Nay, is it too much to say that the education which should embrace these subjects and no others would be a real education, though an incomplete one; while an education which omits them is really not an education at all, but a more or less useless course of intellectual gymnastics?

For what does the middle-class school put in the place of all these things which are left out? It substitutes what is usually comprised under the compendious title of the "classics"—that is to say, the languages, the literature, and the history of the ancient Greeks and Romans, and the geography of so much of the world as was known to these two great nations of antiquity. . . . And what is to be said of classical teaching at its worst, or in other words, of the classics of our ordinary middle-class schools? It means getting up endless forms and rules by heart. It means turning Latin and Greek into English, for the mere sake of being able to do it, and without the smallest regard to the worth, or worthlessness, of the author read. It means the learning of innumerable, not always decent, fables in such a shape that the meaning they once had is dried up into utter trash; and the only impression left upon a boy's mind is that the people who believed such things must have been the greatest idiots the world ever saw. And it means, finally, that after a dozen years spent at this kind of work, the sufferer shall be incompetent to interpret a passage in an author he has not already got up; that he shall loathe the sight of a Greek or Latin book; and that he shall never open, or think of, a classical writer again, until, wonderful to relate, he insists upon submitting his sons to the same process.[19]

With the great increases in wealth among the middle classes, resulting from industrialization, there were by the middle of the century more families that could afford to send their children on into secondary school than there were schools to accept them. Moreover, the type of school desired differed from that above condemned, except as parents wanted to ape the great public schools for purposes of prestige. In 1870 local school boards began to establish high schools to meet this new educational demand. These new schools made one more addition to the motley array of educational institutions. By 1891, then, the English had a system of sorts, but there were still a number of schools that escaped even inspection, and the state had not yet taken entire responsibility for education. It merely inspected, examined, and helped.

D. COMPARISONS

As can readily be appreciated from the foregoing account, the countries of Europe progressed at different rates, in different ways, and for different motives toward a state system of education. What is true of the three countries studied was also true of smaller European nations. Prussia, Switzerland, Holland, and Denmark were in the lead in the establishment of centralized control. All of them accepted the principle that the state was responsible for public, free, primary education, and since the early decades of the nineteenth century all of them have maintained a more or less adequate number of schools in which attendance was, in theory at least, compulsory. In France, education came under state supervision fairly early, if not under state control, but attendance was not compulsory. Religious instruction was included in the elementary schools and met with little opposition, since the population was strongly Catholic, but each commune was allowed to provide whatever religious instruction accorded with the wishes of the majority of the parents. In German-speaking countries, the question of religious instruction had been settled by the provision of denominational teaching by the clergy, from which, however, any pupil might be exempted if his parents claimed that such instruction was against their conscience. England had the least centralized sys-

[19] T. H. Huxley, *Collected Essays,* Appleton-Century-Crofts Company, 1896–1902 (9 vols.), Vol. III, condensed from pp. 92–101.

TABLE 14: COMPARATIVE GROWTH OF STATE CONTROL

Years by Decades	Germany	France	England
1710	Advisory order (1717).		
1720			
1730	Some government aid to schools (1730).		
1740			
1750	Centralization of control over elementary school instruction (1750).		
1760	Education compulsory; teachers licensed; seminars for training teachers (1760).		Free education for pauper children in London (1767).
1770			
1780	State control of secondary schools (1787).		Sunday schools opened (1780).
1790			Monitorial schools (1797).
1800	Department of Public Instruction created (1808).	Each commune to have elementary school; superior elementary schools, lycées, communal colleges established (1802). University of France established (1808).	Ragged schools and infant schools (1800).
1810	Exams for all secondary teachers (1810). All students examined (1812).		
1820	School boards in each province (1825).		
1830		State inspection and certification of teachers (1833).	First government aid to schools (1833). Inspection of schools (1839). Privy Council on Education appointed (1839).
1840		Uniform plan for schools (1840).	Teacher-pupil system established (1846).
1850			

TABLE 14: COMPARATIVE GROWTH OF STATE CONTROL—(*Continued*)

Years by Decades	Germany	France	England
1860			"Payment by results" inaugurated (1862). Endowed school supervised (1869). License from church no longer needed (1869).
1870		Normal schools for women	Board schools opened (1870). High schools authorized (1870).
1880		Primary education free (1881) and compulsory (1882).	Primary education compulsory (1880).
1890			Education free (1891). Central board for elementary and secondary schools (1899).
1900		Teaching orders suppressed (1904).	State responsibility for all schools under local boards (1902).
1910			National school system established (1918).
1920			

tem of all and did not succeed in divorcing religion from education for fifty years after a solution had been reached in both Germany and France.

In order to summarize and make clearer the developments in the three major countries the diagram in Table 14 has been constructed. As may be seen at a glance, the school system of Germany was complete before any real beginning had been made in England. France had a system of schools under state inspection and centralized control by 1833, although attendance was not both free and compulsory until near the end of the nineteenth century, nor wholly secular until 1910. The developments that led to a modern educational system in England did not start until about 1880, and the system was not complete until after the First World War.

READING REFERENCES

Adamson, *English Education, 1789–1902,* chaps. 1, 5, 6, 8–10.
Alexander, *The Prussian Elementary Schools,* chaps. 1, 12, 14.
Allen and McClure, *Two Hundred Years: History of the Society for the Promotion of Christian Knowledge, 1698–1898,* chap. 40.

Arnold, M., *Popular Education in France,* Longmans, Green and Co., 1861 (294 pp.), chaps. 5–8.

Barnard, H. C., *A Short History of English Education,* University of London Press, 1947 (400 pp.), chaps. 1–3, 6–8, 12, 13, 19, 23.

Bartley, George C. T., *The Schools for the People,* Bell and Daldy, 1871, 582 pp., any 25–30 pp.

Birchenough, *History of Elementary Education in England and Wales from 1800 to the Present Day,* chaps. 2–7.

De Montmorency, *State Intervention in Education,* chaps. 6, 7.

Eby and Arrowood, *The Development of Modern Education,* chaps. 16, 18.

Farrington, *French Secondary Schools,* chaps. 4–8, 14–16.

———, *Public Primary School System of France,* chaps. 2–7, 9, 10.

Graves, *Great Educators of Three Centuries,* chap. 12.

———, *A Student's History of Education,* chaps. 12, 18.

Harris, J. H., *R. Raikes: The Man and His Work,* E. P. Dutton & Company, 1899 (335 pp.), chaps. 9, 13, 16.

Marique, *History of Christian Education,* Vol. III, chaps. 4, 9.

McCormick, *History of Education,* chap. 29.

Owen, R., *The Life of Robert Owen by Himself,* Effingham, Wilson Company, Ltd., 1857 (2 vols.), Vol. I, any 20–25 pages.

Paulsen, *German Education: Past and Present,* Book iv, chaps. 1, 2.

Podmore, F., *Robert Owen,* Hutchinson and Company, 1906 (2 vols.), Vol. I, chaps. 6, 7.

Roberts, R. D., *Education in the Nineteenth Century,* Cambridge University Press, 1901 (274 pp.), chaps. 3, 13.

Russell, J. E., *German Higher Education,* Longmans, Green and Co., 1910 (rev. ed., 489 pp.), chaps. 5–7, 10, 22.

Salmon, *The Practical Parts of Lancaster's Improvements and Bell's Experiments,* pp. vii–xli.

PART EIGHT

CONCLUSIONS

CHAPTER XXII

EDUCATIONAL PRINCIPLES

This book has centered around the ideas of great teachers in previous centuries, the kinds of schools that existed, the subject matter presented to the pupils, the methods of instruction, and the results achieved. There have also been incidental comments on the aims and theories of education at different periods and on the nature of the curriculum. In this concluding section it seems advisable to trace certain developments in educational thought, stressing especially those elements that have thus far received relatively little attention. The present chapter will contain material on two topics: the aims of education, and the various theories of education that have been advanced at one time or another.

A. THE AIMS OF EDUCATION

Ever since the first adult began to pass on his knowledge to his or to other people's children there has probably been more or less discussion as to what the training was really for. Such primitive groups as still exist show a diversity in their thinking on this point. A man may teach his son to chip an arrowhead as a technique to be employed at once by the boy in hunting or in self-defense, as a means of preparation for adulthood, as a form of artistic expression, as a training in patience and self-control, as a step in the training for leadership, as a means of coming in contact with a divine power, or as training in a trade. The ends would, in these various instances, be utilitarian, preparatory, aesthetic, disciplinary, social, religious, or vocational. All of these objectives have existed for centuries, often simultaneously, but the emphasis has usually been on only one or two at once. The main end of education in any single period of history is the one that best reflects the needs of society at the time, but less popular objectives have some followers. In short, mankind has never been able to make up its mind for long about the proper aims of education, and since there are relatively so few of them, one finds the same ones cropping up in different centuries whenever the environment is appropriate for each in turn.

Among the Greeks, three aims of education seem to have been predominant—the attainment of perfection, the development of a cultured man, and the preparation for citizenship. As Plato wrote, "Education consists of giving to the body and the soul all the perfection of which they are susceptible."

The Romans were a very practical people, with a genius for government, law, organization, building, and mechanics. They were doers rather than thinkers, and the striving for human perfection did not interest them especially. Their aims were mostly social and preparatory, with some admixture of cultural interests. An educated man held public office and took an active part in public life. The school years were thought of as a preparatory period, during which a boy got ready to play his adult role. As the Romans assimilated more and more ideas from the Greeks, a few writers began to stress the cultural aims of education and the making of a gentleman.

In the period of decline, the cultural aim blossomed into grotesque forms. Whatever was of no practical value was acclaimed as best, and young men were educated in the most elegant and artificial forms of general uselessness. Of this decadence, Ausonius is an excellent example. The practical aim of training orators for the guidance of the state was no longer operative because the state was guided by the emperor without help from orators, except as he made use of them to write fulsome and undiscriminating panegyrics in his honor.

The early Christians founded schools of their own to educate converts and the children of converts into a new concept of life that was inspiring men and women throughout the Roman Empire. Christian education had two closely related objectives: the training of character in this world and the gaining of heaven in the next. The former has been an objective in almost every system of education. The latter became the main objective of education during the Middle Ages. As Christian education developed, it went to extremes and regarded all of life on earth as merely preparation for immortality.

During the Middle Ages, however, there were some strictly vocational schools for the training of letter writers, clerks, notaries, and shorthand writers. As the towns recovered from the devastation of the barbarian invasions, the trade guilds came into being and were soon maintaining apprentice schools, in which the objective was strictly vocational. At the very end of the Middle Ages a few secular schools with secular teachers were established by municipal or royal authority, with aims that were largely cultural. The vocational and cultural objectives did not, therefore, completely disappear during the Middle Ages, although they were overshadowed by the religious.

The main effect of the Renaissance upon educational aims was to give renewed predominance to the cultural objective. Renaissance education was aristocratic and aimed at the production of the perfect gentleman. It also fixed the means by which one became "cultured": study of ancient languages, ancient literature, art, and history, plus the healthy development of the body. This model persists for the education of a gentleman to the present day, with some modifications. The Renaissance revived the Greek ideals of perfection and balance, of truth, and of individual development. One finds in the writing of the period rather strong hints that the aim of education is the unfolding of the individual and the development of his talents to their highest level. The "unfolding" motif was to recur in subsequent centuries.

When the Renaissance moved northward, it took on a moral and humanitarian trend that it never had in Italy. Soon it fused with the revolt against church domination and turned into the Reformation. The new schools founded by the Protestants began with a combination of cultural and religious objectives, but the latter soon repressed the former. While the content of education remained humanistic, the aims changed from the self-development and perfectionist ideals of the Renaissance to the combined religious and civic aims of the Reformation. Luther expressed the purpose of the new schools in the following words: "The object of education is the preparation for more effective service in church and state."[1] One is back again at the preparation for leadership and public service that was the objective of Roman education.

The narrowly religious aim lingered on for another hundred and fifty years, although other motifs were combined with it. Thus Comenius, living more than a century later than Luther, wrote: "Education is the development of the whole man and the ultimate end of man is happiness with God."[2] This definition keeps the cultural and developmental objectives but subordinates them to an ultimate religious goal.

During the seventeenth and eighteenth centuries, the ideals of education, as expressed by outstanding writers, turned from narrow, religious aims to the formation of character and preparation for adult participation in the life of the times. Some of the formulations appear below:

> I call, therefore, a complete and generous education that which fits a man to perform justly, skillfully, and magnanimously all the offices, both private and public, of peace and war.[3]
>
> The attainment of a sound mind in a sound body is the end of education.[4]

Both statements emphasize the production of men who can take their places in this world.

In the latter half of the eighteenth century, the idea of education as the gradual and natural unfolding of a child's abilities became dominant. As Pestalozzi wrote:

[1] M. Luther, *Address to the Mayors and Councilmen of the German Cities,* 1527.

[2] M. W. Keatinge, *The Great Didactic of John Amos Comenius,* A. & C. Black, 1910, (2d. ed., 319 pp.), p. 53.

[3] John Milton, *Tractate on Education,* 1673.

[4] John Locke, *Some Thoughts Concerning Education,* 1693.

> Education consists in developing, according to the natural law, the child's various powers, moral, intellectual, and physical, with such subordination as is necessary to their perfect equilibrium.[5]

This objective differs from the perfectionist aim in that it emphasizes the unfolding of such abilities as an individual has, whether or not the result approaches perfection. The ideals of perfection, happiness, and participation in social activity still found expression, however. For instance:

> The purpose of education is to train children, not with reference to their success in the present state of society, but to a better possible state, in accordance with an ideal conception of humanity.[6]
>
> The end of education is to render an individual as much as possible an instrument of happiness, first to himself, and next to others.[7]
>
> To prepare us for complete living is the function which education has to discharge.[8]

The great teachers who have been described in previous chapters varied considerably in their objectives. Only a few among them expressed themselves directly. Since most of them did not, one has to infer their aims from their writings and actions. Usually, each man had more than one objective, although one might be more important than the others. Table 15 is a tabulation of objectives, insofar as the writer is able to estimate the beliefs of other people.

Modern education has inherited practically all the objectives of previous centuries. Public education, of course, has been forced to eliminate any religious aims, but these still influence the work in church schools. The argument concerning the relative values of cultural and vocational objectives still continues. Teachers in private schools and colleges and professors in graduate schools are still dedicated to the training of leaders for the next generation. In recent decades the cultural objective has been relatively less powerful than the vocational, but at present the belief in the value of cultural education is becoming stronger again. The ideal of the educative process as a gradual and natural unfolding has been widely accepted and has formed the basis of the modern progressive movement. At the moment a heated discussion is in progress between those who believe that schoolwork should consist largely of a preparation for adult life and those who believe that it should give children what they need right now, leaving the future to look after itself in due course. Few people now urge perfection as an aim, perhaps because modern man knows too much psychology to believe in its attainment but not enough to

[5] R. de Guimps, *Pestalozzi: His Life and Work,* Appleton-Century-Crofts Company, 1892 (432 pp.), p. 375.
[6] Immanuel Kant, *Essay on Pedagogy,* 1779.
[7] John Stuart Mill, *Article on Education,* 1840.
[8] Herbert Spencer. *Education,* 1861.

TABLE 15: THE AIMS OF EDUCATION

Teacher	Perfection	Truth, knowledge	Balanced development of all powers	Preparation for life	Preparation for public service	Preparation for eternity	Development of character	Happiness	Development of mental powers	Unfolding of innate abilities	Preparation to earn a living	Service to others	Culture	Control over nature	Erudition	Elegance	Training for leadership
Socrates		√					√		√								
Quintilian					√								√		√		√
Ausonius													√		√	√	
Origen		√					√						√		√		
Jerome						√							√		√		
Alcuin						√	√										
Abélard		√							√								
Vittorino	√		√				√	√					√				√
Melanchthon					√		√						√			√	√
Ascham									√				√		√		√
Mulcaster		√		√			√				√						
Loyola					√		√					√					√
Comenius						√	√										
De la Salle				√	√		√				√	√					
Francke				√	√		√				√	√					
Basedow								√	√	√	√						
Pestalozzi			√				√	√	√	√		√					
Herbart		√					√		√				√		√		
Froebel	√						√	√	√	√							
Seguin														√			
Binet		√															
Montessori			√	√			√		√	√							

perfect himself. In America, at least, happiness is a common objective, and so also is the formation of character. Perhaps the most popular aim, however, is the development of each child to the limit of his capacities.

Of such divergent opinions is democracy made. It is probable and desirable that no one objective should ever so dominate education as to crowd out the others. The result of such concentration would be likely to throttle not only competing aims but education itself. As long as educators continue to put their eggs in different baskets, the prospect for schools in the future will remain bright.

B. EDUCATIONAL THEORIES

In the course of the last twenty-five hundred years, mankind has evolved a number of theories about education. A given theory is often connected with the name of a writer who first popularized it, but it is a mistake to suppose that he was its inventor or its sole defender. He got his ideas from his predecessors, shared them with his contemporaries, and left them behind him for his descendants. In some instances, the philosopher or writer whose name is connected with a given theory was also a teacher, but quite as often he was not. Perhaps teachers become so absorbed by the minutiae of their work that they fail to see the educative process as a whole and do not, therefore, often produce theories about it. The enlightened, thoughtful, public-spirited outsider has a better chance to survey the education of his times, to evaluate it, and to write about it.

In any particular age and country, one or more of the theories to be presented shortly were dominant, because they fitted best into the current cultural pattern; but all the theories, in their elements at least, have existed side by side in almost all, if not all, cultures. They have been contradicting each other for many centuries, and will probably continue to do so. In education, as in politics, there seems always to be a party of the opposition. Indeed, more than one such party commonly exists. For purposes of clarity, the ten commonest theories have been grouped into pairs, the first member of which contradicts or is in contrast to the second.

(1) The first pair of opposing theories may be called the public-service and the individual-development principles in education. Both are very old. The advocates of the former believe that education should fit men to take their places as enlightened citizens. The state or society as a whole is regarded as of supreme importance, to which each member should be adapted by means of his education. Such a theory produces a curriculum that contains those elements needed to make a good citizen. It favors a relatively severe discipline as a means of subjugating the will of the individual to the good of society.

When carried to extremes, as in ancient Sparta or Nazi Germany, it reduces men to robots who exist merely for the state. The theory is not, however, to be judged by its excesses. In moderation it has its values. Since each individual child in a community will grow up to become an adult member, he should learn to take his place in society and to do his part in improving the world around him. Among the great teachers, Quintilian is perhaps the clearest advocate of education for service to society.

The defenders of the individual-development theory regard the growth of each person as the important objective of education. They argue that if teachers develop all children to their highest level, then these children, as adults, will create a satisfactory society. Current society in any age has its defects, and if it is allowed to dominate education, it will merely produce such adults as will fit into it, and therefore it will never improve. Hence the emphasis should be upon individual development. This theory produces a curriculum that contains whatever elements the pupils will need for growth, regardless of possible social usefulness. The discipline is likely to be mild, since there is no need for more conformity among the pupils than is required to keep a schoolroom in order. This concept of education has its merits, but if carried to extremes, it would produce a generation of individualists who could not live together, and society would be worse off rather than better. Presumably the ideal education would combine social and developmental features, but a balance between them is difficult to maintain. Among the great teachers there are several who stressed personal development over social adjustment—Vittorino, Basedow, Pestalozzi, and Froebel—although none of them were as extreme in their views as the philosopher Rousseau.

(2) The second pair of theories consists of the utilitarian versus the cultural principles in education. The believers in the former want education to be of obvious practical value. They argue that since most people have to earn their living, their education should prepare them to do it. The average man finds this theory of education more acceptable than most. All vocational and prevocational schools exist because there are so many believers in a training that is practical. The guild schools of the Middle Ages were expressions of this same interest, as were the Roman schools for training clerks. In Europe, vocational education or even practical education has not been highly regarded, in spite of its obvious value. Perhaps the attitude is a relic from earlier days when manual work was done by slaves, and a gentleman would hardly so demean himself as to learn a trade. American schools have done more than others to support and dignify utilitarian education. A training that is exclusively practical would, of course, be narrow and would not fit the learner to take an intelligent part in the life of his community or to spend his

leisure hours in a satisfying way. Few of the great teachers have upheld the utilitarian theory; however, both Francke and Pestalozzi gave more or less vocational training to orphan children, and Basedow accepted a number of lower-class pupils, who learned personal service by waiting on their classmates.

The cultural theory of education is very old. It has been associated with the aristocratic tradition in those countries that developed a dual system of schools. The work of the people's schools was supposed to be largely utilitarian —enough reading and writing for literacy, enough arithmetic for business, enough religious training for morality, followed by entrance into either a trade or a vocational course—while that of the upper-class school was supposed to be cultural. It is always difficult to explain what is meant by culture, but so far as schoolwork is concerned, it may be thought of as the complex of ideas about the world, life, and people that has been passed down from previous generations. It is not devoid of practical value because it contributes much to an understanding and appreciation of life, but its utilitarian values are only incidental. The curriculum produced by the cultural theory contains courses which cover the history of mankind and the choicest products of the human mind. In modern American life, the undergraduate arts college is the institution devoted to the continuance of cultural education. The same theory is responsible for the recent introduction of survey courses in the early college or university years. These courses are supposed to set before the student a summary of his cultural heritage in literature, science, or art and to act as a common basis of ideas among educated men and women. By this means, the prospective mechanical engineer, the prospective social worker, the prospective wholesale buyer, and the prospective farmer will share in their common heritage of ideas, despite the differences in their specialties.

There have been times in the world's history when an aristocratic, cultural education has been carried to a senseless extreme. In the fourth century after the birth of Christ, Ausonius taught a curriculum that was largely unreal, artificial, and useless. The humanistic program offered by Sturm in the sixteenth century was on a high academic level, but it had little contact with the practical world. In recent times, the best example of extreme emphasis upon culture can be found in the public schools and colleges in England.[9] As one Cambridge don* is supposed to have said, "God bless the higher mathematics, and may they never be of use to anybody." Until the beginning of the present century, the endowed schools of England offered a course of study that had little relation to life outside the schoolroom. When cultural education is carried to such an extreme that it becomes dissociated from reality, it wastes the stu-

[9] See quotation on pp. 610–613.

dent's time, and it may fill him with ideas that will make his later adjustment to the world unnecessarily difficult.

(3) A third pair of concepts offers a contrast between the content and the disciplinary theories of education. Adherents of the former believe that the content of the curriculum is all-important, on the principle that knowledge is the source of power. When and where the content theory is dominant, the materials in the course of study are chosen with great care, since the value of the training rises or falls in proportion as the content is rich or inadequate. The modern detailed analyses of the curriculum have been carried out in the belief that what goes into the curriculum is at least as important as the method by which it is taught. In former times, the best example of this theory in practice was the work of Comenius, who labored long and hard to decide just what should go into each of his textbooks. Mulcaster, Basedow, and Herbart were also concerned over what was to be taught.

The disciplinary theory of education is held by those who, in any age, have contended that the pupils should gain mental power rather than knowledge from their studies. The main question about a given course thus becomes the extent to which it will train the student to think. This theory has become so much a part of everyday thinking that its phraseology appears in common speech. People talk about "training the mind," "acquiring the power of concentration," "improving the memory," "educating the imagination," or "developing the ability to reason," even though it is extremely doubtful if any of these mental capacities exist as separate entities, or if any of them can be trained to function independently. In order to understand the hold that this theory has upon educational thought, it is necessary to go back to the seventeenth century and observe the reasons for its development in its modern form.

At that time, the humanistic curriculum, inherited from the Renaissance was still in force, although a few schools with less emphasis upon the ancient languages had already been founded. Because of the changed conditions and the extensive use of the vernacular, however, the value of Latin in everyday life, or even in academic life, had greatly diminished. Yet the traditional school had a curriculum based on Latin and a corps of teachers trained to teach the language. In fact, there was such a degree of vested interest in the subject that it simply could not be abandoned, although by the end of the seventeenth century it was no longer serving a directly useful function. The highly linguistic curriculum might have disappeared some time before it did, since it was under constant attack from mathematics and the sciences which were pushing their way into a course of study already full, had not the study of Greek and Latin received support from the disciplinary concepts of John

Locke. This educational writer formulated the theory of mental discipline and applied it especially to the study of Latin and mathematics. To both subjects he attributed the power to train the pupil's memory and reason.

The idea that one can learn to think, reason, memorize, and concentrate by the study of Latin or any other subject has now been thoroughly exploded; but if one only could, the use of a single subject for developing mental power would certainly be a short cut. As it is, one has to plod through many subjects, and at the end one can think only in terms of the subjects studied. One can, to be sure, develop a memory for verb forms, or for glacial periods, or for the bones and organs of the body, by studying each; what one cannot do is to develop one's memory in one subject and then simply apply it to another. Transfer of judgment from one field to another is even more difficult. Thus the physicist who reasons superbly about physics may be a nincompoop when he tackles a political problem, or the eminent historian may reason like a child in mathematics, or the most critical and skilled linguist may be completely baffled by a simple problem in geology. When Locke first proposed the doctrine of formal discipline, no modern proof of its inadequacy existed, and the theory was believed until such proof had had time to accumulate. As long as it was accepted, it furnished a defense for the teaching of Latin. It was not until the Classical Investigation* in 1925–1930 that belief in the disciplinary value of Latin received its deathblow. If memory, accuracy, and reasoning cannot be trained by study of languages so that they will function not only in school but in any subsequent walk of life, then languages, like any other subjects, must be justified on grounds of their intrinsic value. Unfortunately, they do not train mental abilities once and for all, so that these can be used anywhere, anytime, on anything—and more's the pity! Although there is some general training in methods of work in any subject, provided it is hard enough to require real effort from the student, there does not seem to be any one subject that is better than another for the purpose.

(4) A fourth pair of theories contrasts repression with naturalism. The former idea was dominant throughout the Middle Ages and at other periods during which religion was an important element in education. The repression theory assumes that human nature is innately bad and can be improved only by proper training. It produces a curriculum that is well loaded with subjects appropriate for inculcating religious and moral attitudes. Discipline is severe because badness must be beaten out of children before goodness can be poured in. The subject matter in the courses is not made attractive to the learner: the less pleasant it is the more opportunity there is for the growth of will power and moral character. None of the world's best teachers subscribed

wholeheartedly to this theory, presumably because they had too much affection for their pupils and because they could arouse so much interest that harsh discipline was not necessary. It is, however, probable that Alcuin, Loyola, Francke and De la Salle all believed in the natural badness of children and the need for their redemption. Certainly, most of the lesser teachers of the Middle Ages and Reformation accepted the repression theory and willingly combined dullness and harshness for the good of their pupils' immortal souls.

The naturalistic theory of education received its best expression in the writings of Rousseau, who assumed that human nature was innately good and would remain so unless contaminated by society. An adherent of this theory believes in letting children behave naturally and develop naturally, guiding them only just enough to prevent them from actual injury. The curriculum that is produced on the basis of naturalism contains, in principle at least, study of everything that arouses childish interest, whether or not the material is divided into instructional units. Discipline is practically nonexistent. In its most extreme form, the naturalistic theory would dispense with schools altogether and let the children just grow, educating themselves by asking such questions as occur to them in regard to the world about them and their place in it. The few people who have tried extensive freedom for children have not, however, been well pleased with the result, except possibly when a skillful tutor has been able to remain for years with one or two children. When applied to a group of pupils, liberty has sooner or later produced more chaos than education. Most of the great teachers of the past have allowed their pupils some degree of freedom to grow as they would, and have tried to guide development rather than to force it. Those who have accepted naturalism as a main principle of procedure are Basedow, Pestalozzi, Froebel, and Montessori. The modern movement in progressive education is an outgrowth of this theory.

(5) The last pair of theories is concerned with the question of whether the schoolwork of children should be designed primarily to prepare them for their adult lives, or to explain to them the questions that arise from day to day at their successive stages of development. The teacher who accepts the preparatory theory teaches children to compute simple interest, not because they have a present need to do so, but because they are likely to need the skill after they grow up. On this principle, the curriculum of the elementary school would cover whatever skills are commonly needed by adults and are simple enough to be learned by children. A teacher would hope to motivate the necessary mastery by use of childish interests, if possible, but the connection is usually indirect. For those children who lack interest, the teacher must resort to a personal appeal, asking them in effect to learn the material because he wants them to do so. In spite of one's best efforts, some pressure is normally

needed, and some degree of discipline, since pressure generates disciplinary problems. In the past, most courses of study have been preparatory, even in periods during which few pupils stayed in school long enough to reach the level for which the preparation was intended. The pupil who dropped out of school when he was halfway through Latin grammar could do little with his education. The same criticism applies to any course of study that is mainly preparatory. For instance, if the first year of high school physics is designed as a basis for a second and third year, the two students in a class who go on into advanced courses profit by the preparation, while the thirty who stop have not derived the benefit that would have been possible had the course explained to them the things about their immediate environment that they wanted and needed to know, instead of giving them a basis for the advanced work they do not take.

In contrast, the here-and-now theory restricts schoolwork to those items that will explain the children's daily lives. Children learn to add 6 and 7 when they have six of something and wish to add seven of something to it; they learn to spell "perhaps" when they are writing a letter and want to use the word; and they learn the meaning of new words as they stumble upon them in reading matter of their own choice. If the work of a school were based on nothing but children's present needs, it would be necessary either to keep all children in school until they were adults, or to develop in all of them such good methods of work that each could attack and master new material when, where, and if it was needed. This theory is relatively new in education. It adds a needed element of immediate interest on the part of the children, but it has not yet won complete acceptance. Of the teachers described in this book, only Pestalozzi, Seguin, and Mme. Montessori show even a partial belief in such a theory.

The student should not suppose the above-mentioned ten theories are independent of each other. They often combine. The cultural, disciplinary, and public-service motifs make a common syndrome,* as do naturalism and individual development, or content and utilitarianism. Most teachers believe in a combination of various principles. In a rudimentary form at least, all the theories have been believed by someone, sometime, somewhere; and most of them have a long history of alternate prominence and neglect. Any one of them, if carried to excess, leads to an education that is too one-sided and inadequate to last for long. The teacher of today would do well to steer a middle path and to get from each theory whatever of value it may have.

CHAPTER XXIII

THE CURRICULUM IN RETROSPECT

Throughout the ages, the three R's* have furnished the absolute minimum that separated the literate man from the illiterate. Above this elementary level, however, the subjects studied have changed more or less with the centuries. Even during relatively long periods of stagnation, when the same subjects continued to be taught, the emphasis shifted from one to another. The curriculum at any particular time is a result of many contributing causes, such as the existing amounts of knowledge in different fields, the power of tradition, the needs and structure of society, the stability of the social group, the currently accepted theories of education, the adequacy of teacher training, and the financial support—however derived—given the schools. The curriculum enlarges as the horizons of knowledge expand and new subjects are introduced. It changes faster in an unstable society than in a settled one, and fastest during or just after periods of upheaval. It spreads out in one direction or another in response to the dominating modes of educational thought. Its natural expansion is often blocked by traditional attitudes, by inadequacies of the teaching staff, or by insufficient funds. The curriculum at any point in time is thus the composite result of many pressures; but as one looks back through the centuries, one can see certain trends in its growth. With these developments the present brief chapter is chiefly concerned.

The Greek boy of the fifth and fourth centuries B.C. began his education by learning to read, count, and write. Then he studied literature, music, and gymnastics, but the literature course included instruction in language, ethics, history, and geography. If he continued into secondary school and university, he studied rhetoric, philosophy, and science.

The Roman boy also spent his first school years in learning to read and write. Counting was learned in the elementary school along with a little arithmetic, but mathematics did not go far with Roman numerals. Then the boy went on to the study of grammar in both Greek and Latin, including a little reading of the classics. Some boys studied Latin before Greek, but in later Roman times it was more fashionable to study the languages in the reverse order. The work in literature and grammar included training in speech, composition, history, mythology, geography, and ethics. The boy studied also a little geometry and astronomy. In the next school, his work consisted almost wholly of oratory and rhetoric. If the scholar went on with his education, he studied law, medicine, architecture, mechanics, rhetoric, or philosophy at a university.

Once a student had progressed beyond the level of literacy, the curriculum of antiquity centered about further training in how to speak effectively, the reading of Greek or Roman authors, and the study of philosophy and mathematics, with, among the Romans, the addition of some practical subjects at the highest level.

The pagan schools of the transition period between antiquity and the Middle Ages imitated the same curriculum, but the imitation lacked the vitality that had characterized the original. Gradually, the study of Greek dropped out, and the emphasis was put upon rhetoric, which spread out to form most of the curriculum, with grammar filling what space was left.

Christian schools at first taught only the principles of Christianity to adult converts, but soon this curriculum, if it could be called such, was extended in two directions. The children of converts were taught in Christian schools to read, write, count, and sing, because their parents feared to expose them to paganism. At the other end of the training, the course of study had to be enlarged to include philosophy and an embryonic theology, as adult converts who had already been well educated in pagan schools were added to the ranks. These men and women demanded a synthesis of ancient philosophy and Christianity.

For two or three centuries the rivalry between the pagan and Christian systems of education went on, with Christianity winning mainly because it had something to say and paganism did not. Eventually the two curricula fused, and the typical course of study during the Middle Ages arose from the combination. For a thousand years the curriculum consisted of the seven liberal arts: grammar, rhetoric, dialectic, arithmetic, astronomy, geometry, and music, with philosophy at the top. During the darkest of the centuries, the curriculum consisted of little more than reading, writing, a little arithmetic, singing, and some religious instruction—sometimes only the Lord's Prayer, the Creed, and a psalm or two. A few scholars went on to reading and commenting upon the writings of the church fathers, but that was about all, although reading of the Latin classical authors never completely disappeared.

As the darkness lightened and some learning from the East, via the Arabs, filtered into Europe, the emphasis within the seven arts changed, with dialectic assuming the dominant position in the trivium; arithmetic, which grew rapidly after the introduction of Arabic numerals, dominated the quadrivium. The amount of material to be learned also increased, as men recovered the books of the ancients and discovered new things for themselves. The accretions were so great that schools higher than those then in existence were needed, and the university appeared in response to the demand. The curriculum then expanded at the top to establish courses in law, medicine, letters, philosophy, and theology.

The Renaissance and Reformation did not alter the academic curriculum greatly, except to add Greek. Literature, grammar, and declamation became the outstanding subjects, with rhetoric taking a lower place. History as a subject to be pursued by itself was introduced during the Renaissance. For the first time since antiquity, the curriculum included training in manners, games, sports, and dancing. In Protestant countries, however, the study of church doctrine soon overshadowed that of literature and history. The curriculum of most elementary schools included reading, writing, counting, physical education, singing, religious instruction, and vocational training. Those who attended these schools usually went no farther. Schools on the next level gave Latin, Greek, Hebrew, literature, rhetoric, dialectic, history, music, physical education and mathematics. The university curriculum continued, as before, to provide professional training. The Jesuit schools established during the Counter Reformation did not differ greatly in their curriculum from the Protestant schools, except in the nature of the religious instruction and the inclusion of geography in the lower schools and logic and metaphysics in the colleges.

By the seventeenth century, the sciences, their practical applications, modern languages, and certain utilitarian subjects had begun to appear. Thus, in the Dissenters' schools in England one finds surveying, drawing, French, mechanics, and science added to the usual basic work in Latin. Court schools throughout Europe developed their own curricula to include such subjects as would fit young aristocrats to their position in life. The curriculum gave no Latin or Greek, no rhetoric or grammar. Instead, it included history, politics, geography, law, heraldry,* a little mathematics, fencing, riding, games, and dancing.

During the seventeenth century, the pattern of European education became stabilized, and with it, the nature of the studies in each school. The school attended by the children of the common people offered reading, writing, counting, religion, a little work in history, geography, nature study, and music. All subjects were taught in the vernacular. Children of the upper classes learned at home to read, write, and count. The school they then entered was either a Latin or a Real school. In the former the curriculum consisted almost exclusively of Latin and Greek. In the Real school, the same two languages were taught, though less extensively, and the "real" subjects—science, mathematics, and modern languages—occupied a prominent place. The curriculum of the first high schools for scientific and technical work included

German, French, Latin, mathematics, history, geography, nature study, drawing, mechanics, architecture, bookkeeping, and anatomy. The higher technical schools and universities extended the same two types of curricula, the former having courses of study that led mainly to work in applied science by means of laboratories and workshops, and the latter offering subjects that led into the professions. Various trade schools, descendants of the old guild schools, which had existed continously on the fringe of the educational system now began to multiply and to offer work that led to specific occupations.

At this point, the modern curriculum had arrived, in its essentials. Subsequent developments consisted of splitting up the existing subjects into smaller pieces, as more and more knowledge accumulated. The course in natural science became differentiated into courses in astronomy, physics, chemistry, anatomy, physiology, zoology, botany, and so on. The modern languages increased in number, the courses in each language being commonly divided into those in grammar, literature, or composition. The ancient languages took their places with the others and in time became relatively unimportant. The social sciences—economics, sociology, and political science—split off from history. Geography developed many subdivisions, among them geology. Mathematics continued to include arithmetic, algebra, and geometry, but continually added more advanced work as mathematicians developed their field of learning further and further. The curriculum of today is thus a logical outgrowth of curricula in past centuries, although most of the differentiation has come within the past two hundred years.

CHAPTER XXIV

SOME CONCLUSIONS

It may be profitable to look back over the previous chapters and to consider what has been said about the twenty-three teachers described, in order to find out, if possible, what makes a great teacher great. A comparison of the teachers with each other may also help the prospective teacher to see his own future work in a clearer light.

It seems worth while also to point out to the prospective teacher the value of history to him if he is to use what he has learned in an appropriate way. This application of the past to the present is, unfortunately, not always specifically made in texts dealing with historical developments, and it has been the writer's experience that not all students are able to make it unaided. A second section of this chapter will therefore deal with this point.

A. THE GREAT TEACHERS OF THE PAST

The teachers who have been described might be expected a priori, to resemble each other in a number of ways. They might have similar traits of personality or similar intellectual attainments; they might have received roughly similar educational training themselves; or they might belong to closely allied schools of thought concerning the basic principles of education. These possibilities should all be considered, if only briefly.

First, as to personality. The student should have noted by now that the great teachers of the world have been of different and often contradictory types. Abélard attracted students by his vivacity, Origen by his serenity. Pestalozzi was passionate and incoherent, while Herbart was cold, remote, and logical. Basedow was an ill-mannered man of the people, De la Salle was an aristocrat, and Ausonius was an elegant aesthete. The geniality of Socrates is in contrast to the quarrelsomeness of Jerome; a similar contrast appears between the timidity of Alcuin and the brashness of Abélard. Quintilian's outstanding characteristic was his courteous dignity, a quality that Froebel lacked altogether. As near as one can estimate from historical records, Jerome, Abélard, Melanchthon, Mulcaster, Herbart, and Binet had extremely high I.Q.'s; the others were, however, well above average in intellectual power. Ingenuity in small matters all the teachers showed, but the outstandingly ingenious were Socrates, Comenius, Seguin, and Montessori.

Not all the great teachers lived lives of faultless rectitude, and several of them had serious personal faults and shortcomings. Froebel was unscrupulous about money, Loyola was a fanatic, Basedow drank to excess, Abélard was a braggart, Comenius was stupidly credulous, Pestalozzi was eccentric and often foolish, Ascham had a wide streak of the sycophant in him, Ausonius had a wider one, and Mulcaster was harsh and irritable. The most lovable members of the entire group were Alcuin, Origen, Socrates, and Pestalozzi. Those who had the best emotional balance were Quintilian, Vittorino da Feltre, De la Salle, Binet, and Socrates; so far as known, none of these men became fanatically aroused over anything. For sheer driving power and determination, it would be hard to surpass Jerome, Loyola, or Mme Montessori. Melanchthon and Comenius were the worriers of the lot, while in color and dash, Jerome and Abélard led the field. There is, indeed, so little similarity among the great teachers that one is inclined to wonder if such a thing as an "ideal" teaching personality exists.

Perhaps the type of individual who becomes a successful teacher is related to the characteristics of the period in which he lives. Thus a man who quarrels does not arouse antagonism in a world in which all thinking men are at the moment quarreling. A braggart does not stand out against others of similar character, nor is a drunkard noticeable among drunkards. On the positive side, a well-balanced man is demanded by a well-balanced general public, an erudite man in a generation that admires learning above all else, a stern disciplinarian in a community that believes in harsh discipline for children, a gentle man by a peaceful and contented public, a fighter in a time of intellectual revolt, or a brilliant man in an age of invention and discovery. A teacher who was greatly admired in one century might not, therefore, be as highly regarded in another. Today, Socrates might be arrested as a general nuisance when he buttonholed busy people on street corners, and Alcuin's passion for preserving every book might be regarded as a harmless but obvious eccentricity. But in their respective ages their personalities and methods were what people wanted and needed. A teacher, no less than any other man, is influenced by his culture.

Although the great teachers varied in personality, they shared a surprising number of ideas, as indicated in Table 16. They believed in a close personal bond between teachers and pupils. They kept discipline by love, not force, and they condemned corporal punishment. Most of them studied each child, analyzing his abilities and interests, and then tried to train him in whatever way and toward whatever goal seemed best. A few made classifications of pupils into types. All seem to have been sensitive to the needs of children and to have adapted their teaching to childish mentalities. Several devised materials for the improvement of teaching: dialogues, grammars, picture books, graphs, maps, materials for sense training, and so on. Except for the few who lived in times when a gloomy religion dominated mankind, these leaders in education wanted schoolwork to be interesting, exciting, and so much fun that children would love it. With the same few exceptions, they encouraged good health, physical exercise, games, and sports, as necessary to the work of a proper school. As a group, then, these men believed in a nucleus of sound ideas that have come down from them to the present, and have formed the basis of what prospective teachers now learn—attention to the human potentialities of each child, adaptation of teaching materials to his needs, guidance of his growth, encouragement of play as a natural and useful element in childish behavior, and insistence upon love and reason as the guiding principles for discipline. These similarities would suggest that great teachers share ideas rather than personal traits.

The ideas listed in Table 16 represent the nucleus of the modern teacher's heritage from the past. The discouraging thing about this heritage is that the basic ideas have been discovered, lost, rediscovered, and relost, century after century. Perhaps this phenomenon arose from lack of books, poor means of communication, and neglect of teacher training. It is to be hoped that the central core of useful ideas and principles, produced with much effort by many people, has now become so integral a part of every teacher's thought about education that there will be no danger of loss in the future. The teacher of today who incorporates into his teaching the best ideas of past centuries will be well equipped for his task of guiding the next generation into the hoped-for era of peace and prosperity, in which education will play an increasingly important part.

B. THE VALUE OF HISTORY TO A TEACHER

A familiar argument for the study of history is that "history repeats itself" and that a knowledge of what has already happened in the world will provide an understanding of what is now occurring. Of course, history does not repeat itself in the way a carbon copy repeats an original, but similar social, economic, and moral forces do tend to produce situations that are similar in different centuries and people do tend to react to such stimuli in somewhat the same way. For instance, the totalitarian state is not new; it was tried out several centuries before Christ by Sparta in response to much the same forces as existed in Germany in the 1920's and 1930's. It was no more successful in the long run than the modern effort, and again for the same reasons. The totalitarian state has never yet been able to maintain itself, perhaps because it trains men to be robots, and robots can do only what they have done and

TABLE 16: FUNDAMENTAL IDEAS ABOUT EDUCATION

TEACHER	Materials adapted for children	Attention to individual differences	Discipline based on love and interest	Personal bond with pupil	Analysis of abilities	Classification of pupils	Education to be fun	Development of both mind and body	Education as guidance of native abilities	Education as a science	Emphasis upon moral growth
Socrates				√				√			√
Quintilian		√	√	√	√	√		√	√		√
Origen		√	√	√	√	√					√
Ausonius				√			√				
Jerome	√			√					√		√
Alcuin	√	√	√	√	√				√		√
Abélard				√			√				
Vittorino	√	√	√	√	√	√	√	√	√		√
Melanchthon		√	√	√							√
Ascham		√	√	√	√	√	√	√	√		
Mulcaster		√			√	√		√	√	√	
Loyola		√	√	√	√	√		√	√	√	√
Comenius	√	√	√		√	√		√	√	√	√
De la Salle		√	√	√					√		√
Francke		√	√	√				√	√		√
Basedow	√	√	√	√			√	√	√	√	√
Pestalozzi	√	√	√	√	√	√	√	√	√	√	√
Herbart			√		√	√				√	√
Froebel	√	√	√	√	√		√	√	√		√
Seguin	√	√		√	√	√		√		√	
Binet	√	√			√	√				√	
Montessori	√	√	√	√	√	√	√	√	√	√	√

cannot therefore adjust themselves to change. It is regrettable that Adolf Hitler had a violent distaste for history.

In the field of education history also repeats itself, in a general sense. Mankind has discovered several times over that children learn better if they are treated with kindness and encouragement than if their efforts meet with harshness and punishment. The modern psychologist can prove by controlled experiment the exact extent of the differences in mastery of subject matter by pupils who are praised for their successes over those who are punished for their errors, but all he is adding to traditional knowledge is exactness. At least as far back as Quintilian, teachers were told to be kind to children, not only on humanitarian grounds but in the interests of efficiency in teaching. Similarly in the matter of individual differences. Modern tests show how great such differences are, but they were not needed to show that variations exist. To be sure, modern techniques of investigation occasionally prove tradition to have been wrong. However, if one were to list the outstanding principles of teaching and learning that form the heritage from the past, one would find that most of them have survived the ordeal of modern scientific investigation with flying colors.

Another point that the thoughtful student may have noticed is that periods of progress and periods of retrogression seem to alternate in education as in other fields. A teacher and his immediate followers blaze a new trail; then their successors go enthusiastically so far along the newly formed path that they reach an extreme, from which the next generation recoils. The reaction to the new movement may be so strong that it may return to the point at which it started; but after the first period of excess and the first reaction, it moves forward again a bit farther along the new pathway than it had been before the trail was discovered. At the time of this writing, the United States is returning to the center after two decades of movement to the left, away from tradition. This progressive movement exerted an excellent influence on educational practice, but it led to the establishment of some ultraprogressive schools in which the children were allowed to unfold their personalities to suit themselves. The results did not seem to suit anyone else. The extremes have disappeared, however, and the schools of the country have accepted, to a moderate degree at least, the fundamental principles of the progressive movement. Education has thus consolidated another of its advances. Similar periods of excessive enthusiasm followed Rousseau and Pestalozzi. In some localities, the conservative forces were so strong as to be reactionary, and the schools experienced a decade or more of retreat to the "good old days," before they commenced on a more modest scale to reap the benefits of the enlightened methods outlined by Rousseau and given form by Pestalozzi. Thus, history moves forward two steps and back one.

It is the nature of young people to make discoveries and inventions which to them are novel and unique. What they often do not know is that their discoveries have already been made several times over. Since a school consists basically of a teacher, some pupils, and a curriculum, the same situations and problems continue to rise, generation after generation, and teachers are likely to think up the same answers to them. Perhaps a main objective of a course in the history of education is the prevention of those solutions that have already been tried many times and found wanting. It seems a waste of energy for a teacher to put his youthful enthusiasm into a "new" idea that was thoroughly exploded in the third century B.C., as well as in the twelfth, fifteenth, and nineteenth centuries A.D., unless the times have so changed that the idea may be worth trying again in modern surroundings; but even so, it might be well to season an experiment with a dash of history as an insurance against disappointment. Since teaching rests essentially upon the human relationship between teacher and pupil and since human beings do not change much, the treatment recommended by Jerome in the fourth century for teaching a small child to read—"let her work be play"—is still good advice, because children are still children. Most of the successful ways of teaching pupils have already been tried by someone, and usually tried repeatedly. What the successful methods need is not discovery, but modern scientific proof of value, adaptation to modern conditions, and systematic use.

Finally, history should be of value to a young teacher because it furnishes him with a treasure trove of the world's best thoughts about education for well over two thousand years. In it he should find a number of valuable ideas that will help him in his daily work. One does not progress by ignoring history but by using it. Naturally, it is not necessary to regard mere age as of value in itself; such an attitude is no more sensible than that of the ultra-progressive who thinks that the older something is the worse it has to be. The prospective teacher is advised to go back over this text, his own notes on it, and his notes on his teacher's lectures—since these will include many items not in the text—and make for himself a list of the sound ideas with which he has come in contact through his acquaintance with the great teachers of yesterday. This summary will then contain, in concentrated form, his own cultural heritage from those who have gone before but have left behind them a path of glory in which he may tread the more easily because they lived first.

GLOSSARIES

GLOSSARY A: PEOPLE

ADELARD OF BATH (12th century), English scholastic philosopher. Studied in France, Spain, Italy, North Africa, and Asia Minor. Translated Euclid's *Elements*. He was familiar with the astrolabe (a forerunner of the compass) and the abacus.

AESCHYLUS (525?–456? B.C.), Greek tragedian. As a young man he fought in the Persian Wars, at both Marathon and Salamis. He wrote over seventy plays of which only seven have survived entirely, among them *Seven against Thebes, Prometheus Bound,* and *Eumenides*. His dramas revolve about the problems of human destiny and are both powerful and majestic.

AESOP (620–560 B.C.), writer of fables which are still read today.

ALBIGENSES, a group of reformers in southern France, in the 11th to the 13th centuries. Their name comes from the Latin *alba,* meaning "white," because they wanted to purify the church. They were exterminated by the crusade against the Albigenses and by the Inquisition.

ALCIBIADES (450–404 B.C.), a wealthy, high-born, able, but dissolute and erratic young kinsman of Pericles. He alternated popularity in Athens with betrayal of his city to her enemies. He contributed to the downfall of Athenian power.

ALEXANDER THE GREAT (356–323 B.C.), son of Philip of Macedon and pupil of Aristotle. A military genius. He conquered Asia Minor, Syria, Palestine, Egypt, then marched eastward into India, spreading Greek language, culture, and religion wherever he went, and at the same time establishing contacts with the East that eventually led to much borrowing of Oriental ideas.

ALFRED THE GREAT (849–899?), king of one English kingdom. He defeated the Danes and preserved England as a largely Anglo-Saxon country. He was greatly interested in education and brought scholars to England from the Continent. Under his orders many Latin authors were translated into the Anglo-Saxon dialect of the period. Some of the books he translated himself.

AMBROSE (340?–397), one of the church fathers. Early bishop of Milan.

APOLLINARIS, *see* SIDONIUS.

ARABS, members of the Semitic race with an original home in Arabia. Since the days of Mohammed they have spread into Europe, Asia, and Africa. They remained for centuries in Spain, where they left many traces in Spanish customs and in the styles of architecture. They were fanatic Mohammedans and spread their religion throughout the countries bordering on the Mediterranean.

ARCHIMEDES (c.287–212 B.C.), a famous mathematician who lived in Syracuse. He wrote a number of papers on geometrical measurement, but his greatest achievements were (1) his discovery of the laws of floating and submerged bodies and (2) his work with levers. He still lives in the popular mind as the man who focused the sun's rays on an enemy fleet and set it on fire.

ARISTOPHANES (c.450–c.375 B.C.), the greatest writer of Greek comedies. His plays are political or social attacks or satires on the life he saw about him.

ARISTOTLE (384–322 B.C.), the greatest of the Greek philosophers. About 40 of the 140 works he is known to have written are still extant. He wrote on logic, physics, metaphysics, psychology, ethics, and politics. With the possible exception of Christ, no other one thinker has exerted so strong and lasting an effect upon European modes of thought.

ARIUS (c.280–336), an early heretic who did not believe in the Trinity or in the absolute divinity of Christ. He was condemned at the Council of Nicaea in A.D. 325.

ARNOLD OF BRESCIA (d. 1155), an ascetic and scholar who vigorously protested against the temporal power of the popes. He was condemned at the same council that condemned Abélard but found refuge in Rome under the protection of the Roman Senate. Later he was seized by Frederick I and executed.

ATHANASIUS (c.298–318), Alexandrine follower of Origen. Saint, and bishop of Alexandria. His creed rather than that of Arius was recognized at the Council of Nicaea.

ATROPOS, the eldest, grimmest, and most inflexible of the three Fates, who, according to Greek mythology, were supposed to control human existence.

AUGUSTINE (354–430), a church father. After a somewhat dissolute youth, Augustine was converted to Christianity and lived to become bishop of Hippo and one of the church fathers. His chief writing—*The City of God*—is an outstanding piece of Christian literature.

A second St. Augustine was the first Christian missionary to England during the sixth century. He became the first archbishop of Canterbury.

AUGUSTUS (63 B.C.–A.D. 14), title bestowed upon Julius Caesar's nephew by adoption—Octavian, the first emperor of Rome. He died in the month of August, which still bears his name.

AVERROËS (A.D. 1126–1198), an Arab philosopher who lived in Spain. He was one of the most famous commentators on Aristotle.

BACCHYLIDES (5th century B.C.), Greek lyric poet, of whose poems only fragments are extant.

BACON, FRANCIS (1561–1626), an English philosopher and statesman. He wrote eloquently in defense of the scientific method and in attacks upon scholasticism.

BARZIZZA, GASPERINO da (1370–1431), a Greek scholar who came to northern Italy, where he stimulated great interest in the study of Greek. For many years he taught at Padua.

BASIL (329?–379), bishop of Caesarea,* a Greek doctor and scholar.

BEDE, THE VENERABLE (673?–735), English monk in Northumbria who wrote hymns, epigrams, grammars, and history. His chief work, an ecclesiastical history of England, was translated into Anglo-Saxon at the order of Alfred the Great.

BELL, ANDREW (1753–1832), a Scottish teacher and clergyman, who lived in America and in India, where he developed his monitorial system of teaching.

BENEDICT (480–543), an Italian monk, founder of the Benedictine order about 530. He composed the first "rule" by which communities of monks were to live.

BENEDICTINES, those monks who lived by the Rule of St. Benedict, who established the monastery of Monte Cassino* (A.D. 529). The monks were travelers and explorers, and founded hundreds of monasteries in Europe. They were distinguished as teachers, missionaries, and theologians. The order still flourishes.

BERNARD OF CLAIRVAUX (1091–1153), preacher and organizer. He preached the second crusade in 1146, healed the worst schism of the Catholic Church, hunted down heretics, and founded many monasteries.

BISMARCK, OTTO EDUARD LEOPOLD, PRINCE VON (1815–1898), soldier, statesman, diplomat. After a career in the army he became a member of the Prussian lower house, where he attracted the attention of the king. Presently he was appointed to various diplomatic positions and eventually became the most powerful man in Prussia. His great ambition was to unify the Germanies. To this end he provoked three wars: with Denmark, Austria, and France, in all of which Prussia was victorious. In 1871 Germany became a single nation with Bismarck as chancellor. He made alliances with Russia, Hungary, Italy, and several Balkan countries. In 1890 he resigned, largely because he was unable to get on with Wilhelm II (kaiser during World War I).

BOETHIUS (c.480–524), Roman scholar and statesman, often called the last of the Roman scholars. He translated some of Aristotle's works into Latin and wrote several textbooks for schools.

BONIFACE (680–755), an English monk who spent most of his adult life among German tribes trying to Christianize them. He is called the Apostle to Germany. After an adventurous life he was killed by a pagan whom he visited to convert.

BONHOMME, JACQUES, used to mean the average Frenchman; corresponds to the American John Doe.

BRAILLE, LOUIS (1809–1852), inventor of the Braille alphabet by which the blind can read by touch. He was himself blind from the age of three.

BÜRGI, JOBST (1552–1632), mathematician and astronomer. One of the inventors of logarithms, which he derived by a different method from that used by Napier, so that there is no question of the two men having made independent discoveries.

CAESAR, JULIUS (100–44 B.C.), Roman military leader and statesman. Conquered the territory from the Pyrenees to the Rhine, and subdued revolts in all parts of the empire. He seized the government as a dictator, weakened the Senate, and carried through many governmental and social reforms before he was assassinated by his enemies.

CALVIN, JOHN (1509–1564), French Protestant leader, who spent most of his adult years as an exile in Switzerland. His theological doctrines profoundly influenced the ideas of the Puritans. Geneva, the "city of Calvin," was for decades a refuge for persecuted Protestants from many countries.

CAMBDEN, WILLIAM (1551–1623), English scholar and historian.

CASSIODORUS (c.480–575), Roman statesman and writer. In his later years he became a monk in a monastery that he founded in Spain. He wrote on penmanship, as guidance for his monks in their copying of manuscripts, and on history.

CATILINE (c.108–62. B.C.), leader of a conspiracy to overthrow the government of Rome and become dictator. Cicero so aroused the Senate against Catiline that the latter fled for his life, and the conspiracy was crushed.

CATO (the Elder, 234–149 B.C.; the Younger, 95–46 B.C.), the Elder tried to enforce laws that would prevent Greek influences from undermining the virtues of the early Romans. In his later years he continually urged the Roman leaders to destroy Carthage. He was also the first important prose writer in Latin. He wrote on agriculture and on the early history of Rome.

CATULLUS, GAUIS VALERIUS (c.84–54 B.C.), greatest Roman lyric poet.

CEBES OF THEBES, disciple of Socrates and one of the speakers in certain dialogues of Plato.

CHARLES V (1500–1558), Holy Roman Emperor at the time of the Protestant Reformation.

CHAUCER, GEOFFREY (1340?–1440), author of the *Canterbury Tales,* stories told by pilgrims en route to Canterbury Cathedral.

CHRYSOLORAS, MANUEL (c.1355–1415), a Greek scholar from Constantinople who became professor of Greek at Florence, where he translated parts of Homer and Plato. He influenced many early Renaissance scholars.

CHRYSOSTOM (347?–407), patriarch of Constantinople. One of the Greek fathers of the church.

CICERO, MARCUS TULLIUS (106–43 B.C.), Roman orator, writer, and philosopher. He was first a lawyer and was so successful as to gain one public office after another on the strength of his reputation. As a senator he exposed the conspiracy of Catiline. In the civil war that followed, however, he vacillated so much that he lost friends on both sides. Augustus tried to save him, but could not keep Cicero's name off the list of those to be killed. Cicero was slain by political enemies as he was trying to escape from Italy.

CLAPARÈDE, ÉDOUARD (1873–), Swiss psychologist. Founder of the Rousseau Institute in Geneva for experimentation in educational and abnormal psychology.

CLEMENT (150?–215?), Greek father of the early church. He immediately preceded Origen at the catechetical school in Alexandria. He was well educated in Greek philosophy, which he tried to fuse with Christianity.

COLET, JOHN (1467–1519), English scholar, graduate of Oxford, who studied in Florence and returned to England as an enthusiastic humanist. In 1510 he refounded the cathedral school of St. Paul's and introduced a humanistic program. It was largely through him that the new studies were introduced into the English secondary schools.

COLUMCILLE, ST. COLUMBA, or ST. COLM (521–597), Irish missionary. After founding several monasteries in Ireland, he went to Scotland, where he converted the Picts, an early group from whom the Scots are descended.

COLUMELLA (1st century), Latin poet and writer whose extant works deal with the cultivation of plants.

CONSTANTINE THE GREAT (c.286–337), Roman emperor who established Christianity as the favored religion of the Empire and moved the capital of the Empire from Rome to Constantinople.

COPERNICUS, NICOLAUS (1473–1543), Polish astronomer who first formulated the theory that the earth, like any other planet, revolves around the sun.

CORDERIUS or CORDIER, MATURION (1479–1569), French schoolmaster and famous teacher of children. Among his pupils was Calvin, whom he followed to Geneva, where he was put in charge of an extensive educational program for both children and adults.

CORNEILLE, PIERRE (1606–1684), French dramatic poet. His greatest work was *Le Cid*.

CRITIAS (d. 404 B.C.), Athenian orator and politician. After many turbulent years, he became one of the Thirty Tyrants and was noted for his cruelty and greed.

CROESUS (590–546 B.C.), last king of Lydia, an ancient kingdom in Asia Minor. His wealth was enormous, and his name has become a symbol for wealth.

CYRIL (376?–444), archbishop of Alexandria. One of the Greek fathers of the church.

DANTE (1265–1321), supreme poet and outstanding national figure of Italy. His greatest work was the *Divine Comedy*, a long narrative poem that describes his trip through Hell, Purgatory, and Heaven.

DA VINCI. See VINCI.

DEFOE, DANIEL (c.1650–1731), English writer. He came of a Dissenting family and was educated in the schools of the Dissenters. In adult life he was a prolific writer of pamphlets on political and religious subjects. Much of his work while of high quality, was closely connected with ideas and movements current during his lifetime. He is now best known as the author of *Robinson Crusoe*.

DÉMIA, FATHER (17th century), a priest who conducted the first classes (in 1672) for training teachers. He did not have a school, only small groups. The first training school for teachers was that of De la Salle.

DEMOSTHENES (c.384–322 B.C.), Athenian orator and patriot, who inspired his fellow citizens to resist Philip* of Macedon.

DESCARTES, RENÉ (1597–1650), French mathematician and philosopher. Inventor of analytical geometry, a means by which algebraic and geometric facts and relationships may be transferred, thus permitting two types of proofs and two methods of dealing with mathematical problems.

DIDEROT, DENIS (1713–1784), a leader during the Enlightenment. One of the editors of the *Encyclopédie raisonée des sciences, des arts, et des métiers.* With Voltaire, Rousseau, and others he tried to awaken the French people to the existing abuses in church and state.

DINTER, G. F. (1760–1831), Superintendent of Education in Prussia and Director of Teachers' Seminars in Saxony. He helped to spread Pestalozzi's methods in Prussia and to reform German schools.

DIOCLETIAN (245–313), Roman emperor under whom the Empire was divided into Western and Eastern halves, with an emperor for each. He took the Eastern Empire, with his capital in Asia Minor, where he abandoned republican forms and ruled as an Oriental monarch. There were many persecutions of the Christians during his rule.

DIOGENES, LAËRTIUS (3d century), an obscure Greek who produced a series of anecdotes and sketches of famous men. His data are not always reliable but are usually interesting. (NOTE: He is not the Diogenes who lived in a tub.)

DISSENTERS, name given to a group of people who withdrew from the Church of England in 1668. For some time they were persecuted, but gradually they came to be accepted as one more Protestant sect. They are often called Nonconformists.

DOMINICANS, members of a preaching and begging order of monks, founded in 1215 by St. Dominic. They were very austere at first, and emphasized poverty, fasting, silence, a simple diet, and woolen rather than linen clothing. Among them were many theologians, notably St. Thomas Aquinas. They played an important role in defending the church against heresy and took an active part in the Inquisition.

DRACO (1) reputed author of the first Athenian written code of laws, in about 620 B.C. (2) A constellation.

DUNS SCOTUS, JOHN (1265?–1308), Franciscan monk and scholastic philosopher, professor of theology at Oxford. Founded a school of philosophy, members of which were called Scotists.

DÜRER, ALBRECHT (1471–1528), a German painter, engraver, and writer.

EDWARD VI (1537–1553), son of Henry VIII. He ruled only six years. He was an ardent Protestant, and during his brief reign the Anglican Book of Common Prayer was published.

ELIA, name derived from a Greek city where there was a famous school of philosophy.

ELIZABETH (1533–1603), queen of England and daughter of Henry VIII. Established the Church of England on a permanent foundation; encouraged both trade and literature. Her reign was one of the greatest in the history of England.

ÉPÉE, CHARLES MICHEL ABBÉ DE L' (1712–1789), Catholic priest who was canon at Troyes until he was dismissed for holding heretical views. He became interested in two deaf-mutes and subsequently devoted his life to teaching the deaf. He devised the "finger" language still in use and founded the first school for deaf-mutes.

ERASMUS OF ROTTERDAM (1466–1536), a famous Dutch humanist. See pp. 222–223.

ERIGENA (c.815–c.877), one of the earliest medieval philosophers. He contended that the universe must be a rational system and that reason was all-important. His works were condemned as heretical.

ESQUIROL, JEAN ÉTIENNE DOMINIQUE (1772–1840), a famous French doctor who did much work with insane, epileptic, and defective people.

EUCLID (3rd century B.C.), a Greek from Alexandria who wrote on geometry. The modern textbook in plane geometry is based upon his work and uses his form of proposition and demonstration. In fact, little has been added to his work since his lifetime.

EURIPIDES (480–406 B.C.), one of the three great Greek tragic poets; author of about 90 plays, the plots of which involved studies of character and of emotional crises. His best-known works are *Andromache, Hecuba, Medea, Electra, Orestes,* and *Iphigenia.*

EUSEBIUS (264?–349?), bishop of Caesarea in Asia Minor, later of Arles. Wrote the first history of the church.

FELLENBERG, PHILIPP EMANUEL VON (1770–1844), Swiss educator who worked for a while with Pestalozzi but separated from him because of incompatibility. He founded a school of his own near Bern, Switzerland, where he made the practice of agriculture the basis of his curriculum.

FICHTE, J. G. (1762–1814), German philosopher and lecturer. He helped found the University of Berlin and was a leader in the struggle for German freedom against Napoleon. He was also an early physicist and psychologist and an interesting writer.

FRANCIS OF ASSISI (1182–1226), an Italian monk who founded the Franciscan order. He lived a life of singular purity and went about the countryside begging and preaching.

FRANCISCANS, members of the religious order founded by St. Francis in 1212. They took vows of poverty and chastity. To support themselves they imitated their founder by begging. Although the Franciscan order degenerated eventually, it was a powerful influence for good, both among the people and within the church. It was one of many movements to rid the church of abuses and to return to the simple Christianity of Christ.

FREDERICK THE FIRST (1657–1713), first king of Prussia and father of Frederick the Great. He initiated many internal reforms. One evidence of his interest in education was his founding of the University of Halle.

FREDERICK THE GREAT (1712–1786), a very talented man with a great interest in culture and the arts. He organized the Academy of Sciences, recalled exiled scholars, encouraged industries, developed agriculture, rebuilt villages, reduced taxes, granted religious tolerance, drained swamps, built up a sizable merchant marine, fought several successful wars to establish Prussia as a major European power, enacted legislation to reform the schools and to make education free and compulsory. He was an excellent example of an enlightened despot.

FREDERICK WILLIAM I (1688–1740), king of Prussia who doubled the size of the army, liberated the serfs on the royal land, and instituted preliminary reforms in the schools.

FRONTINUS, SEXTUS JULIUS (c.40–103), Roman author and soldier. He wrote on such practical topics as military strategy and the construction of aqueducts.

GALEN (131–201), a Greek physician and philosopher.

GALILEO (1564–1642), Italian astronomer and physicist. He was professor at both Pisa and Padua. He discovered the laws of motion of a pendulum and of falling bodies. He invented the thermometer and built a telescope through which he discovered the satellites* of Jupiter, the phases of Venus, spots on the sun and mountains on the moon, and the fainter stars of the Milky Way. He defended the revolutionary ideas of Copernicus about the universe, for which, in his old age, he was called before the Inquisition and forced to recant.

GALLAUDET, THOMAS H. (1787–1851) and EDWARD M. (1837–1917), American educators, father and son. The father studied methods of teaching the deaf in Europe and opened the first school for the deaf in America. He was also professor of education at New York University. His son carried on the work.

GARLAND, JOHN (?–1252?), teacher of the late Middle Ages. He was known chiefly for the grammar and rhetoric that he wrote.

GERBERT (953–1003), scholar and monk who later became Pope Sylvester II. One of the first men to study with the Arabs in Spain. He discovered the works of Boethius on geometry, including some excerpts from Euclid, and re-established geometry as a science and an important school subject.

GILBERT DE LA PORRÉE (1075–1154), scholastic theologian, teacher at Chartres and Paris. Suspected of heresy and attacked by Bernard of Clairvaux, but was acquitted.

GOETHE, JOHANN WOLFGANG VON (1749–1832), great German poet and writer. He began as a romanticist, but ended as a classicist of great austerity and beauty. His masterpiece was *Faust*. He was also the minister of state for the tiny duchy of Weimar, and a scientist, artist, and philosopher. One of the world's great geniuses.

GOLIATH, the giant whom David slew with a rock from a slingshot.

GONZAGA, Italian princely family that ruled Mantua from 1328 till late in the 17th century. Its power was reduced, however, after the 16th century.

GOTHS, members of Germanic tribes that overran the Roman Empire in the third and fourth centuries A.D. They traveled all over the areas now included in Southern Europe, and into Africa via Spain. They established temporary kingdoms, but within two or three centuries they had been absorbed into the population.

GRATIAN (359–383), Roman emperor of the western half of the Empire from 359 to 583.

GREGORY (538?–594), bishop of Tours, where he was most conscientious in caring for the sick and poor and in guarding the rights of the church. He was also a historian and wrote a *History of the Franks* which has remained a chief source of information on the customs and life of a Germanic tribe while it was adapting itself to Roman culture.

GREGORY NAZIANZEN (328–389), a Greek orator, scholar, and theologian. One of the Greek fathers of the church. He was an outstanding theologian, but he put the greatest emphasis upon the spiritual values of Christianity.

GREGORY THE GREAT (550–604), the first great pope. He extended and unified the church, built up its prestige, sent out many missionaries—among them, Augustine to England and Boniface to Germany—made friends with the rulers of barbarian kingdoms, and wrote voluminously. He was one of the church fathers, and is usually known as St. Gregory.

GREY, LADY JANE (1537–1554), English noblewoman who spoke and wrote Greek, Latin, and several Oriental languages. She was the best-educated woman of her day.

GROOT, GERHARD (1340–1384), a preacher and mystic who founded the Brothers of the Common Life. He tried to follow the precepts of early Christianity and to live a holy, simple, and industrious life. He opposed scholasticism as being complex and artificial.

GUARINO (1374–1460), head of famous schools in Venice and Ferrara (1429–1460). The latter was a court school, similar to that of Vittorino. The boys lived at the school from 9–10 years of age to 20–21. Guarino emphasized physical activity, manners, morals, and humanistic studies.

GUIZOT, FRANÇOIS PIERRE GUILLAUME (1787–1874), French statesman, historian, and philosopher. As minister of public instruction he was instrumental in preparing and enacting the School Law of 1833, which gave the foundation for French elementary education.

HAKLUYT, RICHARD (1553–1616), English historian and geographer; author of two books of *Voyages*.

HEGEL, GEORG WILHELM FRIEDRICH (1770–1831), German philosopher of great influence, especially among Protestants. Professor of philosophy at the universities of Heidelberg and Berlin.

HELLENES, The Greeks.

HÉLOÏSE (c.1101–1164), Abélard's wife. One of the most gifted women of her time.

HENRY VIII (1491–1547), the English king who separated the Church of England from Catholic control. His motives were not, however, religious. His first wife had only one living child, a girl, and he felt that he must have male heirs. Since the papal court would not annul his marriage, he set up his own church with himself as head. His three children were all rulers of England—Edward VI, Mary, Elizabeth. *See also* Tudors.

HESIOD (8th century B.C.), ranks with Homer as the earliest of Greek poets. His main extant work is a long poem called *Works and Days,* which consists of fables, myths, proverbs, and practical advice.

HIPPOCRATES (c.460–c.370 B.C.), a great physician. He separated medicine from magic and established it as a science. He was the author of the Hippocratic oath—a code of ethics—still taken by every doctor when he graduates from medical school.

HIPPOLYTUS (3d century), a martyr of the early Catholic Church and a prolific writer, but most of his work has been lost.

HOMER, by Greek tradition, an old, blind, wandering singer who composed the *Iliad** and the *Odyssey.** These poems, probably not written by any one man, were composed in about the 8th century B.C. and are tales of events which took place, if at all, in about the 12th century B.C. and were already mythical in the time of Homer—if there ever was a Homer! There is, however, no doubt as to the permanent interest and value of the two long poems ascribed to him.

HORACE (65–8 B.C.), celebrated Roman poet, friend of Virgil and of the Emperor Augustus. His most important works are his *Odes* and *Epodes*—quiet, masterly poems of great charm, lucid thought, fine expression, and quotable lines.

HUSS, JOHN (1369–1415), a Bohemian preacher and reformer; he followed an earlier reformer, Wycliffe*, and was himself a forerunner of Luther. He was burned as a heretic after being given a safe-conduct by the Catholic Church.

HYGINUS, bishop of Rome in the second century.

INNOCENT III (1198–1216), pope under whom the medieval church reached its greatest power. He maintained that his position as pope made him ruler of the world and that all temporal rulers were subject to him. No pope since his time has wielded as much power as he.

IRENAEUS (130?–202?), early Christian martyr. As a young man he was converted to Christianity by Polycarp. He went as missionary into what is now southern France, where he became bishop of Lyons. He was killed in one of the persecutions ordered by the Roman emperors.

ISIDORE OF SEVILLE (c.570–636). *See* pp. 114–118.

ISLAM. *See* MOHAMMED.

ISOCRATES (436–338 B.C.), an Athenian orator, philosopher, and teacher of rhetoric. The main thing to remember about Isocrates is that he was *not* Socrates.

ISRAEL, "God's Chosen People," the Jews. Originally the collective name of the twelve Jewish tribes; later used for those who came back after the Babylonian captivity, and subsequently for their descendants.

JEANNE D'ARC (1412?–1431), a girl who, inspired by the "voices" she heard, donned male clothes, won the support of the Dauphin (the French crown prince), and led an army to victory over the English. Subsequently she was less successful. Enemies jealous of her power over the Dauphin accused her of heresy and witchcraft. She was condemned and burned at the stake.

JEREMIAH, one of the four major prophets.* He attacked violently the Jewish religion of his period. A vehemently written attack is still called a jeremiad.

JOB, minor prophet of the Old Testament, who lived in about the 8th century, B.C. The book of Job tells the story and gives the philosophical reflections of a man overtaken by great misfortunes and trying to find an explanation for the evil in the world. He is renowned for his patience in the face of calamity—the "patience of Job."

JOHN THE BAPTIST (5 B.C.?–30 A.D.), the last of the Hebrew prophets; a desert preacher and an immediate forerunner of Jesus, whom he baptized and whose birth he foretold.

JOHN THE EVANGELIST (d. A.D. 99), one of the twelve apostles; often called "the disciple whom Jesus loved." Writer of the Gospel according to St. John, the most sympathetic and penetrating account of Jesus' life.

JOHN OF SALISBURY (1120?–1180), English scholar and churchman. He spent many years on the Continent. During his last four years of life he became bishop of Chartres. He traveled much during his lifetime and left a record of some of the things he saw.

JONSON, BEN (c.1573–1637), English dramatist and literary dictator of the Elizabethan Age. He wrote both comedies and tragedies, as well as a number of lyrics.

JOVE, another name for Jupiter.

JUGURTHA (d. 104 B.C.), king of Numidia, a country in northern Africa. For some years he was an ally of Rome, but his cruelty and dishonesty eventually led to a break. The war against him dragged on ineffectually for years, but he was finally conquered.

JUPITER, the supreme god of the Romans. Identified with the Greek Zeus. Also the name of a planet.

JUVENAL (c.60–c.140), Roman writer of satires against the ugliness and decadence of life about him. Although often cynical, he never lost his moral indignation.

KANT, IMMANUEL (1724–1804), outstanding German philosopher, professor of philosophy at Königsberg—the city in which he was born and spent his entire life. His writings center around the three questions: What can I know? (ANSWER: Phenomena only.) What should I do? (ANSWER: My duty.) For what may I hope? (ANSWER: Immortality.)

KRÜSI, HERMANN (1775–1844), the first assistant teacher in Pestalozzi's school at Burgdorf. He also taught at Yverdon and was Pestalozzi's staunchest supporter. He was a man of no formal education and from a very poor part of Switzerland, but he had great natural talent for teaching and a deep love for children.

LANCASTER, JOSEPH (1778–1838), co-inventor of the monitorial system (*see* pp. 607–609), which he devised because he could not find enough teachers.

LAVATER, JOHANN KASPAR (1741–1801), Swiss mystic. A gentle-spirited, ascetic, deeply religious man who became interested in what he called the "art of physiognomy" or the art of reading character.

LEEUWENHOEK, ANTONY VAN (1632–1723), inventor of the microscope; first man to see germs; gave first accurate descriptions of red blood corpuscles, of the lens of the eye, of spermatozoa in animals, and of many other micro-organisms.

LEIBNITZ, GOTTFRIED WILHELM (1646–1716), German philosopher and mathematician. Co-discoverer of calculus. In 1698 he founded the Scientific Society of Berlin, which subsequently grew into the University of Berlin.

LILY, WILLIAM (1468–1522), early English humanist who studied in Italy. He was co-author of *Lily's Latin Grammar,* which was used for about two centuries in the English schools. This grammar embodied the new humanistic approach to language and became a means of introducing classical culture into English education. Sometimes spelled LILIE.

LIVY, TITUS LIVIUS (59 B.C.–A.D. 17), Roman historian, who wrote a *History of Rome* from the city's foundation to A.D. 9. Only 35 of his original 142 "books" are extant. His most important work covers the Punic Wars.*

LOCKE, JOHN (1632–1704), English philosopher, champion of religious toleration, early psychologist, defender of the rights of man, opponent of tyranny, writer on education, and proponent of the theory of formal discipline. *See* p. 626.

LOMBARD, PETER (1110?–1160), a scholastic who began the work of reorganizing theology by the aid of Aristotelian logic. His *Book of Sentences* completely changed the character of instruction in theology. He was a student of Abélard and used Abélard's method of reasoning.

LOUIS XIV (1638–1715), the "Grand Monarch" of France. A despot, a firm believer in the divine right of kings, a patron of the arts, king of France for 72 years. His reign was "glorious," but at a terrific cost to his people.

LOUIS XVI (1754–1793), a good man with good intentions, but weak. He had the misfortune to be king during the French Revolution, and he was quite unable to cope with the emergencies that arose. He was deposed, then reinstated, again deposed, arrested, and eventually executed.

LUCAN (39–65), a Latin epic poet who incurred the jealousy of the Emperor Nero, against whom he later conspired. Lucan's epic describes the struggles between Caesar and Pompey a century earlier.

LUCIAN (c.125–c.190), Greek sophist, philosopher, rhetorician, mathematician, and satirist. He traveled widely in Greece, Italy, and southern France. He wrote declamations, biographies, romances, and satirical dialogues; seventy-nine of his works are still extant.

LUKE, author of the Gospel according to St. Luke and of The Acts of the

Apostles—two books of the New Testament. He was an early missionary of the church in the first century.

LUTHER, MARTIN (1483–1546), German religious reformer and leader of the Protestant Reformation. *See* chap. ix.

MACAULAY, THOMAS BABINGTON (1800–1859), British author and statesman. Brilliant in conversation and in writing. Especially noted for his *History of England.*

MARCUS AURELIUS (121–180), Roman emperor. Opposed Christianity because he thought it weakened the unity of the Empire. In his *Meditations* he told of his thoughts about life and the world generally. He is usually classed as a Stoic philosopher.

MARENHOLTZ-BÜLOW, BERTHA MARIA VON (1810–1893), a German noblewoman who developed a great admiration for Froebel's work. She spent many years traveling about England, Italy, Switzerland, and France, giving lectures and courses and demonstrating Froebel's teaching materials. In 1870 she founded a Froebel Seminar where she trained kindergartners. She had great influence in spreading Froebel's methods throughout Europe.

MARLOWE, CHRISTOPHER (1564–1593), Elizabethan dramatist and poet. Author of *Tamburlaine, Doctor Faustus, The Jew of Malta,* and *Edward II.* He would have been the most remarkable dramatist of his age had he not been a contemporary of Shakespeare.

MARTIAL (c.38–104), Roman writer of epigrams, of which nearly 1200 are extant. Besides being of high literary merit, his epigrams throw much light upon Roman society in the 1st century.

MARTIANUS CAPELLA (5th century), Latin writer from North Africa. *See* p. 145.

MARY (1516–1558), queen of England for five years, during which she conducted a counter reformation in England in an attempt to restore Catholicism after her father, Henry VIII, had established the Anglican church as the state religion. Her program of repression and extermination was so severe that she has been known as "Bloody Mary."

MATTHEW, one of the twelve disciples of Jesus, author of the first book of the New Testament—the Gospel according to St. Matthew.

MAXIM, HUDSON (1853–1927), inventor of the first smokeless powder, of heavy ordnance powder, and of the Maxim Silencer, which reduces the explosion of a gun or pistol to a slight pop.

MERCATOR, GERHARD (1512–1594), a famous maker of maps. His map of Europe in 1554 was the first accurate map of the area. He devised the Mercator's projection for laying out a curved surface (the globe) upon a flat sheet of paper. Most maps of the world are still projected in this way.

MILL, JOHN STUART (1806–1873), English author, philosopher, economist, and liberal.

MILTON, JOHN (1608–1674), English statesman, writer, poet, and irreconcilable Puritan. Best known for three epic poems written in his old age—*Paradise Lost, Samson Agonistes,* and *Paradise Regained.* For two years he maintained a small school and became greatly interested in education—a field in which he was influenced by Comenius. His *Tractate on Education* is still well worth reading, 300 years after Milton wrote it.

MOHAMMED (570–632), Arabian religious and military leader. Author of the Koran and Founder of Mohammedanism, or Islam, which is one of the three great religions of the world—the other two being Buddhism and Christianity.

MOLIÈRE (1622–1673), pen name of a famous French dramatist (Jean Baptiste Poquelin). By many he is regarded as the world's greatest comic genius. His best-known plays are *Tartuffe, Le Bourgeois Gentilhomme,* and *Le Malade imaginaire.*

MONTAIGNE, MICHEL DE (1533–1592), born in Bordeaux, where he later became a lawyer and member of Parliament. At the age of about forty he inherited his family's fortune and retired to devote himself to a life of writing. He produced three books of essays on a large number of topics, among them, education. He is credited with having invented the essay as a form of writing. His work is humorous but without being bitter or satirical.

MOSELLANUS, PETRUS (1493–1524), author of a set of colloquies between two university students about their daily life and work. It gives a good picture of student life, especially at the University of Leipzig. The book was printed sixty-four times between 1518 and 1708 because it was so popular.

MÜNCHHAUSEN, KARL FRIEDRICH HIERONYMUS VON (1720–1797), a German nobleman who told extravagant and highly improbable stories of adventure.

NAPIER, JOHN (1550–1617), Scottish mathematician and minister. He wrote theological treatises but is most famous as a supporter of the decimal system and an independent inventor of logarithms. His tables were published in 1614.

NAPOLEON I (BONAPARTE) (1769–1821), military genius who became consul, director, and eventually emperor of France. Best known for his military successes, he was equally efficient in internal affairs, especially education and law. He created a school system for France under government control (1808).

NAPOLEON III (LOUIS NAPOLEON) (1808–1873), nephew of Napoleon I. Emperor of the French from 1852 to 1871. Abdicated after the Franco-Prussian War and died in England.

NEPOS, CORNELIUS (1st century B.C.), a Roman historian whose works are not great literature but are interesting. He is the easiest to read of any of the classic Roman authors.

NEWMAN, JOHN HENRY, CARDINAL (1801–1890), English priest, writer, and philosopher. Originally a Protestant, he later joined the Catholic Church and wrote an account of his reasons in a book called *Apologia pro Vita.*

NEWTON, SIR ISAAC (1642–1727), English mathematician, physicist, and astronomer. He developed the binomial theorem while still a college student, and later on conceived differential and integral calculus. His greatest scientific contribution was his discovery of the law of gravity, by means of which the motion of the universe could be explained.

OVID (43 B.C.–A.D. 17), one of the classic Roman poets. His best-known work is the *Metamorphoses.*

OWEN, ROBERT (1771–1858), a Scottish millowner and philanthropist. He tried to improve the physical, educational, and moral condition of his workers and especially of their children. He practically abolished child labor in his mills and instituted many other industrial reforms, such as a co-operative sharing of responsibility and profits.

PASCAL, BLAISE (1623–1662), French philosopher and mathematician. He carried on numerous scientific experiments, and was the first man to prove that the height of the column of mercury in a barometer would decrease if the instrument were carried upward.

PAUL (d. A.D. 69?), saint and missionary. Before his conversion to Christianity, he actively persecuted the Christians. On the road to Damascus* he saw a sudden burst of light and heard himself called by Jesus to become a disciple. He spent the rest of his life traveling, preaching, and writing. His letters to his sundry little groups of converts have been preserved as nine books of the New Testament.

PAULINAS OF NOLA (353–431), bishop of Nola in southern France. Pupil and friend of Ausonius. He distributed his wealth among the poor and lived for many years as a hermit. He was one of the most cultured scholars of his generation.

PERICLES (490?–429 B.C.), Athenian statesman, orator, leader, and director of the foreign policy that established Athens as the head of an empire. He initiated many social and legal reforms. Under his leadership Athens experienced a development that is unique in world history. Great architects and sculptors beautified the city, while great dramatists, historians, and philosophers made it a center of as high a culture as has ever been known.

PETRARCH, FRANCESCO (1304–1374), an Italian scholar and poet of the early Renaissance. He is most famous for his 300 sonnets to Laura, a woman whom he loved but never married. His chief significance for history lies, however, in his prodigious efforts to popularize the study of the classics. He was so successful that he established a humanistic trend in culture that is still evident today.

PHAEDRUS, a writer of fables in the first century; 97 of his fables are still extant.

PHIDIAS (500?–432 B.C.), an Athenian architect and sculptor who designed and supervised the carving of the sculptures of the Parthenon in Athens. The most famous sculptor of antiquity.

PHILIP of Macedon (382–336 B.C.), an able king of Macedonia,* a country just north of Greece. Father of Alexander the Great. He organized his country for war, devised a new method of military offensive, trained an army, instituted a fifth column in every important Greek city, and conquered the Greeks by a combination of attack, bribery, deception, and misdirection that would have been a credit to Adolf Hitler.

PHOCYLIDES. (?–1560? B.C.), an early Greek poet.

PIETISTS, name given to a group in the seventeenth century that emphasized the appeal of religion to the emotions rather than to the intellect. The movement arose from the human need to derive inspiration and solace from religion.

PINDAR (522?–443 B.C.), the chief lyric poet of Greece. He was a prolific writer with a magnificent style, beautiful diction, and rich imagery which made him one of the great figures in classic literature.

PLATO (427–347 B.C.), Greek philosopher and pupil of Socrates. Founder of the "Academy" in which he taught for forty years. His writings, preserved in his *Dialogues,* are matchless for their beauty of expression. In four of them, the main character is Socrates, whose life and teachings are thus expounded.

PLAUTUS (254–184 B.C.), a Roman writer of plays that were extremely popular.

PLINY the Elder (23–79), a Roman writer of books on history, military tactics, grammar, rhetoric, and natural history. His encyclopedia of the sciences was compiled from over 2,000 different sources. He was killed in Pompeii* when Mt. Vesuvius erupted and destroyed the city.

PLUTARCH (46?–120?), a Greek biographer. He wrote *The Parallel Lives,* the biographies of 46 great Greeks and 46 great Romans, arranged in pairs. He was not as much interested in historical accuracy as in presenting the character of his subjects.

POLYCARP (69?–155), an early Christian missionary and teacher. He became bishop of Smyrna, a city in Asia Minor. After a long and active life he was burned at the stake during one of the Roman persecutions.

PORPHYRY (233–304?), a philosopher of Syrian origin who opposed Christianity.

POUNDS, JOHN (1766–1839), a simple man with a kind heart and a love for children. He was a philanthropist in a humble way and divided his time between his trade and the rescuing of the most destitute and degraded children in his neighborhood.

PROMETHEUS, a character in Greek mythology who stole fire from heaven. As a punishment he was chained to a rock where every day an eagle tore out his liver, which grew again each night. He is credited with being the founder of civilization because he furnished mankind with fire.

PROPERTIUS (50 B.C.?–A.D. 14?), a Roman poet, famous mainly for his love poems.

PTOLEMY, CLAUDIUS, a geographer, astronomer, and mathematician who lived in Alexandria (Egypt) in the second century. He developed the Ptolemaic system of the universe, assuming that the earth was the central body around which the sun and planets revolve. His system was accepted until the sixteenth century, when Copernicus proved that the sun was the center of the universe.

PURITANS, a sect of English Protestants who advocated popular rights, simplicity in religion, and strictness of morals. Since they opposed the Church of England because of the lack of simplicity in its services and because it was too similar to the Catholic Church, they were driven from England. Many groups made settlements in New England, where they led scrupulously moral and austere lives.

PYTHAGORAS, A Greek philosopher of the sixth century B.C.

QUIRITES, the citizens of ancient Rome in their civil capacity as voters. In their military capacity as soldiers they were called *Romani.*

RABELAIS, FRANÇOIS (c.1495–1553), by profession a physician, but often in difficulties with the authorities and with his colleagues. His two main pieces of educational writing are called *Gargantua* and *Pantagruel.* They purport to be stories about a family of giants, but in them he expresses his ideas about a proper education and his violent criticism of existing schools. His humor is broad and his language often coarse, but his ideas are generally interesting, modern, and sound.

RATKE or RATICH or RATICHIUS, WOLFGANG (1571–1635), an educational reformer who devised a rapid method for teaching languages and tried a number of brief experiments in teaching. He had progressive ideas, but he was so difficult to get along with that his work had little permanent effect, except as later educators borrowed from him.

RICHELIEU, ARMAND JEAN DU PLESSIS, DUKE AND CARDINAL DE (1585–1642), a French churchman and statesman, prime minister of Louis XIV. During his last twenty years he was the most powerful man in France. His ambition was to make the king the dominant force in France, and France the dominant country in Europe. After many years of cleverness and intrigue he lived to see his ambition fulfilled.

ROUSSEAU, JEAN JACQUES (1712–1778), one of the greatest of French writers. His three best-known works are the *Social Contract, Émile,* and *La Nouvelle Héloïse.* His life was in sharp contrast to the beauty and refinement of his writing. For long periods he lived as a vagabond or sponged upon some rich person. He was suspicious even of those who helped him most. At one period he was exiled from France because of his revolutionary writings. He returned to the city of his birth, Geneva, but soon became unwelcome there. Much of his life he was either unemployed or unemployable, but he left his mark upon the intellectual life of his times, and he holds a high place among the world's writers.

SAINT-SIMON, CLAUDE HENRI, COUNT DE, (1760–1825), founder of French socialism. He advocated the state ownership of all property and the distribution of earnings in terms of the amount and quality of work done by each man.

SALLUST (86–35 B.C.), a Roman historian. His extant works include an account of Catiline's conspiracy and of the Wars with Jugurtha.*

SARACENS, in ancient times, the name used for wandering Arabs, who were later converted to Mohammedanism. They became fired with religious enthusiasm, spread across North Africa and into Europe via Spain, where they became the Moslem enemies of Christianity. They were defeated by Charlemagne's grandfather at the battle of Tours, but they remained in Europe for about seven hundred years.

SAVONAROLA (1452–1498), Italian monk who achieved a profound political as well as religious domination over the people of Florence. Eventually the populace turned against him. He was tried for heresy, condemned, and executed. As a speaker he was magnificent.

SAXONS, one of the German tribes that, with the Angles and Jutes, conquered England in the fifth and sixth centuries. Part of the tribe remained in Germany north and east of the Rhine.

SCHELLING, FRIEDRICH (1775–1854), German philosopher and outstanding representative of romantic idealism.

SCHILLER, FRIEDRICH, VON (1759–1805), German poet and dramatist. His best-known plays are *Wallenstein,* which has the Thirty Years' War as background, *Die Jungfrau von Orleans,* and *Wilhelm Tell.*

SENECA THE ELDER (c.54 B.C.–A.D. 39), writer of ten books of *Controversiae,* which contain seventy-four imaginary cases, with the arguments that might be presented in court.

SENECA THE YOUNGER (3 B.C.–A.D. 65), Roman Stoic philosopher, writer, and statesman. He was born in Spain but educated in Rome. He became the tutor of the future Emperor Nero, who eventually ordered Seneca to kill himself. Seneca's writings are all of a highly moral character and include many letters and essays on philosophical problems, education, and natural science.

SEVERIANUS, JULIUS (4th century), author of a widely used textbook of rhetoric.

SHAKESPEARE, WILLIAM (1564–1616), the greatest English dramatist; perhaps the greatest playwright in the world's history. His plays, now 350 years old, are still produced regularly. He wrote both comedies—*Midsummer Night's Dream, Taming of the Shrew, Twelfth Night, Merry Wives of Windsor*—and tragedies—*Hamlet, King Lear, Othello, Macbeth*—to mention only a few.

SIDNEY, PHILIP (1554–1586), English soldier, courtier, and author, who wrote sonnets and other poems. Regarded as a model of gentlemanly grace and unselfish chivalry.

SIDONIUS, APOLLINARIS (c.430–487), Christian writer and bishop. He wrote panegyrics, letters, and poems, all very stilted, elaborate, and artificial.

SOLON (c.638–558 B.C.), Athenian statesman who made many economic and legal reforms. He enacted legislation to relieve debtors, to establish courts, to admit the lowest class of people to the Assembly, and to open most public offices to the second and third classes.

SOPHISTS, Greek teachers of philosophy in the fifth century B.C. They were masters of rhetoric and persuasion, but their honesty was sometimes questioned and their reasoning was demonstrably poor. From these faults comes the word "sophistry," for inaccurate and insincere argument.

SOPHOCLES (495–406 B.C.), one of the three great Greek tragedians (with

Euripides and Aeschylus). He is noted for his purity of style and the power of his compositions. He wrote only tragedies: *Electra, Oedipus The King,* and *Antigone,* are his best-known plays.

SPENCER, HERBERT (1820–1903), English philosopher who wrote extensively on organic and social evolution.

SPENSER, EDMUND (c.1552–1599), English poet, author of *The Faerie Queene,* a romantic narrative and national epic glorifying both England and Queen Elizabeth.

STOICS, members of the Greek school of philosophy who sternly repressed emotion and condemned both pleasure and ambition. They were ascetic, intellectual, indifferent to personal comfort, puritanical, and moral. At their best, they were among the "good" men of antiquity.

STURM, JOHANNES (1507–1589), German educator who reorganized the schools of Strasbourg so that they became models throughout Europe. His system was highly humanistic.

SYNESIUS (c.367–412), an early bishop of the church who lived in Asia Minor. He wrote many letters that are still extant. He was a well-educated man in Greek philosophy and seems sometimes to have been about half pagan and half Christian in his opinions and point of view.

TERENCE (195–159 B.C.), Roman comic poet. Six of his plays are extant, among them the one upon which Shakespeare based his *Comedy of Errors.*

TERTULLIAN (c.160–222), a fiery Christian writer of the second and third centuries. Unlike most early religious writers, he was Roman, not Greek. He wrote in the colloquial language of his day, and his writings reflect his own passionate, stubborn, uncompromising nature.

TEUTONS, members of any of the German tribes that poured into Europe during the third to sixth centuries.

THEOGNIS (?–492 B.C), a minor Greek poet.

THIRTY TYRANTS, a body of men who ruled Athens under the domination of Sparta, after Sparta conquered Athens. Their rule was very harsh and many people were executed by their orders. Their rule extended from 404 to 403 B.C.

THOMAS À KEMPIS (1380–1471), an Augustinian monk, author of *Imitations of Christ.* This book presents a rule of life that stresses seclusion and renunciation. It has become a book of devotion for all Christians.

THOMAS AQUINAS (1225?–1274), the greatest and most influential of the scholastic philosophers. His reconciliation of philosophy and religious doctrine has never been surpassed. His most important work is still accepted by the Catholic Church as the authoritative statement of its religious beliefs.

THUCYDIDES (471?–399? B.C.), an Athenian statesman and historian of the wars between Athens and Sparta. A terse and vigorous writer. Often called the "Father of Historical Criticism," because he was careful to ascertain facts and objective in presenting them.

TIBULLUS (54?–18 B.C.), a Roman poet who wrote charming, simple, graceful elegies.

TOBIAS, the chief character in the Book of Tobias, one of the apocryphal books of the Old Testament. It is the narrative of a holy man.

TUDORS, members of an English royal line from 1485 to 1603. It included only five rulers: Henry VII, Henry VIII, Edward VI, Mary, and Elizabeth, but these monarchs had a profound effect upon the development of England. The English Reformation and Renaissance took place during their reigns.

TULLY, TULLIE, nicknames for Cicero, whose full name was Marcus Tullius Cicero.

UDALL, NICHOLAS (1506–1556), English dramatist and teacher. He was master of Eton and later of Westminster School. He wrote *Ralph Roister Doister,* the first comedy of everyday life in England.

VINCI, LEONARDO DA (1452–1519), artist and scientist. He was a military engineer and an expert on hydraulics; among other things, he designed an airplane. At the same time he was a great artist. His line drawings are unsurpassed, and his two greatest pictures—"The Last Supper" and the "Mona Lisa"—are known the world over. Many people regard him as the greatest universal genius the world has known.

VIRGIL (70–19 B.C.), a Roman epic poet and author of the *Aeneid,* a long poem in several sections relating the adventures of its hero, Aeneas.

VIVES, JUAN LUIS (1492–1540), Spanish philosopher and logician. Friend of Erasmus. Vives traveled a good deal, and studied and lived in many places, including London.

VOLTAIRE (1694–1778), pen name for François Marie Arouet, French philosopher, dramatist, satirist, and historian. His brilliant, satiric writings fill 99 volumes. He was at times immensely popular, but he often aroused so much feeling that he had to leave France for a while. He fought valiantly against official intolerance and ecclesiasticism. He wrote several plays, of which *Candide* is the best known; important volumes of history; and an avalanche of pamphlets and letters. Perhaps his most typical work was his *Dictionnaire Philosophique,* in which he expressed himself brilliantly, forcefully, and wittily on a great many topics.

WILLIAM OF CHAMPEAUX (1070?–1121), French teacher, scholastic, and bishop. He is often called the First Dialectician because of his skill in debating. An outstanding member of a school of philosophy that was opposed to that represented by Abélard.

WYCLIFFE, JOHN (1324?–1384), English reformer, and translator of the Bible into English.

XANTIPPE, the wife of Socrates. She has come down in history as a shrewish, disagreeable woman.

XENOPHON (434–355? B.C.), a Greek soldier and historian. He commanded the famous and successful retreat of 10,000 Greeks across Asia

Minor. His account is called the *Anabasis*. He was also a friend and admirer of Socrates.

ZEUS, the supreme god of the Greeks.

ZWINGLI, HULDREICH (1484–1531), Swiss reformer. After being educated at Vienna and Basle he was ordained as a priest at the age of twenty-two. He began studying the Gospels in the original Greek, in order to fulfill his duties as well as possible. He soon found that many practices of the Catholic Church were not founded directly upon the Bible. He presently began to attack the customs of fasting, worship of saints, celibacy of the clergy, and the Mass. He took part in several public disputations in Zurich and was remarkably successful in bringing his fellow townsmen to his point of view. Attempts were made to amalgamate his reform movement with that of Luther, but both men disliked each other and refused to co-operate. Eventually Zwingli was killed in a battle between the Protestant northern cantons of Switzerland and the Catholic central cantons.

GLOSSARY B: PLACES

This list contains the names of places, other than those associated with famous teachers or schools, that are mentioned in this text. The names of cities in the list below are followed by symbols: for instance, *Altona,* E, II. These symbols refer to the map inside the back cover and mean that Altona is in the column headed *E* across the top of the map and in the row labeled II down the left side. To locate it, look across the top letters until you reach **E**; then follow this column down until you are opposite **II**. Proceed in the same manner to locate other cities.

The large map has over 100 cities and a few islands and areas. The smaller map, inserted in the upper right corner, shows certain areas, such as Saxony or Provence, plus a few rivers and mountains. In the list these areas are designated as follows: *Champagne,* (S = small map), B—C, II. These symbols mean that the district appears on the small map and that it spreads across squares B-II and C-II.

Aix-la-Chapelle, town in southwestern Germany. Also known as *Aachen,* D, II.
Altona, city in northeastern Germany, 15, E, II.
Amsterdam, city in the Netherlands, D, II.
Anhalt-Dessau, district in central Germany, (S) E, II.
Annecy, town in southern France, D, III.
Antioch, two cities by this name were well known in ancient times: Antioch in Asia Minor, I, V, and Antioch in Syria, J, V. The latter still exists.
Arles, a city in southern France, C, IV.
Asia Minor, a large land area, H-I, V.
Attica, another name for Greece.
Augsburg, city in southern Germany, E, III.
Autun, city in central France, C, III.

Babylon, ancient city in the Tigris-Euphrates Valley, K, VI.
Bagdad, city in the Tigris-Euphrates Valley, K, VI.
Barcelona, city in Spain, C, IV.
Bavaria, area in southern Germany, (S) D-E, III.
Berlin, capital of Prussia; later, capital of Germany, E, II.
Beasançon, city in eastern France, D, III.
Blankenburg, town in central Germany, E, II.
Bologna, city in central Italy, E, IV.
Bremen, city in Northern Germany, D, II.
Bucharest, capital of Rumania, H, IV.

Cæsarea, there were several cities and towns by this name, which means "city of Caesar". The two shown on the map are Caesarea in Palestine, J, VI, and Caesarea in Asia Minor, J, V.
Carlyle, city in northern England, B, II.
Carthage, ancient city in northern Africa, E, V.

Champagne, district in northern France, (S) C-D, III.
Champs de Mars, former drill ground in Paris; now a park near the Eiffel Tower.
Chartres, city in central France, C, III.
Chartreux, city in southeastern France, D, III.
Clermont, city in central France, C, III.
Cluny, town in central France, C, III.
Constantinople, city in Eastern Europe, across narrow straits from Asia Minor, H, IV.
Cordova, city in Spain, A, V.
Corinth, city in Greece, G, V.

Damascus, city in Syria, J, V.
Deventer, city in the Netherlands, D, II.
Dresden, city in central Germany, E, II.

Edessa, there are two cities by this name, one in Greece, G, IV, and one in Asia Minor, J, V.
Elbe, river in Germany, (S) D, I.
Ephesus, city in Asia Minor, H, V.
Erfurt, city in central Germany, E, II.
Eton, seat of Eton College, B, II.

Far East, term used to refer collectively to such Oriental countries as China, Japan, Mongolia.
Ferrara, city in northern Italy, E, IV.
Florence, city in central Italy, E, IV.
Frankfort, city in central Germany, D, II.

Gascony, area in southwestern France, (S) B-C, III-IV.
Gaul, province of the Roman Empire. It included what is now France, southern Germany, and Spain, plus the southern part of England.
Geneva, city in Switzerland, D, III.
Glaucha, town in central Germany, E, II.
Gotha, city in central Germany, E, II.
Grand Chartreuse, La, monastery of the Carthusian monks, in the Rhone Valley. See *Chartreux.*

Hamburg, city in northern Germany, E, II.
Heidelberg, city in southern Germany, D, III.
Hellas, classical name for Greece, used by the ancient Greeks, who called their country *Hellas* and themselves *Hellenes.*
Helvetia, another name for Switzerland.
Herborn, town in western Germany, D, II.
Hippo, ancient city in North Africa, D, V.

Jena, city in central Germany, E, II.
Jura, chain of mountains between France and Switzerland, (S) D, III.

Karlsruhe, city in southern Germany, D, III.
Kiel, city in northern Germany, E, II.
Koblenz, city in western Germany, D, II.

Leipzig, city in central Germany, E, II.
Loire, river in southern France, (S) B-C, III.
Low Countries, Belgium and the Netherlands.
Lyon, city in southern France, C, III.
Lübeck, city in northern Germany, E, II.
Luneberg, town in northwestern Germany, E, II.

Macedonia, ancient kingdom north of Greece, G, IV.
Magdeburg, city in northern Germany, E, II.
Manresa, town in northern Spain, C, IV.
Marathon, place about 25 miles from Athens. After the battle of Marathon, in 492 B.C., a soldier ran all the way to Athens to tell the Athenians of their victory. Hence, *marathon* for a long race. G, V.
Marseilles, city in southern France, D, IV.
Milan, city in northern Italy, D, III.
Monte Cassino, monastery in southern Italy, Founded by St. Benedict in A.D. 429; destroyed by American bombing in 1944, E, IV.
Montmartre, section of Paris on a hill to the north, overlooking the city.
Montpellier, city in southern France, C, IV.
Mont Ste. Genvième, a slight rise of ground on the Left Bank of the Seine, a district where schools are still concentrated—the Sorbonne, the Collège de France, the Lycée Louis le Grand, the Lycée Henri IV, the École de Droit, the École Polytechnique, and many others.
Moravia, district formerly in eastern Germany, now included in Czechoslovakia, (S) F, III.
Moselle, river in northern France, (S) D, III.
Münchenbuchsee, village in Switzerland, D, III.
Munich, city in southern Germany, E, III.

Naples, city in southern Italy, E, IV.
Narbonne, city in southern France, C, IV.
Netherlands, formerly used to designate the "low countries" along the northwestern coast of Europe, including Belgium and Holland. Now used only for the latter, (S) C-D, II.
Nevers, city in central France, C, III.
New Lanark, small manufacturing town in Scotland, southeast of Glasgow, B, I.
Nicaea, city in Asia Minor where the Council of Nicaea was held in A.D. 325, at which many important church doctrines were decided upon, H, IV.
Nice, city in southern France, D, IV.
Northumbria, area in north eastern England, (S) B, II.
Notre Dame, great cathedral in Paris, built in the twelfth and thirteenth centuries.
Nuremberg, city in southeastern Germany, E, III.

Oberweissbach, town in central Germany, E, II.
Oldenburg, city in northern Germany, D, II.
Olympia, city in Greece where the Olympic Games were held, G, V.
Orleans, city in central France, C, III.

Padua, city in northern Italy, E, III.
Palestine, country in Asia, J, VI.
Père Lachaise, huge cemetery in eastern section of Paris.
Philippi, city in northern Greece, G, IV.
Poitiers, city in central France, C, III.
Pompeii, ancient city near Naples, covered in A.D. 79 by an eruption from Mt. Vesuvius.
Potidaea, place in northern Greece where the battle of Potidaea was fought in 357 B.C., G, IV.
Provence, area in southern France, (S) C-D, IV.
Prussia, state in northern Germany, (S) E, II.

Rheims, city in northern France, C, III.
Rhodes, island off the coast of Asia Minor, H, V.
Rhone, river in southern France, (S) C-D, III, IV.
Rotterdam, city in the Netherlands, C, II.
Rugby, town in England, seat of Rugby School, B, II.

Salamis, island near Athens, where Persian fleet was destroyed during the Persian Wars, in 480 B.C., G, V.
Salernum (Salerno), city in southern Italy, E, IV.
Salpêtrière, La, large hospital in Paris, founded in 1656, and used mainly for the care of insane, feebleminded, and epileptic persons.
Savoy, district in southwestern France, (S) D, III.
Saxe-Gotha, district in central Germany, (S) E-F, II-III.
Saxony, district in central Germany, (S)
Seville, city in southern Spain, A, V.
Sicily, island off the coast of Italy, E, V.
Sorbonne, the University of Paris.
Sparta, city in Greece, G, V.
Stanz, town in Switzerland, D, III.
Strassbourg, city in northeastern France, D, III.
St. Gall, Abbey of, in St. Gall (St. Gallen) a city in northeastern Switzerland, D, III.
St. Paul's Cathedral, great cathedral in the east end of London.
St. Petersburg, capital of Russia under the czars. Later called Petrograd and now called Leningrad, I, I.
Surö, town in western Denmark, E, I.
Syracuse, city in Sicily, F, V.
Syria, country in Asia, J, VI.

Tasmania, island south of Australia.
Thermopylae, narrow passage between mountains and ocean where the battle of Thermopylae was fought in 480 B.C., G, V.

Peter, Philip, Bartholomew, Matthew, Thomas, James son of Alpheus, Simon, Judas Iscariot, Jude. (NOTE: Paul was *not* an apostle.)

APOSTOLIC CONSTITUTIONS, two very ancient Christian documents, thought by some to have been written by the apostles, giving regulations and directions concerning church services and proper Christian conduct.

ARCHBISHOP, the chief bishop of an ecclesiastical* province, containing several dioceses* or sees.*

ARTICLES OF FAITH, an item of religious belief or doctrine, especially when it is part of a basic statement of religious beliefs, as the Thirty-Nine Articles of the Church of England.

ASCETIC, one who practices extreme self-denial, foregoing all kinds of pleasure or indulgence.

ASCETICISM, the mode of life adopted by those who renounce the world and voluntarily live a life of privation and hardship.

ATLANTIS, a legendary island that was supposed to exist just beyond what is now Gibraltar. Ancient writers peopled it with various kinds of idyllic communities. It is supposed to have sunk into the Atlantic Ocean, leaving a large area of shoals.

AUGSBURG CONFESSION, a statement of Protestant doctrine originally formulated by Melanchthon in 1530.

AUGUSTAN AGE, period from 27 B.C. to A.D. 14, during which Augustus was emperor; the most brilliant age in Latin literature.

AURA, a supposed subtle exhalation from a body, surrounding it with a charged atmosphere that can be felt though not seen.

AUTOHYPNOSIS, self-hypnosis.

AUTONOMY, the right or condition of independent self-government.

BACCHANALIA, drunken revelries, held in honor of Bacchus, the god of wine.

BARIC, sense of weight.

BAROMETER, an instrument for measuring the pressure of the atmosphere.

BEADLE, a parish officer with various small duties connected with a church; also a minor university official.

BEATIFY, to declare a deceased person worthy of respect; beatification is a recognized step in the conferring of sainthood by the Catholic Church. (NOTE: This word is not the same as *beautify*.)

BINOMIAL, an algebraic expression having two terms, such as $(a + b)$ or $(a - b)$.

BINOMIAL THEOREM, a rule by which a binomial may be raised to any power* without performing the multiplications.

BISHOP, a clergyman who is the spiritual overseer of a district called a diocese or see or bishopric.

BLACK ARTS, all forms of magic, witchcraft, or sorcery.

BRIDEWELL, a house of correction, a jail.

CALLIGRAPHY, good penmanship. Used loosely and inaccurately for hand writing of any quality.

CANON, a member of the chapter of a cathedral; he belongs to the bishop's council and performs certain assigned duties. Also, a rule or decree of the church.

CANON LAW, the law of the Roman Catholic Church.

CANONIZE, to place a deceased person in the catalogue (or canon) of saints, thus declaring him or her to be a recognized saint of the Roman Catholic Church.

CAPILLARY ATTRACTION, the attraction of a liquid to the solid sides of a narrow tube, causing the liquid within the tube to rise higher than the liquid in which the tube is immersed.

CARDINAL, a high church official who is a member of the electoral college that selects a new pope.

CASA DEI BAMBINI, House of the Children.

CASUISTRY, the resolution of doubtful questions of right and wrong on the basis of authority rather than upon grounds of moral reason.

CATECHISM, a brief manual of instruction by question and answer; specifically, the church catechism.

CEPHALIC INDEX, figure that indicates the ratio between the greatest breadth and greatest length of the skull.

CHANTRY, a chapel in or attached to a church or monastery, endowed for maintaining daily Masses for the founder. The boys of the chantry schools sang during the services.

CHEF-D'OEUVRE, masterpiece.

CHROMATIC, pertaining to color or to musical intervals.

CHURCH FATHERS, numerous early Christian writers widely accepted as authorities on Christian teachings.

CITY-STATE, a state governed by the free citizens of an independent city with sovereignty over more or less territory beyond its own limits.

CLASSICAL INVESTIGATION, an extensive study made by Latin teachers, twenty-five years ago, of the effect of Latin upon English. As Latin was then taught, there was very little effect.

CLERGY, the entire body of men set apart by having been ordained for the service of God in the Christian church; includes everyone from the village priest to the pope. As a collective noun, *clergy* is contrasted with *laity*.*

CLERICS, men who are clerks in holy orders; CLERICAL, however, may refer either to the clergy or to the functions of a clerk.

CLIENT, a person who was dependent upon a ruler or wealthy person for support or favor.

CLOISTER, a monastery or convent, so named from the covered walk along the walls of the main building around an enclosed quadrangle.

COCKNEY, a person born and bred within the sound of the bells of St. Mary-le-Bow church in Cheapside, London.

COGNATE, allied or related, belonging to the same root, derived from the same source. In language, the English *three* is a cognate of the French *trois;* note that neither is derived from the other.

COMMENTARY, a systematic explanation, as of the Bible or any of its parts.

COMPENDIUM, a brief, comprehensive summary.

CONGRESS OF VIENNA, the conference after Napoleon's defeat, in 1815, for the purpose of bringing Europe back to normal.

CONSTRUE, to state the syntax of a sentence; that is, to tell what is the subject, the predicate, the main clause, any subordinate clauses, the subject and object of each verb, and so on. The grammatical relationship of every word is given.

CONSUL, in ancient Rome, a chief magistrate. Between 1799 and 1804, the French government had consuls, of whom one was Napoleon Bonaparte.*

CONVENTUAL, belonging to a convent.

CORINTHIANS, the name of two books of the New Testament, Corinthians I and II. They are letters from Paul to the people of Corinth.*

COSMOGRAPHY, the science that describes the universe; it includes geology, geography, and astronomy.

CREED, a formal, authoritative, official statement of religious belief.

CRUSADE, any warlike expedition launched with the sanction of the pope. Specifically, the thirteenth-century expeditions of the Christians of Western Europe for the recovery of Jerusalem from the Turks.

CUBIT, an ancient unit of measure, supposed to be the length of the forearm from elbow to wrist; about eighteen inches.

DARK AGES, a period in the history of Western Europe given by different authors as (a) from the fall of Rome (5th century) to the Italian Renaissance (14th century), or (b) the earlier part of this period.

DE AMICITIA, *Concerning Friendship;* title of an essay by Cicero.

DEBACLE, literally, a breaking up of ice on a river, or a flood carrying masses of debris with it; used figuratively for any violent destruction.

DECADENCE, a process of decline, decay, or deterioration.

DECLAMATION, a speech or other selection recited from memory.

DECRETAL, an authoritative letter, especially from a pope, determining some point of church law.

DECURION, originally, the lowest officer in the Roman army; he commanded ten soldiers. Any person having the oversight of ten others.

DE SENECTUTE, *Concerning Old Age;* title of an essay by Cicero.

DICTAMEN (plural, DICTAMINA), literally, something that is dictated. Usually refers to letters or legal documents.

DIDACTIC, pertaining to instruction.

DIFFERENTIAL CALCULUS, a branch of analysis by algebra which investigates infinitesimal changes of quantities when the relationships between the quantities are given.

DIOCESE, the land or the churches under a bishop's jurisdiction.

DISPENSATION, special exemption from a rule or obligation, especially an exemption granted by the Roman Catholic Church.

DIVINE RIGHT, the right of a king to govern; the power is derived directly from God and is inherited in the royal family.

DOCTRINE, that which is held to be true by a religious group; a belief or basic principle.

DOGMA, a statement of religious truth as formulated by a body of official representatives of a church.

DON, a professor in an English university

DONATZ PROENSAL, a "donat" or grammar written in Provençal, the language spoken in southern France in the twelfth and thirteenth centuries.

ECCLESIASTICAL, of or pertaining to the church.

ECLOGUE, a poem containing discourses with or among shepherds.

EGO, the self.

ELECTOR, one of the princes who had the right of electing the emperor of the Holy Roman Empire (twelfth to eighteenth centuries).

ELEGY, a funeral song; a meditative poem with a sorrowful theme.

ELIMINATION RATE, the rate at which a group of children who begin school together becomes smaller as the children progress through the grades. Thus, of 1000 first-grade children in 1940, only 600 may still be in school in 1950. The other 400 have been "eliminated."

EMPIRICIST, one whose methods are based on experience, observation, and experimentation.

ENCOMIUM (plural, ENCOMIA), a formal expression of praise.

ENCYCLOPEDIST, specifically, an editor of or contributor to the French *Encyclopedia* produced about the middle of the eighteenth century; of the many contributors, the best known are Voltaire and Rousseau.

EPIC, a long narrative poem that tells the adventures of heroes.

EPIGRAM, a short, highly condensed, and often witty saying. For instance, "Haste makes waste."

EPISTLES, formal or public letters; specifically, the letters of Paul to his various groups of Christian converts. These epistles appear in the New Testament, as the Epistle to the Romans, to the Ephesians, to the Philippians, and so on.

EPITOME, a condensed, abbreviated summary.

ESTATE, a social or political class. The French Estates-General included the clergy, the noblemen, and the common people—the Third Estate.

ETYMOLOGY, the study of the derivation of words.

EUCHARIST, the Lord's Supper. A solemn celebration of the communion service, or Mass, which commemorates the dying of Christ.

EULOGY, spoken or written praise of a person's character and attainments.

EUTHANASIA, painless, peaceful death brought about because a person is incurably ill.

EVANGELISM, EVANGELICAL, related to or based on the four gospels (Matthew, Mark, Luke, and John) in the New Testament and their interpretation by the individual. Evangelical churches stress spiritual experience as the essential of religion, rather than belief in a particular set of dogmas. Evangelists are often so moved by their own reading of the gospels that they become missionaries to convert others. The emphasis is upon the emotional rather than the intellectual elements in religion.

EXCOMMUNICATION, the expulsion of a man from church membership, cutting him off from any privileges that result from such membership.

FACTOR, one of two or more quantities that, multiplied together, produce a given quantity. Thus $3 \times 2 \times 5 = 30$; 3, 2, and 5 are factors of 30.

FELLOW, a trustee or member of the governing body in some educational institutions.

FEUDALISM, a social system in force throughout Europe from the ninth to the fifteenth century, founded on the tenure of small plots of land rented to the common man in return for military service.

FIGURES OF SPEECH, an intentional deviation for effect from the usual modes of speech—metaphors, similes, and so on.

FLAGELLATION, a beating of oneself with a whip.

FORUM, a place of public assembly in ancient Rome.

GALATIANS, one of Paul's epistles.*

GALAXY, an irregular band of stars encircling the earth (i.e., the Milky Way). By derivation any group of brilliant people.

GASCON, a native of Gascony.*

GEORGICS, poems on husbandry or rural affairs.

GLOSS, a set of marginal notes and explanations concerning a piece of writing.

GORDIAN KNOT, Gordius was a king of Phrygia (in Asia Minor) who tied a hard knot about the yoke of his chariot; according to a prophecy, the man who loosed the knot would rule all of Asia. Alexander the Great loosed it by cutting it in two with his sword. The phrase is used to refer to any difficulty that can be overcome only by bold measures.

GOSPEL, a biography of Jesus Christ in the New Testament. There are four gospels—Matthew, Mark, Luke, and John.

GRACE, a short prayer said before meals.

GROSCHEN, a former silver coin of Germany, worth about three cents.

GUILD, an association of persons engaged in similar pursuits who banded together for mutual protection during the Middle Ages.

GULDEN, a coin formerly used in Germany and Holland; worth about forty cents.

GYMNASIUM, a classical Latin secondary school in Germany, preparatory to the university.

HABIT, specifically, the distinctive costume of a religious order.

HELLENIC, Greek.

HELLENIZE, to make Greek, to adopt Greek language or customs.

HERALDRY, the science concerned with the meaning and history of the devices used on coats of arms.

HERESY, a belief at variance with the official doctrines* of the church.

HETERODOXY. *See* HERESY.

HEXAMETER, a verse of six metric feet. Many Greek and Latin epics were written with six feet to a line.

HIERARCHY, the entire body of clergy arranged according to their rank; also, government by those with the highest rank.

HOLY ORDERS. *See* ORDERS.

HOMERIC, pertaining to Homer* or his period.

HOSPICE, a place of shelter, as a convent in an Alpine pass.

HUMANISM, *see* pp. 202–203.

HUMANISTS, specifically, those scholars during the Renaissance who studied and revived interest in the classical writers of Greece and Rome, emphasizing especially the ideas rather than the style. More broadly, those who center attention upon human interests and ideals rather than upon scientific or religious matters.

HYDRA, a many-headed serpent; when one head was cut off, two grew in its place.

HYPERBATON, the transposition of the words in a phrase from their usual order; for instance, "the hills among" for "among the hills."

ILLUMINATI, those who have or claim to have unusual enlightenment and discernment.

ILIAD, an ancient Greek epic poem describing the siege of Troy* ascribed to Homer.*

INDICATIVE MOOD, the forms of a verb that state or question directly. In such sentences as "I see him," "He threw the ball," or "Is he here?" the verbs are in the indicative mood. In such sentences as "Would that I might see him," "He may have thrown the ball," or "I wonder if he be here," the corresponding verbs are in the subjunctive mood. The forms "See!" or "Throw!" are in the imperative mood.

INFALLIBILITY, the state of being unable to make an error. The Roman Catholic Church is regarded by Catholics as infallible because it is kept from error by divine power. Since 1870, the pope has also been regarded as infallible.

INFIDEL, a person who is not a Christian.

INFLECTION, the changes made in words in order to express plurals and gender of nouns, tenses or persons of verbs, or the interrelationships of words within a sentence.

INQUISITION, a court for the trial and punishment of heretics.

INTERDICT, to exclude a person or group of persons from the religious privileges of a church.

INTROVERT, to turn inward upon oneself, to be interested primarily in one's own thoughts and feelings.

ISAGOGE, an introduction to a literary work; generally used for writings that deal with the history, inspiration, authorship, and genuineness of the books of the Bible.

JURISPRUDENCE, the science of law and its administration.

LACUNA (plural, LACUNAE), a space from which something is missing; a gap.

LAITY, the people as distinguished from the clergy. All those who do not belong to the clergy.

LAY, secular, nonreligious (adj.).

LAY BROTHER, a serving brother in a monastery, under vows and wearing the dress of the order but not a priest or a monk.

LENT, a forty-day period of fasting, just preceding Easter. It is supposed to commemorate Christ's fasting in the wilderness, plus the period of his trial, condemnation, and death.

LEVIATHAN, a large, aquatic, but unidentified animal mentioned in the Bible. (Job 41:1; Isaiah 27:1; Psalms 104:26.) Hence any large animal or anything of huge proportions.

LIBERALISM, the advocating of liberty of thought, speech, and action; opposed to conservatism, but less extreme than radicalism.

LIBERATION, WAR OF, wars against Napoleon, from 1813 to 1814. Through them Germany was liberated from French domination.

LICENTIATE, a university degree intermediate between bachelor and doctor; a person licensed to exercise a profession.

LIGHT REFRACTION, change in direction of a ray of light as it passes from air into water, for instance, or from any medium into another that is of different density.

LIVING, in the Church of England, an ecclesiastical endowment, or the income from it.

LOGARITHM, an exponent or power of a number. Usually, 10 is taken as a base. The logarithm of 100 is therefore 2, because 100 is the second power* of 10, or 10×10. It may also be written 10^2, with an exponent. The logarithm of 1000 is 3; that is, $10 \times 10 \times 10$ or 10^3. Tables of logarithms permit very rapid calculations with large numbers.

LOGIC, the science of correct and accurate thinking and reasoning.

LUDUS, Latin for school.

LUDUS LITERARIUS, elementary school.

LYCÉE, a French intermediate and secondary school that corresponds in general to the German Gymnasium. Its curriculum is largely classical.

LYRE, an ancient stringed instrument, like a small harp, with five or seven strings.

MANOMETER, an instrument for measuring pressure. The instrument used to measure blood pressure is a sphygmomanometer.

METAMORPHOSES, narrative poems by Ovid, in which one or more beings pass from one form to another (a metamorphosis), usually through some magic power.

METAPHOR, a figure of speech in which one thing is likened to another. (*See* p. 77).

METAPHYSICS, systematic study of first principles of being or of knowledge; speculative philosophy.

MIDDLE AGES, the period of history from about A.D. 500 to 1500.

MNEMONIC DEVICE, some way of aiding the memory, such as (a) associating numbers of hotel rooms with already known dates, or (b) remembering the kings of England by learning a poem in which their names appear in serial order.

MOHAMMEDAN. *See* MOHAMMED and MOSLEM.

MONASTERY, a building or set of buildings occupied by monks or others under religious vows of seclusion and separation from the world.

MONASTIC, pertaining to monasteries or to the monks who live in them.

MONASTICISM, western Christian monasticism took the form of a secluded, holy life in communities located in the country. The monks' duties consisted of prayer, reading, and manual labor. The communities were self-sufficient, based upon co-operative labor.

MONITORES, senior pupils placed in charge of classes or living quarters.

MONITORES IMMUNDORUM, bath monitors.

MONK, one of a company of men vowed to separation from the world, to poverty, to celibacy, and to work; a member of a monastic order.

MOOD. *See* INDICATIVE MOOD.

MOSLEM, a Mohammedan (also called a Mussulman). Mohammedan peoples use the word *Moslem* to describe themselves. A follower of the prophet Mohammed.

MOUNT, Mont Ste. Geneviève.*

NEOPHYTE, a recent convert; in the early Christian church, one recently baptized.

NOVITIATE, the period of probation during which one is a novice; used specifically for the trial period of one who enters a religious house.

ODYSSEY, an epic poem, supposedly by Homer, relating the wanderings of Ulysses (in Greek, ODYSSEUS) on his way home after the fall of Troy.

OLIGARCHY, a form of government in which the power is in the hands of only a few people; also, the name given to a state so governed.

ORDERS, HOLY, a group—usually monks, priests, or nuns—belonging to a religious body. The Order of Benedictine monks. To *take holy orders* means to be ordained as a priest or to be admitted to a monastery.

ORTHODOX, holding the sound, correct, officially accepted faith; the opposite is *heterodox* or *heretical.*

ORTHOGRAPHY, the mode, system, or science of spelling.

PÄDAGOGIUM, a secondary school for boys.

PÄDAGOGIUM REGIUM, a school having royal patronage and approval.

PAGAN, non-Christian. All classic Greek and Latin literature was necessarily pagan because it was pre-Christian, although certain writings are definitely of high ethical character.

PAIDAGOGOS, a slave who accompanied a Greek boy wherever he went.

PANEGYRIC, a formal, elaborate piece of writing, usually a poem, heaping praise upon some public figure.

PAPACY, the office of the Pope of Rome.

PAPYRUS, a water plant with a stem six to ten feet high, from which a kind of paper was made throughout the period of antiquity.

PARADIGM, a model giving the different forms of a noun or verb, such as

I do	we do
thou doest	you do
he does	they do

or a pattern for a single form from all tenses of the same verb, such as

he does	he will do
he did	he had done
he has done	he will have done

PARALLELOGRAM OF FORCES, a general principle that states the resultant direction in which an object will move and how rapidly it will move when it is acted upon simultaneously by two forces that urge it in different directions.

PARCHMENT, the skin of sheep, goats, or other animals treated and polished so that it can be used to write on. A diploma, originally written on parchment, is still known as a "sheepskin."

PARISH, a religious congregation including all those who worship in one church; also the district in which members of the same congregation live.

PARSE, to analyze a sentence according to the rules of grammar, showing the grammatical relationships between the words.

PATENT, obvious, clear to everyone, (adj.); a government protection of an invention, a government grant, or the certificate of such a grant (*noun*).

PATRICIAN, a member of a noble or aristocratic family. Opposed to *plebian*. During the centuries of the Roman Republic, the patricians were a hereditary aristocracy that controlled the government.

PATRON, a person who protects or supports or fosters the career of another. A patron saint is regarded as the peculiar protector of a person, group of persons, or place; thus St. Christopher is the patron saint of travelers and St. Patrick is the patron saint of Ireland.

PEACE OF AUGSBURG, a religious peace signed in 1555 between the Catholic and Lutheran princes. By its terms, each ruler was to decide what religion was to prevail within his borders and was to give any subjects who wished a different religion time enough to move into another district. This peace ended the wars of the Reformation in Germany.

PEACE OF WESTPHALIA, the peace that ended the Thirty Years' War in 1648.

PECCATUM, Latin word for *sin, crime, offense, fault.*

PENANCE, the performance of some specific act, undertaken voluntarily, as an expression of sorrow for one's sins and of atonement for them.

PENULTIMATE, the next to the last. Usually, the next to last syllable of a word.

PERI HERMONEAS, title of one of Aristotle's works on logic.

PERIPATETIC, walking or moving about; used to describe the teaching of Aristotle and others who walked up and down while they taught.

PHENOMENON (plural, PHENOMENA), something directly observable, as an appearance, action, or change of any kind—especially an unusual occurrence or one that cannot be immediately explained. A phenomenon is always the appearance as distinguished from the underlying force causing the appearance; thus, one speaks of the phenomena of falling bodies—meaning how fast they fall, what factors affect the rate of falling, and whatever else may be directly observed.

PHRENOLOGY, a system that assumes each mental faculty—such as memory or arithmetical ability—is located in a certain area of the brain; that such areas, by being over- or underdeveloped, affect the shape of the skull; and that abilities may therefore be determined by careful examination of the skull's contours.

PIETISM, a religious awakening in the Lutheran Church of Europe during the last half of the seventeenth century.

PLAGOSUS ORBILIBUS, a schoolmaster who is fond of flogging. The phrase was used by Horace, whose teacher—Orbilibus—thrashed him often.

PLATONIC IDEAS, these were forms or images which were supposed to be the original models or patterns that existing objects embody only imperfectly. Thus any given horse may be imperfect, but the idea of a horse is a true and perfect image.

POLYNOMIAL, in algebra, an expression having two or more terms, such as $(a + b + c)$.

POOR BOX, a collection box put up in a church or chapel for voluntary offerings, the proceeds to be used for helping the poor.

POWER, in algebra, a number multiplied by itself any specified number of times. Thus the second power of 3 is 3×3, or 9; the third power of 3 is $3 \times 3 \times 3$, or 27; the fourth power is $3 \times 3 \times 3 \times 3$, or 81; and so on. The powers are usually written as exponents; thus 3^4 means 3 to the fourth power, or the fourth power of 3, or $3 \times 3 \times 3 \times 3$, or 81.

PREBENDARY, a person who receives a stated income from the revenues of a cathedral.

PRECEPTOR, a teacher.

PREFECT (NOTE: This word is not *perfect.*), a Roman governor or administrator; the prefect of a Catholic college is its superintendent or manager, not a teacher.

PREHENSION, the act of grasping.

PRELATE, a member of the higher ranks in the clergy, such as a bishop or abbot.

PRESCRIBE (NOTE: This word is not *perscribe;* neither is it *proscribe.*), to give authoritative directions, as when a doctor *prescribes* a medicine. There is no such word as *perscribe.* To *proscribe* is to outlaw someone, to exile him, or to condemn him.

PRIOR, an officer in a monastery, with a rank below that of an abbot.*

PRISTINE, earliest, original, first.

PRIVILEGE, a favor, advantage, permission, or exemption that arises from one's social, economic, or legal position. Thus a French nobleman before 1789, by right of his noble birth, had the privilege of hunting over the lands farmed by his tenants, whether or not he ruined their crops in the process.

PROBABILITY, in mathematics, the ratio of the chances favoring an event to the total number of chances; thus if the death rate at a given age is 4 in a 100, the ratio is 4:100 and the probability is that in future groups of the same age, 4 in every 100 will die.

PROËNSAL, same as PROVENÇAL, of Provence.*

PROFESS, to join a religious order by vow. The "professed" members of an order are those who have taken all the vows.

PROGRESSION, ARITHMETICAL, a series of numbers each of which differs from its predecessor by a uniform difference. EXAMPLES: 2, 4, 6, 8, 10, 12, etc.; or 1, 4, 7, 10, 13, 16, etc.; or 45, 40, 35, 30, 25, 20, etc. In the first case the difference is 2; in the second, 3; in the third, —5.

PROGRESSION, GEOMETRIC, a series of numbers each of which differs from its predecessor by a constant ratio. For instance, 2, 4, 8, 16, 32, etc., is a progression in which the ratio is 2, since each number is multiplied by 2 in order to produce the next; for 5, 25, 125, 625, etc., the ratio is 5.

PROJECTION, (1) type of emotional reaction that consists in putting the blame for one's own shortcomings onto someone or something else, thus freeing oneself from a sense of guilt or remorse, since the responsibility for failure or defect has been "projected" to another. (2) The representation of something on a given fixed plane, such as the representation of the earth's surface on a map.

PROLETARIAT, in ancient Rome, the lowest economic groups; the rabble or mob; in later usage, those people who were destitute; in modern usage, the wage workers collectively, regarded as the true creators of wealth.

PROPHET, one who foretells the future or interprets God's will. In Christian usage "the Prophets" refer to the four major and twelve minor prophets in the Old Testament. (The former were Isaiah, Jeremiah, Ezekiel, Daniel; the latter were the authors of the last twelve books of the Old Testament.)

PROSODY, the science of poetic forms, including such topics as meter, accents, and versification.

PROVINCE, a large, administrative division of a country with a permanent local government, as the provinces of the Roman Empire. In church matters, a province is the district over which an archbishop* presides. The "provinces" refer to those areas of a country remote from its capital.

PSALM, a sacred song, especially those in the Old Testament Book of Psalms.

PSALTER, the Book of Psalms in the Book of Common Prayer used in the Church of England and the Episcopal Church, or the Latin collection of psalms used in the Roman Catholic Church.

PUBLIC SCHOOLS, this phrase is used in Great Britain to mean the private, endowed schools which give a liberal education or prepare pupils for the universities. Eton, Rugby, and Harrow are among the best known.

PUNIC WARS, wars between Carthage and Rome during the third and second century before Christ. The first Punic War (264–241 B.C.) was a stalemate; the second (218–201 B.C.) began as a triumph for Carthage but ended with defeat and exhaustion of the Carthaginians, largely because they could not be adequately supplied. The third war (149–146 B.C.) was a triumph for the Romans and ended with the complete destruction of Carthage.

RAPPORT, harmony of relation between two people.

RATIONALIST, a person who forms his opinions on the basis of reason, without dependence upon authority, inspiration, or belief.

REACTIONARY, one who is very conservative and wants a return to former conditions (noun); tending to revert to a former or contradictory state (adjective).

READINESS TEST, a test given before a child enters school (or begins a particular subject) to determine his readiness to start it.

REALGYMNASIUM, a German secondary school, parallel with the Gymnasium, in which the pupils do not study Greek, for which work in the sciences is substituted. Its curriculum is between that of the Realschule and that of the Gymnasium.

REALSCHULE, a six-year secondary school in Germany. Its curriculum contains no work in the classics and consists of modern languages, mathematics, and science.

RECANT, to withdraw publicly a belief that one has previously held.

RECUSANT, as a noun, a nonconformist, specifically to the Church of England; much the same as Dissenter.*

REFRACTION OF LIGHT, the change of direction in a ray of light as it passes from one medium to another, such as from air into water.

REIGN OF TERROR, the period of the French Revolution from May, 1793, to August, 1793, during which thousands of people were guillotined (killed), including the king and queen.

RENAISSANCE, a rebirth or revival; name given to the revival of art and literature beginning in Italy in the fourteenth century and spreading to other countries and marking the transition from medieval to modern history.

RETARDATION, as used in education, the holding back of children by non-promotion. The higher the degree of retardation, the older and more intellectually mature the children are in each grade.

RETREAT, a period of religious retirement, in seclusion and solitude.

REVELATION, the last book of the Bible.

RHAPSODE, a man who went about, in ancient Greece, reciting selections from Homer before audiences.

RHAPSODY, in ancient times, an epic poem, especially the *Iliad* or the *Odyssey*.

RHETORICAL FIGURES. *See* FIGURES OF SPEECH.

ROMAN LAW, the entire body of legal codes set up by the Romans. These became the basis of modern law, especially in Europe.

ROMANTICISM, in literature, a movement in the late eighteenth and early nineteenth centuries away from both classicism and realism and toward the mysticism and emotionalism of the Middle Ages; a substitution of intense feeling for purity of form and harmony.

ROTE LEARNING, or LEARNING BY ROTE, to memorize words by repetition, with slight attention to the meaning.

SARACENIC, Arabic.

SATELLITE, a secondary planet that revolves around a larger one.

SCAPEGOAT, in ancient Hebrew custom, a goat upon which the sins of the people were symbolically laid in a ceremony; the goat was then driven out into the wilderness. Hence any person who is made to bear the blame for others. (NOTE: This animal was not a *scrapegoat.*)

SCHISM, the division of a church into two or more groups, usually antagonistic. During the Great Schism (1378–1417), there were two popes, each opposing the other.

SCHOLASTICISM, the teaching of classical logic and philosophy as applied to the beliefs of the Roman Catholic Church, during the twelfth and thirteenth centuries (*see* p. 153 ff.).

SECT, a group of persons who differ by peculiarities (usually minor) of belief or practice from other groups of the same general point of view.

SECTARIANISM, fanatic devotion to a particular sect.

SECULAR, worldly, as contrasted with religious.

SEE, the place from which a bishop or pope exercises his authority.

SEMITES, literally, pertaining to the descendents of Shem, one of the sons of Noah. Among the Semites are included the Arabs and the Jews.

SENATE, in ancient republican Rome, the state council, which consisted of 300 members; it had extensive powers until these were taken over by the Empire.

SENSUAL, unduly indulgent of bodily pleasures.

SENSUOUS, appealing to the senses; keenly appreciative of beauty or refinement.

SENTENCE, specifically, an authoritative opinion, formally expressed.

SENTENTIAE, axioms or morals expressed in brief phrases.

SINE QUA NON, literally, "without which not"; that which is absolutely essential.

SLOUGH OF DESPOND, a swamp through which Pilgrim had to wade in *Pilgrim's Progress*.

SPECIFIC GRAVITY, the ratio of the weight of any given substance to the weight of an equal volume of water (for solids or liquids) or of air (for gases).

STATUS QUO, the existing state or condition.

STOIC, a member of a Greek school of philosophy that sternly repressed all emotion, all personal ambition, and most types of pleasure or enjoyment.

SUBJUNCTIVE, the form of a verb that is used to express a future possibility, a supposition, a hope or wish, a contrary-to-fact statement, a doubt, or a concession. (EXAMPLES: "If he *were* here." "Lest he *be* discouraged." "*Had he not been* careless, he *would not have* died." "Though it *were* twice as far." "Whether or not he *arrive* in time.")

SUFFRAGAN, an assistant bishop; this word means "assisting" or "auxiliary" and has no connection with "suffering."

SWISS REPUBLIC, began in 1291 and in continuous existence ever since.

SWISS REVOLUTION, after Napoleon became consul of France, he set up a directory in Switzerland modeled upon the French Directorate. The intensely democratic Swiss revolted against this government in 1798. The revolution was short and local.

SYLLOGISM, the regular, logical form of reasoning; it has three parts—a major premise (or assumption), a minor premise, and a conclusion. For instance:

All men are mortal; (*Major premise*)
Socrates was a man; (*Minor premise*)
Therefore, Socrates was mortal. (*Conclusion*)

SYNDROME, a group of symptoms or other single features that commonly occur together.

SYNTAX, the part of grammar that deals with the construction of sentences.

TACTILE, pertaining to the sense of touch.

TAWSE, a whip made of a leather strap cut into strips and mounted on a a handle.

TENET, an opinion, belief, or doctrine that a person or group of persons maintains as being true.

TEUTONIC, Germanic. *See also* TEUTONS.

THALER, a former monetary unit of some German states; in 1907, worth about seventy cents.

THERMIC, pertaining to heat.

THESIS, (plural, THESES), a proposition or statement of opinion, to be defended by debate.

THIRD REPUBLIC, of France. Established after the Franco-Prussian War in 1871 and continued until the fall of France in 1940, under the attacks of Hitler's armies.

THIRTY YEARS' War (1618–1648), long, exhausting struggle which began as a war between Catholics and Protestants, but was prolonged by various political and personal issues, until the religious question almost disappeared from view. By the end, Germany, the battleground, was exhausted. The war finally convinced people that religious opinions could not be changed by force, and the Peace of Westphalia in 1648 gave freedom of conscience and tolerance of varied religious forms.

THREE R'S, "readin', ritin', and 'rithmetic."

TITAN, in Greek mythology, one of a race of giants who rebelled against the gods and were vanquished by the latter; any person of gigantic strength or power.

TOGA, the outer mantle worn by Roman citizens; TOGA VIRILIS, the toga put on boys when they were fourteen as a symbol of manhood.

TRIGONOMETRY, a branch of mathematics dealing with the relations of the sides and angles of a triangle and applying them to other figures involving triangles.

TRINITY, the threefold nature of God—God the Father, God the Son, and God the Holy Ghost—each of which exists separately but all of which are of one divine being or substance. If the student does not find the concept of the Trinity understandable, he will merely be like most people!

TROPE, a word or phrase that is used in a meaning different from its apparent meaning, usually figurative. The term is often used interchangeably with "figure of speech."

TWILIGHT PHENOMENA, the effect of fading light upon different colors and upon other characteristics or features of vision.

UNFROCK, to remove the gown from a monk or priest; hence to take away his ecclesiastical rank.

UNIVERSALS, a concept in the logic and philosophy of the Middle Ages; it is too complex to explain here. A "universal" idea may, however, be thought of as not too different from a Platonic idea.

VELLUM, the finest parchment.*

VENAL, said of persons who are willing to sell honor or principle; mercenary, influenced by sordid considerations of gain or reward.

VERBALISM, wordiness, meaningless profusion of words.

VERNACULAR, one's mother tongue; the language one learns to speak by imitation as contrasted to languages subsequently learned from books.

VIA DOLOROSA, the road of anguish, pain, and sorrow. The expression is derived from the "dolors"—or occasions of great grief—of the Virgin Mary.

VIENNA, Congress of. *See* CONGRESS OF VIENNA.

VISITATION ARTICLES, a *visitation* is an official inspection of foundations or institutions; these particular articles were written by Melanchthon after an inspection of schools and churches in the Protestant areas of Germany.

VOLKSSCHULE, literally, the school of the people. Name used for the elementary schools of Germany.

VULGATE, St. Jerome's Latin version of the Bible, still used—with some modifications—as the authorized version of the Roman Catholic Church.

YEOMAN, a freeman who owned and cultivated his farm; his rank, in England, was next below that of gentleman. The yeomen formed the upper middle class in English rural society.

INDEX

A

V

W

X

Y